PROPER PEASANTS

VIKING FUND PUBLICATIONS IN ANTHROPOLOGY

Number Forty-Six

PROPER PEASANTS

TRADITIONAL LIFE IN A
HUNGARIAN VILLAGE

by
EDIT FÉL
and
TAMÁS HOFER

Subscribers' edition
distributed through
CURRENT ANTHROPOLOGY

for the

WENNER-GREN FOUNDATION FOR ANTHROPOLOGICAL RESEARCH, INCORPORATED

1969

This volume comprises one of a series of publications on research in general anthropology published by the Wenner-Gren Foundation for Anthropological Research, Incorporated, a foundation created and endowed at the instance of Axel L. Wenner-Gren for scientific, educational, and charitable purposes. The reports, numbered consecutively as independent contributions, appear at irregular intervals.

Edited by SOL TAX, *University of Chicago*

Library of Congress Catalog Card Number 77-77651

Published in cooperation with the Corvina Press, *Budapest*
and printed in Hungary at the Kossuth Printing House, Budapest

CONTENTS

LIST OF FIGURES

LIST OF PLATES

(Plates will be found between pages 418 and 419.)

LIST OF TABLES

PROPER PEASANTS

INTRODUCTION

HUNGARIAN ETHNOGRAPHERS IN A HUNGARIAN VILLAGE

This study was written by Hungarian ethnographers about a Hungarian village, and it therefore belongs to the class of village monographs in which the researchers are compatriots of the people they are studying. The difficulties and advantages characteristic of such an investigation are well known. While the identity of language and the similarity of cultural tradition facilitate the researcher's acceptance into the community studied, they render objective and comparative portrayal more difficult. In the case of this study a further factor plays an important part in shaping the relationship between the ethnographers and the village investigated: the fact that rural Hungary is the regional specialization of the authors and the area of their most intensive training. This kind of ethnographical research is characterized first of all by the fact that it is conducted by Hungarian scholars who do their field work among peasant communities in their own country and, second, by the fact that they present their findings to a largely Hungarian audience. As a result, these ethnographers belong to a distinctly "Hungarian school" of ethnographical research which has its roots in the larger fabric of Hungarian society and national culture.

English and American anthropologists, in describing how their science has "discovered" the peasantry, look for precursors in monographs written on tribal communities and attempt to discover how the methods and ideas contained therein were then, beginning in the thirties and forties, applied to the investigation of an increasing number of peasant communities. Such surveys rarely mention that numerous European nations possess independent traditions of scientific investigation into their own peasant cultures, with the result that over the last hundred years or more a copious body of relevant literature has been produced, and numerous periodicals and university chairs devoted to research on the peasantry have been established. This omission is easily understandable, since the European or, more precisely, Central and Northern European studies made in the "Volkskunde" tradition did not contribute to the development of the concepts of "peasant culture" and "peasant society," and their findings have rarely been incorporated into anthropological literature dealing with the peasantry.[1] For this reason we shall attempt to clarify the point of view

[1] E.g., Redfield, 1956: 19–20; Arensberg, 1963: 76.

3

of the authors by giving a very rough outline of this European—or, specifically, Hungarian—ethnographic tradition.

Using an expression from Robert Redfield, the birth of Hungarian ethnography may be described as a particular case of the relation between the "great tradition" and the "little tradition," which took place early in the last century in the context of the national reform movements. Interest in peasant culture was far from being solely devoted to the gathering of scientific information. The language reform movement incorporated several hundred words collected from peasant dialects into everyday language, the poets made use of the metrical forms of recently published folk songs and ballads, and "folk plays" that put village scenes, customs, and rural songs on the stage became fashionable.

This movement was basically derived from the idea that the rural "little tradition" is inherently valuable: not only do folk poetry and art have high artistic merit, but they also preserve ancestral, "original," national features more faithfully than the "great tradition," which is subject to rapid changes and the influence of foreign fashions. Accordingly, ethnography in European countries explored the traditional culture of their own peasantry, conceived as a coherent system. Even at the outset of this research the obsolescent peasant culture was already being steadily reduced and assimilated by the processes of urbanization and industrialization. From the beginning, researchers were encouraged to seize their last opportunity to record old tradition before it was annihilated without a trace. The attention of these workers centered on regions and villages maintaining the old-fashioned way of life—or, as an increasing number of modern elements was adopted, to the survivals of this way of life—in an attempt to piece together the traditional elements so as to reconstruct the original cultural system characteristic of the nation.

Just as Hungarian, Polish, Croatian, Austrian, and other folk cultures were considered self-contained units, so Hungarian, Polish, Croatian, Austrian, and other ethnographies were regarded as essentially separate branches of inquiry. Scholars were aware of each other's findings, and they kept abreast of the progress of world ethnology, but Hungarian ethnography considered itself as confronted with its own special set of problems and so developed its own outlook and set of techniques to meet them, in part independent of outside influences.[2] Research workers dealing with

---

[2] The ethnographers were certainly aware of the fact that most elements of the peasant cultures they studied had a wide distribution which extended beyond national boundaries. Comparative cross-cultural studies have a long tradition in the ethnographic research generated in Hungary and other Central European countries. These studies usually aimed to throw light on the distribution, history, and development of special cultural phenomena—e.g., types of plows or other agricultural implements, styles and motives of decorative art, types of folktales, etc. With these comparative studies as a base, ethnographers were able to outline synthetic pictures of their national peasant cultures, differentiating historically between the different layers of tradition and geographically between the regional sub-cultures (cf. Bátky, Győrffy, and Viski, n.d. [1934]). The attention of the ethnographers was drawn at an early date to the contacts between and coexistence of different ethnic groups. The first general ethnography of Hungary (J. Csaplovics, 1822) contained a comparison of the different national and regional groups represented in Hungary at that time and an interpretation of a multitude of national stereotypes. Moreover, the distinction between ethnography (conceived of as the study of one's own peasant tradition) and general ethnology (which was much wider ranging) was always ill defined

Africa or the Polynesian Islands, though they came from various parts of the world, established international contacts with each other at an early date, accumulating the knowledge gathered by each in a common ethnographic treasury. Ethnographic research on the European peasant was far from being similarly integrated into a unified tradition. Instead of developing general concepts and common themes of rural life, research workers devoted their efforts to the description of discrete regional characteristics and local developments; instead of seeking to outline general evolutionary trends, they concentrated on the illustration of particular concrete phenomena.[3]

The fact that the endeavors of Hungarian ethnographers were directed to this purpose is largely due to the original inclusion of ethnography among the humanities. Its closest connections were with the history, literary history, history of music and art, and linguistics of Hungary, as well as with anthropogeography. Each of these disciplines explored aspects of nonrecurrent processes in Hungary, and their causes and interrelationships, and occasionally members of the different disciplines have worked together on a common enterprise. As did the other disciplines, Hungarian ethnography tried to describe, to characterize, and to explain the single and singular complex of cultural features which was typical of the Hungarian peasantry. Recently the necessity of integrating Hungarian ethnography into the general body of research in social and cultural anthropology has been emphasized.

On the other hand, an ethnographer trained in Hungarian ethnography, setting out to prepare a village monograph, has quite different opportunities from those a social anthropologist without similar training would have. Merely by being a Hungarian, the compatriot ethnographer is familiar with numerous customs and institutions in the village where he intends to work. Moreover, this preliminary knowledge is supplemented by the body of information gathered by several generations of ethnographers, possibly including his own previous researches. (For example, the authors had done field work in more than one hundred Hungarian villages before their research in Átány.) The numerous studies published on various cultural phenomena—e.g., the structure of the plow, the different shapes of the bonnet, the texts of wedding and funeral rites, etc.—furnish him with a special observational sensitivity to variations in cultural forms.[4]

---

in Hungary due to the peculiar historical background of the Hungarians. Hungarians were connected, through their semi-nomadic ancestors, with Finno-Ugric and Turk tribes in Siberia and Eastern Europe. As a result, some outstanding ethnographers conducted field work not only among Hungarian peasants but also among linguistically related tribes.

[3] This endeavor is represented by the expression "regional ethnology," proposed by Sigurd Erixon and accepted by the Arnhem Committee in 1955 "as an adequate name for the whole of international European folk culture research. Erixon thinks that regional ethnology deviates in two respects from general ethnology: it avoids large generalizations, and it is more historically directed because it has recourse to rich documentary source materials. In the latter condition lies the strength of this discipline, he argues" (Hultkrantz, 1960: 203).

[4] This sensitivity is related to that of the villagers to a certain degree. In the eyes of the peasant, the way a woman ties her kerchief under her chin may reveal the village to which she belongs; the various cuts of female blouses may express that some women have married children while others have none.

In planning the Átány research, we intended to make use of ethnographic methods developed specifically for the observation and analysis of discrete cultural elements. We wanted to use the advantages of our position to make complete detailed descriptions of these elements, while at the same time endeavoring to reveal their interrelationships. For example, we tried both to describe the various implements, techniques, concepts, and values associated with labor, and, on a more general level, to discuss the various economic structures of the peasant holdings and the system of peasant agriculture.

Átány people often refer to themselves as "proper peasants," by which they underline the traditional peasant characteristics of their way of life as contrasted with other communities of the area where the traditional way of life has been more dissipated. (See Epilogue.)

Our choice of a village to study was influenced by the traditions of Hungarian ethnography. We wanted our research on the structural relationships among cultural elements to contribute to a better understanding of the same old, "traditional" Hungarian peasant culture which has been the main object of Hungarian ethnographic research for generations. We were looking for a village in which the operation of social institutions and the patterns of interpersonal relationships might preserve much of the ancient peasant culture, with relatively few signs of transition and culture loss. We wanted to avoid any "average" village belonging to the postpeasant type, living in the advanced phase of assimilation characteristic of the majority of Hungarian villages. In observing and recording the culture of the village, our attention was focused primarily on the more antiquated features. Later we shall explain this in more detail, in an attempt to define the essence and the cause of Átány's relative archaism. Here it will be singularly important to fix the "ethnographic present" of the descriptive analysis which follows. Except where an earlier or a more recent period is specifically referred to, descriptive statements in the present tense refer to the period at (and immediately preceding) the time when the investigators first began their research in Átány in 1951. (The subject of the "ethnographic present" and the changes which have occurred since 1951 are treated in more detail in the Epilogue.)

THE RESEARCH AT ÁTÁNY

Being Hungarian ethnographers, the authors were able to adapt themselves to the community relatively quickly and easily. The people of Átány read books and newspapers, and at least some of them have some concept of history and of a museum (an important point, since the researchers are members of the staff of the Hungarian Ethnographic Museum in Budapest). They regard the interest in the history of their own village and in their ancient customs as a sign of esteem. Furthermore, several families have relatives or friends who have moved into town, and some have acquaintances among educated people; it was this latter type of relationship which more or less characterized that of the authors to the village.

From the outset, the status of the authors in the village was twofold. On the one hand, they were regarded as the esteemed and more or less official guests of the whole community, through its communal and ecclesiastical leaders. On the other, they were guests of two Átány families, and as such they were included in the relations of kinship, friendship, neighborhood, etc., of these families. (If, for example, they attended church, they were entitled to the seats reserved for honored official guests: Edit Fél could sit at the side of the pastor's wife, Tamás Hofer among the church officials. But they could also go to church with a member of the host family; in this case Edit Fél could sit beside her hostess in the appropriate women's pew, while Tamás Hofer could go up to the gallery of bachelors.) A further differentiation of perspective was provided by the fact that the financial situations, social positions, and compositions of the two host families were quite different. Generally the authors were permitted to take part in the everyday labor and to attend celebrations in the company of the host families. (To give an example, a relative of the host of Edit Fél, Ferenc Orbán, died. She went out with the women to see the deceased. Her hostess warned her beforehand that her age and the situation demanded a "coffee-colored" kerchief on her head and lent her one for the purpose. As the author stood at the foot of the bier, the circumstances of the deceased were recited to her as to an esteemed relative. [See Chapter 11, "The Funeral."])

The relationship between the authors and the people of Átány is one of mutual consideration. The authors are invited to pigsticking or receive a taste of the result, and they offer hospitality to the villagers who come to the capital for shopping or for medical care. The years of interviewing have established a very close friendship with fifty or sixty families, but all the inhabitants of the village greet and receive the authors in their homes as friends. When the research had reached an advanced stage, a relationship with the village as a whole was established by the exhibition we organized at Átány, consisting of objects collected in the village, as well as by the series of lectures we gave on the history of the village. These lectures had to be repeated several times in order to enable everyone to attend.

Research was begun in February, 1951, and was continuing as of 1967, except for a few interruptions. One or both authors would spend four to twelve days at a time in the village. The short stays were made possible by the fact that Átány is only 120 kms. from the capital, and is easily reached by train or bus in a few hours. In all, we spent about five hundred days in the village (till 1963). Each visit had a definite purpose: participation in a certain type of work or in a festival, or collection of interview material on a definite topic.

The structure of the research team also proved to be advantageous. The rules of propriety of the village admitted the presence of Edit Fél on some occasions and that of Tamás Hofer on others. For example, participation in a vigil beside the dead is permitted only to women, whereas only a man can sit with the males at a *tanyázás* in the stable.

The high degree of conscientiousness, organization, and motivation observed in some of the people of Átány in describing their own social institutions deserves special mention. Ferenc Orbán, for example, seated for the first time before a map of the inner holdings of the village, was able to recite the owners of more than a thousand holdings and a generation of their former owners without a break.

Research was extended to some families which had moved to the capital from Átány, as well as to former officials of the Átány administration who are currently employed elsewhere.

In addition, numerous written sources on the life of the village have come down from past decades, and even centuries. Among them can be found records written by local people, such as the journals of the local council; church records; registries of births, deaths, and marriages back to the early eighteenth century; and other documents preserved by some of the peasant families. There also exist records of public and manorial administration, lists of tithe collectors from the sixteenth century on, documents registering the size of the *jobbágy* (serf) population and listing their possessions and obligations, a few records on criminal proceedings, judicial papers on the consolidation of land strips (executed on several occasions), and finally land registers. For about the last hundred years, the Central Statistical Office has collected data on the population and economy of Átány. These sources, preserved in various archives, are accompanied by a copious scientific literature, interpreting and explaining the source material on the Átány region.

Although the authors attempted to collect historical data regarding Átány, it was not their purpose to draw a coherent picture of the village as it existed in past centuries. Historical data are quoted in the present study only in those instances in which they may help us in interpreting the impression gained by ethnographic field methods and presented as an ethnographic study.[5]

Numerous people helped the authors in both the local and the archival research. In the field work itself we have only one permanent collaborator: Benjámin Rajeczky, who gathered the material on folk music and prepared it for publication. In opening up historical sources we have been assisted by Imre Soós and Béla Bottló; in their interpretation, by Imre Wellmann. Statistical data were collected and the tables designed by József Orlicsek; their interpretation and graphic presentation were facilitated by the advice of István Kiss and Dezső Dányi. Professor Albert Kiss provided us with instructions and some computed data regarding the sources and tables of agrarian statistics.

Both authors are on the research staff of the Hungarian Ethnographic Museum in Budapest. All of the field work and the preparation of the study were done under the auspices of its research program and with its financial support. The Museum administration has been extremely sympathetic to our efforts in the course of the research and has given a free hand to both of us throughout our

---

[5] In several cases we were enabled by the records to make a direct check on statements made by the peasants. For example, some former town officials have pointed out features of the organization and development of the village self-government. We were able to compare these data with journal records of the activities of the village self-government, as well as with information furnished by the former notary of Átány, now living in another village. Both latter sources have verified the data of the peasant informants entirely.

protracted labors. We would like to express our heartfelt thanks to the Museum both for meeting the expenses and for permitting us to publish the study in its present form.

THE PRESENT STUDY

This study was conceived and written from the beginning for publication in the Viking Fund Publications in Anthropology series. In 1962 we had the opportunity to acquaint the editor, Sol Tax, with our research project, and he invited us to publish a study of Átány in the series. At that stage we already realized that we could not present an overall picture of the village in a single study. We then decided to portray the social organization of Átány life. We went beyond the traditional concerns of Central European ethnography, and so our study has a transitional character. It raises questions usually asked by social anthropologists, but in answering them it utilizes concepts and styles partly derived from Hungarian ethnography. We wrote the manuscript for an English-speaking, mostly American, audience, trying to make it understandable for them by using terms and concepts of social anthropologists and by adding special explanations not needed in a Hungarian or Central European edition. On the other hand, in the content and main approach of the study, we wanted to keep our identity as Hungarian ethnographers.

Sol Tax encouraged us to make this experiment and to express ourselves in our own terms regardless of the usual conventions of American community studies. Without him this study would not have been completed. Needless to say however, responsibility for all the interpretations advanced in this book lies with the authors alone.[6]

Aldine Publishing Company, Chicago, and Corvina Press, Budapest, through joint effort have produced this book out of our manuscript. We express our heartfelt thanks to both of them for their patience and careful work.[7]

The translation of the original Hungarian text was completed by György Bónis in Budapest. The English text had to be polished and adjusted to current anthropological usage, however. This painstaking and tiring work was done by Dr. and Mrs. A. Richard Diebold, Jr. Their selfless contribution exceeded the usual limits of such assistance. They came to Hungary to cooperate with the authors and visited Átány to acquire firsthand experience for the restyling of the text. We thank them both as well as our original translator.

In addition to the present study, the authors plan to publish other studies on the village, some of which have already been completed. A monograph on the agriculture of the village, based on an analysis of the equipment and technology, is ready

[6] The manuscript of the present study, including the text of the introduction, was drafted in 1963 and in the spring of 1964. While preparing it for publication in 1965, we added supplementary data from some recent works dealing with the history of Hungarian peasantry.

[7] Thanks are also due to our illustrators. The maps published here were drawn by Magda Schöberl, the sketches on architecture by Ferenc Mendele and Mrs. Dóra Mendele, the diagrams by Mihály Török. (The photographs were taken by the authors.)

in manuscript and has been published in part.[8] Our research has also embraced the world-view, the system of values, the folklore, and other aspects of the ethnoscience of the village; we hope to publish this material as well.[9]

The data were collected during a crucial period of change in the life of the village. The life of the inhabitants had already been deeply affected by national and world affairs shortly before our research was begun. During World War II, in 1944, fighting occurred about the village, causing much damage to manpower, equipment, and livestock. Land ownership was reshuffled by the agrarian reform of 1945. Soon after our research began, the state agricultural policy of the 1950s radically modified the peasant economy. In the following years there were further changes in directives, and the rural economy was obliged to change accordingly. In 1959 the population of the village, along with the overwhelming majority of the Hungarian peasantry, became part of the system of agricultural cooperative farms.

We observed these changes and their results. Our main objective, however, was to study and describe that traditional peasant culture which still thrived at Átány in its original undiluted state.

Our purpose was not simply to depict the situation in the village at the time of our research. A period of fifty years is embraced in the immediate experience of Átány's adult population, and some of our elderly informants could accurately remember even more remote days. In the course of our research we intended to explore and to record this accumulated wealth of experience. Besides adapting ourselves to the everyday activity of the village, we wanted to penetrate the way people thought in Átány. The vivid, immediately observed life of Átány, the spontaneous conversations, and the memories awakened—supplemented by analysis of objects, records, papers, and statistical data—served to portray the vicissitudes of the village over the course of two or three generations. Thus we attempted to outline the nature and function of the various social institutions for this entire time span.[10]

[8] The aim of the research on agricultural equipment was to make a comprehensive survey of all the tools in the village, including the design of the various implements, their uses, and the knowledge and values attached to them. We tried to describe the objects in use in the village as a cultural system, with its own rules, classifications, and "grammar." The study of the agricultural equipment is part of this program. Partial publications of the manuscript, based on this research, are in print (Fél and Hofer, 1961a, 1962, 1964, 1965).

We have also described the branches of rural agriculture (Fél and Hofer, 1961b) and summarized a few implications of this inquiry for the history of peasantry (Fél and Hofer, 1962).

As this manuscript goes to press, another is nearing completion, dealing with the agriculture and household economy of the peasants. It is primarily concerned with calculations made by the peasants —the traditional measures and ratios employed in the use of resources and the energy of men and animals, and the ways of dealing with time.

[9] The description of the Átány mourning ceremonies has been published in Vol. V of the *Magyar Népzene Tára (Collection of Hungarian Folk Music)*, which also contains the melody and the text of a lament contributed by B. Rajeczky (Kiss and Rajeczky, 1966: 30–36, 93–100, 433–436, 807–808).

[10] With reference to these changes, we should further specify what we mean in this study by the term "ethnographical present." The large manorial estates near the village were abolished by agrarian reform in 1945 and, as a result, the traditional way of life of the farm hands, sharecroppers, and day laborers formerly employed on the estates came to an abrupt end. Descriptions of these traditional patterns of employment (sometimes described in the "ethnographical present") always refer to the pre-1945 period. Similarly, the system of local government also was reorganized during 1950–1951. Thus, references to the mayor, the local board, and the magistracy are to be understood in relation to the period preceding the reorganization.

During this period there were sharp differences among the people of Átány, both in financial situation and way of life. We describe these divisions, the interrelationships of the various strata, and their dynamics in Part Four of this book. At the time of our survey a considerable amount of the work and life of the landless agricultural laborers and farm hands fell outside the village. It is among the land-holding peasants that the traditional culture sought by the authors and looked upon as a model by all the population of Átány has been preserved the most tenaciously. Therefore this study deals principally with the world of the farmers while trying also to define the relationship of this world to the village as a whole.

To what extent are the data gathered on Átány society characteristic of the surrounding villages and of Hungarian peasantry in general? We have tried to answer this question in several ways. As an introduction, we endeavored to locate the position of our village among the various types of Hungarian villages and to demonstrate its special and individual features in relation to the general history of the Hungarian peasantry. In our descriptions we have tried to distinguish features typical of the region and the country from purely local characteristics. In the statistical tables we have included indices for the immediate environment, more distant regions, and the country as a whole, along with the indices for the village. (These statistical data and correlations also provided a way of verifying and controlling our statements. The continual comparison between the observations at Átány and the surrounding region, on the one hand, and the ethnographic and historical knowledge on the Hungarian peasantry, plus the experiences of the authors themselves in other Hungarian villages, on the other hand, served as a safeguard against undue generalizations from atypical phenomena.)

A NOTE ON THE USE OF HUNGARIAN WORDS

Assuming that many readers will be unfamiliar with the Hungarian language, some liberties have been taken in citing Hungarian nouns in text: With few exceptions in the pages that follow, the noun is cited as it would appear as a dictionary entry—i.e., in the "uninflected" nominative singular form—even in those contexts where Hungarian grammar would require, for example, a plural or accusative "inflected" form. This convention accounts for those numerous instances where an italicized Hungarian noun appears with an unitalicized (-s) suffixed to it. This is simply to signal plurality by using the English plural ending in order to avoid the possibility of a confusing array of inflected variants of the Hungarian base form. Thus, one "son-in-law" is cited *vő;* "sons-in-law," however, is cited *vő*-s, rather than in the grammatically correct nominative plural form *vők.* Similarly, the possessive has been indicated by suffixing unitalicized English (-'s) or (-s') to the uninflected form of the Hungarian noun.

Notes on Pronunciation

The following synopsis, however wanting in detailed phonetic description, will serve as an introduction to the pronunciation of the Hungarian forms cited in text. The great virtue of Hungarian spelling is that there is an almost perfect one-to-one correspondence between any written letter and the respective phone-type of the spoken language which it represents. Unlike English or French, for which one written symbol may have many pronunciations, Hungarian spelling is relatively consistent, and a guide to pronunciation of this sort is more useful for Hungarian than it would be for some other written languages.

The Hungarian alphabet is as follows: *a, á; b; c; cs; d; e, é; f; g; gy; h; i, í; j; k; l; ly; m; n; ny; o, ó; ö, ő; p; (q); r; s; sz; t; ty; u, ú; ü, ű; v; (w); (x); (y); z; zs.* Note the existence of seven digraphs, e.g., *cs*, which are unit symbols. The graphemes *q, w, x, y* occur only in the spellings of recent or learned loanwords. In addition, *dzs* is used to write the non-Hungarian sound [dž] in some loanwords, e.g., *dzsungel* "jungle," although it is not listed separately in dictionaries.

Word Stress: Practically without exception, the strongest stress falls on the word initial syllable in Hungarian, whether the word is morphologically simple (e.g., *LEves,* "soup") or complex (cf. *LEveshús,* "soup-meat"; *HÚSleves,* "meat-soup"). Note that many "words" in Hungarian are in fact compounds of the type exemplified by *húsleves,* "meat-soup." Within the word, intervocalic consonants (V*C*V) belong to the second syllable: V-*C*V; e.g., *leves* ['lɛ-vɛš].

Consonants: (Sound equivalences selected from English and other languages are only approximate.)

	Voiced	*Voiceless*
Stops:	*b* – [b] cf. Eng. *b*ed	*p* – [p] cf. Eng. *p*et
	d – [d] cf. Eng. be*d*	*t* – [t] cf. Eng. pe*t*
	gy – [d'] cf. Russ. день	*ty* – [t'] cf. Russ. брать
	g – [g] cf. Eng. *g*ill	*k* – [k] cf. Eng. *k*ill
Affricates:	*(dzs)* – [dž] cf. Eng. *J*ill	*c* – [ts] cf. Ger. *Z*eit
		cs – [tš] cf. Eng. *ch*ill
Fricatives:	*v* – [v] cf. Eng. *v*at	*f* – [f] cf. Eng. *f*at
	z – [z] cf. Eng. *z*oo	*sz* – [s] cf. Eng. *s*ue
	zs – [ž] cf. Eng. plea*s*ure	*s* – [š] cf. Eng. *sh*ell
		h – [h] cf. Eng. *h*ill
Nasals:	*m* – [m] cf. Eng. *m*et	

n – [n] cf. Eng. *n*et (with a velar variant [//], as in Eng. *sing*, when *n* precedes *g* or *k*).

ny – [ñ] cf. Span. cu*ñ*a, Fr. di*gn*e. (*ny* is often pronounced as *ni* or *nyi* when it occurs as the final consonant of personal names, but elsewhere it is [ñ], cf. *Átány* ['a:ta:ñ].

Liquids: *l* – [l] cf. Eng. *l*et (but not like te*ll*).

  r – [r] cf. Span. ca*r*a (but not trilled like Span. ca*rr*o).

Double consonants like *tt* are pronounced like the similar geminate consonant clusters in Italian (e.g., It. *notte*) even when these occur at the end of a word, e.g., *ott*, "there."

Semivowels: *j* ⎫
  ⎬ [y] cf. Eng. *y*et
  ly ⎭

Vowels: All vowels are "pure," i.e., they are not diphthongized unless immediately preceded or followed by *j* or *ly*, as in *jó*, "good," or *olyan*, "such." Note that accent marks are used as in French rather than to mark stress differences as in Spanish. Accent marks represent either longer or different vowel sound.

There are fourteen vowels, orthographically grouped as seven pairs. The contrast between sounds in four of the pairs devolves principally on length or quantity. (Sound equivalences selected from English and other languages are only approximate.)

Shorter		*Longer*
i – [i]	and	*í* – [i:] cf. Ger. s*ie*ht
o – [o]	and	*ó* – [o:] cf. Ger. B*o*den
u – [u]	and	*ú* – [u:] cf. Ger. T*u*be
ü – [ü]	and	*ű* – [ü:] cf. Ger. M*üh*le

In the remaining pairs, there is a more marked contrast in articulatory position as well as in quantity:

e – [ε] cf. Eng. b*e*d   *é* – [e:] cf. Ger. S*ee*

a – ⎡ when stressed, [ɔ] cf. Brit. Eng. T*o*m ⎤   *á* – [a:] cf. Ger. *Aa*l
   ⎣ when not stressed, more like [ʌ] in Eng. c*u*t ⎦

ö – [ö] cf. Ger. G*ö*ttin   *ő* – [ö:] cf. Ger. S*öh*ne

Archaic Spellings: Spelling reforms and language standardization account for the observed consistency in Hungarian spelling. Exceptions and archaisms do sometimes occur, however, in the spelling of personal names and, more rarely, in place names. The most common of these are:

  gh, in word final, pronounced as if *g*

  y, in word final, pronounced as if *i*

  ch, *ts*, pronounced as if *cs*

  cz, usually pronounced as if *c*, rarely as if *cs*

  ss, pronounced as if *s*

  th, pronounced as if *t*

  w, pronounced as if *v*

  aa, *aá*, pronounced as if *á*

  oo, *oó*, pronounced as if *ó*

  eö, pronounced as if *ö*

Other than these exceptions in personal (and some place) names, the only other important spelling idiosyncrasy is final *h* in uninflected words, e.g., *juh*, "sheep."

This *h* is not pronounced, i.e., *juh* [yu], unless a suffix is added; cf. *juhok*, "sheep (Pl.)" ['yuhok].

Phonotactics: There are certain important assimilatory changes which affect the pronunciation of some consonant clusters (CC) *but which are not indicated by the spelling*. These can be summarized in two general rules: (1) If a voiced consonant is followed by a voiceless consonant, the first (voiced) consonant becomes voiceless; thus *dobtam* is pronounced as if it were written **doptam*, i.e., ['doptʌm] (and not **['dobtʌm]). (2) If a voiceless consonant is followed by a voiced consonant, the first (voiceless) consonant becomes voiced; thus *képzel* is pronounced as if it were written **kébzel*, i.e., ['ke:bzɛl] (and not **['ke:pzɛl]). There are no such morphophonemic changes if the two consonants are either both voiced or both voiceless.

PART ONE
THE VILLAGE AND ITS PEOPLE

CHAPTER 1. THE VILLAGE

ÁTÁNY'S PLACE AMONG THE HUNGARIAN VILLAGES

József Kakas, one of the hosts of the authors at Átány, related that as a schoolboy he often loitered around the village on summer evenings with his friends. They went to the church and talked as follows: We know that Hungary is in the center of the world, Átány in the center of Hungary, the church is standing in the very center of the village. Thus we stand in the center of the world. They observed that the sky is highest above the Átány church, sloping in a circle all around: this must in fact be the center of the world!

Throughout the community the idea that Átány is located at the center of the world is prevalent. Adults mention it jokingly and remember that other villages nearby make the same boast. There is a song beginning with these words:

"The village of Átány lies in a fine place,
Since it is at the center of the world,
The most beautiful girls in the world live there..."

Otherwise the Átány people have fairly broad and accurate knowledge of the world outside the community. What with fairs and outside jobs on farms or in offices, etc., most of the adult inhabitants have had ample occasion to visit other regions, near and far. The two World Wars took Átány soldiers to foreign countries and brought strangers into the village as well. In defining the location of their village to strangers, the Átány folk mention first that they are Hungarians, then that they live on the Great Hungarian Plain, and, finally, that they belong to Heves county (see Fig. 1).

Hungary occupies an area of 93,000 square kilometers in the center of the Carpathian Basin. This territory consists mainly of plains and hill country with a few moderately high mountain ranges, reaching an altitude of not quite one thousand meters. (The elder Átány generations, however, were born and brought up in what was still "historical Hungary," coterminous with the whole Carpathian Basin. The present frontiers of the country were defined by the Treaty of Versailles [Trianon] in 1920 and the Treaty of Paris in 1947.)

The Hungarians consider their country as divided into three large regions. East

17

of the Danube lies the Great Hungarian Plain, commonly abbreviated to "the Plain." West of the Danube is Transdanubia, a more hilly region extending to the foothills of the Alps. The mountainous and hill country beyond the northern edge of the Plain is the Highland. Budapest, the capital, which contains one-fifth of the Hungarian population, is situated at the point where the three regions meet.

The inhabitants of the three regions are almost all Hungarians (Magyars make up 98.1 per cent of the present population). They speak mutually intelligible dialects; they are not divided by ancient tribal distinctions; and they have been continuously brought together by the frequent wars in the centuries of Hungarian history and by the "melting-pot" effect of modern economic development.

However, public opinion associates specific characteristics with the populations of the various regions. As early as the eighteenth century poems existed in which the plain-dwellers boasted of being more genuine Magyars than the Transdanubians, since the latter mixed foreign words into their speech and occasionally adopted the western fashions from Austria. With its endless wheat fields and herds of cattle grazing in the wide pastures (though these pastures have been reduced to a fragment of their former size, as will be exemplified in the discussion of Átány határ), the Great Plain was regarded as the most "Hungarian" region, as it were. The beauties of the Plain were eulogized in the poems of Sándor Petőfi,[1] who regarded the openness of the lowland as the symbol of Hungarian freedom. The main city of the eastern Plain, Debrecen, "the Rome of Calvinists," is the capital of the Reformed Church, a counterpart of the Transdanubian center of the Roman Catholic Church in Hungary at Esztergom.

Transdanubia, with its varied topography, was a Roman province of old. Several Transdanubian cities were built on Roman foundations, and viniculture, which lends a characteristic appearance to many of its fields, may be a legacy from that period also. The cathedrals, castles, and walled cities of the region are a reminder of past centuries and a striking contrast to the populous, rural towns of the Plain, where stone is rare. Also here the art styles of the "great tradition," to use Redfield's term, were most easily accepted and incorporated into the art and taste of the local peasantry. The feudal ties of peasant life were less loosened in Transdanubia by the wars of the sixteenth and seventeenth centuries than they were on the Great Plain, with the result that of the three regions, Transdanubia was (until 1945) most typified by large estates, tiny villages of former serfs, and clusters of manorial outbuildings inhabited by servants.

Among the mountains of the Highland the peasant villages were generally poor and backward, preserving an archaic type of peasant culture. Since the latter part of the nineteenth century, mining and industrial districts have grown up rapidly in this region.

Within the populations of these three regions, smaller or larger groups are distinguished according to their origin, the geographical unity or character of their locality,

---

[1] Sándor Petőfi (1823–1849) is regarded as the greatest figure of Hungarian national poetry.

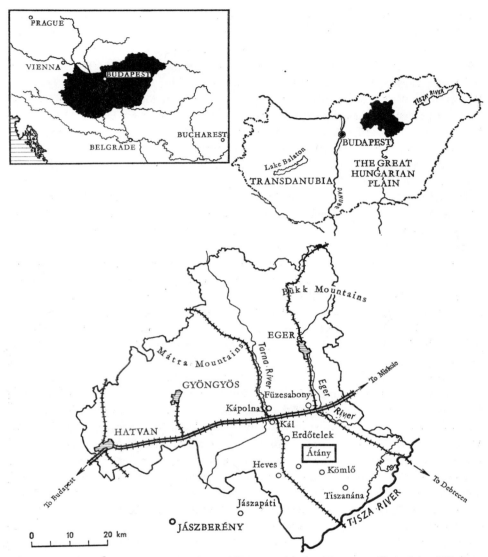

1. The location of Átány. (a) A map of part of Europe showing Hungary. (b) A map of Hungary showing Heves county. (c) A map of Heves county showing Átány, mountains and rivers, principal towns, some villages, and railroad lines in the neighborhood of Átány.

and their customs, attire, or dialect. Some groups consist of only five or six villages, others of as many as forty or fifty communities. Today north of Átány the name "Palóc" is used to refer to the population of three counties, which include several hundred villages speaking North Hungarian dialects; the word is partly the term for a regional group and partly a nickname. At the beginning of the last century only the peasants living around the Mátra mountains were called by this name. Again, the

3

term "Matyó" refers to the peasant population of the borough Mezőkövesd. From the latter half of the last century they have become known all over the country for their especially colorful attire and embroidery. They were well known to the Átány folk, because the latter frequently went to the Mezőkövesd fairs. The settlements of Jazygia (Jászság) to the southwest are bound together by different ties. The Jazygians, along with the Comans, migrated to Hungary in the thirteenth century and were a fragment of a nomadic people of the steppe driven west by the Mongolians. As early as the Middle Ages they were amalgamated with the Hungarians. Later, owing to flights and immigrations during the wars of the sixteenth and seventeenth centuries, their descendants became mixed with the population of other Hungarian regions. After the wars, however, the administrative boundaries of the former Jazygian settlements were restored, establishing a privileged district for the new mixed population. The consciousness of their common heritage and privileges unites the Jazygians even today; they are acknowledged by the people of Átány as superior in agriculture and handicrafts.

Átány does not belong to any of these ethnic, cultural, or geographical groupings. Geographers include the village in "the Tarna region" (referring to the Tarna River), but this is purely an artificial definition. Thus, when introducing themselves, the people of the village mention no regional unit smaller than Heves county; at the most they may allude to the Heves district, an administrative subdivision of the county. Átány is similar to its neighbors, as we shall see, but at the same time is clearly distinguishable from all of them.

Of Hungary's nearly 3,300 settlements, 63 were classified as cities and some 3,200 as villages by the government in 1960. Villages may be of widely differing sizes: 45 per cent have a population under 1,000, many with but a few hundred inhabitants, while the remainder are almost equally divided between the categories "1,000–2,000" and "over 2,000."[2] Large and small villages are not distributed evenly over the country. In Transdanubia and in the northern Highlands the network of settlements is denser but the villages are small. On the other hand, very populous settlements are typical of the Great Plain. The best example for this structure of settlements is Békés county. In 1930, in an area of 640,000 hectares there were only 28 communities with an average population of 11,800 and an average area of 22,840 hectares.[3] The phenomenon of settlement in numerous distinct small villages, typical of the other Hungarian regions, is also found in neighboring regions of Central and Eastern Europe. The settlement pattern of the Great Plain, however, is unique.

It was brought about by particular historical circumstances. The Turkish wars of the sixteenth and seventeenth centuries and the prolonged Turkish occupation of a large part of the Great Plain (to be discussed in connection with the history of Átány) annihilated the medieval network of small villages in this area. The diminished population resorted to larger, and therefore safer, settlements as a means of survival. Later, after the expulsion of the Turks, the eighteenth-century resettlement also pro-

---

[2] Radó, 1963: 62.
[3] Warriner, 1939: 114.

moted large aggregations. As the amount of land tilled increased, thousands of abodes (simple structures for the protection of people and draught animals) were constructed in the wide fields of the villages. Beginning in the nineteenth century, these gradually became places of continuous residence. So the characteristic settlement of the Great Plain is the giant village or peasant city, surrounded by an extensive circle of several thousand *tanya*-s, isolated units of human dwelling.[4] A considerable part of the population, sometimes almost 50 per cent of the inhabitants, used to live in these *tanya*-s.

Átány lies at the border of the region of settlements typical of the Great Plain. It belongs to an area of transition where the number of the inhabitants and the extent of their fields are intermediate between the tiny villages of the northern Highlands and the "peasant cities" of the Plain. In the last one hundred years the number of its population has fluctuated between 2,600 and 3,000, with a territory *(határ)* of 9,172 *hold*-s (13,024 acres).

The same regional features and historical developments which created the special pattern of settlement of the Great Plain also endowed its rural society and culture with special characteristics. Its economy is predominantly agricultural. Here we find the largest proportion of the country's plowland and the largest share of its wheat and maize production. The amount of livestock is below the national average; there are few cattle, but the number of horses and pigs is significant. Naturally one may find regional differences within the Great Plain too: e.g., the central Tisza region is the center of wheat production; during the last decades the territory between the Danube and the Tisza developed a thriving production of fruit and wine in its sandy soil; horticulture is prevalent along the Danube, etc. As a whole, however, the Great Plain is characterized by a less intensive agricultural economy than other regions; it still produces the bulk of the country's wheat and maize and most of its agricultural exports.

The techniques of this agriculture spread all over this region with the settlement of *tanya*-s. During the eighteenth century, when the central tracts of the land were repopulated following a long period of war and devastation, a new, common culture grew up with amazing rapidity among settlers of widely differing origins. In the formation of the new "peasant culture of the Great Plain" the primary influence was from those old Hungarian peasant towns which had managed to preserve both their populations and the age-old traditions characteristic of the region during the Turkish wars. The methods of herding and cereal crop production, both widely prevalent in the Plain, the physical arrangement of the villages, the types of houses, and the costumes were all similar throughout the Great Plain.[5] This "lowland culture" (consisting of agricultural techniques, methods of farm management, forms of architecture, attire, etc.) spread so rapidly that by the beginning

---

[4] István Györffy, 1943: 49–77; Mendöl, 1943; Den Hollander, 1960–1961.

[5] Immediately after the Turks were expelled there occurred a simultaneous migration of Hungarians from the densely populated neighboring northern region, as well as from the western regions, to the sparsely populated fertile areas of the Great Plain. The period of migration also brought some foreign groups (German and Slovakian) to the Great Plain. These people were assimilated to the way of life and material circumstances of the Great Plain but preserved the ethos of their old tradition.

3*

of the twentieth century elements of it had penetrated into the dales and downs of the surrounding hill country, and even into the settlements of neighboring ethnic groups.

The peasant cities had a more lively economic life than the tiny villages; the production of goods for the market was rooted in an old tradition, and economic and social stratification was further advanced and more emphasized. In the eighteenth century, as the system of serfdom was re-established in the areas reconquered from the Turks, the peasant towns could defend their autonomy better than could the villages. Several peasant towns managed to revive their traditional privileges; others converted their feudal obligations into the payment of an annual rent in money, thereby escaping immediate seignorial jurisdiction. In the Great Plain the feudal estate had relatively little power, compared to its influence in the country as a whole, and a well-to-do "*civis* peasant" stratum—a developing bourgeoisie—grew up in the peasant towns. Likewise, cultural change in the peasant towns occurred at a more rapid rate. While the lowland type of peasant costume was maintained in the bordering areas, the people of the peasant towns began to adopt bourgeois styles. Thus Átány, being a village on the periphery of the Great Plain, preserves a local variety of the "lowland peasant culture" which is more traditional than that of the giant villages. For example, ornamental pieces of furniture with painted flowers were not manufactured in the towns later than the 1850–60s, whereas in Átány a bride still received a painted chest of this type as her trousseau at the turn of the century. As late as 1951 similar painted pieces of furniture could occasionally be seen in Átány houses.

The economy and the culture of Átány are unambiguously rooted in the Great Plain. However, the larger administrative unit, Heves county, is only partially included in this region; its northern half is situated in the mountains. Although the county has long been an administrative unit, it is not a geographical one. The county seat, Eger (pop. 42,000), which lies at the foot of the Bükk mountains, is one of the most important towns in the life of Átány. Its fortress was one of the keystones of the defense against the Turks; it is the seat of a Roman Catholic archbishopric; and due to its schools and colleges, it is a significant cultural center. When the railroads were constructed, however, Eger was bypassed by the main line, and its industrial development has been rather slow; thus its earlier leading role in the northern mountain district has been considerably impaired by the rise of new industrial centers. The other city in the county, Gyöngyös (pop. 31,000), which lies at the foot of the Mátra mountains, is also a storehouse for the memory of a rich civic past. Its industry, however, like Eger's, is weak, and it is connected to the main railroad only by a branch line.

The main railroad line mentioned above connects Budapest and Miskolc. Both cities are well known to the Átány folk; they traveled to the Pest fairs during the last century, and from the turn of the century it offered them the most opportunities to get seasonal and even permanent work outside the village. Also, the tendency in emigration is primarily toward the capital. Miskolc, the rapidly developing industrial city of the northern region (pop. 175,000), also provides jobs for the people of Átány.

The nearest station on the Budapest–Miskolc railway line, Kál-Kápolna, is 16 kilometers from Átány. There one may take the southeast branch line as far as the town of Heves. Heves (pop. 11,500) is the seat of the district, the immediate administrative superior of Átány, and is useful to the people of the village in many ways outside the official connection. The Átány folk sell their goods in its market, purchase in its shops, and place orders with its craftsmen.

Átány is only 7 kilometers from Heves. This distance may be traveled by bus, bus service having increased continuously over the last twenty years. The bus enters Átány by the "Bodi road" and stops in front of the town hall, not far from the church. The visitor alighting here finds himself in the center of the village; in the old days the community meetings were held here, and from here the roads of the village radiate.

THE PAST

The first appearance of the name "Átány" occurs in a document dated 1407,[6] but the village may have existed long before this time. Today the community occupies the same site on which it was constructed by its medieval founders. If a pole is set up for electric wires, or the foundations of a house are dug in the center of the village, near the church, the spade often turns up bones from the graves of the medieval cemetery. Even today it is evident from the landscape why the founders had chosen this site. The spot occupied by the village is the highest in the vicinity and therefore the most protected from inundation. (A considerable part of the Great Plain as well as the majority of the territory of Átány was exposed to recurrent floods until the control of the riverways and inland drainage executed in the last half of the nineteenth century.) In the old days, the situation of Átány had another advantage too. The so-called "Great Road," the most important highway leading from Pest[7] to Debrecen and Transylvania, passed close by the community. Old people of Átány still remember that before the railway lines were constructed in the early and mid-nineteenth century, the villagers used to cart goods between Debrecen and Pest. In the eighteenth century the chief mail line (by means of stagecoaches which also carried people) between Pest and Transylvania had a relay station at Átány.

Except for its name, its site, and a part of its population, has Átány inherited anything from the centuries of its past? The sparse medieval data do not reveal any features that might distinguish it from other Hungarian villages. In general, its story was probably similar to that of other communities of the region.

Half-nomadic Hungarians entered the Carpathian Basin from the direction of the steppes of southern Russia in A.D. 896. A century later, in 1000, Stephen, the son of their pagan tribal leader, was crowned as a Christian king and the adoption of the Christian faith accelerated the process of assimilation to the neighboring peoples,

---

[6] As far as we know, this is the earliest documentary evidence mentioning Átány (Dezső Csánki, 1890–1913). However, the network of villages in this region was already well developed in the tenth and eleventh centuries, according to Gy. Györffy (1959), *Az Árpádkori Magyarország Történeti Földrajza (The Historical Geography of Hungary in the Árpádian Age,* vol. *II.* [in preparation]).

[7] Pest and Buda were separate cities in the Middle Ages, united in 1873.

settlement in permanent abodes, and the transformation of the people into land-cultivating peasants. The influence of the ancient half-nomadic way of life, however, was felt for a long time, especially in the Great Plain. As late as the twelfth and thirteenth centuries the villages of the Plain consisted of only a few houses, and moved about frequently. Archeological research on this period has uncovered mainly one-room dwellings, partly dug into the earth, which would be lived in for about six to eight years, after which the inhabitants would move on.[8] At this time the people occupied numerous different social and legal statuses and engaged in various types of economic activity. It was not until the thirteenth and fourteenth centuries that the various groups of free people and servants were amalgamated into the unitary class of serfs and the class of nobles took shape.[9]

At this time the serfs' way of life was agricultural, they lived in permanent villages, and the land they tilled was owned by the king, the church, or a member of the landed gentry. The serfs' use of the soil was regulated by the system of *telek*-s *(mansio, fundus, sessio)*. The *telek* consisted of a plot in the interior of the village, where the house stood, and to it was attached the right to a share in the plowland, the meadow, the common pasture, and the forest. Throughout the country the concept of the *telek* became the standard of a peasant's land holdings. The size of this unit was predetermined, though it varied from region to region. Through inheritance it was often divided into smaller parts.[10] For the use of the *telek*, the serf owed the landlord feudal services. Taxes and obligations demanded by church and state were also based on the *telek*. By the fourteenth century the system of these dues became more uniform, some being regulated by statute. Over the whole country the church exacted a tithe of the grain, wine, lambs, and even the new beehives, and the landlord took the ninth part of the residue. Aside from these, the landlord demanded various "gifts" in kind and "census" in money and also had the right to call a corvée of manual labor or draft animals. The serfs had to pay in money direct taxes to the state and war subsidies, almost continually levied from the fifteenth century. The lawsuits of the serf were decided by the seignorial court, attended by a representative of the county, which was the administrative organization of the gentry.

Átány was one of several thousand villages inhabited by serfs in this period. The oldest sources mention it as a member of a dominion of more than one hundred villages owned by aristocratic families and high dignitaries of the country.[11]

Elements of this system of serfdom have influenced the life of Átány for almost five hundred years: the *telek* system, the limitation of land rights by the jurisdiction of the lord, and the feudal dues and taxes. A prominent part has been played by the

[8] Méri, 1952–1954; Makkai, 1958: 64–68; Váczy, 1958.

[9] Szabó, 1940, 1965.

[10] The serf society embraced also the *zsellér*-s, who did not own a *telek*, though they were not necessarily excluded from the use of land. According to a settlement reached in the second half of the eighteenth century, the category of *zsellér*-s contained all villagers living under the jurisdiction of a landlord who lacked any land or owned less than one-eighth of a *telek*. From their earliest appearance, the *zsellér*-s were mainly people who earned their living as hired labor. Szabó (1963) assessed the proportion of *zsellér*-s at 20 to 30 per cent of the serfs during the fifteenth and sixteenth centuries.

[11] Soós, n.d.: 84–85.

village government, which was sometimes an organ of rural self-government and sometimes an instrument of state and manorial administration, depending on the circumstances of a given period.

In the history of Átány we have been unable to document the social movements of the peasantry in the fourteenth and fifteenth centuries. There is little local evidence concerning the attempts of the peasantry to raise and improve its position by acquiring new privileges and the countermeasures of the landlords, or concerning the bloodily suppressed great peasant revolt of 1514. The severe statutes passed after this revolt was crushed deprived the serfs of the right to change their residence, completely bound them to the soil, and tightened the hold of the manorial jurisdiction on villages all over the country, including Átány. Thus the peasants' condition was already deteriorating when, soon after the suppression of the rebellion, an even darker shadow fell on them—the Turkish wars.

In 1526, following a century of defensive wars, the Hungarian army suffered a crushing defeat, including the death of their king at the hands of the Osmanli Turks at Mohács. In 1541 Buda, the capital, fell into the hands of the Turks. Two years later the first Turkish troops passed near Átány. In 1548 the village and all the surrounding region surrendered to the Turks and began to pay tribute to them. In the following decades the population was decimated year by year by pillaging armies marching through. In one generation the population of Heves county was reduced to one-third of its former size. The people of some villages were killed or dragged away into servitude; others fled before the Turks. Their heavy taxation became another incentive to flight. The Turkish Empire allotted the villages in fief for a limited time to military officers, who endeavored to squeeze the largest possible income out of them in the shortest possible time. The people of Átány fled several times, leaving the village uninhabited, but later returned to their former home.[12]

The history of Átány during this period is elucidated by the rolls of the Hungarian royal tithe collectors. In fact, the jurisdiction of the Hungarian state, the county, and the landlords over the territory subdued by the Turks did not cease, though their functioning was impaired. Soldiers of the Hungarian border fortresses even traveled hundreds of kilometers in the area controlled by the Turks in order to collect taxes. Nor did the feudal dues fall into abeyance, though they often decreased to token payments. Eger, the seat of Heves county, fell in 1596; county authorities, however, continued to function outside their former territory. Peasants of the county brought their lawsuits to temporary county seats, since statutes imposed severe penalties on those Hungarians who dared to sue their adversaries before the Turkish courts in the captured territory.

If the people of Átány want to explain the antiquated character of some of their customs or the old-fashioned disorderly layout of the village, they often allude to the fact that they are "an old community," one of only three villages in the region that managed to survive "the Tartarian and the Turkish wars." All of the other commu-

---

[12] Soós, 1955.

nities are later settlements. Everyone knows the story of the young woman who saved the village. According to the legend, the Turks pitched their tents in the neighborhood of Átány and their leader caught a glimpse of the pastor's wife. He sent a message to the villagers that if she would come to him in the camp, he would spare the community; otherwise he would destroy it. The pastor's wife was unwilling to go and the villagers unwilling to allow her; however, a young woman of similar appearance offered to go to the camp, wearing the robe of the pastor's wife. It is also alleged that she bore a son to the Turk. Some purport to know that this boy, having come to age, migrated to Turkey with the whip his father left behind. According to others, his descendants are the family called Török (Turk) who live in the village to this day.

During the Turkish period, judging from the tithe conscriptions,[13] Átány possessed an exceedingly numerous and constant population compared to other villages, more resistant to the dangers, threats, and catastrophes of the age. To a certain extent the village even benefited by the ruin of the neighboring settlements. It is recorded, for example, that in 1672 the Átány folk harvested more wheat and barley on the land of Kömlő, a devastated neighboring village, than in their own fields.[14]

During the Turkish era two important changes were effected in the life of Átány, and their impact is still felt, contributing special features to the character of the village. The first is the fact that in the mid-sixteenth century Átány, together with the Hungarian people of the neighboring Great Plain, adopted Calvinism.[15] This was typical of the population of the region, but when the Counter Reformation and the villages which arose in the eighteenth century changed the surrounding population to an overwhelmingly Catholic one, Átány remained Protestant. Thus the Calvinist church has become a most important distinguishing feature of the village. Not only is Calvinism noticeable in the puritan moral attitude and world view of the village, but it also brought the community into contact with a particular system of societal relations and a particular cultural tradition. When thousands of peasant families migrated to the Great Plain after its liberation from the Turks, only members of the Reformed Church settled in Átány; the Catholics marched further. Marriage ties outside the village and the resulting bonds of kinship and friendship connect Átány with the Protestant villages of the neighborhood. The cultural tradition centered in the convents and schools of Eger, the seat of the Catholic archbishopric, spread the religious practices of the Counter Reformation and the Baroque style of art to the Catholic communities; but Átány maintained its participation in the Calvinist system of churches, schools, and cultural intercourse, with Sárospatak as its center.

The other important change was the appearance of a class of nobles in the Átány population. In the county assembly of 1658 the Lord Lieutenant of Heves county

---

[13] In the Hungarian National Archives, Budapest. Some tithe conscriptions relating to Átány have been published by N. Kiss (1960).

[14] Balássy and Szederkényi, 1890–1897: III, 337.

[15] Protestant preachers were active in Eger from 1540 and in the peasant towns of the Great Plain, south of Átány, from 1545 (Révész, 1938: 72, 132, etc.). The earliest document on the Reformed Church of Átány is the record of a canonical visitation held in 1596—evidence for the long-standing existence of Calvinism in the village.

protested that Átány, claiming personal privilege of nobles for its inhabitants, had neglected to pay tithes for years on shallow legal grounds.[16] These "petty nobles" were not landowners; they lived on peasant *telek*-s owned by distant landlords and performed the services and paid the state taxes on these *telek*-s while they enjoyed the personal privilege due to nobles. They were exempt from personal taxes and services as well as from the jurisdiction of the manorial court; their rights were safeguarded by the county, which used to include them in its yearly assemblies. The Átány people relate that in the first half of the last century, when men were recruited to the army by force, a bachelor who fled to the court of a noble escaped recruitment, since soldiers and police were barred from following him there. A judicial record of the eighteenth century reveals that the Átány postmaster, flying into a violent rage, attacked the village mayor, who was a serf, with a stick. When a nobleman stepped in front of the mayor, the postmaster did not dare to touch him but had to try to reach the mayor over the nobleman's shoulder.[17]

The "Tripartitum," the very influential Hungarian lawbook written in 1514 (after the peasant revolt was crushed), divided the population into two categories, noblemen and serfs, making an exception only of the citizens of fortified privileged cities and of the clergy. The burdens and duties of the serfs were standardized through the country. At the same time, the lawbook proclaimed the principle that all nobles enjoyed the same degree of privilege *(una eademque libertas)*. Though the following centuries adhered to this principle, within the nobility clear-cut strata were distinguishable. At the top there were the "magnates," proprietors of huge domains and holders of the high offices of the country; from 1608 on, they deliberated separately at the Upper Table of the feudal assembly. Next followed the members of the "landed gentry," who owned medium-sized estates, one or two villages, or even only a few *telek*-s. At the bottom was the widest stratum of the noble society, the "petty gentry." The members of this stratum were nobles who possessed but one *telek* (or a fragment of one); they tilled its land themselves and did not rule over any serfs. One finds numerous villages in Hungary which are inhabited exclusively by such "petty nobles." Others of the "petty gentry" lacked even a single *telek;* having no possession, such people lived and farmed on *telek*-s owned by other nobles and were subject to feudal services and taxes; they enjoyed noble privileges of their persons only. They occupied an ambiguous position between nobility and serfdom, and for this reason some official records used to call them "half-nobles."[18]

This populous stratum of nobles who worked the land is a special feature of Hun-

---

[16] Balássy and Szederkényi, 1890–1897: III, 305–306.

[17] Eger State Archives, Civil Proceedings, 1736: 163.

[18] The Hungarian gentry was very numerous compared with that of the other European countries. At the beginning of the nineteenth century there was one noble for every twenty non-nobles in Hungary, whereas in France this ratio was 1 : 180, in Bohemia 1 : 828. On the other hand, the Polish gentry was even more populous than the Hungarian, with a proportion of 1 : 10. In the mid-nineteenth century the census recorded 136,093 noble households, of which about 100,000 owned only a single *telek*, or none, and thus did not rule over serfs. In Ugocsa county, for example, 304 of the 400 noble families lacked serfs. According to a comprehensive estimate, only 25 to 30 per cent of the Hungarian gentry owned land (Szabó, 1941). After the abolition of serfdom in the mid-nineteenth century, two estimates of the number of villages inhabited exclusively by petty nobles were 906 and 786, respec-

gary. It was made up of the people of those agricultural villages which managed to secure the privileges of nobles for themselves in the course of the great social changes of the thirteenth and fourteenth centuries. During the Turkish wars in the sixteenth and seventeenth centuries, they were joined by such serfs as were granted the title of nobility. The history of membership in the nobility could be ascertained for twelve Átány families.[19] Two of them have never been serfs, and derive from villages having an age-old nobility; ten of them were raised from the status of serfs by letters patent of nobility between 1609 and 1669. At this time a number of such letters patent were granted as rewards for military and other services, mainly to those people who lived in the territory subdued by the Turks.[20]

The "petty nobility" played a significant role as cultural mediators between the peasantry and the landed gentry. Most of them performed the same manual work as the serfs. This was true of the Átány nobles too: in 1828 Átány's 26 noble families owned only thirteen telek-s.[21] On the other hand, they took part in the administration and the political life of the county; some of them went to secondary school; and their attire, their manner, and sometimes also the design and furnishings of their houses followed the style of the nobility. Forms of greeting, address, polite behavior, Christian names, etc. in Átány frequently recall the culture of the landed gentry during the first half of the nineteenth century, as well as that of the "civis-peasant" strata of the populous peasant towns of the Great Plain. This may be explained by the presence of petty nobles in the community. Probably it was partly due to the privileged position of the petty gentry that the authority of the landlords weighed less heavily on Átány than on the neighboring villages.

Buda was recaptured by the Christian armies from the Turks in 1686; Eger was returned to the Hungarians in December, 1687. After 138 years of Turkish supremacy, Átány was uninhabited. In the entire Heves county, where there were more than two hundred villages in the sixteenth century, only one village was still inhabited at this time. The peasants sought refuge in the forests, in the flood plains of the rivers, in the cities, and in more distant regions.[22]

After the expulsion of the Turks, peace was still not restored for many years.

---

tively, out of the ca. 9,200 communities of the Hungarian territory at that time. On the basis of their way of life, these petty nobles, or the overwhelming majority of them at least, could be regarded as peasants. The society of noble villages was characterized by a polarization more pronounced than in the serf communities generally: the majority of the inhabitants became impoverished more rapidly; at the other extreme, families amassed more than the average amount of land more quickly (Für, 1965: 55–57; István Orosz, 1965: 100–107).

[19] Endre Orosz, 1939.

[20] This is related to the special double administration of the area. In the peace treaty of 1606 the Turks agreed to respect the exemption from taxes of the Hungarian nobles in the territories occupied by them. Thus the serf living under Turkish rule had much to gain by acquiring noble privileges. The king was willing to ennoble serfs living under alien rule in a far-away part of the land, since the taxes which he resigned by granting the privilege were not very certain anyway. This granting of large numbers of letters patent irritated the Turks, who lodged an energetic protest against it at the renewed peace talks in 1642 (Makkai, 1958).

[21] The "Conscriptio Regnicolaris," the national census of 1828. Hungarian National Archives, Budapest.

[22] Soós, 1955: 6–7.

Skirmishes of the fight for national independence, led by Ferenc Rákóczi (1703–1711), swept over this region several times.[23]

The people returned to Átány in 1695. Soon a considerable number of new settlers joined them. After the expulsion of the Turks, peasants from all over Hungary set out on a large-scale migration toward the almost uninhabited areas of the center. In the northern and western parts of the country the landlords and the county administrations soon became anxious about the emigration of their serf population and endeavored to regain the peasant families which had left their estates. Generally their efforts failed, but the records reveal interesting data on the migration of serfs. We are informed by one of them, for example, that from the northern county of Gömör alone, fifteen families joined the ranks of immigrants to Átány between 1705 and 1720.[24]

From the 1730s on, the spontaneous movement of the peasants was followed by the planned action of the large estates, which enlisted groups of new inhabitants by contract. The settlement was directed by three mighty landholders: the archbishopric of Eger, the collegiate church of the same city, and the Count Grassalkovich. Their actions brought Catholics exclusively to this area, including the vicinity of Átány. In several communities the landlords removed the Protestant inhabitants and replaced them with Catholics. In this way the region assumed a new composition during the eighteenth century that was quite different from both the devastated period after the expulsion of the Turks and the medieval period that preceded it. Within a radius of twenty to thirty kilometers from Átány there were eight or ten medieval settlements which had not been rebuilt. Some of the ancient settlements were revived under the great landholders—not as villages, however, but as manorial granges. (One of these is Szárazbő, a locality within the administrative boundaries of Átány where noble families of minor possessions founded seven granges near their estates.[25])

The Reformed Church was merely "tolerated" by the statutes of the eighteenth century; its functions were limited, while the Catholic Church enjoyed a privileged, advantageous position. Seizures of Protestant churches, and harassment of Protestant ministers and schoolmasters remained a source of grief for most of the century.[26]

[23] From the middle of the sixteenth century the Kingdom of Hungary and Austria were connected by a personal union. The Hapsburg ruler, Emperor of the Holy Roman Empire and King of Hungary, held his seat in Vienna. Revolts and movements for national independence broke out against the Vienna government (which had surrendered Hungarian interests to those of the dynasty and the Austrian territory) as early as the era of the Turkish wars and the decades following their expulsion from Hungary.

[24] Eger State Archives, Administrative Records, 1695: 89; 1721: 58.

[25] In the eighteenth century a considerable part of the rural population of Heves county consisted of tenants on the manors of the landlords and laborers employed on estates. Some of the latter were true servants, but others were peasants who were granted plots from the manors by personal contract. Thus they became exempt from state taxation because they owned no *telek*-s, but the landlord could demand more service from them in its stead. Later a considerable number of the manorial settlements were transformed into villages, and their inhabitants were classified as serfs (Soós, 1955: 16–17).

[26] The harassment of the Protestants ceased with the "Tolerance Patent" *(Edictum tolerantiae)* of Joseph II, issued in 1781. This did not, however, grant full equality of rights to the Protestant persuasions; for example, a Protestant church was not allowed to have a door opening to the street even after the patent. But it permitted the founding of new congregations and the building of new churches. It was in this period that the Átány Reformed Church, after a series of petitions, was given the opportunity to enlarge. The tablet commemorating Joseph II may still be found in the building.

In 1765 the people of Átány were forced to defend their church against the mighty bishop of Eger, Lord Lieutenant of Heves county, when he came in person to seize it for the Catholics. The protests against the oppressive, anti-Protestant policy of the Hapsburgs often gained inspiration from the struggle for national independence, and especially from the memory of the freedom revolts of the seventeenth and early eighteenth centuries, which were fought for both national and religious liberty at the same time.[27]

As the region became repopulated and the economy began to thrive, the ties of serfdom were re-established gradually. The *telek* organization had deteriorated during the centuries of war. Arable land was used by the peasants on the principle of free occupation or on the basis of periodical division by the village authorities. Instead of the *telek*-s, lots were meted out in proportion to the number of oxen owned by each family, as an indication of the ability of each family to till the soil. From the end of the sixteenth century the corvée and, a few decades later, even a part of the state taxes were assessed in proportion to the number of oxen. Thus a peasant who lost his oxen was deprived of his right to the soil, but at the same time his services were lessened.[28]

For several decades after the expulsion of the Turks the manors increased the burdens of the serfs very cautiously for fear of losing the recently settled population. Seignorial domestic economies, destroyed during the Turkish occupation, were gradually reconstructed. The establishment and extension of these manors had a strong impact on the life of the villages. The area of the manorial farms was continually increased at the expense of peasant farmland. In addition, the duties of the serfs were increased in order to provide more labor, more corvée, for the tilling of manorial lands.

The fate of individual peasant villages depended largely on who the landlord exercising jurisdiction over them was and how energetically he exacted his dues from them. In this respect Átány was more fortunate than most of the neighboring villages.

The large domain of which Átány was a part in the sixteenth century had been partitioned by inheritance during the Turkish occupation and by the end of this period Átány itself was divided among five families. None of them lived in the village. Not

---

[27] This dual struggle is illustrated by the spontaneous peasant upheaval of 1753, which blazed forth in two large Protestant "peasant towns" of the Great Plain, Mezőtúr and Hódmezővásárhely, against the Hapsburg government, and failed soon thereafter due to lack of organization. One of the incidents behind the upheaval was the arrest of the Reformed preacher of Mezőtúr and the harassment of the church, but the peasants took to arms with slogans of national independence.

In this period Heves county, along with Szolnok county (on the Tisza), was administered from Eger, the two being governed as a single county. Mezőtúr, one of the focuses of the movement, belonged to this county. As was typical of the period the news of the movement resulted in an inquisition by the sub-prefect of the county at Átány, which was one of the wealthiest and most significant Protestant parishes of the county. After the pastor had been subjected to a rude inquiry, the two flags and drum, bought by the Átány church for the school "in order to make the children more inclined to frequent it," were confiscated, though the sub-prefect admitted himself that they did not serve the aims of war (Wellmann, 1952; Eger State Archives, Administrative Records, 1753: 148; Assembly Journals, 1754: 254).

[28] Soós, n.d.: 9–10, 19; Juhász, 1936: 69–71, 74–79.

until the middle of the eighteenth century did a landlord live in the community, and
then only for a few decades; he was the owner of a small fragment of the area and the
master of few serfs. Hardly any of the Átány fields were administered under seignorial
domestic economy; in 1848, at the abolition of serfdom, only 214 *hold*-s (ca. 304 acres)
out of an area of 9,172 *hold*-s were used by the landlords. Átány's lords also possessed
lands in the neighboring villages of Heves and Erdőtelek, and it was there that they
established their manorial farms. The serfs and *zsellér*-s of Átány had to travel to
these places for their corvée. The landowners did not want to increase the income
from their portions of Átány by placing their lands under manorial management;
they preferred to allow the expansion of peasant holdings and the founding of additional *telek*-s so they could demand more corvée, more rents in kind, and other
services. Each lord possessed a stackyard in the village, where his serfs had to bring
the "ninth part" of their cereal produce.

The court rolls of Heves county have preserved complaints from the Átány peasants
protesting the forcible acts of their lords[29] and the excessive services, on the one hand,
and the burden of state taxation, on the other.[30] But in spite of this, owing to the lack
of expansion of seignorial domestic economy, the arable land of the Átány *jobbágy*-s
(serfs) increased to a degree which was almost unparalleled in the county.[31] Under
these favorable circumstances there was a constant increase in the population of the
community. According to the register of 1778–79, Átány was one of the most populous
villages in the southern part of Heves county.

At the beginning of the eighteenth century the possession and authority of the
Átány coproprietors was defined only vaguely. From the 1730s on, the landlords of
an increasing number of villages agreed to partition the whole area of their holdings,
and they subjected all the serfs on these lands to their immediate seignorial jurisdiction. In 1743 the coproprietors of Átány also reached such an agreement. They did
not actually make physical divisions in the *határ*, however. So the individual landlords
had less occasion to interfere directly in the lives of their serfs, and the use of
the *határ* remained a unified system under the control of the Átány self-government.[32]

Between 1767 and 1772 a national standardization of serfdom took place. In the
face of resistance from the gentry and the county administrations, the royal government pushed through the regulation in a desire to make *telek*-s uniform throughout
the land and to preserve them from the encroachments of the landlords. The government was interested in keeping intact the *telek*-s since state taxation was based on

[29] Eger State Archives, Assembly Journals of Heves county, 1711: 50; 1712: 146; 1716: 859;
1718: 1012; 1770: 541; etc.

[30] In the eighteenth century the heaviest state burden on the peasants was the obligation to provide
sustenance and transport for the numerous troops stationed in the villages. We know of several
Átány complaints of peasant teams being ruined by doing cartage for the army. Cf. the data of
J. Varga in Spira, 1952: 49–76.

[31] For a comparison we include the proportion of the lands of landlords and peasants in the two
neighboring villages in which the majority of the Átány landlords based their manorial economies.
At Heves there were 1,730 *hold*-s of peasant plowland against 8,317 *hold*-s of the landlords in the
year 1788; and at Erdőtelek the ratio was 1,708 to 2,997 (Soós, n.d.: 4–5).

[32] Soós, n.d.: 84–88.

them. The ordinance also standardized the obligations of *jobbágy*-s to their lords.[33]
In 1771 a nation-wide census recorded 40 $^1/_8$ *telek*-s in the hands of 77 families at
Átány, as well as 53 *zsellér*-s who did not own any *telek*.

In spite of the regulation of 1767–1772, during the following decades serfs in
numerous villages lost a considerable amount of land. In the course of the redistribution of the fields their plowlands were exchanged for lands of a worse quality; in
places the number of *telek*-s was decreased. Although at Átány there was an opposite
trend in that the number of *telek*-s became larger, the growing number of *telek*-s was
surpassed by the increase of population. When serfdom was abolished in 1848, the
Átány peasants possessed 86 *telek*-s instead of their former 40, but these holdings
were partitioned among 203 families, and there were also 225 *zsellér* households with
no *telek* at all.[34] Thus the division of the *telek*-s was accelerated and the landless
stratum of laborers became more numerous.

The revolutionary movement resulting in the statutory abolition of serfdom began
on March 15, 1848, in Pest, prompted by the news of the revolutions of Paris and
Vienna. On the day of the upheaval a fair was being held in Pest. According to local
tradition, Átány people were among those present at the fair, and they took home
firsthand news of the impending changes to their village. After a few weeks the Átány
jobbágy-s (serfs), according to their descendants, were working on the spring plowing
of the landlord's fields in Heves, fulfilling their corvée, when they received the news
that this obligation had been abolished. They ceased work at once and returned home
with kerchiefs tied to their prods.

In effect, the system of serfdom was abolished by reform from above. The land
which the peasants had used in return for services became their own. However, the
numerous *zsellér*-s with or without houses remained deprived of land even after the
liberation of the serfs. The statutes of 1848 were put into effect over several years,
but this long process did not alter the fact that the agricultural area of the country
consisted of much-divided peasant holdings and large seignorial manors or estates.
In the course of the settlement of property relations, the peasant fields became somewhat smaller and the large estates were increased still more. (In the Átány *határ* the
peasants lost 800 *hold*-s, i.e. 1,136 acres.) About half of the agricultural area of the
country was peasant property; the other half was the land of "gentlemen." One-third
of the total was made up of latifundia greater than 1,000 *hold*-s (1,420 acres). Instead
of benefiting from the servile corvée, these great estates now had to hire labor.

The system of serfdom of the eighteenth and early nineteenth centuries, regulated
by uniform statutes and ordinances throughout the country, left a lasting influence

---

[33] According to the ordinance, a serf who owned a whole *telek* was bound to the corvée once
a week with a team or twice with manual labor. He also had to give a ninth of his grain, his new
hives, lambs, flax, and hemp, and a house tax of one *forint*. Further, he was obliged to "make presents" to the lord: two hens, two capons, twelve eggs, one *icce* (i.e., one-fifth of a gallon) of butter;
and for every thirty *telek*-s, the village had to contribute a calf. The service due on a fragment of
a whole *telek* was proportionally less. The *zsellér* owed one *forint* as a house tax too, besides eighteen
days of manual labor a year. The houseless *zsellér* (living with another peasant) owed twelve days
of manual labor a year.

[34] Soós, n.d.: 114–115.

on the life of the village, an influence which in some respects is felt to this day. This system interfered with the hitherto customary manner of division and tillage of the fields. Not only was the serf obliged to give up the "ninth part" of the produce of his *telek* to the lord, but also the kinds of produce he could raise were more or less defined in a three-stage rotation system of agriculture. In the eighteenth century this system and manorial jurisdiction over the peasants were instituted in Átány at the same time. The obligatory crop rotation regulated the proportion of each type of crop raised and established a common rhythm in the sequence of agricultural labor for the whole community. Land transactions were permissible only in terms of the *telek* and fractions thereof. The order of inheritance and opportunities for social mobility were regulated by this system too. The stratification by property could also be expressed in terms of the *telek*. Accordingly, there were *telek*-owner serfs (in Átány this included having anywhere from $1/4$ to $1^1/_2$ *telek*-s), and there were *zsellér*-s, who had no land but possessed a house and the right to a share in the communal pasture, and finally *zsellér*-s without a house. The people of a village had to perform agricultural labor as a group on occasion to fulfill their duties and services, and they had to follow detailed prescriptions for ordering the affairs of the village. So the feudal system of the eighteenth and nineteenth centuries regulated not only the relations of individual landlords to individual serfs, but also the inner order of the villages.

The peasant community structure was an important element of the system of serfdom. Serfs have always been regarded as members of such a community. The local administration was an executive organ of the manorial and state authorities but, within the limits of its legally well-established authority, could also function as an organ of peasant self-government to a certain extent.

The statutory abolition of serfdom altered the traditional order of life established during the long period of the serf system, but this change was gradual. Subsequent chapters of this study deal with these changes as they relate to the agriculture, family organization, stratification, community autonomy, and so forth of the recent past. The perspective of the antecedent background conditions thus goes as far back as the liberation of serfs.

THE APPEARANCE OF THE VILLAGE

Átány lies on a plain. In summer this plain is a mosaic of grain fields and plots of potatoes, sugar beets, and lucerne, interspersed with pastures and meadows. Only the lines of trees along the roads and a few sweep-pole wells rise above the straight line of the horizon. Northward one sees the bluish silhouette of the faraway Mátra and Bükk mountains.[35]

Roads lead to Átány from several directions. Two of them are macadam, the others

---

[35] The Átány people figure the exact north from the "Eger mountain." If they go out to the fields without a watch, they recognize noon by the fact that their shadows point directly toward that mountain.

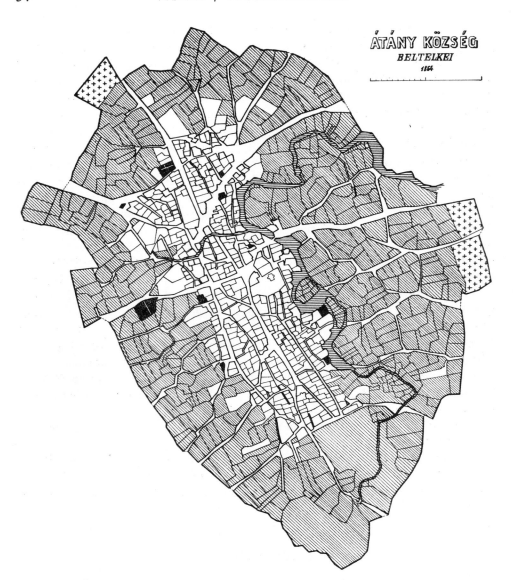

2. A map of Átány in 1864. The dwellings (white areas), situated in the center of the settlement, are surrounded by a wide, continuous belt of farm lots (hachures). The black areas indicate sheep folds in the possession of associations of *gazda*-s.

are dirt roads in which the cart wheels cut deep ruts in wet weather. The roads are lined on both sides by rows of acacias or mulberry trees. As one approaches the village, it appears in the distance as a silhouette made up of the crowns of trees and the roofs of houses, with the pointed spire of the stout church tower in the middle.

From whatever neighboring village the visitor may come, the way leads into the center of the settlement, where all the roads meet in a star. This place is the site of

3. A map of Átány in 1927. The area of the community is little larger than it was in 1864. In center of the village the buildings are still denser than in the old belt of *kert*-s, though an increasing number of houses appear in the outer ring. On the east and west edges of the village the building sites measured out in course of the 1920 agrarian reform are visible; and on some of these sites houses have been built.

the market where the community used to meet of old. The church, the town hall, the school, the rectory, and the post office are here. In the center, surrounded by a grove planted in 1896 to commemorate Hungary's millennial, stands the war memorial of the people of Átány who fell in World War I. The people of Átány describe the division of the village and its lands with reference to this center. The village is divided into the Upper End, *Felvég* (to the north), and the Lower End, *Alvég*, by the east-west

4

line highways leading to Heves and to Kömlő. Public buildings situated in the center are not included in this division. The church, for example, "could not be in any part of the village but in the center, as it belongs to the whole community."

Besides the clear-cut system of highways and roads leading out of the village, one finds an irregular and complicated network of smaller roads. It is by no means easy to find one's way. The roads leading to one of the neighboring villages are generally named after the place which may be reached by them: Egri (meaning "to Eger"), Bodi, Hevesi, Vezekényi, Kömlői, Szárazbői roads (see Plate 2). The names of the less important lanes, the köz-s, are rather uncertain; they are usually referred to by the name of some family living there who has kinship ties with the person speaking. As the wife of József Kakas explained to us: "I say, for instance, the köz of Mari Rózsa. This is significant for us as she is our relative. Other people may use the name of another." Some streets were given names by the village magistracy as early as 1894. In the 1950s all streets and köz-s were allotted new official names, but they are gaining ground rather slowly. The people of Átány get a good deal of enjoyment at the expense of strangers who lose their way in the confusing web of roads. They recall the answer of an Átány peasant to a man from neighboring Kömlő who had lost his way: "With us even the pigs are more clever than your people, as a piglet driven to the grazing field for three days finds its way home afterward, whereas you get lost, although you cross Átány many times."

Along the roads stand irregularly spaced houses, whitewashed one-story buildings with red-tiled or thatched roofs darkened by age. Near them are larger or smaller outbuildings: pigsties, poultry houses, stables, cart houses, and various sheds.

The tenements and yards of the interior of the village are quite different from those in the outer regions. Yards in the interior are narrow (see Plate 4), and some of the houses are not even fenced. In the outer regions the yards are more extensive, sometimes ten times as large as those of the interior. In 1951 there were still 87 tenements which contained only stables and small buildings associated with husbandry but no dwellings (see Plates 3 and 14). These separate farmyards were owned by peasants who lived in the interior of the village but had no farm buildings on their interior property.

In the 1930s many more families possessed dwelling houses and farmyards which were separated from each other. In 1864, when the first cadastral map of Átány was drawn up (see Fig. 2), this was the general system. The interior of the village was occupied only by dwellings, surrounded by an outer belt consisting of farmyards. In this outer region farmyards were owned by the pastor, the notary, most of the zsellér-s who lacked fields, and even by the community itself (stud animals belonging to the community as a whole were kept there).

Elderly Átány people remember a time when the houses in the interior of the village were still unfenced and there were no defined streets between them. "In dry weather people drove their carts across the flat places between the houses; in the muddy season they opened a way in the higher parts. There were roads everywhere." Pedestrians could move about even more freely. Leaving the church, the girls would stop and look around: "They were not looking for a street but for the straightest way home."

Even in those days the farmyards in the outer belt were already fenced in a traditional way: hedges, walls made of clay or dung, or ditches marked their boundaries. These outer farmyards are called in Hungarian *kert;* the word means a garden in the language of today, but originally it stood for "a fenced site." Between the *kert*-s the roads were wide, for flocks were driven to the pasture and back through them.

On the eastern side the *kert*-s were divided from the dwellings by a natural boundary, the Hanyi Brook. This is a slowly flowing stream which spreads out into small lakes in several places (see Plates 1 and 13). It is bordered by reeds, club rushes, and bushes, and the villagers' flocks of geese and ducks swim on its surface. The brook may be crossed by two bridges. (According to tradition, the one over which the Kömlő highway passes was built by the Turks. In 1944 the ancient stone bridge was destroyed by the war; a concrete bridge has been built in its stead.) Pedestrians may also cross the stream by means of several banks which have small covered openings through which the water flows. The narrower stretches of the brook may be crossed on foot by means of planks or boards.

The ancient structure of settlement not only defined the grouping of buildings and yards, but also specifically ordered the villagers' use of them. The activities of the families in the village were divided between the dwellings and the farmyards. Males were almost constantly bound to the stables by the work in the *kert*-s, especially the care and supervision of the livestock. The house was a place for women, children, and old people; the whole family assembled here only for meals and festive occasions. This system separated the economic roles in space, designating the *kert*-s as the sites of cultivation and stock raising; at the same time it separated the living and working areas of the sexes and generations. (For more detail, see Chapter 4, "The *Kert*.")

The ancient pattern of settlement presupposed a special system of ownership of lots and yards. Before the registration of land in 1864–1866, the interior of the village where the houses stood was practically a common property of the community. In those days "a person who wanted to build chose a site for himself saying: 'there is room for my house here,' and there he constructed it." Also at Átány is told the story, known all over the Great Plain, that a peasant built his house at the site where a brick happened to fall out of his cart. In a lawsuit of 1736 the witnesses from Átány testified that anyone was free to build a house on any unoccupied site in their village if the new construction did not come nearer than three steps to an existing one.[36] Thus the house someone constructed did not give the right of ownership over an area larger than a few steps around it, even for the time when the peasant actually occupied it; afterward the site became free again. In the fenced *kert*-s, property boundaries were fixed in a more permanent manner. However, in areas not yet occupied, especially along the brook, free occupation was possible as late as the middle of the last century.

In 1864, when the cadastral map was drawn up, many of the Átány people did not

[36] Eger State Archives, Administrative Records, 1736: 57.

4*

understand that the interior would henceforth be divided into lots owned by single peasants and separated by fixed boundaries. When the engineer asked the families whether he ought to add the empty space beside their houses to their holdings on the map, many of them said no. The descendants still regret the chances lost in this way.

In fact, even the drawing-up of the land register and the map did not fix the boundaries of the holdings for good. In 1927, when the community was again surveyed (see Fig. 3), the surveyors found that 28 *hold*-s (almost 40 acres) of the 317 interior *hold*-s (450 acres) had not been assigned during the 1864 survey but had slowly been taken over by the extension of former holdings. It was a general practice of the peasants to "push the fence a bit further," extending their holdings at the expense of the indefinite roads without opposition. Also, the small *köz*-s were altered incessantly: old ones were barred and new ones were opened. Even the main street was used for private purposes as late as the 1950s; for example, wheat was deposited there until all was threshed, or the thresher itself was set up in the street.

Since the end of the last century the government of the community has endeavored to regulate the streets and holdings. The highways and several roads in the interior have been paved. There was an attempt to straighten the boundaries of the holdings. In 1920, under a general program of the government, new homesteads at the eastern and western ends of the community were given to poor families who applied for them. The symmetrical situation of the two groups of lots is evidence that the people of Átány intended not to spoil the proportions of their "round" village: they measured out lots at two sites at an equal distance from the centrally situated church, in an arrangement similar to that of their two cemeteries, which are located opposite each other at either end of the village. On the new homesteads poor, landless families started to build with the help of credit offered by the state; their constructions marked the appearance of a new style of architecture at Átány.

At the time of these changes the system of having two separated properties was also gradually transformed. More and more people built houses in the *kert*-s beside their stables. Old people say that "formerly people were drawn to the interior from the outlying regions; now everyone migrates out." The movement was begun by the well-to-do *gazda*-s. Other peasants took advantage of the fact that the interior dwellings were becoming few and far between; acquiring the released houses and land, they rounded out their property so that they could place their stables and haystacks next to their houses in the interior. If an inheritance was divided so that one brother received the house and the other the *kert* with the stable, each endeavored to consolidate all his activity on his own lot: one built a stable beside the house, the other a house beside the stable. Sometimes poor families transformed a stable into a dwelling.

The old pattern of settlement observed at Átány is not an unparalleled one. Historical sources and ancient maps showed us that in the seventeenth and eighteenth centuries the majority of settlements (villages and boroughs) of the central and northern parts of the Great Plain had similarly separated dwellings and farmyards. The wide distribution of this pattern suggests that we ought to look for the origin of the system in a more remote period. At the beginning of the seventeenth century the populous peasant towns that came into being at the boundaries of the area occupied by the Turks—settlements of mounted and foot soldiers (the so-called Haiduks)—adopted the same system.[37] This predominant settlement system of the region was also adopted by several new communities founded in the following centuries. Since the end of the eighteenth century, however, the settlement pattern has changed: the more recent communities have a ground plan which was laid out by engineers in unitary and regular sections.

The *kert* structure of settlement involved extensive cultivation and animal husbandry and a very mobile organization of labor. As agriculture and this organization of labor changed during the nineteenth century, the dissolution of the *kert* system began, first in the populous peasant towns and later in the villages.[38]

---

[37] István Györffy, 1942: 153–215; Den Hollander, 1960–1961; Mendöl, 1943.

[38] The separation of the dwelling from the farmyard is also known outside of Hungary. We know of examples of this system in the peasant villages of the Polish, Moravian, and White Russian Plains, and in the mountain settlements of the Alps, the Carpathians, and the Balkans, where actual agricultural practices are quite different. The peasants of today find it generally incomprehensible and burdensome to have some regularly used farm buildings situated far away from the house. Everywhere the trend is to consolidate all buildings in one area (Hofer, 1965).

CHAPTER 2. THE LAND: THE HATÁR OF ÁTÁNY

THE FIELDS

The name of Átány refers first of all to the village, the houses, and the people living in them. But it also refers to the exactly delimited tract of 9,172 *hold*-s (13,024 acres) which has been used and tilled by the people of the community for centuries: the *határ*. The usufruct of this land is one of the bases for the unity of Átány society.[39]

The boundaries of the Átány *határ* are precisely defined. At the corners boundary stones are embedded in the soil or artificial mounds; at other places ditches mark the boundary line. With one step you are in the *határ* of another community, Heves or Kömlő; with a second, you return to Átány.[40]

---

[39] Examining the eras during which the countryside experienced war proves almost as if by experimental method how the *határ* held together the population. During the Turkish wars villages were easily demolished and the inhabitants fled; but it was the fields which eventually made them return after a period of years. In this epoch several communities not far from Átány left their *határ* for up to twenty or thirty years, settling in more secure locations in the vicinity. They did not mingle with the local peasants, however, but rather continued to live from the income of their own now distant fields until they were ultimately able to return.

Even though a village might cease to exist, the identity of its *határ* did not. There is a special term, "*puszta*," meaning the fields of a ruined and uninhabited village. Some of them have been repopulated after a span of 100 to 200 years of being deserted, as has happened in Kömlő, near Átány, devastated in the sixteenth century and repopulated in 1770. If the village was not re-established, the fields in many cases have preserved the name of the medieval village. This occurred in the case of Szárazbő, a former village; after the expulsion of the Turks the old settlement was not re-established, but manorial farms were founded on its *határ* and it has been administratively attached to Átány. (But within the administrative boundaries, the fields of Átány and Szárazbő are strictly divided.)

In the system of serfdom the statute forbidding the free migration of the serf bound him unseparably to the fields, the land and "the glebe." This prescription was declared by the severe statute of 1514; it was valid for only a few decades, but even thereafter the counties vigorously hindered migration by the serfs. (Cf. Szabó, 1948: 65–158.)

[40] Ancient records yield a lively picture of the significance of boundary lines. The people of neighboring villages and the men of neighboring landlords would engage in battle over a debated and uncertain boundary. Less violent confrontations have also been recorded in which the adversaries, facing each other over the boundary line, taunted the people beyond it: "Come and cross the line, if you dare!" However, both parties remained in the territory of their own village.

The maintenance and declaration of a correct boundary was a moral duty, divinely sanctioned. In lawsuits over boundaries the judges would receive testimony on oath. Throughout the country various stories are told of witnesses who perjured themselves for the interest of their own community, but they were punished for it thereafter and could not rest at peace even after death. A false witness might, for example, put a clod of soil from his own *határ* into his boots and go to an alien field to swear: "I stand on the soil of my own village." As the Átány people well remember, their *határ* used to be more extensive of old, but portions have been fraudulently taken away.

The territory in which the people of Átány worked and tilled the soil extended beyond this line. Thus, the people of Átány possessed vineyards in the *határ* of neighboring Heves, on a sandy soil suitable for growing grapes, from at least the sixteenth century. In the period of serfdom this was made possible by the fact that vineyards, planted in a suitable soil and nurtured with great care, enjoyed a specially privileged, an almost "extraterritorial," position. The tithe and the "ninth part" were due from the wine itself, but the vineyard did not belong to the *telek;* it could be bought, sold, and inherited freely, independently from the *telek*, and the landlords generally did not prevent their tenants from extending their vineyards.[41] Communities which had no suitable land for viniculture grew grapes in the area of another village, often at a considerable distance, and sometimes in common enterprise with the people of ten to twelve other villages. At Heves the vineyards belonging to the people of Átány were not mingled with others, so their area formed a discrete tract. And it was the duty of the Átány administration to keep order, to hire a field guard, and to fix the date of the harvest and processing of the grapes. These vineyards were thus an extension of Átány lands in another community. The vineyards owned by peasants of Átány were mostly small, and the produce filled only the scanty needs of their own households.

Formerly, between the seventeenth and nineteenth centuries, the people of Átány used to lease appreciable tracts of land outside their *határ*. Thus they secured grazing land for their cattle in the communities near the Tisza River[42] and acorn grounds for their swine in the oak woods in the Mátra mountains to the north. This older custom survived until the most recent decades in the practice of some rich *gazda*-s' acquiring pasture on lease for their young cattle from the villages along the Tisza River.

The neighboring estates, including those of Szárazbő, which belonged to the Átány administrative area, provided some security to the Átány poor by engaging servants and seasonal workers or day laborers from among them.

Turning now to its physical environment, we note that Átány lies in an area of Holocene sedimentation. The surface meadow soil is mingled, often in small patches, with poor alkaline and fertile black (lowland) soils.[43] The people carefully distinguish the characteristics of the various kinds of soil, choosing the method of cultivation, the plants, and the date of sowing accordingly.

The different types of soil require different amounts of rainfall to optimize their productivity. This is why it is said at Átány that rain cannot fall in a way useful for all; if the black soil needs rain, the alkaline should have sunshine. The average amount of rainfall is 500–550 mm. per year; the average number of sunny hours is 1,950–2,000. Owing to the variable weather of the Great Plain, dominated either by the continental weather masses or by atmospheric motions from the ocean, usually every third or fourth summer is extremely dry (extremely "continental"), which

---

[41] Szabó, 1947.
[42] As we have mentioned, the *határ* of the demolished village of Kömlő was used in part by the Átány folk until Kömlő was repopulated in 1770.
[43] Stefanovits, 1963: 253–254, 260–266.

significantly reduces harvest yields.[44] On the other hand, every eighth or tenth year is extremely "oceanic"; it rains too much and the yields are reduced by the high level of underground water and by floods.

The appearance of the Átány fields has changed considerably in the last one hundred years. The map of 1859 (Fig. 4), drawn before the redistribution survey, shows a very complicated picture because the *telek* boundaries had to avoid numerous small lakes and brooks and patches of reed and marsh. Old people still recall former conditions when "there was a reed bank from Heves to Átány, inhabited by foxes and wild duck," and when reed-wolves sometimes came near the village itself. Most of these waters have disappeared, but left behind are several shallow lakes without outlet where bullrush, sedge, and reeds are cut even nowadays.

The extent of the wet areas throughout Hungary has decreased considerably since the middle of the past century. As a matter of fact, the transformation of the Átány *határ* mirrors on a small scale the change in appearance of the whole Great Hungarian Plain. Since the middle of the last century, the Danube, the Tisza, and their tributaries have been regulated for flood control and drainage. The work of several decades has made dry land from ca. 1,800,000 hectares of the flood plain of the Tisza which previously was either permanently or periodically inundated.[45] With the receding of these waters, agriculture has gained ground: one-time marshes, water meadows, and pastures have become arable land.

In the Átány area only a few smaller channels were dug, but the danger to Átány fields from the flooding of far-away rivers (the Tisza and the Tarna) has abated. At the same time the water table has generally fallen. However, in the two years of flooding of 1940–1941, the earlier conditions of the area reappeared: for a short time drained places were covered by water again, and marsh vegetation sprouted anew.

AGRICULTURE

For centuries the people of Átány lived principally by the use of their *határ*. By following changes in the modes of cultivation, in the plants cultivated, and in the herds grazing in the pastures of the area, we get a synoptic sketch of the development of Átány's agriculture.

In the sixteenth and seventeenth centuries the war-ridden Great Plain was used preponderantly for extensive stock keeping on pasture. Because of the miserable condition of the roads, the most salable produce was cattle, which could be driven to market. In Átány too, a moderate amount of grain production was supplemented

[44] The region of Átány exemplifies the most extreme continental climate of the Carpathian basin. Ranges are widest here, and the record rises and falls in temperature were noticed in this region in particular. During the year the absolute fluctuation in temperature is between 55 and 60° C., while the median temperature is 10 to 11° C. Against the warm sunshine and hot summer, there are on the average 160 to 180 days with frost. This is the driest part of the country. (Cf. Bacsó, 1959.) The changeable climate, which evinces striking variations from year to year, significantly affects the life of the peasantry (see Chapter 13, "The Rise and Decline of Individuals and Families").

[45] Bulla and Mendöl, 1947: 220.

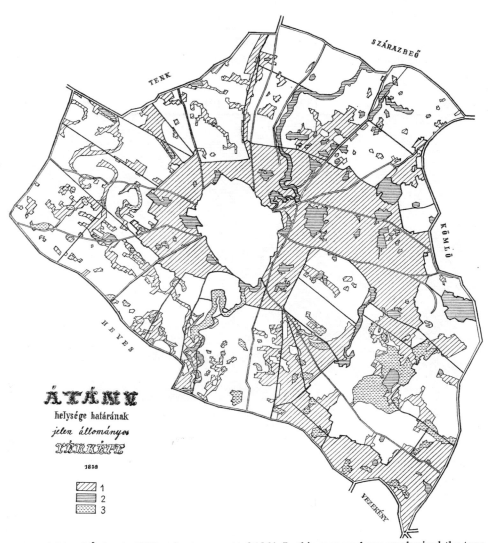

4. The fields of Átány in 1859, prior to survey of 1864. In this map we have emphasized the topographical characteristics and land usage, working from the original large map. Many parts of the fields are permanently or occasionally covered by water, and grassy patches are also extensive. The boundaries of the holdings follow topographical features faithfully. Key to symbols used: (1) Grassland: pasture and meadow. (2) Water: brook and lakes. (3) Marshy places, occasionally covered by water.

by extensive livestock breeding. Practically all the land was grassland, used as pasture and meadow. Small plots of land were cultivated from time to time but became grassland again after the soil became impoverished, and the land usage was rotated.[46] Of types of animals kept, the accounts of the tithe collectors recorded only sheep breeding, since the tenth of lambs was collected. According to these sources Átány possessed an outstanding number of sheep for the region during the period of Turkish

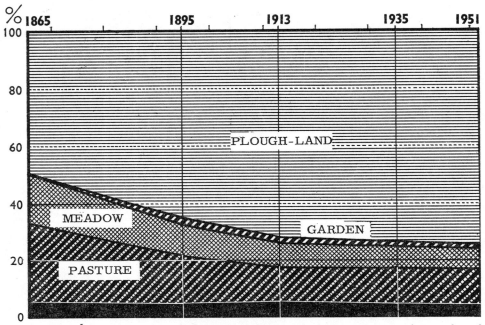

5. Land use in Átány from 1865 to 1951. The black stripe at the bottom represents the area free of land tax (roads, etc.).

occupation. The village was famous for its sheep farming in the last century as well. A survey of the economy of Hungary in the 1840s emphasized that a characteristic of Átány was that "having ample pastures, sheep breeding is widely practiced."[47]

In the seventeenth and eighteenth centuries the draft animals were oxen. Six were regarded as a full team for the heavy wooden plow. But since the end of the eighteenth century the horse has been replacing the ox as the chief work animal. In 1828, 435 horses but only 67 oxen were recorded at Átány. The large number of horses and the fact that all the minor gazda-s who held small portions of a telek owned teams of horses suggest that the Átány people participated with their horse-drawn wagons in the cartage on the "Great Road," which was situated in their vicinity. For a share of the produce, they also undertook to thresh grain with their horses, sometimes even

[46] Wellmann, 1961: 344–370.
[47] Fényes, 1836–1840: III, 212–213.

in distant regions. Our aged informants remember the last phase of these enterprises. The changeover to horses meant more for Átány than new occupational opportunities. The stables mentioned in the last chapter were constructed primarily for horses. The men felt bound to the stables mainly because they were anxious about the horses. A fine horse or a fine team became the main indication of affluence and prestige at Átány. But this chiefly "equicentered" husbandry was no heritage from the distant past; it developed probably around 1800.

According to the oldest statistics on economy, in the middle of the nineteenth century about 42 per cent of the total land belonging to the village was still grassland (mainly pasture), and the total arable land remained below 50 per cent (see Fig. 5). (It was in this period that the region was criss-crossed by many brooks and wet patches.) The plowland was divided into three sections, one-third of it lying fallow and serving as grazing fields. Thus, permanent and temporary pastures, together with the hayfields, made up about 60 per cent of the cultivated land.[48]

In the following decades the ratio quickly altered in favor of plowland. By about 1900 it constituted 65.1 per cent and reached approximately its present size of 71.7 per cent before World War I.[49] By then only the soil totally unsuitable for plowing remained untilled. In the last four decades inland drainage has brought an increase of only 2.6 per cent.

The oldest people remember the appearance of the ancient *határ* in this way: "Surely, my son, looking around we saw a flock of sheep here, a herd of cattle there." From early spring until late autumn the animals were grazed, and in winter they were fed on meager meadow hay, straw, and chaff. By spring the cattle were weakened to such an extent that some of them could hardly go out to graze. The chief object of this extensive keeping of livestock was to acquire young animals; in the case of sheep, both the progeny and the wool were wanted.

As the arable land actually cultivated increased, grazing diminished in importance. The smaller pastures could feed fewer animals and then only for a short time. Earlier the herds of horses, swine, and sheep lived on the grazing fields from spring to late autumn, and even the horses and oxen were driven to the pasture for the night after their daily work as draft animals. After the turn of the century ever more herds were

---

[48] For more detail see Fél and Hofer, 1961b.

[49] This period was one of rapid expansion of plowlands throughout Hungary. From 1869 to 1913 the area of agricultural production grew by 1.6 million *hold*-s, while during the same period 2.6 million *hold*-s of meadows and pastures were converted to cultivated lands. Owing to the cereal boom, lasting with some interruptions from 1853 for two decades, the expansion of the amount of land tilled resulted in increased areas being devoted to grain, especially wheat. Between 1847 and 1867 the quantity of wheat exported grew from 1.5 millions to 10.5 million *mázsa*-s. In the same period the number of head of livestock decreased. The expanded wheat production was terminated ultimately by the appearance of cheaper Russian and American wheat in the market and by the fall of cereal prices in the 1870s. These factors decreased the importance of cereal production and contributed to a more complex crop structure through a series of very slow modifications and crises. In 1870 wheat occupied 68.7 per cent of all sown areas, but this proportion decreased to 60.9 per cent by 1900. At the same time the average harvest yield per *hold* improved considerably. In this period, the second half of the nineteenth century, the main area of wheat growing shifted from the southern part of the Great Plain to the central Tisza region, in the environs of Átány (Balogh, 1965a: [esp.] 385–417; István Orosz, 1965: 108–111; Szilágyi, 1961).

driven home in the evening, a fact revealing that they were already then receiving fodder in the stables as a supplement.

So not only the ratio of animal keeping to cultivation changed, but also the character of both these enterprises. The transformation of the livestock keeping is shown by the rapid decrease in the area of pastures and meadows and, at the same time, the spreading of roughage and fodder in the fields. The more intensive character of stock raising is also reflected in the change in kinds of animals reared at about the turn of the century. The old breeds of cattle, horses, swine, and sheep were hardy ones, able to endure the vicissitudes of the long stay in pasture and the meager foddering in winter. The gray-colored cows yielded little milk, but the young bullocks could be reared to be stout, able-bodied oxen. The sheep gave ample but coarse wool. These were supplanted by more delicate and more valuable horses of larger stature, by equally more delicate brindle cattle yielding more milk, and by merino sheep growing finer wool. To serve the needs of these less hardy animals, the buildings constructed for them and the manner of looking after them changed. For the old "Hungarian breed" of sheep, to cite an instance, open corrals were erected in the grazing fields; the merino sheep needed the covered folds.

Most recently the ratios of kinds of livestock have again changed. The number of draft animals has decreased somewhat, but the quantity of milk-producing and meat animals has increased, especially cows, revealing an endeavor to raise commodity production. On the other hand, the once famous sheep flocks of Átány have been reduced to a fragment of their former size.

These changes have modified the distribution of livestock on the single farms. Earlier, when animals were mainly pastured, even poor people owning little or no land could have cattle, since they too were entitled to use the communal grazing fields. As the keeping of animals increasingly utilized fodder produced on plowland, the number of cattle a peasant could support depended on the extent of his holdings. On the average, three *hold*-s (4.26 acres) are necessary to keep a piece of livestock. This figure represents a balance between the number of head which can be supported by the food from a given tract and the labor and fertilizer which they in turn produce for it.

In the period of serfdom the proportions of the plants cultivated in the plowland were defined by the three-section rotation system. One-third of the land was seeded in winter crops, i.e., wheat or "double" (a mixture of wheat and rye). This planting gave the people their basic food, bread. The second section, sown in the spring, provided food for the livestock, mainly barley, of which even the straw was used as fodder. Oats and maize played a subordinate role compared to barley. The third section lay fallow and served as grazing land for the animals. The herds driven to it manured it and kept down the weeds to some extent, thereby rendering it more suitable for the next sowing of wheat. (This was followed by a spring crop and then left fallow again.)

In order to accommodate the changing composition of crops, the fields had to be divided anew. An occasion for this was presented by the engineering survey of 1868, when the lands of the landlords and the peasants were separated and the plots of the former serfs were remeasured (see Fig. 6). At this time, however, the majority of *gazda*-s retained the system of three-section crop rotation. The plowlands measured in this year were allotted to them in three sections of two lots each, i.e., in six lots all together. The division of a section into two lots was necessary because half of the fallow had been sown already with a mixture of oats and vetch. Thus the full cycle of cultivation spanned six years: after the autumn and the spring sowing each plot of land yielded fodder in the third year, then after repeated autumn and spring sowing it lay fallow in the sixth year. Besides the plowlands subjected to crop rotation, each peasant received "small pieces" of land, not bound to the rotation system, at the border of the village. It was on those pieces that several new crops gained ground, such as lucerne and cattle turnip (fodder), which were destined to become very important in the economy.[50]

Following heated discussions and conflicts, the three-course rotation system was dropped in 1901. Henceforth all fallow land became sown and everyone decided for himself which plants he wanted to cultivate. In 1927 a further step was taken: the holdings were consolidated, and the plowland of each peasant was regrouped into one (or two) plots.

However, the freedom to cultivate by individual choice did not quickly and decisively alter the statistics of which crops were actually planted. The part of the plowland which formerly was left fallow was used for fodder crops, a small quantity of plants raised for commerce and industry, and for plants that had to be hoed regularly (this group, including maize, potatoes, turnips, etc., was distinguished from cereals and fodder plants by the peasants and the agricultural administration primarily through the seasonal hoeing involved in their cultivation).[51] At the same time the traditional cereal crops retained their dominant status: in 1870–1871, the proportion of cereal to other crops amounted to 57 per cent and sixty years later, in 1931, to 57.3 per cent. Earlier, owing to the obligatory communal system of cultivation, each part of the area was sown either with a winter crop or a spring crop, and thus one could gain a clear, comprehensive view of the relative proportion of plants cultivated. After 1901 this clear-cut pattern was upset, and the picture of the single parts of the land became patched. But analysis of statistical data shows that the older pattern of spring and winter crops did not disappear and that their areas have not diminished; rather, they have fallen into tiny plots with a scattered distribution. This was because the people of Átány continued to sow autumn wheat in one third of their holdings

[50] Eger State Archives, "Átány's proceedings for the separation of the rights of the landlords and peasants." The wavering of the Átány peasants between the rotation system and consolidation of holdings and the majority vote cast for three-term rotation are in accord with the attitude of the peasantry of the Great Plain and of Hungary in general in this period. Even after a generation, in 1912, 28.9 per cent of the communities cultivated their *határ*-s by adhering to the three-term rotation system, although most of them have also sown into the fallow tract, at least in part, as have the peasants of Átány (Balogh, 1965a: 397–399).

[51] In 1870–1871, hoed crops (cultivated plants that needed seasonal hoeing) occupied only 18.8 per cent of the tilled land, whereas in 1931–1935 their proportion was 23 per cent and in 1957, 32.1 per cent. In the same period the planting of rough fodder increased sixfold, from 2.1 to 12.6 per cent. (Cf. Fél and Hofer, 1961b.)

and barley or some other spring grain in another third even after the dissolution of the rotation system.

This stability of the relative proportions of crops raised, in spite of repeated changes in the system of cultivation, is explained by the fact that the aims of cultivation remained practically unchanged for nearly one hundred years. The main object of the peasant households remained subsistence farming, beside which market production played only a secondary role.

The Átány peasants cultivate the land to secure subsistence for the people and the animals of their households. "First is wheat for bread; second, barley for the animals," said a *gazda*. "We have to feed the animals for six months [i.e., in winter] and feed ourselves throughout the year." It was this tradition of subsistence farming which preserved without change the primary importance accorded to bread-yielding wheat and the secondary importance of roughage and fodder. At Átány it is considered more or less regrettable and even shameful if someone has to buy a commodity he could produce in his own household—e.g., to purchase bread in the shop or "to stand at another's door to get a jug of milk." The saying goes: "If you buy bread for money, you never eat enough." The well-to-do *gazda* boasts of the fact that he never bought "either a piece of fodder or a grain of cereal" in all his life.

As for market production, the chief object is to produce for the market a surplus of the plants used primarily for subsistence. Better-off peasants, owning more than 25 to 40 *hold*-s (35.5 to 56.8 acres), whose needs were amply filled even in the leanest of seasons, could afford to experiment on one parcel of land or another with plants grown exclusively for sale. At the end of the last century this was done with malting barley, and later with sugar beets, legumes of various sorts, sunflowers, fodder crops grown for seed, etc. In the overall picture these plots accounted for a very small percentage of the crops grown for commerce and industry: in 1870–1871 it was 2.4; in 1931–1935, 3.5; in 1957, 8.2 per cent.

The growing impact of a market economy in the last decades of the nineteenth century caused increasing specialization in the production of rural areas. Whole regions developed well-defined branches of agriculture and brought large quantities of uniform produce to the market. So—in addition to their subsistence economy— the peasants of certain regions began to raise wine or vegetables for the urban markets, others specialized in dairy production or pig fattening, etc. Átány lies on the border of the grain- (especially wheat-) growing region along the Central Tisza River. The peasants of this region deliver mainly wheat to the national market. Since for centuries wheat was the main crop of the Plain, increased wheat production demanded comparatively little structural change in the management of peasant farms. In these areas the organization of family estates remained relatively unchanged.

Rearing livestock was another way to produce a "cash crop" for the market. In the Átány view, stock breeding used to be the mainspring of material gain. The value of young cattle is increased by the mere fact of its maturing, and more profit is gained if the *gazda* breeds and rears the animals himself. Crops could be most advantageously transformed to cash "through the animals," i.e., by letting the animals being reared for the market eat the fodder and provender grown on one's land. Limited only by the capacity of his farm, anyone could raise horses, cows, sheep, swine, geese, ducks, or chickens. As mentioned above, raising livestock was an essential part of the traditional system of farming—to provide draft power for tilling the soil, dung to conserve its fertility, fat, meat, milk, and eggs for the family to eat, and feathers for the eiderdown quilts and pillows of their beds. (Earlier in the last century the women of Átány still spun wool from the sheep and reared lambs of the "Hungarian breed" in order to obtain the necessary material for their long and short sheepskin coats.)

In the 1930s and 1940s all agricultural work except threshing was done with the help of horse and (more rarely) ox teams or by hand. Machine threshing was widespread by the turn of the last century. Sowing machines have gained ground slowly. The fertility of the soil was conserved almost exclusively by spreading manure and by rotating crops. Only the large estates and a few well-to-do *gazda*-s experimented with chemical fertilizers. The technology of agricultural work, however, underwent rapid change even within the framework of the traditional yoke and manual labor. Instead of the heavy wooden plows used in the middle of the nineteenth century (having wrought iron only on the colters and front half of the shares) repeated changes of plow types resulted in the adoption of factory-made iron plows with steel moldboards. After plowing, the final preparation of the soil for planting was made with either the ancient, simple harrows made of thorny twigs (thorn bush) with a log fastened across them, and later by various kinds of iron harrows, rollers, and disks.

As the implements changed, so too did the organization of work done with them and the annual cycle of labor, e.g., even more people used the new steel plows to perform autumn deep plowing in the fields of the spring grain.

As a consequence, both the quantity and value of the products of the Átány *határ* increased in the period surveyed here. Cultivation became more intensive. The amount of work the Átány people had to invest in cultivation of their fields increased. The reason was partly because of the increased production of plants "that had to be hoed regularly" and of plants grown for commercial and industrial purposes, which require much work, and partly because of the introduction of improved methods of cereal production. The quantity and value of goods destined for the market also increased, although they were the traditional produce of subsistence farming.

LAND TENURE

Over the last two hundred years the *határ* of Átány has been redistributed several times. Patterns of land tenure and property titles have also changed. In a village where the well-being, the financial independence, and the way of life of each family are determined mainly by the size of their land holdings, the distribution of land vividly reflects the stratification of the local society. By comparing the changes of property boundaries on the maps of the Átány *határ* drawn up in various periods, one may get a glimpse into the dynamics of social stratification.

The system of land tenure and use was established by statute, administrative measures, or, in a more remote period, the landlord. Thus changes in the distribution of land reveal how state and manorial regulations interfered with the land tenure of the village and how changes were thereby effected in its society.

Until the middle of the eighteenth century the Átány magistrate was accustomed to distribute land to those who applied for it. By receiving a holding, the possessor was subject to state taxation and feudal dues, so there was no unregulated tenure even at that time. The *határ* was regarded as the unalienable property of the landlords although in the use of the Átány people. This use was controlled by the magistrate, who redistributed the plowland according to the actual needs and number of draft animals of the single peasant.[52] Naturally their claims could be satisfied only to a degree in practice. In this period some inhabitants of neighboring villages complained bitterly because their magistrate almost defrauded them of access to land.[53]

The periodical redistribution was supplanted by the system of fixed *telek*-s. Henceforth the size of the arable holding allotted to a serf no longer changed: the plots were fixed in the various parts of the area and were subject to three-term rotation. At Átány this division did not hinder the establishment and development of new *telek*-s. Between 1767 and 1848 the number of serf holdings doubled. In their petition of 1838 the peasants of Átány complained that recent seizures of plowland had progressively diminished the common pasture.[54]

The grazing fields were used by the inhabitants of the village and the landowners in common. It was this common pasture which gave rise to a movement in 1837 aimed at a change in the system of land tenure in the village area. According to the then recent acts on serfdom passed by the feudal assembly in 1836, the *jobbágy*-s could ask for the separation of their pasture from the domanial one. Átány peasants made use of this option at once: in their petition they averred that the multiplying

[52] The records of the Eger State Archives have preserved several depositions of Átány peasants in which were described in detail the manner of periodical division of land (Administrative Records, 1731: 9; 1734: 125; 1736: 57). According to these records, members of the local board, headed by the mayor, visited the plot of land destined for cultivation. Land was allotted to those who submitted their claims beforehand, according to the order of the houses and in relation to the feudal services undertaken by each *gazda*. The site for beginning the partition was decided by drawing lots. The plot of arable land cultivated by the community for the minister and the land allotted, for example, to the postmaster were measured out among those of the peasants. (The testimonies were taken in the interest of the postmaster; being a stranger, he did not want to abide by the rules of common farming, perhaps being ignorant of them.) This periodical division was still practiced at Átány in 1770 (Soós, n.d.: 36).

One might suppose that even prior to the system of periodical redistribution during the unstable era of the Turkish wars, free usufruct was customary at Átány. We have no proof of this from the village, but there is other evidence from the vicinity, e.g., from neighboring Tiszanána. (Cf. Soós, n.d.: 24–29; 1958: 6–8.) According to a description from 1743, in the fields subjected to free occupation, "the land is undivided... both nobles and peasants would break the soil where they wanted and as much as they wanted; they would sow in the autumn and in the spring [i.e., in two successive years], then anyone arriving first could plow it for himself."

[53] E.g., in 1743 the Tiszafüred magistracy was denounced for having allotted much land to the wealthy but little to the poor claimant, asking the latter: "Did you bring a satchel?"—meaning that he would be given as much land as a satchel could contain (Soós, n.d.: 35).

[54] Eger State Archives, "Átány's Proceedings for separation of the rights of landlords and peasants": Petition, November 20, 1838.

sheep flocks of the lords left hardly any room for their animals in the grazing fields.[55] Discontent and excitement rose to such a pitch in the community that authorities arrested two Átány serfs on the charge of "incitement."[56]

The suit for the separation of pastures lasted for a long time. In the meantime serfdom was abolished in 1848. It became a statutory prescription that in every formerly serf village the plowlands and pastures of the onetime landowners and the former serfs should be separated one from another and carefully redistributed. Átány's request became one of these "separation lawsuits."

In 1864 the Átány *gazda*-s were asked what system they wanted to have for the redistribution of land which was their due. As we have said, only a few of the former serfs opted to drop the old system of crop rotation and the obligatory cultivation. This minority, consisting of 28 peasants, received their entire due—i.e., plowland, meadowland, and a share in the pasture—all contained in one plot for each family. The majority, 171 former serfs, had their plowlands measured out in three tracts, each consisting of two equal parcels of land. These *gazda*-s kept their common pasture in a single unit of 954 *hold*-s (1,355 acres). The *zsellér*-s, who possessed no land in the period of serfdom but who had a share in the grazing fields, received a part of the ancient community pasture. They partitioned off half of this for plowlands or into small lots for gardening, keeping the other half as common pasture.[57] Finally, a part of the ancient common grazing fields was allotted to the former landowners, as well as a portion of the land which was found to exceed the holdings established by the laws on serfdom and measured out as such by the surveyors. Thus the share of the landlords totalled ca. 1,000 *hold*-s (1,420 acres) of the Átány land.

After the measurement and separation, the use to which the Átány fields were put, did not change much at first. Most of the plowlands continued to be cultivated on the basis of the earlier crop rotation plan, and beside them lay the wide common pastures. However, the communal system of agriculture and the common use of grazing lands now rested on a quite different basis; these were no longer controlled by state and manorial ordinances but were rather based on the voluntary common consent of the peasant landowners. Hitherto the order of common cultivation had been regulated by the village magistracy; now this task fell to the body of the associated landholders. Which inhabitants of the village were entitled to the use of pasture and in what

[55] They were wary of the settlement made by surveyors and protested against the division of the fields to be allotted to them by the engineers in the course of the surveying of the area, claiming that they (being the best experts on the qualities of each plot of land) would partition the arable land among themselves. And thus they drafted their petition.

[56] Eger State Archives, "Átány's Proceedings for separation of the rights of landlords and peasants": November 30, 1837.

[57] According to the statute, eight *zsellér*-s were entitled to use the pasture of a single serf *telek*. The size of this grazing land, and consequently the size of the plots allotted to the *zsellér*-s, varied considerably from village to village. At Átány, eight "small *hold*-s" (1,200 square fathoms each) of pasture were given for a serf *telek*. Thus each *zsellér* received one "small *hold*." The *zsellér*-s decided on the use of this area themselves. In numerous villages it was entirely converted to arable land. At Átány a compromise was reached: the *zsellér*-s retained half of their due as grazing land, letting the other half be measured out as plowland or gardens. The name of this parcel of pasture and arable land, let out by one *zsellér*, is *massza*.

proportion was defined in detail. The grazing lands of the former serfs and the former zsellér-s were separated. Formerly all inhabitants of the village (serfs, zsellér-s, or even newcomers) were entitled to use the pasture. Now grazing rights became independent of these categories; they were transformed into a share, as it were, which could be bought, sold, and inherited in various portions. The pasture was no longer owned by the community but by two "corporations."

The antiquated agricultural system, with the obligatory rotation of crops, was soon challenged. The 1894 act on agriculture made the abolition of the rotation system easier, and it could be initiated by a minority. Public controversy began to grow just as it had two generations earlier in the matter of the division of pastures. The affair was taken to court, and in 1901 its decision ended three-term rotation, the pattern of cultivation inherited from the period of serfdom. (See also Chapter 18, "The Law of the Land in Átány.")

In the next year the fallow areas were sown, and thus the grazing land decreased considerably. The number of herds and the grazing period had to be reduced. Thus, for instance, immediately after the change, in 1901, the grazing of horses and the existence of the horse herd came to an abrupt end.

With the abolition of the common system of cultivation it became senseless and unjustifiable to have the plowland of each gazda scattered in six different places at considerable distances from each other. People who purchased land or inherited it from different persons possessed as many as fifty to sixty plots. Some parcels of land were so narrow that there was hardly room for a harrow. Consequently a movement for consolidation was begun, ending in a redistribution: in 1927 each gazda obtained all his land in one or two parts, according to his wishes.

This marked the end of a process by which land possessed by the community and used in a collective way for two hundred years was fragmented into exactly measured and independently used parcels of private property. The ancient communal ownership and use was preserved in the pasture only.

In these decades the Átány peasants also managed to acquire new portions from the former landowners. As early as the close of the last century, the old vineyards had been devastated by phylloxera, and they had been gradually sold to strangers. In their stead, in the 1910s, the peasants acquired lots of sandy soil, suitable for horticulture and grapes, in the nearer portions of the Heves territory. The land of the Átány peasants was increased in these years by a further 500 hold-s (710 acres), owing to the parcelling out of further estates at Heves and Szárazbő. In the early 1920s national land reforms of limited scope allotted even further hold-s to the inhabitants of Átány in small plots and at a reduced price. In 1938 additional state credit enabled them to acquire the "Prince's lot" too, the largest part of land originally allotted to the former landlords in 1866.

After these changes the distribution of the fields of the Átány peasants was radically altered by the land reform in the spring of 1945. A considerable part of the onetime manorial possessions at Szárazbő, 1,991 hold-s (2,827.22 acres), were distributed among the peasant families of the village; 301 hold-s (427.42 acres) were allotted to

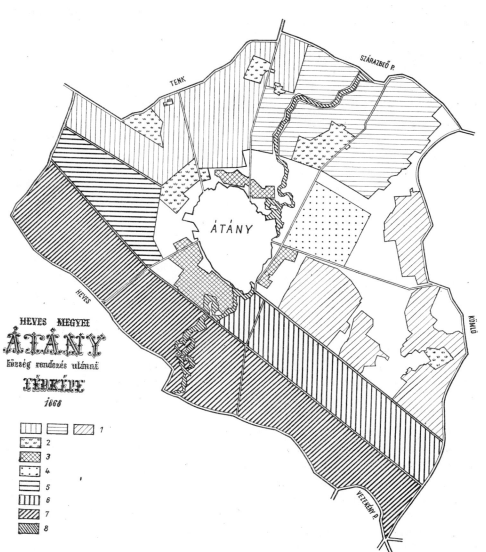

6. The fields of Átány in 1868, after the survey. This map shows the system of land ownership. Key to symbols used: (1) The plowlands of the peasants, divided according to the three stages of crop rotation (autumn sowing, spring sowing, fallow). (2) The pasture land of the peasants. (3) "Small pieces of land," gardens at the border of the village, exempted from the rotation system. (4) The pasture and plowlands of the *zsellér*-s. The empty space beside them represents the pasture of the former serfs. (5) Lands allotted to the community and to the village secretary, the Reformed church, the minister, the teacher, etc. by virtue of their office. (6) Peasant holdings measured out in one piece, exempted from the rotation system. (7) Estates of the landlords. (8) The Hanyi brook.

Kömlő applicants; while a further part of the expropriated manorial lands were attached to a state farm.

We might inquire as to how this quantity of land, the use and the territorial changes of which have been surveyed above, was distributed among single families.

In the period of serfdom land was measured by fixed units: one serf *telek* (36–42 *hold*-s, i.e., about 50–60 acres), one-half of that, and one-quarter. A tendency to divide up the holdings prevailed. This is discernible in the registers of *telek*-s drafted in 1770, in 1828, and in the course of the legal process for separation in 1866. In 1770 there were a considerable number of holdings (about 35 per cent) larger than a half-*telek*. By 1828 this number had almost entirely disappeared and the majority of the serfs (52 per cent) owned only a half-*telek*—or even smaller parcels. By the time of the property settlement at the end of the period of serfdom, the category of half-*telek* holdings had become insignificant, the majority (56 per cent) consisting of lots equal to a quarter-*telek*. But even this rapid fragmentation of holdings could not keep pace with the growth of the population, and the number of landless *zsellér*-s increased.

The data of 1866 also show the influence of the liberalizing of succession rights in 1848, which accelerated the breaking up of land holdings. (This process was not offset by the fact that some peasant families could increase their property, even surpassing the ancient measure of one *telek*.) A new type of miniature holding appeared in 1866: tiny plots called *massza*-s measured out for the *zsellér*-s.

The social developments of the decades following the drawing up of the land register in 1866 will be dealt with at another place. (See Chapter 13, "Mobility in the Last One Hundred Years.") The process of breaking up land parcels continued, while only a thin stratum of well-to-do *gazda*-s managed to increase their possessions. The 1935 statistics on the distribution of landed property show the result of these trends.

Table 1 embraces all of administrative Átány, Szárazbő included; it does not distinguish between the land of peasants and "gentlemen," or that held ex officio, etc. More than half of the 715 farms registered (435 holdings, 60.7 per cent) do not attain the size of five *hold*-s (7.10 acres). However, a comparison with the district, the region, or the country proves that the distribution of land at Átány is slightly less extreme than elsewhere: the extremes of miniature holdings, under one *hold* (1.42 acres), and the large estates are both somewhat under the average, while the independent medium-size peasant holdings are a little over the average.

This was the structure of land tenure when altered by the land reform of 1945. As of that date, 376 Átány applicants, more than half of the agricultural population, benefited from ca. 2,000 *hold*-s (2,840 acres) of expropriated land. And among them, thereby 178 day laborers and 25 former manorial servants became "new *gazda*-s," and the miniature plots of 159 tenants were filled out.

The statistics on landed property of 1949 are an accurate commentary on the redistribution of land. The number of miniature holdings below five *hold*-s and especially below one *hold* (7.10 and 1.42 acres, respectively) diminished, while the

Table 1

Comparative Distribution of Number and Size of Farms according to 1935 and 1949 Land Registers

On the basis of the 1935 Register:

Size of farm	Total Number in Átány village	Total Area* in Átány village	% of Total Number					% of Total Area				
			in Átány village	in Heves district	in Tisza region	in Great Plain	in area of contemporary Hungary	in Átány village	in Heves district	in Tisza region	in Great Plain	in area of contemporary Hungary
Under 1 cadastral hold (1.42 acres)	91	43	12.7	37.4	37.3	42.0	40.5	0.5	2.2	1.3	1.6	1.8
1— 5 cadastral hold-s (1.42— 7.10 acres)	344	791	48.0	37.6	32.9	31.6	33.5	8.6	10.5	8.6	9.0	9.4
5— 10 " (7.10— 14.20 ")	112	803	15.7	10.6	11.4	10.7	11.4	8.8	9.3	8.6	8.8	9.3
10— 20 " (14.20— 28.40 ")	97	1,383	13.6	7.9	9.5	8.3	8.5	15.1	13.5	14.1	13.5	13.5
20— 50 " (28.40— 71 ")	48	1,434	6.7	4.3	6.7	5.4	4.5	15.6	15.5	20.9	18.6	15.0
50— 100 " (71— 142 ")	7	445	1.0	1.2	1.4	1.2	0.9	4.9	9.3	9.7	9.3	6.7
100— 200 " (142— 284 ")	7	916	1.0	0.5	0.4	0.4	0.3	10.0	8.0	5.8	6.3	5.4
200— 500 " (284— 710 ")	7	1,867	1.0	0.3	0.2	0.2	0.2	20.3	9.5	6.8	8.0	8.6
500— 1,000 " (710— 1,420 ")	2	1,490	0.3	0.2	0.1	0.1	0.1	16.2	12.6	6.1	7.2	8.4
Over 1,000 " (Over 1,420 ")	—	—	—	0.2	0.1	0.1	0.1	—	9.6	18.1	17.7	21.9
TOTALS	715	9,172	100.0	100.0	100.0	100.0	100.0	100.0	100.0	100.0	100.0	100.0

On the basis of the 1949 Register:+

Size of farm	Total Number in Átány village	Total Area* in Átány village	% of Total Number					% of Total Area				
			in Átány village	in Heves district	in Tisza region	in Great Plain	in area of contemporary Hungary					
Under 1 cadastral hold (1.42 acres)	43	‡	6.5	8.4	19.1	11.7	13.2					
1— 3 cadastral hold-s (1.42— 4.26 acres)	93	‡	14.0	26.8	21.6	22.4	21.8					
3— 5 " (4.26— 7.10 ")	127	‡	19.1	23.3	20.4	20.1	18.3					
5— 10 " (7.10— 14.20 ")	206	‡	30.9	24.2	26.6	26.4	27.6					
10— 15 " (14.20— 21.30 ")	99	‡	14.9	8.7	10.3	9.7	10.7					
15— 20 " (21.30— 28.40 ")	31	‡	4.7	3.5	4.5	4.0	3.8					
20— 25 " (28.40— 35.60 ")	29	‡	4.4	2.1	2.7	2.3	1.9					
25— 35 " (35.60— 49.80 ")	23	‡	3.5	1.5	2.2	1.9	1.5					
35— 50 " (49.80— 71 ")	9	‡	1.4	0.9	1.0	0.9	0.7					
50— 100 " (71— 142 ")	4	‡	0.6	0.6	0.5	0.5	0.4					
Over 100 " (Over 142 ")	—	‡	—	0.0	0.1	0.1	0.1					
TOTALS	664	‡	100.0	100.0	100.0	100.0	100.0					

* *In cadastral hold-s*
+ *Individual farms only.*
‡ *No data available.*

peasant holdings of ten to twenty *hold*-s (14.20 and 28.40 acres, respectively), generally regarded as medium peasant holdings in Átány and in Hungary, became more numerous. This readjustment of property relations in favor of the medium-size holdings is especially conspicuous if one compares the indices of the village with the averages of the region and the country. The land reform radically changed the distribution of landed property all over the country, but it did not increase the ratio of medium-size peasant holdings to such a degree as at Átány.

One can view land succession, beginning in the period of serfdom and accelerated after 1848, as resulting in a process of polarization. A small number of better-off peasant households were able to thrive, but an ever larger number of holdings, originally capable of supporting independent agriculture, were broken up into such miniature parcels that they no longer sufficed to secure the subsistence of the respective families who owned them. At Átány the lower limit in size necessary for independent subsistence of a peasant family, without additional income or employment, may be drawn between fifteen and twenty *hold*-s (21.30 and 28.40 acres). In 1935 ca. 80 per cent of the Átány holdings fell below this limit, and at the same time 47.8 per cent of the agricultural population had no land at all. By expropriating and dividing the large estates within the administrative boundaries of Átány, the 1945 land reform transformed the structure of property holding; its impact, however, was principally in the allotment of land to landless groups of day laborers and manorial servants, and in the filling out of some of the minuscule holdings. After the agrarian reform, almost 90 per cent of the Átány population owned land. However, the overwhelming majority of these proprietors (more than 70 per cent) needed some supplementary income to what could be produced by working their own land.

In the course of the last two centuries the relation of the Átány peasants to the land has changed significantly. During the first half of the eighteenth century land was a commodity within the reach of anyone who was able to obtain a team of animals and the necessary agricultural equipment. Then, in the period that followed, the population grew, and the amount of available plowland per person diminished and became ever more difficult to acquire. The pattern and character of the rural economy and the well-being of individual families became dependent on how much land they possessed or inherited. The primary goal of economic and social achievement became the acquisition of land or enlargement of what was already held.

WORKING IN THE FIELDS

The fields are more than just soil, property, and where they work for the Átány people. They spend a large part of their lives there. From spring to late autumn, most of the able-bodied people set out for the fields at dawn, leaving the village almost deserted and quiet until their return at sunset. They take their meals to the fields in satchels.

In former times they did not even return for the night during the time of the hardest work, rather sleeping outside in the fields, in order to be able to work longer into the evening and to start earlier at dawn. Harvesters used to improvise shelters with the shafts of tools and sheaves or canvas. Those who did their plowing with the cumbersome oxen stayed in the fields too; they released the oxen to graze, and they lay down in the body of the cart. During threshing time the bachelors went out with the horses at night to graze them; they snatched a brief nap "awake," leaning on one elbow.[58] During these periods of demanding work the peasants were almost ashamed of spending any time at rest in the village. Before dawn they made preparations for starting, vying with one another to be on their way soonest. Some covered the window of their stable in order to prevent their neighbor from noticing that they were awake and preparing for work. And if it turned out after the start that there was no trace of a cart in the road, they were proud of having preceded everyone.

There were also eleven *tanya*-s in the *határ*, the dwelling places and farmyards constructed at the site of the plowlands. However, five of these belonged to people from either Heves county or Jazygia who "sneaked in" when manorial fields were parceled out and sold to peasants. Only six were owned by local Átány families, who were regarded as more or less eccentric because of their settling directly on the *tanya*-s. Nevertheless, several Átány *gazda*-s possessed temporary abodes on their distant plots. Most of these consisted of only a single room; a stable was added to some. During the day they served as shelters from the rain, and at night one could sleep in them if it became necessary. In the vineyards similar simple buildings served for protective storage of implements and as shelters when it rained. Those who were allotted land in the remote Szárazbő area during the agrarian reform of 1945 could return to the village daily only with great difficulty, and so some improvised huts with wooden frames for summer use and took the materials home every autumn. In the pasture the herdsmen erected shelters for the duration of a grazing season. These included the folds used to keep the herd together during nighttime and the huts (made of reeds in the shape of a tent or a cone) which served for protection of the herdsmen and their equipment.

"One ought to love the earth, not only to work it," said one of our informants. Especially in winter one hears much of the beauties and the joy of work done in the fields and little about the fatigue involved. Be it man or woman, adult or child, everyone is happier in the fields than in the home. "As spring approaches, children are buzzing already, the fine weather is near, one would like to move about and to plow in the fields." People praise the spring most, when there is warmth again and the flowers are blooming; as they say, "It is splendid to be in the fields in spring."

Being in the fields does not imply solitude or separation from the people of the village; on the contrary, it presents more occasions to meet other people. In the village the houses conceal activities, but in the fields one may see who is there on his plot and what he is doing, as far as one's eyesight permits. Movements, the rattle of

---

[58] Sleeping in the open became more rare after the turn of the century, and it ceased altogether after World War I. Popular history explains this fact with reference to summer thunderstorms and deadly thunderbolts: "since then people began to fear."

a cart, the smallest sound enable the peasants to discover even from a great distance who is passing by on foot or driving along, and on what errands. People passing each other or working near also greet each other and often begin to converse. During the winter one often hears: "When we go out for the spring work, we'll know better what's going on in the village; we shall hear more of it."

Elderly people consider the peasantry as "the people of the soil," i.e., those who work in the fields, till the soil, and live by its produce. Whenever the Átány people talk of themselves as peasants, they recall the scenes of the work done in the fields. The peasant is also mentioned by the name of "plowman." When a poor man, a landless hired laborer, tried to summarize in a single sentence his desire to be better off, he said: "My goodness, how happy is a man plowing his own land"—i.e., a man who has land, plow, and draft animals and is in good enough health to till his soil. This devotion to the soil, and especially to the *határ* of Átány, was expressed by Ferenc Orbán in the following words: "It is fine to be in the fields, to work there; one is drawn outside by his desire. This is my favorite work, I was born into it, I grew up in it, I would like to do it as long as I live."

CHAPTER 3. THE PEOPLE

THE POPULATION OF ÁTÁNY

In the course of the 1949 census, 2,934 inhabitants were recorded at Átány. The authors found approximately the same population in 1951.

This number seems to have varied little in the last hundred years. Hungarian census material from 1869 is at our disposal. Taking 100 as a base to represent the 1869 figure, the population has oscillated between only 93.6 and 111.4 since then (see Table 2 and Fig. 7). It reached a peak at about 1900 and in the period between World Wars I and II. There was a decrease in 1880 and a slight decrease between 1910 and 1920, followed by an accelerating diminution after World War II.

These data refer to Átány as an administrative unit: besides the population of the village itself, they include the inhabitants of domanial manors situated in Szárazbő and to the south. Only from 1900 can the population of the village itself be distin-

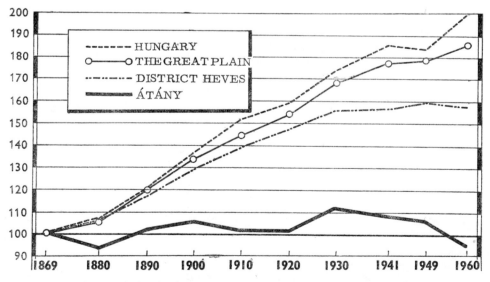

7. Changes in the population in the censuses from 1869 to 1960. Index: population of the year 1869 = 100.

Table 2

Comparative Changes in Size of Population Revealed by Censuses between 1869 and 1960

Year of Census	Number of inhabitants in Átány village*	Index of Changes in Size of Population (1869 = 100.0)				
		in Átány village*	in Heves district	in Tisza region	in Great Plain	in area of contemporary Hungary
1869	2,738	100.0	100.0	100.0	100.0	100.0
1880	2,603	93.6	106.2	106.4	105.2	106.4
1890	2,829	101.7	116.7	120.9	119.2	119.9
1900	2,933	105.4	129.1	134.0	133.6	136.8
1910	2,814	101.1	138.7	139.9	144.5	151.9
1920	2,812	101.1	147.0	151.0	154.3	159.4
1930	3,094	111.4	155.6	161.5	168.2	173.4
1941	3,011	108.2	156.8	166.9	177.2	185.8
1949	2,934	105.4	159.8	166.0	178.1	183.9
1960	2,610	94.0	157.8	169.3	185.8	199.0

* *Administrative unit; includes outlying areas*

guished from that of the outlying areas (Table 3). If only the people of the village itself are counted, the oscillation of population size is even less. The inhabitants of the manorial farms were more mobile; for example, we notice a considerable decrease in 1920, following the war and the revolutions of 1918 and 1919. We conclude that the decrease after World War II also resulted largely from the scattering of the manorial inhabitants.[59]

The stable size of the Átány population is especially conspicuous when compared with population changes in the vicinity and in more remote regions. In the hundred-year period in which the population of Átány remained practically the same, the

Table 3

Distribution of Átány* Population in Its Interior and Outlying
Areas, by Census Period, 1900 to 1960

Year of Census	Total Number of Inhabitants	Inhabitants of Interior Village		Inhabitants of Outlying Areas	
		Number	Percentage	Number	Percentage
1900	2,933	2,238	76.3	695	23.7
1910	2,814	2,274	80.8	540	19.2
1920	2,812	2,487	88.4	325	11.6
1930	3,094	2,585	83.6	509	16.4
1941	3,011	2,542	84.4	469	15.6
1949	2,934	2,663	90.8	271	9.2
1960	2,610	2,568	98.4	42	1.6

* *Administrative unit*

[59] In the course of the 1945 agrarian reform the large estates were divided up. The farm hands living in the manors were entitled to claim land from the estates of the *úr*-s; most of them claimed it, however, in neighboring villages, mainly at Tenk and also at Kömlő. Having received a household plot, the claimant settled in these villages as soon as possible. The Szárazbő land was allotted to the Átány and (to a lesser degree) the Kömlő poor or was handed over to the state.

population of the country as a whole doubled, and the rural, mainly agrarian population of the Heves district increased by almost 60 per cent (Table 2).[60]

What was the index of natural increase in the population of Átány? The registers of the Calvinist church reveal detailed data on births and marriages from 1727, on deaths from 1778.[61] Unfortunately we know only the number of the total Reformed population for the years 1786, 1846, and 1872.[62] In Table 4 we assumed that the

Table 4

Births and Deaths by Decade between 1780 and 1940 according to the Registers of the Reformed Church at Átány

Period	Actual yearly average			Per 1,000 yearly average*		
	Births	Deaths	Natural increase	Births	Deaths	Natural increase
1780 to 1789	82.8	46.7	36.1	47.8	27.0	20.8
1790 to 1799	74.3	57.4	16.9	41.7	32.2	9.5
1800 to 1809	80.3	59.5	20.8	43.9	32.5	11.4
1810 to 1819	87.1	58.2	28.9	46.3	30.9	15.4
1820 to 1829	87.5	64.7	22.8	45.3	33.5	12.8
1830 to 1839	78.1	73.9	4.2	39.4	37.3	2.1
1840 to 1849	84.4	81.6	2.8	41.5	40.1	1.4
1850 to 1859	88.5	65.6	22.9	42.4	31.5	10.9
1860 to 1869	86.6	72.1	14.5	40.6	33.8	6.8
1870 to 1879	92.7	89.0	3.7	42.4	40.7	1.7
1880 to 1889	86.6	76.2	10.4	38.7	34.1	4.6
1890 to 1899	87.8	72.1	15.7	38.3	31.4	6.9
1900 to 1909	77.3	64.1	13.2	33.6	27.8	5.8
1910 to 1919	56.8	56.1	0.7	24.0	23.7	0.3
1920 to 1929	77.1	63.8	13.3	31.0	25.6	5.4
1930 to 1939	61.1	46.7	14.4	23.0	20.6	6.4

* *Estimated from 1780 to 1900; based on state census figures from 1900 to 1939*

population varied uniformly between the dates of the known census figures, so we compared the average of the registered births and deaths to the estimate of the Reformed population at the middle of each decade as the method for calculating population indices between 1780 and 1900. From 1900 we based our conclusions on the denominational data of the state census taken every tenth year. From 1780 the birth rate remained at a uniformly high level for one hundred years, although some uncertain indications of a slight decrease can be noticed from 1830. A decisive fall in the birth rate began in 1880. The death rate was raised by the infectious diseases

[60] L. Thirring has calculated the increase in the population of towns and villages in the contemporary area of the country between 1869 and 1949. Whereas in these 80 years the population of Budapest increased by 426 per cent, that of the towns increased by 175 per cent, and that of the villages by only 54 per cent. Átány lagged far behind the general population increase of rural settlements (Thirring, 1963: 256–262).

[61] The data of the registers were collected by Márta Szabó, assistant minister of Átány, for which the authors express their heartfelt thanks to her.

[62] In 1786 the Reformed population totaled 1,732; in 1846, 2,415 (Fáy, 1854: 47); in 1872, the church recorded 2,453. From 1890 the denominational data of the censuses are published by village as well. The 1890 census recorded 2,280 Reformed inhabitants at Átány.

of the 1830s, 1840s, and 1870s. (The strikingly low death rate of the 1780 decade may be the result of a mistake in recording, or possibly a different system of registration.)

According to the registers of the period of serfdom, Átány's population grew more rapidly in the eighteenth century than did that of most villages in the surrounding Plain region. Also, the growth rate seems to have begun to slow down earlier than in most of the other communities. Thus in the nineteenth century several villages of the region overtook Átány in population.

Table 5

Births, Deaths, and Marriages of Átány Village*, 1901 to 1960

Year	Number of live births	Number of deaths	Natural increase or decrease (−)	Number of marriages	Year	Number of live births	Number of deaths	Natural increase or decrease (−)	Number of marriages
1901	87	65	22	.	1931	81	42	39	31
1902	91	85	6	.	1932	86	63	23	23
1903	92	70	22	.	1933	88	45	43	14
1904	88	57	31	.	1934	74	53	21	22
1905	79	84	− 5	.	1935	86	59	27	20
1906	110	62	48	.	1936	55	61	− 6	24
1907	91	72	19	.	1937	58	36	22	23
1908	85	83	2	.	1938	60	51	9	21
1909	110	85	25	.	1939	54	36	18	15
1910	97	51	46	.	1940	71†	50†	21†	21†
Total between 1901 and 1910	930	714	216	270	Total between 1931 and 1940	713	496	217	214
1911	70	67	3	27	1941	61	45†	16†	26†
1912	91	72	19	22	1942	58	45†	13†	26†
1913	78	54	24	18	1943	60†	45†	15†	26†
1914	85	64	21	11	1944	64	54	10	6
1915	57	66	− 9	5	1945	47	80	−33	20
1916	44	56	−12	10	1946	64	37	27	42
1917	44	74	−30	21	1947	62	44	18	19
1918	36	62	−26	17	1948	57	35	22	21
1919	90	43	47	68	1949	55	33	22	40
1920	104	82	22	40	1950	76	34	42	34
Total between 1911 and 1920	699	640	59	239	Total between 1941 and 1950	604	452	152	260
1921	108	70	38	30	1951	52	37	15	21
1922	90	69	21	24	1952	68	29	39	30
1923	83	55	28	27	1953	57	33	24	29
1924	94	83	11	24	1954	58	23	35	23
1925	81	47	34	30	1955	55	28	27	20
1926	91	58	33	25	1956	49	32	17	21
1927	95	85	10	30	1957	38	35	3	31
1928	90	60	30	39	1958	36	25	11	37
1929	91	73	18	19	1959	46	38	8	25
1930	96	58	38	41	1960	58	35	23	12
Total between 1921 and 1930	919	658	261	289	Total between 1951 and 1960	517	315	202	249

* Administrative unit; includes outlying areas.
† Estimated

State registration was introduced by law in 1894, and population data have been published by the official statistical bulletins from 1901 (see Table 5).[63] These data reveal that in Átány during this period the birth rate and the population increase in general were lower than the national averages and much lower than in the Heves district (see Table 6). From the turn of the century the birth rate has continued to decline; it fell especially in the years of World War I (Tables 4 and 5). The death rates as well as the birth rates of Átány, the Heves district, and Hungary as a whole all fell, but Átány's at a faster pace—especially its birth rate.

Analysis of the death-rate data reveals a general prolongation of the average life span. András Fáy, one of the founders of demography in Hungary, recorded the age categories of the inhabitants of Átány who died between 1837 and 1846 among the data of numerous other settlements.[64] Comparing his data with those of a hundred years later, the striking decrease in infantile and juvenile mortality and the increase of people dying in old age are immediately apparent. These changes are even more dramatically represented by mortality data of the last decade.

Emigration also has contributed to keeping the size of Átány's population virtually

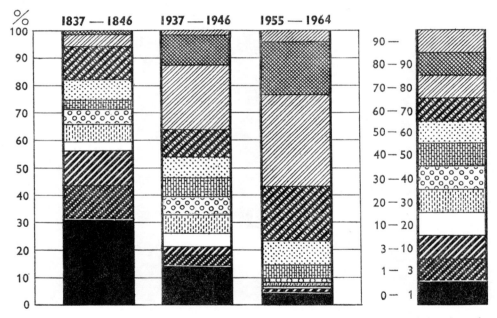

8. Átány mortality ratios according to age for three decades between 1837 and 1964 (taken from the material published by András Fáy and the data of the village registers).

[63] Figures for gross number of live births taken from the registers of the church (in Table 4) and those taken from the state censuses (in Table 5) differ because the census included the Catholic inhabitants of the Szárazbő farms in the data for Átány. However, the list of christenings in the church registers includes children born outside the parish, in hospitals or maternity nursing homes (in recent years). Thus the Reformed peasant population of the village is better represented by the data collected from the church registers.

[64] Fáy, 1854: Table E.

Table 6

Comparative Population Increase or Decrease, Natural and by Migration,
by Census Period, 1900 to 1960

| Period | Numerical Population Increase or Decrease (−) | | | Percentage Population Increase or Decrease (−)† | | | | | | | | |
| | in Átány village* | | | Natural | | | by Migration | | | Actual | | |
	Natural	by Migration	Actual	in Átány village*	in Heves district	in area of contemporary Hungary	in Átány village*	in Heves district	in area of contemporary Hungary	in Átány village*	in Heves district	in area of contemporary Hungary
1900 to 1910	216	−335	−119	7.4	15.6	12.2	−11.4	−7.2	−1.1	−4.0	8.4	11.1
1910 to 1920	59	−61	−2	2.1	7.3	4.8	−2.2	−0.5	0.1	−0.1	6.8	4.9
1920 to 1930	261	21	282	9.3	12.8	9.7	0.7	−6.7	−1.0	10.0	6.1	8.7
1930 to 1941	217	−300	−83	7.0	9.7	6.4	−9.7	−8.7	0.9	−2.7	1.0	7.3
1941 to 1949	88	−165	−77	2.9	4.3	3.6	−5.5	−3.0	−4.8	−2.6	1.3	−1.2
1949 to 1960	243	−567	−324	8.3	9.6	10.0	−19.3	−11.3	−1.8	−11.0	−1.7	8.2

* Administrative unit; includes outlying areas.
† Population shown by census for first year of each period used as base.

constant. However, the indices calculated in Table 6 for Átány as an administrative unit are misleading; they should be viewed in the light of the varying population distribution between interior and outlying areas as shown in Table 3. If the relatively large population fluctuations on the manorial granges were deducted, the differences between the Átány and the district indices in Table 6 would be reduced to almost zero. (The fluctuations of population in the interior village and on the outlying manors, such as shown in Table 3 [e.g., in Szárazbő], cannot be attributed to any significant degree to migration from the manorial *tanya*-s to the village or vice versa; the majority of personnel on the estates were not Átány people, and they did not migrate toward the village.)

Population tendencies are reflected in the age structure of the people of Átány (see Table 7). We have data on the individual communities from 1900, but unfortunately they divide the population into major age groups only. As was true also of the district and Hungary at large, at the beginning of the century the population of Átány

Table 7

Comparative Distribution of Population by Age Group, by
Census Period, 1900 to 1960

Year of Census	Area	Total Population		Age							
				0 — 14		15 — 39		40 — 59		60 or over	
		No.	%	No.	%	No.	%	No.	%	No.	%
1900	Átány village*	2,933	100.0	952	32.5	1,036	35.3	658	22.4	287	9.8
	Heves district		100.0		38.0		36.6		18.4		7.0
	Area of contemporary Hungary		100.0		34.9		38.7		18.9		7.5
1910	Átány village*	2,814	100.0	875	31.1	989	35.1	622	22.1	328	11.7
	Heves district		100.0		38.1		35.9		18.2		7.8
	Area of contemporary Hungary		100.0		34.7		38.6		18.7		8.0
1920	Átány village*	2,812	100.0	847	30.1	1,028	36.6	580	20.6	357	12.7
	Heves district		100.0		34.2		38.7		17.9		9.2
	Area of contemporary Hungary		100.0		30.6		41.3		19.1		9.0
1930	Átány village*	3,094	100.0	995	32.2	1,162	37.5	578	18.7	359	11.6
	Heves district		100.0		31.3		40.4		18.4		9.9
	Area of contemporary Hungary		100.0		27.5		42.6		20.1		9.8
1941	Átány village*	3,011	100.0	936	31.1	1,059	35.2	670	22.2	346	11.5
	Heves district		100.0		30.5		36.9		21.5		11.1
	Area of contemporary Hungary		100.0		26.0		40.6		22.7		10.7
1949	Átány village*	2,934	100.0	761	25.9	1,097	37.4	675	23.0	401	13.7
	Heves district		100.0		26.0		37.6		23.5		12.9
	Area of contemporary Hungary		100.0		24.9		38.7		24.7		11.7
1960	Átány village*	2,610	100.0	667	25.6	904	34.6	590	22.6	449	17.2
	Heves district		100.0		26.3		35.3		23.1		15.3
	Area of contemporary Hungary		100.0		25.4		36.7		24.1		13.8

* *Administrative unit; includes outlying areas.*

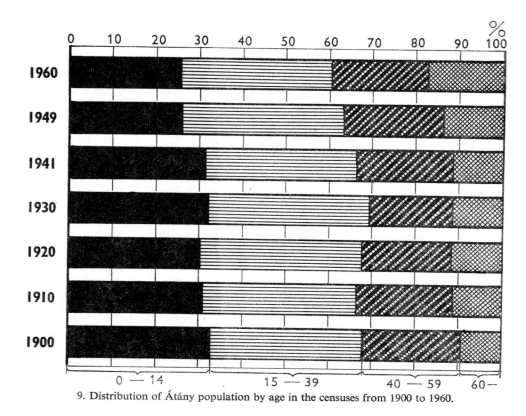

9. Distribution of Átány population by age in the censuses from 1900 to 1960.

was fairly young. At this time the population was still heavily weighted with numerous children and the younger generation of the working-age groups. In the succeeding decades the proportion of older people, in the village as throughout Hungary, has gradually grown.

This change was not brought about solely by the decreasing death rate and increasing longevity that increased the population. It was in these years that the village lost

Table 8

Comparative Proportions of Sexes, by Census Period, 1900 to 1960

Year of census	Total population of Átány village		Males		Females		Number of Females per 1,000 Males		
	No.	%	No.	%	No.	%	Átány village	Heves district	Area of contemporary Hungary
1900	2,933	100.0	1,453	49.5	1,480	50.5	1,019	1,014	1,012
1910	2,814	100.0	1,388	49.3	1,426	50.7	1,027	993	1,007
1920	2,812	100.0	1,389	49.4	1,423	50.6	1,024	1,048	1,062
1930	3,094	100.0	1,539	49.7	1,555	50.3	1,010	1,030	1,044
1941	3,011	100.0	1,455	48.3	1,556	51.7	1,069	1,083	1,042
1949	2,934	100.0	1,433	48.8	1,501	51.2	1,047	1,068	1,081
1960	2,610	100.0	1,284	49.2	1,326	50.8	1,033	1,056	1,073

Table 9

Comparative Distribution of Population by Principal Occupation*, by Census Period, 1900 to 1960

Year of Census	Area	Total Population		Principal Occupation											
				Agriculture		Industry		Commerce		Transport		Civil Service		Other	
		No.	%	No.	%	No.	%	No.	%	No.	%	No.	%	No.	%
1900	Átány village†	2,933	100.0	2,676	91.3	168	5.7	13	0.4	3	0.1	33	1.1	44	1.4
	Heves district		100.0		83.2		7.6		1.1		0.8		1.8		5.5
	Area of contemporary Hungary		100.0		60.8		16.0		4.8		2.9		3.6		11.9
1910	Átány village†	2,814	100.0	2,529	89.9	146	5.1	13	0.5	2	0.1	31	1.1	93	3.3
	Heves district		100.0		82.8		8.3		1.2		1.4		1.6		4.7
	Area of contemporary Hungary		100.0		55.9		19.3		5.4		3.8		3.6		12.0
1920	Átány village†	2,812	100.0	2,609	92.8	122	4.3	21	0.8	7	0.2	17	0.6	36	1.3
	Heves district		100.0		84.1		7.6		1.3		1.6		1.4		4.0
	Area of contemporary Hungary		100.0		55.7		18.6		5.6		4.3		4.3		11.5
1930	Átány village†	3,094	100.0	2,845	91.9	151	4.9	14	0.5	7	0.2	36	1.2	41	1.3
	Heves district		100.0		81.2		8.9		1.8		1.6		2.0		4.5
	Area of contemporary Hungary		100.0		51.8		21.0		5.9		3.7		4.6		13.0
1941	Átány village†	3,013	100.0	2,682	89.1	218	7.2	15	0.5	7	0.2	42	1.4	47	1.6
	Heves district	...	100.0	...	...	...	...	...	...	...	...	...	...	...	...
	Area of contemporary Hungary		100.0		49.1		23.1		6.0		4.0		4.5		13.3
1949	Átány village†	2,934	100.0	2,533	86.4	136	4.6	35	1.2	85	2.9	56	1.9	89	3.0
	Heves district		100.0		78.6		8.8		1.8		2.4		2.7		5.7
	Area of contemporary Hungary		100.0		49.1		23.1		4.8		4.8		7.0		11.2
1960	Átány village†	2,610	100.0	1,697	65.0	433	16.6	53	2.0	109	4.2	‡	‡	318§	12.2§
	Heves district		100.0		59.0		20.0		3.5		5.7	‡	‡		11.8§
	Area of contemporary Hungary		100.0		35.5		33.0		5.3		7.0		6.8		12.4

* Including dependents
† Administrative unit; includes outlying areas
‡ Included in "Other"
§ Including "Civil Service."

to the towns, to less populated agricultural regions, and to foreign countries hundreds of young people old enough to earn a living. Throughout Hungary the rural population grew older, while in the rapidly growing cities the ratio of the able-bodied age groups exceeded the national average. At the same time, the overall proportion of older generations was increasing. Átány, compared with the district and the country, shows a more protracted and more balanced line of change.

Published statistics distinguish between sexes but not by age categories (see Table 8). In the decades of the present century Átány, like the district and Hungary at large, has had a surplus of women, but its sex ratio has generally been more evenly balanced than in either the immediate neighborhood or the country as a whole.

In the twentieth century the proportion of farmers and agricultural laborers in the working population of Hungary gradually decreased (see Table 9). The absolute number of the agricultural population has been diminishing only since 1949. In Átány the dwindling of the agricultural population began somewhat earlier; it is evident as early as 1941, following a peak in 1930. This diminution, however, is in part an expression of the decrease in the personnel of the manorial farms.

Nonetheless, the Átány population is characterized by its rural, agricultural features. The ratio of the people living by agriculture fell under 80 per cent only after 1949. The percentage shows the village to be an outstandingly agricultural one even in the predominantly agrarian population of the Heves district, to say nothing of the entire Hungarian population.

A SUNDAY CHURCH SERVICE:
HOW THE PEOPLE OF ÁTÁNY SEE THEIR OWN SOCIETY

At Átány life goes on in small groups, usually in the family circle. Rarely do even as many as twenty or thirty people gather together. There is only one building in the village where every inhabitant of the community from school age on has a place and this place is exactly defined: the church. For church, the people set aside their everyday working clothes and put on festive attire, symbolic in its color and style of age, rank, and family status. On the way to church the members of the family part and find their places according to a general classification which embraces all the people of the village. This classification corresponds to the family status of each person. In the church married men and bachelors, married and unmarried women, old and young people all sit in different rows. Also, the designation of pews separates the inhabitants of the two parts of the village, the Lower and the Upper End. It expresses the rank and wealth of the individual families and allots a place of honor to the village officials and the non-peasants living in the village. Thus the order of pews is an expression of the Átány people's view of the structure of their own society.[65]

[65] This order of seats was not prescribed by the church. Backed by higher church authorities, ministers tried to reform it several times (in 1883, 1914, 1940), but the congregation maintained the old custom. It is a wide-spread custom of Hungarian Reformed congregations to partition the pews according to age groups, sex, and local units of settlement.

The members of the family do not prepare for the service at the same time. Houses are busy on Sunday mornings as the women boil water for washing and prepare the festive costumes. First of all the unmarried girls are dressed and the bachelors made ready. Then come the married men, and last the married women. They start for church in the order of preparation. The members of the family leave the house one by one, but they avoid going to church alone. Each one goes with a friend, the person living farther away calling for the one living nearer. Dignitaries of community and church might go together if they live along the same road.

The girls gather in the churchyard near the two gates of the church and form several rings according to age groups. The bachelors meet in the open space in front of the town hall. Schoolboys and schoolgirls gather in the classroom, the village officials in the council chamber of the town hall. (Recently the church officials have been meeting in the council room of the rectory.) Married men without any office also stop near the church in order to exchange a few words with their contemporaries. Older men and women go right into the church to their places and start singing.

A protracted ringing of bells, consisting of three "verses," marks the beginning of the service. At the first tolling the schoolchildren take their places, led by their teachers. At the second, other waiting groups enter: first the girls, then the bachelors and men. Each age group reaches the entrance at the same time and file to their seats one by one. Only people who are late arrive during the third tolling. (As the bell-ringer rings the last "verse," he looks out from the spire to see whether there are any of the more respected faithful hurrying late to the service. A widow of a well-to-do *gazda* whose son-in-law is a Reformed pastor frequently arrives a bit late; for her the bell-ringer tolls once or twice more so that she can reach the churchyard while the bell is still ringing.) At the end of the bell-ringing the village officials march in, led by the village mayor, and the pastor enters too, followed, according to a recent custom, by the body of church officials. Then the gates of the church are shut behind them.

The present form of the church building is a result of several extensions (1783, 1801). It is a single large irregularly shaped hall with a broad choir running around three sides (see Figs. 10 and 11). The steeple stands on one side of the building; on the other side a narrow annex, the so-called "small church," joins the hall. One entrance to the church opens below the tower, and a door leads to the porch under the tower and thence to the hall itself. Through this enter the faithful of the *Felvég*, the Upper End, as well as the village magistracy and the pastor. Another door stands on the southern (right) side, below the choir; this is the entrance of the people of the *Alvég*, the Lower End.

The table of the Holy Communion stands in the center of the church, between the tower and the small church; behind the table, at the corner of the annex there is the pulpit, with the "Moses seat," the place of the pastor and his assistant, at its foot. Both on the ground floor and in the choirs the simple soft-wood pews are arranged so that from all three sides they face the pulpit and the table. On the fourth side, in the small church, there are also a few narrow benches turned toward the pulpit.

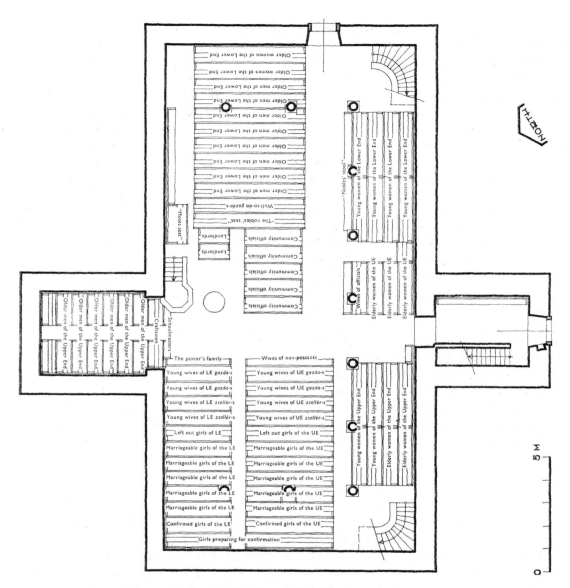

10. Plan of the ground floor of the church and the order of seats in the pews. At the bottom, below the tower, one sees the entrance of the people from the Upper End (UE), to the right that of the Lower End (LE) people. Opposite the tower is the so-called "small church," the pulpit, and the communion table.

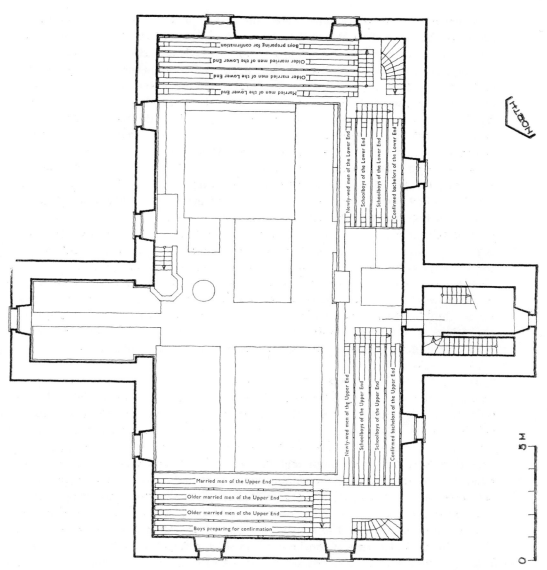

11. Plan of the organ loft (choir) of the church showing position of benches.

People entering the church are divided into two large groups by the two entrances: people of the Lower End and of the Upper End. Inside the doors the groups break up as individuals move off to pews appropriate to their age, sex, and family status.

The place of the men is on the right side of the main hall, in the small church, and in the choirs. Schoolboys sit in the second and third pews at both sides of the central organ loft, opposite the pulpit. The choir is divided into two parts by the organ; the right side belongs to the Lower End boys and the left side to those of the Upper End. When the boys leave school and begin preparing for their confirmation, they move to the back rows on both sides of the organ loft. After they have been confirmed they move back up next to the organ, behind the schoolboys, since they are now classified as bachelors. They remain in the choir after marriage too. The place of newly-wed men is the first row of the choir on either side of the organ. This row is called the "rail." On both sides of the organ loft the "rail" belongs to men who have been married for more than ten years. The rows above them are occupied by men older than they, those "who were not squeezed into the middle of the church yet." At the top the boys still preparing for confirmation are located, as mentioned above.

Below, the seats of the men consist of ten rows of long benches, one behind the other, in front of which are two ranks of short benches. One of these ranks, the two short "stools" (benches) beside the "Moses seat," used to belong to the landlords of the vicinity. The general superintendent of the church was one of them, and he sat in this place. Beside the landlords the male members of their families and their guests could be seated.

The six pews of short benches in the other rank is a place of eminence as well, formerly occupied by the community officials, and now by church officials.[66] In the corner of the first pew, near the table of the Holy Communion, sat the village mayor, beside him the village judge and the secretary, and in the other corner the church-warden. In the second row the village treasurer had a place behind the mayor; his neighbors were the public tutor and the two oldest counsellors. The other short benches were occupied by the remaining counsellors in the order of their ages. In the last short pew the *hadnagy* (cf. footnote 35, Part Five) and the former mayor sat.

Going backwards the first of the long rows is "the nobles' seat," the second belongs to the well-to-do *gazda*-s. The others are occupied according to property and rank, mainly by the older men of the Lower End. In the "small church," the first pews belong to the schoolmasters, the second pews to the craftsmen; behind them older men of the Upper End sit, those who own less and have a lower rank.

Men stay in the choir as long as they can, only moving from one part of it to another. From the rail of the newly-weds they move to that of the men married for a decade at least, then they move backward. Usually a man comes down to the floor only if his father dies and he may occupy his seat, or if he is elected to some office and has to take the appropriate place. Otherwise they come down only if the number

---

[66] Formerly the members of the church council sat in the pews of the older men, each according to the rank of his person or family. Since 1948 the village officials do not go to church in a body, therefore their places are occupied by the church officials in the order of age.

of young people grows and there is no room in the choir. It happens that even men married for twenty-five or thirty years go up to the choir. Propriety demands that they settle into the "aged" pews, however. If a man's father-in-law has a more elevated rank than his own father and enjoys more esteem on account of his office (e.g., being a church official) he may occupy the pew of his father-in-law instead of that of his own father. However, there are people who, out of modesty, stick to the place occupied by the previous generations of their family. Said Ferenc Orbán: "When the term of my church office is over, I shall sit in the third pew from the back. My father and my elder brother occupied it and I shall do the same. I do not intend to go ahead; I shall stay in the place of my grandfather."

In the age groups of the schoolboys and bachelors, the division between the inhabitants of the Lower and the Upper Ends is a sharp one, with each having their separate places in the organ loft. With older people, the boundary line is not as sharp. Should a bachelor of the Lower End marry into a family of the Upper End, he might remain with his old companions in the choir. The rows of the dignitaries, nobles, and wealthiest gazda-s are not partitioned according to locality.

Girls and married women have their places below, in the rows of the left side and also in the three groups of pews directly underneath the choir.

Schoolgirls do not sit in pews. There are benches in front of the left-hand pews for them; if there are too many girls, some stand in front of the benches. When they leave school and prepare for their confirmation, at the age of twelve, they are allowed to sit in the twelfth (rear) row of the left side. The rows are divided into two blocks here: the "short benches" on the pulpit side are "assigned" to the females of the Lower End, the "long benches" next to them belong to those of the Upper End. In both columns unmarried women sit in rows 5 to 12. After their confirmation, the girls move forward from row 12 to row 11. Year by year as they grow older they move closer and closer toward the front. In rows 6 to 10 one finds marriageable girls, in row 5 those who were "left out"—the spinsters.

After marriage a woman moves out of this section of age-graded pews into a new seat. The first row of the short benches, opposite the former pew of the superintendent, belongs to the wife of the minister, the female members of his family, and his guests. In enumerating the rows, the people of Átány do not count this pew; they call the pew behind the pastor's wife the "first stool." It may be occupied by the young wives of the most esteemed, wealthiest gazda-s of the village. The second row belongs to those of a somewhat lesser rank. The young wives of the Lower End poor or zsellér-s occupy the third and fourth rows. (Behind them one finds the unmarried women.)

Beside them, in the first row of the "long benches" sit the wives of the schoolmaster, the village secretary, and other non-peasants. Behind them, in the "first, second, and third bench" according to the Átány reckoning, the young wives of minor gazda-s have their places, then those of the Upper End zsellér-s, and behind them the unmarried women of the Upper End.

The young women may occupy these seats for six to eight, rarely ten years. Then they have to cede their places to younger women and move to the pews below the choir.

Both of the front rows of benches situated to the left of the tower porch, below the choir, are occupied by Upper End young women who have moved on from the pews of the newly wed; behind them are the elderly women of the Upper End. To the right of the porch, the first pew "below the organ" is a place of distinction; here the midwife, the daughters-in-law of the mayor and the churchwarden, and the wives of craftsmen have their places. Behind them there are also elderly Upper End women. The seats of the Lower End women follow in a similar order in the block of pews below the choir on the right. The first row is the "nobles' stool." Behind it is the place of younger women. There is no more room here for the old women of the Lower End; they occupy two or three rows behind the men in the right-hand section of pews. A woman moves from below the choir to the place of the older ones as soon as one of her children gets married. As the saying goes: "She may sit under the choir until her daughter calls her out"—which means that custom requires her to move into the block of the old women as soon as her daughter moves under the choir from the young women's pew.

Between the back rows of the Lower End and Upper End women there are two "paid stools" reserved for the female members of the Szilágyi family. (One of their ancestors was unable to sit in the normal pew on account of a physical deformity, so they had a separate pew made.) There is a long bench without a back in the porch too. Decrepit old women of the Upper End sit here because they have "bad feet" and do not want to go farther to the front. Beggars may also find a place here.

Unmarried girls and bachelors change their places every year. On the Sunday following confirmation, which is held at Whitsuntide, both girls and boys move forward into the benches for those recently confirmed and their former places are occupied by those who are preparing for confirmation in the following year. The older girls and bachelors change their places in order to make room for them. Introduction of the newly wed into the rows of the young married women or men is accompanied by special solemnity. Especially for the young women, occupation of this new place signifies not only age and the new marital status, but also rank. The wedding usually takes place on a Thursday. The following Sunday the young wife appears in the attire of a married woman. She wears the white kerchief of the newly wed to the church for the first time, and both she and her husband occupy their new seats. The young wife is accompanied and led to her seat by a near kinswoman of her husband; he also is escorted to his seat by a kinsman. The relatives are asked in advance to perform this act. The place where the young woman should sit is discussed beforehand too. She is usually assigned her place in the church according to the rank of her husband's family, but should her own family have a higher rank, she may choose a place in accordance with that. When, for example, a *földes* (landowning) girl married a man of less property, she still sat in the first pew, "because she decided on the basis of the *ág* (lineage) she was descended from." The grandmother of one woman came from the rich noble *ág* Vajda, but the man she married was not a wealthy man—only the son of the cowherd. Nevertheless, the descent of her mother entitled her to sit in the first pew.

The young wife arrives in the church accompanied by the kinswoman asked to perform the introduction; this woman ushers her into her future place and sits at her side for this occasion. It may happen that the young woman finds the place allotted to her by the family of her husband unsuitable. If, for example, the family of the husband is ambitious, placing the young wife in one of the first pews where, even if the others welcome her, she is not at ease, she may change her place at the next occasion at will, choosing a more modest one instead.[67]

The place allotted to the newly wed woman is discussed all over the village. People consider whether the choice was too ambitious or too modest. To capture a "distinguished" pew may be the goal of a concerted family effort, since it would amount to the recognition of a social rise. Even in the beginning of the 1950s one could hear young women quarrel in this way: "After all, I married better than you, as I was led into the first pew and you into the second only."

Also, seating changes act as statements made to the entire village. Whether a woman stays in the pew of the young longer or modestly moves to the old ones' place earlier depends on family circumstances and characteristics. Generally one's seat in church is a means of recording one's age. Should a doubt arise regarding someone's age, people ask: with whom does he (she) share the pew in church? The symbolic meaning of one's place in church is illustrated by the fact that in 1948 the secretary of the local Communist Party organization occupied the seat of the village mayor in all solemnity.

At the end of the religious service females leave the church before males. The schoolgirls lead the march, then the unmarried girls in the last row rise at once and follow in single file: those of the Lower End to the Lower End door, those of the Upper End to their exit. Thus age categories follow in order; and when the old women have gone, the bachelors and men leave the church.

Members of the village magistracy go over to the town hall to discuss official business. Schoolchildren, girls, bachelors, elderly men, and married women form several groups and then scatter in the roads leading in various directions. The women have to hurry home to prepare the festive lunch. At the table the Átány families gather again and take their seats in the established order.

---

[67] In 1940 the church council passed a decision against this ushering-in of young women according to rank. Three young wives of zsellér-s sat down in the first row, but only for two Sundays. They gave up their experiment on the third Sunday, as the other women "were bursting" at the sight of them.

PART TWO

THE FAMILY

CHAPTER 4. THE HOUSE AND THE KERT

THE HOUSE

Houses at Átány are one-story buildings, like those of other Hungarian villages. The walls are constructed of adobe and the roofs are thatched with reeds. Traditionally these houses consist of three or four rooms: a living room (which is also used for sleeping), a kitchen, a pantry, and a loft above. Usually one end of the building faces the street. The rooms are arranged linearly with the living room, "the House," at the street end and the pantry at the other end with the kitchen in between. Many houses have a veranda on the entrance side of the building; thus people do not enter directly from the yard but through the veranda. From the veranda (or from the yard if there is no veranda) one enters the kitchen. The kitchen itself is divided into an inner part, the real "kitchen" with an open chimney, and an outer entrance hall, the *pitar*, with an archway between them (see Figs. 12–14). In this "front hall" is a door to the living room on one side, one to the pantry on the other, and the ladder leading up to the loft.[1]

Since the 1860s we find changes, but these have not supplanted the traditional design; in 1960 there were still 473 houses consisting of a living room, a kitchen, and a pantry.[2] The reasons for the changes are manifold, but they always result in elongation of the buildings by addition of another living room, or possibly a cooking room. In the new houses a small living room, the "small house," takes the place of the traditional pantry while the traditional living room, the "parlor," is reserved for special occasions. Now the pantry is built as a continuation of the "small house"

---

[1] The division into living room–kitchen–pantry (the type of ground plan presented here) is generally typical of the Hungarian rural house. Differences are found partly in the heating devices, partly in the building materials utilized (earth, adobe, wood, stone), which influence the proportions and outside appearance of the house.

The dome-shaped oven of Átány, located in the living room but stoked from the kitchen, the vaulted open chimney, and the open fireplace like a platform of adobe or mud are all characteristic features of the Great Plain. These heating devices have spread to neighboring regions with the advance of the culture of the Great Plain. They are now found in the northern, mountainous, part of Heves county too, where long, prism-shaped stoves located in and stoked from the living room were formerly in use (Bátky, Györffy, and Viski, n.d.: 124–245).

[2] That number constitutes 64.9 per cent of the houses of Átány. In addition there were 246 dwellings with two living rooms (33.7 per cent) and ten with three or more rooms in addition to kitchen and pantry (1.4 per cent).

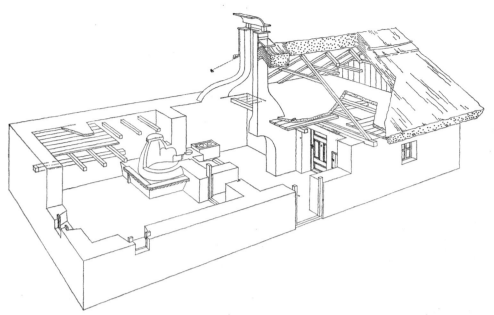

12. A cutaway view of the house of Sándor Rózsa, built in 1876. Behind the entrance door one sees the *pitar* and the kitchen. The kitchen is topped by a vaulted "open chimney." In front of the door of the dome-shaped stove one sees the open fireplace (a small elevation of adobe), on which people used to cook over the open fire. In the corner is an adobe kettle holder. Beside it is a kitchen-range constructed later, the smoke of which also escapes by the open chimney. The crossbeam runs the length of the building from the living room to the pantry; thinner beams laid across the crossbeam support the boards of the ceiling, which are covered with a thick layer of plaster. The thatched roof is supported by rafters.

and is entered through it. In such buildings the ladder leading up to the loft is removed from the *pitar* to the new pantry. If ancient houses are rebuilt, the pantry is turned into a "small house" and a new pantry is constructed as an annex. The breaking up of the extended family may also result in reconstruction or elongation of the house. If the parents are unable to build a new house for a married child starting an independent life, they add a room and a kitchen to the end of the old house. These general types of rooms are common to all Átány dwellings, although their sizes may differ according to the size and status (in terms of property) of the family. Since the purpose of the house is to provide shelter for the whole family as well as storage for the produce they will consume during the year, the local rule generally holds that a large family needs a large house, a small family a small one.

Populous families, consisting of two or three married couples with their children, needed a living room 5 or 6 meters wide by 6 or 7 meters long; the kitchen and the pantry had the same width, with a length of 4 to $4^{1}/_{2}$ meters. In Átány an increase in the number of family members never used to result in construction of additional rooms or even of a single room; growing families preferred to occupy new houses. The pantry never has been used as a bedroom for a young couple, as was true among several Hungarian groups north of Átány, nor has it ever been customary to add

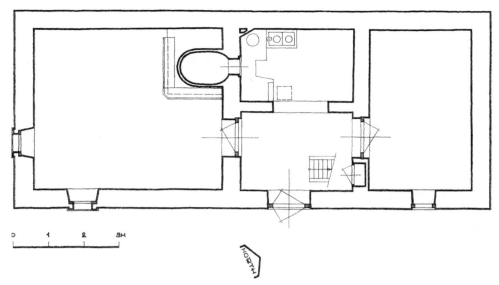

13. The floor plan of the house of Sándor Rózsa. Immediately behind the entrance door is the *pitar*, separated from the kitchen by a wall with an arched doorway. From the *pitar* doors open to the living room (left) and to the pantry (right). From the *pitar* one may ascend to the loft. The stove in the living room (heated from the kitchen) is surrounded by a bench.

annexes to the old house to serve as sleeping places for each young couple, as was done in the southwestern regions of the country. Thus the Rózsa family, living in a joint household at about the turn of the century and not separating until 1927, consisted of five married couples and their children. They inhabited three separate houses, each containing a living room, a kitchen, and a pantry, built close together on one holding. (See Chapter 5, "The Forms of the Family and Its Division of Labor.")

Small families have a living room 4 meters wide by 5 meters long, and a kitchen 3 to 4 meters long; the pantry has a length of 3 meters in the homes of *gazda*-s, 2 meters in those of *zsellér*-s. Houses built to shelter a solitary widow are the smallest. The back living room found in recently constructed houses does not exceed 3 meters in length.

During construction a bottle is often hidden in the "first corner," the corner of the house between the street and the yard. It contains a record of the date of construction and the person for whom it was built; some people record also the prices of cattle and grain or any notable event of the year—a comet in the sky, drought, plague, epidemic, war, etc.[3] Sometimes coins are put into the bottle too. This "first corner" is a spot of ritual importance. Old people believe that the white domestic snake, the good spirit of the house, lives there and leaves its place only at the death of the *gazda*. Inside this corner of the house stand the table and corner benches rimming the two walls (see Plate 7). It is usually a large, expandable hardwood table, big enough to

[3] When the community constructed a new home for the notary in 1901, a bottle containing the names of the village magistracy was placed in the corner of the foundation (see Appendix B).

seat twelve or fourteen people. In addition, trestles and planks are kept in the house for an occasional extension of the table and benches at festive meals. The kerosene lamp which lights the house is hung over the table.

In the center of the wall on the street side a large mirror hangs between the two windows, and around it the photographs of near relatives who are still living; photographs of deceased kinsfolk are hung over the beds. In the other front corner of the room, opposite the table, stands the "first bed," an ornamental bed which is not ordinarily slept in, piled almost to the ceiling with eiderdowns and pillows (see Plate 8). In front of the bed there are chairs, at the foot a painted chest. The baby's cradle usually stands beside the chest. One of the interior corners of the room is occupied by the large adobe oven, fed from the kitchen; this domed structure heats the house and is used for baking and cooking as well. It is surrounded by a bench (see Plate 9). On the very short wall between the oven and the door to the *pitar* hangs a towel rack with an ornamental handcloth embroidered with the name of its maker, the year it

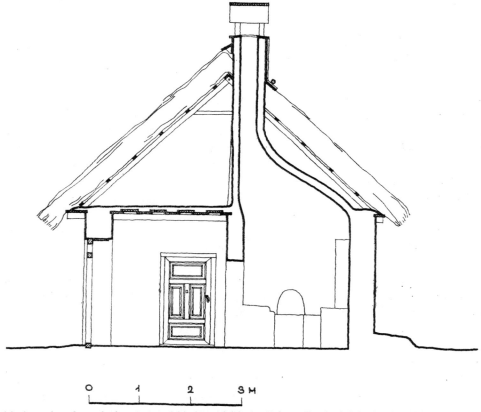

14. A section through the *pitar* and kitchen of Sándor Rózsa. To the left is the door leading to the living room, to the right is the oven door and, in front of it, the open fireplace made of adobe. At the top the brick vault of the chimney is shown in longitudinal section. The part below the vault is the kitchen; the part below the loft, the *pitar*.

was made, and a legend such as "Welcome," "Good morning," etc. The towel hangs on the rack only as long as there is a young woman in the house. In the houses of old people the towel rack is empty. On the other side of the door, in the other interior corner, on the yard side, stands the bed for everyday use.

In more "modern" arrangements the table is no longer in the corner, but in the center, and the furniture is placed symmetrically. In this case both street-side corners of the room contain an ornamental bed; between them, below the mirror, stands a chest of drawers or a bench, in front of which are placed the table and chairs. There are chairs in front of the ornamental beds too. Recent fashion has replaced the chest by a wardrobe with a glass door. The oven and the everyday bed remain unchanged. There are trundle beds under the beds and stools under the benches which are pulled out when needed. Curtains have been hung on the windows since 1885. Those who initiated this fashion were suspected of having something to conceal. Ancient rules of propriety demanded that one should be able to see the interior of the house from the street unhindered. The watchmen, patrolling in the village at night, would enter houses where they saw light after the usual time, in order to offer help. If they found a bachelor inside who was still courting at that late hour, they marched him off to the town hall.

As can be seen from the above description, the walls of the living room are lined with furniture, leaving the center empty from the door to the table. Remembering the large rooms of former days, old people say that the empty space in the middle was spacious enough for a cart to turn around. The *pitar* is also essentially empty; there are niches cut into its side walls, and a narrow cupboard or a bench for water jugs, but that is all. Only the pantry and the loft are crowded.

At Átány a hundred-year-old house is very rare and is regarded as ancient. Adobe houses disintegrate relatively fast, though they are plastered over and whitewashed twice a year. Most Átány families do not live in the old family house for generations; except for a small minority, they sell, exchange, demolish, or extend their homes (see Figs. 15–17). If a young woman is brought to an old house, there is hardly any change in the furnishings; the chest or wardrobe of the young wife is simply added to the old ones. Should a *vő* (son-in-law) move into the house, there is no change at all, since his clothing is put into the chest of his young wife. A poor man, beginning his independent life and moving into a new home, has first to acquire a table and a bed. If he buys an old house, he finds the corner bench in it, as it is not customary for the vendor to remove it. The rest of the furniture must all be paid for, but no one asks or gives money for the benches. It is unusual to sell a house with a full set of furniture; ordinarily only a few superfluous pieces are left in it. Often people leave minor objects behind, if they cannot use them any more. Family photographs, souvenir cards, quotations from the Bible (usually hung on the walls) must always be taken away. In 1963 the public was shocked by a middle-aged couple who, selling their inherited house, left not only the corner bench behind, but also the portraits of their ancestors in the loft.

The activities which take place in the house vary with the season but also with the

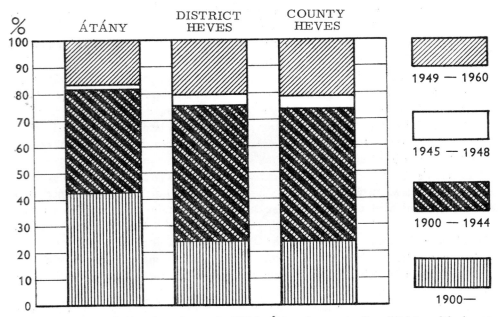

15. The percentage of old and new houses in 1960 in Átány, the surrounding district, and the larger county, dated by period in which they were built, based on census data. The relatively large proportion of old houses at Átány is explained partly by the fact that its population has not greatly increased, and so there was only a slight need for building new houses.

size of the family. In winter, traditionally the family takes its meals in the living room. Women stay in this room all day long, spinning or sewing, and here they set up the loom when the time of weaving comes, usually in late winter. Children play and learn here. The child is born in this room, the gravely ill person dies here; this is the place where the body of the deceased is laid out and mourned over. This is the place for feasts, including the wedding party. In houses where there is also a small living room, people celebrate their festivals in the large "parlor" and spend their workdays in the small room.

The kitchen is the place for cooking and baking bread, the source of heat for the living room, and the place where washing and various other messy tasks are performed in winter. Niches or cupboards contain the kitchenware, the spices, and the milk and other dairy products. The pantry is used for keeping flour, grain, wine, bread, and processed fruits and spices (see Plate 10).

In the loft, which extends over all three rooms, corn is stored as well as some of the other grain if there is not enough room in the pantry, the supply of smoked meat and bacon for the whole year is hung, and peas, beans, nuts, and the seed-grain are kept (see Plate 11). Crockery and baskets which are rarely used and old household utensils are stored here. The dirty linen is thrown across a rafter in the loft until washing.

The different parts of the living room and the pieces of furniture fit into a hierarchy.

The most honored spot in the house is the corner table with its two benches. The highest ranked place is the "head of the table," which is opposite the entrance and below the mirror; the person sitting there not only can take in the whole room with a single glance but may also look out to the yard and the street through the windows. This is the place where the *gazda* and the most esteemed guests of the house sit. From there, the rank of the other places around the table gradually decreases; the chairs with their backs toward the door are the least in rank, belonging to the unmarried girls. The chairs placed in front of the ornamental bed are also esteemed ones, where relatives, female guests, or a desirable suitor may sit. The seat lowest in rank is the platform of the stove by the door. Old women crouch here, and it is also the place for the neighbor's wife or a female day laborer.

At a wedding, the corner of the table is still the most important place; this is where the *násznagy*-s (the marriage sponsors) and the esteemed guests are seated. The bride bids farewell standing beside the table, and bartering for her or for her bed goes on here (see Plates 53 and 54). It is customary to place the bier of the dead member of the family where the table usually goes. In rooms with the new symmetrical arrangement the honored place is no longer the corner, but the center of the "better" part of the room, below the mirror. But the order of seats around the table remains the same. In such a symmetrical arrangement the bier is still positioned in the place of the table, lengthwise in the middle of the room.

When heating is no longer necessary, the family stops having meals in the living room and moves into the kitchen, or, more precisely, to its front part, the *pitar*. A small table is laid here, brought out only at mealtimes, and the members of the family sit around it on low stools. In summer the family has only the evening meal in the house; on workdays lunch is taken in the fields or in the *kert*.

There is a status gradation among the sleeping places too. The ornamental bed or beds piled up with pillows and situated in the front part of the room do not serve as sleeping places for the family. They are used only for an esteemed guest or a person who is gravely ill, and women lie there after giving birth. There is just one permanent sleeping place in the room: in the corner behind the door; this is called the first place. It belongs to the *gazdasszony*, and the *gazda* sleeps there too when he spends the night in the house.[4] The chimney corner is the resting place of the children. All the other sleeping places are temporary and are made up before going to bed and dismantled in the morning. Beds are made on the corner benches and the one around the oven or on a straw mattress on the floor. Low, wheeled trundle beds, kept under the beds in the daytime and drawn forth in the evening, are very common. In the evening when the beds are made, the appearance of the room is completely altered. If the family is a large one, the otherwise empty center of the room is so filled up with bench-beds and mattresses that one can hardly move around. The room regains its customary daytime character in the morning when it is tidied up and the trundle beds are put away.

---

[4] Married couples always sleep in the same bed, even if one of them is gravely ill. It is usual to put children of the same sex into the same bed, and a mother may sleep with her grown-up daughter or small child.

Traditionally a young woman bears her child on the floor, lying on a piece of sackcloth or canvas. Should she follow the recent fashion, she may give birth on a trundle bed or even on the bed in the back of the room. Only after her delivery is she transferred to the ornamental bed, which is transformed for this occasion into "a bed with a mosquito-curtain"; this, at least, was the custom in the old days. The "mosquito-net" is a large, white, ornamental curtain which hangs from the ceiling and surrounds the bed on three sides. Its purpose is to protect the woman in childbed from the evil eye. It is customary to remove the curtain after six weeks' time, after the young mother goes back to church for the first time, where she is blessed. Then she returns to her old place and her baby is laid in the cradle, brought down from the loft.

In summer the family does not sleep in the living room. Sleeping is transferred to the pantry or, like meals, to the front part of the kitchen, the *pitar*. In the pantry people sleep on benches or mattresses placed on the floor. In the *pitar* they lie on a *suba* (traditionally) or a canvas stretched out on the floor in such a way that their heads are supported by the threshold. Old people often say: "It is splendid; I like to sleep on the earth." Those who are afraid of not waking up in time rest the back of their heads on a small stool instead of the threshold. Younger people may also lay a straw mattress down at the door of the *pitar*. Sickly old men, forced to move into the house from the *kert*, lie on planks placed across trestles, a trundle bed, or a straw mattress placed for them on the veranda as long as the weather permits. Very rarely the loft may also serve as a sleeping place. The newly-weds spend their first night there and sometimes even a whole week.

The Átány house provides its inhabitants with warmth in the winter and coolness in the summer. It gives each member of the family the seating and sleeping accommodations due to him, both for everyday and for special occasions. Its status-differentiated arrangement expresses the role of each member of the family, while at the same time it allots to the visiting outsider the place which is due to him in this hierarchy.

But the house provides a definite status framework for even more than the workdays and celebrations of the relatively small circle of persons who inhabit it; it may hold a hundred or more guests at festive occasions so that the place of each guest is indicative of his rank and position relative to the family or even to the community as a whole.

Most domestic activities are performed in the living room in winter and in the kitchen or the yard in summer. Some housework, such as everyday cooking, is considered the intimate affair of the family and is performed inside the house; even the next-door neighbor does not know what is prepared. Other kinds of work, however, like boiling soap, making plum jam, drying fruit, rendering fat, pigsticking, and cooking for the festive meals are all done outside. Newly woven linen is bleached in the yard and spread out there after being washed, giving people a look at some of the household's supply. However, a number of agricultural activities in Átány are done neither in the house nor in the yard, but rather in the *kert*. Thus the house does not represent an organic unity in itself; it becomes one only if we add the *kert*.

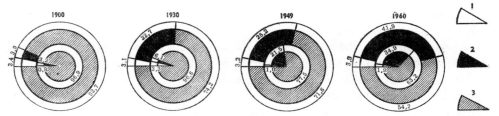

16. Change and traditionalism as reflected by materials used in house construction between 1900 and 1960. Key to symbols used: (1) Stone or brick walls. (2) Adobe on a foundation of stone or brick. (3) Adobe or mud. The outer circles represent Heves district; the inner circles, Átány. The increase of stone or brick foundations and the decrease of brick walls are an indication of the adoption of bourgeois fashions. A comparison of Átány and the Heves district bears out the conclusion that the village has changed with its surroundings, although slightly more gradually. Átány has remained more old fashioned than the district as a whole.

The use of the house has been altered by the partial closing over of the open chimneys, which transforms the hitherto cold kitchen into a warm one suitable for occupation in winter as well as summer. (This process was begun at the turn of the century; the last open chimneys were covered in the 1960s.) Accordingly, a number of activities moved to the kitchen from the living room, enabling the family to save it for more special activities. The transformation went even further. It is now customary to build separate summer kitchens, attached to the house or in its immediate vicinity. Cooking is done in these throughout the summer, and people often sleep there too. So in summer the whole house is spared everyday use; it is tidy and neat all the time, in preparation for the rare visitors.

THE KERT

The *kert* is a farmyard which is separated from the house (see Fig. 18 and Plates 12–22). Its size varies between 200 square fathoms and one *hold* (1.42 acres). Its main building is the stable. (The *kert* of a well-to-do *gazda* might contain two or three stables and sheepfolds.) The cart shed and the tool house used to be under the roof of the stable; now they may be housed in a separate building, to which a shed for the chaff and fodder may be added. Since the dry climate of the Hungarian Plain makes

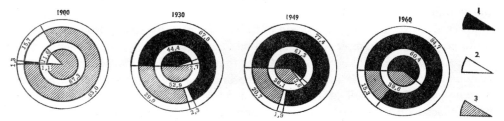

17. Change and traditionalism as reflected by materials used in roof construction between 1900 and 1960. Key to symbols used: (1) Tile, slate, sheet-iron. (2) Shingle, plank. (3) Reed and thatch. The outer circles represent Heves district; the inner circles, Átány. The increase of tile and slate roofs is an indication of the disappearance of ancient building techniques.

it possible to stack cereal crops, fodder, and straw under the open sky, the *kert* is full of ricks and stacks. The stable stands near the entrance from the road, and in front of it is an open space, the actual yard of the *kert*. Until the end of the last century, and occasionally even in this one, the grain was threshed out by the horses in this stable yard. At the side stand the cart house and the shed, farther back the ricks and stacks. Behind them are the vegetable garden and a few fruit trees. The *kert* rarely lacks a well with a watering trough, which is usually located near the entrance.

The stable is no rival to the house. Valuable furniture, bedclothes, important documents, and the money of the family are all kept in the house; the photographs of the living and dead members of the family are hung on its walls, and grain and other provisions are stored there. The house is the site of family celebrations and social gatherings. The stable has no part in these functions. A *gazda* once built a granary in the *ólaskert*, keeping not only grain, but also meat, fat, and eggs there and occasionally bringing some of them to the women for cooking; this was an exception, and was considered exemplary of disorderly family life. It is also considered improper for a *gazda* to hide his money in the *kert*, though it happens more frequently. For one thing, if the *gazda* has buried the money, he might not be able to reveal the hiding place when he is dying.

The stable is built and equipped primarily as a shelter for the animals. Although it is true that men sleep there throughout the year and spend a considerable part of their time there, especially in winter, there is no equipment similar to that in the house. For example, the stable lacks bed and bedclothes; rude beds are improvised from doles and planks and covered with straw or a mat woven of rushes (see Plate 18). When the men spend the night in the stable, they are supposed to be taking care of the animals even in their sleep. Old people, even if they have been going barefooted in the hot summer days, pull on their boots before going to sleep in order to be ready in case anything needs to be done quickly for the animals during the night. (If someone catches a cold, people often tease him by saying he probably slept barefooted.) A fire is kept burning in the stable in order to give light and heat, but there is no stove for it as in the house—it simply burns on the floor.

Like the house, the stable is a one-story adobe building with an entrance on one of the long sides. Its size varies according to the number of animals. Poor *zsellér*-s build small stables for one or two cows, while wealthy *gazda*-s keep as many as thirty animals and the building is so large that it requires two doors (see Plates 16 and 17). Even such a big stable could not hold the entire livestock of the most well-to-do *gazda*-s. For example, the Rózsa family kept its livestock in three stables.

The walls of the stable are usually lower than those of the house. It used to be customary to dig out the inside so that the floor was below ground level. Stables have no lofts. Traditionally, forked poles from the floor, more recently scissor-shaped props placed on crossbeams, serve to support the ridgepole. The roof is always thatched with reeds; even if the roof is tiled, a layer of thatch is placed below the tiles for insulation. The inside of the stable is a single room; one end might be partitioned off to form a wagon shed (see Figs. 19 and 20). A partition at the other end of the

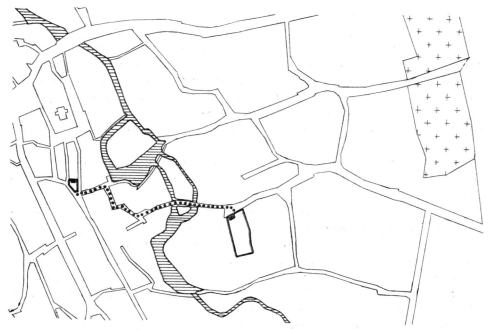

18. Location of house and *kert* of József Kakas. A part of the surveyor's map of the village (cf. Fig. 3), to which we have added J. K.'s house (on the left) and his *kert*. The dots show the path taken by the members of the family across the brook to their *kert*.

building used to form a tool shed, where the peasant kept his work implements and the harness or set up his carving board or workbench.

The stable usually has double doors; sometimes the door is divided across the middle so that the top part can be opened separately, and sometimes there is a small door, waist-high, directly in front of the large one. All this has the object of admitting fresh air and light. The initials or brands of several generations are burned into the door. When livestock are branded with the mark of the owner, the branding iron is usually tested on the door; its mark may serve as an "authentic document" in case of any doubt about the origin of the brand on the animal. Records of crop yields and birth dates of animals may be found on the doors, and in some instances even historical records—for example, the day on which the new bell was put up in the church tower.

Like the house, the interior of the stable has an established arrangement. The manger runs along the back wall. At one end the horses are tied, at the other the cattle. The horses' end is the more distinguished, and is also designated as the end for the men. This end of the building is usually closer to the road and the entrance of the *kert* and has windows on both the end wall and the long front wall. (These small windows cannot be compared to those of the house; in old buildings they are hardly larger than the palm of the hand. Earlier they were made of parchment or greased paper instead of glass and were stopped with straw in the winter.)

Also at this end of the building, "at the croups of the horses," is a plank-bed along the wall or two are placed at right angles to each other in the corner for the men. A few other modest furnishings for the comfort of the men are a rack on which to hang the worn hats and jackets used for work in the stable; a shelf or niche to hold the brush, scraper, and comb for grooming the animals as well as a bottle of brandy and possibly a razor; a mirror hung or stuck on the wall for shaving; and a pipe rack. A wooden holder for the night light also hangs on the wall, with a glass lamp about the size and shape of a small round apple inside; next to it a container for oil is hung on a nail.

In the early part of this century an open fire fed with straw was the only light in the stable (see Plate 21). A shallow pit circled by bricks or stones served as a fireplace in the middle of the open space in front of the beds.

In the old days the fire played a central role in the life of the stables. Usually the old men would keep it going with a metal rod to one end of which a copper ring was attached; it clanked as they directed each piece of straw toward the fire, holding the rod between their legs. When the men awakened at dawn, the first act of the old man would be to strike a light. His son or the servant would take care of the horses in the glimmering light of the fire. If visitors entered the stable, the fire would be relit. It burnt long in those stables where groups of males staying in the *kert*-s—sometimes as many as thirty or forty of them—would gather to talk on winter mornings and evenings (see Plates 19 and 22). In these stables the smoke would be rising to the thatched roof almost constantly, so it was to such places that bacon and meat would be taken to be smoked after pigsticking. In such *tanyakert*-s one could sometimes see thirty or forty sides of bacon hanging above the heads of the group of men.

The guests would sit around the fire on small stools or, in the manner of earlier times, on clumps of earth plastered with mud. The place of honor was the plank-bed. The *gazda* would sit there or on a low stool in front of it, poking the fire. This seat would be offered to special visitors whom the *gazda* wanted to honor, while each member of the usual group of guests had his own stool and place. The stools were hung in a row on the crossbeam or the edge of the fodder box. As the guests arrived, they took their stools one after another; if the beam was high, they reached for them with a fork. This large supply of stools was the single difference between the furniture of the *tanyakert*-s, where these gatherings were held, and the ordinary *kert*-s.

The males, entering the house after being in the stable, always brought a strong smell of smoke with them, and the long white hair of the old men was yellowed by smoke. When the fire was not being used, it was kept going by covering up the embers with a piece of wood, so it could be rekindled easily if a light was needed in the night.

The other side of the stable contains the cattle. The boxlike poultry house is usually built under the roof of this end. Outside, under the eaves, was a ladder for the poultry; inside was one for gathering the eggs. On the wall opposite the livestock is a place for tools and a pen for newborn calves.

Boys began to frequent the *kert* quite young. Some of the old people of Átány

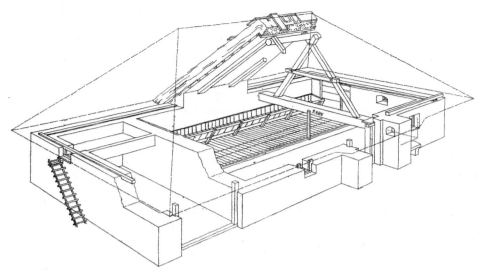

19. Cutaway view of the stable of János Kusper, built in 1888. To the left, over the cart shed, is
a poultry roost in the rear, with a ladder for the chickens on the outside. The thick thatched roof
is supported by a ridgepole and scissor-shaped props, one set of which rests on the partition wall
of the cart shed, the other on a strong crossbeam.

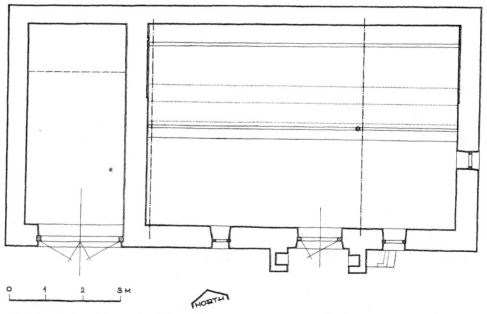

20. Ground plan of the stable of János Kusper. The large space at the right houses the large animals;
their feeding trough runs along the rear wall. To the left is the cart shed. The entrance is protected
by a small roofed entryway in the walls of which are niches for small objects (matches, key, etc.).

remember being brought there for the first time on their father's backs. While the men carried on their conversation around the fire in the evening, as many as eight or ten boys would be snug in the box in which the fodder is stored at the back of the stable. If they were noisy or misbehaved, the *gazda* would clear his throat; this was usually enough to restore calm. If not, "the low stool flew to mete out justice."

When a boy left school at the age of 12, he was given his permanent sleeping place in the stable. If there was no free resting place, a new plank-bed was set up for him. This change was a very welcome one for the boys because it allowed them a great deal of freedom compared to the rather severe discipline of the house. As boys and bachelors, they were able to stay out with their age-mates in the evenings, and later they could court the girls freely. Ferenc Orbán said, "I would not have stayed at home, even if they wanted to keep me. All the other boys came out too, and we became friends. Our fathers went to sleep, while we were roving round. We were glad to have left school." The band of bachelors gathered in a stable where the *gazda* was not spending the night. Sometimes they got hold of some liquor; sometimes they roasted poultry acquired by dubious means, or baked eggs and sang until morning. If they had nothing to do in their own *kert* and they were in the mood, they could sleep in the stable of a friend's family. The fodder box or the manger could be used as a resting place.

The grown-up bachelors and adult men were bound to the good by work and responsibility for the care of the animals. Nor did marriage bring them back to the house for long at a time. People say: "I could not sleep quietly inside, one has to be with the animals all the time, to listen if they make any noise." They have a general principle: "If one has livestock, his place is in the stable. A man who likes the white bed in the house does not take much care of the animals." The good *gazda* was restless even during the short mealtimes in the house, nervously wondering whether his beloved animals might hurt themselves, or whether a man of evil intentions might be trying to force open the stable door.

Elderly people had fewer chores in the *kert*, but many were unable to part with the stable. It was their job to keep order. Many men remember their youth and complain of the old *gazda* who, being a light sleeper, awakened them several times to set something right with the animals. In numerous stables horses were fed at night as well as in the daytime. The life of care-worn, resourceless elderly people was bound even more to the *kert*. Food and clean linen had to be brought to them, for they did not return to the house for weeks at a time. We are told that "these ancient old men experienced illness as an extra punishment, since they had to go to the house." Even as late as the time of our field work we met such old men who lived in the stable, but they represented an extreme case. Coming and going in a regular rhythm between the house and the *kert* (to be dealt with in the next section in detail) was the general way of life.

From spring until late autumn the life in the *kert* was regulated by agricultural work. In a hot summer both men and animals left the stable: the animals were tethered at outdoor stanchions, and the men slept near them, often on a pile of straw in a cart. If the livestock remained in the stable, the *gazda* would sleep in the open door, if only for the sake of caution.[5]

In late autumn the livestock were no longer put to pasture and the people no longer worked in the fields. The program of the day was more comfortable as all activities took place in the *kert*. There was then time to groom and brush the horses with loving care. It is said that at about the turn of the century this was more a passion than a duty. Men swept the floor of the stable behind the horses carefully, then painted it black and formed stars and flowers or the name of the horse out of the white dust they had gathered in tidying it to show off to visitors.

During the long rains of the autumn and the snowstorms and frosts of the winter, the daily intercourse with the house was sometimes interrupted, and the men did not return from distant *kert*-s for a week at a time. Sometimes they could get to the village through the slush and mud only on horseback. On Monday they brought out a large loaf of bread and bacon; milk, eggs, and sometimes a chicken were available in the *kert*-s. They baked eggs and ate curdled milk. This was the real time of *tanyázás*, conversations around the fire. The day was spent caring for the animals, weaving baskets, making brooms, and carving tools. Neighbors sometimes brought their work to the *tanyakert*-s, and the *gazda*-s of these stables left them open, even if they went to the house.

---

[5] Even so, toward the end of the last century, sometimes thieves would lead a horse out of the stable right over the head of the sleeping *gazda*, by covering the floor with straw to muffle the noise.

CHAPTER 5. THE FAMILY

A WORKDAY IN THE FAMILY OF JÓZSEF KAKAS

Before dawn of an early summer day, at about 2 A.M., the cowherd walked through the village and "piped for milking."[6] The women all opened their eyes and got up, and those who did the milking dressed hastily and went out to the *kert* so that the cows would be ready in good time to go out to the pasture when the cowherd "piped for driving."

Thus in the house of József Kakas, both the old *gazdasszony* and her young daughter-in-law got up and made their beds. The younger woman washed, dressed, and went out to the *kert* to milk.

The sound of the horn also wakes the men, who have spent the night in the stables (see Fig. 18). And so in the stable of the Kakas family both *gazda*-s, the old and the young, got up. They put on their clothes[7] and set their sleeping places in order. They cleaned out the scant stable litter from the short night, the old *gazda* from behind the cows, the young one from behind the horses. Together they carried all the dung on a two-man rack. There is no feeding at this time, since fodder was given the animals for the night; eventually the cow gets something, in order to make her easier to milk. In the meantime the young woman arrives, greeting them with the words: "God give you a good morning." They return the proper greeting: "God give you." She begins milking at once. The young *gazda* wipes the horses clean (in summer they are brushed only on Sundays), then he tidies up the stable with his father. Finally they load up the wagon which they will ride to the fields with the necessary tools for the day and with feed for the horses. They wash their hands and faces from the trough or from a bucket, put better hats on, make other preparations, and harness the horses to the wagon.

Meanwhile the old *gazdasszony* has kindled the fire in the house and has looked after the piglets and the few poultry kept there. She has prepared a satchel for those going out to the fields, which she now carries to the *kert*. She greets her people

---

[6] What is actually played is a reveille which is known with numerous variations in the village. One of the texts attached to them runs: "Get up, get up, you *gazdasszony*, or the cow will be left behind." The tune is given in Fél and Hofer, 1962b: 174.

[7] The men always slept with their shirts and under-pants on. In summer they put on their trousers and their hats; in cool weather they would don a vest or a short jacket also.

as did the young woman and is greeted by them in turn. They take the satchel and outline their tasks for the day: which part of the fields they will go to and what they will be hoeing. The wagon departs with the men and the young woman. The *gazdasz-szony* feeds the numerous poultry in the *kert* and gathers the eggs. Since the cowherd has begun collecting the cows, she herds hers out to the road for him to pick up. She collects fuel, packs it into a bundle that she lifts to her back, and with the milk can in one hand and the egg basket in the other, she starts for the house.

The swineherd is blowing his horn for the pigs by the time she gets there, so she quickly drives them out of the yard. Then she wakens her grandchild, dresses, combs, washes her, feeds, and sends her with the geese to join the gooseherd at the end of the village. Now she tidies up the kitchen, and sweeps the yard (and also the road in front of the house, if necessary). Finally she washes herself, changes her head shawl and apron, and sits down to have breakfast. She takes coffee with milk, sour milk, eggs, and fruit together with a generous portion of bread; if she is inclined to have bacon or sausage, she cuts herself some. After breakfast she goes to the well for drinking water, and takes the extra milk to the dairy. On market days she stands in line with the eggs, dairy or other products she wants to sell; having "made a couple of *pengő*-s," she buys the spices she needs. She often stops en route to chat with neighbors, relatives, or friends and hear the village news. On her errands she may also pay a call on some sick relative before she hurries home. On Mondays or Tuesdays she washes the dirty linen of the past week; on other days she may churn butter, make curd, dry fruit, or do just ordinary housework. She may check the *kert* at least once and sometimes twice. "Being at home, she hears a whisper in the *kert;* being outside, she hears one in her home"—she cannot rest anywhere. There is poultry to be cared for, young calves, and sick animals; there are ripened fruits or plants to be laid out for drying in the garden.

At noon, if not sooner, her grandchild will come home. They may have only a cold meal for lunch; at the most, they may bake some eggs, bacon, or sausages. However, the principal items are dairy products and fruit, again eaten with much bread, or some kind of pastry if any remained from breakfast. After lunch the house-wife goes again to the *kert*, this time gathering from the adjoining kitchen garden greens and potatoes needed for her cooking. At 3 P.M. she must begin cooking for dinner. For this she always prepares two courses: soup, possibly with meat, and often with noodles boiled in it—this is the main dish, "the first kind." For the "second kind" she prepares vegetables, tomatoes, and cake or noodles. While the dinner is cooking, she has to herd in the geese, gather the ducks from the brook, and pen up the pigs when they are driven home. Then she tidies up the kitchen, sweeps, "puts herself in order," and awaits "the men for dinner."

To return to the men and the young woman, we find that they have driven to the fields at a trot. The Kakas family have good registered horses and easily overtake the other carts on the road. But they address everyone in a friendly manner: they greet young people jokingly and elderly ones with respect. At this early hour one sees a line of wagons spaced some 200 to 300 meters apart driving toward the fields and beside them larger or smaller groups of pedestrians. A decent man does not want to be one of the last nor to linger behind, especially when going to the fields. As our people reach the wagon trail they pay particular attention to the lands sown with grain, noting their condition, and amicably "shout at" other people who happen to be already working in the fields.

They arrive at their holding at about 4:30 A.M., stopping near a hut, since the Kakas family have a small building or shelter on each part of their land. They tether the horses in the shade and give them fodder from the wagon. The young woman, Zsófi Rózsa, changes her dress and kerchief and the men take off their jackets and vests. They find a good place for the satchel with the food and set the jug with the drinking water in the shade and then all gather in the corner of the land which is to be worked. The *gazda*, being the "first hoer," takes the first row, his son the third, with his daughter-in-law between them, so the men can help her should she lag behind. Before turning the first sod, Zsófi Rózsa utters a prayer she heard from her mother; "My Goodness, we attack this large piece of earth now," and they start briskly hoeing along the rows. The old *gazda* sets the pace. He has already checked the dimensions and decided upon the length of the row. (At hoeing time the people divide their ribbon-like strips of land crosswise into several sections, since short rows make the work seem easier.) Only at the end of a row is one allowed to stand upright and stretch a little. (Their short-shafted hoes make them work in a strongly bent position.) Together they turn and start new rows. Softly talking, humming, perhaps singing, they continue hoeing until 8 A.M. and then, after finishing the particular rows they are on, they gather near the hut to have breakfast. Zsófi Rózsa lays a blanket on the ground, places in its center the emptied linen satchel, and spreads out on it the food they have brought: bread, bacon, sausages, etc. Including the time taken to eat, they rest for about half an hour; some lie down on their backs or sides in order to straighten their backs. Then they hoe again until 10 A.M., when they halt at the end of the tract and the old *gazda* lights a pipe, the young one a cigarette. Such a rest at the end of the section offers a good opportunity to chat with the neighbors, for work is planned so they will meet at the ends of rows. Leaning on the handles of their hoes, they talk as long as the pipe of the old *gazda* stays lit. The next break comes at lunch time, usually between noon and 2 P.M. They eat the same food as in the morning and stretch out their limbs comfortably; most take a short nap. Then they fodder and water the horses and continue working till 4 P.M., when the men light up again as a sort of afternoon rest. If their task is not too pressing, they stop hoeing at 6 P.M. at the sound of the bell, the "field tattoo," change their clothes, climb into the wagon, and drive back to the *kert*.

The young woman hurries home to help her mother-in-law; the men unharness and feed the horses. The old *gazda* milks the cow. They water the animals and go to the house between about 7 and 7:30 to have dinner. There they greet the women respectfully, "Hi, God give you...," the latter returning their greeting. The women prepare water for the men to wash, and they all sit down at the table. The *gazdasszony* serves everyone. It is improper to talk during the meal, but afterward they tell one another the events of the day from the fields and from the village. After this exchange they discuss the schedule for the following day so the *gazdasszony* will know what sort of food to prepare for the satchel. The young woman is told whether she has to join the men again or whether she may stay at home. However, they do not linger long at their talking. The old *gazda* slices bread for the foals, the dogs, and the cats and wraps it in his apron to carry to the *kert*. Sometimes he takes a small jug of soup for the cats. Finally the animals in the *kert* are given fodder, the bell rings for bed time at 9 P.M., and everyone goes to sleep, both in the house and in the *kert*.

The most trying summer work for the Kakas family is gathering the harvested wheat sheaves into the *kert*. Harvesting itself is laborious too, but that work is done mainly by hired sharecroppers; the members of the family do not actually participate in it save for five or six days.

During gathering time the men do not go into the village; they move back and forth between the *kert* and the field, and their food is carried to the *kert* by the women. The men rise at 2 A.M. and quickly water and brush the horses and harness them to a prepared wagon, for they are anxious to be on their way by 3 A.M. If they have two teams of draft animals, one carries the old *gazda* with the sharecropper who is to be the loader, the other carries the young *gazda* and his wife. They work until 6 A.M. transporting the sheaves, then have a hurried "stand-up" breakfast in the *kert*, and make two more trips before noon. Lunch, which is usually an ample hot meal, is taken in the *kert* on a blanket laid on the floor of the wagon shed, after the animals are watered and foddered. There is no time for a rest now, however sweltering the heat may be. At 4 P.M. they return for another load, have another "snack" as hurried as the morning's, and then generally are able to make two more trips before evening. When the bell sounds for bed time at 9 P.M., they are unloading the sheaves from the fifth or sixth round-trip of the day. Only then do they feed the animals, wash themselves, and have dinner on the floor of the wagon shed. They water the horses and cows, throw some fodder in front of them, and retire. This demanding pace usually lasts for two weeks, except for the rest offered on Sunday. The *gazdasszony* assumes all the burdens of caring for the *kert* during this time, not to mention cooking twice a day and delivering the food to the men.

In fall, after all crops have been brought in, the fields lie unworked under the first snow. The livestock are kept in the stables and sheds, and the men also take to warm shelter to rest and pass the winter. The long nights are spent in long slumber. The short days are broken by only two meals. Animals likewise are fed only twice, for both man and beast must live on the reserves from the summer. After a year of bad crops, both may feel need in winter. But this is the time to eating sparingly, for the body at rest does not require abundant food. People work at handicrafts and the animals are seldom harnessed; at the most they are used to cart manure to the fields when the weather permits. Sometimes the horses are "paced" to prevent their becoming flabby from standing in the warm stable.

There is no early sounding of horns; rather, the men are awakened about 5 A.M. by the stirring of the hungry animals. The young *gazda* lights the lamp and busies himself around the horses, the older around the oxen and cows. They give them fodder, gather the litter from under the horses and cattle, and together carry it to the manure pile. The animals are "cleaned" after the second feeding. Horses are brushed with special care now. The old *gazda* milks the cows. They put out fresh bedding, sweep the stable carefully, and then water the animals. The old *gazda* gathers the eggs laid the previous day. They change their hats, put on warm jackets, and at about 8 A.M. go to the house for breakfast.

At the house the women also rise at 5 A.M. Each makes her own bed. The old *gazdasszony* kindles the fire in the stove and for breakfast kneads the dough for *pogácsa*, mixes a *pite*, or molds a leavened loaf. She places the dough in the oven to bake along with some potatoes. A jar of water is placed in the oven to heat for washing. In the meantime the young woman looks after the piglets and feeds the poultry, if any are kept near the house. She sweeps the house, including the kitchen and even the yard in front of the house and the street beyond when necessary. She awakens her little daughter, dresses and feeds her, and sends her off to school. She herself washes, changes her head shawl and apron, and then goes to the village well for drinking water and to the grocery to buy supplies. She returns with the latest news of the village, heard at the well, in the shop, or on the road. The old *gazdasszony* also washes and changes into better clothing. With the meal ready, the house and themselves neat and tidy, the women await their men.

"God give you good morning," the men say as they enter the kitchen, and their greeting is respectfully returned. The *gazdasszony* takes a small jug of brandy from a niche in the corner of the kitchen and pours out one "portion glass" for each of the men. (The "glass" is both a measure of one-half deciliter roughly equivalent to one fluid ounce, and a drinking vessel.) While the men drink the brandy, the young woman pours out water for washing, first for the old *gazda* and then for the young. The whole family then take their places at the table for breakfast. The Kakas family eats the first course, baked potatoes, at the table in the living room, where they have been served hot from the stove. (Many families used to eat baked potatoes from a basket put in the middle of the room around which they sat on small stools.) The second course, usually simple bread dishes, is always served and eaten at the table. If it is after pig slaughtering, breakfast would include pork scraps, chitterlings, or sausages. The family sits together at breakfast until about 10 A.M., and then the men say good-bye and leave for the *kert*. They feed the horses again, the old *gazda* gathers the new droppings, sweeps again, and then lies down on the plank bed to rest. The young one brushes the horse and combs its mane and tail and then sets to work making baskets, brushes, or brooms. This is also the time for overhauling the implements damaged in work; the young *gazda* mends them or manufactures new ones.

Tanyázás in the *kert* (visiting one's neighbor) could be started before 8 A.M. already; those who have fewer animals and who have finished earlier with them may drop over to another *kert* for a chat. The Kakas people, especially the young *gazda*, are not very fond of such visiting; they prefer to receive passing neighbors, friends, and relatives in their home. József Kakas is very clever at making baskets and is actually a master at producing wicker bottle covers. People often call on him in order to learn his technique.

At 2 P.M. the men finish work. They rest and smoke and feed the animals. The young man looks after the horse, the older the cow. After the first feeding the young József Kakas goes out to the barn yard and binds the "ropeful of straw," tying the straw, which serves as fuel for the next day, in a bunch. He throws fodder to the cattle for the second time, and then both he and the old *gazda* water them. The old *gazda* milks the cow. By 4 P.M. they are finished with the animals and cleaning the stable. On winter days the old *gazda* sweeps "the place" at least ten times, picking up every stalk of straw. They prepare for the start home. They change their caps, and the old man takes the milk can in hand, puts the eggs in his pocket, and goes out. His son follows him, with the "ropeful of straw" across his shoulder. The neighbors start at the same time. Each of them carries the same burden: the old men the milk and the eggs, the young men the bunches of straw. They do not form groups, rather moving toward the village in single file.

In the house the women, having finished breakfast, take the spinning wheel and begin spinning. Some neighbors and relatives living nearby join them with their spinning wheels, until sometimes there are four or five women gathered together; they converse quietly while spinning. Only the young woman of the house pauses from this work when her little girl returns from school at noon. She feeds her, washes and combs her hair, encourages her to learn her lesson, and then sends the little one back to school for the afternoon. At 3 P.M., at the sound of the bell, each woman lays aside her spinning wheel. The guests leave, and the *gazdasszony* begins cooking while the young one feeds the pigs and the poultry. Then both women sweep the kitchen and the living room, tidy themselves, and wait for the men. This meal is preceded by an eager anticipation surpassing that before breakfast. It is usual to have boiled food, perhaps soup with noodles, for the first course. Since the noodles become soggy if too long in the soup, the young woman or the girl watches the road for the men, and the *gazdasszony* puts the noodles in the soup only when the men turn in toward the house.

The men do not necessarily arrive punctually, however. Sometimes conversation with a neighbor keeps them on the road; on other occasions a name-day *(névnap)* or some unexpected celebration turns their *tanyázás* into a merry one indeed, and they may arrive home two or three hours late. When this happens, the *gazdasszony* sends the little girl to call them home, with the message that the meal will be spoiled; similarly it may happen at breakfast that baked potatoes "become stiff" (they get cold and cannot be eaten) while the women wait for the men to arrive.

When the men do arrive, they enter with a greeting, wash, and take a seat at the table. Dinner is followed by a long conversation, the men telling the news they have heard in the *kert*, the women what they have heard in the village. This is the time to talk over family affairs: going to the market, buying and selling, purchasing provisions are all topics of discussion. Having finished dinner, the women again take up their spinning wheels and bid the men stay: "Hi, stay a while, let us converse, we are

8

awake now." Once a week the young *gazda* spends the night with his wife in the house. When the time comes for the men to depart, if the young man wishes to remain, he lays the key of the stable on the outer corner of the table. The old *gazda* understands this sign and, lighting his lamp, he jogs along to the *kert* alone, to have another chat or to rest.

Those farming families in Átány which still maintained a separate dwelling house and *kert* in 1959 lived according to the same daily round as that in the Kakas family. Their days were similarly divided up by the bell and the sound of the horns, and caring for the livestock followed a comparable schedule. Thus, in winter, feeding and watering the horses and cattle generally took two hours.

The relative number of men and women in a household would be reflected in differences between farms. Women were spared considerable labor if there were more men in the family, but they would have to share the work with the men if there were relatively few. If a family contained numerous male members, they milked, brought fuel to the house, and looked after the poultry in the *kert* both summer and winter.

Slight differences were observed between more traditional and more progressive families. In the former, the *gazda* exercised greater authority. When returning home from the *kert*, the young *gazda* marched behind him at a distance of at least two steps, while their servant was allowed to jog after both another two steps behind. Such a *gazda* gathered the eggs into a basket and, in the old-fashioned way, carried them home only when the basket was full. Another difference arose from the custom of the older man sleeping in the house at night and visiting the *kert* during the day in order "to frighten" his son or his servant. Whereas this had usually been the case only with those well-to-do *gazda*-s who, for example, had some function on the village board or with the Hangya Cooperative, more recently sleeping in the house implied some degree of urbanization.

During the time of our field work, however, the great majority of the Átány farmsteads were concentrated on single holdings, which eliminated the continual trafficking between the house and *kert*, relieving both the *gazda* and the *gazdasszony* of considerable drudgery. Otherwise, the daily round for those families which had consolidated their holdings was much like that of the family of József Kakas. Although the importance in the daily routine of the men's return from the stable has decreased, and the formalities surrounding the occasion have lessened, still a decent *gazda*, having finished his work in the stable, tidies himself in preparation for entering the house. He changes or dusts his jacket, puts on another hat or cap, and grooms his moustache. Equally important, the division of activities by sex and generation within the family has become looser. Earlier the typical chores of men and women were physically removed from one another by the distance of several hundred meters between the two parts of the farmstead. But with males and females working in the same locale, their spheres of activity may overlap more.

Recent times have not changed the mealtimes, but people rise and leave for the fields later. The industry of "the ancients" is illustrated by the extreme example of a farmer setting out for plowing so early, when it was still dark, that he had to kindle a fire to look for the furrow. Now people wait for all the herds to be driven out, and only afterward do the wagons and the pedestrians move out. Beginning later in the day meant ending later. Thus József Kakas, Jr., used to return from the fields at about 8 P.M., if he was not instructed by his father to come back at 6 P.M.

THE FORMS OF THE FAMILY AND ITS DIVISION OF LABOR

At Átány a house is usually inhabited by one family. Those who live in the same house are called a *háznép*, "household" ("the folk of the house"), more rarely a *ház*, "house," or a *ház-család*, "house-family." The expression *család*, "family," in local terminology does not identify merely those persons living under the same roof. The children of the head of the family who have left the house and live under another roof belong to his family just as much as the children living with him. On the other hand, a more distant relative invited to live in the house or a servant are not members of the *család*. They "belong to the house," the *háznép*, only.

The other meaning of the word *család* refers to the children. "He has many *család*-s" or "he has a large *család*" means that he has a number of children. "A man of a small *család*" has few children.

A man and a woman contracting a marriage are not yet a *család;* they are "a pair of *cseléd*." When a child is born to them, "they become a *család*."[8]

As a rule, each person lives within such a family at Átány. The child is born and reared within a close family circle; the adult works within the framework and for the benefit of the family; it is desirable that he should die in the family circle, to be lamented and buried among its members.

People who are unable to begin a family of their own, owing to some physical or mental deficiency, stay in a family circle too. And an elderly person who remains alone, through losing his or her consort or having no offspring, also looks for shelter in a related family.

It is mainly widows who choose to lead a solitary life—those who refuse to join their children because of their unsociable nature or out of wise consideration and whose financial standing enables them to live alone. Apart from these there are a few solitary men in the village whose families have either died or emigrated and who could not find relatives to take them in. Even they try to join a family. Thus, János Kaja, a bachelor forty years old, joined the household of his near relative József Kakas. He lends a hand in the work of the family, and they reciprocate by cooking, washing, and cleaning for him.

Some males are solitary for spells because they are drunkards and "good for

---

[8] In contemporary colloquial Hungarian, the word *család* means "familia" (i.e., "family"); the word *cseléd* means "domesticus," "famulitium" (i.e., "servant"). The present minimal phonetic distinction developed only at the beginning of the nineteenth century, owing to the impact of the literary language reform. But the folk language still uses the various phonetic forms of the word without distinction, as to meaning, sometimes even with three meanings: (1) "familia," family; (2) member of the family, child; (3) servant, farm hand (Kniezsa, 1955: vol. 1/1.: 119).

8*

nothing," having been turned out by their families. They often form a liaison with women of ill repute who come from other places, fitting companions for their time of debauchery.

Since 1900, the censuses every ten years have differentiated the population according to family status (see Table 10). Compared with the population of both the sur-

Table 10

Comparative Family Status of Population Age 15 or Over,
by Census Period, 1900 to 1960†

Year of Census	Area	Total Population Age 15 or over		Status							
				Single		Married		Widowed ‡		Divorced	
		No.	%	No.	%	No.	%	No.	%	No.	%
1900	Átány village*	1,981	100.0	330	16.7	1,431	72.2	218	11.0	2	0.1
	Heves district		100.0		22.7		68.1		8.7		0.5
	Area of contemporary Hungary		100.0		29.0		61.7		9.1		0.2
1910	Átány village*	1,939	100.0	311	16.1	1,395	71.9	227	11.7	6	0.3
	Heves district		100.0		21.5		69.9		8.5		0.1
	Area of contemporary Hungary		100.0		28.7		61.8		9.1		0.4
1920	Átány village*	1,965	100.0	330	16.8	1,371	69.8	256	13.0	8	0.4
	Heves district		100.0		22.3		67.4		10.1		0.2
	Area of contemporary Hungary		100.0		30.9		58.5		10.1		0.5
1930	Átány village*	2,099	100.0	354	16.9	1,502	71.6	240	11.4	3	0.1
	Heves district		100.0		23.8		66.1		9.8		0.3
	Area of contemporary Hungary		100.0		30.1		59.3		9.7		0.9
1941	Átány village*	2,075	100.0	404	19.5	1,429	68.8	238	11.5	4	0.2
	Heves district		100.0		22.0		67.8		9.9		0.3
	Area of contemporary Hungary		100.0		28.5		60.8		9.6		1.1
1960	Átány village*	1,943	100.0	291	15.0	1,392	71.6	249	12.8	11	0.6
	Heves district		100.0		17.0		71.3		11.0		0.7
	Area of contemporary Hungary		100.0		20.3		67.8		9.9		2.0

* *Administrative unit; includes outlying areas*
† *Published figures from the 1949 census do not give data on family status*
‡ *Male and female*

rounding district and the entire country, Átány has had a larger ratio of married people throughout this period and a conspicuously smaller proportion of bachelors and old maids. But there were relatively more widows and widowers during this period at Átány than in either the Heves district or the whole country. Divorced people constituted an insignificant fraction. In 1869 the percentage of married people in the population was exceedingly large in Hungary. But, as a result of the immigration of the rural inhabitants to the cities and the spread of industrialization, this percentage decreased gradually until the period between the two wars. It then rose to a European record high after World War II. During the same period the proportionate number of divorces increased.[9] We have seen the remarkable stability of the population at Átány. There was a similar stability in the traditional rural marriage pattern in general—to such an extent that the indices do not vary by more than 3.4 per cent within the sixty-year period from 1900 to 1960. The national and regional proportionate decrease of number of married people hardly involved the parish at all. But after World War II, the generally increased proportion of married people in the population can be noted at Átány too; the proportion in the village even exceeded the proportion in the region. The village stayed far behind the national average as regards divorces.

In the period under investigation the nuclear family was common at Átány; however, the village was actually characterized by various forms of the extended family. Neither the Átány people nor the Hungarian peasants of other regions employ distinct words for the nuclear family as opposed to the various kinds of extended families. They express the difference by contrasting families in which the sons "married in the home," "remained in a cluster," or "share the same bread" with those whose descendants "were scattered" or "took wing on their own."

To insure maintenance of a family's economic base and the traditional life cycle—which, among other functions, provided the parents a secure old age—at least one son would have to "marry into the home." Such a stem family would be a minimal form of "ordinary" family life. In earlier times it was thought desirable that several sons should "marry into the home." During the period of our field work there was a family at Átány in which two married sons and their children lived with their parents and tilled the soil together. Among the landowning gazda-s such an extended family was necessary to provide manpower on the farm and to keep the family property intact. Such extended families were also found among landless people at Átány, but less frequently. (See Appendix F, "Forms of Family Units at Átány between 1942 and 1945.")

Descriptions of Hungarian peasant families in the last century mention families of thirty to forty members.[10] In the past several decades, however, extended families of this size have disappeared in Hungary. The largest extended family which could be directly observed in 1943 consisted of fourteen members.[11] At Átány it was possible only to reconstruct from the memories of our informants the life of such a large joint family and its division of labor. The Rózsa family, numbering 24 people, was an outstandingly large one at about the turn of the century. However, data corroborate our belief that such large families were not at all typical in Átány or in other regions, either then or in earlier periods. It is almost certain that most of the population lived in smaller types of extended family groups.

According to nationwide traditional custom, the sons take their wives to the house of their parents on the day of their marriage, wherein the wife becomes integrated

---

[9] Cf. Thirring, 1963: 292–294.

[10] A family of 48 members lived in the 1860s in Szuha village in the northern part of Heves county (Istvánffy, 1898: 305). For further data on large extended families see Gönczi, 1914: 136–140; István Györffy, 1942: 241–242; and Fél, 1944a (the last containing additional bibliographical data).

[11] Fél, 1944b.

into the family as *meny*, "daughter-in-law." The presence of the young wife in the house does not really effect a change noticeable from the outside. The furniture remains in its usual place and is augmented by just the single piece belonging to the *meny*, her hope chest. The young wife sleeps either on a trundle bed (which is pushed under the bed in daytime) or on a place improvised every evening on a bench (which leaves no trace in the room during the day).

But it was not always the girl who was brought into the household of her parents-in-law. In the case of families having a daughter but no son, the daughter was obliged to reside with her parents, and the *vő*, "son-in-law," came into her family to give it manpower. A son ideally did not leave the extended family before the death of his father; if he nonetheless opted to leave, he was, according to custom, given only a hatchet,[12] however wealthy his father might be (see Chapter 13, "The Order of Succession").

Within the extended family each member had specific roles which were defined by his or her sex, age, and rank in the family and which varied with the seasons. We can cite for example the Rózsa family (nicknamed "big," "frightful," or "mighty"), comprising 24 members. Its head, András Rózsa, lived together with his four married sons and their children. In the final two decades of the last century the Rózsa family occupied two houses built close together on the same holding. One served as the living and sleeping place of the women and children; the other was called the "eating house," in which the food was cooked, the common meals taken, and also the grain, meat, and other provisions stored. Because of the growing number of children, at the turn of the century yet a third house was built next to the other two. Two families (the *gazdasszony* and the wife of the oldest son) then lived in the old house, and the three others (the three younger women with their children) in the new one. All of them took their meals in the "eating house." The men stayed and slept in the stables built in the large *kert*. There were stalls for the horses, a place for the cattle, and a separate fold for the sheep. The oldest son looked after the horses, the next two cared for the cattle, and the youngest one tended the sheep.[13] Each son slept near the animals entrusted to his care, although the youngest one, responsible for the sheep, spent the night near the horses. The old *gazda* used to sleep there too and occupied the principal place.

As soon as his sons were grown up, old András Rózsa did not work any more; he gave orders and directions as *gazda*. He could not be in the *kert* constantly, as he held the office of village mayor for years and was obliged to be in the town hall

---

[12] Cf. Istvánffy, 1898: 315.

[13] The division of labor in an extended family by which work with the animals is assigned according to a hierarchical age-ranking among the men was an important factor in other regions as well. E.g., a description from southwestern Hungary gives the following names and roles of the male members of an extended family: (1–2) "great driver" and "small driver," since "in ancient times four horses were set to work, therefore two individuals were needed at their side"; (3) the "oxen farm hand," working with the team of oxen; (4) cowman, looking after the cows; (5) one man tended the calves, since there were six to eight of them in a wealthy house; (6) finally one of the bachelors and boys was named "swineherd," keeping care of the pigs of the extended family, which often amounted to a considerable number. If there were not enough male members to perform all the tasks, one or the other was done by a hired man (Gönczi, 1914: 136–140).

all day. He possessed five *fertály*-s of land, four horses, four oxen, three or four milking cows, and fifteen or sixteen young cattle and horses. The sheep totaled eighty and the number of swine varied between twenty and twenty-six.

In both the house and the *kert* the members of the family were ranked by seniority: the execution of the orders of the old *gazda* fell to his eldest son, to whom all the others (except the *gazda* and his wife) owed obedience—men, women, and children. Sons and *meny*-s worked as field hands and maids on the property, the old *gazda* and his wife directing all their activities. Selling, buying, planning, and finance were their concern; the young ones simply had to obey their orders.

Every woman had her appointed sphere of activity in the household (see Chapter 6, "The Members of the Family"). The old *gazdasszony* was responsible for cooking and baking and was helped by the wife of the eldest son, who assumed the old woman's role in the event of her absence or illness. The other women tidied up, laundered, and attended to the children, but their main occupations were spinning, weaving, and sewing.[14] They were seldom required to work in the fields since, with many strong men in the family, their help was not needed.

Except for the harvest, the men did all the work themselves. The oldest son worked with the horses, the next two performed those tasks for which the oxen were used, and the youngest helped the particular brother who most needed assistance at the moment. The presence of four strong men not only freed the women from working in the fields, it also enabled the family to accomplish all the tasks in time. When it was necessary, all four men worked in a team. For example, in threshing the eldest drove the horses while the other three turned and shook the sheaves. Winnowing the grain thus threshed also involved teamwork by the four. At other times the men could do different jobs simultaneously because they had separate teams of horses and oxen. András (the oldest son) went to the vineyard with the horse cart while Mihály and Sándor (the next two oldest) plowed with the oxen and Gábor (the youngest) drove the sheep to pasture.

As the children grew, they too were set to work. A boy or girl four or five years old makes a good enough gooseherd, so the *gazdasszony* kept a number of geese. When older, the boys looked after the piglets, drove the horses at plowing, and grazed the animals at night during the threshing season. Boys thus found occupations with the animals and in the stable; girls worked at the side of their mother in the house.

When the old *gazda* died in 1910, the four brothers did not divide the property into four parts. With his share—a house, *kert,* and plowland—Mihály started an independent farm with both his married sons, Mihály and Sámuel. But the remaining three brothers continued to work their undivided shares in common. In 1915, how-

---

[14] In conservative families, such as the Rózsa-s, as recently as the first part of this century the underwear of men and women, their summer clothing, and the textiles for use in the household and on the farm were all fashioned of hemp linen spun, woven, and sewn at home. To supply the linen for five males, the house, and the farm was a perennial task that required the efforts of all the women, spinning in the winter, weaving and sewing in the spring. It took one person working for three whole winters to spin the yarn for a tarpaulin necessary for the farm.

ever, they "went to separate breads"—each of the three families got a separate house, and thenceforth the three *gazdasszony*-s cooked and baked their bread independently. The work done on the common property was directed by András, the oldest brother, and all the members of the family followed his word. In the evening the men gathered around the fire of the large common stable and discussed the schedule for the following day. They harvested the crops in common. From the wheat yield they first selected the seed grain and then divided the rest among the three families. Each of them had ground to flour as much as was necessary and were free to sell their surplus and use the proceeds "for the needs of the house," such as the purchase of clothing. The livestock was retained in common, the brothers keeping only some of the pigs for themselves. The milk from the cows was allotted to the three families alternately from day to day. Selling and buying animals were András's responsibility. He saved the profit thus gained as "*tőke*" (capital). This money in his care was for the farm to purchase the necessary implements, animals, carts, etc. for its common economy. Hemp fields were worked and the hemp retted and broken as a joint enterprise. Then it was divided and each woman did her own weaving and spinning. Each looked after the trousseau of her own children, and also the costs of weddings were paid by each family from its own purse. This common farming operation continued until 1923, when the three brothers felt the increasing burden of old age. András resigned the leadership, and subsequently the property was divided into three parts. Their descendants living today, like Sándor Rózsa, the now eighty-year-old grandson of old András Rózsa, relate that the grandparents "died out of the same house" and the parents, the three brothers, "died out of the same stable," after living 57 years together.

In the other Rózsa house the head of the family, the older Mihály, soon died. His two sons, Sámuel and the younger Mihály, remained in a common household and continued farming in common. Sámuel worked by his brother's orders "like a real hired man," but there was strife between the women. Their girls had grown up, and it was time to think of their trousseaus. It happened that each of the women thought the linen destined for the child of the other was too much. In the meantime the old *gazdasszony* also died. So in 1927 they decided to part, to "go to separate breads." The land was partitioned and a new house was built for Mihály in the *kert*.

The sketch of the Rózsa family's history exemplifies a favorable balance between the size of the family and the size of holdings at the given level of agricultural technology (mainly wooden implements, sowing by hand, using horse teams to thresh grain, etc.). There was ample manpower available for agricultural work, sufficient even to relieve the women from work in the fields. Except for the help of four pairs of harvesters during harvest time (reapers and swath-layer), the members of the Rózsa family did all the work themselves.

This favorable balance between size of land owned and members of the family available to cultivate it did not exist in every case. Sometimes the holding was too small for occupancy by all members of the family, such that a surplus of manpower remained "lying." In such cases, increasing the size of the holding was the primary goal, in order "to have property for the family." Until such equilibrium was attained, the women produced more than needed for the household—e.g., of linen, sackcloth, canvas, bread, butter—and sold the surplus. The men rented land by tilling the soil for half the resulting profit *(métayage)*, or they took their horses to other areas nearby and hired out for threshing after finishing their work at home. In such a household an older child who was not needed for work at home was sent to hire out, for the summer season at least, as a swineherd or assistant to tobacco growers. Occasionally he was ordered to do specific tasks for others, e.g. driving the horses at threshing. Sometimes he might even be employed for the whole year as a young hired man by a *gazda* of the village who had more work to do than manpower at hand.

In families which lacked labor power because their boys were too young to do men's work, the *gazda* employed field hands; depending on his property and social status, these included a senior farm hand or a plowboy, or eventually both. A *gazda* in this position did all he could to increase the number of able-bodied people in the family itself. If he had only a daughter, he would not let her marry into another house, but rather brought a *vő* to his own; if he had young sons, they could supply the manpower when they grew up. We quote an example of yet another solution (see Chapter 6, "Children," "Girls"): a wealthy *gazda*, having only daughters, set them to agricultural work until he could bring *vő*-s into the house and thus relieve the females of part of their unusual burden.

The large joint-family variant of the extended family, illustrated by the example of András Rózsa, was no longer to be found at Átány at the time of our field work. However, we were able to observe directly a smaller version of a joint-extended family. This was the household of József Szilágyi, which united three married couples: the parents and their two married sons and wives with their offspring—ten persons altogether living on undivided property, under the same roof, "sharing the same bread" on one farm. Whereas the Rózsa family had communal property only, with private ownership by the women restricted to their personal clothing, in the Szilágyi household the individual property rights of the young women were apparent. Each of them was given a cow-in-calf at the time of her wedding. These animals were kept together but the profits they produced went to the individual women to cover expenses of their own and their children's clothing. Otherwise life in the Szilágyi family was similar to that in the Rózsa family. The wife of the *gazda*, the eldest woman, was similarly the *gazdasszony;* cooking and baking fell to her sphere, and all members of the household used her linen. She was at this time helped by one of the young women, who had recently had a baby and needed care at home. Otherwise, both young wives were obliged to work in the fields regularly in this family. The work of both the men and the women in the fields was directed by the old *gazda* who, being still quite physically fit, actually participated in the work as well as supervising it. Because the Szilágyi-s had a house and a *kert* on the same plot, the *gazdasszony*, besides doing the cooking and other household chores, was able to look after the poultry and the pigs, kept in the same yard, and even the cattle in the stable were entrusted to her care. This family possessed two teams of animals: a pair of horses and a pair of oxen. The horses were groomed by the elder son, who also took them out to work. Work done with oxen was the task of the younger son, who also foddered them and looked after them. The old *gazda* joined the son who most needed help on any particular occasion. When necessary, this family all worked together too.

Since the Szilágyi-s owned only twenty *hold*-s (28.4 acres), their labor force could have worked much more land. They owned a sowing machine and new, light agricultural tools of metal enabled them to work more quickly than the Rózsa-s with their cumbersome wooden implements. Therefore they either leased land, undertook *métayage*, or they performed all sorts of occasional labor with their teams. Whatever work a member of the family undertook, he had to contribute all its profit, even gratuities, to the common purse. As for women's work, the importance of spinning and weaving had much decreased by then. The household used ever more factory-made cotton material, and the women manufactured little more than the burlap bags and canvas equipment for farming. Nevertheless, there was no superfluous female labor in the family, since they produced the industrial plants: sugar beets and tobacco.

The pattern of economic activities just described was disturbed by the death of the father of one of the young women—or rather by the fact that she inherited two *hold*-s (2.84 acres) of plowland upon his death. The family tried to till this additional property separately, keeping account of its taxes and its profit separately. However, the separate property caused strife, which was worsened by the fact that one of the younger couples had three children, the other just one. (This fact in itself accounted for disproportionate needs of food and clothing.) Thus the family decided to break up in 1952. According to tradition, a man seceding from the family in his father's lifetime would not receive inheritance; but in this case the father divided everything into three parts, keeping one for himself. The land, the draft animals, and the farm and household equipment were all divided similarly into three equal parts, but the three families continued to live together under one roof. And as the division left each of them with a rather scanty collection of tools and animals, they continued to lend mutual aid to one another. Thus their land was worked almost as before, except that the produce was stored in separate granaries.

In the 1950s the family life of the Szilágyi-s was regarded as anomalous, however, as a fashion of the early years of the century. The stem family may be taken as the typical contemporary mode: one married child living with the parents, the undivided holding being farmed in common, "on one bread." We presented the daily round of such a stem family in the example of the Kakas household (see Chapter 5, "A Workday in the Family of József Kakas").

The family of József Kakas is but a shadow of the extended family described above, because of a low birth rate. (This did not disqualify it as a type case, since a small number of children has been typical of the *gazda* homes for many decades.) The Kakas family was unable to cultivate its property of 24 *hold*-s (over 34 acres) alone, even when their only child grew up and was able to work since, being a *gazda*'s daughter, she was exempted from labor in the fields. They took on the bachelor son of a relative to help with certain tasks. He lived in a separate house, and the women cooked and washed and tidied up for him in repayment for his services. The Kakas-s did not try to increase their property holding; they wanted just to preserve it. They did all the work in the household and *kert* themselves, never employing a servant. In the fields, however, they usually needed a helping hand. Over a period of many years they hired a pair of harvesters who not only performed this task but also helped to transport the harvest from the fields to the village and did hoeing and other chores as well when necessary.

The Kakas-s and other small families call upon their brothers to help at those times when the agricultural work needs more manpower and pay for these services in kind. The more hands that are needed for a particular task (e.g., threshing, harvesting the grapes, or maize husking), the wider the circle of the kinsfolk called upon— on the basis of reciprocity.

The three different ways of life described above, represented respectively by the three families—Rózsa, Szilágyi, and Kakas—in themselves represent a span of several decades. These decades saw fundamental changes in the farming life of Átány. First to appear and most important were technological changes in the farming implements. At the turn of the century efficient steel tools were rapidly supplanting the cumbersome wooden implements. The heavy wooden plow required three men (one to hold the plow, another to lead the animals, and a third to scrape the mud off the shares) and three to four horses or oxen. A modern steel plow can be managed by only one man with only two horses. This explains why after the turn of the century teams of three and four animals almost entirely disappeared, supplanted by teams of two (in 1895, 47 per cent of the teams were triple or quadruple ones; by 1935 their proportion was below 3 per cent). Accordingly, the organization of labor among the men altered: the two drivers that always accompanied a team of four were reduced to only the one needed for a team of two. Also at the turn of the century threshing machines were becoming popular. Such a machine could thresh the grain crop of a holding of five *fertály*-s in one or two days, work which had previously required three to four weeks at least, and the collective effort of four horses and three to four men together with several women. Before the advent of machine threshing, a family of four workers and two teams, for instance, could thresh much more than twice as efficiently as a small family of only two workers and one team. Thus with the old technology, the larger family was distinctly advantageous. With the new technology, it was not.[15]

In brief, in the middle of the last century a *gazda* with his wife, or even a couple plus a son and his wife, were deficient in manpower and had to depend on others for help at several times during the year. By World War I, however, new implements enabled a small family to cope successfully, and two married couples living together even more so.

Another fundamental change that dates from the turn of the century was the tendency to locate both house and *kert* at the same place and concentrate the activity

---

[15] Fél and Hofer, 1963. The threshing techniques typical on the Great Plain were dealt with in detail for the first time by István Györffy (1928). A comparison of performances of larger and smaller groups in threshing and the associated work patterns has been made recently (Hoffmann, 1963).

of the whole family there. The changeover to improved agricultural tools happened rapidly, but the concentration of holdings was a protracted process. Thus, at the beginning of our field work 87 stables were still in use in the outer circle, i.e. 87 families lived on divided holdings. This pattern of farming made the extended family functionally necessary.

Since the turn of the century a new residential pattern has thus evolved: only one married child resides with the parents. Should there be several sons, the older ones leave their parents' household. As before, each son may bring his wife home to the house of his parents, but the first of these young couples may stay in the household only until the marriage of the next younger brother. More frequently nowadays, the eldest son or sons reside as *vő* in the household of the *gazda* whose daughter he marries. There is security gained by doing so, and the couple may continue the life of the team-owner *gazda*-s. In the other case, they could have an independent but poor existence until the son comes into his paternal inheritance (see Chapter 13, "The Order of Succession"). At the same time, the spreading custom of allotting shares of land to girls has made possible an increase of ever more independent farms. This custom militates against the survival of joint families because land allotted to a *meny* is actually a separate property, and such separate property is incompatible with the traditional communal land tenure associated with the joint family. In most cases it leads to a breaking up of these family units, as was shown in the instance of the Szilágyi-s.

Providing a "dowry" for their daughters now weighs more heavily on parents. The reason is a custom, appearing in the 1940s and becoming widespread in the 1950s, that furniture for one room be included, and (since the middle of the 1950s) even some kitchen equipment, with the traditional trousseau.

Recent modifications of the traditional family pattern place heavier burdens on non-resident kinsfolk as well. Since the latter half of the 1950s it has been customary for relatives invited to the wedding to give the bride kitchen utensils and household pottery along with the traditional gifts of a hen and some pastry. The equipment gathered in this way enables the newly-weds to begin a self-sufficient household. (When formerly the young couple remained in the parental house, separate equipment was not needed.)

Nevertheless, the Átány people consider it customary and decent for the newly-weds to stay with the parents for a varying period of time; this was still the case at the beginning of the 1960s. Landowning families worked out many arrangements for first living together and later parting, as some of our examples have suggested. Separation commences with the formation of a separate household. The young couple lives together with the old one, but they cook for themselves separately and take their meals apart. And the poultry, pigs, and cows, at first reared in the same yard and kept in the same fold or stall, eventually are separately cared for. Another way of "parting" is to contrive a sharper division in the house so that the old and the young couple have separate rooms; the former occupy the larger, more formal one. Sometimes in these cases an annex consisting of a room and a kitchen is added to the old house, or a new house may even be constructed nearby for the young couple. In this phase the property may still not be completely divided; the couples living in the separate households work the land in common and merely divide the produce into halves.[16]

A further step toward separation is the division of the property—equipment and livestock as well as immovables. We saw in the case of the family of József Szilágyi how such a division may make farming more difficult. So long as three couples worked together, the teams of two horses and two oxen were adequate—even more than was needed—for tilling their own soil. After the livestock were divided into three portions, no one man was able to cultivate his plot alone any more. So the members of the divided family were forced to continue to work jointly still: they harnessed their individually owned animals into teams again and went on tilling the soil as a joint enterprise. But crops were gathered into the larder of each one separately.

The last phase of separation is attained if the young people acquire sufficient equipment to cultivate their lands. Then not only the household but also the farm becomes separate and independent.[17]

As was mentioned above, the extended family was not only typical of landowning households at Átány, it characterized some landless households also. For landowning gazda-s, the principal motivating factor in keeping the family together was property (with the associated need to have sufficient manpower to till the soil, and the concern to assure continuity of the estate represented for example, by refusing to give land to a son who chooses to leave the household). For landless people, the principal motivating factor was their very lack of property, i.e. poverty. The newly-weds lacked not only a dwelling place, but also the bare essentials to equip one, like furniture, kitchen utensils, and linen. Many families stayed together in hope of saving a sum sufficient to enable them to found a new home during their lifetime. Others were kept together by "paternal love," according to opinion at Átány. One often heard: "I'd never let my children go, they'll stay with us, we'll help them, we'll share our poverty." But more recent attitudes disapprove of thus binding oneself to poverty in the family. It is said that they "are afraid of life"—afraid to work individually to make ends meet: "Then they devour everything together; they might have something if they went their own ways." A poor man, Sándor Galvács, says: "My sons are struggling

---

[16] Even the stable and the *kert* may remain undivided. Such was the case of Imre Kakas. Until 1959 he shared the paternal *kert* with his brother; but each stored and used his own produce, and even his own manure, separately. In the stable one end housed the animals of one brother, the other housed those of the second.

[17] Numerous transitional types may be found between the fully developed extended family and the separate and independent nuclear families in other villages. Thus at Tiszaigar, some 35 kilometers from Átány, the following six varieties could be distinguished: (1) Extended family living under the same roof and "on common bread," farming in common. (2) Common farming and living under a common roof, but "separate bread" (i.e., separate households). (3) Nuclear families living under separate roofs and "on separate bread" but farming together. (4) Nuclear families living under the same roof but "on separate bread" and farming independently (the estate and the livestock are divided), although they perform agricultural tasks cooperatively. (5) Nuclear families living under separate roofs and "on separate bread" farming independently but performing the agricultural work cooperatively. (6) Nuclear families living under separate roofs and "on separate bread" farming independently (Fél, 1959b: 85–91).

to make their way alone. We could not stand together, for the needs are less if they live apart."

To sum up the changes in the Átány family unit over the first sixty years of the century, illustrated by the several examples above, we notice first that the extended family embracing several generations and several married couples has given way to the stem family. We have sketched the development of this kind of family unit in relation to the forms of settlement and land tenure and the changes in technology. In the stem family we observed a division of farm labor according to seniority, which bound the activity of the elder couple more to the *kert* or the house and laid the burden of the field work on the younger couple. If an accident deprived the family of a working member, a great increase in the tempo and amount of work resulted for all others and either the *kert* or the house became neglected. They were thus forced to unite the stable and the house in the same unit within a short time.

The existence of a house and *kert* separated from each other implies the presence of two couples. On the other hand, if house and *kert* have been united on the same lot, the need for two couples to manage them is less pressing. Even if the extended family is preserved, the division of labor according to age and sex becomes looser. For example, Károly Bedécs, having united his house and stable in 1948, now brings water from the well to the kitchen for his wife, remarking: "I do her a favor by bringing the water for her." The new protracted residence of men and women under the same roof has led to some overlapping in the older sex-differentiated categories of labor.

And thus has evolved the pattern of the nuclear family. In Átány more and more young people now leave their paternal household to eat their own bread and to use their own strength. However, as the extended family dissolves, the necessity of seeking the "help" of scattered members and married couples arises more frequently. Brothers, *sógor*-s, thus lend one another a hand without being paid; they receive a good meal and sincere thanks and later are repaid in kind. So for at least some large-scale enterprises, as many adults are united around the table as in the days of the old extended family.

CHAPTER 6. THE MEMBERS OF THE FAMILY

The position of each member of a family is defined by his sex and age.

Men consider themselves superior to women: "Woman is merely the helper of man, man is always the first. As we know, man is the masterpiece of creation. God created Adam, shaping Eve from his rib. We feel ourselves above the women." Their respective economic roles reflect this precedence. As Károly Bedécs says, "I am the creator, for I am in charge of the production. It is my task to create everything for the family, to bring all the provisions into the house. But inside the woman is the first one." Man is raised above woman also by his strength. "Woman is of less value than man; they cannot even be compared. She is weaker, for she is unable to perform man's work." The special tasks of man are thought to be first warfare, then plowing, reaping, and most other agricultural activities. Even in begetting children the role of the male is considered the more important; old István Czákó says that "this is but natural." And he takes the lead in bringing up the children as well. Though women take care of the children, his authority and power make the man the agent of discipline.

The members of an Átány family are the *gazda*, the *gazdasszony*, and the children. There may also be *meny*-s and *vő*-s and solitary relatives. Servants also are regarded as part of the family.

THE GAZDA[18]

The head, lord, and ruler of the household is usually the oldest married man or widower, the *gazda*, "the head of the family." This position is due to him on account of his sex, since "man is the first person in the house—its esteem depends on him,

---

[18] Besides its usage as "the head of the family," the word *gazda* is also used to distinguish a stratum of wealth. It connotes a peasant who owns 20 to 24 *hold*-s (28.40 to 34.08 acres) or more—i.e. one-half *telek* in the terminology of the period of serfdom and thus "one who is able to live by his own estate" (see Chapter 12, "Team-owners"). There is a third meaning, which expresses expertise in peasant life. In this sense of the word, for example, it is said that "he who has not drawn a foal from the mare or has not reared a calf up to be a dam is no *gazda*," even if he happens to own land.

and he is the head of the family," and also because he is the owner, the proprietor, of the family estate.

It may happen that a male child or a woman becomes *gazda* because of the death or military service of the father. We know of a boy of eleven who became *gazda* because his father died early and there was no elder male in the family. His kinsmen kept on telling him: "Now you are a man, for your father has died, and you are the *gazda*." Helped by his mother, he farmed, went to the market, and bought and sold livestock as befits the role of *gazda*. Likewise, a woman may assume the position of *gazda* if the head of the family dies or goes to war leaving no male successor or only small children at home (see Chapter 6, "The Gazdasszony").

Gazda is also the term for a woman who wields the authority in the house instead of her weak husband. People say of Gy. K.: "The woman is the *gazda* there. When the bailiffs came, the man just sat without speaking. His wife accepted the challenge instead."

There can be only one *gazda* in a house. József Kakas characterized the family of one of his neighbors in this way: "I don't think it is a proper sort of family life—everyone is *gazda* there. Both the man and the woman give orders, and each of them has a separate purse."

Sex and title give the *gazda* authority over the whole household. Everyone in the house depends on him and fears him. He may strike anyone with impunity—his wife, son, daughter, *meny*, *vő*, or servant. This does not happen, however, in a decent family; an angry look on his face and a warning, "chastising by word," are enough to keep order.

The *gazda* is expected to preserve his authority. "It is sad if the man occupies the second place in the family, and one should be sorry for them. Only a weak man, a coward, takes orders from his wife." The story goes that the wife of A. K. slapped a tax collector in the face. The men scolded the tax collector: "Then you are no man at all, since a woman remains a woman, even if she is twice as big as you are." (The officer was small in stature while the woman was tall and strong.)

Authority must be maintained in relation to all members of the household, including the children. Károly Bedécs says, "Being a man, I was strong among them; I preserved order as a policeman does." The task is especially difficult in the case of a second marriage if there are children "of different kinds" in the house. To quote Gábor Varga: "We had children of three kinds; what would have happened without my strength?"

The careful education of the children—by spending time in their company, assisting them in their work—is considered one of the paternal virtues. Some people say: "I never drove my children to the harvest, as some *gazda*-s do; I worked with them." A good *gazda* spares the child, not allowing him to do hard work before his time, and keeping him at his side in the course of hoeing, for example, in order to help if necessary.

A strong, hard-handed *gazda* should also be able to show tenderness. There are few who would not smile at their children, though believing that they "ought to be loved unnoticed"; usually the head of the family speaks affectionately to his small children, calling them "my little daughter," "my little son," and giving them a small present now and then.

With older children he may be more severe. He may order them to leave school if he wants them to work; on the other hand, he may send them to a secondary school in town if he plans the career of a "gentleman" for them.

His is the decisive word when it comes to choosing a spouse for a son or daughter. The daughter of József Kakas was courted by a young man who was favored by the girl but mistrusted by her father, and he separated them, "having both might and right to drive them apart." The father may disown and drive from the house a child who opposes his will, saying: "You are no son, no daughter, anymore." This means that he will not give him or her a share in the family estate. Disinheritance occurs about once in eight or ten years. At the beginning of the century the daughter of K. M. was disinherited when she married against the will of her grandfather, the *gazda*. The young couple moved to a *tanya*. Whenever the young woman came back to the village, she could not pass the plot of land she had hoped to inherit without embracing the boundary stone and loudly bemoaning her sad situation in the manner of one lamenting the dead.

The *gazda* also has absolute authority over the property of his family. Everything they earn, even from work done outside the farm, has to be handed over to him, so as to come ultimately into the possession of the *gazdasszony*. Around 1940, J. Sz. had dissipated all his property, and finally the family had to live on the wages of the unmarried son, who worked as a day laborer. When the son reached the age of twenty-one (full age according to old Hungarian law), he refused to hand over his income, wanting to save it for himself. The father lodged a petition with the court, but the case was decided in favor of the son. In response to this verdict the father disowned his son and drove him out of the house.

Among the various concerns of the *gazda*, one of the most important is to secure the succession in order to "pass on the family name" and to have descendants who will care for him in his old age and bury him decently when the time comes. This concern may lead to adoption. If the *gazda* has no children or is deprived of them by early death, he looks among his relatives for a family having little wealth and many children, one of whom they might be inclined to entrust to his care. The form of adoption customary in the western parts of Hungary, where the child is given the name of its foster-father, is unknown at Átány and would be unacceptable to the parents.[19] Actually, the child is taken into the foster-home only on trial, his behavior as a young man determines whether the old *gazda* will make him heir to the estate in his will. The child is given over to the custody of the *gazda* while still very young, and an oral, sometimes written, agreement is reached with the parents, securing the inheritance for the foster-child on the condition of his good behavior.

[19] Adoption is especially prevalent in regions where excessive birth control, the "one-child system," often leaves families without an heir (see footnote 22 in this Part). In these regions it has also been customary to adopt grown-up, married people.

Since the custom of leaving the paternal house has become more common among newly-weds of the village, cases occur in which the grandparents rear one of their grandchildren. Thus István Török used to live with his wife's parents, being a *vő* married into the family. In 1956 he built a new house and moved in. He had two daughters at this time. The grandparents, who were not yet fifty years old, kept the elder girl in their house with the intention of bringing her up and giving her in marriage when the time comes.

Some solitary *gazda*-s adopt even grown-up poor relations who have their own families. Such was the case of János Gacsal in 1950. His wife had died, and there were no children. So he took in the married daughter of one of his brothers along with her husband and numerous children; they had originally been live-in servants, and later had lived in a rented house. They looked after the "grandpa" well, and took care of his burial. He in turn willed them his house, its furniture, and the small plot of land he possessed.

Besides ensuring that there will be successors, an important task of the *gazda* is to preserve his inherited property intact, and if possible to add to it. Nobody is spoken ill of because he did not enlarge his holdings in the course of his life, but a man who dissipates the inheritance of his father or grandfather commits a grave offense against his family duties. One hears several elderly *gazda*-s say, as though justifying their lives: "Never was I a squanderer, I have preserved all that was bequeathed to me."

Both the landed *gazda* and the manual worker are expected to produce or to acquire all the necessary goods for their households in a measure befitting their social and economic situation. The good *gazda* provides a sufficient quantity of food, earns the cash needed for decent clothing for the members of his family, sees to it that they have a good dwelling, and is expected to augment the family wealth, if possible, and enlarge the holding.

Furthermore, the *gazda* has to look to the well-being of his descendants, in order that they "should not be left with nothing after him," i.e., that they should inherit from him. This is especially the concern of the well-to-do *gazda* who possesses a piece of land. A poor manual worker is contented if he is able to provide his daughter with a meager trousseau. To a son, starting his own life as a manual worker, the father cannot give anything but a small ax. (See also Chapter 13, "The Order of Succession.")

Whether rich or poor, the *gazda* is the chief representative, guardian, and keeper of the rank, authority, and honor of his household. Should anyone of his family misbehave (his wife, children, or grandchildren), the warning is addressed to him, as it is his duty to chastise them. Both the praise and the censure evoked by the members of his family fall on his head.

Should the *gazda* rise to some office in the village government or the church council, the resulting honor and esteem would be extended to his whole household. On the other hand, they would have to enable him to fulfil his official duties by relieving him of certain chores.

The *gazda* as the representative of the family arranges all their official affairs and pays the taxes. He does the marketing and buys and sells the livestock and the produce. He is present at the fair when clothing is purchased or ordered for the members of the family, and in fact often does the purchasing himself.

In the house the *gazda* is entitled to the place of honor at the table. The family does not start eating until he is seated. He slices the bread and hands each one a piece in turn. He serves himself first, and the choice bits are reserved for him.[20] He pours out the wine if there is any. He recites the prayer before the meal or orders the smallest member of the family to pray. The best of the sleeping places is also reserved for him. In the stable his bed is situated in the highest ranking place, near the horses; if he spends the night with his wife in the house, they occupy the only real bed aside from the unused ornamental bed.

The main share of the farm work is also his responsibility. So long as he is in good health, he is the first in mowing or hoeing; he leads the work, sets the pace, and helps the weaker ones.

If the head of the family is over fifty years old and has a trustworthy grown-up son under his roof, he "makes himself a *gazda*" sooner or later according to the circumstances. This means that he lets his son do the hard field work while he himself retains the direction as his main task and works in the *kert*.

The *gazda* maintains his position until his death. At Átány, as throughout the country, the *gazda* does not hand over his estate to the young people during his lifetime, nor does he resign the right to give orders. But as he feels the burden of years, he becomes increasingly intent on reaching a just settlement for the division of his property—one that would be accepted by his children after his death.

THE GAZDASSZONY

The *gazdasszony*, the wife of the *gazda*, shares his troubles and is a companion to him. "I have a helpmeet in my wife, she made fourpence of the tuppence I gave her"— thus several men have praised their wives. The *gazda* bears the burden of the agricultural labor, but the *gazdasszony* has that of the house. This is expressed in the saying that one pillar of the house is held by the *gazda* but the three others by the *gazdasszony*. It is the wife's duty "to keep the family well." "The *gazda* only asks what we shall eat; he does not care where the food comes from. Whether the household has killed two hogs during the year or only a piglet, it is up to the *gazdasszony* to make ends meet."

---

[20] Sometimes a *gazda* would allow his youngest child to be favored in his stead: "Here is this little girl—she has still to be reared. I am willing to go along with her mother if she wants to give the choice bits to her," said Károly Bedécs. I. B., who when he became a *vő* would leave the choice bits for his beautiful wife, is referred to by the humorous and slightly derisive remark: "Eat, my wife, so that you will be beautiful." On the other hand, we may quote the extreme example of the *gazda* who to this day devours the breast and both legs of the chicken, leaving the remainder for his wife and two children.

Women do not lose their maiden names with marriage, but retain them all their lives. Thus the wife of József Kakas is never called Mrs. Kakas but is referred to by all as Zsófi Rózsa. A *gazda* who wants to honor the *gazdasszony* does not refer to her by her Christian name or as "my wife," "the woman," etc., but by both her Christian and her family names. János Egyed, an elderly *gazda*, is an object of praise because he always refers to his wife as Mari Török.

If the husband is a decent *gazda*, the *gazdasszony* knows everything that happens in the *kert* and the fields. They will say, "We are of the same will." When the man asks for a satchel, he is expected to state the reason, saying, for example, "Prepare the satchel, we are going to plow." It is right that the *gazdasszony* should know where the men are and what they are doing. The *gazda* talks over his affairs with his wife after supper, frequently after they go to bed. When they have slept for a little while, he awakens his wife and discusses his plans with her. The *gazdasszony* also tells him her problems regarding the members of the family or the household expenses.

In the house the *gazdasszony* is entitled to the next most honored place after the *gazda;* she sits at his side at the table and sleeps in his bed. Should there be *meny*-s in the house, her precedence would be emphasized by her right to cook and bake. The younger women would work as her helpers in this task. Likewise, all the women and girls cooperate in making the household linen, but it is the privilege of the *gazdasszony* to cut it out and to decide how it will be divided. It is her right and duty to carve the meat at the table and to allot the slices; she decides the quantity of bacon and sausages put into the satchel, taking into consideration the needs and provisions of the family.

When they are walking along the road, the husband walks on the right side and the wife walks some distance behind him on the left side. However, she never has to carry any equipment, such as her hoe; the *gazda* or his occasional companion carries it on his shoulder. One indication of the esteemed position of the *gazdasszony* is that all the cash of the household is entrusted to her care. As Károly Bedécs says: "I always hand the money over to my wife; then she gives it back to me when I go to the fair. When I return, I render an exact account of it to the woman; I tell her what I have sold and for what price." The proceeds from the sale of livestock and grain constitute the *tőke* (capital), the money for farm expenses. The *gazdasszony* must not touch this money without the consent of the *gazda*. In order to cover the expenses of the house—supplies, oil for lamps, etc.—she has to raise a separate fund herself by selling poultry, milk, bread, linen, and other items in the market. A clever housewife is able to earn enough money to pay for the clothing of her daughters and herself. Moreover, the *gazdasszony* provides her bachelor son with money to spend at taverns and on gypsy musicians, and she buys the tobacco for all the male members of her family from this fund. In exceptional households the *gazda* keeps the *tőke* himself, and sometimes even takes the household money earned by the *gazdasszony*. As Károly Mérten relates: "My father used to give my mother money from his hand; then she stole wheat and sold it for half-price." Thus some *gazdasszony*-s make up for the lack of money by selling some of the grain stored in the house.[21] Obedient women, however, make do without money; in some families the supper is served up unsalted, since the wife cannot get even the price of salt from the *gazda*.

The Átány woman lives for her family and stays out of the community administration buildings, saying: "I do not know the town hall, for women never go there. This is the business of the men." She is the first to get up in the morning and the last to go to bed in the evening. She keeps the house and all the people in it clean and neat. Her main task is to allocate the household supplies with fairness and foresight. Whether the harvest is copious or meager, it is her job to provide enough food, drink, and clothing for everyone. On the average, a family of four has sufficient meat, fat, and bacon from a pig weighing 160 to 180 kg. to last for a year, provided that poultry is raised also so that the lack of fat in the autumn months before pigsticking can be supplied by ducks and geese. However, in a year of a good harvest the same family may consume two pigs of that weight, and in other years they may have to make do with a pig of only 100 kg. In either case it is up to the *gazdasszony* to make the meat last, saving enough so that the members of her family do not lack the necessary food in the periods of hard work. During the winter she will cook with a minimum of meat, bacon, and fat in order to be able to provide sufficient food in the season of hard work.

Clothing is partly homemade from the linen woven by the women and partly bought at the fairs or ordered from tailors, shoemakers, etc. The *gazdasszony* has to keep in mind which members of the family need new clothing and when. The broadcloth suits and footwear (mainly boots) worn by the men may be purchased out of the *tőke;* female attire, however, should be bought from the household fund. A frequent cause of family quarrels is the attempt of the *gazdasszony* to use money from the *tőke* for girls' clothing. Brothers strongly protest against this, being convinced that the work of their sisters is less valuable than their own, since girls do not earn money that will enlarge the *tőke* of the family.

Therefore the *gazdasszony* who has a daughter has to plan her economic activities with an eye to events in the distant future. She begins to raise geese from the first birthday of the child in order to save up eiderdown for the trousseau featherbeds. Since a girl's trousseau is supposed to include linen sufficient for her whole life, the *gazdasszony* grows hemp and weaves diligently year after year in order to have enough ready by the wedding day.

Since a son does not need either feathers or linen, but rather pocket money for his bachelor's life, the *gazdasszony* tries to sell as much milk and eggs as possible to get extra money for her son without depriving the rest of the household.

It is the duty of the *gazdasszony* to bring up and care for her children and grandchildren. She is the teacher of the family. Children and sometimes even adults learn

---

[21] In order to prevent such "thefts," some *gazda*-s deviate from the traditional order and build a separate pantry in the *kert*, thereby avoiding the use of the loft as a storeroom. These are the "miserly," "niggardly" *gazda*-s. Two men who store the fat and meat of the slaughtered pig in the *kert* instead of the house were mentioned as examples. They would bring a piece of meat or sausage home each morning for the woman to cook.

songs, prayers, and rhymes of greeting from her. She defines good behavior in her preachings; she knows the Golden Alphabet (see Appendix D) by heart and quotes lines from it several times a day for the benefit of those who deviate from its precepts in her house.

Not only does she educate her children and grandchildren, but also her *meny* or *meny*-s, since in Átány (and for that matter in most Hungarian villages) girls often do not learn from their mothers how to cook or bake bread; at least custom does not demand that they know these things at the time of their marriage. Some of the girls are so spared at home that they are not taught how to do any of the tasks of the household or the field. Many brides of Átány have had to learn milking from their mothers-in-law in the first days after their wedding, as this was to be one of their daily tasks. Many mothers-in-law have to teach their *meny*-s how to tie up vine tendrils and how to lay grain in swaths and bind it into sheaves. This instruction is not always free from discord.

The *gazdasszony* also nurses the sick. Throughout the summer she collects herbs, plants, and flowers that can be used to prepare medicines, compresses, or baths for man and livestock.

Just as the *gazda* must protect the family from outside threats, the *gazdasszony* must prevent dissension within it. "The *gazdasszony* has a wide apron in order to cover everything with it" is a saying heard in Átány. She is expected to smooth out family quarrels and troubles and to prevent the world outside from noticing them. Sometimes she deals out a blow to the children, but more often she relies on threats, especially to relate their misbehavior to their father when he returns in the evening. But she herself may also be somewhat anxious about the homecoming of the *gazda*. The unanimous opinion of the village is that this "female fear" is more typical of the houses which are separated from the *kert*-s, where the men live apart. "A woman is always afraid of being scolded when the *gazda* returns home. If he finds the house yard unswept, that is reason enough to censure the *gazdasszony* at once."

Whereas the esteem in which the family is held by the village is a function of the status and character of the *gazda*, friendly relations with neighbors and kin are maintained largely by the *gazdasszony*. Her daily interest, small acts of kindness, and participation in the custom of widespread lending and borrowing are the components of good social relations and a guarantee of help in case of need. The *gazdasszony* has to keep track of all the relationships so as to comply with the requirements resulting from kinship at the appropriate times. From the moment when she is presented to the relatives of her husband as a bride she attends to the kinship ties on her husband's side as much or more than to those on her own. She visits the sick relative, cooks for the woman lying in childbed, and keeps vigil and laments for the dead. She prepares feasts for church and family celebrations, always trying to make them elaborate and plentiful enough to live up to the expectations of her family.

Since the proper place of the *gazdasszony* is in her house and in the village, she spends at most a few hours daily in the *kert* during the summer. She goes to the fields only so long as she is without a *meny* or a strong daughter, or while her *meny* is nursing a baby. All the women prefer the work in the fields to that in the house: they say they prefer the quiet regularity of work in the fields to the multiple duties that are constantly demanding their attention at home—and besides it is nice to be outside. The *gazdasszony*-s like to spend one or two days there in the spring or in summertime, and on these days their place is taken by their *meny*. It would be improper to spend more than two days in the fields. When the mother-in-law of Zsófi Rózsa wanted to go to the fields for the third day, her *meny* would not agree to it: "I would have been ashamed to have people find me at home instead of my mother."

Sometimes the *gazdasszony* has to find a substitute and travel outside the village, called by her duties as a relative, especially as a mother. It is her lifelong duty to take care of her daughter or daughters when they are sick, especially when they are lying in childbed. If a daughter who lives outside the village has a baby, the *gazdasszony* leaves home for a week, entrusting the household to her *meny*.

A *gazdasszony* is just as indispensable to a household as is a *gazda*. If the *gazda* is left a widower, and there are still young children, he would marry a second, and, if necessary, a third time. If the *gazdasszony* dies when there is a *meny* in the house and the *gazda* wants to stay with his family, he does not marry again but accepts his *meny* as a *gazdasszony*.

The strong *gazdasszony* retains this role till her death; she does not hand the "wooden kitchen spoon" over. However, it is proper for the *meny* to gradually relieve her of the heavier work. Zsófi Rózsa became a *meny* in 1927, but the bread was still being baked by her mother-in-law in 1960. Neighbors and relatives used to scold her, saying, "Are you not baking yet?" Her father-in-law was very annoyed and for years kept saying to her, "Learn how now. Aren't you ever going to learn how?" So now she has finally begun to bake, but her mother-in-law still stands over her while she is kneading. The elder woman had handed over the chore of cooking several years ago because she was sickly and her *meny* wanted to be *gazdasszony*. Says Zsófi Rózsa, "That was all right, I was glad to do the cooking." But when she soon found it tiring work and offered to give it back, her mother-in-law would not agree: "You have taken the wooden kitchen spoon, now go on cooking." So now all the chores have been handed over to the *meny* by the seventy-eight-year-old mother-in-law; their roles are exchanged, and the old woman has become a helper. However, her *meny* finds it prudent to ask her opinion on everything in advance.

Although the *gazda* cannot act as a *gazdasszony*, a woman acting as *gazda* is not infrequent. In such a case a well-to-do *gazdasszony* engages a servant or tries to get a *vő* into the family to do the men's work; however, some *gazdasszony*-s are forced to drive the horse and do hard work in the fields, even harvesting. People watch such a widow with compassion and esteem, helping her as much as they can. So it has become usual for smiths to sharpen the implements of a widow without pay. (This would ordinarily have been the husband's job.) Women are not expected to be competent in farming, nor to be able to exercise the authority of a *gazda*, but widows do so often enough so that Átány men often cite, with astonishment, the saying: "A widow brings up the most handsome bachelor; a widow rears the best foal."

A woman carrying out the duties of a *gazda* is entitled to his rights. In the 1940s the wife of J. Gy. was widowed. Her son and three daughters quarreled constantly because the son demanded all the property for himself, though she had planned to divide it equally. She ended the quarrel by disinheriting her son and, except for the portion legally due him, allotting all the property to the daughters.

CHILDREN

The children are the "ornament" of the house, of *gazda* and *gazdasszony*. Says Károly Bedécs: "For me my children are worth more than any fortune. All of them were able-bodied; there was no cripple. This is happiness indeed. They were worthy of esteem and honor before God and man. It is a plague on a family if the child is disabled. It makes one's heart ache." Thus János Győr "had no pleasure in his children. One of his daughters is nearsighted, the other is lame, and his son is puny. He says, 'God has given the children in vain; I have no pleasure in them.' "

A son is more welcome than a daughter. When J. B. had four daughters and no son, he resigned himself to it saying, "If God has given like this, we must not protest against it." The reason for the preference is that the son carries on the family name, while it is lost at the marriage of the daughter, for her children take their father's name. Besides maintaining the family name, the son will take care of his parents in their old age. The male descendant is needed "in order to have someone who will think of me and take care of me when I'll be an old man." When he becomes an adult, the son takes on his father's work: He knows how to harvest the crops, and in Átány this is the single most important agricultural labor "which earns one's bread." (The landless laborer hired for harvesting could earn his year's bread with his scythe.) The daughter usually "goes out of the house" when she gets married, so she cannot take care of her aged parents. Besides, since she is unable to harvest, she "does not earn her bread"; "she is a girl after all—she can hoe but cannot reap."

The girl becomes a "wife" by childbirth, not by marriage. Julis Madarász, the wife of József Sárközi, did not bear a child in the year following her marriage as was desired. Several elderly men asked her, "When will you be a wife, you Madarász girl?"

There are various opposing considerations in deciding the right number of children to have. A child is a gift of God, and a large number of descendants is a source of joy and means security for the aging parents. Also, the role of the father as paterfamilias can reach its fullest development only if he has a populous circle of offspring. Children, grandchildren, and great-grandchildren ensure his honor and glory in the eyes of the village. The life of a childless family is considered irregular, lacking an object. Such a *gazda* is less interested in agriculture, less motivated to enlarge his property. Some of them even dissipate their inherited estate.

On the other hand, bringing up numerous children is a considerable financial burden on a family of moderate means. As Samu Kiss said: "A small child is a small problem, a grown one is a big problem." "An example is Károly Sárándi, a *gazda* of small fortune who had six children. It was hard work for him to keep his children as well dressed as the other children of the village; he brought them up with great difficulty. But when they grew up, his cares ceased. Wherever he touched, he found money in each pocket, since all his children earned their bread." However, this is only for a short period, as the grown-up sons soon marry and "take to their wings." Rearing children was no such strain for the well-to-do *gazda* household, and, besides, the farm ever needed manpower. Parents eagerly waited for their children to grow up, to work, and to make servants superfluous. But to satisfy a large number of children demanding equal shares of the inherited property would mean the partitioning of the estate and the impoverishment of the descendants. *Gazda* families try "to avoid the breaking up of the property."

Taking all these considerations into account, the general view is that "two or three children are needed in a decent family." One child is not enough. "One child is almost nothing; if it dies, it is as though the family were barren. One cannot know God's intentions, but if one has two or three children, the death of one still leaves one or two behind—as for five or six children, people find them too many."[22]

This does not mean that the peasants of Átány regard the regulation of the number of children as wholly within their control. "Man is unable to plan; it happens as God gives," they say. "Everyone could not have his heart's desire." In some families, like the Varga-s, the birth of one or two children in each generation is regarded as an inherited family trait. Others are, on the contrary, of a prolific "race," which by Átány standards is undesirable. The Varga-s say proudly, "Valuable things are always rare."

The children are brought up by the grandparents, but they belong to their mother in their early years. Traditionally they are clothed by their mother or their maternal grandmother until they reach the age when their work is "profitable." From this time, they are claimed by the father's family.

In a joint family or a stem family the young mother stays at home with her baby for only three to four months, and even that is considered a relatively long time. The baby is taught to eat solid food early so that the mother can go back to the fields. Then it is entrusted to the care of its grandmother during the day and suckled

[22] Compared with the views common in other parts of the country on the proper number of children, public opinion in Átány is intermediate between those groups which prefer many children and find their large number a source of honor, and those groups which have introduced a strict birth control, the "one-child system." At the turn of the century and between the two wars the people of Mezőkövesd and the Jászság (both Catholic regions) were characterized by many children; both are fairly close to Átány.

The most conspicuous examples of strict birth control are furnished by some Calvinist groups living in the western half of the country. Near the Drave and along the southern stretch of the Danube the birth rate showed a rapid decrease as early as the middle of the last century; in some villages birth control appeared even earlier. Owing to the "one-child system," by the 1930s the original population of several settlements had decreased to a small fraction of what it had been a century before and the communities had been filled up by poor families from other regions. In these areas the "one-child system" gave rise to a specific moral standard: a young woman having two or more children was deemed immoral and universally condemned. Social structure was profoundly influenced by this system (see Note 26 in this Part) (János Jankó, 1902; Elek *et al.*, 1936).

by its mother only in the morning and the evening.[23] In a nuclear family living apart the young mother carries her baby to the fields on her back. In the old days especially, a mother did not leave a fretful child alone, but hoed with the baby on her back.

Should the young wife feel that she cannot get along with her husband, she would go back to her parents, taking the children with her. (A mother of numerous children never leaves her husband.) If there is a son among them and "seven summers, seven winters" cannot reconcile the couple, the boy is sent back to his father at the age of twelve, in accordance with the custom of this and other Hungarian regions.

Illegitimate children are also brought up by their mothers, or, to be precise, by their maternal grandparents. Should the mother marry the father of the child, she takes the child with her. But if she were to contract a marriage with another man, the child would remain with the grandparents. A boy of ten or twelve years of age, already able to work, is a frequent exception.

In wartime, or if the husband goes to work in town and remains there for a long time, it may happen that the young wife bears a child to another man. Old people still remember the ancient Hungarian saying: "No matter who owns the bull that sired it, the calf belongs to the owner of the cow." This means that the husband has to accept such a child, to let it bear his name and call him father, though everyone knows the begetter. (The child will know it soon himself, since other children will mock him in school saying, "You are not of your father's make but of So-and-so.")

The absence of children may be a reason for divorce. The husband who prefers other women or girls to his barren wife is not blamed, nor is he criticized if, having begotten a child outside his home, he leaves his wife and moves in with the mother of his child.

Both grandmothers are usually present at the birth of a child. No male may enter the lying-in room, but a good husband will be found somewhere near the house. The midwife bathes the baby, then hands it first to its mother, then to its paternal and maternal grandmothers to be kissed. When the mother has been attended to and laid into the curtained bed, the father is called into the room and may take the baby in his arms.

The first child is usually named after its paternal grandparents, the second after the parents or a well-loved close relative who has recently died, if there is one. According to a countrywide custom in the Calvinist villages, many names are taken from the Old Testament: Rebeka, Zsuzsanna, Eszter, Sámuel, etc.[24]

Baptism usually takes place a week after the baby is born. Traditionally the baby,

---

[23] The infant is usually breast-fed by its mother for nine months. According to tradition, the cherished only child is nursed for ten to twelve months. Lately the fashion has been to wean the baby to solid food at six months. Women who had to work in the fields and leave the care of a baby to their mothers-in-law would adapt the child to normal food early. There is no special food for the baby; it gets a share of the family meals.

[24] A major change in Christian names has been brought about by World War I. Átány boys named Sámuel who were recruited were thought to be Jews and mocked for it. The people of the village decided never to christen another child Sámuel. Károly and Gábor (Charles, Gabriel) have come into fashion. With female Christian names, the tradition has been dropped in the past ten to fifteen years; the fashionable names now are Hajnalka, Ibolya, and Erika (Aurora, Violet, Erica).

covered by the wedding shawl of its mother, was taken to the church by the midwife and the godmother. Recent ecclesiastical requirements have demanded the presence of the parents. Each household takes the baptismal water from its own well in a special jug reserved for this purpose. After the ceremony, the midwife used to lay the christened baby at the side of its mother with the words, "We took a little heathen and brought back a little angel."

From the date of the baptism the baby is called by both its Christian and family names by everyone except the parents. Traditionally the young mother lies in childbed for six weeks. This is made possible by the custom that her visitors—parents, sisters and sisters-in-law, first and second cousins, baptismal *koma*-s *(keresztkoma)*, and neighbors—cook and carry the meals for the whole household during this time. After six weeks the young mother leaves home for the first time and goes to the church to be blessed.

In 1958, Mihály Papp's wife, who had not yet visited the church, took her five-week-old baby and went to pay an unexpected call on her mother. Noticing her as she approached down the street, her grandmother warned her severely to return. Her mother ran up to her and accompanied her back home.

After churching it is permissible and also proper for the young mother to present her baby to the kinsfolk, neighbors, and godparents who have "cooked for her" and carried the meals while she lay in childbed. When she makes her first visit the elderly women make a circle round the face of the baby with a shapely egg, saying: "Be as round, as beautiful, and as healthy as this egg."

Each person who sees the baby takes it up and addresses loud and kind words to it. It spends much of its time in the arms of its grandmother, especially if the mother is working in the fields. If there is a great-grandmother alive, she cares for the baby, or sometimes an older brother or sister will rock the cradle. If there are none of these persons in the family, the adults free themselves for work by calling one of the neighbor children to rock the cradle.

The father seldom takes a child into his arms while it is still in swaddling-clothes: "There is nothing to love in it." By the time it is six or eight months old, however, he holds it willingly and so does the grandfather. If the child is a boy, father and grandfather can hardly wait for it to toddle so they can take it for a short ride on the driver's seat. At this age both boys and girls wear nothing but long shirts, but the father buys a small hat for his boy as soon as possible so people will know that he has a son.

When the child begins to toddle, people start calling it a "little boy" or "little girl." It no longer sleeps in the cradle but in the chimney corner or on a small plank bed with its brother or sister. Up to this point it has eaten in the lap of its mother or grandmother; now it takes meals on the bench around the oven. In good households the women feed the children before the men return for meals, so that the little ones will not disturb them.

The father, grandfather, godfather, or another male relative manufactures a small whip or a horse team of animal bones for the boy so that he can "play horse"; the girl is given a small doll, a small rolling-board, or a miniature distaff with which she can learn to work in the form of play, helped by her mother or grandmother. Children of four or five years are already useful as messengers. They know their relatives; they are taught the proper form of address for each (mistakes are not infrequent, but they are corrected with care—e.g., your *ángy* Balog, the wife of your *báty* János Kiss); they are acquainted with the neighbors; they know the houses of those who are often visited by the family; they can find the shop, the post office, the church, and the school. At this age children may be taken with one of the grandparents to a field near the village, where they may be entrusted with some minor task such as dibbling. We have seen a girl of three help her grandparents plant maize by dropping the grain into the prepared holes.

At six the child becomes a schoolchild, referred to as "one who is big enough to go to school." At this time they learn how to comb their own hair and to wash and dress themselves properly. They are expected to greet people decently and to keep quiet in the company of adults. Girls are warned not to roughhouse with the boys, to pull their skirts below their knees, etc. The same precepts are enjoined by the schoolmaster, who also tries to get them to spend more time studying and less time playing. In some families an intelligent schoolchild is already allowed to sit at the table of the adults. But if he (or she) speaks except in response to a question, he is reprimanded with the words: "You are a child, keep quiet." On holidays the child is asked to say grace; on Sundays he has to recite the text on which the pastor has preached in church. A child "not taking the Word home" might go without dinner.

In summer the schoolboy spends his whole day in the stable and sleeps there with the men if he is allowed. A ten-year-old boy can be very helpful. In *gazda* families he is given a small pitchfork so that he can learn how to pitch hay; he also gets a used hoe, the "training hoe," in order to learn this work. During school holidays the boys from poor families are sent to drive horses or to watch *kert*-s or are engaged as help by tobacco growers; girls work as nurses or goose-girls. These jobs bring no significant profit to the family. The children of both *gazda* and landless families are put to work mainly at herding geese in the summer. A boy will herd geese when he is young, but as he grows he becomes "disillusioned with the geese," leaves the work as unfit for his sex, and herds piglets, calves, and cows instead.

When the child reaches the age of twelve or thirteen, having finished six years in school, he (or she) prepares for confirmation and is mentioned as *iskolahagyott* (one who has left school). From now on the girl is *eladó* (marriageable), the boy is *suhadér* or *suttyó* (a youth). Traditionally both boys and girls were given new clothes for confirmation; until that time (mainly in poor families) the used clothes of the parents or older brothers and sisters were cut down for them. Poor children sometimes went to school in their father's boots and wore the sheepskin jacket of one of their parents in winter. Since about 1910 children have been better clothed; eight-year-old boys who sing at funerals with the choirmaster receive the full men's attire that usually came only at confirmation.

After leaving school the child is considered a young adult, though the different status of boys and girls is marked in the saying: "The girl is marriageable while the boy is nothing yet." Both boys and girls know everyone in the village, they are aware of the connections of their families with relatives, neighbors, and friends and extend these by the ties of their own associations. Faulty or incorrect use of terms of address (e.g., calling an elderly person "thee") is no longer condoned. They know all the equipment of their own household or farm and are familiar with all the animals. They are informed of the size and location in the fields of the family plot and of the produce which will grow on it. They are prepared for the life of adults now.

Boys

After they have left school and been confirmed, boys move to the *kert;* from now on they will live there with the men and animals all year round. Most of the elderly Átány men say, "As soon as I left school, I moved to the *kert*. I did not sleep in the house any more." The few men who "disliked" the stable and avoided sleeping in it are exceptions. Their kinsman would keep asking them, "What will become of you, Józsi K., if you do not long for the *kert*?" Károly Bedécs characterizes the life of a *gazda*'s son after his school years as follows: "As soon as I left school, I sat at the croup of the horse [i.e., on the driver's seat of the wagon] and my father let me stand at the stilt of the plow." Other youngsters are engaged as shepherd boys or day laborers. After confirmation the lives of boys from *gazda* and from *zsellér* families are differentiated, whereas before this time all boys "could be used as gooseherds only." As soon as the boys grow older and stronger and are able to work, the advantages or drawbacks of the economic and social situations of their families come to light. "One stays at home on his father's farm, while the other is sent to find work as a swineherd, a shepherd, or a day laborer on a manorial estate." Those who were fortunate to remain with their fathers on the family farm relate with pride, "Nobody gave me orders but my father." Those who became young shepherds or day laborers were directed by strangers and "got their bread from [another's] hand." This is not to say that the youths who stayed with their fathers were given easier work. Ferenc Orbán, the son of a *gazda* having 24 *hold*-s (34 acres), recalls his youth like this: "Having passed twelve years of age, I became a veritable servant on our own farm. But my father would not have given me for two servants, since he ordered me about as he pleased, while a servant performed just the task for which he was hired."

During the first months when the small "servant" returns home with the men for meals, he is asked by his anxious mother and grandmother, "Aren't you tired, my boy?" But he shuns the caressing hand and answers, "Not in the least," though he is often so tired that he cannot really enjoy the meal; he knows that a man should suffer fatigue without uttering a word. Some of the sons of *gazda*-s or families who have plenty of manpower can expect some consideration. They may work with lighter "training" implements until they are fourteen or fifteen and are expected to accomplish only half as much work as an adult. Poor boys of the same age are sent to perform day labor with adult tools.

Although a boy may be started out on hoeing, reaping is considered the real work of men. As soon as he can find a chance, the boy gets hold of one of his father's worn scythes and tries to reap in secret. There is always a man, a relative or neighbor, who notices his efforts and comes over to him to demonstrate the correct handling and use of the scythe. In order to encourage the beginner and to stir his ambition, the adult generally gives him some implement used in mowing: a whetstone sheath, a hammer, or a hand anvil. He also tells the father the good news that his son is reaping already; this means that the boy will be a full-fledged worker in a short time. Having learned the techniques of reaping, the youth continues it alone for a while. In a few years, however, he may be tried out with the team of men as a harvester. If he passes his test, his father usually lets him smoke in public and serve himself at the table, since now he is regarded as a bachelor, a scythe man. A bachelor deserves a fine suit and good boots, and in former times he also was given on this occasion the embroidered peasant cloak, the *szűr*, which he would keep all his life.

Learning to reap is not the only way a youth can get a good suit of clothes, plenty of pocket money, and permission to smoke, slice the bread, and talk at the table. He may also go to war. During World War I several youths volunteered as soon as they reached the age of seventeen, in order to be free from their hard-handed fathers. One of our Átány acquaintances mentions such a case: "My liberation came when I joined the colors. My father's hand did not fall on me, and nobody hit the pipe out of my mouth if I lit one. I relied on my own strength thereafter." This, however, is an exceptional case. Sons usually bear paternal severity, even tyranny, without a word of rebellion.

This period is made easier for them by their "bachelor's life," a time of irresponsibility for all of them. However strict paternal direction and supervision might be, the sons do not look further ahead than the fulfillment of the task at hand, thinking, "My father is the farmer, it is all his business." Bachelor life means roaming around in groups, dancing, drinking, courting, conversing almost daily with one's friends, and, last but not least, brawling. Men of fifty and sixty still recall: "When we were bachelors, we never went to sleep at the usual time. Both in summer and in winter we went to the village; a group was standing at the corner every night. Even if the police caught and arrested us [for disturbing the peace], we went out again the following evening. We circled the village, singing, and then we entered the tavern. On summer nights we sang under the walnut tree and didn't come home till dawn. In the morning we went to work without having slept." Because they needed money for their revelry, and their mothers could not satisfy all their desires from their household funds, they used to "steal from their fathers"; they brought wheat, corn, or some other produce from their homes to the tavern, where it was easily exchanged for drink.

In this period the bachelor was not interested in the progress of the family farm. He knew the extent of land and the number of animals, but he never asked about the size of the family *tőke*, the possibility of debts, or the endeavors of the *gazda* "to make two out of one." This juvenile irresponsibility sometimes resulted in *gazda*-s' preferring hired men to their sons; they would discuss the actual work with the servants and let them sit beside them at the table, though tradition holds that the sons should have the seats to the right of their father in order of age and hired men should sit on the other side of them.

This situation changes with the end of bachelor life. When he is eighteen the youth is enlisted for two or three years of military service, from which he returns greatly sobered and matured. Now his mind is occupied with getting married and his family helps him to accomplish this as soon as possible.

When he is married, the young man changes entirely and behaves as if he had never been a bachelor. "Now that he has passed the tests, he thinks otherwise. While he was a bachelor, he stole even God's two eyes at home to spend in the tavern; as a married man he forgets the inn." The thoughts of a husband revolve round his family. Even if he remains at home under the rule of his father, he knows that he will inherit the estate in time and feels that he is working for himself. The difference between the attitude of a bachelor and a married man is well illustrated by the following example. Ferenc Orbán and János Kakas worked together in Budapest for six years. Ferenc Orbán had a wife and a daughter at home; János Kakas was unmarried. During all this time Ferenc Orbán, "since he was already married," avoided all sorts of entertainment, while János Kakas, being a bachelor, visited the zoo, the city park, and other places of innocent amusement.

Likewise the father changes his attitude toward his earnest son. He discusses the affairs of the farm with him willingly, and some fathers listen to the opinions of their sons. Others refuse to listen to their sons even after they are married, and this sort of behavior often results in quarrels between father and son.

Should the *gazda* treat the horse cruelly, striking or kicking it, his son would warn him, "Don't hurt it, father, I am working for its welfare too." But if the *gazda* fails to heed the warning, the son is forced to stand and watch even if he beats the animal to death. He always has to give in; should he rebel against paternal discipline or the way he is treated, he may leave the home empty-handed.

In a peaceful family life the father lets his married son go with him to fairs in order to make him familiar with the sale and purchase of animals; he also lets him work more and more independently in the fields.

According to modern custom, if there are several sons, they all leave the house except the youngest one, who remains with his father. This son is called the "young *gazda*," and he gradually takes over from his father the reaping and all the other tasks. The old *gazda* hands over the tasks of the fields to him one by one, taking up his abode in the *kert*, where he finally remains as a fire-poking old man.

Till the death of his father the young *gazda* has second place in the house; the enfeebled old *gazda* retains his authority and the direction of the farm to the last.

As the coffin of the old *gazda* is carried out of the house, his son, no longer a servant to anyone, becomes *gazda* and takes over the leadership of his household.

Girls

When she has finished school, a girl helps her mother or grandmother and performs her allotted tasks in their company. Whether her participation in the work of the fields starts at once or is assumed gradually depends on the status and the requirements of her family. If possible, the parents "spare the girl," expecting her to hoe only one row in the time it takes an adult to finish two. She is given easy work in the vineyard or during haying. Parents keep a daughter at home if they can, letting her do household chores. They do not teach her to cook, since this is the duty of older women; instead she picks up, cares for the little ones, spins, weaves, sews, and works on her trousseau in preparation for marriage.

It may happen, however, that a girl has to do a man's work. This was the case, for example, in the family of János Kádár, who had three daughters and no son. The *gazda* ordered the girls to work in the fields just as if they were boys, the only difference being that they did not spend the night in the stable. In wartime more girls were obliged to do "man's work" owing to the lack of manpower. Those who learn to reap, sow, or plow are admired. These cases are exceptional, however. The usual work of a girl is considered of little value, since its object is to have her trousseau ready for her own future rather than to preserve and enlarge the family estate.

This is why girls are the least valued members of the family. They occupy the last places at the table, they are the last to have a share of the meals, and, like children, they are not allowed to participate in the conversation of men. Brothers often quarrel with them and their parents if they are well dressed, arguing that since she doesn't work for them, a girl does not deserve fine clothes.

The situation is different for girls from families who do not own any draft animals. After their confirmation these girls regularly worked by the day. The surrounding manorial farms gave ample opportunities for hoeing sugar beets, working in the vineyards, and gathering turnips. From the 1920s, when teams of contract workers *(summás)* began to be recruited to work on distant estates (see Chapter 12, "Teamless Farmers"), women were in more demand for hoeing, picking, and cultivating vegetables. During hard times it happened occasionally that men were unable to find work and the family lived on the wages of the girls.

A girl of fourteen is allowed to receive suitors; by the age of seventeen or eighteen she should be married. A girl of twenty is regarded as an old maid, "one left out," and has to sit conspicuously in the spinsters' pew in church. Such girls are no longer free to choose a husband on their own; their family hastens to "give them out of the house" in marriage to anyone who will take them.

VŐ, MENY

"My *meny* is no daughter, my *vő* is no son"—so runs the saying at Átány, and in all of Hungary. "Whatever kind of *vő* you may have, he is never a son of your own blood." Inquiring about the behavior of an elderly woman toward her sick *meny*, a man asks his neighbor: "Does Aunt Maris favor Rebeka?" "Well, just as her *meny*," is the answer.

From the moment he enters his new home, a *vő* calls his in-laws "Father" and "Mother," and they call him "thee" and "thou" and address him by his Christian name. The same is true for a *meny*. If a *vő* or *meny* acquires favor, he or she may be called "son" or "daughter" as are the real children and referred to as "our daughter" or "our son"; otherwise they are just "the *vő*" or "our *meny*."

In Átány a daughter's husband is called *vő* whether he takes her to the home of his parents or moves in with hers. In the latter case he is also called a "married-in *vő*." In spite of the identical names, the situations of the two types of *vő* are very different, as expressed by the conversation of two villagers watching an old man driving a flock of geese along the street (a job for women and children). "I wonder if there is a meaner situation than this," says one of them. "There is one," answers the other; "to become *vő* in another's house."

Nobody wants to become a "married-in *vő*." A young man is always forced to do so by circumstances or tempted by the "desire for property." A poor bachelor may marry a well-to-do but sickly girl (who is unable to get a mate of her own rank), or the girl he loves may not be allowed to leave the house because her parents are trying "to bring a *vő* into the property." Among several brothers all but the youngest have to leave the paternal house, since it is the youngest who stays with his father. Such elder brothers, obliged to move, resign themselves to assuming the undesirable position of a "married-in *vő*" because according to the custom of succession, they do not receive their share of the family estate until the death of their father. By working on the farms of their fathers-in-law they can make more headway than they could by "taking wings" and earning their living as *zsellér*-s, a hard fate for the sons of a *gazda*.

In the house of his father-in-law the life of a *vő* is a humiliating one. It is true that he is provided with clothes, since a shabby-looking *vő* would be a disgrace to the family, but he is not necessarily fed regularly, and a mother-in-law may even start a quarrel with her *vő* at the table in order to take his appetite away. It happens that some *vő*-s are not even allowed to go near their wives. If such a *vő* wants to harness the horses to the cart in order to drive somewhere, his father-in-law may remark, "Harness the horse you brought from your father," reminding him that he did not bring any. Sometimes the mortified *vő* leaves the house of his father-in-law and works for his room and board at the home of some relative. The family usually manages to lure him back, since they need his labor. In one such case the father-in-law gave a piece of the *kert* to his *vő* by way of appeasement.

Other "married-in *vő*-s" are more fortunate. J. K. married the daughter of a *gazda*,

10

but she died after only four years of marriage. Since they had no children, he left the house, receiving as a reward for his services a full set of bed clothes, a few sacks of wheat, and some cash.

I. J. married the daughter of a *gazda* and moved in with his wife's family. After five years his wife died, leaving a child. The mother-in-law "allowed the *vő* to take a wife into the property"—in fact she even chose a girl for him. The new wife became a full-fledged member of the family, addressing everyone according to the status of her husband (as if she were a *meny*), and she brought up the child as her own.

In some instances the *vő* who joins his wife's family is a servant who marries the daughter of his master. This type of arrangement was more frequent before it became the custom for the girl to receive a share in the inheritance. In recent times it is often brought about by adverse circumstances: when the daughter is pregnant, or the son is useless and the *gazda* thinks the former servant will be more likely to keep the property of the family together than his own spendthrift son.

There are only a few "married-in *vő*-s" in Átány; their number fluctuates between fifteen and twenty in *gazda* families.[25] Although they find their position very humiliating, this is true only by local standards. The treatment of a "married-in *vő*" in Átány and on the Great Plain in general is only moderately severe compared to custom in other regions of the country. In the northern and especially in the western regions, the proportion of *vő*-s is much higher (owing to the widely practiced birth control, there are a lot of female only-children who need them),[26] and their situation is much more degrading. In Transdanubia, for example, the children bear the name of the wife's father instead of that of their own father, the *vő*. The position of *vő* is such an established institution in these regions that there is a certain day of the year when these men come together to tell each other their complaints and to drown their sorrows in drink.

In Átány the more frequent arrangement is for a man to bring his wife to the home of his parents. He has some duties toward his wife's parents too, but these are based on the principle of reciprocity. Usually he helps his in-laws in their work, but only after he has finished the chores on his father's farm.

A few hours after her wedding the young wife, now a *meny*, is led in a solemn

---

[25] One has to distinguish between the kind of unfortunate *vő* described in the text and the kind who were sons of well-to-do *gazda*-s and married into families of equal wealth (see Chapter 13, "The Order of Succession," "Mobility in the Last One Hundred Years"). Since they were frequently heirs to a considerable amount of property, they held an esteemed position in the house of their fathers-in-law (cf. Appendix F).

[26] In communities which adhere to the "one-child system" a *vő* from a poor family may be able to found a rich family by marrying a wealthy girl. If there is only one daughter, she cannot be allowed to leave the house, but the bachelors (also mostly only children) are not eager to marry her and become a *vő* in her house. In the 1930s a detailed investigation was made of the marriages in Kemse, a very small village which had adopted the "one-child system." Even in the last century 60 to 80 per cent of the girls born in the community were married to poor *vő*-s from other villages, and from the turn of the century all the Kemse girls have contracted marriages with men from outside the village, who then became "married-in *vő*-s" (Elek *et al.*, 1936: 34–36, 47).

The *vő* often secured his future by making a contract with the family of his wife. There is a clause in most of these contracts which states that the *vő* is entitled "to the average wages of a hired man in this region" for the duration of his marriage, should he leave the house (e.g., on account of the childless death of his wife) or be sent away.

procession to her future home, the house of her husband's parents. On the morning after her wedding the *meny* has to work beside her mother-in-law and henceforth carry out her orders obediently, "as if she were a real servant-maid." She must give up the household techniques learned from her mother and assume those of her mother-in-law instead. "Living with a dog, you must become one," and "where the dog is, there his tail belongs," are sayings that express the fact that the new couple, including the *meny*, will become like the in-laws they live with. A woman of fifty told us, "I forget all the habits I used to follow at home; instead I take up those of my mother-in-law. I do the cooking as she does, even my speech is adapted to hers." The *meny*'s relationships with other people are also influenced by her in-laws; if her mother-in-law is on bad terms with somebody, she must be cross with that person too.

Julis Madarász was married to József Sárközi in 1902 and went with her husband to the home of his parents. They lived in the house for a week and then it was time for the husband to move out to the *kert*. Occupied with the spring and summer agricultural work, he visited the house only on Saturday nights and Sundays. Since the mother-in-law carried the meals to the men in the fields and the *kert*, the young wife hardly ever had a chance to see her husband. "How bad it was," she remembers. A new *meny* "behaves bashfully" at first. She may be ashamed of eating: "I dared not eat my fill; the family of my mother-in-law was a strange one." Zsuzsi Kálósi says, "I lived with my mother-in-law for five years before I dared touch anything. I could not get into the habit of taking up the bread myself." This is the reason for the saying that the *meny* or the *vő* "gets the bread from hand," like a servant; thus it is also an expression of misfortune. On Sunday afternoons young married women visit their mothers, who have saved choice things to eat for this occasion and let them eat their fill. J. S. told us at the age of sixty, long after the death of her mother-in-law, that sometimes she did not get a bite for two days running, since she was not handed food. Those *meny*-s who could pass their old homes on the way to the fields were fortunate. They could drop in more frequently to see their mothers and eat what had been saved for them.

The young wife brings all her troubles to her mother. If she is ill, she goes home and is put to bed there. According to ancient custom she would also go back to her mother's house to give birth. As soon as she went into labor, however, the mother-in-law received notice, since it was proper for her to be present for the birth. Should the young wife have a baby in the house of her husband, her care would still be the job of the maternal grandmother, who would also provide the baby clothes. The mother-in-law usually gave only a swaddling bolster.

The *vő* who marries into a family is accepted even if he has nothing but a suit of clothes. The *meny* must have a trousseau which will last her for life, comprised of underclothes, outer garments, and bed linen. The mother is expected to supply her daughter with an entire set of bed linen for everyday use, and more well-to-do people add another to put on the ornamental bed. The only furniture the bride brings with her is a chest for her belongings; after the turn of the century wardrobes were used instead of chests. In both instances she could lock up her things and keep the key with her. The young wife uses only her everyday bed clothes and keeps the rest of her trousseau in the chest, since the household uses the linen of her mother-in-law, the *gazdasszony*. Often she leaves the better bed clothes and her nicest articles of clothing in the keeping of her mother; this is possible only if she has no sister. A fifty-year-old woman whose mother-in-law was still alive complained to us that she had not yet been able to be a *gazdasszony* for even a single day, and on holidays she could not lay her cloth on the table since her mother-in-law still kept all her own things in use. The *gazdasszony* guards her place of honor at the table and among the sleeping places "as long as she bears her age well." As mentioned before, the bed of the young wife is made on a bench or on a plank bed which is hidden under the bed in day-time.

Under the supervision of her mother-in-law the young woman does everything she is told. She may be ordered to milk the cows on the first day of her marriage, even if she never learned how to at home. During her girlhood she may have spent little time in the fields, but now she will be sent almost every day if necessary. She has to take part in breaking and spinning the hemp and in weaving the household linen. If this work is done to the satisfaction of the mother-in-law, she may cut out an apron or something else for her *meny* from the finished material. If an animal or some pro-duce is sold successfully, it is customary to reward her with a pair of slippers or an apron, while the real children may receive a full suit of clothes. The reason is that the young wife's work is supposed to be rewarded by board only, plus an occasional piece of clothing when she has worked herself "out-at-the-elbows." It is not per-missible to use the farm money to buy a more valuable garment for her, nor for her children until their work is "profitable."

At her marriage a well-to-do girl gets a cow-in-calf from her father; the animal is housed in her father-in-law's stable, but it grazes on the pastureland of her own father. In this case the money made by selling the milk and the calves belongs to the young wife, who uses it to buy clothes for herself and her children. If the father does not give a section of his pasture and the cow grazes in the pasture of the father-in-law, the money would go into the common purse, but the animal itself would still belong to the young wife. If the family cannot afford to give her a cow, her mother may allot two or three geese to her use for a couple of years, provided that the mother-in-law will allow them to be fed at her house. In this case any money made from them will be saved for the future baby, and the feathers will be kept for his bed. If the young wife has brought some property into the family (if her parents have died and she has inherited their property, if she has been given the portion of her deceased mother, or if she has inherited property from some other relative), the land is worked by her father-in-law or by her husband with the father-in-law's implements and animals, after the labor necessary in their own fields is finished. If the husband is an only child, the profit from this piece of land goes to the common purse too; if he is one of several children, however, the income is saved by the young couple for their own use.

In well-to-do houses the *meny* is spared for a couple of years. She only has to sweep, sew, weave, and tidy up. She is getting accustomed to the household. The mother-in-law does all the real work: baking, cooking, carrying the food to the men in the fields, and so forth. The young wife is gradually trained to do the household chores. In the homes of the poor, however, she cannot be spared; she must help with every kind of work as the occasion arises.

As the mother-in-law grows older, the *meny* helps her more and more; first she supplants the old woman in the field work, then gradually in the household chores. It is her duty to take care of aging, sickly in-laws and to lament them properly after their death.

When the coffin of the mother-in-law is carried out of the house, the *meny* takes her place and becomes *gazdasszony*, and she will keep this position all her life unless her father-in-law remarries.

OTHER MEMBERS OF THE HOUSEHOLD

Solitary Relatives

In most cases this type is represented by the "old *szüle*," the aged widowed mother of the *gazda*, who has resigned her position as *gazdasszony* to her *meny*, the *gazda*'s wife. She is called "a fire-poking old woman," and she is usually surrounded by love and esteem. Not only her family and her kinsfolk, but also the people of the *zug* address her as *szüle*, e.g., "Orbán *szüle*."

The *szüle* busies herself mainly in spinning, later in sewing and mending. She does as much household work as her strength will allow. Also, depending on her physical condition, she may look after the house or care for the poultry; some of these old women still herd geese. If she is able, she feeds and takes care of the children of the house, and not infrequently those of the neighbors. She teaches them songs, verses, and rhymed greetings. She tells them stories of "her time," passing on the traditions of her youth to her descendants.

In winter the *szüle* sits on a small stool in the chimney corner, where she can stay snugly warm and spin quickly. In the other seasons she uses a special low armchair manufactured for her. This is necessary because she no longer sits at the table, but crouches in her little chair in front of the bed with her plate on her lap. She does not participate in the conversation any more, though if she wanted to speak, she would be listened to reverently. If asked for advice, most *szüle*-s only say, "Just do it; you know better. I do not know how to any more." She devotes much attention to her belongings, her clothes and linen; these are left after her death and by these she will be remembered.

Other solitary relatives are formally received into the household. They may be men or women suffering from some physical or mental deficiency which excludes them from the normal life of the community and prevents them from ever marrying. Their situation is more fortunate if they have some property, in return for which people will take them in willingly. It is even better if they are able to perform some manual work which makes them useful in the house or in the fields.

A relative whose spouse has died and who has no children at home may be received into the household. Warm-hearted relatives would not leave such a person to live alone; there are usually very few belongings, so it is possible to take the lonely kinsman into the house and provide him or her with proper care and a decent burial.

"Little Servant," "Old Servant"

"Little servant" and "old servant" are distinguished according to age and family status. The "little servant" is usually a youth of twelve to sixteen years; after this age he is usually just called a servant. The "old servant," "old farm hand," "old hind" is a man who is married or one who is helped by a little servant.

Until World War II even a *gazda* owning only a *fertály* of land used to engage a servant while his son was young or because he wanted to spare both his son and himself. If he owned two *fertály*-s of land (20 to 24 *hold*-s; ca. 28 to 34 acres), he had room for two little servants, and if he had no adult son or if he held some office which prevented him from working in the fields, he might also hire an adult farm hand or perhaps an old servant.

Both little servants and old servants were hired for one year, beginning January 1. They were given their bread, payment in kind (wheat and barley, a piglet), and some cash. At the beginning of this century the wages included also a *szűr*, a sheepskin jacket, boots, and other garments; later these were supplanted by payments in cash. In a decent *gazda* family the servants take their meals with the *gazda* and his family at the common table, getting a share of every dish which is served. Nor do terms of address differentiate between *gazda* and servant.[27] Whereas in numerous parts of Hungary a hired hand addresses the head of the family as *gazd'uram*, in Átány the form of address is regulated only by the age differences. The servant addresses the *gazda* as *bátyámuram*, the *gazdasszony* as *nénémasszony* (i.e., uncle or aunt) if they are his elders, and the other members of the family according to their sex and age, using the same terms of address that would be used by an unrelated villager. Should the hired man be a relative of the *gazda*, the terms of address would be defined by that relationship. Also a *gazda* sometimes calls an esteemed servant "my little brother" or "my son" and uses his Christian name and the familiar pronoun.

As we have mentioned above, in some cases the *gazda* esteemed his old servant higher than he did his bachelor son. In a household where there is an old servant, the *gazda* does not sleep in the stable, but just visits the *kert* during the day. In such cases the servant directs the work on behalf of the *gazda*.

---

[27] The Golden Alphabet (see Appendix D) contains a special verse regarding terms of address for servants; also a book very common in Átány called "Christian Instructions," which was published in several editions in the eighteenth and nineteenth centuries, and which contains domestic services and prayers, has a special chapter admonishing the *gazda*-s to treat the servants humanely.

The little servant is usually a boy who has finished school and whose parents are landless villagers who also earn their living by working for others. A *gazda* with little land and many children may also seek employment for at least one of his sons, so that the boy will be fed by his employer and clothed by his own earnings. If possible, he is given as a little servant to a relative or a friend, so that the father will feel free to ask the employer not to overstrain the boy with work unfit for his age. This little servant lives in the stable but he takes his meals in the house, where he goes with the *gazda* or his son. He is allowed to visit his parents once a week, on Saturday evening, when he receives fresh linen for Sunday.

The old servant was generally a poor man who had been employed as a hired man from his early years and "has been accustomed to the horse" (unlike the hired men on the manorial estates, who worked with oxen, or day laborers in the village, who were not accustomed to the horse). Working as a servant in one household was considered preferable to performing the manifold tasks of harvester and day laborer in several places. The income of the old servant was no less than that of the harvester and day laborer. If he was esteemed by the *gazda*, he grew old in his service, since such a servant "is a servant till the end." In 1944 there were only three old servants in the village. Their well-being depended on their families. If there was a hard-working thrifty wife and healthy sons, the family could not only live comfortably, it could also succeed in acquiring something. An old servant who was married entered service with his own implements and used them until the end. One of the old servants in Átány returned to his family every evening, but this was possible only because there was another man spending the night in the stable. Others went home once a week, on Saturday evening, and returned to their service on Monday morning with fresh linen.

Otherwise, neither the little nor the old servant had any vacation. Whether he would get time off when he asked for it depended on the mood of the *gazda*. But a church-going servant had to be given the opportunity to attend the service on Sundays and holidays. The *gazda*-s liked a religious and pious servant and did not object to his going to church, but it was hard for the servant to find any time to spend with his friends and relatives.

CHAPTER 7. MARRIAGE

CHOICE OF MATE

Everyone knows each other in the village, especially the young people of the same generation. They spend time together in school, at play, and at dancing. During winter five evenings of the week are "spent with the girls," the bachelor bands going round the houses and courting the marriageable daughters.

A little boy may become attached to a little girl as early as the age of four or five years. They are often together, and the boy gives the girl his candy or apple. They are called "lovers," as if they were adults, and their parents are mentioned as "*nászos*" (those linked by the marriage of their offspring). However, such liaisons are usually forgotten after the juvenile years and only rarely lead to marriage.

Looking for a mate begins with the "bachelor days." Some boys begin courting at the age of fourteen, others at seventeen or eighteen. Each boy looks for a girl suitable for his age, i.e., one who is two to four years younger, although bolder youths sometimes visit girls older than they (see Chapter 10, "Activities of *Koma* and *Mátka* Groups," "Courtship"). The bachelor chooses his lover himself, "lover" meaning the girl whom he courts, with whom he dances, to whom he makes presents; but his future wife is chosen by his parents in the majority of cases.

The old men of today relate that a custom of "the ancient times," remembered from the time of their parents, sixty to eighty years ago, was for a bachelor returning from military service to be greeted by his mother with the words, "Well, my son, you are married." He asked, "Whom did I marry, mother?" and received the answer, "The daughter of the Szórád-s, Maris, you may have her for certain."[28] Neither did the girl know in advance who her husband would be. A seventy-year-old informant told us that her mother, when still a girl, one evening noticed a lot of people entering

___

[28] As early as 1857 a characteristic story of the Mezőkövesd marriage customs was noted down. "As the son returns from the pastures where he tends the family flock, he is surprised by the following news, communicated by his father or mother: 'Well, Bera [Albert], you were married.' The son answers with the question: 'Whom did I marry?' Being informed of the name of the girl selected for him, he acquiesces whether he knows the girl or not, as this was the custom followed by his father and his still-living grandfather" (István Györffy, 1942: 263). Among similar stories related in other parts of the country, we are told that in the village of Uppony (situated in the Bükk mountains north of Átány), in the 1910s there lived many men who "did not know their wives before marriage" (Istvánffy, 1911: 163).

their yard and called to her mother, "Look, dear, how many people are coming here!" The mother explained, "Because you are married, my dear daughter." "With whom?" "With János Rózsa." The suitor had already entered the house when the girl first was informed of her impending marriage.

This custom had not changed much during the youth of today's old people. As they recount it, there would be a family gathering in some house and some old woman would observe with a sigh that the son of the family had not yet chosen a wife. Another woman retorted, "God will command one for him." Finally the father muttered, "Before God could notice it, two old women put them together." This situation did not really change until the 1950s. Among well-to-do families "the land boundaries were fitted together" by parents and female relatives deciding whom their young people should marry. Landless youths were more free in choosing a mate. Several Átány men remember: "I courted my lover for three years but came to a wedding with my wife in six weeks' time." Parents and kinswomen often "dissuade" the bachelor from a present romance and make him marry another girl.

When the bachelor has done his military service, returning to the village at age twenty-one or twenty-two, his family intends him to marry, and if his mother is sickly and a female hand is needed in the house, his father would press him quite soon: "If the condition of your mother does not improve, you will have to marry, my son."

Girls too are pushed toward marriage. A girl is given as soon as she is asked for, to avoid her becoming a spinster. As soon as she has finished school a girl becomes eligible and may be courted, and her family watches eagerly for a suitor to appear. Juliska Gulyás had hardly turned thirteen when her grandmother asked each Sunday when she returned from her walk, "Have you got a lover yet? Your mother had one at your age." Girls are warned not to be choosy, "since the bachelor may ask, but the girl may not." The advance of the unmarried girls one row in church each year places a twenty-year-old in the pew of "those who are left out," marking her as already old. Proper families try to marry a daughter before she has to sit in this pew.

In the traditional order of the village everyone might find a mate and have a chance of founding a family, although it is easiest for those girls and young men who approach the ideal of desirability. But even persons physically disabled or morally disapproved of find a mate. The well-known saying that "one in frieze clothes fits another in frieze clothes" alludes to the rule that everyone has to seek an appropriate mate: a person of low rank who wears inexpensive clothes should marry another of the same rank. In the last century—in fact, until World War I—the son of a *gazda* could marry a poor girl, since all daughters, even those of wealthier families, were allotted a minimum of the inheritance. In these cases personal qualities and family circumstances were taken into consideration.

Among personal qualities, physical fitness ranked first. Among persons of equal status even the slightest defect of sight—e.g., near-sightedness—might be an obstacle, since physical deficiency "makes the girl wholly valueless." Beyond physical fitness, the girl should be "beautiful and *fájin* [fine] too." A round and ruddy face and dark eyes are desirable, and a build that is "strapping, quick, and nimble." White-skinned, blonde Átány girls (very few in number) are "not looked for"; young men prefer brown-haired girls. Also, silent, lifeless girls or those who do not dance well are relatively neglected. But essentially, it is asked whether the girl is "good at work," is active in the fields, and knows the art of spinning and weaving. And as for the bachelors, the *fájin*, strapping, healthy, ruddy-faced good workers are most sought after.

The majority of Átány girls correspond to the ideal of beauty in both face and figure. But the men tend to be short and lean more often than tall and broad-shouldered. If the girl has the choice, she favors the strapping, robustly built man even if he has less property.

Besides fine stature both boy and girl are expected to be pure, honest, and honorable, if they are to win a partner of their rank. If a bachelor makes a girl pregnant, he has to share the shame and to marry her, whatever her rank. So it happened that S. R., a scion of one of the most respected families, married a servant-maid. This was regarded as just, even by the parents of S. R., but they did not receive the young woman into the family. Among others, it was thought that a son should not thus bring his wife into the paternal house, as he would have done in other circumstances, but that they should start out on their own at once.

But physical attributes such as beauty and fine stature are not enough. The genealogies of both the suitor and the girl are carefully scrutinized. The large wealthy independent families are especially concerned about comparable social standing; the origin, rank, prestige, and also behavior of the other family are carefully scrutinized. They ask whether the father leads a moral life and the mother is chaste: in short, just "what breeding" the future mate represents. They try to find out whether there is some latent disease in the family which has been kept secret, or whether the girl herself is ill. When G. C. wanted to marry Zs. L., an old female relative put in a word, saying: "Listen, Gábor, you won't be a husband for more than a year; after this time Zs. L. will die. She has a wound of the size of a crown on her neck, concealed by her family; this will be her fate." Consequently G. C. changed his mind. The girl married a youth of lower standing and in a year's time she died in childbirth. The C. family was eternally grateful to the old woman for having thwarted the marriage.

Young people suffering from some physical or moral defect or "unsought" girls over the marriageable age are paired with mates of lower rank. Girls with defective sight or hearing and lame ones marry young men of a lower social standing or those who are in some way socially stigmatized. A case in point was S. O., who shot and killed his grandfather when he was sixteen years old. He was convicted and served a nine years' term in prison. When he returned to his family, though he was a son of a *gazda* possessing 24 *hold*-s (ca. 34 acres), he knew that it would be useless to court a girl of his own social rank. So he courted and married a girl who was "unsought." He now lives with his wife like any other person and time is gradually "washing his sin away."

Recently, and especially since World War I, family troubles, physical defects, and social stigma are mitigated and canceled out by the possession of land. One often hears: "They stick inheritances together"; "they fit the ridges to each other"; "property buys property"; "property makes it easy for one to marry." Deficiencies in rank, prestige, esteem, or physical ability loom less important if the other family is assured of adding a few acres of land. If a female relative of the prospective bridegroom were to raise the traditional objection about some physical or other defect in the chosen girl, she might receive the answer: "Property will cover it up."

One of the historical consequences of these efforts to balance status and maximize property is the intermarriage of relatives. Until the turn of the century, marriage to kinsmen as distant as fourth-degree collaterals was out of the question and would have been regarded as incestuous. Since then the incest boundary has narrowed, extending only to marriage of second cousins. Quite recently, however, the feeling "that the inheritance should not be parceled out" beyond the family has resulted in the marriage of even first cousins. Two such marriages were contracted in the village in the 1940s. There is discord in these families, which is attributed to their close relationship, and it is believed that the future descendants would be cripples.

It is the unanimous local opinion that everyone should choose a fitting mate in the village, except perhaps widowers, who may have difficulty finding an acceptable companion. Nevertheless, every year several bachelors acquire brides in another village or some Átány girls marry out. Analysis of the causes of such exogamous marriages forces us to attribute a considerable number to fortuitous circumstances. For example, in the mid-twenties, two Orbán daughters were married to bachelors in Tiszanána. Their father owned a *félhely* at home and enjoyed universal esteem; the daughters were pretty and industrious. Once the elder daughter accompanied her father when he went to Tiszanána to trade animals in the market. There they put up in quarters of a family they knew. The bachelor son of the house took a liking to the girl, and the suitors came to Átány soon thereafter. Since the girl had no committed lover in the village yet, her family consented to the marriage. However, the two sisters did not want to part, so their acquaintances in Tiszanána sought a mate there for the other as well. Although the second bachelor was rather shiftless, regarded as only "fit to be a guard of melon fields" (helpless old people used to guard the melon fields), he was chosen to be the husband of the other daughter so that a relatively less costly double wedding ceremony could be held (see Chapter 7, "Forms of Marriage").

Occasionally families would find husbands outside the village for girls who have been insulted by the bachelors at home (e.g., "danced out" of the room; see Chapter 10, "Activities of *Koma* and *Mátka* Groups," "Dancing") or who have passed the marriageable age and are not "sought for" at home.

Naturally, a son of a poor farm hand married outside the village far more often than did a son of a landed *gazda*. Such a bachelor often contracted a marriage while working in another village. As hired man to a *gazda*, he may marry a daughter he is "serving in the place of," or he may take a fancy to another girl in the alien village. Thus the Átány bachelor became an inhabitant of his adopted village as a *vő*.

Some choosy bachelors might think that they could not find in Átány a girl worthy a son of a *gazda* and therefore looked for a mate in the more "urban" Tisza-nána.

Exogamy was more often the case in a second marriage. Widowers were almost obliged to look for a second wife outside the village, partly because of the high-handedness of Átány widows, who by custom demanded a written contract as surety in the event of the husband's dying before her. The law guaranteed to a first wife but not to a second a life-long benefit from the use of a husband's property. The second husband used to assign the proceeds of two to three *hold*-s (2.84 to 4.26 acres) of land, or a parcel of vineyard or garden, or even the use of a house to assure his second wife's maintenance in the event he predeceased her. It was rumored that the widows of Átány *gazda*-s used to demand more surety than women from the outside.

If a proposed marriage is between young people who are both of the village, the family of the prospective bridegroom does not go out to reconnoiter the girl's family or even to pay an official visit prior to opening negotiations, because almost everyone knows the circumstances of other people. However, if the prospective bride lives in another village, the parents, married brothers, and godparents of the future bride-groom used to drive out to have a look at the house of the girl, after the first inquiries but before the formal proposal. According to custom, the visitors were shown the court and ushered into the stable, where they could judge the standing of the *gazda* by his livestock. Simultaneously, the family of the girl would judge the family of the bridegroom by their team of horses.

If the young man's family found the girl acceptable, an elderly female relative would be sent to inquire about the intentions of her family, in order to avoid their later open refusal. If such inquiry is unexpected, the family of the girl would ask for one or two weeks' time for consideration. For a bachelor not to their liking, they would refuse very tactfully, averring that the girl is too young, her trousseau is not ready yet, or the family is not prepared "with mutton and wine" for the wedding as is proper. But if they looked favorably on the offer, they would agree on a date for the wedding outright.

Families of higher social standing used to send a number of people to make the proposal, for the sake of decorum: the married brothers, uncles, and godparents of the future bridegroom, all accompanied by their wives, and by the suitor too. Very circumspectly, using humorous and metaphorical phrases, the delegation would allude to the object of their visit: they are looking for an escaped bird, they saw it fly into this house, etc. Finally they would make their proposal. The parents would then call their daughter into the room and ask her whether she is willing to marry the bachelor who has thus proposed to her. It is proper for the girl to answer, and if her parents find it all right, she generally does not object. The bridegroom then hands over a few *forint*s to the girl in a small envelope as "kissing money" and he kisses her in front of the guests. The families then agree on a date for the ceremonial engagement, usually a few days later.

They hasten to make the preparations and, if possible, to keep them secret especially in the case of a favorable match since they fear that the young couple will be "dissuaded" in the meantime. The bridegroom and his mother, accompanied by the bride, go to Eger to buy the engagement ring. (As in other regions of Hungary, the bride wears only an engagement ring at Átány.) Then the *jegy* is prepared in both houses. The *jegy* of the bridegroom consists of money placed inside a small pearled purse. The bride buys as a *jegy* a fine, ornamented silk shawl or headdress and puts it into a box, often heart-shaped, together with six to eight other kerchiefs. The box is decorated with ribbons and artificial flowers. On the evening of the betrothal the respective godmothers carry each *jegy* to the other family in exchange.

The engagement is celebrated in the bride's home in the presence of the nearest kin and the godparents. At the beginning of the century betrothals equaled a minor wedding in preparation and elaborateness. Later, cooking was omitted and the guests were served only bacon, sausages, and wine. Finally the ceremonial engagement ceased to be celebrated altogether.

Until World War I the bridegroom used to parade on holidays during his engagement with the fancy shawl tucked into his belt. On his hat he wore the artificial flowers which embellished the *jegy* box and which had originally adorned the bonnet of the bride's mother. The bride wore a bunch of flowers, natural or artificial, pinned to her breast and turned upside down as a sign that she was a bride-to-be. Should the engagement be broken off (this happened not infrequently, either as a result of a quarrel or because of "dissuasion"), the girl would fasten her flowers right side up, and the young man, by way of contrast, would wear his upside down. He might also tear the fancy shawl in two and tuck the pieces into his boots like foot-rags, with the tassels hanging out, or tie them on his horse's harness near the ears and drive around the village with some friends, his *koma*-s, thus informing everyone that he was no longer betrothed.

After the formal engagement, if the couple did not part, the banns were published in the church on three successive Sundays. In these three weeks both families prepared for the wedding.

Besides readying the house and procuring food and drink, the preparations included manufacturing additional *jegy*-s. The bride would sew and embroider a white shirt as the groom's wedding shirt. He would wear it only twice—at the wedding ceremony and for his burial. The material was purchased with the bridal money (given by the bridegroom at the engagement) and the costs of the manufacturing (sewing and embroidery) covered by the girl's godmother. The two betrothed would also send gifts to six or eight persons in each other's family: headshawls, handkerchiefs, sometimes even material for a whole suit of clothes for a child. (If the immediate family of either bride or groom were less numerous, the presents would be distributed to first cousins as well.)

FORMS OF MARRIAGE

The bachelor who has proposed to a girl says, "I have married"; the girl whose parents have agreed to the match is referred to as a "married one." The young couple are often together, and one might help the parents of the other in their work. They are not reproached for sexual union. The actual wedding ceremony adds only a final solemn sanction to their marriage.[29]

At Átány the newly-weds rarely set up a household by themselves. Usually the young wife settled into the house of her husband's parents immediately after the marriage, to work there like "a veritable servant-maid" under the command of her mother-in-law. More rarely, the young husband moved into the house of the bride's parents, busying himself there like "a veritable farm hand" under the direction of his father-in-law. The several varieties of these two fundamental forms of marriage are explained in detail in the preceding chapter on "The Members of the Family."

The more frequent patrilocal form of marriage is symbolized most conspicuously by the custom of "transferring the bed." The bed (i.e., the bed clothes) of the bride is brought to the house of the groom in a solemn procession on the eve of the wedding. A few decades ago the bed, the pile of cushions and eiderdowns, and the ornamental bride's chest used to be loaded on a cart and transferred in daytime accompanied with loud singing, as if to exhibit these exquisite articles of the trousseau to the whole village.

The other form of marriage, in which the *vő* moves into the house of his bride, has not evolved as much ceremony around it. Division of property or lodgings is generally out of the question here, since the *vő* is brought into the house because his labor is needed on his father-in-law's farm. (See Chapter 6, "*Vő, Meny*.")

All the wedding ceremonies are linked to that form of marriage in which the young husband leads his wife to the house of his parents. An outstanding event of the day is the bride's farewell to her parents, brothers, sisters, and neighbors as she leaves her girlhood home to take her place in the family of her husband. Even if the young woman is to stay with her parents and a *vő* is brought into the house, she takes leave of her parents and kinsfolk and is accompanied to the house of the parents of her husband as if she were to settle there. The people of Átány are of course aware of this formal contradiction.

It is perhaps to soften the fact of the less desirable uxorilocal arrangement that the *vő* does not move to the bride's house on the same day as the wedding (as the *meny*

---

[29] There are both civil and ecclesiastical forms of marriage. Civil marriage became obligatory in Hungary in 1894. Marriage in the church can be contracted only after the registry marriage. The wedding party marches to the parish hall first and then to the church (see Chapter 11, "The Wedding"). It happened for the first time in 1964 that an Átány couple contracted a civil marriage only, without the benediction of the church. Marriage in the church follows three weeks after the day on which the parties have presented themselves officially; in the meantime, on three successive Sundays, the persons to be married have the banns read from the pulpit. It has happened that ill-informed families have fixed the date of the wedding and made all preparations but that the minister was unable to bless the young couple for lack of the threefold publication of the banns. In such cases a wedding was celebrated anyway so that the preparations should not have been in vain, and the church marriage performed later.

does in the case of the patrilocal form), but rather a week later. The *vő* has no bed
and therefore no ceremonial transferal can take place. Recently, since sons of *gazda*
families as well as of poor people assume the role of *vő*, their belongings are transferred by cart. But this happens without any formality and is unrelated to the wedding
ceremony.

A brother and sister often have a joint wedding with another brother and sister.
People say that they "married in exchange." And we may note that a double wedding
saves a lot of money in both households. But the folk description is misleadingly
applied also to a double wedding of two siblings of a family even if their mates are
from different houses, which is not "marriage in exchange"[30] in its technical sense.

If a spouse dies, the survivor frequently remarries. An elderly man having a daughter
or a *meny* in his house to take care of it may well not marry again, and an elderly
woman would be even less likely to. Younger people thus bereaved, however, soon
look for a new spouse according to the circumstances of their families. A young
widow may marry a bachelor, even if she has a child by her marriage. But, in fact,
the parents of the bachelor "are not glad" about such a bride. Also, a young widower
may marry a maiden. In the case of young people marrying again, the wedding is
almost as solemn as the first one, the single difference being that in the house of the
widow or the widower the merry-making is somewhat less noisy. At the wedding
ceremony the widow stands in front of the pastor in a dark costume, a kerchief on
her head instead of a veil, her attire not revealing that she is a bride. Nor does the
widower fasten a bunch of flowers to his hat or to his breast to mark his being a
groom. Should the widow have one or more children, they might stay at her side on
the wedding day.[31]

If a widow or widower has children, there is a strong tendency in Átány to look
for the second spouse from the family or from among the kinsmen of the deceased.
The sororate is just as frequent in the village as the levirate. Átány people explain
that this is a widespread Hungarian practice because a brother or sister is more
kindly disposed toward a deceased sibling's children than a stranger would be. The
families involved arrange such marriages even if the sister of the deceased wife or

---

[30] It is widely held that one match of such double marriages turns out to be unfortunate. Nevertheless, only once, in 1963, did a young girl protest in public against a double marriage because of its
bad omen. Ferenc Török intended to give both his son and daughter in marriage on the same day,
but the bride of his son wanted a separate marriage, and so it happened. This example was followed
by Károly Együd, who gave separate weddings for his son and his daughter a few months apart.
Within a year of the marriages Károly Együd met with a fatal accident, and public opinion reacted
by pointing out that the two weddings were celebrated in vain, that bad luck in the form of the
accident befell the family nonetheless.

[31] Zsuzsanna Kiss, the wife of István Kálosi, remained as a widow with her small daughter in the
house of her father-in-law after being married one and a half years. Ferenc Orbán, who was a bachelor,
wanted to marry her and sent a kinswoman to ask if he might visit her. She was ready to receive
him, but only in the house of her own parents. The bachelor continued to visit the young widow and
on each occasion she returned to her parents' house to receive him. There was no solemn proposal,
in view of her widowhood. Ferenc Orbán himself asked her if she would marry him and also asked
her parents whether they would give her in marriage. After a favorable answer the young widow
informed her in-laws of her intention to marry again. She was allowed to go in peace, and all the
brothers of the deceased first husband were present at her wedding. Only the former parents-in-law
were absent, not because they harbored resentment, but because "it would have hurt them to see it."

the brother of the deceased husband is ten or more years younger. In *gazda* families particularly the wish "to avoid the property falling into strange hands, to keep it together," often leads to considerable pressure to assure these ends. If no brother or sister is still unmarried, the new husband or wife is sought from among the cousins of the deceased; only when no suitable person can be found among near or remote kinsmen, will the family turn to a stranger.

Often in the case of levirate or sororate the couple, finding the number of children enough, does not want to have more. But in other cases, if the new spouse is a stranger, it is desirable that he or she have children too; in fact, if the newly-weds are still young, they are glad to have children of their own. It is said of such families that "they have children of two or three sorts."

The wedding ceremonies for elderly widows used to be quite modest. The saying goes that preparations for the first wedding take three weeks, for the second one, less than a day. It was considered improper to celebrate a second wedding with revelry when it takes place a few months after the death of the first spouse. Thus in houses where the *gazdasszony* has died without leaving an adequate substitute, need for a woman in the house does not allow the widower to wait out a year of mourning; custom requires only the passing of three months. If a remarriage does then ensue, only a modest supper is prepared, and the parents and godparents are invited to it.

A remarriage does not end the relationships established by the former one. Opinion holds that these former ties "cannot be cut"; "we do not cut the kinship." So Gábor Varga had two wives, and he buried both of them. However, he and his children foster the ties with both of his wives' families.

Remarried couples having children from their previous marriages often bring up these children in the expectancy of their marrying a stepsibling. Thus the widower Sándor Juhász found a second wife at Tiszanána. He had two sons and the woman three pubescent daughters. When the oldest pair of stepsiblings reached marriageable age, their wedding was celebrated. The younger pair were similarly betrothed, but the young man became fatally ill. His stepsister, destined to be his wife, sewed the wedding shirt for him in which he was buried, and she mourned for the deceased youth as if he had been her bridegroom. In the 1930s J. K. and his wife each had two children by previous marriages; they let the young people marry each other. It was said of them: "They became three couples." The wedding of the two stepbrothers and step-sisters was celebrated on the same day, and thus they were married "in exchange."

Since 1894, marriage and divorce have been under the jurisdiction of the civil courts. Divorce is, however, quite alien to Átány values about family life. Married people who cannot live together in peace used to "resign themselves to their fate." They acted so that "the smoke of the fire should not be seen," concealing the discord from the world. The fire metaphor is used to refer to marital difficulties on other occasions as well. One woman said, "It was no life, it was burning." Another lamented her dead husband, who had insulted her frequently in life, as her "burning fire" when he lay on his bier (see Chapter 11, "The Funeral").[32]

[32] Kiss and Rajeczky, 1966: 31, 94.

Marital harmony is most often disturbed if the man (more rarely the woman) becomes a drunkard, if he beats his wife, dissipates the property of the family, or if one of them (mainly the man) "makes digressions," i.e., philanders. The old people living today remember three murders among married couples. In two cases elderly women killed husbands who had become addicted to drink and maltreated them; in the third case a jealous young husband killed his wife.

A divorce might be initiated at the prospect of another marriage. The first divorce in the village occurred at the end of the last century because a young woman who was barren had become mentally ill and her husband wanted to begin a family with another. In the present century several divorces have occurred on the grounds that the young people had been forced by their parents to marry and were "perfect strangers to each other," not even having consummated their marriage. A story is related about a young woman who had been married against her will before World War I. She tried to poison her husband the day after their wedding. She did not succeed in killing him, but they were soon divorced. However, the number of recent legally divorced people did not total ten until 1960 when it became eleven.

More frequently the partners just "separate" or "go apart." This can happen in the case of newly-weds and it usually results in only a few months of separation. The young wife may "run away" from the house of her mother-in-law and return to her mother. A severe mother does not take her daughter in but sends her back saying: "You are a *meny*, be silent"; or, "You are a *meny*, you have to endure it." If she lets her daughter in, she sets the condition that the latter not do "the disgrace" of parting one day and returning the other. A soft-hearted mother would receive her daughter and wait patiently until word came from the house of the mother-in-law, or until the husband fetched her personally. It also happens that the young wife returns of her own will.

Some married couples "go apart" for good. In the 1920s a woman left her husband, learned midwifery, and settled in another region. The man settled into the family of his brother, but he committed suicide in his old age. Another separated couple simply found new consorts; they "went together" with another and became "married over a broomstick."[33]

---

[33] There are a few people living "irregularly" in Átány. A stepmother lives conjugally with her stepson. It is said that their relationship dates back to the time when the father was still living. A widowed mother-in-law lives with her widowed *vő*, and a widowed father-in-law cohabited with his widowed *meny* until he died recently. Cohabitation between the members of an aged and a young couple living under the same roof is also known; the father-in-law having sexual intercourse with his *meny*, the mother-in-law with her *vő*.

11

PART THREE
THE NETWORK OF SOCIAL RELATIONS

CHAPTER 8.
CONSANGUINITY, AFFINITY, AND FICTIVE KIN-TIES

An old aunt of László Varga was so feeble that she was unable to pay calls in the village, but sometimes her son would harness his horses and take her by cart to visit a kinswoman of her own age. What was the subject of their conversation? "They recalled bygone times. Who is this person? He had another brother too... what has become of him? Where did he live? He had his house along the Eger road but does not live there any more; another man has bought the house, while he has constructed another in front of the Bedécs-s." Keeping track of the inhabitants of the village and who everybody was are favorite topics of conversation. And as her son drove the aged woman home, she would say, "How well we chatted, how well we spent the time."

When elderly people are together, sitting in the yard on a Sunday, and they see somebody not immediately recognized, they instantly ask each other: "Listen, who was that? Whose son or daughter?" If the father is not known either, they range further back: "This is the grandson of Jóska Kiss, you know, the one who dwelt in front of the pub of the Jew."

A person is thus identified primarily by his position in a kinship network. Every Átány peasant uses extensive genealogical knowledge whenever he inquires about one of the many hundreds of villagers. He uses a variety of concepts about larger and smaller kin groups which express descent or a combination of descent and affinity. Some of these groupings are conceived as ego-centered networks and others are based on descent from a common ancestor. Belonging to one of these groups sets guidelines for behavior toward the other members of the group.

The terms and concepts of these kinship groups are known by the Hungarian peasantry all over the country. Why some of these terms have rather variable meanings while others have more definite and fixed meanings is not yet completely understood. Some terms and concepts complement one another, whereas others seem to overlap. Some terms for kinship groups have a long history; old sources reveal that they referred centuries ago to organized, corporate groups, and in some traditionally rural regions one can still find survivals of the older kin groups.

151

GROUPS OF CONSANGUINES

Ág: Lineage and Its Ramifications

The word *ág* means both the branch of a tree and a lineage. Hungarian peasants visualize the structure of the lineage as a branching tree and refer to its parts as they refer to a tree's parts. When the man fathers children, it is said that he "branches out" and that his line is divided into several *ág*-s. "As we have branched out, we have divided up into several *ág*-s"; "ours is a large *ág*"; "the Varga *ág* is a small *ág*, it is much broken off, only the trunk has remained." In this last case the father, the trunk, agrees: "They have been torn from my *ág*. I am the trunk; my two sons and my grandsons are my *ág*-s. These are not far-reaching branches; it is not a fertile *ág*. The Barát-s, the Barna-s are prolific; my mother-in-law comes from the Barát *ág* too... Also at Rimaszombat there is one who belongs to my *ág*." "People become ramified, the branches of kinship are intertwined."

When reckoning back, the father (who is the trunk) is in turn classified as the branch of some earlier *ág*. Most people record their *ág* through three generations in the ascending line; some reckon even more. One finds some Átány people who know that the trunk, the origin of their *ág*, was settled in the village in the early eighteenth century, and sometimes even the Christian name of the ancestor is kept alive. Most, however, cannot trace back their *ág* further than 80 or 100 (at the most 120) years; thus it appears that parts of the pedigree are forgotten even by these relatively new settlers. (Elderly people recall that their father or some other predecessor was able to reckon back the whole *ág*.)

The husband belongs to one *ág* and the wife to another. She remains in her *ág* to the end of her days. Children belong to the *ág* of the father, although illegitimate children belong to that of the mother. Daughters are considered essentially irrelevant to the *ág*, since "the *ág* goes after the name"; "the *ág* is led by the sons."

The *ág* is also reckoned collaterally. Among the *gazda*-s it is reckoned as far as the fifth grade in the collateral line, and tradition holds that the village ancestors recorded it as far as the seventh grade. Younger and poorer people restrict it to the third. (The concept of collaterality here used is the native one, not that incurrency in technical anthropological usage; it is elucidated below in discussion of the meaning of *íz*.)

Many related families bearing a common name have segmented into several *ág*-s by now, but memory of their "once" existing unity does not disappear. For example, there are three Bedécs *ág*-s in the village. Károly Bedécs (63 years old) enumerates the members of all three *ág*-s but adds that in his childhood all the now diverged families invited him to weddings. This means that they expressed their unity as a single *ág* at that time. But as a new generation grows up, the people born into the same *ág* are separated by an additional grade *(íz)*. Kinship is not recorded collaterally beyond the fifth (more recently the third) *íz*. Hence fission of the *ág*-s is inevitable.

Members of the separating *ág*-s who bear the same family name are distinguished either by surnames or by nicknames. An *ág* of the Kakas family, mentioned as Deme Kakas, is known from the last century. (The surname Deme comes from the wife of the *ág*'s ancestor, this woman having belonged to an ancient Átány family, the Demeters; although the Demeter family became extinct in the male line, the family name is preserved by this sobriquet.) However, as the Deme Kakas people multiplied, this *ág* also divided into two: the *ág*-s are called Kis (Small) Deme Kakas and Nagy (Big) Deme Kakas. These names were derived from two brothers, one of whom was small, the other big. (Our much-cited informant József Kakas belongs to the Kis Deme *ág*.)

The above example illustrates two characteristic types of surnaming. One involves attaching the family name of the wife to that of the husband. Besides the Deme Kakas *ág*, we may cite another example, Vajda-Kálosi. This is the *ág* of the Kálosi-s, the ancestor of whom married a daughter of the well-to-do Sámuel Vajda (see Chapter 13, "Mobility in the Last One Hundred Years") and acquired considerable fortune by the woman's inheritance. The other type of surname derives from a personal quality, as in the case of the Kis and Nagy Deme Kakas *ág*-s. Similarly, one *ág* of the Együd family is called Okos Együd (i.e., Clever). The surname came from the grandfather (he died in the 1930s), a very ingenious man who constructed machines, planned a novel type of house for himself, etc. His son, János Együd, at the age of more than seventy, still carried the nickname "Okos," although it had not been given to his sons. A sobriquet of this sort, alluding to a personal quality, usually becomes extinct in the third generation. One of the Madarász *ág*-s is called Nyalka Madarász (i.e., Jaunty) because some sixty years ago Antal Madarász acquired this surname by dressing very smartly as a young man. The other Madarász *ág* has the nickname Köcsög (i.e., Jug), which is explained by an anecdote about the founder. Coming from the *kert*, János Madarász carried a milk jug in one hand and a dead cat in the other, planning to throw the latter into the brook as he passed by. But he threw the jug into the water instead of the cat. Since that time he and his children have been called Köcsög. Besides this *ág*, we also know of the branches Füles Madarász and Nagy-bajuszú Madarász. One of the heads of these families received the nickname because of his large ears, the other because of a big moustache which he kept neatly groomed at all times.

Grade of relationship within and between the *ág*-s is expressed by the word *íz*. For example, József Sárközi remained *íziglen* (i.e. a solitary *íz*) since he had only sisters whose offspring did not belong to the Sárközi *ág*. "The *íz* is my son, the second *íz* is my grandson, the third *íz* is my great-grandson." Contrary to the nomenclature used in the Hungarian cities, but in accordance with usage of the Hungarian peasantry, the "first" collateral *íz* is the sibling bond; the "second" *íz* designates first cousins: i.e., "If our fathers or mothers are the offspring of the same parents." "If our grandfathers are brothers, their children are our cousins in the third *íz*." "The children of our great-grandparents are our cousins in the fourth *íz*. The more remote ones have no such name."

Atyafiság

Atyafiság refers to a wider category of consanguinity than *ág*. While *ág* embraces blood relatives on the father's side only, *atyafiság* includes those on the mother's side as well. One counts as his *atyámfia* all consanguineals to the third or fifth degree of collaterality, both uterine and agnate.

Atyafiság is also an expression used for blood relations generally: "Being a *sógor* (brother-in-law) or baptismal *koma* (godparent) is no *atyafiság*"—so goes the saying in the village and all over the country. This means that ties established by marriage and by fictive kinship are not equal to those of the kindred. One hears older people say: "He is *atyafi* by my wife," but this means less than to say: "He is *atyámfia*;" the latter expression is used only to refer to persons to whom one can trace filiative links through one's father or mother. In this respect the group comprising one's *atyafiság* resembles those types of "bilateral kindreds" reckoned only through consanguineal linkage.

Whereas the word *ág* (or *ágazat*) is used only as reference terms, one may address another as *atyámfia*. One often hears the question: "Where are you going, dear *atyámfia*?"; but one could not ask: "Where are you going, my dear *ág*?" Older people often greet blood relatives in this way: "Welcome, dear *atyámfia*"; "how do you want it (i.e. 'where are you going?'), dear *atyámfia*?" This is comparable to the equally usual, old-fashioned addresses "brother" or *vérem* ("my blood"). All three address terms are used for blood relatives in general, irrespective of the degree of relationship: "One has an *atyafi* by the ties of blood only." We should take note that although *atyámfia* refers to relatives on both the father's and the mother's side, a distinction is made between these two. "Children of an uncle on the father's side" are considered more closely related to one than are cousins on the mother's side; a "child of a father's brother is nearer than one of a mother's brother." Thus we can discern a strong patrilineal emphasis even with this bilateral grouping.

Had

The expression *had* designates a group of descendants in the male line, potentially larger than the family but smaller than the *ág*. Its reference is rather uncertain at Átány today and seems to persist as a survival. It is used much less frequently than the word *ág*, and some give it a pejorative meaning: "That Vince *had* is an ugly *had;* they are a race of fools." "They are an affected *had*, a bad race." Older people do not hear this pejorative overtone in the expression *had* and themselves use the term as follows: "There goes the old Varga with all his *had*," meaning that Gábor Varga is going by with his sons and grandsons. They regard the word as an old-fashioned one.

Thus *had* appears to have meant a living male ancestor together with his sons and grandsons. József Sárközi at the age of seventy-four said: "I have no *had*"; "all the Sárközi-s [his brothers] had daughters so they did not propagate the *had*." This

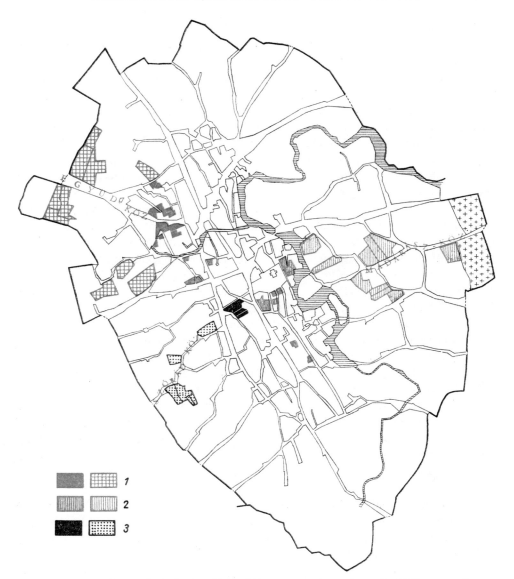

21. The location of three *had*-s in the village. This map was drawn from the 1864 surveyor's map and the land register and shows the house lots and *kert*-s of the Együd, Madarász, and Szórád families. Related families form clusters but not closed units. According to old street-naming custom the *köz*-s were called by the names of the families and *had*-s in their neighborhood. Key to symbols used: (1) Dwellings and *kert*-s of families called Együd. (2) Dwellings and *kert*-s of families called Madarász. (3) Dwellings and *kert*-s of families called Szórád.

means that the *had* cannot be perpetuated in the female line, since daughters get married and their children then belong to the *had*-s of their respective husbands. There is a strong implication that besides the father and his descendants, the father's brother and his descendants are also counted as belonging to the *had*.

People speak of the bier of old György Orbán surrounded by his kindred and the neighbors all day long. In the evening, when strangers and many others had gone, "nobody but the Orbán-s, the Orbán *had* remained there." In this case the deceased's brother and the brother's children were included in the *had*. This is considered the correct interpretation of *had*, since in other parts of the country it means the group of living descendants in the male line, offspring of the same grandfather. It embraces three generations: the stem (the grandfather) and his brothers plus the male descendants of these and their male children.

"The *had* multiplies after the name" means that the husband belongs to his own *had*, his wife remains in hers. Only illegitimate children are assigned to the *had* of their mother; all others belong to the *had* of their father.

Figure 21 shows the residential groupings of some old families. If we examine it closely, we can see that several blood relations settled immediately next to their kin, forming a cluster of related households. (This was made possible by the ancient privilege of choosing the domicile [cf. Chapter 1, "The Appearance of the Village"].) This settlement pattern is not rare in the Great Hungarian Plain, and is known in the ethnographic literature as a "*hadas* settlement." Elderly Átány people recall the "ancient," "one-time" custom, which still existed at least in a fragmentary condition in the 1860s and 1870s. They affirm that the kindred did not live widely scattered, but that people constructed new dwellings in the immediate vicinity of the old home if it were possible. (Until quite recently, among several Hungarian groups, sons, upon leaving the paternal house, habitually built their houses on the father's property as long as available space permitted.) Aged inhabitants of the village claim that these earlier *had*-s settlement units have been dissolved by the recent practice of *vő*-s often marrying into a family; thus families with different names came to be settled among those having the same name, i.e., the *had*. Nevertheless, members of the populous Barna and Barát *had*-s are still living near one another on the Alvég; and the Rózsa, Madarász, and Bedécs folk also have preserved their ancient seats with one *ág* each, as did the Horváth-s with their *had*.[1]

In some other rural Hungarian regions we were able to observe the *had* as a still functioning corporate group. The people of any one of these *had*-s, settled in the same vicinity, form a closed group of kinsfolk, lending mutual help and fulfilling other special duties to one another. These viable *had*-s thus resemble localized clans.

Nemzetség

The *nemzetség*, like the *ág*, is no longer actually a corporate group at Átány, but now only an old-fashioned, obsolescent kinship classification concept. The *nemzetség*

---

[1] The *hadas* settlement pattern is widely known in the Great Plain and among the *palóc* groups living in its northern mountainous fringes. Its archetypical realization was nonetheless possible in such an unregular settlement system as that of Átány. Young people tried to construct their houses in the neighborhood of the "ancestral" one, near their kinsfolk. Thus the *had*-s were based on spatial proximity as well as kinship (Györffy, 1942: 61–62, 405).

includes all the *ág*-s bearing the same family name. Like the *had*, the *nemzetség* is patrilineally extended, "it goes after the name, after the son." However, while the *had* embraces only living relatives in the male line and is thus an actual kin group, the *nemzetség* comprises both known and unknown predecessors.

At Átány, everyone who traces his descent from the village, "who is aboriginal here," is included in a *nemzet* or *nemzetség*, "People who just happened to come here or whose father settled in the village have no *nemzetség*."

"My *nemzet*"; "he belongs to our *nemzetség*"; "he is not of our *nemzet*"; "that woman is a shame to her *nemzetség*" (because she is lean)—these are some of the sayings which mention the *nemzetség* in everyday speech. In today's usage it is often synonymous to *fajta* (race), *família* (family), *had*, and sometimes even to *rokonság* (relationship, group of relatives). Each *nemzetség*, like each *fajta*, has special qualities: for instance, the Orbán *nemzetség* is clever and excels in singing; the Bedécs *nemzetség* is keen on having a leading role in the village, "not because they are more clever, but because this ambition is in the blood of that *nemzetség*."

The main difference between all other concepts of groups of kinsmen and the *nemzetség* perhaps lies in the feature that this latter is the most solemn one.

With some Hungarian groups the *nemzetség* is still a corporate group, which fact we noticed during field work in the 1940s.[2] Its existence may be traced in Hungarian history, with the help of records, from the Hungarian Conquest up to the fourteenth century, and in some groups even to the seventeenth century.[3]

Elderly people still use the obsolescent expressions *fajta* and *família*, but with rather uncertain and faded meanings approximately equivalent to *ág*. These words refer to smaller groups than *nemzetség*, at any rate. None of them is usual as a comprehensive label for this or that particular group of kinsmen; they are, rather, used in conversation when the characteristics of some families are being discussed. In the course of time both expressions have acquired a somewhat pejorative connotation;

[2] Among the Székely-s of Bucovina (a Hungarian ethnic group which removed in the eighteenth century from Transylvania to Bucovina and then in 1942–1945 immigrated to the present Hungary), it was still customary in the 1940s for the people of a village to be partitioned into sections, as it were, according to *nemzetség*-s traced from a common ancestor who had migrated in the eighteenth century. Each *nemzetség* was directed by a council of elders and the chief of the clan. The decision in some economic affairs and also in the feuds between the various clans rested with them. The membership of the village magistracy was drawn from the *nemzetség*-s in a traditionally established ratio (Fél, 1959a).

Discovery that the *nemzetség* is in this form a still functioning institution has furnished several insights into the overall structure of our entire kinship system. Thus we can see that the *had* is a more recent development than we had hitherto suspected and has almost no function or is entirely unknown in a village community where the *nemzetség* is a viable institution. Another correlation is that the nuclear or the stem family is the preponderant residential form where the *nemzetség* exists, whereas the "joint family" is found in villages which evince the *had*.

[3] There is some research comparing the clan system of the Hungarians who occupied the Carpathian basin in the late ninth century with the similar clan system of the contemporary nomadic peoples of the steppe. When the foundations of the modern Christian state were laid at the turn of the tenth and beginning of the eleventh centuries, it came into conflict with this clan system. But later territorial organization of the whole country, particularly the system of counties, has been shaped in relation to the areas of settlement of these early *nemzetség*-s. This persisted alive and active among the Székely-s for the longest time. (The Székely-s played the role of frontier guards, and their privileges protected them from the fate of serfdom for a long time.) It was from this Székely group that the settlers of Bucovina, mentioned in the preceding footnote, are derived (cf. György Györffy, 1959).

they are appropriate, for instance, when someone is being disparaged. They often come up when a marriage is being considered, and one might hear words like: "I will not let my daughter be married to this man; what *fajta* is this? We do not want any of this *fajta*; there is tuberculosis among them." "The Mikó youth are a *fajta* of brawlers; I will not give my daughter to one of them. All their *fajta* is like that; all their *família* was like it." "The *fajta* throws back even into the seventh grade."

In the speech of Átány, *fajta* means the unchangeable attributes of a consanguineal group, their inherited qualities, as distinct from kinship *per se*. The latter implies mutual duties between persons of the same kin group, but the link is a kind that can be cut off. "They are of the same *fajta* but not relatives anymore"; so they say, "People split away from each other; their fathers used to be great *atyafi*-s, but they do not cultivate the relationship any longer."

ROKONSÁG

The expressions *rokon* and *rokonság* ("relative"; "relationship") have several meanings in the speech of Átány. One interpretation, the strict one, is that they refer to the connections established by marriage, i.e., affinity. Interpreted in a wider sense, *rokonság* is a comprehensive notion, connoting blood relationship as well as ties of affinity. When people speak in general of relatives, without special reference to the linkage involved, they most frequently use the word *rokon*. "Our neighbor and a distant *rokon* died at the same time. We could not join those who mourned for the neighbor, since we had to go to our *rokon*."

It seems that the wider sense of *rokon*, *rokonság* prevails in recent usage. Thus younger people (under forty) say *rokon* for "relative" almost to the exclusion of *atyafi*, *ág*, *nemzetség*, etc.

But older men do distinguish their circle of *atyafi*-s (blood relations) from their wives' even today. "My relatives and the relations of my wife, these are two [different] things." A "relative" of the wife is actually no relative; "we know it but do not specify it." To avoid offending the women, as it were, men do not tell their wives that they do not regard her relatives as theirs. The kindred of the *meny* and the *vő* receive the same short shrift. "A relative after my *vő*, a relative after my *meny*—these are a grade lower than my relations, since blood is thicker than water."

By this narrow reckoning of one's *rokonság*, marriage brings the *meny* or the *vő* and their respective parents closer to one's family, not their brothers and sisters. However, the address terminology normally used only to *rokon*-s is extended to the brothers and sisters too, but without implying any obligation or service. If the marriage is an advantageous and amicable one, affinals greet and address each other in a more friendly fashion than before; if not, they express their disaffection and inject social distance by omitting these complimentary terminological extensions.

Reckoned out to the fifth degree, the *rokonság* of any one person may embrace as many as 240 to 280 people. In large families the number might be increased by forty to sixty, in smaller families the number might be some 100 less. The 260 members of the *rokonság* of Samu Kiss, for example, include 182 on his father's side and sixty on his mother's side, while eighteen are attached by "blood affinity," being relatives on his wife's side or the husbands of his sisters.[4]

More than half of such a group of 200 to 300 kindred assemble for two family festivals: weddings and funerals. On other occasions and for joint economic enterprises of everyday life, less than half usually participate. This smaller group are called "great relations" or "close relatives"; the larger group includes "distant relatives." When people of the village tell us, "We do not mind having the relatives, but only at funerals or preparing for a wedding," we know that distant relatives are meant, those who are not usually visited. However, if one should meet any of these on the road or at the fair, hardly any urgency can prevent stopping to exchange a few words. The more important events at the home of distant relatives—such as births, illnesses, calamities, casts of fate—are all kept track of. But, in fact, this applies to just about everybody in Átány, and not to relatives only.

At Átány, to say of someone, "We cultivate the relationship," implies that the person is invited to a wedding. Those who are not invited are not really considered relatives any more. The large majority of people who have settled outside the village return for family weddings and, conversely, they invite their relatives living at Átány to their own family weddings.

Relatives, especially older ones, avoid any occasion which might give rise to a quarrel among themselves. Thus if someone is asked to forward a disagreeable message to a relative, he would say: "I don't want to be a postman, otherwise we shall not attend each other's funeral."

Until World War I all relatives to the fifth degree were invited to a wedding, which often meant seventy to eighty families. "We wondered how he is related to us, so as to have the occasion for inviting him." Since that time, however, the circle has narrowed: "relatives in the fourth degree are no wedding guests."

The bier of the deceased is surrounded by the nearest relatives (see Chapter 11, "The Funeral"). Relations of the first and second degrees see him three times a day. Those in the third, fourth, and fifth degrees may also come by day. But the most important thing is to attend the vigil in full number. Every relative, near and far, has to attend the funeral. But only the most closely related are invited to the burial feast.

Fewer relatives are touched by a third kind of event of family life, the birth of a baby. The immediate and close relatives (in the first and second degrees) fulfill the customary obligations of preparing and carrying traditionally ample meals to the house of the young mother for the six weeks she lies in childbed. The closest relatives cook twice, the more remote but once. The christening of the first child only is

---

[4] In the course of drawing up the genealogy presented below, Samu Kiss enumerated 208 blood relatives on his father's side and 105 of their affinals, a total of 313 persons. This number includes dead ancestors and infants as well as persons who have left the village. In the number cited here, these latter were disregarded by Kiss (see Chapter 13, "The Careers of Three Families").

celebrated with much cooking and feasting. The parents send invitations to their parents, grandparents, and siblings on both sides, as well as to the godparents. Only the godparents are invited to the christening of other children, and if a third or fourth is born, even this is omitted: "We do not celebrate the end."

After the young mother's initiation (see Chapter 6, "Children"), she visits those who have "cooked out" for her in order to show them her baby.

The one most prominent perennial meeting of the kindred is the "killing," the "pigsticking." To Átány folk, pigsticking is at least as important as Christmas. This is also the most intimate occasion for the gathering, for only the closest relatives are present; no stranger is admitted.

More than once we have heard people say: "Pigsticking had passed, Christmas was over, still they did not return." (This is said by those whose close kinsmen serving as soldiers in World War II were reported missing; the relatives repeat this year after year.) Pigsticking is scheduled for the time around Christmas and the New Year, and close relatives endeavor to be at home by then, wherever they may be. Those working in distant cities or doing military service try to save their holidays or leaves for this occasion. Children who have married out and settled in remote parts of the country return too. This is the feast of children, parents, grandparents, brothers and sisters, vő-s and meny-s, sógor-s and nász-s. In a smaller family, even relatives of the second degree may be invited.

The women help all day long in processing the meat of the slaughtered pigs and in preparing food for the evening feast, but only two or three of the men join them. The children of the guests and some of the relatives who did not help come for a meal twice a day. In the evening, after the busy day, a copious meal is served. Everyone appears in festive attire and occupies a prescribed seat at the large table. Nász-s sit at the head of the table, then the other relatives according to age and rank, wives accompanying their husbands. The usual number of guests is twelve to fourteen in smaller families, twenty or more in the larger ones.

When a house is built, the family's kinfolk assemble in great number to help carry the building material, lay the foundation, and put up the walls. Each phase lasts for a day. The work is done at a moderate pace, accompanied by continuous serving and drinking of wine, and ending with an abundant feast.

Among the 54 participants at a house-building observed in 1959, forty were relatives, the others were neighbors, koma-s, or friends. When János Boross built his stable in 1933, 65 people helped him, all relatives.

Making fuel out of manure may occupy twenty to thirty relatives in larger families (see Plates 39–46). This perennial task is scheduled for the end of May. (The region is poor in wood and fuel is made by stamping dung and drying it in the sun.) For this occasion only near relatives who are strong are invited. Helpers are kept supplied with drink and at the end of the day are feasted. While the time for repaying help in construction is not fixed, this work is repaid in kind in a few days' time.

Threshing requires thirty helping hands. The mechanic's work is usually done by the owner of the threshing machine, but the rest of the manpower is provided by the farmer. "Everyone is still busy transporting the harvest from the fields to the village —relatives, *nász*-s, *sógor*-s—so we cannot have the machine"; such a statement indicates who are usually to be invited. In this kind of work no distinctions are made between near or remote relatives, *koma*-s, neighbors; all who have time to come and lend a hand are included. This assistance is rewarded by a copious meal and is repaid in kind by the family within a few days' time.

Besides these family projects which mobilize a number of persons, there are several occasional jobs which involve a smaller group of near relatives. On a reciprocal basis, the nearest kinfolk help to harvest and press grapes for wine, husk corn, and harvest cattle turnips and sugar beets. An even smaller group is mobilized for such tasks as helping to wash homespun yarn in lye, hoeing, haying, etc. These usually involve brothers and cousins of the first degree, who may be joined by parents and *nász*-s.

Of the several church holidays, Easter Monday is the one when even distant relatives come to pay respects to the family. It is obligatory for the boys to sprinkle their closely related female relatives on this day; if a more distant relative (beyond the second degree) does so, he is thanked very much "for cultivating the relationship in this way."

NÁSZ-S

In Átány, *nász* is the term defining persons whose children are connected by marriage. This relationship is one of the most solemn of all kinship ties. It is characterized by maintaining social distance and showing the utmost respect.

The mode of address used between *nász*-s reflects this distance. Whatever their social contact may have been before their children were married, from then on the *nász*-s say formal "you" (i.e. *maga* or *kelmed*) to one another and use the respectful address *nászuram* and *nászasszony*. These forms apply not only to the parents of the newly-weds, they are extended also to the grandparents (hereafter called "old *nász*-s") and to the in-laws of each brother, sister, child, and first cousin. In this way, a couple who has but one married child may be related to eight, twelve, or even more *nász*-s. However, there is a distinction between the people addressed as *nász* and the real *nász* in that only the latter, the parents of the newly-weds, are bound by solemn and strong mutual obligations.

The first formal meeting of the *nász*-s occurs on the morning after the wedding, when the guests of the bride's house walk over to the home of the bridegroom, where they are awaited in front of the door of the house. The father of the bridegroom extends his hand to the bride's father with the following words: "Welcome, *nászuram*. I am glad to be able to greet you in my modest abode. May God allow us to be *nász*-s all our lives, to honor and esteem each other, to live in strength and health." "So may God allow, *nászuram*," answers the bride's father. Only then do they relax their handclasp in order to raise the "*nász* glass" which they clink and drain in one draft. The gypsies start playing their tunes and, according to proper tradition, the *nász*-s begin a slow dance with their *nászasszony*-s. From now on they say *kelmed* to each other and use the formal address.

The *nász*-s are frequent guests in each other's homes. At pigsticking the first place at the head of the table is given to them. They are present at all weddings celebrated in the house; the men play the role of *násznagy*, the women *gazdasszony* (see Chapter 11, "The Wedding"). The *nász*-s visit each other on name-days too, to wish many happy returns. The good *nászasszony* often spends all her day spinning in the house of the other woman on such occasions. The *nász*-s greet each other also on New Year and on other festivals. If there is trouble in the family, the *nász*-s hurry to each other. In the event of bereavement, the *nászasszony*-s sit in the first ring around the dead as mourners. In this case it is the *nászasszony*'s duty to cook for the people of the bereaved house. The *nász* helps to dig the grave and then to close the coffin.

The *nász*-s also help each other when labor is needed as long as they are strong enough—in such work as building a house, making fuel from manure, wine-making, garnering, threshing, etc.

AFFINITY

Marriages of one's siblings and even cousins create affinal links. One's sister's husband is referred to as *sógor* and is addressed as *sógor* or *sógorom*. The husbands of one's parents' and grandparents' sisters and of one's cousins are also called *sógor*. If they are ten or fifteen years older (or more) than the person addressing them, the more honorific *sógorom* is used. Sisters' husbands have a special status: they are "blood *sógor*-s" and are addressed as *sógorom* even by those who are of the same age.

One's brother's wife is *ángy*, addressed as *ángyom*: e.g., "Maris *ángyom*," "Kakas *ángyom*." If she is older than the person speaking to her, the address is the more respectful *ángyomasszony*. The same terms are extended to the wives of one's parents' and grandparents' brothers and also to the wives of cousins.

Affinity, as we have mentioned above, is considered something less than blood relationship; "being *sógor* or *koma* is less than being really related."

From the day of their wedding the husband and wife address each other's parents and grandparents as *apámuram-anyámasszony*, *nagyapámuram-nagyanyámasszony*, etc. The brother of one's spouse is called *sógorom* and the sister *néném* if they are older than the person speaking to them. No special words are used for the other relatives linked by the marriage. More distant kinsmen of one's spouse are referred to as "the cousin of my wife," "the uncle of my wife," etc. After their union the husband addresses all the other relatives of his wife as she does and vice versa; thus all the persons whom the husband calls *báty* in his kindred are so addressed by his wife too.

At the turn of the century Átány (like other traditional Hungarian regions) still preserved special terms by which a young woman addressed her husband's brothers and male cousins. Her husband's elder brother or male cousin was *nagyobbik uram;*

a younger brother or male cousin was *kisebbik uram*.[5] She called all their wives *ángyomasszony*.

People who become *sógor*-s offer a drink to each other at the wedding feast and drink a "*sógor* glass" together. On such an occasion we once heard the following conversation: The bridegroom, raising his glass, bids the wife's brother to drink. To his call: "Drink!" the answer is: "I don't want to." Then the husband says: "Drink, *sógorom!*" At this, the new "blood *sógor*" answers: "So I want to," raises his glass, and they both drain the "*sógor* glass" to the dregs.

Within the family circle, the *sógor*, *vő*, and *nász* belong to an equivalent social category in a sense, as evidenced in the case of bereavement. *Sógor*-s and *vő*-s close the coffin and carry it out of the house, and then share the task of digging the grave and lowering the coffin into it. In some cases they may also substitute for absent sponsors (*kəma*-s).

THE BAPTISMAL KOMA

Next to becoming a *nász*, the most honored kinship-like link in Átány is to become a *keresztkoma*, i.e., a "baptismal *koma*." The person asked to be such a sponsor is assured that he will be "first guest" at the wedding of all his godchildren and at other family festivals as well. The local concept of the *keresztkoma* relationship stresses the alliance between the parents and the godparents; or, in a narrower sense, between the father and the godfather. This is a symmetrical relationship: the two couples are reciprocally godparents of each other's children. Residence in the village is an indispensable condition.

The godfather is the favorite *koma*, a close friend from the father's bachelor days or military service. *Koma*-s who are intimate in their bachelor years commit themselves even then to serve as best men at each other's weddings and to be baptismal *koma*-s, equivalent to life-long friendship. Such early commitments, being known to no one except the two *koma*-s, may give rise to complications. Thus István Gulyás had been asked by István Juhász to be his baptismal *koma*. István Gulyás did not want to accept because he was bound by a prior promise to András Szórád, made in his bachelor years. The Gulyás parents, however, did not allow their son to refuse, because it is improper to avoid assuming such an honorable duty. At last István Gulyás promised András Szórád to ask him to be *his* baptismal *koma* even though he (Gulyás) had accepted the same duty in another family. But this compromise was opposed by the parents of András Szórád for the reason that "in this case he [A. Szórád] will not sit at the head of the table in the wedding."

All the children of one couple have the same godparents. It would be improper to refuse to continue sponsorship after several children are born—"to cut the baptismal *koma* relation." This may nevertheless happen if one family has more children than the other. "This is rather costly. One does not know how many babies will be

---

[5] In some regions the address terms *kisebbik uram* and *nagyobbik uram* are extended to the husband's blood relatives as far as the fourth degree.

born when one undertakes to be a *koma*. The third child is not greeted with such great joy. Sándor Czákó undertook *koma*-ship, and then he had one child while his *koma* had nine. It is not nice that he did not go to more christenings than one." Czákó was raised in a *tanya*, so he was not blamed for his improper behavior. But an Átány man, bred in the village, would never do this. For example, the wife of István Gulyás had only one child before her husband was killed in the war, and the family of the baptismal *koma* had four children. "However difficult it is, she still cultivates the *koma* connection; it would make a bad impression to fulfill the duties toward only one child and to cut the link afterward."

It has recently become a country-wide fashion for *gazda* families to ask a brother or some other near kinsman to be godfather instead of somebody unrelated. But Átány public opinion is against this practice: "A stranger is better, because if one comes to loggerheads with a brother, he loses both brother and *keresztkoma*. What sort of wedding there will be!"

The relationship with the baptismal *koma* is stronger than that with one's *nász*. When two families establish affinal relationship as *nász*-s, they drop the form of address used hitherto and use the form appropriate for the new association. But if it happens that the new *nász*-s were also *keresztkoma* before, then the terminology appropriate for that relationship is retained despite the additional role.

Being a baptismal *koma* entails numerous obligations. The duties of the sponsors toward each other and to their godchildren begin with birth or christening and end only with burial of the child or children. But if the baptismal *koma* should die, his son follows in his steps; likewise a dead godmother is replaced by her daughter.

After a child is born it is the midwife who informs the would-be *koma* couple of the event and at the same time invites them to the baptism: "Károly Mérten and his wife honor you as their *komaura* and *komaasszony;* they ask you for dinner on Wednesday." The invited couple knows that this will be the day of the christening. It is the duty of the *komaasszony* to "cook out" at least twice while the young mother lies in childbed, i.e., to provide festive meals for the household. The *komaasszony* carries the meal to them in ornamented vessels. It is also her duty to carry the baby to the church for baptism. She has to purchase a quilted coverlet and a small jacket and bonnet for the baby. Traditionally, the child was carried to the christening ceremony by the midwife and the godmother alone.[6] The godfather used to come only for dinner. As he entered the house, he would halt before the bed of the young mother and greet her with the following words: "May God give my *komaasszony* strength, health, an ample breast, that she may rear this infant to the pleasure of its parents, to the honor of other people, to the glory of our mother church—so I wish with all my heart." Or the godfather might propose a toast with the first glass of wine: "Let us thank God for having formed this infant in the womb of its mother with His strong arm and for having helped it into this world. I wish my dear *komámasszony*, may God

---

[6] In our data there are several cases where the baptismal *koma* is a bachelor. Then his sister or even a near cousin carries the baby to the christening, and continues to play the role of godmother until the godfather marries.

give her an ample breast, that she may rear this infant for the glory of God and the splendor of His mother church. We carried this infant to the bosom of our faith, to the house of God; we bade the pastor christen it Laci, and registered it under the banner of Christ, to the joy of its sponsors and parents—so I wish with all my heart."[7]

After the toast they all drink the "godfather's glass" to the dregs and henceforth address each other as *komámuram* and *komámasszony*, using *kelmed*, the honorific "you." The baptismal feast is the first occasion on which the baptismal *koma*-s occupy the first place at the table. To the christening of the first child, especially if it is a boy, the father used to invite two or three of his favorite friends from his bachelor years; these were also *koma*-s, but just "common ones" *(közkoma)*. After dinner the midwife takes around a plate to collect "money for a spur" for a boy, "money for a silk skirt" for a girl, whereupon the godfather gives 100 *forint*-s, the godmother half of this sum, the common *koma*-s even less. When the midwife takes around the plate a second time, now for herself, the baptismal *koma* gives the largest amount (five *forint*-s).[8]

The godfather watches the growth of his godchild and gives him presents on certain occasions. On Easter Monday the male godchildren go to sprinkle the daughter of their godfather or, in the absence of a daughter, the godmother herself. Small boys then receive Easter eggs and pastry from their godmothers, and perhaps some cake wrapped in a kerchief for them to take home. As the godchild grows older, he receives money too, in ever greater amounts, to cover the costs of further Easter revelry: gypsies and drinks. At the Easter sprinkling people show great tact and discretion in cases where the families have unequal numbers of godchildren. If in one family there are only one or two boys and in the other four or five, the younger boys of the larger family are ordered to stay at home. And if the baptismal *koma* is short of money and the gifts would overtax his means, even the older boys are told not to go.

---

[7] A manuscript notebook dating from 1864 gives the "address of the godfather" in the following form: "Let the name of the Lord be blessed, because He shaped this infant in the womb of its mother wisely and by the strength of His mighty arm He has helped it into the world alive. The parents of this infant did not want to leave it without a name any more, since our Lord Christ has ordered His followers befor His ascension: 'Go throughout the world and teach all peoples, baptizing them in the name of the Father, the Son and the Holy Ghost.' This is why we have taken this infant up in the bosom of our faith and have brought it to the Mother Church of God, and let it be inscribed under the banner of Christ by the minister, calling it by the name of István. Therefore I wish that the Holy Majesty of God may maintain it in the faith and creed, letting him finally enter unto eternal happiness. As for the dear *komámasszony*, may God give her abundant milk, that she may rear this infant up first to the glory of God, to the edification of the Mother Church, to the pleasure of its dear father and mother, that it may serve its close and remote relatives. I wish this with all my heart."

[8] Especially if the first child is male, two or three additional *koma*-s, *közkoma*-s are appointed to accompany the real baptismal *koma*. These sponsors are also chosen from the circle of friends defined by the parents' age group, and their invitation serves to strengthen these earlier ties of friendship. But the connection with these subsidiary *koma*-s is by no means as close and significant as with the chief baptismal *koma* himself.

In some regional groups of Transdanubia in which there are relatively fewer kinsmen, owing to strict birth control and the "one-child system," as many as fifteen to twenty pairs of baptismal *koma*-s are invited to the christening. Thus "missing" ties of relationship are compensated for by the bonds of fictive kinship, which evince a rich and manifold variety (cf. Jankó, 1902: 396).

Tradition demands that the godparents be present at their godchildren's examinations in school. The children show their godparents their notebooks and receive some money from them. The godparents must also be present at the children's confirmation ceremonies. It is then their duty to buy the first psalter for the child. If the godfather is clever at woodwork, he does not wait for a special occasion but manufactures miniature tools for his godchildren—such as a small distaff, a small molding board, or a small beater for a girl; a toy plow, a whip, or a cart with a foal made of bone for a boy. He may make a fine colored hoe handle for the time when a boy begins to learn hoeing. Several young farmers received their first anvil, hammer, and hone from their godfathers.

However, the most important event involving the baptismal *koma*-s is the wedding of a godchild. This is the time when a godfather must give the most presents, but also the time when he is accorded the most honor as first guest of the wedding party. Every person invited to the wedding brings gifts, but the godparents bring the most. The godmother bakes a special cake, the so-called "godmother's loaf." It is the biggest one at the feast, and each guest should receive a slice of it. The godmother also buys the bridal wreath and a dress-length of black material with the appropriate black kerchief. Traditionally, it was not customary to provide anything for a godson, but now he also is given some articles of clothing.

The *koma*-s also participate in the wedding preparations. The godmother is chief *gazdasszony* of the betrothal ceremonies, even if she is quite young and inexperienced. In such case she is provided with good counsel by the other six to ten housewives who participate. On the afternoon before the wedding the godparents accompany the engaged couple to the rectory in order to pass the so-called "little examination"; recently the couple has been going alone. In the evening the godfather begins to act as *násznagy* (best man). Henceforth, throughout the marriage celebrations the godfather occupies the place of honor at the head of the table. His charm, originality, jokes, and, when required, his dignity are important factors in forming the atmosphere of the occasion.

The baptismal *koma* plays a significant role when there is bereavement in the house of his *keresztkoma*. He is asked to act as *bejáró*, the manager of the funeral arrangements. He informs the civil and church officials of the demise and asks the pastor to deliver a eulogy. On the day of the funeral he calls for the pastor, stays with him throughout the proceedings, and stands by his side during the burial. When it is over, custom demands that he "drive in the relatives"—that he ask the grave diggers and the nearest kin to a funeral feast. The *bejáró* raises the first glass and greets the guests with these words: "May God give a quiet resting place in the grave to the deceased; may my God console the bereaved hearts." Another duty of the *bejáró* is to advise the household of the dead *gazda* to divide his inheritance peacefully and to observe his last will. All listen to his words in silence, then they raise their glasses and drink without clinking. The godmother's duty is to buy a bridal wreath and veil for the deceased if it is a girl, for she must be buried with these.

However important and honorable the role of the baptismal *koma* may be, though he is raised to the level of chief actor, even master of ceremonies, at outstanding *rites de passage* of family life, he is nevertheless an outsider and not a "real" kinsman. One of our Átány informants explained the difference between a kinsman and a *koma* as follows: "The *nász*, the *sógor*, the *koma*, they are honorable. One is respectful to them, especially when one talks to them. But if one has to choose, only children are one's real relatives."

Very few married couples in Átány do not have a chance of assuming the role of baptismal godparents, unless they are childless. Even without children of their own they may have this role, since barrenness becomes evident only after a number of years. (Not being godparents is a strongly felt defect; they are saddened by it, and others feel sorry for them. But they are sometimes consoled by those who happened not to choose a very sympathetic baptismal *koma:* "There is not much pleasure in him; he is in vain.") Of course such couples do not themselves need a baptismal *koma*, since, childless, their lives do not include christenings or confirmations or weddings. Only in bereavement are the services of a baptismal *koma* as *bejáró* needed. The order of substitution in such cases is that the role of *bejáró* is assumed by the husband of the sister of the particular spouse (i.e., the blood *sógor*) or by the first cousin of the same.

Except for these few childless couples, every healthy and competent Átány married man and woman is a sponsor and acts as baptismal *koma*, best man, or *bejáró* on some given occasion. For the people of Átány this role is an essential ingredient of a full life. The penniless hired man or the big *gazda* who owns a hundred acres may alike fulfill this task, and thus each one in turn is accorded the highest dignity offered by family life at Átány in the circle of his relatives and friends.

It is but natural to find individual differences in the way this role is played. One man may dominate with his presence the baptism, the wedding, the burial, the funeral feast, being gifted at verbal expression and versed in the traditional formulae. Another man may be so embarrassed that he cannot open his mouth. But these variations in performance do not of themselves detract from the elevated position and the high honor associated with being a *keresztkoma*.

CHAPTER 9. LOCAL TIES

DIVISIONS OF THE VILLAGE

The highway which runs from Heves in the east to Kömlő in the west divides Átány into two major sections (see Fig. 22): the Lower End *(Alvég)* and the Upper End *(Felvég)*.[9] These parts are autonomous in some respects even today, and were even more so before World War II. The majority of large, well-to-do, "aboriginal" families live in the Lower End; one finds more *zsellér*-s' cottages in the winding *zug*-s of the Upper End. Each end of the village has its own cemetery; the Lower End cemetery is about a third larger than that of the Upper End (see Plate 64). The houses of the Lower End are surrounded by the semicircle of their own *kert*-s, those of the Upper End by theirs. Not only are the houses, *kert*-s, and burial places of the two parts of the village separated, but each part has its own craftsmen and tradespeople. Local government used to maintain a different smithy for each end, and both parts of the village had their own wheelwrights. The shops and butchers in the Lower End served Lower End people, those in the Upper End the people of their part. The Upper and the Lower Ends employed different community herdsmen, who drove the livestock of their respective parts of the village on separate routes through their own sides. Since drinking water is bad in the community, there were two public "drinking wells," one in the Lower End, the other in the Upper End. The only church has two entrances; one is used by the people of the Lower End, the other by those of the Upper End. Inside the church, pews also are differentiated according to these divisions. Formerly, places of entertainment were separated too—the fields for ball games, playgrounds, skittle alleys, and taverns, where the bachelors of the Upper and Lower Ends caroused to the tunes of separately hired musicians.

This division extended to local self-government too: each end had an assistant to the mayor and a night watchman chosen from its own people. In the mid 1930s the community was allowed to bore an artesian well. Though the county authorities who were bearing the costs permitted only one well, the village officials decided to sink two, one for each part of the village.

[9] This division has existed for several centuries. According to the record of a 1736 lawsuit a witness from Átány gave testimony on a house built in the Upper End but added that he did not know the particulars since, as an inhabitant of the Lower End, "he rarely visits the Upper End" (Eger State Archives, Administrative Records, 1736: 57).

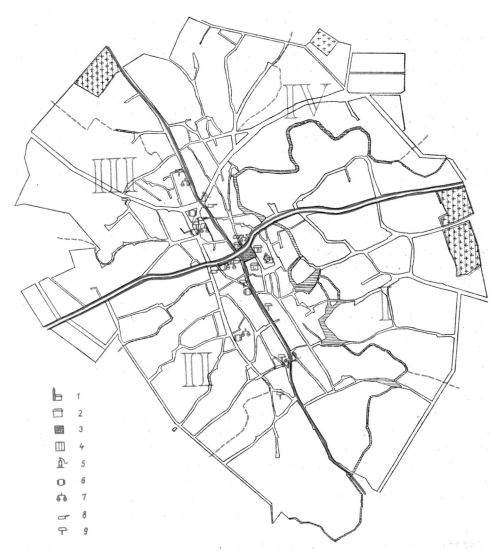

22. Administrative scheme of Átány and location of shops, workshops, and public wells. The thick double line marks the boundary between *Felvég*, the Upper End (North), and *Alvég*, the Lower End (South); the single line, the boundaries of the *fertály*-s (I–IV); the broken line, those of the *hóstya*-s. Key to symbols used: (1) Church. (2) Public buildings (A: town hall; B: rectory; C: school). (3) Market place. (4) Cemeteries (one for the Upper End and one for the Lower End). (5) Public well, "drinking well." (6) Taverns. (7) Shops. (8) Butchers. (9) Blacksmiths.

The local administration divided the Upper and the Lower part into two *fertály*-s each. A natural line of partition was the Tenk-Vezekény road, which crossed the Heves-Kömlő highway. To the four *fertály*-s provided by this division the new settlements were added as a fifth in the early 1950s. Local self-government and administration reckoned the population on the basis of the *fertály*-s, and endeavored to include residents from each in the body of officials and to settle legal cases with the help of councillors from the same *fertály* as the litigants. In the everyday life of the community the *fertály*-s are not used as a reference unless fire breaks out, when the number of chimes struck at the beginning of the alarm indicates in which *fertály* the calamity is.

Where a person belongs is decided by his residence, but it is influenced by where he spent his childhood. For example, Ferenc Orbán's father belonged to the Lower End, but he married in the Upper End and lived there until his death. "I was born in the Upper End," says Ferenc Orbán. "The child belongs to the place where it has grown up." He remained an Upper End man till the end; after his marriage he refused the *kert* in the Lower End offered him by his father-in-law; even now he says, "What would I have done with that *kert* in the Lower End? I don't leave the Upper End." There is no sharp dividing line between the two ends. The population of the *zug*-s adjoining the highway may decide where to belong. When the question is first put to the young people, it is usually answered on the basis of where one's childhood was spent and who one's friends and *koma*-s are.

Unlike the division into *fertály*-s, the division into Upper and Lower Ends is significant in everyday life. Recalling their youth, people seventy or eighty years old repeatedly say: "At that time the guest from the Lower End was offered a meal in the Upper one." This means that they were strangers to each other, meeting but rarely. During our field work we noticed that it was only on Sunday at church that the people of the Lower End were informed of the danger of flood and the struggle with high water which had been keeping the people of the Upper End in suspense day and night for an entire week.

In the evenings and on holidays bands of bachelors from both parts of the village roamed the streets with sticks, almost looking for a chance to fight each other. Opportunities were not hard to find (see Chapter 10, "Activities of *Koma* and *Mátka* Groups," "Fighting"). Finding out that Upper End bachelors are courting a girl from the Lower End, for example, was sufficient provocation for a brawl. Though the authorities punished the fighters with imprisonment, this sanction was not taken seriously. Upon their release from prison, the culprits returned home and went on brawling.[10]

Fights, however, were the business of bachelors and young people only; as soon as they were married (and unions between Upper and Lower End people were frequent) "sworn enemies became relatives and friends."

Both the Lower and the Upper Ends are divided into several smaller units and local groups; these have various names, which refer to the vague boundary lines. A single

---

[10] The division of villages into Lower and Upper Ends is common all over the country. Large settlements are partitioned even further. In Mezőkövesd, a peasant town of about 20,000 inhabitants, the idea of Lower and Upper Ends has become vague, but the bachelors of smaller sections or of single streets form bands all the more cohesive. The bachelor band of each part of the village was at a constant war with all the others; if a bachelor went outside his own part of the community to court a girl, he could be fairly sure that he would be beaten up by the local bachelors. Thus the separation of the parts of the village was most intensively manifested in the life of the bachelor bands.

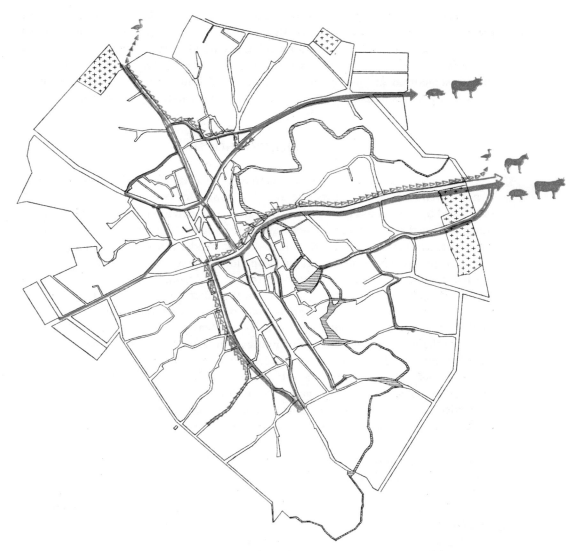

23. Routes by which the herds are taken to pasture. The herdsmen take the cattle and swine by the same routes, of which there are several serving the Upper and the Lower Ends separately. The horses had one herdsman only (prior to 1914), but he sent his boys to gather the horses of the two parts of the village separately. The geese had different gooseherds (women) in the two parts of the village and were driven to different pastures.

row or group is called *zug, köz, rész, hóstya, ment, fél,* or *ódal.* The expressions *ment, fél,* and *ódal* refer to only one side of the street, while *zug, hóstya,* and *köz* mean both sides. Our attempt to define and delineate the individual *hóstya*-s failed, since one of our informants would include ten houses in the same *rész* or *hóstya,* another twelve, and a third perhaps only eight. This uncertainty becomes all the more evident when informants are asked to give the boundaries of their own *hóstya*-s, since each one regards his house as the center, and therefore all the boundary lines are moved over by one house-lot when the next-door neighbor is asked. A further complication is due to the fact that some of the houses are arranged in streets (rows), while others consist of unsystematized groups of various sizes. The delimitation of the unsystematized *zug*-s and *köz*-s is actually clearer because they have natural boundaries.

NEIGHBORHOOD

These *zug*-s and *köz*-s may also be referred to as neighborhoods. A neighborhood is not a well-defined entity; its size and the number of people called neighbors are influenced by numerous factors. "If a cow calves, one neighbor is enough; if we stamp dung, we need six or seven." This statement indicates that the circle of neighbors may be expanded or contracted as occasion demands. Speaking generally, we may state that people whose houses are lined up along a street think of themselves as having five families of neighbors: two next-door, or "front" and "back," neighbors, and three so-called "opposite neighbors" on the other side of the street. Those living in a *zug*, a group of houses which are not laid out on streets, regard all the households of the same *zug* as neighbors, even if there are ten or more (see Figs. 24 and 25). Likewise the *köz*-s, smaller groups of houses built after World War I when lots were parceled out at reduced prices, constitute separate neighborhoods. They are called "proletarians" *(poletár*—for example, "Heves *poletár*-s" or "Upper *poletár*-s"— alluding to the composition of their population).

Besides the neighborhoods of houses, there are also neighborhoods of *kert*-s and of fields. A field neighborhood may arise from the proximity of plowlands or vineyards.

"First we are relatives, then neighbors," goes the saying in Átány, which means that the rights and duties of neighbors are much more limited than those of kinsfolk. Accordingly, if someone goes beyond the ordinary neighborly obligations, giving and taking more than is common, he says, "we have become great kinsmen with the neighbor."

In trouble, it is the neighbor who is the nearest. People say, "We may be dead by the time the brother arrives, but the neighbor is at hand." "The neighbor is here day and night; the brother only if he looks for me." "When we come out of the house in the morning, the first one we see is the neighbor: 'God give you a good morning. How did you sleep?' we shout at each other. In the evening, when we retire to the house: 'Good night, we won't see each other any more today.'"

Some neighbors are better than others. Esteem is due to the good neighbor, as in the saying: "A good neighbor is worth more than a bad kinsman." "Some neighbors deserve to be honored and esteemed, while some ought to be sent to the *puttyantó*" (i.e., to go to hell).

Even in the case of generally good neighborly relations, some neighbors are partic-

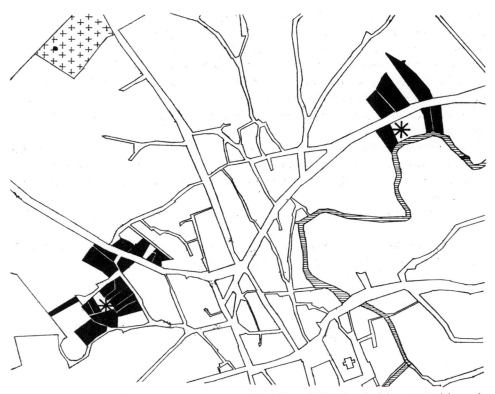

24. The neighbors of Sámuel Kiss and Ferenc Orbán. Sámuel Kiss (marked by an asterisk on the left) lives in a narrow, crooked *köz*, where numerous holdings are crowded together haphazardly. He regards seventeen houses as neighboring ones. Ferenc Orbán (marked by an asterisk on the right), who lives by the broad Egri Road, considers only six families to be his neighbors. Both *gazda*-s dwell in the belt of the ancient *kert*-s. The empty patches between the holdings marked as "neighbors" represent uninhabited vegetable gardens or *ólaskert*-s.

ularly well liked. Each household has one or two favorite neighbors with whom the family is on "daily" terms, while other neighbors are seen less frequently. The "daily" neighbors drop in on each other; the men stop by in each other's stables in the morning and in the evening, and the women run next door or across the street in between household chores. The visits of the women are short; they exchange a few words in the doorway or standing just inside the house. The neighbor is not considered a guest and so is not asked to come in and sit down. The neighbor should know that her presence is desirable only if there is no one else, such as a relative or a stranger, in the house. If another person arrives, the neighbor should leave.

Neighborly relations reflect the rank and fortune of the neighbors. Poor people are more friendly and talkative with one another, while well-to-do neighbors are more reserved.

"A neighbor is not a friend; it is not his business to share my troubles, but to help me in my need." One of the most frequent ways of helping is to lend the neighbor objects and implements; another is to send over someone to help with a task requiring many hands. The third and greatest is to let the neighbor use many objects and persons at once, sometimes even the whole house. Each form of help is based on reciprocity, with every service rendered requited by one of equal value.

One of the chief goals of Átány households is to be self-sufficient, "to have everything." "One strives to avoid borrowing"; nevertheless, "No one can say that he is not dependent on anyone, because nobody can have everything." "One of us has this, the other that, so we lend things to each other."

To illustrate the elaborate network of reciprocal ties that can arise, we list below the borrowing and lending relationships of Sándor T. Juhász, a sixty-eight-year-old peasant possessing a *fertály*, with his twelve neighbors (see Fig. 25). Living in a *zug*, he has many.

1. From Mihály Hajdú, the family borrows the drill planter, giving manual labor in return.

2. Neighbor Mihály Sebők has no cart but his hand tools are good. The Juhász family offers him cartage in return for implements.

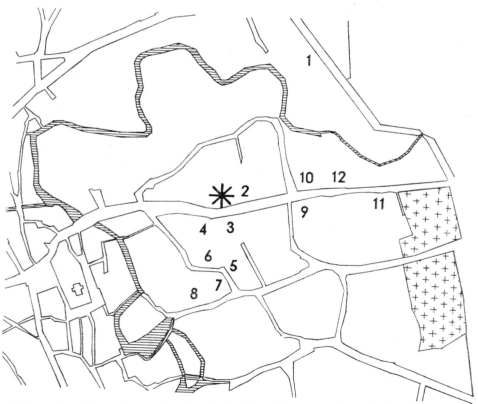

25. The reciprocal borrowing and lending relationships of Sándor T. Juhász (marked by an asterisk) with his neighbors. For the key and explanation of the serial numbers see pp. 174–75.

3. The family of Imre Jámbor frequently borrows household articles and even spices from the Juhász family and lends them the same types of items in return.

4. Sámuel Ötvösi is a *gazda* of thirty *hold*-s (i.e., 42 acres). The Juhász-s work his plowland and receive a third of the profits. The Ötvösi-s used to call Sándor Juhász to tie up the cow or lift a burden.

5. János Kis "has a shoemaker's shop"; "he is a jack-of-all-trades"; "there one may ask everything." He mends the Juhász family's shoes but is unwilling to be repaid for his services done since he is a "believer," a member of the Bethany religious community.

6. János Ötvösi lends his winnower and is repaid with manual labor.

7. From Ádám Bedécs, the family borrows augers and lend him their saw.

8. From Julcsa Barát, the family borrows spices and kitchen utensils, repaying in kind.

9. János Sebők lends his cart when they need an extra one and they do the same for him.

10. Lajos Tót is a man-of-all-work; he mends the corn grinder and uses the cultivator in return.

11. Samu Kálósi is an old man who has only one horse. Sándor Juhász also has a single horse. Since the two farmers are nearly the same age, they harness the animals together. (There is a younger *gazda* with only one horse in the neighborhood, but he chooses someone his own age as a partner.)

12. As for the widow of Mihály Szilágyi, "we have become such good relations that if I told her to cut off one of her ears and lend it to me, she would do it." The family borrows household utensils, a quern, a mortar, and spices from her. Our informant closed the conversation with the following: "Half of Átány village consists of my helpmates; everyone gives me what I ask."

In some neighborhoods individual households purchase rarely used utensils with an eye to the neighborhood reciprocity system. For example, Ferenc Orbán has neither a roller nor any of the large vessels and implements used in pressing grapes. But he has a drill planter, which he lends to his neighbors, receiving a roller from one and the tools of viniculture from another in return. The roller is of less value than the drill planter, so its proprietor supplements the exchange by occasionally giving a handle for a tool or a piece of wood for the head of a rake. The wives participate in the same system of reciprocity. The wife of Ferenc Török has a poppy-seed grinder which is used five or six times a year. The wife of Ferenc Orbán has none, but she does not want to buy one since she has a pair of scales, which she lends to the Török family regularly in exchange for the use of the poppy-seed grinder. Both utensils are rarely used and their values are almost the same.

People willingly lend the objects asked for, but they expect the borrowers to return them in a clean condition after use. If the tool is damaged or ruined by the borrower, propriety would demand that he buy a new one to replace it, but this is rarely done; the borrowers simply report the damage, and the matter is dropped. As a rule, the borrowed object should be returned immediately after use. However, people frequently forget, so it sometimes happens that the owner discovers one of his tools in the house of a neighbor after several years. In this case he tells the neighbor that it belongs to him, picks it up, and takes it home. It is a great nuisance when a neighbor breaks something borrowed, but it is not proper to show anger.

Some implements are not lent, such as a scythe, the good harness, and the branding iron. If a man buys an expensive new tool, he lets people know that he will lend it on demand, but if someone spoils it, he will have to buy a new one or refund the price.

Another large area of neighborly services is personal help. This help may be of short duration, lasting for a few minutes when a burden is to be lifted or an animal held down, but it may also be prolonged and involve several people at the same time. For such group jobs as building a house, digging a well, or stamping the dung, the family asks as many people from the neighboring houses as they will be able to repay. If there are few relatives or they are busy somewhere else, neighbors may also be called to help in transporting the harvest to the village or in threshing. The women of the neighborhood get together in small groups to process the hemp, starting at the house of one and moving on to the others in turn, or they gather all the material in one court. They also assist each other at *lugzás* (washing the home-spun yarn, the bedclothes, etc. in lye).

The services mentioned above are reciprocally equal. But if a *gazda* possessing horses carries the wheat of his horseless neighbor to the mill for grinding (grain should be brought to the mill by cart, and a man with horses would be ashamed if his neighbor had to push his grain on a wheelbarrow), this service is repaid by manual labor. The service done with a horse has an established equivalent in manual work which is just as well known in the village as the rules for the exchange of tools.

There are numerous services which cannot be so equated, however. If a young mother is absent and her baby is left at home, a neighbor may be asked to suckle it. She might even be asked to give prolonged help if the mother has little milk. So Mária Sárándi nursed two neighbors' children besides her own; sometimes she was even awakened at night to soothe the crying baby. Such help may also be asked from a neighbor if the mother is in the field or goes to a fair. (In several regions of the country babies suckled on the same breast become "foster brothers" or "foster sisters." This notion is unknown at Átány, though the child and the wet nurse remember the connection.) If the parents are away, there are numerous ways of asking and giving help in the care of the children and animals left at home.

A good neighbor has many important duties if the house of the other is bereaved. When someone is seriously ill, women from the neighboring family make frequent visits, helping to turn the sick person in the bed and giving whatever other assistance they can. When a person dies, one of the experienced neighbors washes and dresses the body. At least one household in the neighborhood will have a plank bed suitable for a "cold bed," a bier on which to lay out the deceased. (From a poor widow, Mrs. I. T., we tried to acquire an old-fashioned plank bed for the Museum. Though she needed money badly, she would not sell it, since her neighbors counted on her to lend it to them if they needed it.) A good neighbor who has a cart is duty-bound to drive to any town the family should desire, near or far, to buy the coffin. And as long as funeral feasts were in fashion, it was also the neighbor's duty to bring brandy and wine.

While the deceased is laid out, there are times (for example, in the evening) when some of the visitors are unable to enter the bereaved house because it is already too crowded. Then the recent arrivals wait in the houses and stables of the neighbors until they can take the places of those who leave (see Chapter 11, "The Funeral"). On the day of the burial the neighbor fetches his hoes, spades, and other tools so that the male members of the funeral procession can use them to cover the grave and form a mound on it. The neighbor with a team cleans up his wagon and horses carefully for this occasion, as it is his duty to convey the coffin to the graveyard. Another neighbor also harnesses his horses and follows the procession with an empty cart in order to carry the old or sickly members of the procession back to the house after the ceremony.

The good neighbor is also a "door keeper," watching the house whenever the neighboring family is invited to a wedding and so has to be away all day long. The door keeper also looks after the animals. His services are repaid by the parents of the bride or the bridegroom, who send two meals to him.

A marriage in the family is the occasion for particularly important service on the part of neighbors. Not only do they lend utensils, chairs, vessels, tablecloths, etc., but they offer whole houses and yards. One of the neighboring homes provides lodging for relatives living outside of Átány, another is where the bride or bridegroom is dressed, and a third serves as a repository for the extra furniture from the house where the wedding is celebrated. This is perhaps why all the neighbors, though they usually do not attend other family festivals, are invited to a wedding.

Finally, there are times when a neighbor may substitute for a relative. For example, neighbors are not usually invited to pigsticking. But if there is a feud between brothers and there are not enough helpers among the near kinsfolk, neighbors are called in their place. A neighbor may undertake the duties of relatives in other situations as well; for example, if a person is alone and sick and his kinsfolk neglect him, the neighbor may take care of him.

The neighborhood of the house is primarily the domain of the women, while that of the *kert* is the territory of men. A *kert* neighborhood is even more difficult to define than a house neighborhood, since the *kert*-s are usually even more irregularly laid out than the houses. The *kert* neighborhood is based on the same principles, however, but with some modifications, due to the role of the stables as *tanyakert*-s (see Chapter 9, "*Tanyakert*-s").

A good *kert* neighbor receives a taste of the pork, as does the neighbor in the village. He is not invited to the wedding or other family celebrations, but he does visit the bereaved house.

A third kind of neighborhood is established by proximity of plowlands and vineyards. The number of field and vineyard neighbors depends on the division of one's holding, since there are two neighbors to each plot of land. Field neighbors express their relationship by cordial behavior. Lending and borrowing are rare, since everyone brings the tools necessary for his own work to the field.

When work in the fields is first begun in the spring, the field neighbors greet each other with loud expressions of joy after the long winter. It takes some time for both men and animals to get used to field labor again after their muscles have softened during the long winter's rest. Thus at first they often pause in the course of their job, and smokers light up—but never alone; they wait for the arrival of the neighbor, and the two rest together for as long as their cigarettes or pipes burn.

During the spring plowing and the first work in the vineyard, everyone has grilled bacon for lunch. The people of the field neighborhood gather and grill their bacon on one fire or on separate fires near each other. Should any of them have a hut or a shady walnut tree in his vineyard, the whole neighborhood meets there, where it is cool, and eat and rest together. In bad weather the huts and buildings of the *gazda*-s who have them give shelter to near and distant neighbors alike. Even without being invited or asking permission, everyone may seek refuge in them.

In the vineyards neighbors offer the best of their fruit to each other, especially kinds which do not grow on the other's plot, if there are any. They are willing to give a shoot or a twig from a special tree or vine to another for grafting. In the same way, field neighbors often ask for seeding exchange if one of them has produced a better quality.

Neighbors in the fields are not invited to one another's family festivals, but if one dies, it is proper for the others to attend his funeral.

The neighbor relationship begins with proximity in space but may outlast it. In other words, people who change their residence may maintain a "neighborly" relationship, though a looser one, with their former neighbors. For example, Károly Bedécs built a house in his *kert*, beside the stable. But when he celebrated the wedding of his daughter ten years after the move, he invited the people from the old neighborhood. Field and vineyard neighbors do likewise. Thus a funeral is attended by all those who have even had a plot in the neighborhood of the deceased.

A prime criterion of good neighborly relations is whether or not the families send "tastes" (samples) of the new pork to each other at pigsticking. If they do, it is very likely that they also help each other with milk (at times before calving when the cow does not give milk) and invite each other to weddings at their houses. They consider it important to contribute to the good relationship so that it will be maintained. Many people bear real or imaginary insults without a word and try to smooth over difficult situations with small acts of courtesy.

Nevertheless, enmities between neighbors are just as frequent as family feuds. A person who is on good terms with all his neighbors is a rare phenomenon.

In all three kinds of neighborhood (house, *kert*, and field) disputes arise most frequently when one person causes damage to another's land or uses it without permission. The neighbor may trespass on the other's holding by plowing on the boundary line or removing the stone or pole which serves as a marker. Much enmity is caused when a person living on higher ground lets the rain or ground water run down to the holdings of neighbors living on a lower level, especially at high-water. Chickens often wander out of an unfenced or badly fenced yard and cause damage, or quarrels may arise when a neighbor catches a stray chicken and the owner notices the loss.

Gossip is also a common cause of hostility between women neighbors. In the case of such a quarrel the members of the family try not to interfere, and the enmity is generally restricted to the two persons directly involved.

The "opposite neighbors" F. O. and F. T. came to loggerheads because F. T. let the large quantity of water which had accumulated in his yard flow down into the holding of the O. family. A few angry words were exchanged between the two men, and they refused to speak to each other from then on. The women purported to ignore the affair, however, and continued to call on each other, to borrow and lend, and to help each other as good neighbors should. The feud of the men lasted for more than eight years. Then F. O. arranged the wedding of his granddaughter. As neighbors, the T. family were invited, but only the women made preparations. On the morning of the marriage F. O., moved by a sudden impulse, went over to his neighbor's house and invited F. T., too. The latter was so overjoyed at the reconciliation that he harnessed his horses and drove to the next village to fetch the gypsy musicians for the wedding.

Another neighbor on bad terms with the O. family was S. O., one of the next-door neighbors. The row started with the women here, when the wife of S. O. reclaimed her lost hen from the neighbor's yard. The feud had lasted for more than ten years and was so acute that even the wedding could not bring about a reconciliation. J. K. is an "opposite neighbor" of the O. family, with whom a dispute arose over some insinuation of the women. The enmity was primarily an affair of the women, but of such an intensity that no one in either family desired a reconciliation. When there was a wedding in the house of J. K., they chose not to invite a single neighbor in order to avoid the company of the O. family.

The most intense relationships based on residence are those of the neighborhood, but the population of the *zug*, *hóstya*, or *köz* also constitutes an alive and active community. When a new agricultural implement becomes fashionable, as was the case with the spike-tooth harrow and the disk harrow, and even a certain new type of turnip fork, one is sufficient for the whole *zug*, since all the *zugosi* people may borrow it. While the threshing machines were still the property of private Átány inhabitants, the proprietors tried to get orders from all the *gazda*-s of a *zug*. In one threshing season the machine would be used by a whole *zug*, or even two if there was much work.

For several years the thresher came last to the *zug*, where János Boross lived, and by then the optimal time for threshing was long past. Therefore the *gazda*-s dwelling in the *zug* decided to get a machine in from another village, and they sent a representative to negotiate. They then joined together to provide transportation for the machinery and the staff of the thresher from his village and back. Since the threshing machine needed twelve to twenty men and eight to ten women as helpers, the families

13

of the *zug* all worked together on each of their *kert*-s or courtyards in succession; almost the whole threshers' brigade was recruited among them.

The geese from each *hóstya* are driven to the same pasture beyond the village and are looked after by neighborhood gooseherds.

The saying goes that people who like chewing tobacco "walk over all the *zug* for plug." Pipe smokers keep the unburned chewing tobacco from the bottom of their pipes for them.

If a storm breaks out at night, the peasants arise, dress, and go out into the entryway of their houses to see if any damage is caused. Their concern is not only for the safety of their own house and yard, but also for their neighbors, the folk of the *zug*. If trouble should befall a house, the family can count on the help of the neighbors. In the late 1930s, for example, a house in the Upper End was struck by lightning and caught fire. In Átány it is believed that such a fire cannot be extinguished by water, but only by milk. Within a few minutes, people of the *zug* had brought almost eighty jars of milk for this purpose.

People living in the same *zug*, *ment*, or *hóstya*, besides maintaining rather restricted neighborly relations with each other on that basis, cultivate "good friendship" with the ten or more families whose property they pass frequently. Since they use the same road when going to church, school, the town hall, the store, the dairy, and the drinking well, they pass the houses along the road daily or several times a day, and they greet each other in a friendly way. They watch the vicissitudes of those families and show compassion in time of trouble. For people living "in one *ment*" it is proper to stand in the doorway or beside the fence when the wedding procession of one of these families goes by. In the case of bereavement they call on the family and follow the *zugosi* dead to the cemetery.

Also *kert* neighbors who live in the same *ment* are friendly to each other. For example, on winter afternoons when preparations are being made to take a bunch of straw and a jug of milk fresh from the cow home from the *kert*, people will look over into the next *kert* to see how their neighbors' preparations are coming along, in hopes that they can walk home together—although they walk in single file to the village, keeping a short distance between them.

Friendly relations also link a family to the families who live along the *hóstya*-s they take to go to the fields. In summer, when they use this road almost every day and see the families in their yards, they exchange greetings and a few words and know a little of their affairs.

The three kinds of neighborhood (house, *kert*, and field) establish close relations between each Átány family and eventually thirty or more others. Traffic in the *ment* and along the same lane creates somewhat looser but still friendly connections with forty or fifty more families. Thus the residential groupings connect each family with about a hundred others by ties which are less or more close, depending on the degree of proximity and the type of neighborhood involved.

TANYAKERT

Tanyakert or *cékert* was the name given to a stable where a group of men would sit around the fire and talk on winter days (see Plates 20, 21, and 22). The most suitable stables were large, kept warm by numerous animals, and owned by friendly, sociable *gazda*-s who would welcome the assembled crowd and occasionally even neglect the chores on their behalf.[11]

Each *tanyakert* had its habitual guests, mainly the neighbors; first of all people who had few animals and thus finished feeding them earlier. Other habitual guests had no stables of their own and so walked to the *tanyakert*-s from the village, often going back and forth three times a day. The *tanyakert*-s were at their height at the turn of the century, when the poor people of Átány had not yet begun to get winter jobs in the city but simply idled away their time in the village until spring. "They were bored in the village" (i.e., in the houses), people say. "One *kert* puts me out, another *kert* takes me in"—thus they wandered from one stable to another.

Even after the village began to lose workers as men found jobs in the city, the *tanyakert*-s continued to be social centers for the men. In 1953, János Kusper, whose ancestors were craftsmen (who did not raise livestock and kept their only cow in a small shed beside the house), decided to become a farmer and purchased a stable for his animals in the row of the *kert*-s. "We were tight inside," he explains, "and a man finds friends more easily here outside." Until 1959, his "opposite neighbor" Ferenc Orbán visited his stable almost every morning between foddering and breakfast for a *tanyázás*. As late as 1954, 25 neighbors used to go regularly to the *tanyakert* belonging to József Szilágyi (Fig. 26). This was the most frequented *tanyakert* of the village, but there were others as well, visited by smaller groups.

The *tanyázás* centered on the open straw fire which burned in the middle of the stable, usually kept alive by the old *gazda*. When night lights came into fashion and stable fires began to be neglected, many of the older guests protested; they did not want to come to talk if there was no fire. Thus it happened sometimes that when the guests began to arrive the night light was extinguished and the straw was lit, so that the guests could sit around the fire.

The location of one's own stable mainly decided which *kert* one went to. People of the same *zug* generally chose a centrally located *kert*. The deep mud was one reason for avoiding a distant *tanyakert*. The choice was also influenced by "the kind of people gathered there" and by the age of the owner. An aged *gazda* was visited mainly by elderly people, a younger one by the young folk. This was not true of all *tanyakert*-s, however. The *tanyakert* of István Török on the Bodi road was favored by the whole *zug*, old and young people alike, and numerous children as well.

---

[11] In the village, the women of the same neighborhood also had a daily social meeting in the winter. Fifteen or twenty women and girls would gather in the warm rooms of a large house during the day or in the evening with their distaffs or spinning wheels and talk and sing while they spun their hemp. These spinneries had gone out of fashion by the beginning of the present century, however, and now they live only in the memory of the old people. On the other hand, the *tanyázás* of the men survived until the 1950s.

13*

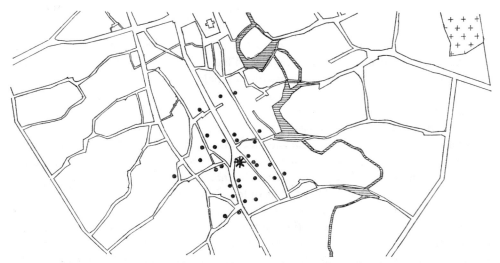

26. Area from which men attended *tanyázás* in the stable of the Szilágyi family. Asterisk shows position of stable; dots indicate homes of men who frequented the Szilágyi *tanyázás*.

The "membership" of each individual *tanyakert* was fairly stable. Regular guests just threw a word of greeting to the company as they came or left, but if a stranger arrived, he had to shake hands with everyone and was treated as a special guest. The people in the village knew which *tanyakert* each man belonged to, and during the winter if someone could not be found in his own house or *kert*, people would go to look for him in the *tanyakert*.

In some *tanyakert*-s a "membership fee" was demanded and the group subscribed to a newspaper with the collected pennies. News was read by the light of the fire or by the night light or lamp, which was lit for this purpose. Sometimes the group played cards.

Regular members had their own places around the fire. Some brought stools from home and left them in the *tanyakert* permanently; some sat on stools manufactured by members who were skillful in wood work. Nobody sat in another's place or on his stool; to do so would have been a grave insult.

The world of the *tanyakert* belonged to men only; no respectable woman ever entered. If the housewife wanted to urge her husband to return home for supper or if she needed him for anything, she sent a child. It is said that women of ill repute were seen around the farmyards outside the village; they did not visit the *tanyakert*-s, however, but rather men who were alone in their stables.

The *tanyázás* began in autumn, "when we finished plowing under spring" (i.e., plowing the fields destined for spring sowing). They lasted until spring, "when the plow enters the earth." They did not then cease altogether, since on Sundays and days when heavy rains or excessive drought hindered agricultural work, the members of the *tanyakert* gathered again, but under a shady tree in the *kert* rather than in the stable.

In winter people generally finished feeding and watering their livestock by 6 A.M. and "then they came together" and stayed in the *tanyakert* till the bell at 8 A.M., when they left to go to the village. Some attended morning service on the way. Men went out again for *tanyázás* after breakfast, at about 10 A.M., and stayed together till 2 P.M., when the animals had to be fed again. In the evening the participants in the *tanyázás* did not linger at supper very long: "We swallowed supper and out we went to the *kert*." The evening bell dissolved the company, except when lively conversation held them there even longer. "They sent the old man to see if the moon was rising. Coming back, he said: 'It rises already,' although it wasn't rising, it was going down before dawn" (i.e., the *tanyázás* had continued past midnight). Some men even stayed in the *tanyakert* for the night, lying down in the straw or an empty manger. This was especially true of groups of bachelors, who stayed awake till the early hours, but sometimes solitary old men would also ask for a resting place in the stable of another.

There was a great deal of laughter and joking, and people seized every opportunity for drinking, for *áldomás*. If one of them sold livestock, an *áldomás* was drunk; if another sold some produce, the bargain was followed by *áldomás*. Then there were people's name-days. Gábor Tóth, for example, did not await the gathering in the *tanyakert* on his name-day; with a glass of brandy in his hand, he went around the stables, saying: "Get up—today is Gabriel's day." They celebrated it until the evening. If there was no name-day or *áldomás*, the men "supplied." This was the word for collecting pennies to purchase brandy for the *tanyakert* meetings.

When there was a new supply of brandy, the women simply had to postpone meals until their husbands finally came home to eat. Some would send the children out with the urgent message that the meal would be spoiled if they did not come. But often the males had their breakfast or supper in the stable, especially in bad weather, when the mud came almost to the top of their boots. They brought bread, lard, and bacon and prepared the favorite food of men over the open fire—toasted bread with lard.

Samu Kiss, recalling his childhood, told us: "Old people discussed important things over the fire. The light shimmered and they sat in a circle, one supporting his chin with his hand, another leaning on his staff, while we children made noise. The eldest, stirring up the fire, would warn us several times, 'Silence: is it useless to tell you?'" First of all, people discussed their personal affairs. "Anyone present shared all the troubles of the others. Well-to-do *gazda*-s helped the poorer members. People were good to each other." The old men recalled past times and events, those who had wandered abroad told of their experiences, and good storytellers entertained their fellows with well-told anecdotes.

During the *tanyázás* the men also discussed the affairs of the community. Here they might decide whom to engage as a herdsmen or field guard. Local and even parliamentary elections were debated in the *tanyakert*-s until a consensus was reached which would represent the public opinion of the village. The inhabitants of the village, including the authorities, kept track of the various *tanyakert*-s and were generally aware of how many men belonged to each and who they were. Before elections the assistants of the candidates made the rounds of the *tanyakert*-s in order to get votes, always bringing an added inducement in the form of a well-calculated amount of brandy (see Chapter 17, "The Local Government").

The officials of the village also had populous *tanyakert*-s. "The *kert* of the Szórád-s [the mayor's] was frequented by the whole *félódal*—as many as forty or fifty people."[12]

Regular members of a *tanyakert* were always ready to assist each other. When the host harnessed his horses in order to carry dung or turnips, five or six of his friends from the *tanyakert* would be there to help. If they were asked, they would go to other *kert*-s to lend a hand as well, or would help with smaller jobs, such as weaving a basket or making a broom.

Some *tanyakert*-s existed for fifteen or twenty years. Several stables were shown to the authors with the words, "This used to be a *tanyakert* in my father's time." Some *tanyakert*-s were particularly prominent and memorable, such as the large stables along the highway, where the hospitable *gazda*-s let even "wandering" people enter. The spacious stable of András Rózsa along the road to Kömlő, at the big stone bridge, was an example. The family kept a separate vessel in the stable, in order to feed the wanderers. The *gazda* would notify the *gazdasszony*, saying "We'll have a guest; prepare some food." These people might be wandering singers or beggars, carrying news from village to village and county to county. Some of them taught songs to their hosts, some told them stories—horrible tales of murder and robbery—but the majority were war invalids who recalled experiences of war and captivity. Sometimes peddlers would come, traveling by cart or on foot, selling earthen vessels, wooden tools, scythes, sewing outfits for women, and all sorts of other things. In return for lodging they would give some present from their wares.

When the *tanyakert*-s were at their height men rarely frequented the taverns, except for the bachelors who made merry there on Sundays. When the *tanyakert*-s began to decline, the importance of the taverns in the social life of the men gradually increased.

---

[12] These meetings of the males around the fire in the stable existed throughout the area where the separate *kert* settlement was found. (Cf. István Györffy, 1942: 241–242; 1943: 61–62; etc.)

According to nineteenth-century descriptions of the peasant towns of the Great Plain, horse-driven mills used to be centers for male gatherings, similar to the Átány *tanyakert*-s. These mills were turned by horses under a round, tent-shaped roof. Átány also had a few of these mills in the last century. The men gathered under the awning or in the mill building, where they discussed the affairs of local administration and listened to the candidates before elections.

CHAPTER 10. AGE GROUPS

GROUPS OF CHILDREN

As soon as they have learned to walk, the small children of Átány begin to wander about in the street on sunny days and look for other children of the same age. Those of the same neighborhood or the same *zug* find each other very soon, and the more there are, the better they like it. They spend all day playing in the sand or a grassy ditch. At this age boys and girls play together, and there may be age differences of up to three years in a group. They are called "small friends," small *koma*-s, and the whole group is a "small band." Some families prefer to keep an eye on the little ones, so they invite the whole band in off the street to their yard. Young lambs, dogs, and cats are given the children, who caress them, and tumble about playing with them.

When the children reach school age, those of the same *zug* wait for each other so they may walk to and from school together, and during recess they play together in the schoolyard. At this age permanent bands of children are formed, consisting of schoolmates, especially those who are in the same grade. In the first and second grades boys and girls sit in the same classroom, but divided according to sex, with a few exceptions made for pairs of very close companions. In winter they go sliding on the ice in groups; in summer they spend most of their time herding geese. And since the various sections of the village have their own separate pastures, the little bands of neighbor children stick together at this time too, spending their whole day together. They tie rings of grass or straw, make toy animals out of thistles, and play with dolls. In spring little boys fly kites, and when they are a little older they begin playing skittles (using a wooden ball and sticks), a game they will continue to play until they are considered bachelors.

Boys in the same grade are all *koma*-s and the girls all *mátka*-s, these being the terms for male and female age-mates. Bands of six to twelve *koma*-s or *mátka*-s are soon formed, which will last throughout the school years. By the time these years are over, each youngster has chosen a best friend from the band, who is almost dearer than a brother or sister and who will remain a close companion when they are adults, through good times and bad. The decisive criterion of membership is still residence; a child from the Lower End cannot belong to an Upper End band, and the neighborhood is so strong a tie that even the age limits of the bands are exceeded for this reason. Bands are usually comprised of those who are in the same grade, but if there is a child in the close neighborhood who is one or two years younger, it is proper to admit him or her to the group.

KOMA-S AND MÁTKA-S

The strongest comradeship of the *koma* relation does not begin until after the school years, however. The bachelors who join together in a group "are all intimate friends, belonging to each other from the time they leave school until they become soldiers. They go to the tavern and they play cards together and this remains so forever: they are *koma*-s." The Lower and the Upper Ends usually have four bands each. There is a band for the "old bachelors," another for the "real bachelors," a third for the "young bachelors," and the fourth for the "youths" *(suttyó, suhadér)*. Each band sits together in a special place in the church, and in the tavern each band has a separate table. "Everyone had a place according to his age at this or that table; the inn was big enough for all."

Each band has a leader. This is someone who seems to be a leader by nature and is tacitly accepted as such by the group; leaders are not formally chosen. Even among the children there are a few whom other children follow. The behavior of the whole band depends on the nature of the leader. A rambunctious and turbulent leader has a rowdy band, apt to get into brawls; a mild and peaceful leader has a peace-loving one. When such a "grown, blossomed leader" suggests a dance, the band follows him; when he says, "now let's go this way," all go with him. "Then if the band gets into trouble, he has to stand in front; if he could not demonstrate his kingship on these occasions, he would fall." Till the twenties, one of the most important tasks of the leader was to organize parties, hire musicians, and collect the money to pay them. The leader was responsible for making sure that the merrymaking did not get out of hand and that nothing but "what is proper" was done. Two gypsy bands from the neighboring community of Kömlő made music for the people of Átány, one for the Upper End and one for the Lower End. Every Sunday afternoon, from the first Sunday after Easter until the recruits joined up at the beginning of October, the bands came over and played for the merrymakers. On the first Sunday the leader of the bachelor group went by wagon to pick them up, but at the Átány boundary the musicians jumped down and walked into the village, playing on their instruments till they reached the tavern. In front of the musicians, the leader of the bachelors walked alone, his spurs jingling. Everyone watched him, even the village officials from the window of the town hall; they appraised his gait and behavior and tried to judge whether he would be suitable for the task.

Every bachelor belongs to a band at Átány; to stay outside is to be like "a bird with its wings clipped." This happens to some "old bachelors" who fail to marry at the same time as the others and are left alone. In order to avoid loneliness in this situation, most of them join the younger band.

As soon as they leave school, members of the same band usually address each other with terms such as "Mikó *koma*," "my dear *koma* Mikó." The younger brother of one's *koma* is a "little *koma*," the elder is "my big *koma*" or "my old *koma*." The sister of one's *koma* is a *mátka*. The members of the youngest bachelor band, the youths, often do not start bachelor life at the same time, even though they belong to the same age group. One of them may begin courting when he is fourteen, another not until he is seventeen or eighteen. Youths stand in front of the musicians to perform the *verbunkos*, the bachelors' dance, at different times because when a youth does so it is a sign to the whole village that he has attained the status of bachelorhood by first fulfilling several conditions. The first of these is the performance of certain agricultural tasks, such as plowing and mowing. Ferenc Orbán, for example, began bachelorhood at an early age. When he was not yet fourteen years old, he bought two bottles of beer with the money he got for some eggs and offered a drink to the elderly hired harvester who was teaching him now to reap. "I felt like a bachelor already," he says, "since I could pay for two bottles of beer." In the same year he also plowed alone, and consequently his father allowed him to cut his own bread. Thus he had already passed several requirements of bachelorhood and was ready to stand in front of the band and perform the bachelors' dance.

"When they get older, they become 'real bachelors.' "[13] These are young men between eighteen and twenty years old, who would go on dancing, making merry, and brawling all day long if they had the chance. On summer nights they loiter about the streets arm in arm, singing loudly, or sit in one of the *kert*-s, roasting purloined meat or sausages, eating and drinking—in a word, baching. Dawn often finds the band still awake after a night spent without lying down or sleeping. In this condition they start work in the morning. In winter they establish their headquarters in one of the *kert*-s, whence they start out in a group for courting or drinking expeditions. As they walk along the road they are on the lookout for a chance to play some practical joke, to show off their strength and skill, or to get into a brawl.

When they become "old bachelors" of twenty-two or twenty-three they calm down; they dance less and let the gypsies play more melancholy tunes. They are already preparing for marriage.

Whereas the bachelors are divided into four age groups, the girls divide into only three. The youngest are the junior girls, next the marriageable girls, and last the elder girls. As soon as they have left school, girls of the same band address each other as *mátka*-s: "Kiss *mátka*"; "Barna *mátka*"; "where have you been, Kollát" or "where have you been, Kollát *mátka*?" The *mátka* relation is a lifelong one, like the *koma* relationship. "They are all *mátka*-s till the hour of their death."

Bachelors meet every day if they can, while the girls meet mainly on Sundays. They start for church together and wait outside in clusters of *mátka* groups for the

---

[13] If someone reached the age of the "real bachelors" (bachelors with full privileges, awaiting their enlistment), he could sit at the table of this age group in the tavern. A ceremony was attached to this transition also; he had to buy wine for the remaining bachelors, and they repaid him by drinking his health.

bell to ring. If there is no dance on a Sunday afternoon, they visit each other and play "take and leave," a game played with dice and nuts. Nowadays spinning rooms are only a memory, but in the old days, on weekday afternoons in winter, the *mátka* groups would meet in a house hired (usually from a widow) for this purpose and would spin and play together until the late hours. By 1920 these spinning rooms had gone out of date. In the spring the *mátka*-s went to play ball, to the *perenge* (an improvised, simple merry-go-round), and to dances together.

Nowadays the groups of girls walk in the main square for hours on end on Sundays and holidays (see Plate 36). If music and dancing are going on, they stop in front of the door of the tavern, waiting for the bachelors to ask them to dance. The young men stand in the doorway or at the window of the tavern or in groups in the street to watch the bands of laughing girls parade in front of them.

ACTIVITIES OF KOMA AND MÁTKA GROUPS DURING ADOLESCENCE

Playing Ball

In spring when the weather grew milder and the deep, heavy mud dried up, girls used to go to the playground to play ball and to swing. Our informants in their sixties, and some of the younger people too, still remember the spring ball playing. The girls of the Lower End had their playground beside the lower cemetery; those of the Upper End had theirs near the mill, beside the farthest *kert*.

Each girl possessed a rubber ball or one made of cow hair rolled together by an older relative or the godfather after brushing the cow. The girls stood on the grass in a circle and threw the ball to one another. They did not play undisturbed for long, however, before the bachelors arrived in bands, wearing *szűr*-s (at the beginning of this century the *szűr* was worn mainly for work or it was thrown on the shoulder when going to the playground). The bachelors stopped and watched the game. Sooner or later one of the girls would throw the ball too far and one of the others would run after it. Now the bachelors were moved to action too, and they would take off after the ball and kick it farther and farther. One young man after another would be left behind, until at last the only one left following the girl was the bachelor who wanted to court her. They would run far away after the ball, returning after a long time, the young man walking with the girl and covering her with his *szűr*. Thereby his affection was made manifest to all. If there was another who wanted to court the girl, "they fought on the spot, on the green grass." Sometimes the girl did not like the youth who held her under his *szűr*, in which case she preferred not to play ball any more. Ball playing continued until the beginning of the summer; "there was work in the summer and they did not play much then."

Another springtime amusement was on the *perenge* or merry-go-round. Several *perenge*-s were set up in empty *kert*-s, the Lower and the Upper Ends each having their own. There was one in the vicinity of the tavern also, so the bachelors could watch the girls from nearby. The base of the *perenge* was a post of about one and a half meters stuck into the ground. A beam was fastened crosswise to the top of the post by means of a big nail, which served as the axle of the whirling movement. To each end of the beam a rope was bound, the other end of the rope being tied around the middle of a short, strong stick which swung free. The persons riding the *perenge* either stood or sat on the sticks and "embraced the rope," holding it tight. Three or four of their friends pushed the center of the beam, turning it as fast as they could—"they were glad if it flung somebody off." Sometimes the whirling *perenge* made the girls' skirts billow and rise. Like the ball games in the playground, the *perenge* belonged to the girls, but they were followed by the bachelors here too. Often the boys turned the swing and some of them even sat or stood on it themselves, enjoying the swift whirling.

If the musicians turned up anywhere in the village, however, both ball game and *perenge* were abandoned and everyone went to dance.

Sprinkling

Easter Monday is a special occasion when the bachelors visit the girls in groups. In Átány and throughout the country this is the day of "Easter sprinkling," when the bachelors douse the girls with water.

On this day, from early morning until the first sound of the church bell, every bachelor and younger boy is in the street with his band making the rounds of houses where there are girls in order to douse them.

After 6 A.M. the little boys, the four- and five-year-olds, begin to sprinkle; at about 7 A.M. boys too small to go alone are accompanied by their fathers. At about 8 A.M. the bands of schoolboys go round, and finally the bachelors. Easter dousing is similar to the early years of courtship in that every bachelor visits every girl. Even small boys are started off by their fathers with the warning: "Go to all the girls or I'll knock your brains out." Little boys may sprinkle girls of all ages, but bachelors visit only grown-up girls.

Before World War I the manner of sprinkling was different from what it is today. In the morning ten to fourteen bachelors, members of the same band, met in the tavern and from there went out into the streets, strolling along arm in arm, singing and feigning drunkenness. They entered houses where there were marriageable daughters, caught the girls, took them to the brook Ér, and soaked them in the water. "They brought every girl they could find to the Ér on Monday—I led the girls into the water up to their waists and I ducked them." Sometimes they dragged a refractory girl to the well, and while two bachelors held her down, a third poured a pailful of water over her face. "If they could catch the girl, they poured water on her until she was as wet as a duck." Others brought a bucket into the house: "Some of the girls hid under the bed but I heaved the water in her direction and it flowed under the bed fast and hard." Some girls were so afraid that they ran up to the loft to avoid the bachelors. The majority, however, submitted to a dousing.

The bands came one after another, and the girls could hardly find time to change into dry clothes. But this manner of dousing gradually became milder. Not much water is used nowadays except in those houses where the family is careless enough not to empty the kitchen pail beforehand. Bachelors entering the house look for the water bucket first of all; if they find water in it, they ladle out a large glassful and pour it into the girl's face. Otherwise they sprinkle her face or hair with perfumed water, brought in their pockets in small bottles.

The sprinkling is witnessed by all female members of the family and often by the *gazda* too, since he is usually preparing to go to church at this time. The girl sits in one of her better workday outfits and waits with her hands folded. The bands of little boys enter reciting the following rhymes:

> "Good morning, good morning, dear lily,
> I sprinkle you with rose water to save you from fading;
> Take then the rose water, my pearl, my lily of the valley;
> Where is the egg, the red-painted egg? I throw it in my pocket.
> Is sprinkling allowed?"

Bachelors do not recite a verse but simply greet the family, wish them a happy Easter, and ask the *gazdasszony* if they may sprinkle the girl. "You may, my son, you may," says the mother or the grandmother. The *gazda* encourages the bachelors saying, "Spray her, my little brothers, so that she will grow." The sprinklers hurry to the girl in a group and sprinkle the perfumed water into her face. The girl does not speak; at most she shows some reluctance and complains if she gets water in her eyes. The little ones stay only a few minutes—time enough to greet the family, reel off the verse, douse the girl, and receive their rewards. A little boy gets money and pastry. A godchild or the child of a kinsman receives a red-painted egg in addition to the pastry. Above the age of twelve, wine is offered too, and money is reserved for god-children. Instead of pennies, however, they receive ten or twenty *forint*-s. Recently the sprinklers have been given a red-painted hard-boiled egg, whereas thirty years ago a raw egg without any paint was customary. Besides wine and cake, each bachelor also receives a red-painted egg. Children are received in the kitchen and are not en-couraged to stay. Bachelors are brought into "the house" and asked to sit down, but they are not supposed to stay for more than fifteen minutes. Though bachelors visit fewer houses than the boys, one Easter Monday supplies a band with between two and three hundred eggs. When it was customary to give raw eggs, the bachelors would sell them in the tavern and use the money for further merrymaking in the afternoon.

Sprinklers hurry to get to every house and to be off the streets by the time the first chime of the bell calls people to church (on Easter Monday the ringing of bells begins half an hour later for the sake of the sprinklers), when only a few broken egg shells are left to indicate the morning's activity.

The Monday sprinkling by the bachelors may be requited by the girls on Tuesday—if they get a chance. One of the Átány men told us the following story: "I was driving home from plowing when J. S. came along. She was carrying a pail of water from the well. 'Are you carrying water, Julcsa?' I asked her. 'I am,' said the girl and she poured the bucketful on me." The bachelor sprinkled in this way makes a point of vigorous repayment the next year. J. A. told us: "Once Sári Kádár sprinkled me on Easter Tuesday. So the following Easter, I grabbed Sári Kádár, took her to the stream, which was drying up and full of puddles, and there I ducked her again and again—she had a fine linen shirt on."

Caroling

On Christmas Eve groups of children connected by kinship, and also the *koma* bands of sometimes as many as sixteen to twenty bachelors, go around the village to extend greetings and to sing Christmas carols. They go into the yards, stop in front of the living room and ask through the window whether they may be allowed to sing. After the encouraging words "you may," they sing a Christmas carol and then one of them recites a Christmas greeting in verse. The family listens to them in silence, while the *gazda* makes preparations; as soon as the greeting has been given, he takes a bottle of wine and a glass to the bachelors and serves them all and thanks them for having remembered him. Should the carolers arrive when the family is already in bed, the lamp is lighted and the *gazda* gets up so as to treat them properly. On this evening one band after another comes into the yard and stands in front of the windows, and sometimes several bands, as many as thirty bachelors at once, meet and sing together. The well-to-do *gazda* Kálmán Kovács, one of the first to unite his house and stable in one place, remembers such a Christmas Eve with the words: "The loud caroling made the horses dance so that they almost kicked the stable wall to pieces."

Maypoles and Hancsikolás

Bachelors used to celebrate May Day also. No bachelor went to bed the night before because from sunset till dawn they rambled around the village, setting up Maypoles and engaging in *hancsikolás* ("digging up")—the term for the acts of vandalism the bachelor bands traditionally perpetrated on that night in the yards of houses where marriageable girls lived.

The first task was to erect a Maypole for each girl who was being courted by one of the members. It was placed in the yard of her family's house near the gate or the well-sweep. A poplar with rich foliage or a lilac was felled and tied to the pole to make it as high as possible. In the evening, before the Maypole was raised, the girl decorated the tree with ribbons and kerchiefs. Then at night the *koma* group set up the pole with the decorated tree on top.[14]

[14] Raising the Maypole and other customs of youth are described very vividly and authentically on a nationwide basis by K. Viski (1932).

Then the bachelors started out for *hancsikolás*, carrying spades on their shoulders. They would demolish the small daubed protrusion at the base of the walls (called a berm) and break up the earthen seat built beside the gate to the street. The earth from the ruined berm would be tossed up in the air and a few spadefuls thrown into the yard. If the yard was not guarded, the bachelors would rush in and wreak havoc to their hearts' content. They would frequently unhook the gate from the fence and carry it to a neighbor's yard four houses away. They might turn the whole yard topsy-turvy and often detach the trough from the sweep-pole well and carry it to the next yard. Large agricultural tools left in the court, such as a plow or a harrow, were dispersed in the same way. Sometimes they even barricaded the road with beams and implements brought from the yards.

However, careful *gazda*-s guarded their property, hiding behind the fences and keeping watch. If the bachelors tried to enter the yard, the *gazda* hit them with a tool he had ready. Samu Kiss related one such night in the following manner: "S. M. knocked me on the head with a flail on May Day Eve. We made *hancsikolás*, myself on one side and Bedécs on the other. We went to scatter the small berm. There was the old man hiding behind the fence with the flail. I was carried home." (The *gazda* dealt such a mighty blow with the flail that Kiss was carried home in a bed sheet.)

On the morning of May Day the *gazdasszony*-s would hurry to look out at the street and see whether there had been any trouble during the night. They grumbled and lamented and abused the bachelors. They would try to find the polterns and implements which have been carried off and would flatten and daub the demolished berms anew. During our field work the small seat in front of an old woman's house was demolished and the village was in an uproar: "What sort of bachelors are they, to have destroyed the berm of an aged woman?" Later it was discovered that a young girl, the old woman's granddaughter, often slept there, and the commotion died down. "What a shame it would be to leave the berm untouched where a girl resides on May Day!"

Today Maypoles are no longer set up for grown-up girls, but only for little girls, by their fathers or elder brothers. Instead the bachelor buys a kerchief for his favorite girl and gives it with a pot or basket of flowers on the eve of May Day. The kerchief and the flowers are now called a "Maypole."

The girls of Átány ordinarily go to church bareheaded, but on the first Sunday of May those who received kerchiefs wear them to church. Thus all the inhabitants of the village can see who has a serious suitor and who has none, just as in the old days they could tell by the Maypole in the yard.

Courtship

"We used to love all the girls, one after the other," the older men say. "All of them have been my sweethearts, every girl in the village. We asked all the girls to dance; today a young man may only love one." On girls' evenings as many as three or four bands of bachelors used to visit the same girl.

Girls' evenings occurred five days a week in winter, every day but Tuesday and Friday. On these evenings the bands of bachelors would gather after supper, as night fell, at an agreed-upon place, and then set out arm in arm, singing as they walked along the street. The bachelors' song heralded their arrival at a house where a marriageable daughter lived. They were allowed to enter only houses where the lamp was lit; a dark house meant that young men would not be received. They entered the yard and one would knock on the front door three times. When the girl heard the tapping, it was her duty to open the door and let the bachelors in. They would crowd into the living room after depositing their sticks in the corner of the *pitvar*. The *gazdasszony* sat in the living room with them, spinning, sewing, or shelling. The girl also was spinning or sewing. The young men sat down and started a conversation with the *gazdasszony* about work, the weather, or the livestock. After a little while, one of the bachelors who was fond of the girl got up and went out into the *pitvar*, leaving the door open behind him. The girl had to follow him, whether she liked him or not. They talked to each other standing in the middle of the dark *pitvar*, and the bachelor might hug and kiss the girl if she let him. Should they stay out of the living room too long, the mother coughed once or twice as a warning. If this was not enough, she called out, "Shall I bring a stool for you?" This was a serious warning and meant that it was time to say good-bye. The bachelor stamped his foot hard on the dirt floor of the *pitvar* and all the others in the living room stood up and took their leave. The girl accompanied them to the gate.

Propriety demanded that all bands be welcomed, even when three or four visited a girl the same evening, but a mischievous girl could show her disfavor by playing tricks on some of the bachelors. If she disliked the one who called her out of the room or if she thought the band too young for her, she chose the least congenial of the bachelors and put a wooden knife and a piece of turf (the fuel made out of dung) in his hand and said, "Cut yourself a slice—you have come from far." Sometimes the girl might give the bachelor a piece of thread and ask him to twist it; as he did so he would have to step farther and farther backward until he reached the door. "Farther, farther," the girl or her mother would say; "Open the door." As he stepped out, the door was slammed in his face. A bachelor ridiculed in this way either took revenge at once, perhaps by breaking the windows of the house with his stick, or he waited for the next dance and then danced the girl out of the room.

Some bachelors would also make mischief. Sometimes one band would be chatting in the living room while another, waiting in the *pitvar*, would steal the meat reserved for smoking out of the chimney, consume any food or milk that was left out, take the plates down from the wall, and so forth. However, this could happen only in the house of a weak *gazdasszony*.

The male members of the family were never present on these occasions. Some old *gazda*-s did not like bachelors in their houses. Sometimes when a large crowd was sitting in the living room, the *gazda* would enter and knock the lamp down with his hat, saying, "This lamp is the kind of lamp that doesn't light unless I want it to." The bachelors would jump to their feet and run, every man for himself.

Group courtship continued for two to four years. As soon as a bachelor made his choice, he left his band and visited the girl's house alone; at most he asked his best *koma* to act as "escort," to provide some support in case a row ensued. When it became known that a bachelor had chosen a girl, the other bands no longer visited her house. If two young men liked the same girl, the bachelor bands fought it out. The victor, however, had no prerogative; the girl simply chose the one she liked better.

Dancing

An eighty-year-old Átány man remembered the Sundays of his youth in this way: "We either danced or fought." At that time the bachelors of the Lower and the Upper Ends occasionally engaged one or two gypsy musicians (for example, on the afternoon of Easter Monday) and chose some ample, shady place in the street to dance. They also used to dance in new houses or new stables, in order to stamp the dirt floors down. After a new building was roofed but before the doors and windows were fitted in, the *gazda* of the house used to invite one of the bachelor bands from his part of the village for a dance. The young men brought the gypsies and the wine and brandy, the girls were attracted by the music, and they would all dance until the floor of the building was smooth.

Since about 1900 people have danced mostly in the taverns. Every Sunday afternoon from Easter to October gypsy bands, engaged by a seasonal contract, played in both the Lower End and the Upper End taverns. The musicians are paid by the bachelors, by each young man who is allowed to stand and dance in front of the band alone—i.e. each fully qualified bachelor—contributing a *véka* of wheat and a liter of wine for the season. Children may learn how to dance at the edge of the group without paying, while youths *(suttyó)* contribute half a *véka* of wheat.

The music begins when the Sunday afternoon service is over. The door of the tavern may not be opened until the church door is shut. After entering the tavern the bachelors stand around in groups for a while, smoking and drinking. Then, at the summons of their leaders, they form a ring and all start with a *verbunkos*, a dance for men only. Sometimes the circle is broken up and they dance individually. At this time the youth who desires to join the young bachelors may demonstrate his intention by standing in front of the musicians to perform a *verbunkos* by himself. When he has done this, he is included in the circle.

The girls go home from church to change their clothes until they hear the music: "We ran there in a hurry—'come on, come on, the band is playing!'" When they get to the tavern the girls stop: "We formed a cluster and stood there. One would push another forward: 'go a bit further, they don't see us!'"

After dancing the *verbunkos*, the bachelors take a rest and look at the girls. As the gypsies tune up again, they call the girls to dance. In a loud voice, each bachelor shouts the name of the girl he wants to dance with, and the girl steps jauntily out in

front of him. After the dance he leaves his partner, and the girls again walk up
and down in their groups. At the sound of the music they stop and wait for a
new call.

Until a bachelor has chosen his special girl, he asks every girl for at least one dance;
afterward he dances with his sweetheart all the time. If a bachelor asks a girl to dance
several times, it is a sign of his affection for her.

However peaceful the dance may be at the beginning, there is no guarantee that
it will remain so. Although it is considered improper to cut in on a dancing couple,
sometimes it is done, and a brawl is usually the result.

If a bachelor asks a girl to dance and she refuses, he may take revenge by "dancing
her out." He may also do this if the girl has ridiculed him or played a trick on him
when he went to her house to court her. "Dancing a girl out" is done by the offended
youth himself or by his best *koma*. The plan is made known to all the *koma* group
and the musicians are warned. The unsuspecting girl is asked for a dance as usual
and her partner makes a few turns with her in the ordinary manner. Then the bachelor
exchanges a glance with his *koma*-s; at this sign they clear the center of the room,
leaving a large open space. The gypsies stop the dance tune and strike up the Rákóczi
march. By this time everyone knows what is going on, and they all move aside. The
bachelor dances through the empty space with the reluctant girl, pushing her toward
the door. One of the company opens the door and the dancer bundles the girl out of
the room. A girl who is "danced out" is not asked to dance again for a year.

Dancing used to go on until "striking a light," i.e., until dark. Then the girls who
had suitors were accompanied home by them; the rest returned home with their
mátka-s.

Fighting

Our elderly informant who said "Either we danced or we fought" did not exaggerate.
Fighting is the most important indication of manly prowess, *virtus*, for a bachelor.
Those who deal out hard strong blows are admired and those who get hit are not.
János Mikó's wife, mother of four grown-up bachelors at the time of our field work,
constantly begged her sons not to start a brawl or get mixed up in any fighting when
they went out courting or to the tavern; nevertheless she would say good-bye to them
with the words: "I would rather see you dead than have you get hit."

Because of the intergroup fighting it was desirable to be a member of a large band—
to have a populous *koma* group to make one strong and invincible. Until the end of
World War I the bachelors of the Upper and the Lower Ends were enemies: "Like
two male dogs, they would start a row at once." The fur would fly when a band from
the Lower End met one from the Upper End. As they passed each other, someone
might drop a word or someone might get pushed, and they would be at each other
with sticks. Bachelors in general, and certain bands in particular, were usually on the
lookout for chances to exchange blows. Little boys used to follow them diligently

14

and watch their fights in order to learn how it ought to be done. For a while the authorities did not allow the young men to take their big sticks into the tavern. The bachelors then entrusted their sticks to the care of the bands of young boys who stood in front of the tavern; they kept the sticks faithfully, ready to hand them over to their owners at a moment's notice if necessary.

Often a trifle was enough to start a row: "Someone told a lie and I said, 'that's not how it is.' I also thought to myself, 'I shall strike first, since whoever deals the first blow wins'"—and the fight was on. A bachelor who wanted to fight "would start bantering until he was hit by someone; then, after him and a terrific row started. But the weaker band ran away as soon as it could and had to bear the shame of either running away or being beaten."

Usually, however, they fought over girls. There was some truth in the saying that "the bachelor dared to enter but he did not dare to come out" (of a house where there was a daughter). If a bachelor from the Upper End courted a girl from the Lower End, he could expect a scuffle, even though it was considered proper for each bachelor to visit each girl during courting and desirable for a man to marry a girl from a distant part of the village.

If a group of bachelors from the Lower End courted a girl in the Upper, "the enemies surrounded the house like a castle." One of these fights between two bands of bachelors is related as follows: "Once the boys from the Lower End entered the house of old Lepe, who had a daughter. But there was a sharp altercation with the bachelors of the Upper End, who had noticed the group entering. So they knocked at the door too and the girl opened it. They did not enter, however, but just reached in and snatched the others' sticks. Then they stood in a row outside. The bachelors inside were frightened to death, knowing that they had lost their staffs and that the others were waiting outside. As they left the house, they saw the Upper End bachelors standing across the road. Now, *koma*, what next? They had no choice but to attack the band barefisted. The Upper End bachelors jumped to both sides and the Lower-Enders ran between them. There was great confusion and they were all gone."

A bachelor who went to court a girl alone was often forced to run. He was chased as far as the town hall, which was the boundary between the Upper and the Lower Ends. Therefore those who went courting by themselves often asked someone to escort them, frequently a married man of their kin. Although married people did not fight (any more), they still kept their sticks. The escort followed the bachelor and waited until he came out, since "he would have been flayed in the doorway if he had had no escort." At Easter sprinkling, a bachelor who went around alone was also beaten.

Bands of bachelors would almost certainly come to blows if they went to court the same girl at the same time. "Whoever was more clever went out [to converse in the *pitvar*] with the girl first, leaving the others to wait for a long time. There was nothing for the other band to do but say good-bye. If that happened, one had to use the *duráng* [big stick]."

But two bands meeting at a girl's house did not always start a row; "They looked at each other and tried to gauge which was the stronger. The band which felt itself weaker was afraid of being beaten, so it quickly said good-bye. But if the stronger band was quick enough, the other group could reckon on being greeted with sticks in front of the house."

Such battles were not innocuous. Some fights have ended with severe casualties and many more with minor injuries. Most bachelors at one time or another suffered severe cudgel blows on the head; "there was one who had 25 cuts on his skull when he got married."

The weapon was a club, much more rarely a pocketknife, and in drunken brawls sometimes a wine bottle. "K. M. dealt me a blow on the head with a stick so that my blood began to flow. I grabbed the one-liter flask and hit him on the head with it, knocking him down on all fours."

After serious fights those who could afford it reached an agreement with the injured ones privately and paid some compensation for the wounds. But the private agreement was in vain if the family took the injured bachelor to the doctor, who was bound to report the case and thus cause the matter to come before the judiciary. Brawlers were usually sentenced to prison for two to nine months. This punishment did not prevent further rows; there were some bachelors who went to prison three times for fighting.

Fighting gave the bachelors pleasure but made their mothers so nervous that they could never be at ease. A man of the Upper End related: "My mother stood outside the house in the evening. In the stillness of the night cries could be heard from afar. She kept listening to hear if there was a row somewhere. She could not rest until her son reached home. She was anxious for me since she knew I was courting in the Lower End; she listened every night in case I would need to be fetched home."

However, bachelors who fought with each other never became permanent enemies; "they beat each other up and then they sit together in prison and become good friends again." It was not uncommon for those who fought and served their term of imprisonment together to become *sógor*-s and *nász*-s later. Gábor Varga related: "We beat up Samu Juhász so badly that he had to be carried home. I did not have a better friend when he became a man."

Military service puts an end to bachelorhood. When the young man returns from the army, "he does not join a band again—he has had enough of that kind of life. Now he gets married." Bachelors who returned from the war were especially silent. "We came from the war," Ferenc Orbán told us. "We passed the test. We were like lambs grown up into sheep. We gave up the ways of youngsters. When the gypsies played their tunes at our table, we sang but we did not dance any more."

Stealing

A bachelor needs money, and the more intensely he lives the bachelor life, the more he needs. He has to pay for tobacco and for liquor and music at the tavern. He needs money also for the small presents he wants to give to the girl he is courting.

However, the rules of family life do not allow a bachelor to have an income of his own. Even if he works as a hired man or a servant, he has to hand over every penny of his wages to the family without spending any of it independently. Now and then his mother gives him a little from the meager household fund, but rarely enough to cover his expenses. He needs more. Bachelors usually get extra money by "stealing" from their fathers. They begin with eggs. They do not tell their parents exactly how many eggs the hen has laid, and each day they hide one or two in a cache they have prepared. When they have collected a few, they take them to the tavern and the bartender gives them liquor in exchange.

However, one cannot acquire a *véka* (about a bushel) of wheat by exchanging eggs and, since that is the contribution each bachelor has to make to the hiring of the gypsies, they resort to stealing whole sacks of wheat or other produce. Like fighting, stealing is also one of the indications of prowess in a bachelor. There is no man in Átány who did not steal in his youth. Even a bachelor who is relatively uninterested in merrymaking or who is already provided with the necessary spending money will steal from his father at least once in his life, in order to be able to say he has done so. A cautious bachelor, accustomed to the rod of a severe father, may dare to take only a hatful of wheat at a time, repeating the operation until his *véka* is full. More audacious ones steal a whole sack at once. The best time to get a sackful is during threshing and winnowing, when the new grain is first poured into sacks. K. M. related the following episode: "My father kept a strict watch during threshing. All the wheat was collected in the barn. I got the key from my sister and crept in stealthily with a sack. When it was more than half full, the old man noticed something wrong. 'Which of you left the barn open?' he asked, and then he came and locked the door on me. I did not say a word; even though I was locked up, I could at least get the sack filled up. I put it near the door. Then Zsófi [his sister] came and said, 'Where is the key, father?' 'Hush, hush, I am in here,' I said. Then Zsófi called my father away: 'Come, my father!' While the old one wasn't watching, we managed to drag the sack out. Casting a glance back toward the barn, my father said, 'Now you have left the place open again—anyone could take wheat!' But by then the sack was outside."

The bachelors need money especially at Eastertime, and "there was much stealing during Holy Week. They stole anything they could from their fathers because they needed the money to pay the gypsies." "Last winter my grandson came to me," an aged informant told us. "'Grandfather, do you want to buy some turnips?' 'Whose turnips are they?' 'My Kakas grandfather's.' 'How much do you want for them?' 'Fifty *forint*-s.' When I had bought them, I found out that my own turnips had been sold to me."

Another kind of theft is also important as a demonstration of *virtus*, a bachelor's manly prowess. In summer bachelors steal flowers from the house gardens and raid the small orchards. This kind of stealing is of no profit, however, since if the flowers acquired in this way were displayed, the theft would be apparent. They are thrown away as soon as they are picked. When they are lucky, bachelors get a chance to eat their stolen fruit, but if they are caught red-handed and beaten or chased off, the fruit gets thrown away. Samu Kiss related the story of a fruit raid as follows: "It was in the autumn and we met in a band in the evening. Some of us proposed to steal apples from the garden of Ferenc Gál. That was Fuder, since he knew exactly where the tree was. So we went and he shook down the apples, picked them up and brought them out of the garden. But old Gál lay under the eaves. As Fuder came out, the old man did not say a word but knocked the boy on the head so hard that he staggered and fell down. With a cry, my *koma* Fuder hurried to get out. When we had left the place, he did not want to eat any of the apples on account of the blow he received from the old one."

The Last Season before Military Service

Suddenly the carefree days of walking in bands, courting, and making merry are interrupted by the summons to military service which will take the bachelor group away from their village for two or three years. (Young men used to be called up at the age of twenty or twenty-one; recently this has been changed to eighteen.) The summons comes in the spring but service does not actually begin until October. Since all the bachelors of the same age are drafted at the same time, all the age-mates of the *koma* company make their preparations and leave together.

On the eve of the day they are drafted, the people who are closest to each young man—grandparents, brothers and sisters, uncles, aunts, first cousins, godparents, older or younger *koma*-s, and close neighbors—all visit his parents, and cake and wine are offered to them. Every visitor brings one or two silk ribbons two meters long. The bachelor goes off to bid farewell to his beloved and does not come home until late, when the party is nearly over. Male visitors usually reminisce about their military or war experiences to encourage the young man; the women try to console the mother. Before leaving they present the gifts they have brought—ribbons for the bachelor's hat.

At dawn the next day the young men are taken by cart to Eger, each one accompanied by his mother or an elder female relative and one or two older or younger *koma*-s of the band. The mother carries her son's best black hat bound up in a kerchief along with the ribbons received as presents. At Eger they wait in the courtyard or the corridors of the barracks until the bachelor has passed the examination. The enlisting officers are familiar with the Átány custom and so when they read out the list of the able-bodied Átány bachelors they let the mothers know when they may decorate the hats. Then each mother ties a ribbon of the national colors (red, white, and green) around the crown of the hat and slips the other ribbons through it one by one so that the ends hang down behind. Usually the streamers are light colored. It is not considered advisable to put on a red ribbon, since it may signify a bad end, especially in time of war. Yellow ones are given by those who do not like the bachelor. Near relatives give one or two black or dark blue ribbons to a bachelor whose father or mother is dead. If there has been a death in his family recently, everyone gives him a black, dark blue, or violet colored ribbon.

As the young men leave the recruiting office, their weeping mothers step up to them, embrace them, and place the beribboned hats on their heads. The older and younger *koma*-s also surround the "accepted" bachelor and string the ribbons they have brought through the red, white, and green bands of his hat.[15] (The bachelor who is found unfit for service returns home in a hat that has no ribbons. At home his mother puts a piece of white ribbon around the crown to signify that he was called up but found unfit.)

The "soldiers" then pile into the carts and gallop the horses back to Átány, drinking wine and singing. "Glory was due to the one whose cart got home first. The soldiers filled as many as nine carts, and there was not much left of the horse shoes. They swore their oaths at Eger at 5 P.M. and they had already reached the village at 8 o'clock." The day ended with merrymaking which lasted till the early hours.

Henceforth the bachelor, being a recruit, parades about in his decorated hat every Sunday until October, when the term of service actually begins. Some of them have forty or fifty streamers hanging from their hats: "the more ribbons he had, the more glorious he was considered; some had so many that their hats could hardly hold them up." From then on the bachelor goes to the tavern with his beribboned hat and wears it while he is dancing; the ribbons stream out behind him as he whirls around the dance floor. The recruit also parades his hat to the church (see Plate 37), but uncovers his head at the church door and winds the ribbons around the hat. At one time it was fashionable to lay the decorated hats on the edge of the organ loft so that the ribbons all hung down over the railing of the gallery. When he greets someone, the bachelor usually does not raise his hat, though he will remove it and press it against his heart with his left hand when he meets the pastor or the magistrate, who n turn are expected to exchange a few words with him.

The last carefree summer is soon over and as October approaches the recruits get ready to leave. On their last Sunday at home they carouse in the beribboned hats for the last time. They bid the gypsies strike up, and they dance wildly, saying farewell to their "bachelorhood." At the end of the revelry they unfasten the ribbons from their hats and give them away as gifts.[16]

The day of departure is a day of sorrow in Átány. Close relatives, neighbors, godparents, and *koma*-s visit the family of the recruit again, to encourage the young man and console the weeping females in the family. The plight of widows is especially

[15] The mustering and enlistment of the young men was also regarded as official business by the town magistracy. Both the mayor and the secretary escorted them to the recruiting office at the Eger city hall and often brought a gypsy band along. The young men from Átány filed out of the office together, wearing their beribboned hats, and the gypsies followed them, playing tunes. They went across the street to the tavern, where the mayor ordered bottles of wine and treated them to a drink. They set out for home after the *áldomás*.

[16] According to custom, the ribbons are given back to the people who originally gave them to the bachelor, if there is a girl in the family who could wear them in her hair. The rest of the ribbons are given to the girl the bachelor is courting and to his sister. (The ribbons are set aside for the wedding, when they will be the ornaments of the best men and their attendants.)

lamentable, since they are often left without a breadwinner for several years. All the recruits then gather at the center of the village, along with their escorts and the ever-present musicians. When everyone has arrived, the recruits, embracing each other, lead the procession, the band marching near them. Then come the women, weeping and wailing, and the older men, jogging along in silence. The people of Átány remember a time when some of the elderly men who accompanied the recruits held their hats in their hands, as is the custom for a funeral procession.

At the edge of the village the procession halts and the young men embrace their kinsfolk. This is one of the rare occasions when males embrace and kiss each other. The gypsies strike up martial tunes as the bachelors board the empty carriages which have followed them from the village center and speed away. Then the music stops and everyone returns home in silence. No music is played in the taverns from that day until the following spring, when a new generation calls forth the gypsies to make music and new bands of bachelors dance the *verbunkos* before them.

MIDDLE-AGED MEN AND WOMEN

Marriage dissolves the *koma* and *mátka* groups, whose members are then reintegrated into the circle of their family and kin. Their days—weekdays and holidays alike—will be spent with their relatives from now on. The age of irresponsibility has come to an end, and acts which used to be allowed and even encouraged are now considered inappropriate and some are forbidden altogether.

On the last Sunday before his wedding the bridegroom bids farewell to bachelorhood. The whole *koma* group meets on this occasion to drink and sing; "the sweet-smelling leaf of the geranium has fallen; the best time of my bachelorhood is gone."

Each bachelor establishes a lifelong relationship with his favorite *koma* by asking him to be the godfather of his future children. As for the other *koma*-s, though a warm sympathy may remain among them, they have no occasion to meet each other regularly after marriage. If they run into each other on the road or in the smithy, mill, or office, they exchange cordial greetings and inquire into each other's doings, but they do not visit each other's houses unless there is a death in the family.

A married man lives entirely for his family and his work. This is the time when the foundations of his life are laid, his way of life is usually decided: to be a poor "teamless farmer," a harvester, striving to provide for his family by his own resources and hard labor; to be a "team owner" under the guidance of his father or father-in-law; or to be an independent farmer fighting for success.

Not infrequently the former leaders of the bachelor bands find the narrow family circle associated with married life too limited for their talents, and they often try to have a say in the affairs of the village too. Some are motivated by family tradition, others by the ambition to enhance their own status and that of their family, and still others by the promise of a small but certain cash income.

In Átány a man is considered "ripe, arriving at the zenith" by the age of forty, when he attains the fullness of his strength, abilities, and knowledge. After the son living in the father's household reaches this age the father "has more trust" in him and repeats more and more frequently, "You do it—you have more strength."

A man who has reached this age has to remove from his hat the night-heron's feather—the sign of rakishness—because "his time has passed"; the prime of his life is over. At this age it is proper for him to descend from the gallery to the ground floor of the church and occupy the pew of his ancestors, or sit beside them if they are still alive. A man of this age may be invited to a wedding only as *násznagy*; he should not join a band of the youngsters, but must sit with the older people.

In Átány the term "middle-aged" refers to men and women between forty and fifty years of age. During this time their physical condition stays about the same. Depending somewhat on the circumstances, real "old age" usually begins to set in between the ages of fifty-five and sixty. An aging man watches himself, noticing the decline of his strength and the weakening of his muscles, and the change is also observed by the people around him. As soon as his increasing weakness is apparent, people begin to say, "He is losing his resources; he feels the weight of his years. He is no longer what a man should be." A man approaching his sixtieth year is "going homeward" toward his grave. In the farm work, a man indicates his recognition of old age by putting down the scythe and ceasing to reap with the group, by which act he hands over his leadership and pace-setting functions in the work. The *gazda* then gives up one kind of field work after another, passing the duties on to his son, *vő*, or servant, and retains only the job of caring for the *kert* and stable and the general supervision. A *gazda* does not lose respect as his strength wanes, and although *he* may emphasize his declining ability to work, no one else does. He continues to be the most respected person in the household and his authority is not impaired by the weight of his years. The *zsellér*'s situation is quite different. He reaps, i.e., does the hard work of males, as long as he is able to. If he can no longer work as a harvester, he looks for an easier job: guarding fields, threshing by hand, or any other task he is still able to perform in his old age.

Marriage surrounds a young woman by even more prohibitions than it does her husband. A married woman may not sing a nonreligious song in the presence of others, and she may sing sacred songs only in her family circle; thus she is not allowed to join in a church choir. She has to avoid the playground and the walking places, and no longer may she dance in the tavern, only at family weddings.

From now on her place is at the side of her mother-in-law and she has to accommodate herself to her new environment. It is considered desirable to bear a child as soon as possible—if a son, to be the pleasure and helper of his father; if a daughter, to be the support of her mother.

Usually the newly-wed woman is considered a young woman for ten years, during which period she may sit in the young wives' pew in church. If she is bereaved in the meantime, or if her health is broken by the birth of numerous children and the rigors of work, she leaves that pew sooner. Occasionally when a young woman would like to remain in the young wives' pew, a bereaved mother-in-law, wanting the young woman to take over some of her sorrows, makes her *meny* give up light-colored kerchiefs and wear dark ones instead and take a seat with the older women.

According to tradition, an Átány woman would not think of taking part in the public life of the village, but would live only for her family. Even the wives of the local shopkeepers who worked in their husbands' stores and the midwives came from other villages or towns. Between the two world wars the more well-to-do *gazda*-s sent their daughters to the higher elementary school (the lower elementary school provided four years of schooling and the higher another four), but nobody thought of letting them go on to further study. Only the social reshuffling of the years after World War II has made it possible for an increasing number of Átány girls to attend high school and even college and to seek positions in skilled professions or village jobs such as assistant in the office of the town hall, saleswoman in the store, or weaver in the local cooperative weaving workshop.

When a woman becomes "middle-aged," after forty, she henceforth wears a rather dark dress and no longer takes communion on the day of a church festival, but rather on the following day, along with the elders: "It is more fitting than to go with the young ones." She hands over the work in the fields to a daughter or *meny*, if she has one, and busies herself around the house.

Though women mature and start to work earlier than men, they give up working later. Under ordinary circumstances a man of sixty no longer reaps. However, one finds numerous women of seventy kneading the bread and cooking for the household. A woman ceases to work only when her strength has failed to the point where she no longer can. Even in her decrepit condition she still tries to make herself useful by feeding the chickens, tending the fire, doing a little weaving, or looking after the children and the house.

OLD PEOPLE

Some of the old women of Átány live out their lives with their married sons or daughters or other members of the family. The widow, who is entitled to all the property of her deceased husband for life, may remain on the holding as *gazda* and direct the farming with her son as long as her physical condition remains good. Only when her strength declines does she retire from the duties of housewife, giving them up one by one. It is up to the young people to provide for her, to take care of her when she is sick and to bury her properly when she dies. Some well-to-do widows do not stay with their children but move to a separate little house "for widows" and lead a solitary life. Such women usually renounce their property in favor of their children, making an agreement whereby the children bring their mother a fixed amount of produce, fuel, meat, and other necessaries. Such a well-off widow, the "old *szüle*," is rarely alone. The family usually sends one of her grandchildren to her, to sleep in her house and help her in the household chores. Also her children—sons, daughters, and *meny*-s —pay calls on her almost every day. Fresh water is carried to her kitchen daily, the snow is swept away from in front of her house, and in the days when straw was still burned for heat, it was the job of one of the male grandchildren to bring this fuel to his grandmother during the winter. Nor does the old woman neglect to repay their services. She reserves all the dainty morsels for her visiting children, not allowing anyone to leave her house without being treated to something to eat. Those who are able to keep a piece of vineyard for themselves are in an especially favorable position, as they can offer wine to their kin in return for the services rendered.

If such an old woman becomes too helpless, she is taken to the house of one of her children for her last days; the family objects to her staying alone, since it would be shameful if she were to die without anyone near her.

In her old age a woman once again seeks the company of the *mátka*-s of her girlhood. Whenever they happen to meet they have long and tender conversations, holding each other's hands (see Plate 38).

An old woman who has no property at all is in a different situation. Usually this is a woman who in her youth found a place in the family of the *gazda* who hired her man for the harvest, her job being to help in washing, cleaning, and spinning the hemp. A good housewife provides her in return with all she needs in her old age. Friendly neighbors also help such an aged woman by bringing food and drink to her and picking up her room if she has no relative to do it.

Once a year, on New Year's Eve, the widows of the parish who are poor and alone are helped by the church; on this occasion the money gathered in the collection is divided among them.

Every old woman, rich or poor, prepares her funeral costume and keeps all the items together: the dress she wants to be buried in, the face-cloth, and the small souvenirs she would keep with her even after death. These may include a braid of hair cut in her girlhood, the tress of her favorite daughter, the portraits of her relatives, and so on. It is a frequent and natural occurrence to hear the old woman preparing for death repeat to the members of her family all her wishes about her funeral and the clothes she will be buried in. If she is too poor to be able to save for it, she grows anxious about the cost and tells her relatives her misgivings, asking what will be done with her after she dies. The authors heard such an old woman consoled by her daughter with the words, "Don't be afraid, mother; you won't be left out on the ground. We shall bury you."

Up to about the age of seventy the *gazda* continues to help the young people in a number of tasks. Gábor Varga at seventy-one told us, "I still do a man's work"— meaning that he looked after the cattle and mowed some of the grass for provender, but only by himself, in the slow way of old people. As long as such an old man is healthy, he attends the weddings of close relatives, dances with his *meny*-s now and then, and may even go to fairs. However, a man of this age retires from any office he may hold in the community, the church, or public life, since he feels himself too old for them.

But the presence of an experienced old man may be extremely useful for the family, the kin group, and even the whole community, especially if he formerly held an office. His advice is asked on questions of inheritance, and when someone dies he is called upon to preside at the division of the estate. A very good example is the case of János Boross, who held office in the village from 1904 to the end of the 1930s. His family had property and authority, and he added to the esteem in which they were held by his long service as "a man of the community." He was sixty-eight in 1944, when the battle line was coming closer and closer to the village. The German military authorities who occupied Átány tried to persuade the population to flee westward ahead of the approaching Soviet army. One evening the leaders of church and community assembled in the presence of a high-ranking German officer, and János Boross was also invited. After drinking for a while in silence, Boross asked the mayor why they had gathered. The mayor answered: "Listen, tutor [this term became attached to him on account of his long service as a public tutor], you are the oldest here; tell us what to do." He related the rumors of the plundering of the Soviet army and the proposal of the Germans that they evacuate. János Boross gave his answer in the following words: "Look here, mayor, the road is open to everyone. I do not want to dissuade anyone from going—let each man do what he thinks best. I, however, am not leaving my house, because I know that if I did I would find only the ashes later." His words became public knowledge, and the population did not move, except for some of the leaders who were not native to the village.

There were some roles and jobs particularly suitable for the old, even the oldest people in the village, such as stoking the fire in the *ólaskert*. Even today, though fires no longer burn in the *ólaskert*-s, a man too old to work in the fields is called "a fire-poking old man" (see Chapter 9, "*Tanyakert*-s"). And some group tasks are led or directed by the oldest guest, whom the company wants to honor. For example, when in 1953 they stamped dung for fuel at the house of Ferenc Orbán, the oldest helper invited was József Sárközi, a neighbor who was seventy-two years old and still in good condition. Before they started to work, the host handed the rake to József Sárközi, symbolically asking him to direct the process. So József Sárközi leveled the dung spread out for stamping, regulating its thickness and directing the women who were stamping it. When he had finished this part of the work, he took the spade and stepped in front of the male group, who were ready to begin cutting up the material into bricks. As the first helper, he controlled not only the pace of the work but also the size of the bricks to be cut.

In Átány a *gazda*, regardless of how much property he owns, spends his old age in honor. He is held in general esteem and is supported by his children willingly, if only in hopes of the inheritance. In the village an old man who is treated badly by his family, who is not given food, or who is not provided for with tenderness, is an exceptional case. It happens sometimes to poor people, but very rarely. Such a case is kept secret; at most only the nearest neighbors know of it, since a family that does not honor an old man is censured severely. One does hear some grumbling about old men, however: "An old horse is worth more than an old man. Why? Because if an old horse dies before autumn plowing, people say, 'What a pity, if only I could have used it for the plowing!' But if the old man dies, they say, 'Never mind; we shall bury him.'"

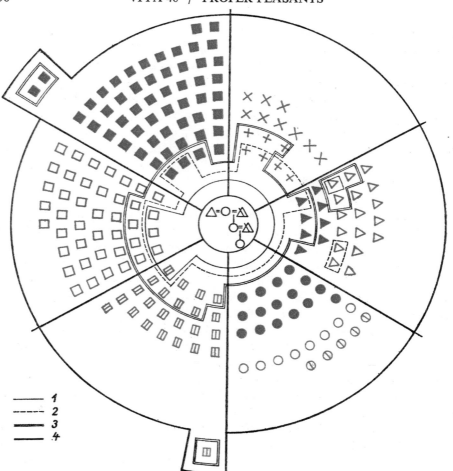

27. Close ties between the family of Ferenc Orbán and other families. This diagram presents a concrete example for the contents of the previous sections: it contains all the families with which the family of Ferenc Orbán had particularly close relations in 1954, on the basis of consanguinal and affinal kinship, neighborhood, baptismal *koma*-ship, friendship, and membership in the same age-grade. Ferenc Orbán belongs to the poor stratum of people who own draft animals, and the circle of his relationships is not especially extensive. For details on the family see p. 390. The symbols are identical to those in Fig. 28. In the upper left corner there are the relatives of Ferenc Orbán. Moving counterclockwise we come to those of his wife, and then to those of his widowed stepdaughter, Zsuzsanna Kálosi, who also lives in the Orbán household. The connections based on age groups come second. Among the *koma*-s of Ferenc Orbán we have listed also the "soldier *koma*-s" alongside whom he fought in World War I. Then come the "baptismal *koma*-s" and "friends," i.e., persons and families with whom there are connections of occasional lending and borrowing, mutual help, etc. Finally there are the neighbors of the house, the fields, and the vineyard.

In order to show how these connections function in everyday life we have drawn boundaries around the symbols of (1) those families which are invited to pigsticking by the Orbán-s; (2) those who help them to make fuel out of dung; (3) those who were guests in 1958 at the wedding of the step-grand-daughter of Ferenc Orbán; and (4) those who would take part in the burial ceremonies should Ferenc Orbán die. The last obligation includes all persons and families in the diagram. On the periphery we have included a few related families living in neighboring villages who were present at the wedding and who would also take part in the funeral ceremonies. Connections with other families living outside Átány are not included. The category of wedding guests is atypical, since the bride was only a step-granddaughter of the *gazda*. Thus fewer of the kinsmen of Ferenc Orbán were invited than of those related to his wife and his stepdaughter, who were kinsmen of the bride as well.

28. Close ties between the family of Ferenc Orbán and other families. The symbols of Fig. 27 are projected on a map. In the preceding diagram the symbols represented families; here they stand for houses. Thus there are fewer symbols on this map since in some cases two families live in the same house. Key to symbols used: (1) Relatives of Ferenc Orbán. (2) Relatives of the wife of Ferenc Orbán, Zsuzsanna Kiss. (3) Relatives of Ferenc Orbán's stepdaughter, Zsuzsanna Kálosi. (4) *Nász*-s of Ferenc Orbán. (5) Baptismal *koma*-s and "soldier *koma*-s" of Ferenc Orbán. (8) The *mátka*-s of Zsuzsanna Kiss. (9) The *mátka*-s of Zsuzsanna Kálosi. (10) Neighbors. (11) Neighbors of the fields and the vineyard. (12) The house of Ferenc Orbán.

People over seventy feel that each day that passes is worth two or three: "One reckons that he has not much left." Deterioration is not only physical but also mental, in "the brain." An old man has "neither eyes nor ears nor brains." He is no good for work; "he has nothing but a mouth." He can say what ought to be done, but he is unable to do it. There is no place for him in the fields; even a stranger, finding him there, may say, "The hoe is no longer for your hands, my uncle"; or "Why are you puttering about in the plowland? Your stride is no greater than a boot's length any more." His place is in the *kert*, in the stable. He may do things like spin hemp fibers, woodworking, and mend tools. If his wife is still alive, she makes him live in the house so that he can be nursed in his illnesses and later die there, since it would be a matter of great shame to the family if the *gazda* died in the stable. If his wife dies before him, however, he stays in the stable. His family bring him food and clean clothing, and he is brought to the house only when he is dying. He no longer goes to church or visits relatives.[17] If his strength permits, he attends funerals and visits the family of the deceased. He looks for his old *koma*-s from his bachelorhood again, since he does not feel too lonely as long as at least one of them is still alive. Having started his children on their career and brought them to an agreement on the inheritance, he has nothing to do but find pleasure in his grandchildren, who represent the continuation of his life, and to prepare for death. The old man says over and over again, "It would be fine to rest now—I am tired. Let it happen this year or next year, but I can't wait for long." The ailing old one likes to compare himself to the grain: "Man matures and ripens to be cut down like wheat." Several have their coffins made in advance of suitable walnut wood, and even lie down in them to see whether they will have a good rest inside. They also try to get acacia wood for their grave markers and to engage a man skilled in woodwork to carve them when the time comes.

---

[17] One of the rare occasions on which a married man leaves his home in the evening is when he has to escort his bachelor relative. It happens especially when the bachelor is courting a girl who receives the attention of others, in which case the married man's presence prevents a brawl. Generally he waits in the street for the end of the visit, then he may enter the tavern with the bachelor to have a drink, but he cannot sit to the bachelor's table, since married men have a separate table in the inn.

CHAPTER 11. TWO FAMILY CELEBRATIONS

The people of Átány are all aware of important events in the lives of the other villagers. Information of certain types of events spreads rather slowly and does not draw much attention, but other kinds of news spread rapidly and are of great interest to everyone. It may be two weeks before word of the birth of a baby reaches every house, but news of a wedding is spread much more quickly, and of a death most quickly of all.[18]

Although a wedding or a death is the concern of almost all the inhabitants of the village, such events are above all an affair of the kinship groups involved. In the whole life cycle, these are the two occasions when the entire kin group gathers and participates as a body. As we have described in Chapter 8, preparing for these events is a constant concern in the daily life of the people; they undertake some tasks and refuse others with the ultimate goal that whenever one of these two occasions arises there should be no impediment to the inclusion of all the relatives in the ceremony. We have noted that in the tasks and celebrations of ordinary life, a man invites only his family and close relatives to help, provide support, and share the fun. People keep track of the wider circles of their kin, but this circle plays no overt role in every-day life.

It is considered good to have a large circle of relatives. When a corpse is laid out, there is great satisfaction in seeing it surrounded by two circles of relatives and in having a house full of wailing kinfolk. Likewise, the sight of a numerous wedding party makes the old men in the family shed tears. When Károly Viski was eighty eight years old, the wedding of one of his grandchildren was celebrated in his house, with 140 persons present. All day long the old man kept expressing his joy: what a fine party; so many friendly relatives; everyone came; none of them are on bad terms with us; all are present. Almost everyone tries to avoid offending his relatives and to treat them in the friendliest way possible. In spite of these efforts, there are

---

[18] It should be noted, however, that not all bereavements generate the same interest. The death of a small child or a poor, solitary widow is primarily the concern of close relatives and neighbors. More compassion is aroused by a sudden or untimely death, a fatal accident, or the demise of an old man who is head of a numerous family.

numerous family feuds, primarily among close relatives, and primarily due to disputes over division of inheritances. Weddings and funerals provide occasions for reconciliation of the hostile parties.[19] "Whatever your relatives are like, that's the kind of wedding you will have," the saying goes, and this is valid for funerals too. The rank, importance, and dignity of the occasion are determined by the number, the appearance, and, most of all, the behavior of the relatives.

Those who are invited to share the feast and the fun of a wedding are expected to requite that invitation by joining the mourners when there is a death in the family. Kinsmen who pay frequent calls to a bereaved household often say, "We are relatives not only when we are invited as tapsters or *gazdasszony*-s to the wedding"—meaning that since they participated in rejoicing, they are willing to undertake the tiresome task of mourning. On the rare occasions when someone invites his friends instead of his relations to the wedding, the kinsmen ask, "Who will grieve for him?" People also say, "We don't want to attend his funeral if we are not invited to his wedding."

In both ceremonies neighbors of the house and the *kert*, fictive kinsmen, and *koma*-s and *mátka*-s from the age group also play a part, though it is secondary to that of the relatives. These are the times when the network of a family's social relations is made manifest, represented in concrete form.

THE WEDDING

A wedding celebration naturally involves two families and their kin groups. But the neighborhoods are also involved[20] to such an extent that the whole population of the village is divided into two groups: the wedding party, those who are "fortunate" because "they eat with a big spoon"; and the others, who watch the activities but are required by decency to stay away.

Both houses designate numerous (and identical) functionaries from the respective circles of their relatives and friends to serve as masters of ceremonies at the celebration and to take responsibility for serving and entertaining the guests.

The role of the godfather of the bride or the bridegroom as *násznagy* is the most honored. In the town hall and the church he is the official witness of the marriage, and at the wedding festival he occupies the place of honor at the corner of the table. He takes care of the timing of the celebration. "When the wedding starts, the *gazda* is no longer *gazda*; it is the *násznagy* who gives orders."

In Átány the bride and groom each have a "best man," who adds spirit to the proceedings. He invites the guests and leads the wedding party from one house to the

---

[19] In the case of a wedding, the wish to make peace is demonstrated mainly by the act of invitation. In the case of a funeral, where invitations are not customary, the kinsman who is on bad terms with the family may demonstrate his good will by attending.

[20] Not only the neighbors of the bride's and the bridegroom's families are referred to, but the neighbors of all the people who are invited to the wedding. When people go off to a wedding their neighbors take over their tasks in the house and the stable and are rewarded afterward with something to eat from the feasting house.

other at the appropriate times, and then to the town hall and the church. He is the first to serve the food, and he acts as chief entertainer of the party with his rhymes. The best man of the bridegroom is his best friend, his future baptismal *koma*; the bride's best man is the son of her godfather or a close kinsman. Godchildren or sons of relatives may also help out as attendants. Children sometimes act as "little attendants" and wear on their breasts the ribbon and the bunch of artificial flowers which are the badges of the best man and the attendants.

The two bridesmaids are favorite *mátka*-s of the bride; they walk on either side of her during the ceremony, and they carry the presents from the bride's house to the groom's house. The godmother, wife of the *násznagy*, acts as *gazdasszony* and takes charge of cooking and serving. Her task is shared by six or eight other *gazdasszony*-s whose husbands figure as *násznagy*-s subordinate to the chief one.[21]

The role of "tapster" is an honorable one, too, usually occupied by a favorite close relative of the family, "one who is trusted." He manages the wine and the bread. The *pados* is an esteemed female relative, usually an aunt or a sister, whose task is to divide and serve the cakes and pastry.

The gypsy musicians are professional entertainers who play from the beginning to the end of a wedding, according to the requests of the guests: dance music for the young people; slow, melancholy songs for the older guests.

Parents play no significant role in the wedding of their children; they have nothing to do but welcome the guests, exchange kind words, and be friendly and polite.

Both families celebrate in their own houses with their own friends and relatives. In the course of the celebration, however, one party visits the other at fixed times and for definite purposes. They usually bring gifts, liquor and milk bread for the other party. At the same time the bride gives presents to all the members of the groom's family, and the bridegroom to all the members of the bride's family.

The usual day for a wedding is Thursday. Ten days earlier, on a Sunday, the bride's and the groom's best men invite the guests of both houses. They each get a list of persons to be invited which indicates the role allotted to each guest, and they communicate these roles in the course of the invitation rhyme.[22]

The nuclear families of the bride and the bridegroom invite each other. For example, the bride's household is invited by the groom's best man with the following words: "So and so begs you, *bátyámuram* [uncle], to be his perpetual *nász*, you, *nénémasszony* [aunt], to be his perpetual *nászasszony*, and Mariska to be his perpetual daughter."

---

[21] Another reason for including all the male relatives who are forty years old or more in the category of *násznagy* (though the ceremony provides a role for only one) is that the wedding party consists of only two age groups: the dancing and reveling youth and the sedate older people. The older men sit in the corner at the table, acting as assistants of the real *násznagy*. Middle-aged men, considered too old to dance and make merry with the young people, are also seated in this group. The wives of this age group act as *gazdasszony*-s with the wife of the *násznagy* in cooking and serving.

[22] Once the circle of relatives to be invited has been decided upon, no discriminations are allowed among kinsfolk of the same degree. Leaving anybody out is regarded as an insult, and may be the source of permanent ill will. The relatives on the father's side must be invited to the same degree as those on the mother's side.

15

From then on the people invited make preparations, the immediate families of the bride and groom preparing most zealously. The guests bake milk loaves and buy gifts and take them to the family sooner or later according to how closely they are related: the closest relatives, four or five days before the wedding; the more remote relatives and the neighbors, not until the evening before.

Each invited couple brings a hen, a few eggs, one or two liters of wine, and five or six trays of pastry (see Plate 47). If the wedding is celebrated by landless families, the guests bring one or two kilograms of flour too. Two decades ago, when pastry was not yet fashionable, each family brought three milk loaves and three round trays of *rétes*. Brothers, sisters, first cousins, uncles, aunts, and grandparents give kerchiefs, dress material, kitchenware, and table sets as well as food. Godparents give most of all: one sheep, from twenty-five to fifty liters of wine, according to their means, twelve large trays of pastry or cake, and the traditional godmother's ten-kilogram cake. The bride's godmother buys the bridal wreath, sews the bridegroom's shirt or has it sewn (the material is bought by the bride with the money she receives at her engagement), and purchases the red polka-dot dress and kerchief which her godchild will wear for the bride's dance.

The day before the wedding is called "noodle-making day," though both families also prepare many other kinds of food on this day. Early in the morning all the *gazd-asszony*-s and other women and girls as well gather for "noodle-making" in white linen aprons specially made for the occasion. The near male relatives come too—the godfather and the *nász*-s. They pitch a tent in the yard to serve as the kitchen, butcher a sheep or other animals, assemble tables, and so on.[23]

The bridegroom, accompanied by his best man, goes to see the bride at least once on this day. In the afternoon the young couple and the *násznagy*-s visit the pastor to take the "censure," an examination in religion. In the late afternoon the *násznagy*-s begin to carry out their duties. A group of female kin, along with the *násznagy* and the groom's best man, come from the bridegroom's house to demand the bed (bed-clothes) of the bride. Protracted bargaining and joking begin, and the *násznagy*-s put riddles to each other and sometimes old, valueless coins are fetched to "purchase" the bed. The women tie the bedclothes onto their backs and, singing merrily, carry them to the groom's house (see Plate 48), where they make up a bed in the loft.

By the morning of the wedding day the house is ready for the celebration. All furniture has been removed except the table with the corner benches, which will be the place of honor and the only furniture used throughout the feast. Each time a meal is served the long tables and benches are brought into the room and placed along the front and back walls; after the meals, when the dancing begins, they are carried back

---

[23] As soon as a daughter is one year old her mother begins to buy and collect earthen plates, bowls, and bottles decorated with roses, so that the girl will be able to set the wedding table with her own crockery. Families who cannot afford to do this may have to borrow cooking utensils and tableware for as many as 120 guests. They borrow first from relatives, turning to their neighbors only if their kinsfolk cannot produce all the necessary utensils.

out to the yard.[24] The *gazdasszony*-s arrive first and start right away to cook food for the numerous meals (see Plates 49 and 50). The *gazda* of the house is a "general factotum"[25] on this day; he and the "tapster" wear working clothes and aprons.

The guests arrive during the morning, first the near relatives, later the more remote ones and the friends and neighbors. The *násznagy*-s take their places. Their table must never be short of wine, since they have to offer some to all who enter.

In the morning each of the two houses sends a cart to fetch the gypsy musicians. Both carts go to the bride's house first, where the horses are decorated with bells, fringes, and colored paper bands. After picking up the musicians, both carts return to the bride's house, where the musicians for the groom's house alight too and play a few tunes for dancing before going on to the house that hired them; the guests who have come from the groom's house ask the *gazdasszony* of the bride's house for a dance. The gypsies play continuously from the time they arrive throughout the wedding festival except for very short intervals. All the young people present begin to dance.[26] The two bridesmaids solemnly carry the bridegroom's shirt from the bride's house to the groom's house, and the groom's best man comes to the bride's house to announce when the ceremony will take place.

All these visits are performed in a state of faked drunkenness and hilarity, which is often quite unconvincing to the onlooker. The groom's best man asks for food and drink, and at first he gets carrots and water, and so on. All the joking goes on in front of the table of the *násznagy*, and the women are often as funny as the men.

After the visits the table is laid for lunch, which is the first meal but not the main one. Only the near relatives have arrived by this time. The food and the way it is served are simple. The gypsies, however, play during the meal.

The women cook food for many other people besides the guests. They send something from each meal to the people who were invited and who sent a gift of a chicken or some pastry but were too old and infirm to come themselves. Food is also sent to the "doorkeepers," the neighbors of the wedding guests who look after their houses during their absence and feed the animals. The sick people of the village are sent some food too, even if they are neither relatives nor neighbors, and a little something is tossed to the mendicant gypsy women as well.

Accompanied by her two bridesmaids, the bride goes to one of the neighboring houses to be dressed. When she is ready, her mother and female relatives come to grieve for her, kissing and consoling her: "This is how it has to be—we went the same way. It is very bad. Don't cry; this is the fate of girls."

---

[24] The houses of the families of bride and groom are used exclusively for the feast, the common meals, and the dancing and merrymaking. For other functions, neighbors' houses are used: one provides lodging for the kinsfolk and *koma*-s from other villages, another is where the bride is dressed, and a third serves as a place for the guests to leave their coats and shawls.

[25] If the father is dead, the mother's brother or another close male relative puts on an apron and undertakes the role of "general factotum."

[26] Mothers use this occasion to teach their children to dance: the small ones in their arms or on their laps, the older ones at the edge of the group of dancers. (They proudly show off the babies in their arms who, still unable to talk, move their arms to the rhythm of the dance.) Besides dancing, other behavior is taught to little boys. We heard a mother tell her five-year-old son, "Eat my boy, eat much. Don't drink until afterwards, so you will not get drunk."

At the appointed time the wedding procession starts out from both houses. The *násznagy*-s march in front, followed in one procession by the bride, her best man, and the bridesmaids, and in the other by the bridegroom. Next come women and girls. Only the *gazdasszony*-s stay at the house, tending the fireplaces and kettles. Bachelors and young people do not actually walk *in* the procession, but rather along with it, arm in arm, singing and embracing each other, and behind them comes the band. They stop at every corner, form a circle, and drink from the wine flasks they have brought with them. They offer a drink to any acquaintance they meet in the road. This is the best chance for people who are not included in the wedding party to participate in the occasion, at least as onlookers. People who live along the route watch the procession from behind the fences and even put chairs outside if the weather is nice. They are joined by their female relatives from farther away who want to get a look at the wedding procession.

The two processions meet in front of the town hall. The young couple and the witnesses go in, and while the civil ceremony is performed the wedding party waits for them outside. Then they all go over to the church for the religious ceremony. In the meantime the young people gather at the tavern and the bachelors from both houses treat each other to wine. The gypsies play and sing, and the girls not invited to the wedding are asked for a dance.

Up until the 1920s the wedding ceremony took place in the morning and afterward the bride and the groom returned to their separate houses to have lunch. Nowadays the two parties of guests still separate after the ceremony, but the bridegroom, along with a few young friends and relatives, accompanies his wife. As soon as they arrive at the bride's house, the music and dancing recommence. An early dinner is served in one of the neighboring houses for the young couple and a small group of their unmarried friends.

Later, at about sunset, the wedding procession from the groom's house arrives, with the *násznagy* in front and the musicians at the rear. The bachelors and young married men walk apart from this procession also, embracing each other and singing. The *gazdasszony*-s greet them in the yard and give them wine.

Inside the two *násznagy*-s start another session of protracted bartering, full of jokes, this time for the bride. They demand that she be presented. At first women disguised as old, lame hunchbacks enter, the real bride waiting until the third call.

When the bride enters, her husband stands beside her and the two best men on either side of them. After the rhymes of the groom's best man, the bride recites her farewell.[27] Brides' farewells are conventional verses supplied by certain women in the village, and all are almost identical in substance: the bride says good-bye to the members of her family one by one and thanks them for their love, not forgetting those who are deceased. Then the groom recites a rhyme announcing that he wants to found a new family with his bride and thanks his father-in-law and mother-in-law for bringing her up. The bride and groom stand in front of the table of the *násznagy*,

---

[27] See Appendix E for the text of a bridal farewell.

surrounded by their parents and all the other relatives from both wedding parties (see Plate 54). It is a touching scene, with many people crying and wiping their eyes. The bride kisses all her relatives good-bye, since she is about to leave them.

Then the wedding party of the bridegroom, led by the new husband, surrounds the bride and takes her to the groom's house. No one follows her from her parents' house except the bridesmaids, her most intimate friends.

The husband's parents wait in front of the door for their arrival. It is proper for the bride to step up first before her father-in-law and then before her mother-in-law, greeting them with this rhyme:

"I wish good evening to all the relatives,
especially to my father and my mother.
So I have come to this honorable house
to be a beloved daughter in this good family.
That you will receive me as a cherished guest
as I step over the threshold of the door now,
I wish with all my heart." [Literally translated.]

Or she utters the words, "May God allow that I be your good and obedient daughter." Her new in-laws answer, "So may God allow. Welcome my dear daughter." They kiss each other on the mouth. (Formerly the bride used to kiss the hands of her in-laws.) She is also kissed on the mouth by all her new close relatives.

Then the main meal is served. The bride's attendants call the guests to the table with rhymes and recite other verses while they serve the trays of food and the bottles of drink. The menu traditionally consisted of three dishes: chicken bouillon, stewed mutton, and mush boiled in milk. Nowadays potatoes or rice are served with the meat, and pastry or tarts are offered after the mush.

The tables are arranged in a U-shape with the open end near the door. The *nász-nagy*-s and male guests of honor sit at the corner, and the young couple sit in the center, facing the door, with the bridesmaids on either side of them. The other guests choose their places so that the close relatives and older people sit near the upper end of the table, close to the bride and groom, and the more distant kinsmen and younger people at the lower end. Husbands and wives sit together.[28] Children are served earlier, in a different place.

Although all the guests are present at this time, they cannot all be served at once, even in big houses. So at the end of the long dinner the table is set again for those who could not find a place the first time. Meanwhile those who have finished eating go off to the neighbors' houses. Bachelors and girls go to a house where young people are assembled, older guests to another. They all take wine with them, and drink and sing.

By this time it has grown dark, and the uninvited bachelors, the *gallér*-s, begin to appear among the gaping children. Wine and cakes are served to them outside, and the musicians go out too and play two or three tunes, for the *gallér*-s may now ask

---

[28] This is a modern custom. Before World War II women did not sit at the wedding table.

the girls of the wedding party to dance. (Formerly *gallér*-s brought their sticks and caused damage if their wishes were denied; housewives had to be on their guard, since they also used to steal food from the tent.)

After all have eaten, the tables are removed and dancing, singing, and merrymaking go on till morning. Should people get sleepy from too much food and wine, games are played to reanimate them.[29]

Singing goes on throughout the revelry. Usually one or two bachelors are standing in front of the musicians, singing and "directing" the music. Other circles of young men gather in the *pitar* or the pantry and link arms and sing together. They drink each other's health, clinking their glasses. Some young men may step forward from the singing groups and perform a new song which the others don't know; pairs or groups may sing songs alternately in competition or sometimes they try to sing each other down. Meanwhile the dancing continues. The traditional manner of dancing allowed an opportunity to show off individual talents, especially when the dancer, letting his partner loose, "made figures" alone.[30] Women are rather passive participants in the merrymaking.

The bride's best man, the host, the "tapster," and the close relatives who have been active in organizing the party see to it that no one is left out of drinking, singing, and dancing. This amiable carousing during the day-long wedding festivities establishes a new relationship among the participants. The sets of relatives from different lineages, *koma*-s, neighbors, and even friends from military service days who are wedding guests often live in different places and rarely meet. These acquaintances recall later that they "were *lakzi*-s," that is, that they attended the wedding together, and they feel closer to each other on account of it.

In the bride's house the feasting goes on after the bride has left. Before midnight, however, the younger men and women of the wedding party, led by the bride's best man, go to visit the new couple at the groom's house. Beforehand, the bride is taken from the groom's house to one of the neighbor's and dressed in the attire of a young wife. Formerly it was customary to put her to bed with the groom as soon as her wreath was removed, and then after a few hours to awaken the young couple with great solemnity. The women then gathered up the bride's hair in a knot, put a bonnet on her head, and led her back into the midst of the wedding party. Now the women merely change the bride's clothes, dressing her in a red dress and putting a red kerchief on her head. The bride's best man introduces the new wife with rhymes, and she offers roast chicken, her husband's wine, and the bridesmaids' milk bread to the guests, one after the other.

[29] One game they play is "stork." A bachelor puts on a white sheet and parades about as a stork with a long wooden beak frightening the young women and blurting out people's secrets. Or a "corpse" is laid out on a bench and a "minister" delivers a mock sermon over him. Drinks are offered in tricky vessels which dribble the liquid down onto the unsuspecting person's shirt or which will not let it leave the glass at all.

[30] One of the standards by which people are judged is their capacity for merrymaking. Just as a good worker or a good reaper is highly esteemed, so is a good singer, dancer, wit, or all-around reveler. At a wedding we heard a *gazda* congratulating his *sógor*; "How fortunate you are to have such a dashing grandson! I heard him sing for the first time; how nicely he does it!"

Then the "young wife's dance" begins. The groom's best man has one dance with the young wife, then allows the others to dance with her, crying, "Bride for sale!" In the old days a sieve was placed on the *násznagy*'s table and each guest bought a dance by throwing some money into it, the best man calling out the sum given by each.[31] Every guest has to turn around once or twice with the bride, even single women. In recent decades the bride has been receiving valuable presents in advance, so payment for the dance has fallen out of use.

The young wife's dance is a high point of the wedding. All the guests of both houses come together at the groom's house at this time, just as earlier they assembled at the bride's house, at the time the groom arrived to ask for the bride and take her away. The dance itself may last for an hour or more, until everyone has at least one short dance with the young wife. Finally the bridegroom asks his spouse for a dance, signaling the end of the young wife's dance.

After the young wife's dance the visitors from the bride's party, the *hőriszes*-s, go back to the house of the bride's parents or leave for home. In both houses, however, the merrymaking continues until the next morning. The *násznagy*-s and best men stay on duty until the end. Departing guests say good-bye to the host with phrases such as, "Thank you for the kind hospitality"; "God bless you, *komámuram* (or *sógorom*)"; etc. The *gazdasszony* tries to persuade her guests to stay, and when they do leave she has some cake packed for them: "she does not let them leave the house of the wedding empty-handed."

The next day is devoted to putting things in order. The families clean and straighten up the house and return the borrowed objects along with some cake as a token of their gratitude. The neighbors help with the rest. Sometimes the family can eat leftovers from the feast for a while, and sometimes they have to start cooking again right away.

Before World War I marriage ceremonies did not end at this point. After a week a "little wedding" was held to which only close relatives, up to two or three degrees distant, were invited. The sequence of dishes was the same as in the real wedding, but more carefully prepared since there were fewer people to feed. The reason given for holding the "little wedding" is that on the actual wedding day the crowd of neighbors, friends, and strangers prevented the family from serving the kinsfolk as much as they deserved; therefore this feast was held for their benefit only. More well-to-do people hired gypsies and made merry till morning all over again.

---

[31] The money collected during the young wife's dance was generally used to purchase a piglet or a calf. The animal was raised by the father-in-law and its milk was marketed for the common household, but the animal itself was regarded as the capital of the woman. For example, if the husband died young and the widow remarried, an animal of similar value was allotted to her by her father-in-law (without any consideration of the number of offspring of the original animal).

THE FUNERAL

The ceremonies surrounding a death may be divided into several phases. The first stage is the farewell visit to the person on his deathbed. The members of the family —parents, grandparents, children, brothers and sisters, *meny*-s, *vő*-s, *sógor*-s, grandchildren, and first cousins—all come to call twice a day and stay for an hour or two each time. Special friends among the neighbors also look in on the sick person several times daily and help take care of him; usually they do not stay long, however, but just enter the room where he lies and leave right away. Second cousins, baptismal *koma*-s, godchildren, and *koma*-s visit the dying person once every two or three days and stay for half an hour. Remote relatives (those of the third, fourth, and fifth degrees) and the house and *kert* neighbors pay only one call, at which they say their final farewell. They stay for half an hour or even less with the sick person. Those who honor him also pay a single farewell call; this group may include friends and people with whom he once held an office in common, or, if the dying man is a person of standing, the village elders themselves. Close relatives bring a present of soup, some hard-to-get fruit, candy, a refreshing drink, or some other special morsel; more remote relatives bring no gift. All day long the sickroom is full of people, crying and lamenting. The aged person endures his fate with calm resignation and even consoles the mourners: "Everyone who is born has to die." "I have lived enough; I am tired now." It is desirable that the whole family be present for the actual death; if someone is absent, he is sent for. Somebody is sent to the bell ringer so that he may ring the bell and call out the news of the death. The bell ringer hurries to the rectory at once and reports to the pastor: "We have a death, the widow of Gábor Szórád." Then he goes up into the tower to ring the bell. For men (and male children) he rings three "verses" of fifty chimes each with the small bell and then repeats the process with the big bell, for a total of 300 chimes. Then he "rings together" the big bell and the small one a hundred times. For women he rings only two "verses" with the separate bells and then "rings together" a hundred times just as he does for men. People hearing the knell who want to know more gather in the garden of the church or just outside the door while the bell is ringing. People in the nearby shop, the town hall, the market, or passing by the church wait for the tolling to end. Afterward the bell ringer stands in the open church door and "calls out, reports the dead": "Julianna Mikó, widow of Gábor Szórád," or whoever it is (see Plate 55). If an Átány man has died in another village and is to be brought home for burial, the sexton says no more; he does not "report" or "call out" the place of the death. If, however, the deceased is not to be brought home but will be buried outside the village, the bell ringer does announce where the death took place: "He died at Miskolc"; "He died in the hospital at Eger."

The deceased is dressed and laid out on a bier, called the "cold bed," in the center of the living room. It is surrounded by benches and chairs for the close female relatives who, as the "keening group," will play the principal part from then on. The bier remains there until the funeral. Until that time the deceased is never left alone and the mourning goes on continuously except for very short intervals.

Only women may stay in the room with the deceased. The keening group—mother, grandmother, wife, daughter, sister, granddaughter, and *meny*—sit around the corpse in a tight circle (a double circle if the family is large), lamenting the deceased loudly until the time of the burial. A constant background to the weeping women is provided by a sympathetic audience made up of friends, neighbors, and other relatives, filling the chamber of the dead (see Plates 56 and 57).

All over the village, as the news of the death is spread by word of mouth and the ringing of the bell, the women make preparations and set out in groups of three or four to view the deceased, especially in winter, when the labor in the fields and at home is less pressing. Until the funeral, the streets are full of small groups of women dressed in mourning, hastening to the bereaved house.

If the immediate family of the deceased is small and there are not enough women to surround the bier, aunts, *nász*-s, *koma*-s, and first cousins also join the circle. If there are enough women to form a full ring without them, these form a second or a third circle behind the closer relatives. Each group of women sits in the room for two hours without a break, tearful and silent, uttering at most a quiet question or a word of praise about the deceased, and then the group rises to make room for the next one. Mourning lasts all day long, but its peak is not reached until evening.[32]

There are short intervals for meals, but no cooking is done in the bereaved house. The *nászasszony*, baptismal *koma*, or aunt usually cooks for the mourners, who leave the deceased and go into the smaller room or the kitchen to eat. Their vigil is interrupted for a short period at night too if the mourners are so worn out from nursing the dying person that they cannot stay awake. In this case they take a short nap lying down, fully dressed, on a bench or sitting on a small stool in the chamber of the dead.

During the day relatives of the first and second degree pay two calls, one in the morning and one in the afternoon. In the evening both close and distant relatives gather in full number. This is the time for the baptismal *koma*-s, godchildren (who sometimes also come during the day), *koma*-s, friends, neighbors, and other devoted villagers to visit. Whereas during the day only women come to see the dead, in the evening men come too, although they do not enter the room where the body lies. When we began our field work there were still fourteen old men in Átány who used to attend the vigil of every single person who died in the village—regardless of age, sex, or social status—in order to sing together with the other male visitors. Benches are set up for them in the kitchen, and until a few years ago they were offered wine. Samu Jámbor was the leader of the male singers; as *diktás* (a man who leads the funeral singing), he "served" at the mourning of 800 persons, directing the men's singing. Ten or twelve men assemble in the kitchen, and at about 6 P.M. they begin to sing dirges and continue until 10 or 11 P.M., alternating with the women at intervals (see Plate 58). The female song leader directs the singing of the women from her seat at the foot of the bier.

The mourning follows a fairly standardized pattern. When a group of visitors enters

---

[32] Should the deceased be laid out for two days, the obligation of a visit was valid for both.

the room of the deceased, the keening group rises and utters loud cries of grief. For ten, fifteen, or twenty minutes, depending on the position and authority of the visitors and the closeness of their relationship to the bereaved household, they chant the sad story of the death, using improvised words and a traditional melody (see Plate 57). When their lament subsides, the women sing alternately with the men.

For example, the visiting women open the door saying, "János Balogh has now retired to rest"; or "He has finished, the poor one"; "He has gone to rest now, the poor one." They step forward and stand at the foot of the bier, bowing their heads and covering their mouths with their handkerchiefs. A close relative such as a first cousin or an aunt enters silently, steps up and finds a place at the "cold bed," grasps the side of the bier, and "utters a painful cry": "Alas, my dear brother János Balogh—oh, you have retired to rest, my dear brother János Balogh." Some say a little more: "Alas, my dear *nász*, the last hour has come; every illness has an end"; or "You suffered much, and now you have gone to rest in the dust of the earth." The visitors' cries of grief are echoed by the keening group.

The closest relative of the deceased, usually the wife (or mother), answers first, from her place at the head of the bier. "János Balogh is no more, alas, alas, alas, János Balogh is dead. Alas, he does not seek refuge from his many troubles any more, alas, alas, alas. Oh János, my dear companion, how much you wanted to stay, but still you had to go. Oh my goodness, alas, alas, alas! Oh, my dear God, why did you not give strength for his recovery?" Her daughter takes up the cry: "Alas, my dear father has died, alas, alas, alas. How hollow-eyed you are, alas. My dear God, how the great suffering can be seen on his face, alas." Then it is the mother's turn: "Alas, my dear son János, here is your large family around you. How he loved us, his family, how he was able to love, to esteem, to honor it. Alas, we did not say an ugly word to him either, alas, alas, alas. Woe to me, my dear dead son—oh, all we did was in vain, nothing was of any use. Oh, how your hard-working hands have grown cold." Lamenting, i.e., the chanting of these "painful words," follows an established melody, though sometimes the chanted cries of pain may alternate with spoken lamentation. All this is the affair of women; men never chant laments.

The length of time that the keening group stands up varies according to how closely they are related to the visiting person or how much esteem they feel is due to him. For example, when one of the authors arrived at the house of the deceased János Tamás and stood at the foot of the bier, the mourners stood up and chanted a lamentation which lasted for almost sixty minutes. Each taking her turn at the proper time, they sang the story of the sudden death—how János Tamás went to visit one of his brothers, and how after the visit he collapsed and died in the street on his way to his sister's house. "Oh, my dear lost one," began the widow. "My dear companion has died, alas, alas, alas." The daughter continued: "My dear father has died, alas, alas, alas." Then the widow resumed: "He washed and shaved before he left the house, alas, alas, alas. My dear companion has died." Like a refrain, the daughter repeated: "My dear father has died." Then the widow came in again: "Oh, if only he had uttered a word before leaving, my dear companion." The niece interrupted her:

"Yesterday my dear uncle was in our house; today he is dead, alas, alas, alas." The sister whom he could not reach: "Oh, my dear brother! Why could not my dear brother come to me, alas, alas, alas. My dear elder brother started out on his way, alas, alas, alas. Oh why could not my dear brother visit me, alas, alas, alas."

Only the tune of the lament and a few standardized phrases, such as the terms of address for the deceased, are fixed. The rest is improvisation and depends on the individual qualities and abilities of the woman. It is improper to leave a deceased person unmourned. Particularly fine examples of lamentation are recalled for a long time. Older women are the experts. The younger ones in their laments often excuse themselves and mourn the fact that they are not yet able to chant and express themselves as they ought to.

In some parts of the country the texts of the lamentations are prepared beforehand, but this is unknown in Átány. As one aged woman told us, "It comes from itself as pain dictates it. One remembers everything on this occasion." "It would be impossible to enumerate, what each one wanted to say. One doesn't know what her relative will say when she prostrates herself on the coffin." (The woman is supposed to respond to the lamentations of her relatives.) When we inquired about the substance of the lamentation—what is usually said about the deceased—we got the answer, "Each one is lamented according to his behavior." In general, the lament is the summary of the life, nature, deeds, and general attitude of the deceased; all these are now revealed, enunciated in front of the entire village, in effect, just as the interior of the house can now be seen by those who could not otherwise have gotten a glance inside. Bodily defects, such as lameness, are mentioned as well: "My husband, my soul, limping almost suited him." Nor is drunkenness or a cantankerous nature concealed: "My blazing fire, my flaring fire," lamented one woman. "Now you have gone to sleep. Your hands and feet are dried up; you won't beat me any more." The lamentation and vigil are the occasion when the households, accustomed to keeping all their private affairs behind closed doors, reveal to the whole village secrets which have been anxiously concealed from all but a few close kinsmen.

The women visiting the bereaved room watch and listen with critical attention. Some even express their opinions in a low voice. On a tape recording made by the authors at one of these lamentations, the most plaintive wailing of the widow was followed by remarks like this: "Woe' is uttered many times but 'my dear husband' not even once"—meaning that the widow could not have liked her husband very much since she failed to use the accepted term of address to him after death; and, "Better to weep where nobody sees you."[33]

Most of the time the chamber of the deceased is full, and in the evening there is not enough room for the crowd of visitors. In good weather they wait in the yard; otherwise they find shelter in one of the neighboring houses until some of the visitors leave the room and they can enter.

[33] A description and a series of photographs of the Átány lament were published in Kiss and Rajeczky (1966: 30–36, 93–100). In the same place the music and words of an Átány lament are given by Rajeczky.

The men who do not sing look for a place in the small room, the pantry, the stable, or even the stable of one of the neighbors. Relatives are bound by politeness to stay outside as long as there are other villagers who want to enter.

The vigil comes to an end at about 10 P.M. when the singing ceases. Acquaintances, neighbors, *koma*-s, baptismal *koma*-s, godchildren, and distant relatives leave slowly, one by one. The close kinsmen stay on for about an hour in order to mourn privately for the dear deceased and to discuss what is to be done next.

The sequence of events in the funeral is directed by the *bejáró*, whose duty it is to choose the resting place in the cemetery. During the vigil he asks three or four middle-aged men—*vő*-s, *sógor*-s, and *nász*-s—to come and dig the grave the next day. Also, an equal number of persons come unrequested to do this. The *bejáró* asks a neighbor with a good team of horses to take the coffin to the cemetery when the time comes, and he asks a close friend who is good at woodwork to carve the *fejfa* ("headpost," i.e., grave marker) and the "footpoles." (The coffin is carried on these latter, which are afterward driven into the ground at the foot of the grave. The grave marker is at the head.)

The funeral itself is the last phase of the proceedings. It begins with the closing of the coffin. Only the closest relatives, the keening group of women, and the *vő*-s, *sógor*-s, and *nász*-s are present when the coffin is closed. They carry it out into the yard, which is the site of the religious ceremony. All the deceased relatives and friends—all who visited the household separately during the vigil—gather there for the burial ceremonies. The old men of the village who go to all the funerals form a separate group, with the middle-aged men, relatives, friends, and respectful acquaintances on the edges. The keening group forms a dense circle around the coffin, prostrating themselves on it and embracing it. At the head of the coffin stand the closest male relatives. A crowd of women surround the group—the relatives nearer to the coffin, and the friends, neighbors, and acquaintances somewhat farther away (see Plates 59 and 60).

After the ceremony a procession forms to take the coffin to the cemetery, the pastor walking in front, followed by the men. Then comes the cart bearing the coffin, behind it the family, and last the crowd of women (see Plate 61). It is a custom peculiar to Átány that when the procession enters the cemetery, distant female relatives do not follow the coffin to the grave site but instead visit the graves of their own dead; the cemetery is filled by the sound of scattered cries. Only the members of the family and the men remain around the new grave. The men sing while some of them, the *vő*-s and *sógor*-s, lower the coffin into the grave and cover it. A dozen or more other men then together form the mound—all the neighbors and friends who particularly want to honor the deceased or to indicate their friendship and support to the bereaved family.

After the burial the close relatives and those who have helped to dig the grave are invited to the bereaved house for a small feast. The *bejáró* utters valedictory words to the deceased and bids the surviving members of the family to respect his last will and to divide the inheritance peacefully.

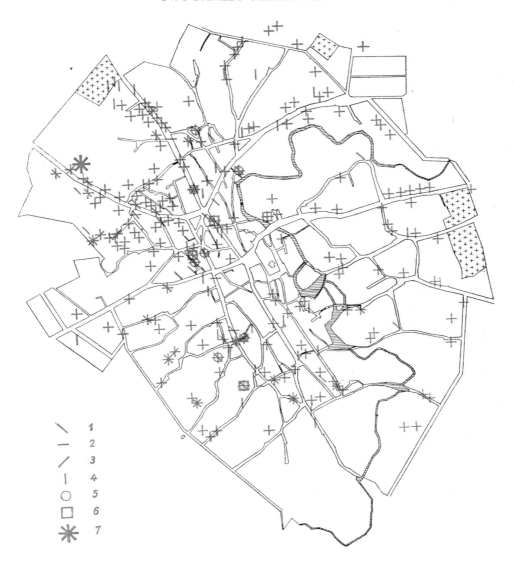

29. Persons attending the funeral of Gábor Varga. This map shows how many families expressed their sympathies with the dying man and in what form, and how many attended the funeral cere-monies. Key to symbols used: (1) Paid a call to the sick person in the Eger hospital or at his Átány house. (2) Went to view the deceased. (3) Took part in the common work of covering the grave. (4) Attended the funeral. (5) Lamented the dead. (6) Attended the burial feast. (7) The house of Gábor Varga.

After a short funeral feast, all the relatives go home except the members of the family, who stay and begin to discuss the division of the inheritance.

According to the Átány view, the dead man becomes a gateman in the Nether World; he waits at the gate until the next deceased person from his village comes to take his place.

PART FOUR
WAYS OF LIFE AND SOCIAL STRATA

CHAPTER 12. VARIETIES AND LEVELS OF SUBSISTENCE

The majority of the population of Átány are peasants who till their own soil, small landowners, landless day laborers, and people who work as farm hands, usually on large estates. Although the people of the village are well aware of the differences in wealth and way of life among these groups, they see them all as belonging to a superordinate category which distinguishes them from other citizens by the fact that all of them live by tilling the soil, either their own property or someone else's. They are "the people of the soil."

There are several strata not included in this category. The first is that of the *úr*-s. Before 1945, this term referred to the landowners of Szárazbő, Tenk, and Heves who lived outside the village but maintained direct connections with its people. Within the village the term *úr* is used for the pastor, the assistant minister, the teacher, and the village secretary. They live in the village but their relationship to it is different from that of the peasants. Their ancestors did not live here and are not buried here, and their descendants will not settle here. They are elected or appointed to a position in the village for the term of their service and they can be removed by a similar act.

The position of the craftsmen is more or less the same. Some of them moved to the village from other regions. They possess special knowledge and equipment and do not work and live like "the people of the soil." Other artisans belong to local families and thus are bound to the peasants by the ties of kinship, age-grading, and so on. They often do some agricultural work in addition to performing their specialized crafts. It would be hard to differentiate them from the "real" Átány folk—the people of the soil—although they do belong to an intermediate category. Railway workers likewise are an intermediate group. Much of the time they work far away from the village, but they take time off to participate in the harvest.

The differentiation between the peasants and the gypsies is of another sort. Though gypsies live in Átány, their homes are outside the village. In the eyes of the Átány peasants the difference is not simply that they make their living in a special way but that they are people of a lower sort, "being created different": they are "no Hungarians."

Table 11

Comparative Distribution of Agricultural Occupational Group by Status of Individual, by Census Period, 1900 to 1960

Year of Census	Status in Agricultural Occupational Group	Átány Village*						Heves District	Area of contemporary Hungary
		Number of			Percentage of			Percentage of Principals	Percentage of Principals
		Principals	Dependents	Total	Principals	Dependents	Total		
1900	Landowners, over 100 cadastral hold-s†	4			0.4			0.4	—
	Tenants, over 100 cadastral hold-s†	3			0.3			0.2	—
	Small-holders & tenant farmers	290	818	1,350	28.3	49.5	50.5	16.3	—
	Small-holder day laborers	50			4.9			5.3	—
	Share-farmers	18			1.8			0.5	—
	Helpers (member of family)	167			16.3			16.8	—
	Employees	1	...	1	0.1	....	0.0	0.4	—
	Servants	160	364	524	15.6	22.0	19.6	15.4	—
	Workers	332	469	801	32.3	28.5	29.9	44.7	—
	Total	1,025	1,651	2,676	100.0	100.0	100.0	100.0	—
1910	Landowners, over 100 cadastral hold-s†	4			0.4			0.3	0.4
	Tenants, over 100 cadastral hold-s†	1			0.1			0.1	0.1
	Small-holders & tenant farmers	100	871	1,456	10.5	55.3	57.6	} 23.8	30.9
	Small-holder day laborers	276			28.9				
	Share-farmers	...			....			0.2	0.7
	Helpers (member of family)	204			21.3			19.4	22.1
	Employees	2	3	5	0.2	0.2	0.2	0.3	0.3
	Servants	79	179	258	8.3	11.4	10.2	13.2	14.7
	Workers	290	520	810	30.3	33.1	32.0	42.7	30.8
	Total	956	1,573	2,529	100.0	100.0	100.0	100.0	100.0
1920	Landowners & tenants	328	543	1,192	25.2	41.5	45.8	20.9	26.3
	Helpers (member of family)	321			24.7			24.3	27.1
	Employees	1	...	1	0.1	....	0.0	0.2	0.2
	Servants	92	170	262	7.1	13.0	10.0	10.3	10.8
	Workers	558	596	1,154	42.9	45.5	44.2	44.3	35.6
	Total	1,300	1,309	2,609	100.0	100.0	100.0	100.0	100.0

Year	Category	No.	No.	No.	%	%	%	%	%
1930	Landowners, over 100 cadastral *hold*†	3			0.2			0.2	0.3
	Tenants, over 100 cadastral *hold*†	2			0.1			0.1	0.1
	Landowners & tenants: 50—100 cadastral *hold*†	5			0.4			0.7	0.5
	:10—50 cadastral *hold*†	102			7.6			6.6	8.3
	Small-holders & tenants: 1—10 cadastral *hold*†	306	{741	{1,514	22.9	{49.3	{53.2	23.0	23.0
	(including small-holder day laborers):								
	less than 1 cadastral *hold*†	14			1.1			0.9	1.3
	Share farmers	3			0.2			0.7	1.1
	Helpers (member of family)	338			25.2			23.7	26.6
	Employees	3	5	8	0.2	0.3	0.3	0.2	0.3
	Servants	134	280	414	10.0	18.6	14.5	10.3	10.8
	Workers: less than 1 cadastral *hold*†	91	{479	{909	6.8	{31.8	{32.0	5.6	4.5
	:landless	339			25.3			28.0	23.2
	Total	1,340	1,505	2,845	100.0	100.0	100.0	100.0	100.0
1941	Landowners & tenants	815	882	1,697	66.0	61.0	63.2	—	—
	Employees: engineers	1		1	0.1		0.0	—	—
	: farm managers	1			0.1			—	—
	: administrators		1	2		0.1	0.1	—	—
	Contractual employees: overseers	77	185	262	6.2	12.8	9.8	—	—
	: servants	2	5	7	0.2	0.3	0.3	—	—
	: attendants	4		4	0.3		0.1	—	—
	Servants receiving board	5	7	12	0.4	0.5	0.5	—	—
	Herdsmen, guards, etc. of village & commonage	10	28	38	0.8	1.9	1.4	—	—
	Field gardeners							—	—
	Seasonal workers							—	—
	Day laborers	313	328	641	25.3	22.6	23.9	—	—
	Other agricultural occupations	7	11	18	0.6	0.8	0.7	—	—
	Total	1,235	1,447	2,682	100.0	100.0	100.0	—	—
1949	Landowners & tenants : 25 or more cadastral *hold*†	28	58	86	2.3	4.4	3.4	1.8	1.6
	: 10—25 cadastral *hold*†	128	266	394	10.5	20.3	15.6	7.5	9.2
	: 1—10 cadastral *hold*†	442	812	1,254	36.0	62.0	49.5	42.1	37.4
	: 0—1 cadastral *hold*†	18	29	47	1.5	2.2	1.9	3.0	3.2
	Other independent agriculturists							0.1	0.1
	Helpers (member of family) of land-owner or tenant having: 25 or more cadastral *hold*†	34		34	2.8		1.3	1.7	1.4
	10—25 cadastral *hold*†	135		135	11.0		5.3	7.2	9.5
	1—10 cadastral *hold*†	318		319	26.1		12.6	27.8	23.7
	0—1 cadastral *hold*†	2		2	0.2		0.1	0.1	0.7
	Employees								0.3
	Workers	117	145	262	9.6	11.1	10.3	8.0	12.9
	Total	1,223	1,310	2,533	100.0	100.0	100.0	100.0	100.0

* *Administrative unit; includes outlying areas.*

† *1 cadastral hold = 1.42 acres.*

16*

"The people of the soil" are divided into two large groups: "team owners" and "teamless farmers." The first group consists of the land-owning *gazda*-s who possess a team as well as a plow, a cart, and the other equipment used with draft animals. These families are able to perform all the tasks of tilling the land, those which require draft animals and those which do not. The opportunities of the teamless farmers are greatly limited. Some of them have a small plot of land which is insufficient to provide for a team of horses. Others are wholly landless but make their living by working for others and receiving wages or a share of the produce.

Beside these two large groups there is a third, which is only loosely attached to the population of the village. This includes the farm hands and tobacco growers who live on manorial farms outside the village. They may be linked to the community by numerous personal ties of descent, kinship, and friendship, and they strive to return to the village with their offspring. (All data on large estates and farm hands refer to the pre-1945 period.)

One finds the same groupings in other Hungarian communities. In the towns and cities, however, the occupations are different. They contain strata which are not represented in Átány. Here there are *úr*-s by profession too, but in the opinion of the local *gazda*-s, the landowner is the only real *úr;* though the attire and way of life of a professional, "a learned man," may be similar to that of a landlord, he is still in another's service and obeys his orders. Likewise, a doctor or a lawyer must serve others. (The authors, especially at the beginning of their research, were also accorded mild compassion: "Poor ones, they have to earn their bread like this, going from house to house." The real bread is growing on one's own land in Átány.) Industrial workers and the poor of the cities are compared to the agricultural wage earners, usually to manorial servants and day laborers. Thus it is degrading for a landowning *gazda* to work in the town. The poor of the village maintain a different view on this point. To them the city means greater mobility and more opportunities, especially for the agricultural laborers and tobacco growers who live in *tanya*-s outside the village, since the ways of rising inside the village society are generally unavailable to them. Compared with the dreary world of the manorial farms, the town environment seems attractive.

This chapter surveys the social stratification defined by property and the means of subsistence in the village.

TEAM OWNERS

Various types of teams are owned by the Átány peasants. Some raise young colts and use them to till their soil, others own valuable adult thoroughbred horses. In some stables oxen as well as horses are found, and a few farmers keep only oxen, though this is exceptional. There are also great differences in the sizes of the farms to which these teams belong. The dividing line between team owners and teamless farmers runs in the category of small farmers of six to eight *hold*-s (8.52 to 11.36 acres). The owners have the choice of keeping a team and tilling their own soil, additionally working for others, or living the life of a teamless farmer, in which case they would get others to do the jobs requiring a team on their land or give it to a *métayer* tenant. A few holdings of approximately eighty *hold*-s (113.60 acres) are the largest peasant farms.

Regardless of the size of the farm, the primary concern is always mixed subsistence agriculture (see Chapter 2, "Agriculture"). However, there are differences in the management of these farms. Type of labor organization tends to correlate with size of farms.

The traditional common principles of farming determine the tasks in relation to the size of the landed property, to the amount and kind of manpower of the family, and to the number of animals owned. Manpower and animal labor are to some extent changeable: the *gazda* may increase the livestock until he reaches the level most suitable for the size of his farm, or he may supplement the manpower of his family with farm hands or wage earners. Thus size of holding still represents the most solid basis for classifying the types of farms. This is the standard used by the people of the village to compare the various farms, although they may add a statement about the "standing" of this or that peasant in his farm.

In most cases the quantity of arable land is still computed in terms of the categories of the feudal *telek* system. People speak of a *fertály* (one-quarter of a *telek;* 10 to 12 *hold*-s; 14.20 to 17.04 acres), a *félhely* (one-half of a *telek;* 20 to 24 *hold*-s; 28.40 to 34.08 acres), or a plot of three or four *fertály*-s (40 to 48 *hold*-s; 56.80 to 68.16 acres), this last being equal to a whole *telek*. For many decades there was no obstacle to fragmentation of plots in the conveyance of property; thus there are now many plots smaller as well as many larger than the units of the *jobbágy* times. However, the types of farms are still characteristically described by the names of *fertály, félhely,* and full *telek*.[1]

In the lowest category of team owner is a *gazda* owning a *fertály* or an even smaller plot. To provide food for the horse and to make the best use of it, he has to find other occupations for the animal besides the cultivation of his own land. The most usual occupations are cartage, cultivation of land for money or half of the produce, and horse dealing.

The "carter" regularly does paid work with his wagon. He makes it known to the community that he will perform this service for all and sundry. Some of them have the town crier announce that they are ready to serve with their carts from that day on. They are then called upon to convey goods to the railroad station, to fetch produce from the fields, to transport persons, and to help in plowing, sowing or harrowing in the spring or fall. The carter has to give up seeing "his horse trot

---

[1] The different *telek* sizes mean not only quantitative differences in the peasant farms but different structures. At the time of the serfdom the proportions of various cultivated crops were prescribed by uniform rules for all peasants. But animal husbandry was exempt from these rules. The 1828 census shows that in Átány different patterns of livestock keeping were joined to the different *telek* sizes. Each serf who owned one-quarter of a *telek* had a team of two or three horses, each *gazda* who owned a whole *telek* possessed four oxen and in most cases a team of two horses, or even four. The different composition of the teams of draft animals reveals that the organization of animal and human work was quite different.

delicately; it was driven each day from spring to autumn and sometimes in winter too." He was paid in cash or in kind for these services.[2]

These people often undertake some major work as a group, led by the "carter *gazda*." Such work may be transporting tobacco from the neighboring estates to the state receiving station in winter; transporting baled fodder to the railway for village merchants; or transporting stone for road construction. These major tasks are contracted for by the leader of the group, the "carter *gazda*," who then enlists participants. They work together and divide their earnings into equal shares.

It is said that cartage yields enough to maintain a family and farm but not enough to increase property. The hard-working horse must be given much provender, and the *gazda* can rarely resist the temptation to stop at the taverns he passes on his errands. It is thus more profitable to take up land on lease or on half profit.

In *métayage* the worker does all the work on the plot and divides the product with the owner in equal shares. The plan of cultivation and the order of tasks are fixed by the proprietor. It is agreed on in advance how many times the corn will be hoed and which part of the land will be manured. The owner often helps in the actual work and he warns the farmer when the date set for some task approaches. (As a matter of fact, the proprietor still directs the farming and is involved in all operations, but through *métayage* he secures all necessary labor in advance.) The half-and-half system is favored by old people or families who have no male children and are not interested in increasing their wealth. Thus the family of József Kakas rented out ten of their eighteen *hold*-s of land (14.20 of 25.56 acres) on *métayage* when the old *gazda* felt the burden of age. On the whole, not much land is cultivated by the half-and-half system—no more than a tenth of all the peasant land.

The amount of land leased out for a fixed sum is even smaller. According to the people of Átány, only lazy people lease out their land, people who won't accept even the task of directing and controlling the work of the sharecropper. Teamless farmers who leave the village to try to make some money by working in Budapest are forced to choose this solution for their land. The property of the community and the church, and sometimes part of the land allotted to the pastor, the village secretary, and the schoolmasters, is also commonly leased out.

The lessee would use the rented land for whatever he wanted to. The rent, fixed in advance, was less profitable for the owner than the half-and-half system but, on the other hand, he was spared the care of farming, and a poor harvest did not affect the amount of rent. Usually the contract covered a period of from three to six years.

It is held at Átány that *métayage* and leasing land were profitable only for those who possessed some land of their own and who used such an arrangement to complete their property, as it were. Leasing land, unlike cartage and horse dealing, has the advantage of securing work for all the family.

The same stratum which produces the carters and *métayers* also provides the

---

[2] For example plowing one *hold* was repaid by a *mázsa* of alfalfa in spring; carrying the straw allotted to a sharecropper in the nearby estates, by one and a half *véka*-s of oats for each turn of the cart. Bringing in the grain from the fields was also paid for in kind, according to the distance traveled.

majority of horse dealers. It is said of them: "Such a man was prevented by his plot and livestock from going to work"—meaning that he did not have enough time left over after his chores at home to undertake work outside the village, as a teamless farmer would have done. "On the contrary, he cultivated his plot with the horse he bought and made a profit on its sale in addition."

Two or three of the well-to-do *gazda*-s also engage in horse dealing. In the course of one journey they buy as many as four to six handsome and valuable horses with the purpose of selling them to the army, to buyers seeking quality, or to foreign merchants. The majority of horse dealers, however, usually totaling thirty to fifty, belong to the stratum of small-holders. They are unable to purchase many horses at a time; in fact, they usually have just two or three at a time, which they use on their farm until they sell them. At the Jászberény or Jászapáti fair, or when peasants from the northern areas visit the village, the dealers sell their horses and then set out for the southeastern regions of the Great Plain to buy new ones. Occasionally two teams are sold in a single week. Dealers may also keep a pair of colts for several months or a year and then sell them at a profit when their value has been increased by growth and training.

Dealers are able to make a profit because horses are cheaper in the south than in the mountain district of the north, where horse breeding is uncommon. Prices also vary with the season; draft animals are cheaper after the fall plowing and more expensive before the spring work. The relation of supply to demand also causes significant fluctuations in price. The value of individual horses varies widely. A shrewd purchaser who can recognize valuable animals can gain much, and an inexperienced one can lose just as much. Astute bargaining also contributes to success. Because of the risks and the demands for bold and shrewd action, alien to the customary activities of rural farming, the rest of the peasants look at the enterprises of the dealers as games of chance; these very risks, on the other hand, establish a close solidarity among the traders themselves. They are referred to as the "people going outside," since they wander in distant regions unknown to the other villagers.

The minimum amount of land necessary for an owner to make his whole living by tilling his own soil is fifteen to twenty *hold*-s (21.30 to 28.40 acres). In the opinion of the people of Átány, "a good [i.e., sufficiently numerous] family is able to live on fifteen *hold*-s of land here. A good family can work this plot and may keep a brood sow, two pigs, two cows, and two horses. Less than this is not enough for subsistence; the family must look for supplementary income." The larger autonomous, self-sufficient farms, of approximately twenty *hold*-s, are in the *félhely* category. The *gazda* of such a property does not undertake work for another, even if he is not using his team for his own work. He makes an exception only "if he has a harvester, a friend [small-holder, teamless farmer], whose work he does along with his own, as it were." This work performed with the team is not aimed at getting money or reward in kind, however. The *gazda* undertakes it so that he may ask the teamless farmer to help in his farming in return. A considerable part of the labor on these farms is done by outsiders. The harvest is entrusted to sharecroppers, as is partially hoeing the cornfield. The male members of the family take care of the livestock, do the plowing, prepare the fodder, and work in the vineyard. Even in poor years such *gazda*-s are able to take a surplus to the market and to store up considerable reserves. Stock breeding is the most profitable aspect of their farming. This, then, is what differentiates the *gazda* from the poor peasant, who has to sell his young animals soon after birth at a disadvantage. The *gazda* keeps and raises his calves and colts and sells them as trained animals at a good profit.

This stratum, "living by its own property," and the owners of larger amounts of land are the ones called *gazda*-s in Átány. Those who have less land are not *gazda*-s, just "medium holders," "middle-class."[3] For the people of Átány, especially the old people, the image of a *gazda* is closely connected with raising foals. "*Gazda* is one who drives a relay horse [a colt or a filly harnessed to the team of horses] or a four-in-hand team with colts." "The *köz* was full of them as they drove out."

However, careful and extensive horse breeding is possible only on holdings of about forty or fifty *hold*-s (57 to 71 acres), equal to the entire *telek* of feudal times. On such farms one or more teams of oxen are kept in addition to the horses, and it is said of wealthy *gazda*-s that in summer they take the horses out of the stall only when it is cool; "they protected them even from the rays of the sun."

Besides the power gained by having two or three different teams of draft animals, these farms have a much wider range of human labor at their disposal. The members of the family are aided by one or two permanent servants whose work is supplemented by harvesters, day laborers, and occasional assistants called in for special services. Most of the produce from such farms is sold at the market.

TEAMLESS FARMERS

The teamless farmers generally own houses and yards in the village, though some of them live in rented houses. Pigsties and poultry coops are visible in the courts of the teamless farmers, and if possible these families keep a pig for sticking and raise poultry. Some houses are joined by small cowsheds. Their plots are equal to the ancient holding of a *zsellér*, the *massza*, originally 600 square fathoms (about 23,000 square feet) of arable soil and the same amount of pastureland. Occasionally they possess a dwarf holding of a few *hold*-s as the result of two or three *massza*-s being accumulated or of ancient *jobbágy telek*-s being divided. Many of these people are landless, however. Their common attribute is that they earn their living by work "on the soil of another."

As we have mentioned, the *gazda* thinks that "the wheat takes first place because of the bread." In his plowland he chooses the site of the wheat first, the most fertile and the best cultivated piece. Similarly, the teamless farmer allots a central place in

---

[3] "Middle-class" is a term used in Átány. It refers to small-holders who have a team but who are not real *gazda*-s because they are forced to work for others on land which is not their own. Thus they occupy a central position between the *gazda*-s and the poor.

his schedule to the work of harvesting wheat in return for a share of the crop; this is a guarantee that he will procure almost all the bread the family will need for the coming year.

The harvester usually reaps the wheat and other grain according to a fixed agreement. He recruits a swath-layer from his family or engages a paid helper[4] who helps to gather and stack up the grain after the harvest. He is paid a tenth of the grain, either in the form of reaped sheaves or in both grain and straw after threshing. Besides these general items the agreement may contain a number of other services and allotments.

There is a difference between harvesting on the large estates and on the holdings of the *gazda*-s in the village. Led by a "reaper *gazda*," groups of from twelve to twenty harvesters contract with the estate. Every year, from 120 to 140 men and women from Átány usually join these bands. At the beginning of the harvest the "band" moves to the manorial farm. They return home Saturday evenings and spend Sundays with their families. The women carry warm meals out to their husbands and the swath-layers every day at noon. To reach the distant manor, the women must walk for one and a half to two hours, with the food carefully covered up to keep it warm. They wait for one another and go in groups. Some of the more remote estates send carts to the village to transport the women.

The band of reapers often works at the thresher as well. Usually the estates engage one band of harvesters for each threshing machine and the men thresh the grain they have reaped themselves. For this service the band receives 3 per cent of the threshed grain, distributed among the members. Generally the estates figure on "one scythe" for ten *hold*-s (14.20 acres) of grain.

The reapers who work for the *gazda*-s of the village have less land to cover,[5] and the fields are near the village so the harvesters are able to return home each day. A *gazda* has enough work for only two or three harvesters at most. On the estates the reapers work quickly but not very carefully, whereas the *gazda*-s expect them to be meticulous and thorough. In Átány it is regarded as an insult if someone is told, "You are reaping like on an estate." The harvesters of a *gazda* do not do the threshing. The thresher is run by special helpers or, more recently, by bands who move from farm to farm with the machine.

The harvesting and threshing last much longer on the estates than on the farms

---

[4] Each harvester is followed by a weaker laborer—a woman, a girl, or an adolescent boy—whose duty it is to gather the reaped wheat into bunches and to prepare it for sheaving. The swath-layer does not receive a share but is paid fixed wages for the entire harvest season: four *véka*-s of wheat and a *véka* of barley. In addition the girls receive enough money to buy a headshawl, paid by the reaper in advance when the agreement is made in the spring. During the harvest the reaper provides the swath-layer with meals.

[5] Aside from the size of the area he reaps, the income of the harvester depends largely on the "quality of the *gazda*," the type of soil, the methods of cultivation, and the development of the crops. The sharecroppers prefer to work on farms and estates where the soil is relatively good and the farming relatively intensive.

Depending on the quality of the harvest and the size of the area, a sharecropper may earn from five or six to twelve or fifteen *mázsa*-s of wheat; eighteen *mázsa*-s is remembered from a year of an especially successful harvest. About two-thirds of this payment is in wheat, one-third in barley and oats.

of the village *gazda*-s and the workers are able to earn more. But the profit is diminished by the necessity of transporting food to the reaper on the distant estate over a long period of time. For two months the *gazdasszony* has to prepare the best food for her hard-working husband and his swath-layer; a considerable part of her day is spent carrying their meals. Many people do not undertake reaping on the estates because they "have no family for the purpose" of bringing them food.

The work of harvesting and garnering for the *gazda*-s lasts for a week or two and proves to be very profitable for those who have a permanent occupation in Budapest and take time off from their jobs in town to work as harvesters. As a rule, those who reap on the estates plan to work there as day laborers throughout the year.

The estates and most of the *gazda*-s allot a half or an entire *hold* (1.42 acres) of corn field to the reaper, allowing him to keep one-third of the produce grown on this area. However, in many instances, he is granted a half—and exceptionally he may take all the produce except the corn stalks, which are kept by the landlord or the *gazda*. In this case the sharecropper is bound by contract to continue working for a number of days without pay. They are usually set the task of mowing for three to ten days, depending on the benefits received. Sometimes the contract obliges the harvesters to do some additional work on the estate in the fall "for the current day-wages."

Whenever some male labor is needed on an estate over and above the work covered by contract, the manors make use of the organized reaper bands. The "reaper *gazda*" is the mediator. From time to time he visits the manor and inquires how many men are needed and for what kind of work and he then enlists workers from among the members of the band. According to our informant, "Because my father was a sharecropper [in a band], he was engaged on the estate throughout the year; he never went elsewhere. Now he was called to mow, then to transport manure, to gather turnips, or to dig out a tree stump in winter." The children of the sharecropper also find work on the estate clearing the fields of weeds and thistles in the spring.

But not all labor needs of the estates can be satisfied by the reaper bands. Some chores are performed for day-wages, others for a share. Mowing,[6] pruning, and digging out stumps are done for a share. Besides the portions of corn field allotted to the reapers on the half-and-half system, other portions are allotted to cultivators for one-third of the produce, the stalks being left for the landlord. Those who work fields on this condition begin with the land already plowed and sown.

The estates usually engage day laborers for weeding the sown fields, carrying manure, and cultivating the vineyards and especially the sugar beet fields. It is said that for eight months, from the first hoeing until the harvest, girls and women can always find work in the sugar beet fields. Sometimes the estates publish the job openings by drum, and when the need for labor is urgent, the landlords attempt to outbid each other. Each big estate has a representative in the village entrusted with the recruitment of the desired number of day laborers.

---

[6] Mowing of alfalfa was paid for by a sixth or seventh of the crop; of hay by a fifth; of the after-grass by a third. The haying on large meadows was undertaken by groups or "bands," who worked together and divided their share of the hay into equal parts.

The day-wage men meet at the end of the village at sunrise and start out for the estates together, sometimes in groups of eighty or a hundred people. Sometimes the crowd "resembled a black cloud." Each brings his own tools as prescribed in the advertisement. Groups of forty or fifty day laborers are organized under the direction of an overseer. When "singling" (weeding out the superfluous plants) or hoeing the beetroot, the workers proceed side by side at the same pace. One day-man works two rows; young boys and girls "take up" one row and receive half wages.

There is work for day laborers on the farms of the *gazda*-s too, though less than on the estates. *Gazda*-s pay the same wages as the estates but provide the worker with meals in addition. We were told that the extra benefit of free meals is offset by extra labor, since the *gazda* leads the work himself, setting the pace and controlling its thoroughness.

With the beginning of winter the job opportunities decrease both in the community and on the estates. Men and bachelors help to transport manure; women and girls may select peas for sowing. There is also the possibility of working with the tobacco growers. Dried tobacco leaves are flattened, classified, and made into bundles from early or mid-November. The work lasts for six or seven weeks. The helpers are engaged for a fixed sum and in addition receive board and a place to sleep in the work room.

After World War I the estates instituted a new method of securing the necessary day laborers by making contracts in advance and for longer periods of time. Agricultural laborers engaged in this manner are called *summás*-s because they receive their wages in a lump sum.[7] The people of Átány consider their situation more favorable than that of laborers hired from day to day because of the slightly greater wages and the more long-range security. There are "spring" and "autumn" *summás*-s who contract to perform the tasks of cultivation or harvesting for two months of the appropriate season. There are also *summás*-s" for four months" and "for six months." The bands of *summás*-s are recruited by the *summásgazda*-s, who receive half a *hold* of corn field from the estates in return for this service.

Between the two World Wars *summásgazda*-s from quite distant estates occasionally came to the village to recruit workers for periods of two months or six months. They sought female labor for hoeing and sometimes male labor for mowing. The groups traveled by train, carrying their implements and their simple personal effects. At their destination they were lodged by the landlord, who also provided food, which was prepared by themselves or by the wife of the *summásgazda* for all of them. Some years as many as one hundred people left the village for this sort of service.[8]

The reapers and day laborers engaged by the nearby estates and, more importantly,

[7] For instance, a *summás* might receive 80 kg. of pure wheat, 40 kg. of rye, 4 kg. of bacon, 1 kg. of salt and red pepper, and some cash for two months' work.

[8] Poor peasants who were forced to undertake work in other parts of the country were more or less specialized according to regions. The peasant towns of the southeastern Great Plain sent bands of pick-and-shovel men throughout the country and even abroad to build dams, railway lines, and roads. Some well-defined relatively small areas specialized in groups of *summás*-s to cultivate and harvest on the large estates. Átány lies at the boundary of one such area whence seasonal workers, *summás*-s, used to travel to almost all regions of Hungary (Schrikker, 1953).

the *summás*-s who travel to remote places are examples of people who have found occupations outside the economic system of Átány. In addition, the number of people who leave the village for a certain period for urban jobs has been increasing since the end of the last century. Since the 1880s there have always been a few people from Átány in the iron works of Miskolc and Ózd, at the sugar factory of Hatvan, building earthworks for flood control in various parts of the country and even abroad, and most of all in Budapest. Átány residents relate that at the turn of the century and especially during World War I, "Átány discovered Pest and also Pest discovered Átány." The villagers recognized the opportunities for work and earning in the capital and were acknowledged by the city dwellers as good workers in certain occupations. Gardening and laying out and repairing sports fields have become their specialities. Groups of fifty to one hundred villagers also worked on the construction of roads and bridges, and during World War I many of them found jobs in war factories.

Formerly most teamless farmers regarded a job in Budapest as only a short-term enterprise suitable for seasons when there were no jobs in the village, such as from late fall through winter and before mowing began in the spring. But over the years more and more of them found permanent jobs in Budapest and returned to the village only for short periods. The majority tried to reserve the right to return for the harvest, however. "At some places they only wanted to engage us for the whole year but we did not accept, since harvest was the most important thing of all. We would not have been able to purchase wheat for money."

Originally work in the capital was a man's job. After the 1908 Balkan crisis, however, girls also were recruited to Budapest to work in cartridge factories. During World War I the war factories of the capital provided jobs for whole groups of women and girls. Like the men, they tried to return home for the harvest, in order to work as swath-layers.

At the turn of the century and between the two World Wars teamless farmers even looked for work abroad. Some tried their luck in the United States; others formed small groups of seasonal workers and went to Germany.

The families of teamless farmers live on the earnings from any or all of these various occupations, according to the circumstances. "In the spring, in March, I went to Pest for a while. But I had to return home in May. The season of hoeing and mowing had begun. On the estate where we contracted to reap we got a *hold* of corn field for the half share; we had to hoe it and we were also obliged to do some mowing on the estate. Then came the harvest and threshing. In the fall we were able to stay in Pest again for two months. We came home when it got cold. In November we took up tobacco bundling; that lasted for six or seven weeks, sometimes until mid-January." This story portrays a good year, but there are still gaps when no work was available. In fact, the teamless farmers are hardly ever employed continuously throughout the year. Between the two World Wars finding a job was a constant cause of concern and anxiety. They tried to gain the favor of *summásgazda*-s with presents in order to be given a place in their bands.

At the end of the last century the families of the teamless farmers were completely provided for by the labor of the males, the household heads, as was also the case with the *gazda*-s; harvesting provided the bread, and a few weeks of day labor supplied money for clothing. After World War I it became necessary for the family to work; they even had to try to get work for recently confirmed girls as *summás*-s. Even so, the financial equilibrium of landless families was unstable. Disease, the breaking of contract, or the failure to secure one would bring almost insurmountable difficulties and often indigence.

Among the teamless farmers there are some "specialists" who are equipped with special knowledge and implements and thus can undertake jobs out of the reach of others. The "flail men," for example, know how to thresh out the grains of rye with their hand flails without destroying the straw, which can then be used for thatching. Thus their work was not supplanted by the thresher. On the estates, and sometimes in the yards of the *gazda*-s in the village, they usually work together in groups of four, five, six, or sometimes even twelve. They received a share of the threshed rye and additional pay in proportion to the quantity of straw.[9] Threshing is seasonal work— with good luck it may last until late autumn or winter. For some reason or other, the "flail men" specialize in making adobe bricks the rest of the year, as well as participating in the usual agricultural occupations of day laborers.

Others supplement their incomes by carving, manufacturing wooden implements and shafts, thatching, and occasional carpentry or basket weaving. János Madarász, who worked for years with a partner as a "house binder" (thatching and mending roofs), related that some two-thirds of his time was spent on agricultural occupations and one-third on roofing, which provided a somewhat higher daily wage than simple manual labor.[10]

Women from this group, particularly lone ones, may also supplement their incomes by performing specialized occupations. There are seamstresses, manufacturers of granulated dried pastry of flour and eggs, and women who help with the spinning and weaving in a *gazda* house for payment in kind. The village also has several market women. They purchase eggs, curd, and poultry in the village and take them to the city market, or buy fruit and sell it for a higher price in the neighboring villages where it is not grown. Some of them fatten or purchase pigs and people come to their houses to buy pieces of the meat and fat. This business flourishes at harvest time, when many households have used up their meat supply.

[9] Every fifth or sixth *véka* of grain threshed out goes to the threshing band. In addition to the money or grain received according to the number of bundles of thatch, they got one liter of brandy for one hundred bundles. If there is enough demand, one "flail" could earn seven to nine *mázsa*-s of grain in a season. If the band is engaged by some large estate to perform a major job which lasts until late winter, very rarely the income might reach twelve to fifteen *mázsa*-s, "but one had to beat a great deal for it."

[10] A common teamless farmer has to pay for one workday of plowing by four days of hoeing. However, three days of thatching are regarded a suitable equivalent.

HERDSMEN

Although herdsmen also work on the land of others (in the community pasture) and receive wages, their way of life is quite different from that of other teamless farmers.

There are several types of herdsman. The herding of horses, cattle, swine, and sheep are separate professions. There is also a difference between herdsmen of "herds going out"—those which are driven to the pasture in the morning and brought back in the evening—and those of "herds sleeping outside," whose keepers roam the pasture continuously from spring until late fall with the animals and live outdoors in simple reed huts.

The estates also engage herdsmen to guard their animals. But the livestock of the Átány peasants are driven to the common pasturage in flocks and their herdsmen are engaged by the community, so that instead of being directed by a single *gazda* they are responsible to the whole village. Their wages are collected from the *gazda*-s whose livestock they watch.[11]

During the era of large-scale stock breeding and herding the profession of herdsman was an esteemed one. In the last century it was even adopted by some landowning *gazda*-s. István Gyenes possessed 24 *hold*-s (about 34 acres) of land in the 1870s but took up herding "because he liked it." Ádám Madarász rented out his fifteen *hold*-s (21.30 acres) on the half-and-half system in order to become a herdsman. His four sons worked as cowhands, riding around the herd on their fine horses.

Herding can be very profitable. The herdsman is employed for a whole grazing season and his wages, paid in kind, are proportional to the number of animals in the herd. His pay might total as much as seventy or eighty *mázsa*-s of grain and, as the peasants add, "he earns all this with a whip." In addition he receives half a loaf of bread for each animal, baked by the families who own them. The peasants of the Hungarian Great Plain bake large loaves of bread, weighing from six to eight kilograms, and 150 of these loaves (payment for a herd of 300 animals) are enough to feed the herdsman, his family, the young cowhands, and the herd dogs for a whole year. The *gazda*-s also pay a sum of money proportional to the number of animals driven out to graze; this is called "sandal money." The herdsman's pay is supplemented by holiday gifts. At Easter and at Christmas the *gazdasszony*-s bake milk loaves for the herdsman, who takes the presents with him in sacks when he drives the herd out. If his family cannot provide him with young cowhands, he is obliged to employ them at his own expense, the number depending on the size of the herd.

---

[11] Flocks of sheep and their shepherds are handled differently from the described system of common pastures controlled by grazing associations. Eight, ten, or twelve sheep-owning *gazda*-s might join together and employ a shepherd to drive their sheep as a common flock, and each *gazda*'s contribution to the shepherd's wages would be proportional to the number of his animals included in the flock.

Another form of shepherding consists of the so-called "self-owning" shepherds who own a flock and rent pasture for their sheep, now in one village, now in another, depending on the circumstances. There is no such shepherd-owner among the people of Átány, but occasionally one of them visits the fields of the village.

In the old days herding was a profession "for life," and was handed down in a family from generation to generation. These "real" herdsmen were inexpert in agricultural work; they neither mowed nor hoed.[12] However, they possessed other types of special knowledge. They knew how to cure the animals. Some of the *gazda* households called in swineherds to stick the pig in winter. The leather-work specialists were herdsmen; they would make whips, sandals for the harvesters, and satchels. Some of them were also good at woodwork.

Today there are fewer herdsmen and most of them do not inherit the profession or learn it in their youth. Herding has become an occasional job for poor people in need of money. It is said that "today's herdsman belongs to the day laborers and is the lowest type of them."

The custodians of fields or vineyards are also poor men of advanced age. They receive a modest payment in kind in proportion to the area of the land or vineyard entrusted to their care.

FARM HANDS AND TOBACCO GROWERS

On the estates the manual work was done by teamless farmers of the village for a share, for day-wages, or on the basis of a *summás* contract. Work requiring draft animals, however, was done by the estate's own teams.[13] A manor's own personnel performed these jobs and took care of the teams. Manors had other employees too —gardeners, mechanics, craftsmen, herdsmen, and domestic servants—but the most characteristic manorial servant was the farm hand who drove and tended the oxen. There were also a few drivers who handled horses and were considered higher in rank than the farm laborers who handled oxen. The liveried coachman was the highest ranking of them; he drove the carriage of the landlord or the keeper, wore a fancy uniform, and was exempted from hard work.

Four oxen were entrusted to the hired man for plowing and transport. There was hardly a day when they could rest, for even when it was snowy they had to carry manure to the fields. They usually worked in teams. The work was led by the "first

---

[12] During the period of large-scale stock breeding in the eighteenth and nineteenth centuries, the numerous herdsmen represented a distinct element in the towns of the Great Plain. They felt a strong cohesive ingroup solidarity. Not only was their profession handed down from father to son, but they also chose their wives from herding families if possible. Owing to the frequent moves imposed by their occupation and to the prevalence of intermarriage between families of herdsmen, this solidarity included the herdsmen of the various towns and villages of a wide region.

The herdsmen engaged by the communities had a sense of personal freedom associated with the responsibilities of their services. They felt themselves to be better off than the hired men of the estates and the day laborers and sometimes even than the *gazda* serfs, who were bound to perform the corvée. The contemporary assembly journals and police records contain numerous charges against herdsmen, stating that they do not go to church, that they keep company with horse thieves and lewd women, or that they brawl. But contemporary records also reveal that the costume and manners of the herdsmen were often the imitated models for peasant youth, who admired the hardy, proud herdsmen holding their ground in the face of any danger (István Györffy, 1941).

[13] Only one large estate owned a steam plow. Even the manorial farms used tractors and steam engines only to drive threshers.

farm hand," or "farm-hand *gazda*," who, for example, made the first furrow while the other farm laborers followed him at an even pace, each leading four oxen. The farm hands were also responsible for taking care of the oxen. They took turns sleeping in the stable for a week at a time, and the tasks of carrying feed and water were similarly arranged. Until the turn of the century the farm hands were also obliged to graze the oxen at night during the summer.

A farm laborer was hired by the year and was paid in produce and cash. He received fifteen to twenty *mázsa*-s of grain for the year, about two-thirds of which was wheat. He also got salt and kerosene and had free use of the straw of the estate for fuel. His wages were paid quarterly in equal shares.

Housing was provided for the servants by the owner and consisted of long buildings located on the estate and divided into apartments. Usually two families shared a room and a kitchen.

The members of the farm hand's family might also find employment on the estate. We were told that a family would begin to prosper when the children had grown up enough to bring home wages. The wives of the farm hands were usually obliged to help on the washing day of the *úr*'s household once a month. Children eight or ten years old could herd piglets, graze sheep, or lead the oxen in front of the drill planter. A twelve-year-old boy could contract as a "young farm hand" to drive the oxen, for which he received half the yearly adult payment in kind. At fourteen or fifteen, he got three-quarters of the adult wage. Children could also work in the beet or potato fields of the estate as day laborers, or they could be used as swath-layers.

It is generally held in the village that the servant of the estate differed from the teamless farmers in that he had to obey the orders of other people all year round, "becoming the hands and feet of another," whereas the day laborers living in the village chose their work themselves. Farm hands were in fact engaged to perform one task all year round, usually tending and driving the oxen. They did not hoe or reap. Instead of the changing, colorful activities of the peasants or day laborers, their life was spent in monotonous uniformity near the stable of the oxen and the dung heap. If an Átány man had a choice, he preferred the hazardous but free and diverse life of the *zsellér*, the independent teamless farmer, to this fate. It was mainly the landless youths who had no place to live who were driven by necessity to the occupation of a farm hand.

Átány *gazda*-s also employed servants,[14] but their life differed considerably from that of the farm hands on the estates. They performed different tasks; and in most cases they worked with the horses. "In the service of the landlord one always had to go out, but in that of the *gazda* the horses were taken out only in good weather." On the manorial farm the hired men were almost exclusively in each other's company, but in the village the servant worked and took his meals with his master. (See Chapter 6, "Other Members of the Household.")

---

[14] According to official records, eleven hired men and five herdsmen were employed in the village in 1942, not including the herdsmen hired by the community. In the same year there were fifty hired men at Szárazbő. (Eger State Archives, Átány Village Records.)

Whether he was a bachelor or a married man, the *gazda*'s servant had a home and family in the village. This was the main feature differentiating him from the hired man of the estate. His situation resembled that of other teamless farmers; he had the chance to exchange his servile condition for the life of a *zsellér*.[15]

"Winter farm hands" were engaged by *gazda*-s of the village from November to April instead of for a whole year. They were employed by wealthy *gazda*-s to feed and tend the animals from the time they were brought back from their summer pasturage by the herdsman until the next summer season. Besides feeding the live-stock twice a day, they were responsible for taking care of the animals at night and for keeping the stable neat. They did not take their meals at the house of the *gazda*, and they were allowed to go home during the day.

Tobacco growers also lived in the servants' quarters of the manorial farms and often had to share an apartment with another family, but in other respects their situation was fundamentally different from that of the farm hands on the estates. Their profession is characterized in Átány as a "dirty but fat" (profitable) job. A tobacco grower contracted with the landlord on the half-and-half system. He was given a plot of four or five *hold*-s (5.68 to 7.10 acres) called a *kukásalja*, or even two if he had a numerous family. The landlord had this piece of land well plowed several times and abundantly fertilized. The tobacco grower performed all the tasks connected with the tobacco from raising the seedlings to drying and classifying the ripe leaves. The marketing and processing of tobacco were monopolized by the state. The tobacco crop was transported to the state receiving station and its price was divided equally between the landlord and the grower.[16]

Since the tobacco plantation did not require the services of the tobacco grower and his family to the same extent throughout the year, the estate provided other occupations for them. Tobacco growers usually contracted to reap also. They were allowed to harvest the crops on the land where tobacco was grown the preceding year. Since this land was excellently worked and copiously fertilized, they secured a good share. They also received corn fields on the half-and-half system, in return for which they did some mowing for the domain. They were also allowed to mow for a share or to perform day labor. On the other hand, when working with tobacco, they needed help themselves. They engaged a boy or a youth as a "tobacco assistant" for the tasks of planting and picking. The jobs of bunching and flattening also required them to hire several people. They usually agreed to pay their helpers seasonal wages in cash.

---

[15] The yearly allowance of grain for a farm hand working in the village is less than on the large estates, since he is provided with full board by the *gazda*. As an example, in the 1930s a hired man received five *mázsa*-s of wheat, one *mázsa* of barley, and half a *hold* of cornfield, to be hoed by his wife and children. He also received a cartload of straw and ten cones of dried dung for fuel, an eight-week-old piglet, and forty *pengő*-s.

[16] However, not all of the tobacco necessarily reaches the receiving station. It is said that a clever tobacco grower smuggles two or three *mázsa*-s of tobacco to the village a year. Here he can market it much more profitably than at the receiving station. Inhabitants of the mountain region to the north of the village (where tobacco growing is impracticable) come to take some of the tobacco, smuggling it farther by ingenious methods. Sometimes Átány carriers would participate in these smuggling trips when they go to the mountains to get stone or wood for fuel.

17

Relatives and friends were often willing to come and help flatten the leaves, their services being requited with tobacco.

The life of the tobacco growers was better and more free than that of the agricultural servants. Their daily tasks were not set by the estate; they did their own work on their assigned tobacco fields and enjoyed the benefits of *métayage*. Once they had transported the tobacco to the receiving station in winter, they had nothing to do until it was time to prepare the hotbeds for the seedlings in the spring; they just sat in the warm room playing cards and drinking wine, a pastime a farm hand could afford very rarely. In addition, they were frequently able to save a considerable portion of their earnings. Around the turn of the century several families rose to the rank of *gazda* by tobacco growing.

The tobacco growers of Átány had a good reputation. Occasionally estates as far away as 100 to 150 kilometers offered to employ them. The travels of some families of tobacco growers could be followed through several villages and two or three counties over a period of thirty years, until they returned at last to settle in their own village as aged people. Some of them settled for good in distant regions. (For this reason it is difficult to estimate the total number of Átány families who earned their living by tobacco growing, although there is evidence that from fifty to sixty families were employed on the neighboring estates.)

NON-PEASANTS IN THE VILLAGE

Craftsmen and Shopkeepers

In 1951 there were six smiths, six wheelwrights (including three unlicensed amateurs), one carpenter, one mason (as well as four or five unlicensed masons and "house binders"), three joiners, three tailors, five shoemakers, two butchers, and three barbers active in Átány. The smiths and butchers represented the oldest and most important of these professions. For centuries the community has maintained two smithies (one in the Lower End and one in the Upper End) and a butcher shop, renting them out from time to time.[17]

These artisans do not all lead the same sort of life. In fact only the smiths, one of the wheelwrights, the joiners, the carpenter, and the mason are able to make a living by their craft; the rest do harvesting or other agricultural work as do the teamless farmers. The amateurs represent an intermediate status between the true craftsmen and the teamless farmers. With some of them craftsmanship is merely supplementary to the usual chores of the teamless farmer. The barbers also lead a dual life: on Fridays, Saturdays, and Sundays they trim and shave the men and on the other days they do rural work. In the old days this was also true of the Átány furriers. Thus

---

[17] The 1828 national census listed eight artisans in Átány: four smiths (who worked all year round), two millers (who owned horse-driven mills), one butcher, and one kosher butcher. There were also two shopkeepers of the lowest class.

János Dorogi was both a furrier and a "reaper *gazda*" on one of the estates. He also held the position of counsellor to the village mayor as a representative of the *zsellér*-s.

The Átány craftsmen do not produce for the large fairs but cater only to the needs of the village. They work to order, using material supplied by the customers and then do repairs. Thus the main tasks of the smiths are sharpening plowshares, shoeing horses, and mending ironwork on carts, tools, and buildings. If they manufacture a new implement to order, the iron is provided by the customer.[18]

The artisans also exchange their special services for produce; specialized manpower is provided for the *gazda*-s, and the necessary amount of grain for the landless artisans. For example, all team owners need to have their plowshares sharpened and make yearly contracts with the smith in advance for this service. The smith receives grain in proportion to the *gazda*'s arable land: one *véka* of wheat and half a *véka* of barley per *félhely*. Wealthy *gazda*-s agree on a fixed yearly wage beforehand, for which the smiths agree to shoe their horses and keep their carts and implements in good repair. These services are repaid with two or three *mázsa*-s of wheat and sometimes a "chain-length" of a melon patch or corn field as well. In the 1940s the smith Pál Ivák usually contracted with eighty to eighty-five *gazda*-s per season to sharpen their plowshares for payment in kind, and he had similar agreements with five or six *gazda*-s covering the repair of all their equipment.[19]

In general, the artisans may be compared with the more prosperous teamless farmers. Because of their knowledge of specialized crafts, they regard themselves as superior to the teamless farmers, but since they own no land, the *gazda*-s look down on them as their inferiors. In view of their special knowledge and their alien background, some of them are addressed as *úr*, but only by the customer; the neighbor addresses the craftsman simply as "neighbor."

Before 1900 there were many shopkeepers, and the majority were from outside the village. They usually sold salt, matches, and spices, as well as dress materials, ironware, tools, and kitchen utensils. They also collected grain to sell to the big grain dealers in Heves, Füzesabony, or Eger. They were willing to accept grain or eggs instead of cash. Most of them kept taverns in addition, connected with the shops.

Since the establishment of the consumers' cooperative (from 1898 the *Hangya*

---

[18] Unlike the Átány smiths, the smiths in the towns of Jászság, Jászberény and Jászapáti, manufacture from their own materials, without orders, and then sell them at the fairs. In cooperation with the wheelwrights, they build new carts and manufacture harrows, cultivators, and turnip cutters. (Often small, smith-manufactured agricultural machines appeared in Átány, even before those produced in the factories. For a time the smiths were able to compete with the factories.) From the turn of the century the number of such hand-crafted implements has decreased. However, peasants were still using a few hand-made tools in the 1950s.

[19] However, the reciprocal relationship between the smiths and their peasant customers is a good deal less formal than the contract might imply. The peasants borrow tools from the smith, and they expect him to perform certain services without pay, such as the delicate first sharpening of a new scythe. But also, many *gazda*-s send a taste to the smith after pigsticking without expecting anything in return. When preparations are being made for a feast, the wife of the smith receives as many as fifteen liters of milk, as a present, as well as other dairy products and fruit. "The world pays its debts," says the smith Pál Ivák, "but I do not like to be a debtor to anyone either."

17*

szövetkezet), the needs of the village have generally been met by this organization. Several tiny grocer's shops survived until the 1950s, providing a scanty supplement to the income of certain teamless farmers.

Úr-s

Those landlords of Szárazbő, Tenk, and Heves who possessed land within the administrative boundaries of Átány before 1945 were thereby entitled to a seat in the body of village representatives; if they were Calvinist, they were also members of the village church. Thus the Átány folk had an official, if rather incidental, relationship with them. These *úr*-s were the descendants of the ancient Hungarian landed gentry who farmed their own estates of a few hundred to a few thousand *hold*-s; their mansions were surrounded by outbuildings and servants' apartment barracks.

The Calvinist minister and the village secretary also belonged to the class of *úr*-s, as learned people, not Átány born, and they played a leading role in the life of the community. On the other hand, since their offices were elective, they were somewhat dependent on the village as a whole. Though an *úr*, the village secretary received instructions from the village mayor, who was a peasant. Likewise, the members of the presbytery did not hesitate to voice their objections and criticisms to the minister, albeit with due reverence.

The livelihoods of the minister and the secretary (as well as the leader of the church choir and the schoolmasters) were provided for by the village in the course of the 1866 consolidation of land holdings by special areas being measured out for them. The fields where these areas lie are not the most fertile ones: "the *úr*-s were allotted the worst land, but at least the sections were large ones, in order to put them in the mood to accept them." These office holders either leased out the land, or worked it on the system of *métayage*, or farmed it themselves. If the minister chose to farm the land himself, he was able to build up a livelihood at least as prosperous as that of the largest peasant farms. At the beginning of this century, when János Illyés was elected minister, the members of the presbytery traveled to his former rectory with thirty carts in order to transport his farming equipment, provisions, and animals to Átány. He engaged three full-time servants and two tobacco growers and kept four oxen, four horses, and fifteen or twenty cows in his stable.

Besides the land, the pastor was entitled to receive the *párbér*, a parochial tax called "the tax of the married couples," about 250 *mázsa*-s of grain.

The village secretary was given 45 *hold*-s (63.90 acres) of land, a salary paid by the community, and a large house appropriate to his office.

Gypsies

The gypsies actually do not live *in* the village but in a settlement of their own located in a public area just beyond one end of the village. They have no yards, and their small, low houses are unlike those of the peasants; the entrance is on the narrow side, the roofs are daubed, and there are no lofts. Most of the houses consist of a single room. There are no outbuildings, not even a pigsty or a poultry pen, since the gypsies have no animals.

The gypsies have occupied their present settlement since 1941, when their former huts were demolished by a flood. The area allotted to the gypsies was determined by the magistracy of the village. "Since Átány gypsies are carrion-eating people," the decision was to place their settlement outside the village. The basis for this reasoning was that until very recently it was the duty of the gypsies to dispose of dead animals. But their "carrion-eating" is not the only difference perceived between them and the peasants. It is said that "they aren't created like us; they aren't fitted for all the types of work that we are." Gypsies do not work in the fields. Some have the special profession of musician. Low-prestige jobs such as daubing, building ovens, and, most of all, making adobe bricks are reserved for them. Larger households have their own "usual" gypsy, who comes from time to time to collect the garbage and perform traditional gypsies' work. Since one gypsy usually visits several houses, they are on the street all day long, continually begging. They go into the yards, but they are not allowed in the houses. They are outside of the spiritual community of the village as well since they are Catholics. The men find no place in the tavern, nor their children in the school.[20]

[20] This description is valid for the 1930s and probably for a long time before that. According to a journal of 1740, gypsies lived outside the village at that time. Old people remember that the ancestors of the present Átány gypsies were settled in the community pasture near the village about 1860. Their number totaled 57 in 1931, 182 in 1964.

Today integration of the gypsies and the villagers is encouraged by numerous allowances of the state. For example, if gypsies want to build a house "in the Hungarian way" inside the village, they receive a long-term state loan without interest, a benefit not available to the peasants. They enjoy free medical treatment and free education for their children. Owing to the effective help of the public administration, by 1964 there were already five gypsy-owned houses in the village. These, however, were inhabited by eleven families, so their housing conditions were not much different from the small crowded abodes built "in the gypsy way." Of the 182 gypsies only twelve are working regularly in the cooperatives, and about ten in industry outside the village.

CHAPTER 13. THE WAYS TO WEALTH AND POVERTY

THE RISE AND DECLINE OF INDIVIDUALS AND FAMILIES

The land of the Átány peasants was bordered by big estates, medium-size holdings of landlords, and plots belonging to peasants from other villages. This frame was generally stable in time and space; generation after generation had roughly the same quantity of land at their disposal. Nevertheless, the borders of the peasants' property have never been completely fixed. In the process of land reapportionings, for example, the Átány peasants were able to carve out considerable tracts from the lands of the úr-s. But land-hunger was greater than the land available so neighboring communities and individual villagers who desired more land resorted to clever means to acquire the parcels, bidding for them until the poorer bidders were passed over. In the last century there were still opportunities to extend one's plowland within the boundaries of the village, e.g., by improving barren soil and by plowing up pastures and meadows. But these latent resources were exhausted in a few decades. The peasants then tried to expand beyond the boundaries of their holdings into the lands of the domains which they could not buy by doing sharecropping on these lands. In this manner they managed to acquire for their own community a fraction of the crop at least of the neighboring estates.

In the period known and lived through by our informants there were other ways open to the Átány peasants to increase their earnings. As a matter of fact, some such opportunities have always been available. Thus, some of the Átány people made animal dealing their profession as early as the eighteenth century, and the 1828 national census reveals that cartage also supplied subsidiary income for some villagers. But after serfdom was abolished, and especially at the turn of the century and thereafter, opportunities for employment outside the village increased considerably. It was in this period that the Átány people began to exploit the opportunities for horse trading between the southern Great Plain and the Highlands and thereby secure subsistence for a sizable number of their group. Recruitment of agricultural labor for remote estates also commenced at this time. And so also the towns which offered job opportunities in industry or construction work attracted more and more people. The chance of finding employment overseas, especially in the United States, remained open for some decades, and groups of people from Átány embarked on the venture of emigration from Hungary.

Nevertheless, the centripetal forces of the community offset at least some of the attractions of the outside world throughout this period. Although fragments of the village population did secede from time to time to take advantage of these outside opportunities, their loss in numbers was balanced by the increase in the remaining population, so the community actually remained constant in size. And many of those who sought their fortune outside did so to acquire the means of rising in their home village; they merely took a very roundabout way toward that goal. Some would work in Budapest for years (all the while eating bread baked at Átány) and save their earnings in order to build or to buy land at home. Men working in America might send money home to their wives for the purpose of purchasing land. Those who hired themselves out as servants or tobacco growers on the estates would plan to return to the home community and there buy a house in their old age. József B. Kovács, who spent 32 years far from Átány as a tobacco grower, told us: "I still longed for home just as those who go abroad."

Whether they farmed at home or worked outside the village, Átány peasants envisaged the possibilities of rise or decline in their wealth and rank relative to the structure of the village. In this section we want to deal with the notions about rise and decline and the "tricks," the ways and means, by which they strove to rise in the society of their village.

The people we conversed with at Átány, even the oldest ones, felt that they lived in an open society which offered opportunities for one to increase his wealth and power, as well as possibilities for decline or ruin. They told us: "The blood in a man makes him strive for the better." "The peasant is born with the desire of enrichment."[21] Nevertheless they think that the village as a whole has become poorer during the past one hundred years. "The community was wealthier in ancient times." As a matter of fact, however, the land owned by the Átány peasants has increased, not decreased in extent, and so has the productivity of the land, while the population of the village has not risen. On the other hand, the number of houses and households has become larger because the number of people within a single family unit has become smaller. Also the number of separate holdings has grown—principally those plots too small

---

[21] Nevertheless, sudden affluence is viewed with suspicion and regarded as more or less irregular. It is rumored that the quickly rising Vajda family of the last century owed its fortune to their ancestor's retaining the taxes collected in the village in the war years; he filled the post of village mayor during the fight for freedom in 1848–49. Similar rumors have circulated concerning the family of the village mayor in the period of World War I.

In other cases the rise of a family to wealth might be explained by a treasure trove: "When the ditch around the land of the *zsellér* association was dug, Sári Veres found money in a jug. It was not quite clear how, but her father purchased land soon afterward ..." At about the turn of the century a *zsellér*, Sándor Sebők, wanted to gain his fortune by a systematic search for treasure. He ordered a thin "treasure-seeking drill" nearly two meters long to be made; then he began discovering treasures in the fields and even in his own yard by some sort of magical formulas.

In the last century there was a widespread belief among the peasantry of the Great Plain that magical charms and witchcraft could be used to draw the milk from another person's cow and add it to the milk of one's own. Átány peasants firmly deny the existence of witches—regarding such as a "superstition" believed only in Catholic villages. But now and then, "unofficially," as it were, such beliefs do in fact emerge. In the Lower End it was said of one successful ambitious man that he had bewitched his neighbors' animals in order to get rich. The ruin of some people was attributed to a curse.

for independent farming. Thus by 1935 there were many more team owners in Átány than forty years earlier (in 1895, 170 teams were counted in the village; in 1935, 237), but in most cases they were small-holders who required supplementary income. In this "middle class," which overlaps at one end the "real" team-owners and at the other end the teamless farmers, individuals have to struggle constantly to preserve their status. The economic and social equilibrium of these farmers always used to be unstable, for there was always the danger of "sliding down" among the poor. Moreover, needs have grown and standards of living have risen, and the number of those who can barely or who cannot live up to the raised norms has increased.

The *gazda*-s used to divide the poor into two groups. One was "the poor of God," who have been impoverished by the blows of fate or nature; the other, "the beggars from their own doing," who suffer the consequences of their own carelessness, awkwardness, or extravagance. Those of the lowest standing, the manorial servants, were regarded as almost unalterably bound to their mean status: "they are stuck in the dung."

Looking at this stratification from below, through the eyes of the poor, the chances for rising seem slim indeed. "One who has begun life as a poor man is followed by poverty until his death"—as a one-time day laborer told us. Among the poor living on the estates, the tobacco growers used to be the most mobile. Their position was intermediate, between the boundaries of two strata, and some fortunate people were able to break through, rising in some cases to the level of well-to-do *gazda*-s. But this "breaking free" was the reward for only a few tobacco growers. Many of them could say: "By growing tobacco we did not acquire a crooked house (*ház*), just a crook-back (*hát*)."[22] This reservation notwithstanding, it was the rapid advancement and the enrichment of some tobacco growers which justified the widely held opinion that one could rise to the level of a *gazda* from an all but destitute condition. Other poor men were able to scrape together as much in the United States, at the beginning of this century, and similarly surmount the barrier that divided them from the *gazda*-s. However, most poor people aspired to more modest improvements of their condition, as will be shown below.

In each stratum public opinion notices those who try to rise and to increase their property. They are said "to bustle about"; "to busy themselves very much." They exert the full powers of their families and themselves. They look for supplementary income. They are young people in most cases, since "a young one is not afraid of anything, he strains every nerve in order to get ahead." Others were content with merely preserving their property; this was characteristic of childless *gazda*-s, for example. Finally there were spendthrifts who sold land in order to live better on the proceeds, to eat and drink. "They put too much under their skin"; they did not work properly, performing their agricultural tasks in a slipshod way.

However, gain or loss did not depend on human calculations and endeavor alone. As the Átány people say, the crop "is in the palm of Goodness," in the hands of God,

---

[22] The "crooked house" means a large dwelling of an L-shape, following the patterns of town and suburbs; it was a symbol of wealth.

who "may give and take." The crop of the plowlands depended mainly on the changeable weather of the Carpathian Basin. In earlier times the shallow plowing of the primitive plows made the grain especially susceptible to the effects of drought. In bad years the crop hardly repaid the seed which was sown, but a good harvest might yield twenty to thirty-fold.[23]

Sickness of men and animals can profoundly influence the life of a family. Summarizing his life, Samu Kiss related as outstanding events the facts that he underwent two operations, that one of his daughters died after a prolonged illness involving much medical care, and that three of his horses unexpectedly perished in succession. His inactivity during his disease, the costs of medical treatment, and the loss of valuable animals meant a setback of at least ten years in his economic progress. This is why he was not able to enlarge his plot. András Együd and Ferenc Együd are the sons of a tobacco grower who later became a "*gazda* of hired men." Ferenc married a girl with a house and settled in the village. He lived as a harvester and "house binder" and in doing so succeeded in acquiring four *hold*-s (5.68 acres) of land. András remained a tobacco grower but he also succeeded in purchasing a house and two *hold*-s (2.84 acres) of land. But in comparing his fortune with that of his brother, he said: "Were it not for my difficulty with the women [he married three times, two of his wives dying after protracted illnesses], I might have ten *hold*-s [14.20 acres] of land and horses too. Everything decayed while the woman [one of the deceased wives] was ill; she had to be treated for six years."

Besides health and disease, good and poor harvests, and individual quirks of fate, changes in the economic situation of the country could affect each farm just as would natural disasters. Agrarian crises and changes in the policy of agrarian price control had a strong impact on the profits of Átány peasant farms. In the present century, since money economy has become widespread and bank loans have become usual, the workings of the money market have affected Átány farming. After each of the two World Wars the villagers lived through a currency devaluation. During these periods some local cash reserves were exhausted; at the same time numerous peasant farms were delivered from the squeeze of their creditors. The periods of prosperity and crisis also affected the estates in the neighborhood of Átány, resulting, for example, in the division of parts of the estates into small plots, which the peasants could buy.

The first goal of a farm hand or a tobacco grower was "to gather for his old age"— to acquire a house where he might find shelter in those years, together with a small parcel of land. The house represented the boundary line between the very poor, who were forced to live "under the roof of others" in the manorial dwellings of farm laborers, and the teamless farmers of the village, who had marginal independence. "It is better to have a house than land," so they say, implying that one's first requirement is to acquire a house. "But a house never gives one land, while land gives a house."

[23] István Balogh, 1965a: 389. A peasant from a village not far from Átány kept a diary for the 73 years from 1793 to 1866. According to this record 16 years produced very meager harvests because of drought, hail, or floods; and several years there was even famine; 25 years brought good harvests; and 32 years produced medium yields, some crops doing well, but others poorly. The diary lists nine incursions of rinderpest and two large epidemics (Varga, 1964).

The prospects of a poor man were somewhat improved if he had numerous children and after they reached an age when they could earn money. Small children, however, hindered both the farm hand and the tobacco grower in their activities because they meant full-time occupation at home for the mother. When the wife was indispensable in the cultivation of tobacco, the *kukás*-s were forced to engage a nurse for the small children. For planting and stripping they employed a "*kukás* boy," and they paid wage-earners to do the bundling. Their lot improved when their children grew up. They were then able to take on even two *kukásalja* of land and employ only a few outsiders to help; their children could earn money as harvesters or day laborers too. After they had completed their tenth year, the children of a farm hand brought their scanty wages home. They received half to three-quarters of an adult's pay over twelve and fourteen years.

Capital could be raised by keeping animals, as this was secured by the estates. One who had the means could keep a cow with calf and raise the young. The animal could be sold, either in case of need or to provide the basis for some major investment. Thus János Madarász, upon leaving his father, received but a single ax. He worked as a house porter and a gardener for a couple of years in Budapest. Returning home, he married and settled in a rented house. He managed to acquire a two-year-old heifer and provision for the winter. Then he heard that a small old house was being offered up for sale. "We'll do nothing else, wife, we'll sell the heifer and the provender and we'll buy the house."

The career of Gábor Madarász, the father of János Madarász, exemplifies the possibilities open to a hired man. He worked as a servant for ten years at Kápolna, on the estate of the Eger Collegiate Church. He had five children. When the two eldest could earn money, the father engaged himself on the "Prince's property" in the environs of Átány, in order to "be nearer to the village" to be able to watch for the chance to settle into the community. After a few years' service he inherited a house in the village, a *hold* of land, and a vineyard. He moved into the village and again engaged himself as a servant, now with the Vajda family in the village. He could serve for only a few years though, because he was growing old, "unable to pull a heavier yoke." He next became a herdsman and then a guard in the vineyard. In the meantime he gave his five children into marriage.

Outside, on the manors, servants could rarely achieve the status of "farm-hand *gazda*." But if they did, it meant more wages, and instead of manual work, their task became overseeing.

The poorest teamless farmers owned only a house or merely rented a dwelling. Their road to prosperity involved acquiring one or two *hold*-s of land, a cow, and grazing rights. Local opinion holds that it is impossible to keep a horse on less than six *hold*-s (8.52 acres); a teamless farmer rarely succeeded in crossing this boundary line. The *gazda*-s held that people of this sort, "not being educated in this way," were afraid of tending horses. To be sure, one had to own land to keep a cow too, but a much smaller amount than for a horse team. The cow gave milk, but even more important were its progeny, as they could be sold. Apart from the work a teamless farmer did for others, his own small plot and cow brought a measure of independence and made his situation more stable. Their farming then rather resembled that of the gazda-s but on a much smaller scale.

A teamless farmer could also become a craftsman. József Gacsal, when he was twelve years old, was asked by his father, who was a day laborer and sharecropper as well as a "house binder" and repairer, "What will become of you, my son?" He replied, "I like crafts. One of my koma-s [bachelor friends] has become a smith." "If your koma has become a smith, be a wheelwright." (There were many jobs in which a smith and a wheelwright could cooperate.) He was apprenticed to a local artisan and then became an itinerant worker for two years; finally he settled in the village as a craftsman.

Before a team owner could think of enlarging his land, he had to "catch himself up." According to the traditional principles of farming, he first had to acquire equipment and healthy, valuable animals in proportion to his land and also to accumulate some reserves. If he managed to do all this and had the fifteen hold-s (21.3 acres) necessary for an independent life, he might cease his efforts toward further achievement. "He drives two good horses; he has his bread and butter too; there is peace in his family." But such a person might easily turn his thoughts to further gain. People used to explain: "It is like that: as soon as one has caught himself up and is full of everything, he still keeps on advancing. Once an animal is fattened, it does not throw off its weight easily." "If there are two horses with young, they fill the stalls very soon; even the partition walls have to be demolished in two years' time." A man of such wealth could wait and sell his produce to best advantage, while the poor had to sell their produce even below the usual price, "in order to grasp the ears of money as soon as possible." If no disaster thwarted them, such gazda-s were regularly able to add a few hold-s to their property.

Some gazda-s had to pursue more mean occupations in order to "catch themselves up." Sámuel Együd was up to his ears in debt. In order to achieve solvency for himself and his property, he engaged himself as a tobacco grower. With his four sons he worked two kukásalja-s of land and also kept his own team of horses on the estate. He returned to the village regularly to cultivate his own plot of land. In a few years he not only paid off all his debts but was able to build a new house and a new stable.

The desire to rise demands of both teamless farmers and the less wealthy team owners self-denial, thrift, and sustained hard work. József Tóth, being a tobacco grower, acquired sixty hold-s (85.20 acres) of land, but "he dared not eat his fill in his whole life." Gábor Varga, as he strove to free his small holding from inherited debts, "wondered even at night how he could make two pengő-s out of one." He went out to work in the dark before dawn. Where his neighbor plowed his plot once or twice, Varga plowed his three or four times, trying to increase the crop by more intensive work. "We took it out of our bellies"; "we went about in rags for it"—this is how people relate the antecedent trials of purchasing land.

The periods in which the people really have to struggle in order to "overtake themselves" and stages after "having caught themselves up" are saliently and accurately recalled when they offer their life histories. Most of them achieved the state of "catching up" only in their later years, faring like old József Tóth (not the tobacco grower described above). He was mentioned in this way: "The old man finally fell sick. Since he no longer had to work hard, he could have stayed in his *kert* peacefully. He could have had a good old age, but he became ill and died soon after."

Besides increasing their property and acquiring valuable livestock, the *gazda*-s used to accumulate cash as well. This is an ancient habit. The villagers frequently tell stories about gold being buried in the *ólaskert*-s by the head of the family, who was then silenced before he could reveal the site to his successors. The advantage of money over other forms of wealth is that it can be readily concealed. Thus the Rózsa family, living in a traditional extended family household, used to accumulate and cache money. They were caricatured accordingly: "They liked money for itself, since it does not need care like livestock." When they had a large sum in their chest, they set out to buy an extensive piece of property which was offered for sale. But halfway there one brother asked the other: "Shall we give the money away? Shall we bring ourselves to nought?" So they returned home. But their cash lost its value in the inflation following World War I.

While some people hoarded cash in secret, a few "circulated" it. As early as in the eighteenth century there was a law suit over the issue of who had provided credit to a peasant dealing in livestock. Between the two World Wars four people used money lent by Viktor Simon, the well-to-do butcher, for horse dealing. But among the villagers credit is only infrequently requested as a rule. Samu Kiss, for example, borrowed money from one of his relatives because his horse died during plowing operations and he urgently had to buy a replacement to continue his work. And a *gazda* was usually willing to lend one or two sacks of wheat free of interest to his harvester until the new crop.

This general lack of credit gave rise to forms of usury. In lean years there were some who would lend wheat until the new harvest but at an interest rate of 25 per cent. The lender could be paid by work. One villager cultivated his creditor's plot of ten *hold*-s (14.20 acres) for years, paying by his work the interest on a loan which initially helped him buy a pair of oxen and property of four *hold*-s (5.68 acres). Some people lent money at a usurious interest rate in a quite businesslike manner, although this was the exception.[24]

Apart from the horse dealing already mentioned, the villagers generally did not circulate money in other commercial enterprises. Between the two World Wars there were some who tried their luck in grain dealing, usually as middlemen for large firms.

Larger sums could be borrowed from the banks. A *gazda* having a large holding (twenty to thirty *hold*-s; 28.40 to 42.60 acres or more) generally was no longer able to increase his property by dint of hard work, self-sacrifice, and parsimony, but

---

[24] We have examined the notes of a wealthy *gazda* on the cash and grain lent by him during the 1860s. He had thirty to forty debtors at the same time; each owed him one to six *korona*-s or one to four *köböl*-s of wheat (one *köböl* = one butt or two hogsheads = four *véka*-s).

rather by cleverly and boldly buying and selling with borrowed money. When the parceling out of estate lands enabled some *gazda*-s to buy ten to fifteen (or more) *hold*-s (14.20 to 21.30 acres) in one piece, it was difficult to pay the price involved out of their own pockets. In the 1920s some wealthy *gazda*-s managed to purchase a number of minor possessions from the *úr*-s with bank credit. In the early 1930s, however, when the economic crisis brought on a decline in wheat prices, almost all of them would have been ruined by their mortgage and interest burdens if some state measures to defend peasant property had not averted legal proceedings against some. Thus local sentiment regards a bank loan as a hazardous enterprise; many people say, "Bank credit devours one's holding"; "It winds round the neck of the *gazda*."

THE ORDER OF SUCCESSION

As one investigates the rise and decline in economic status of individual families over the period of several generations, one encounters a mechanism of primary importance: how each generation hands down its property to its successors.

As we have written above, during the era of serfdom, land dealings in general and the parceling out of specific holdings were restricted by the *telek* system. No division of land was allowed which resulted in a holding below a quarter-*telek*. In practice, this rule meant that land could not come into the hands of teamless farmers, since no small holdings could come into being which would not require a team. The serf who owned but a quarter-*telek* was bound to work for a lord with a team, as did all other land-owning serfs. Consequently, individual families divided their land among as many male successors as there were quarter-*telek*-s in the total of the father's estate. The son who was left without a quarter became a landless *zsellér*, and the proportion of *zsellér*-s in the population increased. For families with large holdings, the principle of succession was that an equal share go to each male successor whenever possible. The impact of this principle was the speedy fragmentation of *telek*-s (see Chapter 2, "Land Tenure," and Chapter 13, "Mobility in the Last One Hundred Years").

The land and the farm equipment passed to the sons, while the daughters were entitled only to their dowry, which consisted mainly of linen—bedclothes and attire—and a chest to keep the clothes in. A poor girl was married off with only a "bed to sleep in"; a rich one got an ornamental bed besides. A really well-to-do *gazda* might also endow his daughter with a cow and a share in the pasture.

After the abolition of serfdom, the division of land became free and the legal order of succession changed correspondingly. In the feudal period, serfs and nobles were subject to different inheritance regulations. For the serfs, no unified, general, country-wide pattern was prescribed; the law actually allowed flexibility for local customs. The bills passed in 1836 and 1840 brought about a uniform regulation of peasant succession. And with the abolition of serfdom, the affairs of the peasant were subjected to the unified Hungarian civil codes. This system provided for equal succession to sons and daughters. The peasants did not then nor do they now find it just that daughters should share equally in the property and farm equipment with the sons since they do not work directly for the sustenance and growth of the farm as men do; moreover, they often take their portion into another family upon marriage. Thus it was but slowly that the law changed the traditional order of succession which favored the sons. Although a girl might institute legal proceedings against her brother and succeed in obtaining an equal share of the estate as early as 1864, most parents continued to favor their sons, and the daughters did not claim an equal division themselves. However, by the 1880s it became general practice for peasants to bequeath a piece of land to a daughter, although not one equal to the share of a son.

In a will made in 1913, the father of Károly Bedécs left all his land to his only son, bequeathing to both his daughters only money. The will of the deceased was still being contested as late as 1927. At that time the favored male heir made an offer to his sisters to divide the plot into two halves; he retained one half and ceded them the other. The farm equipment and livestock remained in his hands, but he undertook to care for and ultimately assume the funeral expenses of their widowed mother. Thus even recently, though the daughters might receive an equal share of house and land, the farm equipment and the *ólaskert* went to the son.[25] Similarly the teamless farmers wanted to secure their immovable property for their sons. Thus in 1905 József Gacsal and his brother were bequeathed by their father all the interior plot and the house, valued at 1,200 *korona*-s. They were obliged to give their sister but 100 *korona*-s. Bowing to changed concepts, they finally gave her 300 *korona*-s, but the villagers took the view: "You have given that girl too much of that *porta*."

Inheritance of land by women also affected the customs for choosing a mate. (See Chapter 7, "Choice of Mate.") In the economy of the *gazda*-s, the wife's inheritance became of as much consideration as the husband's. Married couples worked their property in common and did not distinguish between the respective incomes. If it came to division, however, it was customary for the daughters to inherit from their mother and the sons from their father. But this distinction is not recognized by law. The time for handing over the shares to the successors was also affected. If the mother died, as a rule, her property was actually allotted to those of her heirs who lived apart from the parental household even during the lifetime of the father, before the final division.

This distinction between the property of men and women is colored by concepts about "ancestral property" or "ancestral estate." The law distinguished between inherited (ancestral) and acquired property. The benefactor was free, generally speaking, to dispose of his acquired property as he chose, but his children were legally entitled to at least the "legitimate portion" of the ancestral property, i.e., half of their share in the case of equal division. The ancestral estate was preserved with special care. "I would not have sold a speck of it; my father and grandfather would rise from the

---

[25] If the *gazda* owned a house and an *ólaskert* too, the daughter usually inherited the house with all its belongings and the son the *kert* with all the equipment. As to a house alone a daughter could always claim as her due the bed, her mother's clothing, and the kitchen utensils.

grave if they knew it."[26] The family estate is due "to the person who has inherited the family name," meaning principally the son. This is why people attempted to satisfy the claims of the daughters with the maternal inheritance, to save the "ancestral goods" for the sons.[27]

A peaceful settlement by brothers and sisters is viewed as the correct, the desirable solution. "I would not harm my brother [sister] over a few hundred *forint*-s"— so many people say. One *gazda* told his wife: "Do not bring even a handful of soil here; I don't want to quarrel for it, nor to be on bad terms with your brothers." People blame those who divide the inheritance with such meticulous care that they allot even the shares of scrap iron; "some of them would break a pin into two."

Owing to strictly limited possibilities for acquiring land, inheritance used to have a critical effect on the future financial situation of the descendants. This is why division often did result in squabbling among brothers and other successors—as in a family in which the principal male heir managed to keep a large portion of the inheritance for himself, at the expense of his sisters: "He has the land, but he can hardly find anybody to stick the pig." This means that he is on bad terms with the traditional participants of pigsticking: near relatives, siblings, and *sógor*-s. Two cases were mentioned in which a *vő* flew into such a rage at his father-in-law for having slighted his wife in favor of her brothers that he set fire to the straw yard of the old man.

In this system of succession, a sole heir, lacking brothers and sisters, is in an advantageous situation indeed. This is true for both team owners and teamless farmers. Thus Sándor Együd owned only a *massza*, 250 square fathoms of vineyard, and a small house in a holding of 80 square fathoms. But being a sole heir, he was able to marry the daughter of a *gazda*.

If there are several children, the parents try to arrange for a division during their lifetime. Their aim is to lay the foundation for the economic independence of their sons and to satisfy their daughters. It sometimes happens in the case of such an agreement that even before the demise of the parents one of the brothers or sisters feels himself wronged; therefore "one does not speak to the other for years."

The father often drafts these directives in his will. Either he puts the agreement reached with his successors in writing, or he draws up his intentions secretly. In the latter case, he visits the notary, dictates his will, and then two witnesses are ushered in to sign; the contents of the testament remain secret.

A general principle at Átány is: "Don't undress before you lie down." This means that the *gazda* does well to retain control over his property until his death. According to a desirable and traditional resolution, the grown-up sons fetched their wives to their father's house and resided together with him. But this cannot be done in every

---

[26] Sons would make considerable sacrifices, even to renouncing a more desirable plot of land, in order to retain the ancestral estate. "I don't let out this home; I won't allow another to take over this home. . . . It belonged to the grandfather of my grandfather; it is a most sacred thing to the family."

[27] When an estate was divided among several male descendants, the most centrally located of both the village holdings and the plots in the fields went to the eldest, the more peripheral to the youngest.

case, especially if there are too many brothers. "A man having three sons knew well that two of them had to leave the home, so he acquired houses for them. Then he got hold of a small *massza*, a half share in the pasture, that he might drive his cow out." This account illustrates the attempts to provide the basic means for a secure life for a son who has to leave the paternal home even though his inheritance is not vouchsafed. The father often gives to a seceding son a fairly extensive plot of land "for cultivation"; sometimes he leaves all his property to his son or *vő* on a half-and-half system.[28]

Thus the adult lives of many people divide into two periods: first, having left the paternal home, the young man tries to live by his own resources, often on a lower socio-economic level than he was accustomed to in his youth; and then, having received his share of inheritance, he continues farming on his own, but materially better off. The sons of teamless farmers worked as farm hands until an inherited house (or a part of one) enabled them to return to the village as teamless farmers themselves. Sons of *gazda*-s often hired out to harvest for others or they found occupations in Budapest until they came into possession of the plot. Some people "became *gazda*-s" (team owners) only in their old age.[29]

What is the process and what the consequences of division? Let us cite the estate partition of Ferenc Orbán with his brothers and sisters as an example. The father owned 24 small *hold*-s (25.92 acres) of land, a house, a *kert*, and farming equipment appropriate for a team owner; his estate was divided among two sons and three daughters. Two daughters were given into marriage to husbands in Tiszanána; the third married in the village. When the father died in 1918, the elder son was also married; "he had taken wing" and settled on his own. The younger son, Ferenc Orbán, when he returned from a prisoner-of-war camp, a bachelor still, remained with his mother and continued farming the estate. In 1922 he brought his wife to his mother's house. The partition, which had first been demanded by the sisters, took place in 1924. In the absence of a will, the descendants divided their legacy into five shares according to law. They drew lots for the immovables and movable property, dividing the latter into five heaps in the yard. This was the first partition in Átány in which daughters managed to acquire shares of the farming equipment equal with the sons. Public opinion disapproved of this, and especially of the action of one of the

[28] When the eldest son of Gábor Varga married and, after the wedding in the autumn, settled in with his father-in-law, his father let him have the eight *hold*-s (11.36 acres) of land and one thousand square fathoms of vine, which was the inheritance of his deceased mother. The land was already planted, and he added four sacks of wheat. The father said: "You have worked here during the summer; they shall not say that you went there in order to eat." "If by chance you do not agree with your father-in-law, you just leave him; your land is sown, you have wheat, you have something to set your eyes on."

[29] The division also means a decisive turn in the life of the son who remains with his father. As long as his father lives, he works the land with the latter as an undivided estate; but his brothers take out their shares at the time of the partition. Before World War I, the then more than eighty-year-old grandfather of János Boldizsár just smoked his pipe in the company of other old men and left all practical affairs to his youngest son, with whom he lived. The farm was kept together by his presence, however, and when the man died, their respective portions of the estate had to be allotted to the older brother, then living on one of the manorial farms as a tobacco grower, and to a sister. Thus the holding was reduced to one-third its former size.

daughters, who entered the stable and unhooked the chain of the cow that it might not be forgotten in the course of the partition.

Ferenc Orbán's share consisted of but four small *hold*-s (4.32 acres) and 960 square fathoms of land and meadow, one mare with colt, a cart, a harrow, fifty quintals of turnips, and some grain. Apart from this, he already owned two heifers, bought with the help of his soldier's pay, which were not subjected to division. After the partition he left the paternal house and settled in that of his father-in-law.

Having thus divided the inherited estate, this son of a well-to-do *gazda* (who owned a *félhely*) became a teamless farmer without even a house of his own. Ferenc Orbán reckoned with his possibilities: in the very year of the partition he sold his animals, the cart, and the harrow and managed to build a house on the interior plot allotted to him from the old *kert*, but without furnishings, without a door and windows. Then he rented out his plot, securing support for his family from the rent paid in kind, and left for Budapest to find a job. He worked hard and economized for six years, so scrimping that he never entered a tavern even once. During his short visits to the village he finished the house, built a stable, purchased a plow, some tools, and a cow, which was kept by his father-in-law. In 1929 he returned for good and settled into his own house together with his family. He thereupon purchased a team of horses and a cart and took to cultivating his small plot with his own hands, at the same time undertaking cartage and farm labor for others on the half-and-half system. Thereafter he lived like a proper team owner.

This case illustrates how decisively the economic situation of descendants was conditioned by the partition of the paternal estate. Had Ferenc Orbán been an only child, he would have set out on his career as a well-to-do, independent *gazda*. At the same time, his career is an example of how the fate of the successor is not exclusively determined by the land he inherits. The son of a teamless farmer owning four to five small *hold*-s (4.32 to 5.40 acres) would not have contemplated the acquisition of a team. But Ferenc Orbán grew up with horses in his father's house. By the age of eight or nine, he was harnessing them himself; the horses bent down their heads that the boy might reach them. Having received his modest share, he began planning how he could acquire horses and continue as before farming like a team owner. He succeeded in his plan, an exceedingly bold one by Átány standards, by dint of much effort and self-sacrifice. He recalls those years as follows: "I often wonder how, being a frail man, I was able to do all this."

Quite a number of people shared the initial lot of Ferenc Orbán when their inherited land fell below the necessary amount for a career as a team owner. There were some who "took up the fight," as he did, and who were finally able to claim: "Though my father did not bequeath [land] to me, we secured our sustenance nevertheless." On the other hand, many others slid down into the growing number of teamless farmers. Many of the wealthy *gazda* families of the last century are now described as "having been prolific later"—meaning that the family holdings were divided among several children and that the successors have become relatively poor as a consequence.

18

THE CAREERS OF THREE FAMILIES

The chances for rise and decline in wealth are illustrated by three genealogical diagrams (see Figs. 30–33). They show how the fortune (or poverty) of an ancestor was transmitted to the descendants and how the latter managed to improve upon their legacies by marriage and purchase or how much they squandered of their inherited land. "Fortune" means land in this respect, being the most important and durable component of one's material wealth. Since daughters have been heirs of land for several generations already at Átány, both male and female descendants are shown in the graphs. Below the names of each married couple we have noted the inheritance of both husband and wife, and on the husband's side the amount acquired, or sold and lost, by them. The diagrams also include the younger generations who either have not yet inherited anything or have received but a part of their shares. Neither the land allotted in the course of the 1945 land reform nor the plots given to the state in the 1950s (see the Epilogue) are shown in the graphs.

We have noted the families which have emigrated from the village, but only those who left the village before collectivization. The graphs do not indicate the emigrations beginning with the early 1960s. Nor do they show those lone bachelors among them who were engaged in industrial work in the towns, although they still returned regularly to their parents' house, which was their real home.

In order to understand the emigration pattern better, we indicate spouses' provenance from outside Átány when so, since removal from the village is often the result or precondition of a marriage contracted with a spouse from another locality. We also marked the *vő*-s who have "married into" their wife's family.

Each graph represents a different socio-economic stratum. Each has been prepared with the help of one of our principal informants, who is marked by an asterisk in the respective diagram. Thus the graphs illustrate also the genealogical knowledge of an older person, but only part of it. These graphs necessarily relate to agnatic descent. Besides the relatives "from the father," those on the mother's, wife's, *meny*'s, and *vő*'s sides are also recognized by the people but are not indicated in the graphs.

Information furnished by other peasants corroborated our informants' statements about wealth. Our informants did show some uncertainty about a few families which migrated to other regions. We indicated these points of uncertainty in the diagrams, since they are evidence of the particular relationship having become attenuated. The data on children who died in their early years were also uncertain. We suspect that many of these are missing in the tables, but do not believe that this critically affects the picture of the inheritance of property which emerges.

The Kakas and Rózsa Families

The data in this graph (Fig. 30) were furnished by József Kakas. He traced not only the history of his own estate (inherited from both his father and mother), but also the many second- and third-generation descendants' handling of his paternal and maternal great-grandparents' estate.

Both the Kakas and the Rózsa families count among the most prestigious of Átány; their members have played a leading part in the village for centuries. The diagram shows a comparable number of *gazda* families in each family, some of which are on the level of the wealthiest in the community. The explanation for this is that the estates have been divided into relatively few parts in the course of succession. Only two cases show as many as four heirs; in all the remaining instances the estate has been partitioned among fewer successors. The relatively small number of children may well be an outcome of the desire of well-to-do families "to hinder the division of the property into many parts," as well as being some function of the characteristics of the individual families. The Kakas-s themselves regard the small number of their

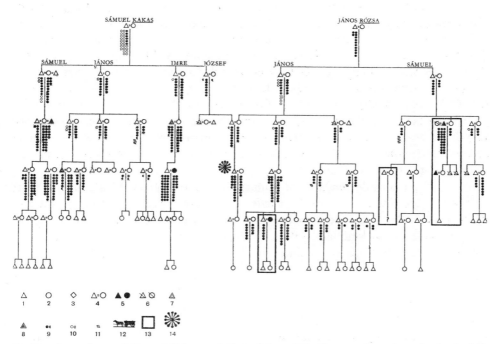

30. The descendants of Sámuel Kakas and János Rózsa. This diagram shows how the land of the ancestors was transferred to the descendants by inheritance and how their material situation was altered. For a more detailed explanation see pp. 261–62. Key to symbols used: (1) Male. (2) Female. (3) Descendant of unknown sex. (4) Marriage relation. (5) Male or female, respectively, deriving from another village. (6) Male or female, deceased at a young age. (7) *Vő* married into the family. (8) *Vő* married into the family from another village. (9) Units of inherited land: 2 *hold*-s or 1 *hold* (semicircle). (10) Units of bought or acquired land: 2 *hold*-s or 1 *hold* (semicircle). (11) Units of sold or lost land. (12) Owner of draft animals, applied in diagrams 31–33. (13) Emigrated from Átány. (14) Informant.

kinship as striking; they explain it by the fact that their family "isn't of prolific stock."

Both Sámuel Kakas and János Rózsa resided on the plots inherited from their fathers. Their wives were not landed. However, the women of the following generation did inherit land, so when marriage was contemplated they ascertained that the prospective husband was correspondingly wealthy. In this system the level of affluence of the parents can be preserved by having but two children. To be sure, the estate is divided into two halves, but the children gain an equivalent half by marriage to someone of the same socio-economic standing. In the case where there are three or four children, however, the descendants probably would "slide down." Conversely, the chances of gain for the single child are enhanced: upon finding a spouse of similar standing, the child may double the paternal estate. Among the Kakas sons, the branches of Sámuel and Imre furnish examples of this development. The two men had one daughter each, whose marriages were advantageous; the grandchildren have risen to among the ranks of the "first *gazda*-s." And among the Rózsa-s, the second son of János succeeded in rising by this same fluke.

Yet the choice of the mate was frequently influenced by factors other than wealth. For example, the grandfather of József Kakas (bearing the same name) married a poor girl. Such was the case because he was struck down by a carriage in his childhood. As a result of the injuries sustained, his shoulder, elbow, and face were disfigured, and although he was a son of a *gazda*, he was not able to marry any but a poor girl.

None of them was able to acquire land on a large scale except the first Sámuel Kakas. His opportunity to increase his fortune came with the favorable conditions for purchasing land in the period following the abolition of serfdom. But the diagram also shows some people who lost much of their property: the third son of János Kakas and several descendants of the Rózsa family. The reason in each case was alcoholism: "they liked the tavern too much."

Among the recent descendants of Sámuel Kakas and János Rózsa, in the fourth generation, there were six wealthy *gazda*-s in Átány plus the second daughter of Sámuel Rózsa, who married a well-to-do widower (as his second wife) and lived at a comparable socio-economic level in Tiszanána. Five more descendants were team owners with minor property holding, and three others were teamless farmers.

The Kiss Family

The ancestor, István Kiss, stood at the same level of wealth as his contemporaries in the Kakas and the Rózsa families (see Figs. 31 and 32), albeit the Kiss family never enjoyed quite the same rank nor esteem that the other two did. Despite the earlier affluence, all the heirs of István Kiss have become demoted in socio-economic status. Practically the only exception in the fourth generation is our informant, Sámuel Kiss. But his independent financial situation is actually the outcome of a fortunate marriage.

The diagrams show clearly how the descendants fell to a lower level through successive generations. There were no spendthrifts or drunkards in the family, however. Rather, the heirs' fall from affluence was determined almost exclusively by partitions among the children and by financially disadvantageous marriages.

Mihály and István, the two sons of the ancestor, were still *gazda*-s, each owning a *fertály* of land. However, their wives inherited nothing. (As we mentioned above, in this transitional period only some families allotted land to the daughters.) And the Kiss-s preserved the tradition, the *fertály*-s of Mihály and István were inherited by their sons; the daughters were satisfied with money and cows. (Fig. 31 does show inherited land under the names of Mihály's daughters, but this came not from their father but from two of their brothers who died without offspring.)

The turning point for the heirs came in the third generation. Mihály's estate was divided among three sons, István's between two. Despite the exclusion of the daughters from the inheritance, all five of the grandsons fell to the lowest level of team owner. And among the five, only the third son of Mihály succeeded in "breaking out," through a favorable marriage. He became a horse dealer and used to have cash at home. He was the relative who lent money free of interest to Samu Kiss when the latter's horse suddenly died and he urgently needed a replacement.

By the fourth generation land was being divided among sons and daughters in equal shares. Sons had a real advantage only in the case of the Madarász *ág*, in which both daughters ceded the house and the *kert* to an only son.

In the fourth generation, the first among the descendants of Mihály was a man, who was killed in World War I. His sister married the small-holder Sámuel Juhász who, because he was unable to keep a horse team, farmed with two cows as draft animals. The eldest Madarász daughter married János Gacsal, a small-holder clever at woodwork; he supplemented his meager income by his craft and was able to keep a single horse. Thus he was not a regular team owner either. Later he purchased a used thresher, and thus fitted out, embarked on a more prosperous course. In his old age he was even able to buy two *hold*-s (2.84 acres) of land and a second horse. A brother, János Madarász, surmounted his difficulties by a fortunate marriage. His wife's paternal inheritance actually amounted to little, since it totaled only two *hold*-s, but a childless uncle of the woman bequeathed her six *hold*-s (8.52 acres). Éva, the third Madarász child, a daughter, unfortunately contracted a bad marriage with Imre Ötvös. He was due to get a few *hold*-s as his inheritance, but he fell from his father's favor and was disinherited. Thereafter he earned his living as a village drummer. Nevertheless, Éva married him, as "he was a bachelor of fine stature; he used to sing beautifully."

The descendants of the Kollát and Kakas families were hard-working smallholders. They undertook cartage and jobbery, and one of them managed to acquire a thresher, just as had János Boldizsár.

We can discern similar events in István's line. His elder son, István (marked "3" on the diagram), was a hauler; he also undertook the threshing of grain with a team of horses for a share and thus managed to acquire two *hold*-s (2.84 acres) of land through his hard labor. Even so, he was unable to leave more than 8.5 *hold*-s

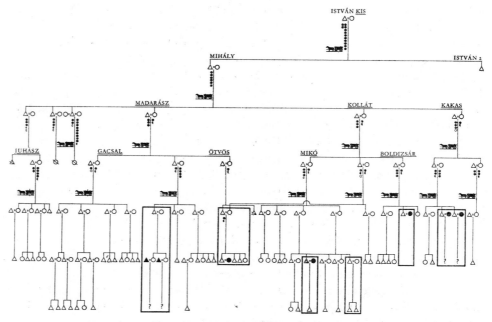

31. The descendants of István Kiss, I. (See explanation of this and the following diagram on pp. 262–63.) The symbols are the same as in Fig. 30.

(12.07 acres) to the three daughters. His first *vő*, Ádám Kovács, worked his small plot with draft cows and earned his living by day labor. The second, Márton Mérten, was a butcher and sausage maker. The third, Albert Mónusz, acquired a team of horses and undertook cartage, eventually managing to buy a small plot of his own.

Sámuel's children were lucky, since there were only two to divide their father's inheritance. Moreover, the younger Sámuel (our informant) contracted a favorable marriage, since his wife not only received the inheritance of her father but that of a childless uncle as well. Sámuel Kiss's sister lost her first husband early in her life; she then married our oft-quoted informant Ferenc Orbán, whose career has been dealt with in detail elsewhere.

In the Barát *ág* one of the daughters married a tobacco grower. They were not able to maintain even the level of teamless farmer. They and the Gönczi descendants shared in the modest acquisition of one or two *hold*-s allotted by the agrarian reform after World War I, but this did not change their status from that of poor small-holders.

Among the younger descendants, one can notice the striking effect of emigration: most of those who left Átány settled in Budapest as factory workers, but two were engaged as farm hands on the estates. The latter lived in neighboring villages at the time of the 1945 agrarian reform, where they settled permanently afterward.

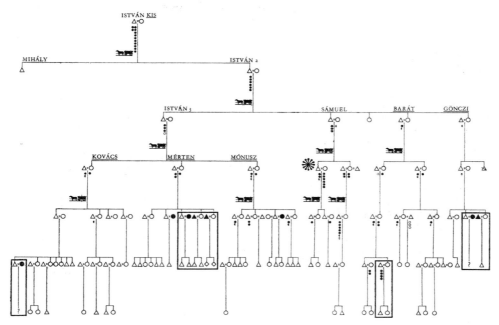

32. The descendants of István Kiss, II. (See Fig. 31, and explanation on pp. 262–63.) The symbols are the same as in Fig. 30.

The Madarász Family

The Madarász ancestors used to be herdsmen, herding horses and cattle for as long as anybody could recall. After the abolition of serfdom they were regarded as *zsellér*-s, and thus their predecessor, János Madarász, was given a *massza*. So János was unable to bequeath property to his five sons. Figure 33 shows how the descendants, starting thus essentially propertyless, managed to sustain themselves. (It should be noted at the outset that our key informant for this *ág*, János Madarász, known as "Madarász with the big moustache" in the village, was unable to remember his ancestors beyond his grandfather. This is significant: generally speaking, the poor peasants can recall one generation less than more affluent families, so their circle of kinsmen is accordingly smaller.)

The ancestor was married twice. He lived in the period when the plowing up of pastures reduced the need for a number of herdsmen. Of the two sons born to his first wife, János became a tobacco grower, while Ádám remained a herder. Both enjoyed similar good fortune: each built a house in the village, each purchased land, and each left his acquisitions to an only daughter. Thus their heirs, contracting favorable marriages, were able to start on the road to becoming team-owner farmers. One of the *ág*-s succeeded in "running in" among the first *gazda* families.

After the death of his first wife, an Átány girl, János Madarász chose his second wife from Poroszló. He had three sons by her, and they were unable to duplicate the

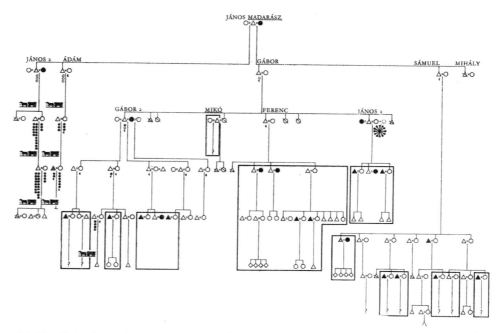

33. The descendants of János Madarász. (The explanation is given on pp. 265–67.) The symbols are the same as in Fig. 30.

fortunate careers of their older step brothers. Gábor became a farm laborer, rising merely to the rank of a "farm-hand *gazda*." He purchased two *hold*-s of land and an old house in the village. He had nine children, five of whom survived childhood. (Gábor has already been discussed above in Chapter 13, "The Rise and Decline of Individuals and Families.")

Gábor's eldest son ("Gábor 2" in the diagram) was a tough and ambitious man. He was known to have litigated with his brothers as well. He was a "farm-hand *gazda*." Purchasing three *hold*-s (4.26 acres) of land, he then settled in the village, becoming a sharecropper. His successors did not have much success. His *vő*-s were poor people living in the village; one of them was a harvester, the other, physically weak, a barber and a builder of ovens. His only son became a farm hand on an estate. One of his granddaughters married into a *gazda* family; the rest of his grandchildren emigrated from the parish. Among these are a factory worker, a soldier, a ship's master, and a tractor driver in a town of the Great Plain.

Another of the elder Gábor's children, Ferenc, owned a house and one *hold* of land at Átány, but he earned his bread in Budapest working in a factory for some 22 years. All of his descendants have left the village, and he joined them in his old age. One of his sons stuck to rural life, settling in Transdanubia in 1945, where he acquired more land than he could have in Átány. The other son became a railway-man. His *vő* was a tram conductor at Miskolc. His grandchildren all became "learned people"; one of them occupies a leading administrative position in his town.

Now follows our informant, "big-moustached" János Madarász. He was first a farm hand, next a harvester, and then finally worked as a thatcher and carpenter. His sons married outsiders and live in Budapest; one is a railwayman, another a driver, and the third a structural steel fitter on bridge constructions.

Turning back to the fourth son of the ancestor, Sámuel, we again see the descendants going off in several directions. Sámuel himself was a farm laborer on an estate, but he acquired a house in Átány and returned there as an old man. His eldest son married into a family of teamless farmers in a neighboring Heves village. Of the others, two became farm hands on an estate, one a day laborer and sharecropper in the village, another a railway employee. Except for the eldest, all lived at home. But the majority of the grandchildren have left the village: one works in a mine, another on construction work in a town of the Great Plain, but most of them have settled in Budapest.

The youngest son of the ancestor, Mihály, stuck to the herdsman's profession, but he was killed as a young man in World War I.

Summing up the quantity of land used by the peasants included in the diagrams, we obtain the following distribution, listed according to the means by which the property was acquired:

Inheritance by men:	862 *hold*-s
Inheritance by women:	710 *hold*-s[30]
Land acquired (purchased):	127 *hold*-s
Land lost (sold):	14 *hold*-s

Although not mentioned in all cases in the histories of individual families, it is important to note the mortality in wars: nine of the men figuring in our sample lost their lives in World War I and seven in World War II.

MOBILITY IN THE LAST ONE HUNDRED YEARS

The form and processes of social mobility during the period of serfdom and after its abolition have been roughly outlined in our discussion of land tenure (see Chapter 2, "Land Tenure"). A main development was the parceling up of large peasant holdings and the increase in the number of *zsellér*-s.[31] The process of dividing up *telek*-s begun in the eighteenth century, in the period of serfdom, accelerated after 1848. The absolute number of farms of course increased. In 1828 there were 186 farms at Átány; in 1866 the number of units, including the dwarf holdings of the *zsellér*-s, totaled 402; by 1935, 715 holdings were to be counted.

---

[30] In the younger generations the estates inherited by men and women are almost equal, but the sum given here includes ancestors whose wives had not received land. In the fourth generation the inherited property of men and women shows a proportion of 159 : 155.5, with a slight advantage to the males.

[31] In 1847 the national percentage of *zsellér*-s in the total population of serfs was 59.5 per cent. In Heves county this proportion was even greater. In some parishes of the county there were two to three *zsellér*-s for each *telek*-owning serf. When serfdom was abolished in 1848, 87 per cent (or, according to another calculation, 83.5 per cent) of the peasants had holdings under one *telek*. The national average held by each land-owning serf was 0.41 *telek* (Orosz, 1965: 56, 59, 73–74).

The period immediately following the abolition of serfdom saw great flux and transition; it was an age of great risk, leading either to quick enrichment or to speedy impoverishment. The various restrictions on the serf's *telek*-s barred an accumulation of wealth, but they also protected the farms. Given the new system of free exchange of land, plus favorable conditions for the sale of cereal crops, people of enterprising spirit and ability acquired fortunes with a speed which before and thereafter was considered unimaginable. This is illustrated by the career of the Vajda family. Péter Vajda appeared in the 1828 census as a miller, not even owning his own house. His son, by 1848, possessed a house, had three *fertály*-s of a serf *telek*, and held the office of village mayor. In the course of the settlement of agrarian relations he purchased the "Szathmáry share" (a minor estate of one of the landlords) and took possession of several hundred *hold*-s in the course of reallocation. But he wore the *gatya* (linen trousers) and still worked in the fields, just like any other peasant. And his daughters were given into marriage to peasants. His son, Sámuel, worked at his father's side and courted the girls of the village, but finally married an "*úr* woman" (a lady). In the years that followed his house and life became adapted to the standards of the country gentlemen. Although he cultivated his kinship and friendship links with the peasants, he was addressed by them as "honorable *úr*." The rural life was ultimately eschewed by the children: his daughters married pastors and a doctor, and his son attended an agricultural college; all of them emigrated from the village.

In the first decades after the change the population did not seem to understand the full meaning of property entered in the land registry under their own names (a similar phenomenon was noticed regarding the new rules relating to possession of interior holdings, see Chapter 1, "The Appearance of the Village"). Nor was the value or price of land fixed definitely. Some *zsellér*-s are recalled who ceded their *massza*, their share in the arable and grazing land, to another for a loaf of bread. Some of the one-time *zsellér*-s amassed as many as five or six *massza*-s, while others remained wholly landless. János Boross recounted: "My mother was born in 1837; she was given a heifer by her father. With the price of that one female calf, they bought 900 square fathoms of vineyard"—an extremely good bargain relative to the subsequent value of such land. Also, the minor shares that the *úr*-s were entitled to were offered for sale if the *úr*-s did not want to farm them.[32]

On the other hand, several well-to-do *gazda* families lost all their property within a few years' time because they were unable to manipulate the new possibilities for buying and selling land by means of mortgaging. One of the wealthy *ág*-s of the Ötvös family, which to this day bears the nickname "half-*úr*" Ötvös, after the genteel customs of their predecessors, sank from the level of well-to-do *gazda*-s to tobacco growers on an estate. Querying the fate of such families, we were told the saying of a *gazda* who was addicted to drink and was selling his land bit by bit; when criticized, he

---

[32] In this period the sale of peasant land was widespread all over the country. According to investigations made in villages in various parts of the country, by the 1860s and 1870s 10 to 20 per cent (and in some parts as high as 50 per cent) of the land-owning serfs who were liberated in 1848 had lost their estates. Rising fortunes like those of the Vajda family, on the other hand, were no great rarity either (Orosz, 1965: 63–72).

answered: "If no one becomes bankrupt, no one can become *gazda*"—observing that the ruin of some people enabled others to increase their estates. In this he was right, for the almost entirely fixed boundaries of Átány land made extension of one's property in effect possible only at the expense of others.

These possibilities for socio-economic mobility were soon changed by the transformation of the national economic situation. At the end of the 1880s, the so-called wheat crisis set in. Hungarian wheat, traditionally sold at a good price in Europe, was undersold and edged out of the foreign markets by cheaper Russian and overseas wheat. Within a few years the price of wheat did not cover the average costs of production in Hungary. The economy of the country survived this crisis only through establishment of protective tariffs at the beginning of the twentieth century. And during the crisis a large number of peasant farms both in the surrounding countryside and in the village were ruined.

At just about the same time farming on the large neighboring estates became more intensive. The hitherto almost exclusive concentration on cereals was replaced by more diversified agriculture. Cultivation of industrial plants, root crops, and especially sugar beets offered job opportunities to an ever-increasing number of day laborers.

The same period witnessed the growing migration to the towns to find work. As industry developed by leaps and bounds, it sucked in manpower from the villages. Within the single decade from 1900 to 1910, one-seventh of the agricultural population emigrated from its ancient home in the rural hinterlands to the towns. Development was quickest in the capital, the pace of its growth surpassing all the large cities of Europe during those years.[33] It was in the same period that emigration of rural labor began and assumed ever growing proportions, especially to the United States.[34]

Átány was in no way exempt from these profound changes in the life of the land. In the 1870s, the Budapest–Miskolc–Kassa railroad was constructed, and in a short time branch lines connected the parish directly with the national communications network. The great loss through emigration, 11 per cent between 1900–1910 (see Table 6), proves that Átány has lost swarms of its inhabitants to the cities and abroad. These statistics include both those who looked for a job opportunity in the towns for only a few months or years and those who settled there for good. During these decades work in the cities, especially in Budapest, became one of the major sources of income for teamless farmers.

[33] The population of Budapest more than doubled between 1890 and 1910 from 500,000 to 1,100,000. Between 1869 and 1910 the population of nine major Hungarian towns similarly more than doubled (Rácz, 1965: 440–444; Lettrich, 1965: 27).

[34] Between 1899 and 1919, 3.8 per cent of the population whose mother tongue was Hungarian emigrated; the proportion who went to North America was by far the greatest (Rácz, 1965: 457). At the beginning of the century two to three thousand peasants left Heves county every year to settle in the U.S.A. Most of them left their families at home, intending to return to Hungary. In 1909, the authorities of Heves county reported that 34 per cent of the former emigrants had indeed returned. According to one national estimate, a quarter of the emigrants to the U.S.A. returned home (Borovszky, 1909: 200; Rácz, 1965: 477). Migration to the towns and abroad profoundly changed the proportions of age groups in the rural population of the whole country by increasing the ratio of the older generation. A correlated change was the diminished birth rate. Rising agricultural wages constituted a further correlated change.

The story goes that when one bachelor returned home to Átány after a season's work in the sugar factory at Hatvan, at the end of the last century, his father refused to believe that the sum of his son's wages could have been gotten in a lawful way. Money earned by industrial work in the cities and the sums sent home from America[35] did much to stimulate mobility among the local society at home and to free land, which was a principal expression of social mobility. By World War I, several domains of the landlords had been parceled out. The new opportunities for acquiring land almost equaled those in the period after the abolition of serfdom. In the course of a few years some families rose quickly to the level of wealthy *gazda*-s. Raising a mortgage played a prominent part in the purchase of land. Thus I. L., being "a man of courage," bought sixty *hold*-s of land with credit, although he had no more collateral than twelve *hold*-s of his own. In order to pay both mortgage and interest, each year he sold a piece of his plot until the devaluation following World War I enabled him to disencumber his property with the price of a single calf. (Similarly, inflation has helped to free other farms from the burden of ever-heavier bank rates.)

After World War I, in 1920, the government initiated a land reform program of modest proportions.[36] Building sites were measured out at the two ends of the village and poor people, the "proletarians," constructed houses on them with the help of cheap state credit. Some arable and grazing land also was distributed, in plots of one or two *hold*-s. As a result, some new small holdings were created while some, already extant were enlarged or strengthened. Parcelizations continued too. When the "Ballai piece" was parceled out, the well-to-do *gazda*-s swooped down on the land offered for sale "like hawks." Many of these purchases were effected with bank credit. Even heavier, then, was the impact of the economic crisis of the early 1930s on encumbered farms. State aid enabled several insolvent peasant farms to survive these years.

During the crisis job opportunities in Budapest also became restricted. Population statistics show a noticeable increase in the Átány population, since many people who were employed temporarily in Budapest lost their jobs and returned to the village (see Tables 2 and 6). According to the census of the village magistracy, in the winter of 1931–32, 158 families with 563 members were destitute, lacking basic sustenance.

---

[35] The changes initiated by the money which emigrants sent home was to be felt all over the country. Speculation in the sale of land and parcelization began (Rácz, 1965: 480–481). In 1906 alone, peasants who emigrated to North America sent home to Heves county almost one and a half million Austro-Hungarian *korona*-s (Borovszky, 1909: 200).
As a result of the parcelizations around the turn of the century (between 1890 and 1914) about two million *hold*-s (2.84 million acres) of land, earlier part of large estates, became the property of small holders, without any state intervention or coercion. (In 1913 the total area of all estates in Hungary over 100 *hold*-s amounted to 26,580,000 *hold*-s. Zagoroff, Végh, and Bilimovich, 1955: 158.)
[36] The 1920 land reform touched only about 5 per cent of the agricultural territory in Hungary, much less than the agrarian reforms of the other Danubian states executed after World War I. The average parcel allotted to one person was only 1.5 *hold*-s. In 1936 a supplementary act ordered the partition of additional but much smaller estates. However, these plots were not divided into dwarf-holdings, but were rather used to augment small properties so that they could be self-sufficient. This was the time when the "Székesgyep," the former "Hercegtag" ("Prince's lot"), the property of the Princes Coburg-Koháry at Átány, was parceled out (see Chapter 2, "The Fields") (M. Somlyai, 1965; Zagoroff, Végh, and Bilimovich, 1955: 40, 113–115, 159–161).

Relief did not come until the late 1930s, when the World War II years again brought a boom.

"The uppermost" of the *gazda*-s owned eighty to one hundred *hold*-s (113.60 to 142 acres). However, the affluence and financial leadership of a family usually did not last longer than two or three generations. In a familiar pattern, either unsuccessful economic ventures or fragmentation by inheritance would push the descendants down into lower socio-economic echelons.

Agricultural statistics from 1930 illustrate the standing of the Átány people. Unfortunately, the table we present (see Table 6) distorts the actual situation in two respects: on the one hand, it includes data on the servants employed on the Szárazbő manorial farms; on the other, it reckons principally with earners in agriculture, with the consequence that the proportion of day laborers and seasonal workers (whose family members are independently gainfully employed) seems to be larger than that of *gazda*-s (whose active family members are counted merely as helpers). The category of helpers for which there is no breakdown as to groups of occupation available makes the estimation of the ratios between the various strata difficult in itself. For this reason below the percentage distribution of the 1,002 agricultural earners of Átány is given, not including the helpers. According to the 1930 register, owners of more than ten *hold*-s (14.20 acres), those who were more or less able to live from the income of their plots, totaled 11.2 per cent. Then follows the category of people owning one to ten *hold*-s (1.42 to 14.20 acres), the poor team owners, and the teamless farmers who were dependent on wages to supplement their income, with a percentage of 30.5. The majority of wage earners were represented by the owners of dwarf-holdings who worked others' land, by day laborers, by agricultural workers, and by farm hands, totaling 58.3 per cent. Among these, 10.5 per cent owned plots under one *hold*, 13.4 per cent were farm hands without land.

This was the stratification as it existed through the war and which was transformed by the 1945 agrarian reform.[37] Átány's 376 applicants, more than 50 per cent of the people with local rural occupations, received shares of the 2,000 *hold*-s (2,840 acres) of land distributed at that time. The 1949 census then found the majority (62.1 per cent) of the population possessing one to ten *hold*-s, a larger number having five to ten *hold*-s than one to five *hold*-s. But the group owning lots of ten to 25 *hold*-s also increased, totaling 20.9 per cent of the population. Only small percentages of the rural

---

[37] The 1945 decree on land reform ordered the appropriation of all estates over 1,000 *hold*-s (1,420 acres) and almost all holdings over 200 *hold*-s (284 acres). The expropriation embraced 34 per cent of the agricultural lands of the country. About 20 per cent was divided among the landless peasants and dwarf-holders who claimed eligibility. A national average of 4.6 *hold*-s (6.53 acres) was allotted each claimant. The size of the allotment depended on the original size of the expropriated estates in the particular village as well as the number of eligible families (M. Somlyai, 1965).

The guide lines used for redistribution in Átány were the following: a family of three members could receive a maximum of four *hold*-s, a family of four members a maximum of five, a family of six members a maximum of six *hold*-s of land (5.68, 7.10, or 8.52 acres, respectively). The dwarf-holders could complement their holdings to the above limits. The Átány poor did not receive all the land of the Átány estates; on orders from above, they had to assign more than 300 *hold*-s (426 acres) to the neighboring village of Kömlő, where the amount of available property was smaller. Finally 1,400 *hold*-s (1,988 acres) were used to found a state farm. In the course of the land reform, 163 building sites were also measured out.

population fell to either extreme: 2 per cent possessed plots under one *hold;* 4.7 per cent owned property over 25 *hold*-s in size. The proportion of landless agricultural laborers fell to 10.3 per cent, and the estate farm hands disappeared entirely.

In the tables not only the statistics for Átány but also the regional and national figures are worth our attention. Prior to the land reform, the statistics show that Átány landholding per capita was slightly above the surrounding areas: there were somewhat more independent *gazda*-s and landowners in the village than in the neighborhood. After the land reform, the large proportion of middle-sized peasant holdings at Átány was even more conspicuous.

The appearance of the "new *gazda*-s" did not change only the proportions of the older village stratification, they also changed the traditional order of founding an independent farmstead. We have illustrated with the example of Ferenc Orbán how a small-holding teamless farmer might pull himself up to the status of *gazda* by well-planned, pertinacious effort. But the new *gazda*-s were given land without equipment, and at a time when the livestock of the entire village had been reduced by the war to a small fraction of the usual numbers. Ignoring the traditional order of farming, they helped each other in various ways, sometimes harnessing a horse and a cow together in front of the plow, or they tilled their soil manually, by hoeing. Some of them later renounced their plots or tried to let them out to team-owning farmers to be cultivated for cash or labor while they themselves continued the way of life of teamless farmers. However, some of them did in fact succeed in establishing an independent farm. In the eyes of the old *gazda*-s, however, these "new *gazda*-s" represented a separate stratum, principally because of their nontraditional farming techniques. As Károly Bedécs said: "We proper peasants know about the horse better, for we grew up at its side; these new *gazda*-s, even if they have a team, work with cattle; they plow with two cows, not daring to begin with a horse."

All these movements upon which we have focused involved "the people of the soil" of Átány. The number of secessions from "the people of the soil" was relatively small as a whole, at least until World War II. No *gazda* family succeeded in imitating the example of Sámuel Vajda in becoming an *úr*. During World War II several of the daughters of the two largest *gazda* families married pastors or schoolmasters. A well-to-do *gazda* founded a distillery and played an active part in a national association of the distilling industry. He abandoned the customs of the peasants, e.g., he did not take a satchel with provisions on his rounds; he tried to behave like an *úr*, but he soon became ruined financially. Some of the *gazda* families built and furnished houses which did not fall into line with local traditions, but rather were adapted from the models of the houses of the pastor, the village secretary, and the *úr*-s.

There are a few examples of people leaving the peasantry through their education. "General Ötvös," the only really famous son of the village, a scion of a peasant family, succeeded in becoming a company officer in the second half of the last century, but his knowledge did not stem from actual academic studies. Another son of a rather poor team-owner family became an engineer before World War I and for a while was active at Átány. Another typical example is furnished by the case of S. Ö. His wealthy parents sent him to study in the famous Sárospatak college, but he flunked out after the fourth form. But even this brief education, and his wealth and rank, raised him to be a director of the local consumers' cooperative (*Hangya szövetkezet*), a post he occupied for several decades. Studies in agricultural schools brought more success. Four Átány youths qualified in these on the medium level before World War I and later filled minor offices on the surrounding estates. One of them rose far above the others, becoming a bailiff, and was able to send his son to an academy. After World War II, some poor teamless farmers urged their sons to qualify for the profession of teacher. Some have been employed in the local school, and one is the present headmaster. Their success has produced a new local "intelligentsia."

Nevertheless, the well-to-do *gazda*-s did not regard the career of a "learned man" as an absolute rise in status. The teacher or the lower administrative official was a "quill driver," obeying orders, lacking independence, and not living off his own land (see Chapter 12, "Non-peasants in the Village"). Elderly *gazda*-s explained why they did not send their children to study: they did not want them "to take the bread from those who have no other sustenance." Industrial work was held in even less esteem. A *gazda* whose son became a skilled worker and built a house in the outskirts of Budapest told us: "After all, my son has become a tramp in Pest."

In most cases the ultimate purpose of tobacco growers, servants, workers in towns, or emigrants to America, was to return to Átány.[38] Since the beginning of the century, however, numerous people have emigrated for good, chiefly to Budapest—to become house porters, school attendants, workers, etc. But these emigrants did not cut the ties with their place of birth either, for they would return to the village on the occasion of family festivals. Finally, those who had sunk to the lowest ebb both morally and financially found refuge in the capital. "He has gone to Budapest; he did not return," often means that the person mentioned was an outcast.[39]

---

[38] Here is the case of a poor man who worked in Budapest for a long time, as told by his neighbor: "Old Imre Tót left his father's house with a loaf of bread, perhaps even without that, and went to a landlord to become a hired man. Six daughters and one son were born to him. He was called up in World War I. He was wounded in the leg and became a war invalid. He left the service and went to Budapest, where he worked on Margaret Island on a sports ground. Being a good worker, he was liked by the foremen. In the meantime his family lived at home; but when his daughters and his son grew up they too found occupations in Budapest, at his side on the sports ground or in gardening establishments. In the meantime he used his savings to buy now a *massza*, then one *hold* of land. As an old man he owned nine *hold*-s [12.78 acres] of land. But they went hungry and toiled terribly for that land. They would take the food from their mouths and sell the porker or the cow in order to buy land. Tót's daughters were given in marriage in the same way: two pillows, one small eiderdown. Everything went for land. He returned home after World War II sixty years old. He thought he could then live off his property, and so he acquired a team of horses too."

[39] In 1908 there was an exodus of *gazda*-s too. They were informed that the parcelization of a large estate in the north offered favorable conditions for buying land, and fifteen *gazda*-s left with their families. There they purchased extensive holdings but some of them did not sell their Átány homes, intending all along to return in a few years. About half of the group did in fact return.

During the 1945 agrarian reform, eight families, all poor teamless farmers, left to settle in the western half of the country, where the distribution of large estates resulted in larger allotments than at Átány.

CHAPTER 14.
THE ROLE OF SOCIAL STRATIFICATION
IN EVERYDAY BEHAVIOR

DIFFERENCES IN WAY OF LIFE

Within the framework of "the people of the soil" differences in the quality of food, clothing, and household furnishings and repair are not necessarily indicative of corresponding differences in financial standing. If the *gazda* has surplus income, he first of all devotes it to obtaining more livestock. When his farm is sufficiently stocked with animals, when he feels that he is "caught up," he will buy any items of farm equipment that he is missing. Not until these things are accomplished is there any relaxation of frugality in regard to clothing and, still later, in regard to food. Expenditure on the furniture of the house comes last of all. However, concessions made toward personal comfort, finer clothing, etc., may come still later if the ambitious *gazda* intends to acquire land, as in the case of the aforementioned *gazda*, formerly a tobacco grower, who owned sixty *hold*-s (85.20 acres) and who "dared not eat his fill once in all his life."

In the morality of the villagers self-denying, careful, and efficient work is esteemed. At dawn the *gazda*-s cut short their hours of rest by competing with each other to be the first to start for the fields. In accord with these norms, purchases serving personal comfort instead of the development of one's agricultural enterprises are regarded with a certain suspicion. It is a general principle in Átány households that spending money is to be avoided; cash is to be saved as much as possible. Fine clothing, abundant meals, and large houses are desirable and respected, but a certain esteem is due to a person who, though able to procure all these, decides to renounce them.

Anecdotes are told about wealthy *gazda*-s who go about in shabby attire. The prosperous Pál Tóth drove his fine horses to the mill in Eger but, being dressed in rags and tatters, he was mistaken for a farm hand from an estate. He was asked about the landlord who owned the beautiful team. He answered with pride, "It is mine; you may buy it at once if you want to and if you have enough money." The old Győr, one of the wealthiest *gazda*-s in the community, is said "to have even been proud of his shabby clothes." "Old Kollát carried money to the savings-bank wearing a tattered frieze cloak, while those in dress boots took money out."

The situation is similar with housing. Some wealthy *gazda* families build large, "L-shaped," "angled" houses following the bourgeois fashion; others, equally

274

wealthy, stay in their simple, old, one-roomed houses, while some of the *gazda*-s of lesser property construct houses which rival the largest ones.

The stable and the *kert* furnish more accurate information on the size of the farm and the property. The man of whom it is said that "the animals leave his stable by two doors" is regarded as a big *gazda* even if he lives in a simple house. Special attention is devoted to the neatness of the yard and the *kert*. They not only reflect financial standing, but also the care and orderliness of the *gazda*. As the villagers say, the yard "reveals all secrets and shows the quality of the family." "If one sees straw and feed thrown about or stumbles over tools, one may assume that the *gazda* is disorderly." The *kert* and the yard of the *gazda*-s are kept smooth, especially the traditional threshing yard, where not a weed or a single blade of grass is tolerated. To say "May your yard be overgrown with grass" was a serious curse, because it implied such dire poverty that there would not even be any animals to tread down the ground.

But the most conspicuous sign of the quality of the *gazda* and of his farm are the team and its equipment, the harness and the carriage. In this respect the otherwise sober and extremely thrifty people of Átány are lured to extravagant investments without any real immediate profit. Besides the wagon used for everyday work, the wealthy *gazda*-s also possessed "parade harness" for the horses and a "light carriage" with fine mountings and paint for festive occasions. It is said that in the 1930s, "Mankind competed fiercely one against the other in the matter of horse trappings." The *gazda*-s followed new fashions every year, trying to surpass each other. The old Győr was famous for his fine horses, and a conversation he had with the equally wealthy Sámuel Galvács lives on in memory. He said to the parsimonious Galvács, "Why do you save money like a miser? No one sees it, no one esteems you for it… but if I drive through the village or into the market, everyone stares at me." In the case of an exogamous marriage when a strange wedding party visits Átány or the villagers drive to another community, the first thing to be appraised is the quality of the horses. "They have come here with three fine horses. They cannot be badly off; horses are not kept on nothing." A scrawny, unkempt horse, however, was mentioned as "a disgrace to the *gazda*."[40]

As signs of status, the people of Átány believe that "it is not the things inside the house that are important, but those outside of it," such as the yard, the property, the livestock, and the quality of the work. For example, they say about the father of I. S., "What a store of books he had—two bookcases full of books with golden covers, but his horses could hardly pull an empty cart." Therefore he was not esteemed at all. On the contrary, everyone knew that "the horses coming out of the yard of the Vajda-Kálosi family are unequaled by any in the village."

Nevertheless, the people of Átány know how much food is sufficient to provide for a family of a given size, and by comparison with this standard they are able to tell which households are well supplied and which ones scantily.

[40] At the turn of the century the proverb still held: "Two horses are poverty, three horses honor, four horses decorum, five horses luxury."

They reckon that two and a half to three *mázsa*-s of wheat are sufficient to feed an adult for a year. This quantity of wheat is the basis of the diet, providing the various forms of bread, cakes, and noodles consumed. The same ration is reckoned for *gazda* and *zsellér* alike and has almost always been secured by the poor as well as the rich. This sufficiency is the foundation of the relative well-being of the people of Átány; this is why they say that "a poor man at Átány is a lord compared with a poor man at Heves," since the latter often lacks even the necessary supply of bread. The difference between a *gazda* and a *zsellér* or a farm hand is better measured by the quantity of fat and meat consumed. "One who does not stick a pig is a real pauper," the saying goes. The nourishment of the family sinks to a lower level if there is no pigsticking; the consequences are felt throughout the year. Even poor teamless farmers endeavor to stick a piglet at least. On the other hand, the household of a wealthy *gazda* kills four to five pigs a year, and sometimes a sheep in autumn too,[41] besides consuming poultry more freely. Poor people take to market the few chickens they raise. The wealthy *gazda*-s are able to celebrate pig slaughtering with large feasts, treating their guests to fresh pork, black pudding, and sausages and sending their many kinsmen and friends a taste. Some of the *zsellér*-s and a few farm hands raise cows, so their diet is supplemented by sweet or sour milk, curd, and dishes requiring milk. However, many of the teamless farmers do not consume milk except when they are given a jugful as a present or as a reward for some work. Vineyards are owned mostly by *gazda*-s, and they can drink wine from their own grapes or have brandy distilled from the fruit or the marc. As a rule, the farm hands of the estates do not taste wine all year round.

The family and the livestock of a *gazda* are provided for mainly from his own crops. He has provisions stored up for at least a year, usually longer. It is said of good crops that they are "not given by God for one year only"; a portion of the produce is saved. Wealthy *gazda*-s are proud of the fact that they have the wheat from the preceding year ground, so as to have reserves for a whole year. Farm laborers, *zsellér*-s, and those team owners who have small plots lack these reserves. But the sense of economy in dealing with given provisions is different too. The *gazda*-s scold the poor for "not practising economy," and there is much truth in their opinion. The farm hands receive their wages in kind quarterly; there is great feasting in their homes when the payment is made, while they live scantily toward the end of the quarter. Occasionally in poor households the wheat and flour run short before the harvest, so they have to borrow at usurious rates until the new crops come in. On the other hand, in the economy of the *gazda*-s, economizing, dealing with resources, and long-range planning of consumption became a highly refined art. They have reserves for a year or two. The poor plan for a shorter period and their consumption is adapted to the resources of the moment; consequently their households suffer from economic instability and they often come into desperate straits and have to resort to loans.[42]

As regards dress, in spite of the examples of *gazda*-s who wear tattered clothes,

---

[41] It should be remembered that workers (sharecroppers, day laborers, and helpers) also regularly took their meals at the table of a wealthy *gazda*.

[42] We deal with this in more detail in our manuscript on Átány agriculture and households.

there are a number of proverbs to the effect that wealth and social standing are manifested in attire. Thus the marriage of people of the same rank is commended by the adage "a moccasined man [i.e., without boots] is the mate of the moccasined woman," meaning that a poor man ought to choose a poor wife, whereas "the mate of the velvet is silk." It is said that even the death knell rings according to the different costume of rich and poor; when a rich man is buried, the great bell says: "*bíborba—bársonyba*" (in purple, in velvet), while at the burial of a poor man the small bell rings: "*suba— guba, ringy—rongy*" (sheepskin coat and tatters).

In earlier times the differences in attire between the various strata of rural society were less conspicuous. "When people wore a cambric *gatya*, the difference was less; rich and poor were more distinguishable when cloth trousers became fashionable." The Átány population has become "more addicted to costume" only in the recent past. Until World War I men generally possessed a single suit of broadcloth; since around 1920 the wealthy have had a light-colored "good" suit made in addition to their light summer "working" suit. Thus in the wardrobe of a *gazda* one finds an everyday suit and a dress suit for both winter and summer, and people who hold a village or church office need a third one too, since "they could not go to collect the dog tax in the same suit which they wore when they partook of the Lord's Supper," nor could they go in their workday attire. The poor cannot afford to have such a differentiated wardrobe; they have no dress clothes, and sometimes not even enough warm ones for the winter. Their suits are not manufactured to order by the tailor, but purchased in the market ready-made. As a contrast to the black broadcloth suits of the *gazda*-s, they wear yellowish-gray, "colorless" ones, the traditional hue of a farm hand's clothing throughout the country. In the winter the *gazda*-s rarely take off their high boots, and the old ones even sleep in the stables with their boots on. Besides their everyday boots they also have stiff shiny dress boots. A farm hand and a *zsellér* in summer often go barefoot, and some of them can afford only ankle boots for the winter.

Like the men, the women of all strata wear "rural" or "peasant" clothes. Only the costumes of the marriageable daughters and young wives are exceptions to this rural style. The young females are said to be "fashioning," imitating the recent bourgeois styles and ordering outfits like those in the fashion magazines. The trends are set by the young wives and daughters of the wealthy *gazda*-s, who have their clothes made by the dressmakers at Heves and bring back the latest styles to the village. The old outfits of the *gazda* daughters are sold to poor people's daughters (such as the daughter of their sharecropper) the next year; it is this year's difference in fashion plus the difference between new and used articles of clothing that distinguish the social strata. An observer might think that this "fashioning" is a sign that the rural style is being abandoned for good. But after the few bright years of their youth, when they are dressed according to Budapest fashions, the young wives don the dark peasant costumes which have earned the name of "crow" for the Átány women in the surrounding villages. (This "fashioning" of the young women has been going on since the end of the last century.) In the rural attire of the elder Átány women the difference

19*

of the strata is the same as with men: their stock of clothes may be ample or deficient, and the material may be more expensive or cheaper.

As regards housing, the farm hands and tobacco growers are "under a different star" than the villagers. In the farm laborers' dwellings on the estates one room is frequently allotted to two families and a kitchen is used by four. The narrow rooms can hold only a few pieces of furniture, and in many cases the beds of the children consist of straw scattered on the floor. Measured by the standards of the village, living on the estates is disorderly camping, by no means an existence "in the Átány way." In addition, such places were unsuitable for the proper celebration of family feasts too.[43]

In the village the dwellings are similar to each other on the whole. In both the large L-shaped houses and in the old traditional *zsellér* homes one living room and one kitchen served the everyday needs. The large houses have one or more additional "good rooms" containing decorated furniture and oleographs on the walls, but these cannot be heated, and the family spends little time in them except for rare special occasions. Otherwise they are simply places where the wealth and rank of the family are exhibited. The ornamental bed with the tall pile of pillows and eiderdown quilts heaped on it is also indicative of the wealth and status of the family. Another pride of the *gazdasszony*-s is the stock of home-made linen rolled up in large bolts, which also represents a kind of reserve.

The daily and yearly work schedules of the members of each family are determined by the way of life implied by the family's social status. A wealthy *gazda* usually gets up at dawn; it is his task to wake up the farm hands. The workday of the team owner is generally longer than that of the teamless farmer, since the former has to feed, water, and clean up the animals at dawn and in the evening, but he also goes out to the fields with the teamless farmers, who do not have to take care of any livestock. The work of the *gazda* is made easier by the fact that the harvest of the cereals and hoeing of corn and sugar beets are done by others for a share, and the stable is kept clean by the farm hand. But he does the plowing, sowing, mowing, and the work in the vineyard himself. With *gazda*-s owning more extensive property, however, work may be suspended for half a day, a whole day, or an even longer period between these chores. On the days when they do not go out to the fields, the men busy themselves in the *kert*, and the women find some occupation in the house. Both the men and the draft animals have a rest. Winter is also a time of rest for them, a period of tending the animals or mending and manufacturing utensils. Those who have medium-sized plots—for instance, carters—cannot afford such relaxation. When Ferenc Orbán was a carter, after a day spent working he would go out in the evening or in the moon-

---

[43] This is one reason why the farm hands of the estates and the tobacco growers strove vigorously, often for most of their lives, to acquire a house in the village. They wanted to live out their old age "in the Átány way," in accordance with a value which was instilled in their hearts in childhood, but which they could never put into practice. In the early 1950s we visited the house of a family of former tobacco growers who had "settled home" into the village. The old man, serene and calm, sat in the chimney corner with his back to the stove, smoking his pipe in his own living room furnished in the Átány way, like a man who has reached the goal of his life.

light with his cart if somebody wanted him; he did not want to miss the opportunity to earn some money. He tried to get carting jobs for the winter too. In the years following World War I the teamless farmers and day laborers had even less chance to rest in winter. Since they had to go to the towns to earn money, they could not attend the *tanyázás* in the stables even during the winter months. For them the time spent out of work meant the involuntary interruption of income, and thus also hardship and anxiety. Nor did the farm hands of the estates have time to rest in the circle of their families; they had to go out with their oxen to perform the required work rain or shine, in frost or in snow.

The people of the village realize that all people do not bear "equal yokes." One's situation is influenced to some degree by one's individual character, ambition, and luck. But a wealthy man can "more easily spare himself"; he is able to live and to provide for his family even if he "does not tear the halter with working." He can choose among various chores and work out his own schedule for cultivating his land. The poor man survives "by the work of both hands"; he has to work if he wants to eat. The Orbáns characterized one of their relatives as follows: "Gyuri Sárándi could enjoy his life. He did his own work, he could spare himself, and he never even caught a real cold. He embarked on horse dealing; things turned out very well for him."

RANK AND PRESTIGE

The expression "rank" is often heard in the conversation of the villagers. "The village mayor had to be chosen from a family of rank, but his property counted too." "There is only rank, no more wealth."

These sayings show that although property and way of life count in determining rank, they are not the only factors. The age of the property is also very important. József Kakas mentioned with pride that his predecessors performed corvée for their land in the period of serfdom; thus they were landowners, team owners, a hundred years ago. "A *gazda* made of a *zsellér*" is a disparaging expression, implying that the owner of the property has not the self-reliance of the "born" or "real" peasant either in farming or in human relations. "Mihály Hajdú worked for eight years in America. He bought a fine house and eighteen *hold*-s (25.56 acres) of land, but he never drew a single foal out of its mother, or raised a calf to be a cow." On the other hand, "He always had a horse with young," is an expression of praise.

The day laborers also keep strict track of which people really belonged to their stratum. When Ferenc Orbán went to find work in Budapest after the division of the paternal inheritance, he was in the same position as the day laborers and teamless farmers who regularly looked for jobs in the capital. However, he was not received into their company: "They knew that I would not be a day laborer until my death; I would not carry the satchel all my life as they would. Even then I belonged to the middle class." When he was looking for a job, they did not advise him: "They did not support me. They would not mix with a man like me. They had enough colleagues.

There was an elderly man who had once owned ten *hold*-s of land; he was the one who found work for me." A "middle-class team owner" is not "pushed" into the third pew in church even if he has become poor, "as long as he behaves himself."

Kin ties between families of rank and wealth create a sort of reaffirmation of the ancient and distinguished existence of the families involved. Marriage, baptismal *koma*-ship, and all sorts of enduring personal relations also connect two groups of relatives. Having high-ranking kinsmen creates a favorable climate for success for the individual, whereas relatives who are recognized as debased or impoverished diminish the likelihood of success. Kinship and descent serve as a certain guarantee for the nature, character, and personal qualities of the individual. As we have mentioned above (see Chapter 8, "Groups of Consanguines"), the villagers, with their widespread genealogical knowledge and interest about the *ág*-s and kinship groups, often attached certain qualities to particular groups of descendants: these are clever, those rich; some are frivolous, addicted to drink; others quarrelsome. It is generally believed that the sort of life to be expected from an individual is more or less determined by who his ancestors and relatives are.

A large circle of kinsmen is desirable in itself, and the lone person without relatives is to be pitied. Thus the big *gazda*-s who can afford it do not regret treating their guests to a large amount of the meat of the slaughtered pig because it means that they are able to invite a great number of relatives. One reason that the poor reckon fewer people in their circle of kin is the fact that they cannot invite as many persons as the rich.[44]

Noble descent is an indication of an ancient and autochthonous family. In 1848 the personal privileges of the nobles were abolished and the heightened esteem for the members of such families became but a reflection of their past standing.[45] The rank of an ancestor generally clung to impoverished descendants for one, or at most two generations, but the rank and distinction of noble titles has faded more slowly. "She married a noble bachelor; she is led into the first pew in church," is the comment of envious young women, even if the bridegroom concerned is a mere day laborer. In some families, such as the Bedécs family, participation in the village administration is closely associated with noble descent. "It is in their blood to manage the affairs of the community; there is the *virtus* (manly prowess) of nobles in them," the saying goes. "A gentleman was more excellent in his speech; he could express himself better."

Nevertheless, the honor and pride of the *gazda*-s are primarily based on their independence. They do not have to work "on another's soil" or to buy provisions in the shop. This autonomous and independent status is indicated both by their attitude of self-reliance and by the respect accorded to them. A *gazda* is proud of "having

[44] The poor generally reckon and cultivate the ties of relationship in a more restricted circle than the *gazda*-s (see Chapter 8, "Groups of Consanguines," "Rokonság"). On the other hand, they are more dependent on neighborhood connections. Their equipment is often in poor condition, and thus they rely more heavily on the borrowing network. In the "proletarian" part of the village a hay cutter is borrowed by as many as ten neighbors, whereas every decent *gazda* has a hay cutter of his own.

[45] In this century, particularly since World War I, members of the noble families discontinued signing the title "noble" before their names. Several of the noble families who have become *zsellér*-s or artisans have voluntarily given up their privileged pews in the church.

inherited a certain breed of horse from his father and bequeathing the same to his children." In other words, he has raised the foals of brood mares to continue the line, whereas the less fortunate team owners are forced to exchange their horses now and then. In the stables of a wealthy *gazda* one sees animals which he has bred and branded with his own sign. Livestock belonging to the poorer members of the "middle class," acquired at fairs, sometimes carry two or three different foreign brands. Since these poorer farmers do not raise animals, they possess no brand of their own.

Among farm hands, tobacco growers, and day laborers it is a step toward independence and enhancing their rank if, for example, they manage to acquire a house or one or two *hold*-s of land. When the farm hand moves into the village and becomes a day laborer, people say, "He has got on his feet"; "he has come to rely on his arms," as if he has become a full man as compared with his former status of being "hands and feet of another."

The lower rank of farm hands and tobacco growers is largely due to the fact that they live on estates *(tanya)* outside the village. The word *tanyasi* is a pejorative expression; many brawls have been started in the tavern when somebody has called the sons of farm laborers come into the village for Sunday "*tanyasi,*" or has made a remark like, "I won't sit at the same table with *tanyasi* people." This scornful term is not only applied to farm hands, but also to the few *gazda* families who live on their own holdings outside the village. In the eyes of the villagers these people are uncouth and uncivilized. Their appearance in church is considered "as rare as a white sparrow." When one of them dies and the time comes for the church hymns to be sung at the bier, "no more than three can sing." They are not familiar with the refined rules of behavior, address, greeting, gait, and facial expression, and they do not learn the art of polite conversation and the words and gestures suitable for festive occasions. A guest is revealed at once as a *tanyasi* by his awkward way of entering a room and taking a seat. "He grew up in a *tanya* like a bird," is said of them with pity, but sometimes the second line of the jingle is added: "He is such an ass!" Villagers who are reduced to the level of farm hands try to send their children to the Átány school so that they will have friends in Átány and will behave like the villagers. But the villagers regard this attempt as futile: "howsoever one pulls the head of a dog up to the table, it still lets it drop."

Besides the *tanyasi* people, who are spatially separated from the village, there are families who live in the village but who are excluded morally. (We disregard the gypsies, who only live "next to Átány.") These are criminals and depraved people from peasant families. The murderer (there have been several of them in the village) loses the place defined for him according to wealth and descent; other villagers avoid his company with a shudder. However, he is not completely excluded from Átány; a bachelor who has served a term of imprisonment for manslaughter can still marry in the village. The road to depravity is marked by alcoholism, "a disorderly family life," later the neglect of one's work and household, and finally financial ruin. Such a man is excluded from the band of bachelors, and the duties of relatives toward him are suspended.

Honesty, morality, fairness, and personality form another level of differentiation among the villagers. Whether or not somebody is a man "as he ought to be" may add to or detract from his rank as determined by family, wealth, descent, and kinship.

The community tolerates a wide range of individual differences. One often hears it said that, "We are not all the same; even our fingers are not equal." The other frequently used formula is, "To do any task, one must be created for it." Thus one man "is born" to be clever at wickerwork, another to buy and sell horses at the fair. A wealthy *gazda* characterized his sons by saying, "One of my sons is an expert on foals, and the other is only interested in oxen, though they were grown on the same tree." No one reproaches Ferenc Orbán because he does not take part in butchering and carving when the pig is killed; it is well known that he does not like to touch raw meat and fat. Honor and esteem are not affected by such idiosyncrasies. In the words of a *gazda*, honor requires "that a man be good at work, keep order in his household and family, bring up his children well, and go to church."

We asked József Kakas what kind of person is the man who is "what he ought to be." He answered, "We may use this expression both for one's outside appearance and for one's inner composition. As for outside appearance a man should be sturdy, well-built, strong, and of a good height. As for the inner character, one ought to be morally clean, leading a sober life, no drunkard, not rough-spoken, not a girl-chaser, not arrogant, not proud. Mentally he should have a good intelligence and a keen mind. He should have a good word for his neighbor, his relative, his fellow man." "A man with sticky fingers or a liar is known by all the village; he is not esteemed much."

In everyday conversation people's moral defects are very rarely alluded to. People try to avoid encountering a murderer who has returned from prison, but if they do meet him in the street, they address him in the terms appropriate to his age and relationship, just as if he were not a criminal. It is improper to talk of other people's vices. The authors were constant visitors in the family of Ferenc Orbán for ten years, but they did not hear that one of the neighbor women was a tippler before noticing it themselves. The Orbáns are on bad terms with these neighbors, but still they never mentioned this failing. In the openness entailed by rural life many things become known, but this knowledge is kept under cover; the information is passed along in secret. "Gossipy" women are reproached. It is even more shameful if a man reveals the hidden vices of others, especially to strangers. The father of Ferenc Orbán, who married into the family of his wife as a *vő*, was sent out of the house and forbidden to see his wife when it became known that he spoke ill of the Átány sexton in a tavern before strangers.[46] People's shortcomings are revealed and discussed in

---

[46] The case was as follows. Sámuel Orbán, the son of György Orbán, lived as a *vő* in the house of Sámuel Csontos. He was sent to the Poroszló fair to buy a calf, then on his way home went into an inn to drink some brandy with an Átány youth and some men from the neighboring villages. The conversation turned to the improper behavior of the Poroszló bell ringer, and Samu Orbán remarked on the carryings on of the Átány bell ringer. At home it was regarded as especially heinous that he spoke ill of this particular man: "the bell ringer is the first man in the church after all; he is always at the foundation of the church," so his shame is that of the church and the village too. The other Átány youth, not being burdened with a calf, reached the village earlier and revealed the indecorous

public at the decisive turning points of human life: at marriage, at burial, or before a church or community election. When the spouse is chosen, the merits and blemishes in the histories of both families are all revealed and inspected. At funerals the deeds and misdeeds of the deceased and the behavior of the family toward him or her are discussed in a similar manner. Candidates for an office are likewise "turned round" by the public.

The most prominent and most esteemed seats in the Átány church were reserved for the members of the village magistracy. This situation corresponds to the rank allotted to them by the community. The occupation of a leading position in the community, village magistracy, presbytery, or positions in the pasturage associations and the consumers' cooperative society (see Chapter 17, "Other Community Organizations") may be said to sum up the rank of the family and the personal qualities and merits of the individual. "People strove for these offices," it is said; "they brought little or no profit, but all of them meant rank." This ambition is again something basic to the nature of some individuals; "one has to be created for it." Some *gazda* families of good reputation and rank do not aspire to these offices; "it is not in their blood." József Kakas, who expresses himself very eloquently in matters of morals and prestige, says, "A man may be honest even if he does not participate in the affairs of the community, but in this case he is hidden, not known by the village." On the other hand, the members of the magistracy and other functionaries are in the floodlight of public attention, revealing both the strengths and the weaknesses of their characters.

As we have mentioned above, wealthy *gazda*-s can afford to wear tattered clothes, to dress below their rank. But the members of the magistracies are obliged by the authority of these bodies to take care of their appearance. One who "gets into the town hall" has a fine dress suit made at once. It may be that holding an office serves as an incentive to make other investments expressing status as well. For example, Imre Kakas was village judge in 1870, and in the same year he constructed a house which was surpassed only by the pastor's home. There was even a song which commemorated the famous big house.

In church the ex-mayor occupies a prominent place, and the other officials are entitled to advance a pew when they rejoin the older men after the term of their office. Their authority persists informally after their active duty. Károly Bedécs says, "I was once a village official, and even now people come and ask me what they should do, since they have seen that I was a just man."

---

speech of Samu Orbán to Orbán's father-in-law. When Orbán arrived in the *kert* of his father-in-law in the evening (he usually slept there in the stable), he looked for his frieze cloak *(szűr)* in vain. Nor could he find his tobacco, the board used to slice it, or his second pair of boots. The *kert* of his father was next door, and he found out in the morning that all his personal belongings had been thrown over into it. His father-in-law forbade him to enter the house and told his daughter not to follow her husband if she wanted to enter her father's house.

The young man was reconciled with his wife and father-in-law only two years later. Both *nász*-s, being on ill terms, went to the fair separately, but there György Orbán noticed that Sámuel Csontos had been cheated with a sick horse. He told his *nász*, and they together returned to the dealer. György Orbán shook him mightily, gave him two boxes on the ear, and so regained the price of the horse for his *nász*. The next day the wife of Samu Orbán was sent to make peace with her husband.

RELATIONSHIPS BETWEEN THE STRATA

Both József Kakas and Ferenc Orbán are members of the presbytery. When they enter the church, József Kakas gives Ferenc Orbán precedence, since he is the elder. He addresses him as "Ferenc *bátyám*." Each regards the other as an honorable and respectable man, and in the opinion of the village they are friends. Still, if Ferenc Orbán had a son who wanted to marry the only daughter of József Kakas, he would be refused (or would not even think of proposing). The reason is that the Kakas family owns 24 *hold*-s (34.08 acres) of land while the Orbáns have only seven (9.94 acres). "This does not matter in friendship but it matters a great deal in marriage."

The modes of greeting, address, and general behavior in Átány express very precisely the relationship between two persons. Aside from differences in conduct based on sex, the tenor of behavior is set primarily by age and the frequency or intensity of interaction. The older person, even if the difference is only two or three years, is entitled to respect. On the other hand, frequent communication lends an everyday easiness to encounters, whereas greater distance requires the formal politeness of ushering in and greeting the guest. When the Orbán family is visited by their neighbor, the wife of the wealthy and esteemed *gazda* Ferenc Török, the *gazdasszony* does not set her kerchief right; the women simply start a conversation in the kitchen. But when a *zsellér* who lived somewhat farther away and was unrelated to the family was expected to visit in order to meet one of the authors, the Orbáns began to rearrange things in the room and straighten their attire, so that the ceremonial reception of the guest would be faultless.

The rhymed Golden Alphabet, inculcated in children at school, instructs them to honor an older person and to greet him or her before being greeted. There is no similar rule prescribing additional respect for those of greater rank or wealth. The wealthy *gazda* addresses an older day laborer in his service as *bátyám;* József Kakas called the sharecropper who was his own age "brother" when he was young. Of course, everyone is completely cognizant of the differences in rank and wealth. This knowledge adds special nuances and emphases to the prescribed forms in conversation. The poor and the rich *nász* greet each other with the proper terms, but the poor one speaks with heightened eagerness and pleasure, feeling honored by the communication. It is considered improper to be offhand with a person of lower standing. Big *gazda*-s are most frequently reproached because some of them behave superciliously toward their subordinates or poor relatives; "he didn't throw a good word to them." The Golden Alphabet also warns that one should treat domestic servants "like men."

There are no "good neighborhoods" in Átány, made up of the homes of wealthy *gazda*-s; the neighborhood links the houses of the rich and the poor. This situation was changed somewhat by the distribution of building sites in the 1920s, in which new developments were constructed by poor people at both ends of the village. No *gazda*-s dwell on these "proletarian" streets. In the *tanyakert*-s, *gazda*-s and day laborers sit next to each other. This was true in 1954 in the stable of József Szilágyi, where we observed a living example of this ancient male social grouping. Nevertheless, the teamless farmers are rarely able to attend these meetings, since more and more they have been employed outside the village even in winter.

Similarly, the *zsellér*-s have been left out of the bands of bachelors, although in principle there is no boundary line between the strata in "making friends." In the beginning of the 1920s the bachelor friends of József Kakas were made up of five sons of *gazda*-s, one son of a "middle-class" peasant of minor wealth, and two *zsellér* boys. He remembers that it was "as if the band had grown together like brothers." However, the two sons of *zsellér*-s found jobs in Átány as farm hands and could not leave the stables of their masters. They were often visited by the band, but still their participation in the walks and singing in the evening was much restricted. The sons of the *tanyasi* tobacco growers and farm hands are even less able to take part in the social life of the young; at most they come by foot to the tavern on Sundays for a dance.[47]

If one constructs genealogical tables and surveys the ties of kinship to the fourth or the fifth degree of collaterality, one finds impoverished relatives in almost every *gazda* family. It is rarer to find rich kinsmen in the *zsellér* families, since upward mobility is much less common that downward. But a "poor relative" is not a full-fledged kinsman, since he is unable to fulfil his duties as a relative reciprocally, and does not add to the prestige of the family. The rich kinsmen may subsidize him, but they also exploit his labor. The most decisive factor in the restriction of kin ties to a single stratum is the custom of marriage between a man and a woman of equal wealth, made possible by the fact that a girl inherits equally with her brother. It is said of some marriages that "she was pushed to him because of the property." There is also a saying that "if the bachelor expects to inherit one *hold* of land, the girl ought to have just as much." While the poor can find suitable spouses in the populous stratum of teamless farmers, the wealthy *gazda*-s have to choose their brides within the narrow limits of their class. This stratum is closely linked together by intermarriages. "Those who own more than twenty *hold*-s [28.40 acres] are all related, all *sógor*-s and *nász*-s."

Besides the groupings based on kinship, neighborhood, and age, occupation also establishes connections between the villagers, linking together those who perform similar jobs. The dealers go out in groups to buy horses at the distant fairs. The carters form a band when they transport tobacco, provender, stone, or other goods, led by the "carter *gazda*." The teamless farmers almost always work in groups. The harvesters and the *summás*-s are employed in the service of the estates in bands, and men

---

[47] The order of seats in church (see Figs. 10–11) clearly divides the villagers into groups according to sex, age, and district, but differences in wealth and rank are expressed in a supplementary way and only in certain age groups. The village magistracy, the elderly nobles and noble women, and the big *gazda*-s are entitled to privileged pews. They do not vie for seats, however, since this rivalry would not befit their rank. The rows of the young are where competition takes place. As the proverb goes, "We esteem a woman by her husband, a horse by its owner"; in other words the rank of the young wives is not defined by their person, but rather by the houses to which they belong by their marriage. In effect the relative rank of these houses is expressed when the young wife is first escorted to her new seat. On the other hand, rich and poor sit together in the rows of single girls, bachelors, recently married men, and old women where only age is a factor.

work in teams on the construction of roads and dams, in market gardens, and so forth. A considerable part of the *zsellér*'s life is spent on such teams. Membership is of critical importance to him, since it provides him with the opportunity to earn his bread.

These groups are held together not only by the common interests of work. The members are originally recruited on the basis of existing ties of kinship, neighborhood, and *koma*-ship. Work teams in which the members are very familiar with each other try to give their association the qualities of kinship. There was a *gazda* who invited his fellow horse dealers to a wedding, for which he was reproached by the villagers, who regarded it as an insult to his kinsmen.

A good example of this is presented by the harvester bands. They are permanent associations, maintaining the same personnel for as many as ten years, with minor changes; in general they are dissolved only when the estate carries out some reorganization. Before and after the weeks of the harvest they are bound together by the fact that they are allotted the same tasks as day laborers and sharecroppers on the estate. They work together—the reapers cut the corn with the same rhythm, standing next to each other, while they take daily turns binding the sheaves, gathering the fallen stalks, and heaping the shocks. For the duration of the harvest they live together on the estate. The estate pays the wages for the work of the whole band in a lump sum, and they divide it among themselves.[48] The estate rewards extra labor of the band leader with the right to use a piece of cornfield; if he tries to obtain more than he deserves, especially at the expense of the members, the band can "depose" him and elect another leader. Before entering the contract for harvest, the band fixes its membership, making replacements for those who have left. A bad worker reduces the income of the whole group. If someone violates the common working rules, the whole band passes judgment on his offence; the usual fine is one or two liters of brandy, which are consumed by the whole team. But the severest sanction is to leave the culprit out of the next year's contract.

How was a harvesters' band recruited? Let us take the list of such a band from the 1920s, noting the connections between each member and the others:

Gábor Madarász, 42 years old, the *gazda* of the band.

János Madarász, 32 years old, the younger brother of the *gazda*.

Gábor Sebők, 33 years old, the *koma* of János Madarász, and a relative of Sándor Sebők.

Sándor Sebők, 32 years old, the *sógor* of János Madarász.

Gábor Sebők, 25 years old, the younger brother of Sándor Sebők, also the *sógor* of János Madarász.

---

[48] After threshing the estate measures out the grain owed to the whole harvesting band. The heaps of wheat, barley, and oats are each poured out onto a canvas. The members of the band surround the canvas, each with his sack in his hand. The leader of the band holds a *véka* measure brought from home or borrowed from the estate. Making the rounds of the band, he measures out one bushel of wheat for each; one of the members levels the top of the *véka* with a strickle. When the wheat, barley, or oats are diminished to a heap which does not seem to be enough for another round of *véka*-s, half *véka*-s are measured out with a smaller vessel; then they divide the rest in cupped hands keeping a watchful eye on the equality of the portions.

János Sebők, 58 years old, a relative of the preceding Sebőks, the father-in-law of Ferenc Kövesdi.

Ferenc Kövesdi, 37 years old, the *vő* of János Sebők.

János Kövesdi, 32 years old, the *sógor* of the band leader Gábor Madarász, a relative of Ferenc Kövesdi.

Mihály Nemes, 23 years old, the *sógor* of János Horvát, the *koma* of Sándor Abonyi.

Mihály Nemes, Sr., 58 years old, the father of the above.

Sándor Abonyi, 24 years old, a "great *koma*" to János Horvát, Jr., and Mihály Nemes.

Mihály Abonyi, 22 years old, the younger brother of the former, a *koma* to Horvát and Nemes.

János Horvát, 60 years old, the father-in-law of the band leader Gábor Madarász.

János Horvát, Jr., 23 years old, the son of the above, thus a *sógor* of both Gábor Madarász and Mihály Nemes, a *koma* to both Abonyi sons.

János Gyulai, 48 years old, the maternal uncle of the band leader and his younger brother.

József Papp, 30 years old, a *kukás* in the farm where the band undertook harvesting.

Kálmán Nemes, 25 years old, also a *kukás* there, and a relative of Mihály Nemes.

Besides the connections of kinship and friendship, all the members of the band lived near each other in the same part of the Lower End. The swath-layers are also recruited on the basis of kinship. Gábor Madarász's swath-layer was his daughter, that of János Madarász was the daughter of his *sógor*, etc. (See Chapter 13, "The Careers of Three Families.")

However, occupation not only connects people of equal status, it also establishes durable relationships between families of different financial levels. The teamless farmers who own a *massza* or even one or two *hold*-s of land rely on the help of the team owners who plow their plots, transport their crop home, or cultivate their soil for half of the produce. Even the landless reaper has to look for a cart to carry his reaper's share home from the estate. On the other hand, the wealthy *gazda* needs the labor of the teamless farmer. Both needs can be satisfied in an impersonal, "business-like" way, by engaging a carter or a day laborer for previously agreed upon wages. But both *gazda* and teamless farmer endeavor to secure the necessary team or manual labor by continued personal relations for their mutual benefit.

János Boross in the 1930s owned seventeen *hold*-s (24.14 acres) of land. He had a harvester and he maintained a labor-exchange relationship with two of his *zsellér* neighbors, two brothers. They also reaped the crops of the Vajda property for a share. But István Vajda had such a large farm that he did not need to waste his time by performing minor jobs with the team for his laborers. Instead the dwarf holdings of the two *zsellér*-s were plowed by János Boross, or he lent them his horses for plowing and brought their share of the crop home from the Vajda farm in summer. The *zsellér*-s did not take home the oats used as fodder, but gave this part of their wage to János Boross. They helped out the *gazda* in their spare time, even if they had only Sunday mornings free. If János Boross and his wife went to the fair, one of the *zsellér* wives spent the night in their house. On the other hand, the harvester could not always help, since he was employed outside the village for a large part of the year, but his wife was a regular participant in the various chores of the Boross family. János Boross said, "The wife of my harvester was at home with us, like one of ourselves. She needed no direction, she saw at once what we were doing. Often she arrived at dawn asking where we were going and whether we were ready to leave. But it was the same on our part; as soon as we finished the hoeing in our fields, we harnessed the horse to the cart and set out to hoe their plot."

In the houses of big *gazda*-s the wives of the harvesters and *zsellér* neighbors often help with the washing and ironing and are active in the spring and fall cleaning and whitewashing.

There is a fixed rate of conversion between work with a team of horses and manual labor; a day's work with a team is worth three days of manual labor, but in return for plowing, which entails the use of various implements and sometimes a sowing machine, the manual labor equivalent amounts to four or five days. But a *gazda* and a day laborer who work for each other as good friends or neighbors are not bound by rules of strict equality. As Boross says, "We never calculate whether the other man has worked more." Besides the exchange of work performed with a team of horses and by manual labor, there is an uncalculated factor in the relationship: the food and drink offered by the *gazda* to his poor laborers. In the wealthy *gazda* households the *gazdasszony* cooks sometimes for five to six workers in the evening. In the 1940s a wealthy *gazda*, János Bedécs, received regular assistance from the wife of his harvester; the woman took her meals in the Bedécs household and so did her husband, even if he had spent the day working for someone else. If the husband did not come, his wife took his food to him. "The service of the woman was unpaid, but she lived there all the time; she took her meals there throughout the winter too." Károly Bedécs is a team owner who provides for his numerous family by hard work; he stressed the fact that any time he uses his team to help a teamless farmer he takes his satchel (i.e., his food) with him, but when the teamless farmer repays his services, Bedécs gives him his meals.

The idea that *zsellér*-s should have common class interests and should act in common against the *gazda*-s or vice versa was alien to the people of Átány. In 1951, Sámuel Galvács, a former tobacco grower, characterized the relations between the strata as follows: "Rich and poor did not hate each other here. If the poor could not make both ends meet, the *gazda* supplied him [wheat] until the new crops. Here the *gazda* did not despise the poor; rather he loved him very much." If a big *gazda* showed insufficient respect, equity, or readiness to help, it was regarded as a personal flaw.

In the course of the 1866 land apportionment the pastures of the serfs and the *zsellér*-s (roughly corresponding to the later "team owners" and "teamless farmers") were measured out into separate units. The use of the two types of pasture was directed by the "minor" pasture association of the *zsellér*-s and the "major" one of the *gazda*-s (see Chapter 17, "Pasture Associations"). The free transfer of grazing rights, however, resulted in mixed membership in both societies; thus the leading positions in the pasture association of the *zsellér*-s were held by *gazda*-s. In the course of the following decades there were hardly any public affairs in which the *gazda*-s and the teamless farmers faced each other as two separate groups. One of these rare conflicts was the movement for abolition of the system of compulsory three-crop rotation started in the first years of this century. It was initiated by the poor against the pasture associations led by the wealthy *gazda*-s (for more detail, see Chapter 2, "Land Tenure," and Chapter 18, "The Law of the Land in Átány"). As their chief argument against letting land lie fallow, they adduced the fact that unfarmed portions are useless (and therefore detrimental) to the teamless farmers, who have no livestock, whereas they are profitable for the *gazda*-s, who can graze their animals on them. They argued that the poor ought to receive an indemnity for their fallow plots.

In the revolutionary period of 1918–1919 there was a movement to put the village government, hitherto monopolized by the *gazda*-s, into the hands of the poor. Nevertheless, there were *gazda*-s on the "Soldiers' Council," and later, during the proletarian dictatorship, in the local "Directory" too. In the late 1920s and early 1930s the community election campaigns witnessed the movement of a group of teamless farmers to get their candidates into the magistracy of church and community. The movement proved to be successful in part. In several boisterous meetings of the village magistracy, the two parties clashed as representatives of the *gazda*-s and the teamless farmers. The *gazda*-s, with their long family tradition in the government of the community, defied the recently elected poor with the words, "Do these *zsellér*-s want to command us?" However, this movement was unable to change the system of village self-government, and after a few years it disappeared. Each of the two opposing parties, the teamless farmers (especially those with regular jobs in Budapest) and the *gazda*-s, also possessed a formal organization at this time: the two reading circles. However neither of the rival book clubs—"the *gazda* circle" and "the civic readers' club"—was able to mobilize more than a fragment of their respective stratum of the population.

PART FIVE
THE COMMUNITY

CHAPTER 15. ÁTÁNY AS A UNIFIED WHOLE

In June of 1964, Károly Együd, Jr., a twenty-four-year-old Átány peasant, was in an automobile accident. He was in the Eger hospital for six weeks before he died. During this time his close and distant relatives visited him every day, bringing him bottles of water from the local well to quench his thirst. Any villager who happened to be in the city visited the dying youth in the hospital, even if he or she had had no former connection with him beyond mutual greeting. Those who could not pay him a call in person went to the Átány bus station to ask the returning visitors how he fared; if there were no such passenger on the bus, they asked the driver himself, who was always able to furnish precise information.

From the day of the accident to the time when the news of Együd's death arrived, the conversation of the villagers was centered on this subject. However, people had different amounts of information on the daily condition of the patient, as the news was passed from one group to another. The dissemination of the news had several centers in the village, corresponding to the members of the young man's numerous kin group: his wife, and the homes of his parents, grandparents, brothers, sisters, and close relatives, whence visitors set out for the hospital almost every day. News was not communicated directly in all cases. The family of Ferenc Orbán lived next door to the parents and was on very good terms with them. The Orbáns shared the concern for the life of the young man, but it would have been improper for them to tell the parents of their feelings, just as any inquiry would have been inappropriate. So Mrs. Orbán listened to the sorrowful words of her neighbor in secret, from behind the fence. Ferenc Török is an "opposite neighbor," but, more important, he is also a first cousin of the Együd family. As a relative, the wife of Ferenc Török was expected to watch in the street until the parents came home from the hospital and to ask them about the condition of the patient. It was from this family that the Orbán-s and other anxious neighbors got the news. The other families of kinsfolk were likewise the centers of information.[1]

[1] The Orbán family was generally very well informed, as they had yet an additional source of news. Juliska Együd, the sister of the patient, worked in the same weaving workshop as the granddaughter of the Orbán-s. Juliska informed her colleagues as to the condition of the patient in the same detailed way as the family did the kinsfolk.

The deceased was laid out and buried at home. As long as he lay on the bier, there was a ceaseless flow of visitors, and the funeral was attended by so many people that the large yard of the paternal house was not large enough to hold all of them.

The example is a specific one. A traffic accident, especially a fatal one, is a very rare, conspicuous, and upsetting event in Átány. In this case interest and compassion were enhanced because of the young age of the victim. The fate of the patient was a matter of concern for the whole village, each man expressing his sympathy as best as he could. Our concern here is this solidarity of feeling and action and its prevalence and significance in less extraordinary cases.

The inhabitants of Átány, at least those belonging to "the people of the soil," are linked by a close network of relations as shown in Part Three. These relations may extend across the differences of wealth and social standing which divide "the people of the soil." Though they are more frequent and tighter within a single social stratum, they encompass the entire Átány population. Furthermore, there are organizations, such as the political community, the village administration, and the church, whose jurisdiction extends to all the inhabitants with minor exceptions. These will be described below. But there is an intermediate layer of relations which connects people just because they are people of Átány, and specifies certain correct types of behavior toward one another.

First of all, Átány's unity is local: the comprehensive entity comprised of the *zug*-s, neighborhoods, and Lower and Upper Ends. Belonging to Átány means living in this compact settlement unit. Both the villagers and the inhabitants of the neighboring villages regard the village as a round thing, comparing it to an apple, and thereby expressing its totality and unity. When new building sites were distributed in the last decades, the community was careful to preserve the roundness of the village area. People who leave this local unity—for example, by moving to a *tanya*—thereby take a place on the outskirts of the village society, regardless of how long their family has "belonged" to the village. As we have mentioned above, this is true for both the *gazda*-s who move to their own property and the tobacco growers or farm hands of the estates. Feeling the drawbacks of their situation outside the village, they entrust their children to the care of relatives living in the parish at least for the time of their schooling, "so that they will have Átány schoolmates." A farm laborer strives to acquire a house and settle in the village by the time his children are ready for school. If at that time he is still not able to, he then tries to move into the village by the time they reach marriageable age, so that they may "be married from Átány." On the other hand, gypsies are not allowed to move into the village, since they can never become real Átány people, being neither Hungarians nor peasants. The location of their houses outside the village corresponds to their exclusion from the community. "Two villagers and a gypsy died when the front was here"; thus the peasants recall the victims of the last days of the war. Whereas the death of the villagers is mentioned with compassion and sadness, that of the gypsy is surrounded with humorous episodes. Nevertheless, gypsies may be buried in the Átány cemetery, in spite of the fact that it belongs to the Calvinist church and they are Catholics, and they are not reproached if they ask the Calvinist minister to baptize their children or to celebrate their marriages.

Strangers who want to move into the closed settlement unit of the village or to acquire land in the *határ* of Átány are also treated with reserve. "We don't want them to squat on our fields." Aliens desiring to settle in the village have to ask for permission from the town hall. The community records reveal that the granting of such permissions was sometimes debated in the village assembly for years. The applicants are usually craftsmen. Even if the village needs the work of the would-be immigrant, the elders conduct an inquiry to find out "whose son or calf he is," what his descent and behavior are like. Numerous applicants have been refused.[2]

What connections are established among people by virtue of living in the same village and working in the same fields? The first consequence is that the Átány people know each other and greet each other. A stranger who happens to come into the village is greeted only if he is known, and if the villagers go to other villages, they greet only their acquaintances. (The *tanyasi* who went to Budapest and raised his hat to every passerby is mentioned with a smile.)

An elderly Átány man who comes across an unfamiliar boy in the road who is neither his relative nor his neighbor asks him, "Whose son are you?" The child is supposed to answer in this way: "My father is Ferenc Barna; my mother is Zsófia Csontos." By the names of the father and mother the inquirer can place the family exactly; he knows "whose son and calf" the child is, to which *ág* and kin group he belongs, and in which part of the village he resides. "Everyone here knows who the grandfather or the ancestor of any other villager was, who his relatives are, and by which *ág*." Several Átány people say, "I know everything about the whole village. A villager knows an entire community better than a city dweller knows a house," meaning the apartment buildings in the towns. "In the open we see each other all the time, both in the yards and in the fields. It is true that we withdraw into our houses in winter, but everything leaks out nevertheless."

The knowledge based on immediate experience, sight, and interaction also includes the livestock of other people. People say with facetious exaggeration, "Everyone here knows everyone else's dog and cat." As a matter of fact, they do recognize horses, as well as harnesses and wagons. People sitting in the house can recognize the person driving by in the street by the tinkling of the bell, or sometimes by the rattle of the wagon or the "clatter" of the axle. The number and the quality of everyone's cows and pigs are generally known, since the animals are driven to the common pasture every day. An acute observer also notices when someone's cow is pregnant, on the verge of calving, or recently a mother.

The size, neatness, and order of the houses, outbuildings, and yards disclose the wealth or poverty of their owners without further inquiry. They reveal whether the inhabitant is a *gazda* or a teamless farmer, or a lone widow. The ricks and stacks of fodder and hay give information as to the crops and the size of the holding. The

[2] On the other hand, the villagers are proud of the fact that a craftsman who is accepted into the village is satisfied there.

number of milk jugs drying on poles enables one to figure out the number of cows. Even the especially valuable, conspicuous articles of clothing are known by the villagers. When János Boross became a community official in 1904, he went to Tisza-füred with the village judge and had an embroidered frieze cloak made. Fifty years later, when we purchased the cloak for the Ethnographic Museum, the older people in Átány all recognized it; they knew that it had been owned by János Boross and the occasion for which it was manufactured. When Károly Bedécs became a village official in 1927, he ordered a fine new black suit of broadcloth from the Heves tailor. This is still his dress suit today. In the winter of 1964 the children were throwing snowballs near the church one Sunday and one of them hit the jacket of Károly Bedécs. The women spread the news that naughty children had thrown snowballs at the well-known "beautiful dress suit" of Károly Bedécs.

Besides these external features, which may be seen by any alien observer, the villa-gers know each other's family connections and relations. They are aware of the ties of kinship and descent and, judging by the traditional qualities attributed to each family, the probable behavior of each member. They know each other's property, wealth, and land; the extent of the arable land, vineyard, and *kert*; and the pasture rights of each—as well as the history of acquisition or inheritance of the family fortune and the incidents of its enlargement or dissipation. Let us repeat the example of Ferenc Orbán, who, faced with a map of the village drawn up thirty years ago, was able to name the owners of all of the more than one thousand holdings and to relate the history of their transferences over a span of two or three generations. The villagers are cognizant of the location of each other's property, the crop cultivated or the seed sown on it, the quality of the work, and the quantity of the harvest.

In addition there is a submerged, secret level of information regarding other people: the knowledge of hidden faults, crimes, and diseases. It is improper to speak of them; even to know about them is considered more or less indecent. No inquiries are allowed, but the facts are known all over the village nevertheless. (See Chapter 18, "The Law of the Land in Átány.")

There are traditional ways of conveying information in the village. A death is announced and the people are called to the funeral by the tolling of the bell. As we have mentioned above, the bell ringer "calls out" the name of the deceased and the circumstances of the death after he rings the bell. The bells also ring out the alarm when there is a fire. The village administration publicizes its notices and injunctions by means of the drum. Early in the morning the town crier makes his rounds, stopping at the prescribed places (see Fig. 34) and calling the neighborhood together and then making the announcements in a stentorian voice. The villagers are allowed to add their own items to the announcements; for example a person might ask for informa-tion about a stray animal or offer something for sale.[3]

---

[3] The town crier receives the announcements written down in the "drumming book." The drum-ming book of 1946 is preserved among the records of Átány village in the Eger State Archives. In this year 1,539 items (official and private announcements) were communicated to the populace by means of the drum.

The outstanding events of family life about which it is important that other villagers should be informed are revealed by well-known signs. If a girl and a bachelor who are unrelated sit together in a wagon and drive through the village, this means that they are engaged and they are on their way to buy a ring. The news spreads through the village at once. An engagement is also publicized by the fact that the girl wears a bunch of flowers upside down on her breast. A bunch of artificial flowers fastened to his hat is the emblem of a fiancé; by removing it or turning it upside down, he lets people know that his engagement has been broken off. Ribbons on the hats of the bachelors who have been summoned before the recruiting commission and found fit signify that they are preparing for their military service. The wedding procession takes a long route to the town hall and the church, choosing the roads that are more important and more frequented if possible, so that the greatest number of people may see it. The young woman is led to her new seat in church before the eyes of the whole community on the first Sunday after her wedding. Likewise, the infant is baptized in front of the entire community, so that everyone may see the child and hear the name given to it at the christening. While the school was still maintained by the church, not only the confirmation "examination" but also the school examinations were held in the church, before the full congregation. Advancing to another age group is manifested by changing pews in the church year by year; everyone may see the girls of marriageable age and the older unmarried women who are ushered into the pew of the "left-out" ones.

The coffin of the dying person or the deceased is carried through the village on an open wagon; the body lies on the bier for days and may be seen by everyone; and the funeral procession marches to the cemetery along the main road.

The examples enumerated above show what an Átány person is supposed to know about the other villagers and how he or she is informed of these matters. Besides responsibility for information, however, there are also mutual obligations.

At the end of the 1950s the crop of maize was very meager at Átány. One market day it happened that two families set out for the Heves market with wagons full of maize in order to sell it. They were severely censured in the village; in fact they were told directly that it was improper to sell the produce in another place while it was so scarce in their own village.[4] When the crop is harvested, the *gazda*-s leave some of the ears on the ground on purpose; this is not only true of the maize field, but also of the wheat and potato fields, the vineyards, and the orchards. The reason is that as soon as harvesting is finished, the gleaners—poor widows and children of large poor families—appear on the fields; they gather the fallen grain, ears of maize, or bunches of grapes. What is left in the fields for the gleaners is an impersonal gift to the poor of the village in effect; people from other villages are not allowed to glean. Also the collection of camomile is free to every villager, though it grows only on the sodic fields of certain

---

[4] Those who have a surplus of wheat or straw, for instance, are supposed to offer it for sale to indigent villagers. On one occasion someone wanted to buy straw from a *gazda* who possessed enough to far surpass his yearly needs. He refused. The would-be customer found it so unfair that he took revenge by setting fire to the *gazda*'s *kert* that night.

farmers. It is the habit of the poor to gather the cobs from the maize fields to use as fuel.[5]

The sick and indigent of the village must be taken care of. The Átány patients in the Eger hospital are visited by other Átány people who happen to be in town, even if they are not usual visitors in their homes. There is no drug store in the village. The prescription is taken to the Eger or Heves bus and handed over to any villager, who then has the medicine made in the pharmacy, brings it home, and gives it to the other villager, who waits for his return at the bus station. At a wedding celebration, where much cooking is required, the *gazdasszony*-s send tastes not only to the numerous neighbors and relatives unable to attend, but also to all the sick, helpless persons who are confined to bed, regardless of their financial situation.

Building a house is a common enterprise in which kinsmen, neighbors, and *koma*-s participate. However, the construction of a new house is more or less an affair of the whole village too, beyond the circle of the aforementioned people. A good example is the building of Ferenc Orbán's house. Brought up as a son of a *gazda*, he received only a meager fifth of the paternal inheritance, so he could not build a home of his own or equip his farm until he had labored hard for six years in Budapest. When he finally started to build his house, he asked eight related team owners, as was customary, to help him in transporting adobe and stone. On the morning of the construction the teams of the eight relatives stood in front of the building site, along with 37 uninvited wagons owned by helpful villagers.

If a villager gets into trouble, he must be helped. This is evident in the case of fire. At the sound of the alarm bell everyone who can move grabs a bucket and runs toward the fire, regardless of whether the owner is an enemy or a friend. Help is especially necessary if a villager gets into a scrape outside the community, among strangers. This is illustrated by the example of the two *nás020*-s who were on bad terms. When one of them noticed that the other had been cheated, he hastened to help him without hesitation (see footnote 46, Part Four). Solidarity also demands that no one denounce another villager, even if he is guilty. If an outside creditor has the land of an insolvent Átány *gazda* sold at auction, no villager could be found to purchase it, nor would any of them take the plot on lease from the new, alien owner. A similar solidarity is manifested by the village magistracy toward the inhabitants. As appraisers, they endeavor to estimate the products and the livestock of the indebted Átány man as advantageously for him as possible, when they have to prepare an auction.

There are twelve or fourteen elderly men in Átány who usually keep vigil and sing at the bier of each deceased. The great majority of the villagers accompany the body to the cemetery. Furthermore, there are *diktás*-s who visit the house of the bereaved family and lead the singing at the vigil. The widow of Samu Jámbor, Julianna Fuder,

---

[5] An Átány man, driving his wagon to or from a strange place, is expected to give a lift to any villager walking on foot. When we escorted József Kakas to the fair, he brought home not only people but also a pig which had been purchased at the fair, carrying them a distance of thirty or forty kilometers without reward, though the buyers were neither his relatives nor his friends, but simply his co-villagers. The villagers also help out those who have sold their horses at the fair by drawing their wagons, left without teams, back to the village.

visited every single bereaved household for thirty years to lead the singing line by line and to begin the funeral chants as a *diktás* of the women. She did not keep track of the number of deceased persons she sang over, nor did her husband, who was a *diktás* of the men until he was very old. Their son, Samu Jámbor, did count the times he performed this function. Before his activity was cut short by his sudden death, he had "served," according to his own testimony, almost eight hundred times. The *diktás* of the men visits the bereaved house only in the evening, while the women's *diktás* goes during the day. According to the testimony of Samu Jámbor, he made a vow to serve every deceased without discrimination at the time he decided to become a *diktás*, and he kept his vow. When asked why he undertook this heavy duty (to go out in the evening after a day of work, regardless of mud, wind, or rain, to sing at another's house from six or seven o'clock until ten or eleven), he answered: first of all for the glory of God, then for the service of his church (he was a churchwarden for several years), and finally for the consolation of the mourners. He explained: "Because if a man of sixty-five years dies, that's all right; but if a vigorous young person dies, the villager should know what we are there for."

Belonging to Átány also means behaving in the Átány way. For a stranger, the differences between the village and its surroundings are not obvious, but the inhabitants recognize the nuances of behavior and attach a symbolical meaning to minute differences. For instance, both the men and the women of Átány walk with a swinging gait. They regard this as a characteristic feature; thus to adopt it may express the fact that somebody has become a real Átány man or woman. The wife of György Barát, a Catholic woman from another village, was told after 25 years' residence in Átány, "Your body is swaying, Rozál, like ours; though you were not born in Átány, you have become an Átány woman." As we have mentioned before, the *tanya* dwellers are distinguished from the real Átány people by such small traits of behavior as the manner of taking a seat, or their offences against minute rules of greeting, address, and polite conversation.

In view of the Catholic surroundings, the Calvinist religion is an important symbol and expression of one's belonging to Átány. Several people told us, "Wherever I go, my faith is with me; I can't put it aside." Átány teamless farmers who have worked in gardening establishments in Budapest related that they had several times been hired by Catholic priests. "I entered with the greeting, 'May God give you a good day'—in order to let that churchman know he was dealing with a Calvinist." In Catholic villages people often greet each other with the words, "Praised be Our Lord Jesus Christ," and a priest is always addressed in this way. The exogamous relations of the Átány people are also influenced by their faithfulness to their religion (see Chapter 18, "Átány among the Neighboring Villages").

The preservation of specific features of the local culture of Átány has a special significance and symbolical meaning for those people who leave the village for a more or less extended period to work in other regions. The people of Átány use a specific variety of the dialect of the Great Plain. A considerable proportion of the villagers who work in the capital retain their own dialect on purpose, even after a continuous stay of five or six years in Budapest. Thus Ferenc Orbán remained faithful to his dialect, all the more so because during all his laborious years in Budapest his thoughts centered on the possibility of returning to Átány and becoming a farmer there.[6] But there are some teamless farmers working in Budapest who have adopted the speech of the capital. Most of them have gone beyond the traditional framework of Átány life in other respects as well, like the industrial workers who have become interested in politics and have joined labor organizations or religious sects.

The attire of the Átány people working in the capital also possesses a symbolical meaning. Most of them wear the same rural costumes worn at home, buying new articles at the local fair. Girls and widows who have jobs in the Budapest factories or seasonal work in the capital also wear their peasant costumes; they gave up the bonnet in Budapest only when it went out of fashion in the village. Only girls who do not intend to return to the village change their attire to the city fashion. The scope of the Átány dressing habits is shown by the striking example of the women who had their hair cut short in the 1950s. In the village they cover their heads with kerchiefs as demanded by tradition, but if they go to Budapest, they remove the kerchiefs when they get on the bus or the train.

Most of the Átány people who work in the capital regard the city environment as a separate world. Many of them have jobs in gardening establishments, but they never bring a seedling or ornamental shrub home to their own yards. Nor do they adopt the special tools or hoes used in the nurseries of Budapest. Mihály Hajdú worked in factories in Chicago for eight years, sending the money he saved home to his wife. The woman embarked on the construction of a house and a stable according to his written specifications. Mihály Hajdú wanted his buildings to be innovations: he ordered an L-shaped house with a veranda and a stable with a loft, such as he had seen in America. Feed could be stored in the loft and thrown down directly to the animals. (The Átány stables have no lofts, the feed being kept in stacks and ricks in the open.) The construction was executed according to the wishes of the husband, but the wife made a modification in the veranda before the return of her husband, since the new-style porch would be an obstacle for the coffin when it was brought out of the house. There was no death in the family at the time of the remodeling, but the woman gave the following explanation for her action: "If one builds to last forever, one has to think of how the deceased is to be carried out." The modern way of storing feed in the new-style stable did not last long either. When Mihály Hajdú returned home, he was "fashioning" for only two years, after which he became accus-

---

[6] People from Átány also try to maintain ties with their co-villagers in Budapest. For example, János Madarász (see for his data Chapter 13 and Appendix A) occupied a very advantageous position as a house porter in Budapest, but nevertheless he left it. He explains it as follows: "I was bored with being alone. My elder brother lived in Csepel Island [a southern suburb of Budapest with large factories for heavy industry] with his family. He said to me, 'Why don't you come with us, all the people are from Átány. You could talk to them; you would not be alone.'" So he left his job and became a factory worker in Csepel Island. "There were really a lot of Átány people. Mező Street was full of Átány lodgers from one end to the other: married women with their husbands, but also girls and children." One motive for his settling there was that he was thinking of marriage. As a matter of fact, he found a wife in the colony of the villagers in Csepel.

tomed to the local habit again and kept the feed in the open, carrying it to the livestock whenever they needed to be fed.

The village and the *határ* represent "the homeland" for the people of Átány, the place to which they want to return if they wander in distant regions. In case they may not be able to return alive, they at least make arrangements to lie in the local cemetery after their death. However poor and helpless the family may be, one who is dying is brought home from the hospital in Budapest or any other town, in order to find a resting place in the Átány cemetery. In 1912 a man from Átány, the "brigand Kása," died in a far-away prison. His body was not turned over to the family. Nevertheless a funeral ceremony was held at home, but instead of the coffin, the frieze cloak *(szűr)* of the deceased was laid out on the washing stool, placed in the center of the yard according to tradition. A similar symbolic burial was arranged in memory of the soldiers who were killed in foreign lands and buried in unknown places. During World War I the pastor held these ceremonies in the yard, and the coffin was replaced by a photograph of the deceased, if the family had one. This was also true at the beginning of World War II, but then some of the villagers raised objections, asking whether the minister was saying farewell to the washing stool (on which the coffin or the photograph is traditionally placed). Under the pressure of such criticism, the bereaved families transferred the ceremony to the living room, remembering the dead in front of their photographs, which were placed upright on the table.

As more and more people have been able to find job opportunities outside the village, the character of the Átány community itself has changed. Besides the villagers who live at home according to the traditional Átány customs, another "membership of the community" has come into being, residing in other parts of the country and following more or less alien customs. These persons and families, living in far-away parts, are linked to the village by the celebration of family festivals: they return for a wedding or a burial and invite their Átány kinsfolk on similar occasions. In recent years some young people from Átány have built houses in Budapest. The construction is done with the help of unpaid assistants, just as it is at home; the close relatives travel to the capital to do their duty. If a baby is born in remote regions, the relatives cannot send food to the mother, so they make a money gift instead. The names of deceased people from Átány who have kept up the ties of kinship from their new homes are "cried out" at the church door just like those of the villagers, and the bell tolls for them as it does for any other inhabitant.

As we have seen, belonging to Átány means, among other things, that one's father, mother, and other relatives are known by the villagers. The person who moves away from the community renounces this claim. The name of the alien wife of an Átány man who has left the community never to return is not known at home; at most, she is mentioned as "that woman from Pest" or "that alien woman," and people are also ignorant of the names of their children. Such people, those who do not let the village know about the changes in their families, no longer want to rest in the Átány cemetery. They renounce the bell ringing and the "crying out" of their names after their death, choosing to be cared for by their new community according to its own customs.

CHAPTER 16. RELIGION

THE CALVINIST REFORMED CHURCH[7]

In 1951, at the beginning of our field work in Átány, and for the following few years, one could hear singing in several houses on winter days after dark. Having finished their work, the members of the family gathered in the warm living room and sang hymns before lighting the lamp. In the houses hymnals and prayer books stood on the window sills, along with the big Bible. As one entered a room on a holiday afternoon, one would see people sitting alone and turning the pages of the Scriptures (see Plate 27). On the walls of the houses were plaques with scriptural texts. The church was full on ordinary Sundays and crowded on holidays. On weekday mornings a group of eight to twelve old women used to attend the service.

The passage of the year is divided up by Sundays and church holidays, which define the rhythm of work and rest and the change of attire. The religious ceremony stands at the center of family festivals: the christening, the wedding, and the funeral. The minister is the most esteemed guest in the people's homes.

The holiday means a break in work. On the first days of the Great Holidays (Christmas, Easter, Whitsuntide, and New Year's Day) even the duties in the stable are hastily performed; the horses are hardly tended. As long as the church door is shut

---

[7] Though the overwhelming majority of the population is Reformed, other denominations were and are represented among them. The Roman Catholic gypsies have been mentioned several times already. As regards ecclesiastical jurisdiction, they belong to the Heves vicarage, but they rarely avail themselves of its services. They prefer to ask the local Calvinist minister to serve at christenings, weddings, and funerals. There are also Catholic Hungarians among the poor, people who have married or moved into the village. Moreover the community of Átány, regarded from the administrative point of view, includes the personnel of the Szárazbő manorial farms as well. Thus the statistical records show 497 Catholics in Átány in 1890, 370 in 1920, 534 in 1930. Basing its claims on this number, the Catholic vicarage of Heves bought a building in the village in 1937 to which the chaplain came once a week to provide religious instruction. However, since the Catholics did not live in the village, scripture classes ceased after a trial period of two years, owing to the scanty attendance.

In 1791 a Jewish family settled in the village. Under the patronage of one of the landlords, it was allowed to rent the community butcher's shop. The inhabitants of Átány protested against their immigration, complaining that they sold bad meat (Eger State Archives, Journal of the Heves county assembly, 1792: 1105). Nevertheless, a Jewish colony was founded in Átány, and the 1828 census mentions eight Jewish families, among them two shopkeepers and a kosher butcher. The statistical record of 1890 shows fifty Jews in Átány. They had a meeting house, the foundations of which are still visible, and their cemetery exists to this day. However, this Jewish colony was scattered after the turn of the century, leaving only one Jewish family by the beginning of World War II.

on a Sunday or holiday morning (i.e., before the service), a cartload of goods may be transported if absolutely necessary, mainly to help another. But even such wagons avoid the main roads, and they return home and unharness before the first chime of the bells. At the first peal of the bells the tavern doors are closed, not to be opened again until the end of the service, when the church door is shut. Bachelors standing in groups in the early afternoon during the second service warn each other, "Hush, hush! They haven't left church yet." On holiday mornings everyone takes greater pains with his or her appearance than on weekdays, and Sundays are also the days of changing into clean linen. Those who go to church put on their best clothes, but even those who stay home put on better clothes than on weekdays. Sundays and holidays also mean plentiful meals and dishes which cannot be served on weekdays because of lack of time and means. If the family can afford it, a bottle of wine is also put on the festive table.

The main service is held on Sunday morning. The head of the family and the children are expected to attend. The *gazdasszony*-s, who are busy with cooking, and poor people with rather shabby attire go to church in the afternoon. The services at which the Lord's Supper is served are celebrated with particular solemnity. These are Easter, Whitsunday, "for the new bread," "for the new wine," Christmas, and New Year's Day. The heads of the families and the young people take Holy Communion on the first day of the holiday, the *gazdasszony*-s and the poor and old people on the second. During the service the members of the church-going families who have stayed home sing psalms aloud; any of them who is not occupied opens the Bible or the prayer book called "Christian Instruction."

A Sunday or holiday afternoon is a time of rest. In fine weather people sit in front of their houses, the neighbors meet each other, the men play cards, and the women have a chat. The newly-weds go to visit their parents, bachelors and girls join their bands and have a good time.

The peasants believe that they live in a world dependent on the will of God. The result of their labor throughout the year, the harvest, "is in the palm of God": a rain or hail storm may destroy it on the very day before reaping. When a soft, "growing" rain falls in the spring or there is a favorable snowfall in the winter, the villagers say, "God did not turn away from us sinners after all." The abundant crop is derived from God too. They mention it in this manner: "It was not given by God for one year only"—therefore a part of it ought to be saved for a possible scanty year. Also illness, a stroke of fortune, an unexpected death, or unhoped-for good luck are the acts of Heaven. "God's poor" is the name given to the indigent people who in spite of their efforts and labor have been thrown into a lower position by misfortune; on the other hand, those whose troubles are their own fault are "their own beggars" (see Chapters 12 and 13). "God may give and take away": He is the absolute master, and human beings should not judge His resolutions or reflect on the seemingly good or bad outcomes of His will. When the son of old Rózsa, the respected village mayor, complained about the drought, his father warned him, "Don't go on like this, my son; it is no business of yours. There is Someone who is directing it."

God's benevolence cannot be secured in advance; His decisions are already formed, beyond the reach of human efforts. In the eyes of the people of Átány, it is senseless "superstition" for the people of Catholic villages to go on pilgrimages to the holy places, to keep holy water, consecrated candles, or other devotional articles in their houses to avert evil, or to hope to recruit God or the saints to their cause by frequent prayers or vows. No one can assure himself against "the visiting of God" (i.e., disaster) even by pious, godly behavior, since it is often aimed at "the trial" of the righteous. On the other hand, a person who commits an offence against the moral order may take it for granted that he will be punished by the hand of God, whether he sinned openly or in secret, whether he has been penalized by human justice or not. The rules enjoining an honest way of life and right behavior often allude to God directly, for example, the first sentence of the Golden Alphabet: "Honour thy father and thy mother, in order to obtain the blessing of God." He does not hasten to punish, but He does not forget, and the people of the village almost wait for divine vengeance to be wrought on the sinners (see Chapter 18, "The Law of the Land in Átány"). Penalties are expected in this life. Though people learn the articles of faith concerning the survival of the soul in the hereafter and recite the "Apostolic Creed," they do not do so with any great personal conviction.[8] Although the mourners who assemble around a bier sing about the soul on its way toward the pleasures of Heaven after the vicissitudes of this world, in their hearts they are convinced that human life is ended by death for good. The only real continuation is provided by the descendants, who carry on the name, the physiognomy, and the characteristics of their ancestor.[9]

God wants men to lead an honest, sober, and temperate life and to treat other people "humanely." Among one's duties to God, participation in the formal religious life—i.e., going to church—does not play a central part. A Catholic commits a sin if he does not go to mass on a Sunday or holiday, but a Calvinist may stay away from church and still be a godly, religious person. As a matter of fact, there have been villagers who have not attended a service for years but who read the Scriptures regularly, know long passages by heart, and even inject phrases taken from the ancient

---

[8] Cf. Balogh, n.d.: 69–75.

[9] It is the "official" view of the peasants, as it were, to reject the religious practices of the Catholic villages for the benefit of dead as mere superstition. However, it is sometimes revealed in confidential conversation that some people in Átány have endeavored to communicate with the deceased. According to the beliefs of the Catholic peasantry of the vicinity, the souls of the dead rove the earth for a time after their death, visiting shrines and places of pilgrimage, and sometimes appearing before individuals. One may hear of "necromancer women" who are able to communicate with the dead and to interpret their wishes to the bereaved family. At the end of the past century and in this one such necromancers have been active not far from Átány, at Novaj, Mezőtárkány, and Dormánd. They were visited by people from Átány whose relatives have died under extraordinary circumstances or were reported missing in the war, so that it was uncertain whether they were alive or dead. Such villagers set out early in the morning to avoid meeting anyone, and they try to keep their journey a secret afterward. In general, the communications of the dead do not reveal anything of the hereafter; they prefer to mention bodily inconveniences: for instance that they have not been buried in the proper attire. Thus a bachelor killed in a brawl allegedly reproached the members of his family for having put his festive suit on over his blood-stained underwear, instead of changing his clothes entirely.

translations of the Bible into their everyday conversation. They are self-contained, unsociable people. It is acknowledged that some people do not go to church and are nonetheless religious, just as some families do not participate in public affairs "by their nature" and yet remain good Átány citizens.

Historically there has been a noticeable decrease in church attendance since the last century. In 1879 the minister of Átány wrote the following: "Except for summer days, the church is full of the faithful, and it has even happened that we were eight hundred in the house of God on a weekday." No such zealous church-going has been observed on weekdays in the present century. However, at the turn of the century the church yard was filled on holidays, and even on Sundays there was not room enough in the building for all of the faithful. In 1910 an addition to the church was planned, but owing to World War I it was not built, and later it became unnecessary.

Besides people who are fundamentally religious but who attend church rarely or not at all, since the turn of the century there has been an increasing number of people who are simply indifferent, owing to their increasing contact with urban life via city jobs. Poor men argue that they have no Sunday clothes, and thus cannot dress in the Átány manner appropriate for church, so they prefer not to attend. However, even these people pay the church taxes regularly and lift their hats to the minister, acknowledging him as the first man of the community. Every newborn baby is christened in church, every marriage is performed there, and all the dead are buried with a religious ceremony. The craftsmen, most of whom moved into the village from other regions, have been acquainted with the ideas of Socialism since the first years of this century, but they are no exceptions to the rule. In the 1950s a member of the 1919 Revolutionary Directory, a professed Communist throughout his life, specified in his will the psalms which were to be sung at his burial. To be an Átány man or woman means living according to the rules of the Reformed Church. This requirement is still generally valid, and in 1963 the daughter of the secretary of the local Communist Party Organization was confirmed along with her friends.

According to the tenets of Calvinism, the most important part of the service is the sermon based on the Gospel. Although the people of Átány admire a fine sermon and expect their minister to be a good orator, they regard singing as even more important. It is believed in Átány that song is a double prayer. Singing in unison is held in a special esteem. A large part of the lamenting of the dead constitutes people singing together. The villagers sometimes sing alone too. During work in the fields or the stables and in the course of household chores one hears more religious than secular songs. A middle-aged man is not expected to sing secular songs. People often "bring home" the songs they heard at the vigil, and one may hear several different men chanting the previous evening's psalms while they work in the stable at dawn.

Another important part of the service is reading from the Gospel. The people of Átány consider the Bible a collection of moral examples which may serve as guides to their behavior and orient them in the affairs of the world. There are several older men who have read both the Old and the New Testament four or five times from beginning to end. Scriptural exegesis was included in the most favored prayer books, with rhymed moral lessons at the end.[10]

THE PARISH OF ÁTÁNY

The Reformation not only changed the articles of faith and the liturgy, it also fundamentally revised the organization of the parishes. The affairs of the medieval rural parish were settled either by the landlord on the basis of advowson or by the bishop. The community had practically no part in the direction of the church; even the tithes were handed over to the tithe collectors of the bishop rather than to the local rector.

In the Protestant villages the minister, the choir leader, the church, and the school were supported wholly or in part by the community. In many villages, including Átány, the parish authorities measured out a section of arable land among the fields of the inhabitants to be cultivated by the parishioners for the minister. Besides the burdens, the community also acquired rights, among them the right to elect the minister. As early as the sixteenth and seventeenth centuries the "entreaty to stay" had become habitual; at the end of the year the minister had to ask the congregation from the pulpit whether they wanted him to stay or to go.[11] In Calvinist villages—at least in the relatively independent, populous, and homogeneously Calvinist settlements of the Great Plain—the local government was at one time identical with the church magistracy. Beginning in the mid-eighteenth century, there was a trend toward separating the ecclesiastical and the secular administration, but true formal and actual separation was not effected until the middle of the nineteenth century, when the church council began to be elected on the basis of popular representation.[12]

---

[10] During World War I the wife of István Vajda (see Chapter 13, "Mobility in the Last One Hundred Years") founded a devotional circle, which at first included only women and girls and later admitted men as well. They wanted to experience a more intimate and personal devotion than the customary local religious practices offered. After a slow beginning, the movement expanded rapidly in the years after the war, and included almost one-third of the population by the early 1930s. The church at first regarded the members of the group, who called themselves "believers" or "contrites," as sectarians and looked askance at their activity. The number of "believers" dwindled gradually during World War II. At the beginning of our field work in 1951 they totaled only 60 and were made up mostly of former *zsellér*-s and farm hands. Their meetings were soon forbidden by the authorities. In the meantime they made their peace with the parish and in 1949 church authorities ordered the local church to receive the group into the fold: its members were even given several leading positions on the church council. The large majority of the population did not favor the "believers"; if one or another stood up in front of the Communion Table and said a prayer after that of the minister, he was frowned upon. Claiming to have a more intimate devotion, the "believers" feel superior to the other villagers; this superiority is not acknowledged by the latter, however, who often raise objections to their behavior.

[11] Szabó, 1948: 224–225, 278–280.

[12] The organization of church councils independent of the village magistracies was begun at the end of the seventeenth and the beginning of the eighteenth centuries in the western parts of the country, but on the Great Plain it lagged far behind. The constitution of the Transtibiscan diocese, dating from 1762, designates only the role of a churchwarden: he was to be entrusted with the care of church property in company with the village magistracy. The Pest church district did not order

Though the forms of administration have changed, the general principle has remained the same up to our day: namely, that the affairs of the church are the concern of the faithful, and primarily of the congregation, and therefore they are the ones who elect the minister, who are responsible for the church and the school, and who support the minister and the church by means of the church tax, assessed by a mutual agreement. In the case of Átány, the Protestant landlords, who lived mainly in distant places or at Szárazbő, made gifts of valuable church vessels, contributed to the costs of church construction, and appointed a general superintendent whose position was for the most part honorary, but they did not interfere with the local government in ecclesiastical matters. According to tradition, at the beginning of the last century one of the landlords, the count Butler, wanted to entice the excellent minister of Átány to be his domestic pastor and promised a large donation to the Átány church in return. The village elders answered: "Our pastor is not for sale," and refused the donation.[13]

The Átány ministers used to be preachers of wide renown. The villagers had an ample choice of candidates, since their parish was the second richest in the whole diocese (227 villages).

The election of the minister is a great event in the life of the village, attended even by those who do not ordinarily go to church. As a parish of rank and standing, Átány usually invites a minister who has already been in a minor parish. As a first step, the church council delegates a few members to gather information and listen to the minister. Then, when they are relatively sure about their choice, they invite the candidate to Átány to deliver a trial sermon. Often they try to get someone they already know something about—a man who has already served as an assistant minister in Átány or preached there as a "legate" (a student of theology at the Sárospatak academy sent to preach on a holiday and to take up the collection).

In electing a minister, people want to know first of all "what sort of a preacher he is, and how he will be able to influence the souls of the people." Then they inquire about his behavior: "How well he is able to speak the language of the people"; whether he is equally understanding of "old and young, man and woman." They assess his singing voice and, last but not least, the dignity of his appearance. They

---

the establishment of church councils until 1804, and even then a part of their membership was automatically supplied by the magistracy (Illyés, 1936: 109–110; Révész, 1938: 37–38, 51–54; Tóth, 1941: 85–98).

Aside from administration, there have been numerous other areas in which both the village and the church have been involved. For example it was found in the course of the redistribution of serf holdings (1864–1866) that the village butcher shop was situated on church property, but had been constructed of village building material with village labor. At the end of the last century the village government undertook the job of keeping the clock tower in repair, the rationale being that though both the tower and the clock belonged to the church, the time is shown to the whole community. As was done in former times, today the community organizes a fire watch from the church tower during the period after the harvest. If a fire breaks out, the population is warned by the alarm-bell of the church.

[13] The independence of the Reformed church of Átány is especially conspicuous if we compare it to the Catholic church of nearby Kömlő, for instance. In Kömlő the Archbishop of Eger was the landlord and consequently the patron, and at the same time the higher church authority. The priest, the assistant priest, and the schoolmaster were all named by him and he had the church and the school constructed according to his own plans, at the cost of the dominion.

endeavor to reach unanimity at the election. After the election and its approval by the church district, the minister may move into the rectory, a six-room house which remains the largest in the village to this day.

The duties of the minister, as the pastor of the Átány congregation, are first of all the performance of the service on weekday mornings (before World War I also in the afternoons), and on Sunday and holiday mornings and afternoons. He conducts another for the children on Sundays and a biblical exegesis for the adults on a weekday. Moreover he has to take care of the administration of the parish, as head of the church council. He serves at christenings, weddings, funerals, and confirmations. As permanent head of the school board, he supervises the schools, and since 1950 he has also given religious instruction to the children. He represents his parish within and outside of the village. As one of the greatest taxpayers, due to the church land, he was a *virilis* (an official member of the village board). Since 1950 he has been elected to the actual council of the community. In addition to all this, he is expected to be at the disposal of the parishioners, who are eager to see him at any hour of the day, to listen to their complaints and to help them when he can.

As the first man of the community, he has to lead an exemplary life. He has to foster good relations with the village magistracy and the landowners of the vicinity. In his work he is aided by his wife as well as by the assistant minister. Though the pastor's wife has no official duties, she is expected to visit the sick assiduously, to provide them and the indigent with food occasionally, and to help with medicine and advice whenever she is asked.

Until 1946 the minister's income was derived from the use of 85 *hold*-s (120.70 acres) of church land and the free use of the rectory.[14] In addition, the families of the village contributed four *véka*-s of wheat each as *párbér* ("married couples' church tax") until 1932, and the minister also received christening, wedding, and burial fees. In 1932 the Átány congregation changed the *párbér* system at the initiative of church authorities, who felt that an equal tax for rich and poor was unjust, and the basic *párbér* was set at 16 kg. of wheat per family, to which the landowners added 3 extra kg. per *hold*. In this manner about 250 *mázsa*-s of wheat were collected each year. Later the *párbér* was converted to cash.

Besides the pastor and his assistant,[15] the parish is directed by the church council. This is a body of 24 men (and six substitute members) headed by the general super-

---

[14] The ministers usually rented out a part of their land and farmed the rest themselves. The minister's land also included a separate farmyard; the livestock was kept and tended by the hired man in the "pastor's *kert*." The ministers modeled their farming after that of the landlords rather than after that of the Átány peasants; thus they were the first to purchase agricultural machines, they have several times introduced new types of seed grains, and they changed from three-crop to four-crop rotation long ago.

[15] The assistant minister is employed by the church district for one to three years and is recruited from would-be pastors who have finished their studies in divinity but have not yet passed their examination. The assistant minister lives in the vicarage, with his board provided by the pastor. Until 1945 the church possessed a separate orchard, the "chaplain's garden," which furnished the assistant minister with a supplementary income. Not infrequently the assistant minister returned to the village after passing his examination and stayed in Átány until he was elected minister somewhere else.

intendent and the churchwarden, the "*kurátor*." The former is actually an honorary position held until 1945 by one of the landowning *úr*-s of the neighborhood. The churchwarden is elected from among those experienced and esteemed peasants who have served for a long time on the church council. His duty is to execute the decisions of the church council. Since the office of the *kurátor* is regarded as equal to that of the village mayor, it is important that only a member of the most honored Átány families should be elected. It has happened more than once that brothers held the offices of mayor and churchwarden at the same time. Like the village mayor, the *kurátor* is not allowed to fill any other post, whereas the other church officials can also be members of the village magistracy, or officials of the grazing association, or all three at the same time.

The churchwarden and the members of the council are elected in the fall, usually in November, in the church or the school. Like the offices of the village magistracy, those of the church council are filled by married men of Átány origin, of adequate wealth and good reputation.[16] But the members of the church council went through more rigorous moral selection than those of the representative body of the village; as the saying goes, "nobody but a just man could enter the church council." Not only was his own family life considered, but also the behavior of his brothers and close relatives. It is said: "This is a just, honest office, since the meeting is begun by prayer and song. One was honored and esteemed, and elected for this reason." To be a church council member is regarded as higher and better than to be a village official.

Membership on the church council lasts for twelve years, one-fourth of the council coming up for re-election every third year. "If the public wanted him [the member whose term of office had expired], he was retained; he was re-elected." Re-election is declined by people over sixty years of age. "The person knew that he could not hold office for another twelve years, so he resigned, saying, 'I feel myself insufficient. I thank you for your kindness, but I am old now—please elect a young man in my stead.'"

The members of the church council try to behave like "the sons of the same father" toward one another. Especially in the old days they addressed each other as brothers: brother Orbán, brother Kiss, etc. They do not tolerate conflict within the group; if one member has a grudge against another, one of them must resign. Similarly a member who proves to be open to bribes—for example, at the election of the schoolmaster—is forced to give up his office. It once happened that one of the candidates for the schoolmaster's job promised S. M. the use of one *hold* of land if he was elected. S. M. dissuaded the electors from voting for the other candidate, though he seemed

---

[16] In the early 1930s the church went deeply into debt, owing to the settlement of the teachers' pay (see Chapter 18, "The School"). A considerable proportion of the public did not understand the serious financial situation of the church, since it owned extensive lands. The dissatisfied elements were headed by Átány *zsellér*-s, usually town workers; at the church council elections, when six members were up for re-election, they voted out five of the unsuspecting *gazda*-s and secured the election for themselves, though formerly they had been the "canvassers" of the *gazda*-s. But when they got acquainted with the complicated administration, especially in the matters of finance, they gradually withdrew; thus the *gazda*-s, having by this time organized their attack, succeeded in replacing them at the next election.

to be the better man. When the facts leaked out, S. M. had to resign. The members of the church council perform small services for each other, each according to his abilities: one who is good at weaving manufactures baskets for his colleagues, and a team owner helps his co-presbyter by transporting stone for the construction of his house. They are not able to invite each other to weddings since 24 families would mean a large additional burden, but if there is a death in the family of a member, all of them come to keep vigil and attend the funeral as a group, led by the minister. The funeral dinner of a deceased member is celebrated by the rest of the group in the church assembly room.

The duty of the church council is primarily to select the lower church officials and to direct their activity. It also administers the property of the church. Until 1948 the church lands were leased by the church council, and they also administered the income. In 1948 church land was taken over by the state. The church tax was assessed and collected by the council too. The council elected a committee of four men for financial business and a controlling group from among its members.

In the course of the reallocation of the fields in 1860, 100 *hold*-s (142 acres) of land were measured out for the support of the Átány Reformed Church, besides the fields appertaining to the offices of the minister, the teachers, and the bell ringer (totaling 152 *hold*-s (215.84 acres). The church building, regarded as the showplace of the village by the inhabitants, and its yard belong to the congregation. Next to the church stand the houses of the minister and the choir leader, along with the granary of the parish. The school buildings and the homes of the teachers were nationalized at the end of the 1940s. The Lower and Upper cemeteries, totaling eight *hold*-s (11.36 acres), are owned by the church.[17]

In the first half of the last century it was still obligatory for any Átány person who committed an offense against the public morals "to do public penance" before the church council and to suffer public humiliation by standing on "the stone of shame" beside the church door.[18] In the present century this form of punishment no longer

---

[17] Though this cemetery is owned by the Reformed church, all Átány residents may be buried there, including non-Calvinists. A grave plot in the cemetery is also provided free for any stranger who happens to die in Átány. The villagers themselves are buried in the cemetery of the Upper End or the Lower End, according to the part of the village where they lived. The graves are dug in a row, in a pattern defined by church authorities (see Plate 64). There are no family vaults in the parish, but one grave may contain three or four coffins (in planked niches dug into the wall of the grave). Thus family members may use the same grave. Married couples are buried one beside the other in any case; a man or woman who dies during a second or third marriage will rest with the first spouse. An unmarried son or daughter is buried in the grave of the father or mother, or sometimes in that of a grandparent.

[18] In order to illustrate the old judgments of the church council, we quote two items from the church journals:

1781: "János Kováts and János Mikus Szabó, having dug out [i.e., broke into] a storage pit, stole the wheat, and after the punishment imposed on them by the county according to their deserts, did religious penance on the 23rd December, though János Kováts threatened the intervention of his landlord." (Although the county court had punished the criminals, the parish did not regard the case as settled until they were also chastized by ecclesiastical censure. But there was disagreement regarding the sphere of the two jurisdictions, or at least the possibility of disagreement between the courts of state—landlord-county—and those of parish—church. Thus the thieves tried to claim the authority of their lord in order to avoid ecclesiastical censure.)

1785: "The girl Panna Marton, having become pregnant by the bachelor István Erős, did public

exists, the only remaining vestige being the role of the church council in occasionally trying to placate quarreling spouses. The council is entitled to forbid parishioners to take Holy Communion (such as the person who agrees to bring up the children in the religion of a Catholic spouse),[19] and it may allow people who do not belong to the congregation to take the Lord's Supper, the latter right being a local speciality.[20]

Traditionally the members of the church council sit in the church in the pews which are appropriate to their age, descent, and residence. Starting in 1948 when the village magistracy stopped going to church, their pews (the first ones on the men's side) have been occupied by the church council members. Before the service they meet in the council hall of the rectory, and then they march to the church behind the minister in single file, in order of age. After the service they return to the council hall in order to discuss and decide current business.

In the old days the relation between the minister and the church council members was similar to that between the secretary and the village officials, except that the pastor possessed greater authority on account of his vocation, which was regarded as more worthy than any other. Nevertheless, on several occasions in the years preceding World War I the minister had to yield to the will of the church council, just as the secretary yielded to the decisions of the magistracy. If the council members feel that their minister is not acting or behaving properly, they elect one of their number to be a spokesman, and censure the minister in their meeting, expecting him to apologize. On the other hand, they endeavor to make him remember the time spent at Átány pleasantly. They do him unexpected services, "that some day he may recall what sort of presbyters he had in Átány." They expect the minister and his wife to visit them and congratulate them on their name-days, and they vie with each other in treating them as lavishly as they can. They invite the minister to wedding feasts in their homes and seat him at the head of the table. Between the minister and his council members an intimate connection, including the members of the families, may come into being, a situation which is unknown in the relation between the secretary and the village officials. Interestingly enough, while the role and significance of the mayor and the village officials has continually decreased, to the benefit of the learned secretary, especially in the last four decades, the church council directs its minister at will up to our day.

Formerly the school board, consisting of five members, was elected by the church council. The pastor held the chairmanship by virtue of his office, and the other members were the headmaster and certain members of the church council. The schoolmaster and choir leader was also elected by the church council. The vacancy was advertised, the applicants demonstrated their qualifications by playing the organ

---

penance on the 18th September, while István Erős traveled to the Bátskaság [the southern part of the country]. But driven by his conscience back to Átány, he undertook the censure voluntarily and did public penance on the 22nd October of the year 1786; both ascended the stone of infamy in church for a week, and then he married Panna."

[19] In the case of a mixed marriage it was ordered by civil law that sons should follow the confession of their father, daughters that of their mother. By letters of concession one party might renounce this privilege for the benefit of the other.

[20] As in the case of the Roman Catholics of the village.

and singing in church, and then the church council made the decision. (Teaching ability was not tested.)

The bell ringer was also chosen by the church council.[21] Until the 1930s this was a profitable job, offering the use of 25 *hold*-s (35.50 acres) of church land. In those years the bell ringer employed an "apprentice" to toll the bells, while he himself only supervised. When the ministers' salaries were readjusted in 1932, the land allotted to the bell ringer was reduced to ten *hold*-s (14.20 acres). It is the section of the "minister's plot" situated nearest to the village, so that he can go back and forth quickly between the bell ringings. The bell ringer has the right to mow the grassy parts and to prune the trees in the cemeteries.

The bell ringer doubles as parish clerk; he keeps the church and its surroundings neat, delivers the letters of the church, and helps to bring the bread and wine to the Lord's Supper.

Important matters which affect the whole church are decided by the entire congregation, with every adult male member who has been confirmed and who pays his taxes having one vote. (In the 1930s there were about 900 voters.) It is the job of the assembly to elect the minister and the church council and to vote on changes in the church tax and major investments.

Certain tasks are sometimes done in common by the parishioners. If a fence has to be repaired or a job involving construction, demolition, or transport arises, the minister calls upon the members of the congregation to volunteer their help. This type of parish action has continued into the 1960s. For weeks there may be fifteen or twenty wagons and twice as many teamless farmers at the site, taking turns every other day. The work is led by the *kurátor*, and the helpers are treated to wine at the expense of the congregation.

The Reformed Church of Átány is an organic unit whose jurisdiction extends to the small Calvinist minorities of a few of the neighboring villages. (Formerly Átány had more affiliated churches, especially at the beginning of the eighteenth century, when even the Calvinist inhabitants of the town of Gyöngyös were under its jurisdiction.) The next level above the Átány church in the hierarchy is the church district, centered in Eger and directed by the archdeacon. The church district conducts annual visits to check the registers and the financial management. The assistant minister is appointed and the minister's election is confirmed by the church district. Several church districts make up a diocese, headed by the bishop, who visits Átány about once in a decade. In former times these visits were outstanding, solemn events in the life of the village, and the bishop was received at the Átány border by a mounted escort.

---

[21] He has to ring the bell four times a day: in the morning, at noon, in the afternoon, and in the evening. The hours of the afternoon and the evening bells vary according to season and the changing schedule of the workday. A former bell ringer noted this order down on a piece of paper and the current bell ringer follows his schedule. The tolling of the death bell is also prescribed exactly, according to the sex of the deceased (cf. Chapter 11, "The Funeral"). The bell is tolled during the funeral ceremony and the burial too. Should the bell ringer not see the ceremony from the tower, his wife signals him when to begin and end the ringing by waving a white handkerchief from below.

CHAPTER 17. ADMINISTRATION AND GOVERNMENT

PASTURE ASSOCIATIONS

Over the past two hundred years the proportion of Átány land owned by private individuals has steadily increased. Nevertheless, large islands of community property remain in use among the privately owned fields. On these patches the customary order of joint ownership has managed to survive, to a limited extent, as a heritage from the period when all the fields were common property and their use was regulated by the village administration.

The largest territory of joint ownership is the common pasture, which is larger than 1,000 *hold*-s (1,420 acres). In summer the majority of the livestock of the village are grazed there.

The pasture land was separated from that of the landowners in the course of the division of the Átány fields, made between 1863 and 1866 when the area was surveyed. Each *telek* entitled the owner to eight *hold*-s (11.36 acres) of pasture, but the owners agreed that this should be increased by a portion of their allotment of arable land. The *zsellér*-s were entitled to 1,200 square fathoms of pasture apiece. But since they had no plowland, they asked for some in exchange for half of their pasture allotment (see Chapter 2, "Land Tenure"). In this way two pastures came into being: that of the former serfs, with a size of 950 *hold*-s (1,349 acres); and that of the former *zsellér*-s, with 110 *hold*-s (156.20 acres). The use of both was regulated by their respective bodies of owners—the former serfs and the former *zsellér*-s. As long as the former serfs still farmed their land according to the compulsory three-crop rotation system, their organization was authorized to deal with both grazing rights and the use of arable land. As a consequence, their association was called the "Rotation Association" (*Nyomásos Társulat*), and that of the *zsellér*-s the "*Massza*-owners' Association" (*Masszás Társulat*). When Act 10 of 1913 reorganized these societies all over the country, the names were changed to "Great" and "Small" Pasture Associations. After the abolition of the three-crop rotation system, the organization of the former serfs was no longer required to regulate the use of plowland. The Associations were regarded as public bodies and passed their own self-governing statutes, which were subsequently confirmed by the organs of public administration; their finances were controlled by the state. The following paragraphs deal with the functioning of these reorganized bodies of commonage up until 1950, when the Pasture Associations were dissolved and their grazing lands became village property.

In 1938 the two commonages mentioned above were joined by a third one, established in the course of the parceling out of a manorial estate with state subsidy. At this time the former "Prince's lot" came into the hands of fifty *gazda*-s. They decided not to divide up the 94 *hold*-s (133.48 acres) of pasture land among themselves, but instead to found an independent body analogous to the other two associations. This they called the "*Székesgyep* Pasture Association." Since in most cases they leased out the pasture, they neither engaged a herdsman nor kept any livestock there, unlike both the older associations.

In 1866, when the grazing lands were measured out, each owner was entitled to an amount proportional to his former *telek*. However, both the arable lands and, independently, the ownership and use of the pasture were subsequently redivided by inheritance and other transactions. In a few decades' time the immediate descendants of the former landowning serfs and of the *zsellér*-s in the membership of the Pasture Associations were joined by newcomers; thus the *gazda*-s acquired some "grazing rights" on the pasture land of the *zsellér*-s, and so on. At the beginning each former *telek* entitled its owner to a section of the pasture sufficient for ten or twelve "big animals" (horses or cattle more than two years old) to graze on. (Generally one *hold* of pasture is reckoned for one "big animal.") The right to drive one "big animal" out to graze later became the unit of property. Some people possessed the right to graze ten or twelve "big animals"; others had only a fraction of a unit. In the 1940s the partitioned rights had to be expressed down to thousandths.

In order to drive a "big animal" out, one had to own one full "pasture right." This unit entitled the owner to graze one cow, or two calves or colts below two years of age, or four pigs or sheep, or forty geese. The number of animals driven out rarely corresponded to the number allowed by pasture right. The owner who sent fewer animals out to graze received a cash bonus for the unused part of his allotment. The one who drove out more animals than his right entitled him to would pay rent for the surplus. The rent was doubled if a person with no pasture rights at all grazed his animals. Everyone tried to acquire a pasture right in order to enjoy the reductions given to the members of the Pasture Association.

In the 1940s the "Great Pasture Association" had 735 members and included the majority of the villagers. Once a year, usually about December 10, the membership gathered for a general assembly, and the financial balance was submitted to it by the officers. Every third year the assembly held elections for president, "pasture *gazda*," treasurer, secretary, and a controlling commission. According to the bylaws, the right to vote was given to those who had at least one and a half pasture rights. However, those with lesser rights were also allowed to attend and speak at the meeting. The officers of the association were recruited from among the medium or smallholders—those who were willing to undertake a lot of trouble for small recompense (one *hold* of pasture land, utilizable as hay field, for the *gazda*-s, and a modest salary for the treasurer).

The use of the pasture was regulated by the associations. Individual *gazda*-s were not allowed to turn their horses, cows, or pigs out to the common pasture separately, but only in common herds, tended by the herdsman engaged by the Association. Sheep were an exception, since the flocks of sheep were owned by individual *gazda*-s or by their own private societies who hired separate grazing land from the Association. Stallions, bulls, and boars were kept by the Pasture Associations. The supply of these studs represented a considerable item in their budget. They were kept in a separate stable, where the herdsmen tended them during the winter. In order to provide food for them, part of the pasture was enclosed as grassland. Furthermore, the Pasture Associations took care of the equipment at the watering wells and cleaned them out in the spring; they erected a simple hut for the herdsmen and a fold for the animals. Formerly the *gazda*-s who owned pasture rights were obliged to go out together every spring to weed out the thorn bushes in the grazing fields; later it was done by day laborers who were paid from the common treasury.

All these functions required a complicated administration. The secretary of the Association kept track of the transfer of pasture rights and also wrote up the minutes of the assemblies and the decisions of the administration. The minutes were drawn up in the same way as in the town hall; but while the village had a learned secretary, the administration of the Pasture Associations was carried out exclusively by peasants. They also kept their own accounts, which often became very complicated due to the parcelization of pasture rights. Károly Bedécs, a former treasurer, told us, "Many times we spent the nights multiplying pennies till midnight by the light of the kerosene lamp. This is how my eyes were ruined."

The Association engaged the herdsmen annually in mid-December, and the majority of the stock-owning *gazda*-s appeared for this occasion. It was announced in advance by means of the drum that the time had come to appoint the herdsmen, and that the candidates for this office should report to the president. The president then listed the applicants by name to the assembled *gazda*-s so that they could choose the most suitable persons. When the decisions had been reached, the *gazda*-s sent for the individuals they had chosen. When they appeared, each one was addressed as follows by the president: "Well, my *öcs* [younger brother], the assembly has unanimously appointed you as [e.g.] head herdsman of the upper herd; what sort of wages do you want?" Though the salary had been fixed for decades (see Chapter 12, "Herdsmen"), the herdsman enumerated his conditions and the president agreed to them. Then the president said, "Well then, give me your hand," and, holding the right hand of the herdsman, he said, "I wish you strength, health, a quick foot, and a good watchful eye, so that you may tend and graze the animals faithfully." The herdsman answered, "I thank you very much." Now each member of the Association board shook hands with the new herdsman, uttering a traditional good wish similar to the one mentioned above, or, if he did not know one, saying, "I wish you the same." The handshake had a binding force, since the appointments of the Pasture Associations did not entail an oath or vow. The term of service started at once. If a new herdsman was engaged instead of the old one (which was relatively rare, since a good herdsman used to be appointed as many as twenty times), he began tending the studs on the very evening of his appointment.

Until the end of the last century, from 100 to 200 horses were grazed in the common pastures of Átány every year, but in 1901 herding horses was given up. Also, 700 to 800 head of cattle were driven out to pasture. Among them 80 to 120 cows belonging to the herd of the *zsellér*-s were turned out daily; 200 to 300 young animals in the herd of the Great Association were kept in the open from spring until autumn; 70 to 80 oxen were herded with them for a few months (from the end of the spring plowing until they were needed to transport the harvest from the fields to the village); about 300 cows belonging to the *gazda* association were driven out daily in two groups (the Lower End herd and the Upper End herd); and 80 to 120 calves were also driven out daily. Throughout the year about 500 to 600 pigs were taken out every day by the swineherds of the Lower End, the Upper End, and the *zsellér*-s.[22] As long as horses were grazed, a head horseman was elected as well as a head cattleman. The Upper End and the Lower End each had a head herdsman for cattle and another for swine. These responsible herdsmen hired boys to help them, usually two for each herd, and paid them out of their own wages.

There was a hierarchy among the herdsmen. The horseman was the first, followed by the herdsman for the cattle kept in the open, the herdsman for the cattle driven out daily, the calf-herd, and last the swineherd. With the exception of the swineherd, the head herdsmen were expected to have some property, in order to guarantee the safety of the animals entrusted to their care.

Between spring and fall the schedule for driving the animals out to pasture, which determined the daily work routine of the peasants in many respects, was the following: at 2 A.M. one of the herdsmen of the "great cattle herd" began to "pipe for milking" all over the village; then he settled himself comfortably in one of the stables near the edge of the village and took about an hour's nap. In the meantime the *gazd-asszony*-s or other female members of the family hastened out to the *kert*-s and milked the cows. During the milking the horses were turned out. When "the dust of the horses was blown away," the cattleman began to "pipe for turning out." The cows of the Lower End were herded together, as were those of the Upper End, and on separate routes were driven out to pasture. The cattle of the "Great Association"

---

[22] The animals driven to pasture were marked. The brands of the individual households and families were known in the village, or at least in the neighborhood; recognizing the brand mark, people would drive a stray animal back to its owner. The *gazda*-s brand the cows and horses they have bred with a special iron made for this purpose, putting their initials on the hindquarters of the animals. They apply similar brands to their tools and paint their marks on their sacks. Recently, in order to spare the skin of the animals, smaller irons have been used, and they are sometimes even applied to the horns or hoofs. Sheeps are marked on their ears with various incisions. Pigs are labeled on their backs with black or red paint. Ducks and geese are marked in a manner which varies from house to house: the webs of their feet or their nails are cut in various patterns, or sometimes a mark is painted on their heads or backs.

The brands used on large animals also served as valid evidence before the authorities; formerly this was very important in cases of theft. The herdsman was able to account for an animal which had died in the grazing field by producing its branded skin. Since the end of the eighteenth century it was required that the brand of the village also be applied to the animals in order to make identification possible. Until quite recently some *gazda*-s still used the brand ÁT, the ancient mark of Átány.

walked first, followed by those of the *zsellér*-s. The *zsellér* cattle also had a head herdsman with two boys, and were also taken out to graze by separate routes, according to which end of the village they belonged to. If there was a herd of calves, it came next. When "the dust subsided" after the calves, the "great herd of swine" of the Lower End and that of the Upper End came, followed by the swine of the *zsellér*-s from both parts of the village. However, in lean years the *zsellér*-s gave up their independent herd and grazed their pigs on the pasture of the *gazda*-s for a fee.

The work of the herdsmen was directed by the officers of the Association, and most of all by the president. He had the right to set the date of the first "turning out" in spring and of the roundup in the autumn, and to decide which part of the pasture land was to be used for grazing. From the first driving out to the "crowding in" (from St. George's day, April 24, to St. Michael's, September 29; formerly to St. Andrew's, November 30) the herdsman and his boys lived with the herd on the open pasture. They took turns visiting the village to fetch food and clean clothes. The other herds were driven out to the grazing fields every morning and back to the village every evening, early on weekdays, somewhat later on Sundays. In the pasture it was the duty of the herdsmen to make sure the animals had enough to eat and to draw as much water as they needed from the sweeppole wells (see Plate 23). They cured the minor ailments of the cattle. During the grazing season the breeding animals owned by the Pasture Associations—six bulls, two brood mares, and four boars— used to follow the herds.

As we have mentioned above, the herdsmen were paid mainly in kind. In order to collect the required quantity of produce, the herdsmen had special measuring vessels, tested by the Associations every year. The "vessel test" took place in the town hall, in the presence of the mayor and the other village officials. The volume of the vessels was verified, and then they were marked with the seal of the community or the association. It was with these vessels that the herdsmen went from house to house after the harvest, collecting the grain due to them according to the number of the animals each household had sent out.

The two field guards were engaged on the same day as the herdsmen. They were usually elderly men of small means, who came to apply for the job together with the herdsmen after the drum announcement. The leaders of the Association shook hands with the newly appointed field guards as well, saying, "Guard our fields well, and report on anything wrong," or, "I wish that you may pass the term you have undertaken to serve in health and strength."

The field guards watched the "living soil," the planted fields, to prevent any damage which might be caused by the herd or by a private person who grazed his animals in secret. In the old days they used to ride armed with a long whip and an ax. If they caught an animal in the enclosure, they drove it into the community *kert*, whence the owner could retrieve it after the payment of a fine. The field guards were obliged to make the rounds of the pasture every day, to visit all of the herds and to inquire whether they needed anything or whether there was a sick animal, in which case they informed its owner. It was their duty to report on defects in the wells, watering pails, bridges, and roads to the president of the Association, so that he could take steps for repair or replacement.

The "Small Pasture Association" engaged no field guard. Its grazing land was so small that the herdsman was able to survey both fields and animals himself.

The parts of the common pasture which are situated in the neighborhood of the village are called "pasture for geese" or "pit" after the numerous wet and dry pits of different sizes which are located there. The "black earth" and "yellow earth" needed by the households for daubing (three to five cartloads a year) are taken from the dry pits, while the wet pits yield the mud used for making bricks. Anyone who had pasture rights in the Great Association was allowed to take earth or have bricks made, provided that he first informed the *gazda* of the Association, who then assigned the spot where he was to dig.[23]

In addition, the pitted parts of the "great pasture" are used by the geese for grazing and bathing in the water of the pits. Before May 1, while the young geese were still weak they were watched by the children of the family, but on that date "the goose-herds stepped forward" in both ends of the village. From then until the harvest, each gooseherd tended the geese from her end of the village in a common flock. Each of these flocks totaled from 500 to 600 fowl. After the harvest each villager turned out his geese onto his own harvested field. The gooseherds were controlled by the *gazda* of the Association, who kept track of the number of geese driven out by each owner and the use of the circumscribed part of the pasture. The gooseherds (widows, girls, and other women) were not appointed by the Associations but by the *gazdasszony*-s whose geese they watched. One day's meals and a few *forint*-s were the wages for herding ten geese.

The reed banks of the village were also managed by the Pasture Associations. After the 1866 consolidation of holdings, both the Great and Small Pasture Associations, and even the *tagos*-s (peasants whose property consisted of a single piece of land [see Chapter 2, "Land Tenure"]), owned undivided areas of reeds which could be used by their members. In the course of the 1927 consolidation the reed bed of the Great Pasture Association was divided up among individual farmers; the remaining two Associations, however, retained the common administration of their reeds. In exceptional cases of damage due to storm or fire, the victim was given reeds by the Association free, so that he could re-thatch his roof. Otherwise those who wanted reeds gathered near the Association's marshland on a prearranged day to buy marsh rights at the outdoor auction. Sometimes several peasants would get together and make a group purchase, after which they would cut the reeds together and divide them equally among themselves.

The Átány vineyards situated in the Heves fields were guarded in a manner analogous to the operation of the Pasture Associations. The older vineyards were considered

---

[23] Those who had no grazing rights in the "great pasture" were not entitled to the use of the pits in its territory (e.g., people who had grazing rights only in the pasture of the *zsellér*-s, or the *tagos*-s, who also received their grazing share in 1866). In some cases the community allowed them to dig pits in the so-called "village land" in order to make adobe or get some earth. Consequently the plowing area of the village was reduced by about three *hold*-s (4.26 acres).

a "colony" of Átány within the Heves boundaries. The work schedule, maintenance of the fence and the ditch, and general supervision were directed by the Átány village government. At the end of the last century the villagers of Átány left these old vineyards, but when they planted new ones, beginning in 1912, they retained a common organization for guarding and management. The *gazda*-s who own vineyards elect a "vineyard elder" from their number and appoint vineyard guards. The people of Átány emphasize the "non-official" character of the vineyard elder. He is not elected in the town hall, nor is the election governed by written rules. The association of the vineyard-owning *gazda*-s is a private association, unlike the "public bodies" under state supervision, such as the Pasture Associations.

In December, at the same time as the other elections of the village are held, the interested *gazda*-s assemble in the house of one vineyard owner, each of them bringing a liter bottle of wine in his pocket. They elect a *gazda* who is willing to fill this post, and then drink *áldomás* from the bottles they have brought. At the same time three vineyard guards are engaged. From March until the end of the season the vineyard guard lives in the vineyard, and during the winter he makes the rounds of the area entrusted to his care to see whether the trees and buildings have been damaged. He is paid in kind in proportion to the size of the vineyard he watches.

The job of vineyard guard is a rather easy one, and often the applicants are old former herdsmen. Like the herdsmen, the vineyard guard collects his pay in a basket, which is tested by the vineyard elder. It is not marked by the seal of the Association, however.[24]

The traditional associations formed by the sheep-owning *gazda*-s for the purpose of appointing a shepherd to graze their sheep in common should also be mentioned here. These were usually groups of from five to ten *gazda*-s who lived in the same part of the village. As a group they leased a pasture from the Associations, where they erected shelters for the herd and the shepherd, and they also constructed more lasting buildings in the *kert*-s to shelter the herd in winter, sharing the cost and the labor in both these enterprises. In the course of the 1866 consolidation of holdings, eleven winter *kert*-s containing sheepfolds were counted and registered as the common property of from five to ten *gazda*-s each. The common ownership served as a guarantee for the duration of such associations. However, they went out of existence at the end of the last century, owing to the decline of the famous Átány sheep breeding.

OTHER COMMUNITY ORGANIZATIONS

The roots of the Pasture Associations reach back to the secular traditions of the autonomous rural government, though their activity has been curtailed by recent statutes. Other community organizations and associations were inspired by outside

[24] Besides the grain he receives, the vineyard guard is entitled to mow the edges of the roads, and he also receives bundles of dead vines to use as fuel, in an amount proportional to the size of the vineyard entrusted to his care.

forces, such as the interference of higher administrative units or the initiative of the "intelligentsia" of the village, i.e., the minister and the village secretary. Yet, whatever their ultimate source, many of the peasants came to be included in their scope; they became the forums of the public life of the community, as it were, the institutions within which public opinion was formed and matters concerning the whole village were discussed. Leading personalities would often begin their careers in minor community organizations. These associations took over activities which had formerly been carried out without any formal organization. For example, in the old days a dance was spontaneously conceived and arranged by informal groupings of the young people who belonged to the same part of the village or age group; later on, several associations and organizations regarded it as their important task to give "balls" in a hired locality—issuing invitations, demanding entrance fees, and asking for licenses—for dancing till dawn in the fashion of the cities.

The Volunteer Firemen's Association

In 1901 the village administration placed a description of the village in the foundation of the new village secretary's house, advocating the cause of progress in enthusiastic words (see Appendix B). The document states proudly: "We have a fine social life; we have ... a Firemen's Association." The pride of the "progressive" Átány citizens in their Firemen's Association was not unfounded. The activity of the Association can be followed from the 1880s on, and since then it has fulfilled a number of tasks besides its duties strictly conceived. At the turn of the century, when Árpád Horkay, the village secretary, held the office of chief, the Firemen's Association rose to such a height that it was able to construct a large new building and to provide all thirty of the members with new uniforms. The uniform of the firemen was highly esteemed; one of the deceased fire chiefs was buried in his uniform, and his fireman's helmet and ax were laid on his coffin. The firemen performed regular exercises with their hoses, and the "firemen's competitions" of the district and the county offered them the chance to go on excursions and to win laurels for the village.

The fire house allowed the Reading Circle to use its premises for a long time, both for its meetings and to house its library. Every year on March 15 the "day of the 1848 revolution" banquet was held in the firehouse. The general assemblies of the Consumers' Cooperative were also held there. Every year the firemen themselves put on several "firemen's balls" and theatrical performances in the building. In the late 1950s one of the first television sets in the village was acquired by the fire brigade; it was placed with the fire-fighting equipment, and anyone was allowed to watch the programs for a small fee. (The firemen used the fees from television viewing, balls, and theatricals to buy new equipment.)

The Úr-s' Casino

Although the exact date of its founding is unknown, the Casino was certainly in existence before the 1880s. At first it was the social circle of the local "intelligentsia," and the membership was recruited from among the úr-s: the secretary of the village, the minister, one or more of the schoolmasters, and the landowners of the vicinity. Of the villagers, the mayor and one or two men who themselves or whose close relatives had studied in the Sárospatak secondary school were the only ones to go to the Casino regularly.

The Reading Circle

Before World War I the Casino changed its name to the Reading Circle and enlarged the scope of its membership. Thereafter the members of the village government, the leaders of the Consumers' Cooperative, and, generally speaking, the peasants who were active in the public life of the village also belonged to it, so that 95 members were included in the banquets of March 15. The Reading Circle subscribed to newspapers and had its own library in the fire house. The úr-s seem to have gradually withdrawn from the circle, leaving the peasants of medium wealth to set the fashion. From then on they subscribed to newspapers and periodicals only in the winter; during the summer work season, when the farmers were unable to find time for reading, the subscriptions were withdrawn. They calculated their expenditures (kerosene for the lamp, fuel, keeping the room clean, subscriptions to papers), and the sum was divided equally and collected as a membership fee.

The membership of the Reading Circle grew during the 1920s and came to include an increasing number of poor people who worked in the towns during the summer and came back to the village for the winter. Owing to differences in world view and conflicting opinions on the affairs of the community, dissension soon arose among the members, and not long afterward things came to a head. In 1931 the Reading Circle split into two groups: the "*Gazda* Circle," which, as the name implies, was made up of people from the higher socio-economic strata, and the "Civic Readers' Club," the poor people's association, made up of those who had summer jobs in Budapest. (For them the Readers' Club assumed to some extent the role of the *tanyakert*-s.) The village government managed to acquire a large building, one wing of which became the seat of the *Gazda* Circle, the other (after heated debates in the magistracy) that of the Civic Readers' Club. This was the period during which "party strife" began in the village (see Chapter 18, "Politics"); before every church, community, or even Consumers' Cooperative election, the "opposition" organized its demonstrations in the Civic Readers' Club. This "party" was recruited from among the day laborers and those who worked in Budapest, and their goal was to oust the wealthy *gazda*-s from their traditional status as leaders. (When the zeal of the opposition subsided, however, the Readers' Club also lost its significance.)

The Hunters' Association

According to the minutes of the village assemblies, as early as 1886 there was a Hunters' Association in Átány which leased portions of the village property suitable for the shooting of small game.[25] However, only one of the Association's members was of local origin, Gábor Czégel, who was descended from an Átány family. He had gone to secondary school for a few years and held the office of secretary in one of the neighboring villages. All the other members were *úr*-s: the minister, the village secretary, and the landowners of the vicinity.

The General Consumers' Cooperative

This organization was founded in 1892 on the initiative of the minister József Fekete. Shares were sold in that year and again a few years later. At that time there were about 150 shareholders, each holding four or five, or sometimes more, shares valued at either 10 or 50 *korona*-s. They bought an ancient peasant house and turned half of it into a store and the other into a tavern. After a while they were able to construct a stately building in the middle of the village, using half of it as a store and half as a tavern as before. The shopkeeper and the bartender received a share of the income in addition to their pay. The shareholders were given a dividend each year, which entitled them to an amount of goods from the shop proportional to the number of shares they held.

Following various efforts to consolidate the rural cooperative societies, a bill was finally passed in 1898. This served as the basis for founding the National *Hangya* Cooperative Society, subsidized by the state. The Átány organization joined it in 1901, receiving credit and aid in purchasing goods from the National Center,[26] and business increased rapidly.

The board of the cooperative consisted of a president, a managing director, a treasurer, a directorate of three members, a board of control likewise of three members, and a committee of five. Later the constitution was changed so that eight members were elected to the directorate and eight to the board of supervision. The leaders were recruited from among the peasants—partly respected *gazda*-s, partly smallholders of intelligence and ability. They were elected for a term of three years, after a campaign similar to that of the election of the village administration. Some thought

---

[25] The right to hunt on the village area was rented out by auction to the Hunters' Association for a period of six to ten years. The income went to the members of the Pasture Associations and was divided among them. Later it was decided that the money, which was so little as to make division difficult, should be laid aside as a community reserve. Once it was given as a donation to the Calvinist school, once as a contribution to the construction of the doctor's house, and afterwards it was added to the fund for drilling artesian wells.

[26] The *Hangya* Cooperative Society soon established a national organization. Even before World War I it had 1,276 member cooperatives. At that time about 25 to 30 per cent of the rural population took part in the activity of the credit and consumers' cooperatives. About 60 per cent of the membership of the latter belonged to the *Hangya* (Gyimesi, 1965: 628–629, 648).

that the posts in the consumers' cooperative were "fat ones," promising financial gain, because the officers received salaries as well as travel allowances for their journeys to procure goods.

Cooperative Dairy

The cooperative dairy was founded in 1913–1914 on the initiative of the village secretary in order to help the Átány gazda-s sell their dairy products. Like the consumers' cooperative, it belonged to a national organization. The members were obliged to buy as many shares as they had milk cows at the time of marketing. The Cooperative Dairy obtained machines from the national organization and built a receiving-processing station on its own. Its work was directed by an elected leadership.[27]

Levente Association

In 1920, by the terms of the Treaty of Trianon, Hungary was no longer allowed to maintain a standing army larger than was necessary to keep internal order. In order to counterbalance this restriction, the government founded the *Levente*, voluntary at the beginning, compulsory from the end of the 1930s. It was supposed to promote the physical education of the youths between twelve and eighteen years of age, and actually provided their preliminary military training. As long as participation remained voluntary, few Átány boys joined the *Levente*, since their parents were opposed to the waste of time, preferring to have their able-bodied sons working. Nevertheless, there were thirty or forty bachelors in the organization. The goal of the leader, an Átány peasant and ex-serviceman, was to make peace between the quarreling bachelor bands of the Lower and the Upper Ends. He succeeded through the *Levente* balls, theatrical performances, and parties organized by and for both groups.

Choir, Orchestra

The first adult choir in Átány was organized by a zealous choir leader in the 1890s. It consisted of young men and girls and totaled about forty members. This choir acquired a good reputation and used to sing at the celebrations of other villages and Reformed congregations as well as its own. With the retirement of the choir leader

[27] Cooperative dairies belonged to the National Center of Dairies. They began to be organized in 1897, and by 1907, 8 per cent of the milk cows of the country were covered by them. In addition to organizing the marketing of dairy products, cooperatives were active in mechanization and the introduction of new processing techniques. After the cooperative was founded a few Átány gazda-s began to experiment with dairy farming. For the rest, the cooperative took what milk was left over from the family cows after the needs of the household were satisfied, and marketed it as butter and bitter curd (Balogh, 1965a: 379; Gyimesi, 1965: 633, 648–650; Szilágyi, 1951: 44–46, 54–55).

the choral society went out of existence. But when a leader can be found, a sweet-voiced youth is often the excuse for organizing a new choir, even to this day. It is taught either by the minister, who takes the group around the village to herald the birth of Christ during Advent, or by the schoolmasters. The village administration also encourages choral activity.

In 1899 an orchestra also came into being in Átány; it was a "Hungarian band" of wind instruments. They played at national festivals and dances. But when one of the leading members died suddenly in 1918 the band went out of existence for good.

THE LOCAL GOVERNMENT

In former times the village had a single local board which served as the organ of both the ecclesiastical and the secular administration and jurisdiction and regulated the use of the fields as well. Even our oldest informants can remember this period only from the stories of their predecessors. They grew up in a time when the administration of church and village and the control of community pasture land had already been separated. Besides its function as an organization for local self-government, the village administration has become the executive organ of state administration to an ever-increasing degree. Its activity has been regulated by statutes: Act 18 of 1871 established the first nationally uniform system of local administration on the basis of the equality of rights. This was modified by Act 22, 1886, which remained the basic law until 1950 except for minor amendments.[28] This is the period that we shall describe here.

Though the authorities of church and state had been separated formally, their former close connection was evidenced by a number of customs even in these decades. In the men's section of the church the first seat was reserved for the village mayor and the second was allotted to the *kurátor*, the head of the church council. Led by the mayor, the remaining members of the local administration occupied the first pews (until 1948). During the service, "as long as the church door was open," the door of the tavern had to be closed. Poor relief was an official duty of the community, but in practice it was the church that raised a collection for the poor of the village.

The political community was headed by two councils—the local board and the body of representatives. The mayor was the president of both. He was assisted by the village secretary, who was entrusted with village administration. The secretary was the only trained, technically qualified official of the local administration; also he was a non-villager, who received a monthly salary from the community supplemented by money from the state.[29] When the Local Government Act was passed, his power was still secondary to that of the mayor. In those days the highly esteemed peasant mayors, acquainted with the rules of law and cognizant of the workings of public affairs, were

[28] Magyary, 1942: 297–326.
[29] In addition to his pay he was entitled to the use of 45 *hold*-s (63.90 acres) of land and the official residence.

able to direct the secretary. Later, as public administration grew increasingly bureaucratic and presented the village board with increasingly complicated tasks, the role of the well-trained secretary became more important from decade to decade. Whereas the mayor and the other officials were elected for a term of three years, the secretary held his post for life. Eventually, through his qualifications and the continuity of his office, he became the first man in the village administration, though in principle this honor remained the mayor's.[30]

Nothing can illustrate the growth of the village secretary's authority better than the house allotted to him by the village. Before 1906 the home of the secretary and the office of the government, "the bureau," were located in the same building as the local tavern (one wing being occupied by the home and office of the secretary, the other by the tavern). In the 1880s and 1890s the building became so decrepit that the mayor, András Rózsa, moved his office from it into his own house, not to return until the construction of a new town hall in 1896. Then in 1901 the village built a fine new "secretarial home" on a property of almost one *hold*. Thus, instead of hiring a bachelor who had just passed his secondary school examinations, the village was able to provide for an authoritative married man with a college education. Soon an assistant secretary was added, followed by another assistant to deal with matters of taxation, while the former secretary advanced to the rank of "chief secretary."

The village secretary takes the minutes of the local board meetings, where he also puts forward new proposals. Along with the mayor he controls the village economy, and he directs the collection of taxes. He keeps a number of records: the registers, the list of livestock, the rate book, and the deeds of title. He has a notary's power of certification and authentication, and the state-controlled labor contracts such as those of the harvesters' bands and *summás*-s are entered before him. With his legal and administrative training, he may also serve private individuals—for instance, by drafting documents or petitions. For the people of the village he is the nearest, most easily accessible representative of the public administration, the offices of which are generally found at the seats of the district or the county.

But let us return to the members of the local board, who are elected from among the Átány peasants and whose role and authority has decreased in comparison with that of the notary only in the last few decades. Their leader is the mayor. He was elected (from the three candidates approved by the chief administrative officer of the district) for three years by the "elective body" of the village, i.e., the adult tax-paying males who had been domiciled for at least two years in the village. His was an honorary office for which only a token salary was paid; after 1940 he became a regular paid official.

---

[30] Magyary, 1942: 320. The position of village secretary was developed in the seventeenth and eighteenth centuries. From the middle of the eighteenth century authorities urged each village to employ its own secretary, but they did not succeed until the end of the century. These secretaries were the "servants of the community," having as their qualifications literacy and an elementary education; they performed the tasks of administration in cooperation with the peasant magistracies. During the 1730s a young noble was the Átány secretary, and contemporary records reveal that he followed the injunctions of the peasant mayor obsequiously (cf. Szabó, 1948: 280–282).

Before the 1870s not only the village but also the surrounding fields were under his direction. He had the right to fix the dates of the various agricultural undertakings, announcing them by means of the drum. Plowing, sowing, transporting the manure, and reaping all were done "after the drum." He set the beginning dates for the harvesting of wheat, oats, and maize, the pulling out of hemp, and the gathering of grapes. Everyone had to obey, since after a fixed period the herds were allowed to graze on all the fields, whether the owners had harvested their grain in time or not. Similarly, he named the day when the livestock were to be driven out to pasture and the day when they were to be rounded up and driven home. In the days when the swine of the village were driven out to beech groves rented in the Mátra mountains, the mayor had the right to force open the pigsty of a *gazda* who did not drive out his swine at the sound of the drum and to put the animals in the common herd, if necessary by force.

In the Middle Ages the head of a Hungarian village government was called the "village justice." In the period described here some of the duties of the village mayor were a heritage from the traditional office of village justice: to keep order in the village and to administer justice. He "had to keep an eye on everything that happened in the village." Any villager could turn to him, whether it was a case of a quarrel with a neighbor over the plowing of a boundary line or the killing of a hen; or antagonism within the family over the division of the inheritance. The mayor, the secretary, and one other village official acted as a court of arbitration.[31] He sent an expert member of the local board to measure the debated border or balk or went with the judge to settle the division of the inheritance, and he summoned the litigants to the court. In the last century he had criminal jurisdiction as well: he had the person guilty of swearing, stealing, or disorderly behavior in church publicly whipped, laying him on the "whipping bank" in front of the church on a Sunday. He ordered the thief to walk through the village with the stolen property tied on his back. He was escorted by villagers, who would ring small bells to call attention to the misdeed. He could arrest a person for rioting and even make him spend a night in the town hall. He retained his right to punish disorderly bachelors or children with his mayor's staff until recent decades. On the other hand, he was obliged to help a man in trouble. For example, if a poor man was too ill to procure a team to cultivate his tiny plot, he could ask the mayor's assistance; when there was no other solution, the mayor placed his own horses at the suppliant's disposal.

The mayor was in charge of the financial affairs of the village. People remember that before 1886 the tax was paid to him; he kept the money in his house and carried it to the county authorities "in the sleeve of his *szűr*"[32] on the last day of the year. When the term of his office expired, he presented the community with an account of the income of the village and the official expenditures. Later he shared the duties

---

[31] According to the Local Administration Acts, the village mayor was not part of the judicial organization; he had jurisdiction only in matters "under the value limit" or where he was accepted by the litigants as a mediator.

[32] Usually the *szűr* was not put on like a coat but thrown over the shoulders. Thus the end of the sleeve could be tied up to form a satchel or pocket.

of tax collection and the budgeting of expenditures with the village secretary, although even at the beginning of the twentieth century some village revenues were still paid to the mayor and budgeted by him.[33]

The mayor was the chairman of the meetings of the village board and the representative body. The body of representatives was an organ of self-government which decided the affairs of the village, while the village board, which met more frequently, was an executive organ which handled current administration. Thus the personality of the mayor had a marked influence on the life of the village. The electors tried to choose a respected, friendly, and honest man for this office. "Popularity and eloquence make one a mayor—the ability to put his ideas into words." Thus some experience and self-assurance in public affairs were desirable. In practice, the office of the mayor was attained almost without exception by people who had held lower offices, such as that of a minor village official or judge. Election to this honor could be sought only by the members of large, wealthy *gazda* families who were supported at the voting by a numerous kin group, a crowd of friends and neighbors, and a number of poor people and laborers who were obliged to them. The candidate was expected to be irreproachable and to lead a chaste family life. Before the election, people were "turned round," meaning that their own hidden faults and those of their families were exposed. People wanted to see the mayor in church regularly. "No man who did not go to church was raised to that rank." If, as happened once in the early 1940s, a mayor was elected who had not previously been a church-goer, he was obliged to become one after the election.

On the village council, the office of judge was next in rank to that of mayor. Whereas the mayor was paid a yearly fee and (after 1940) a salary, the judge received only "honor." Like the members of the village council, he was elected for a term of three years. As implied by his title, his duties were to administer justice, to settle differences, and to hold court days for the settlement of lawsuits below a certain "limit of value," the so-called "bagatelle" suits. Examples of these were cases of trespassers in the fields who had been caught by the field guards or distrained by the proprietor, and the prosecution of petty thefts or verbal or actual injuries. In the case of damaged field boundaries, the task of measurement usually fell to the judge, and therefore he had to be an expert in handling the measuring chain. He substituted for the mayor in cases of absence or illness. Local custom allotted an additional role to the judge. According to local opinion, the mayor was not empowered to contest county ordinances, so when the village administration was discussing an order it did not want to fulfill, the mayor turned over the chair to the judge, who then presided over the meeting and signed any document which protested or disregarded the county ordinance.

The third man in rank on the village board was the treasurer. This post was also usually attained by men who had held lower offices, most commonly after a three-

---

[33] The mayor had to have some financial resources of his own, so that he might be held responsible for the money of the community. "His property was at stake." On the other hand, the house of the village mayor was by law insured against all sorts of damages (larceny, fire, etc.) at the expense of the village.

year term on the village board. The community generally elected a man who was moderately wealthy to this office, one with enough property to serve as security for the sums entrusted to him. He received a modest salary.

Then followed the public guardian, who managed the affairs of the orphan children in the village. He appointed one of the child's relatives guardian, and he and the guardian shared the job of managing the property of the minor—for example, by leasing it out. In the last century he also managed the money belonging to orphans and wards and was entitled to make loans to the villagers under the supervision of the village council. In those days, when credit was hard to come by, the village guardians all over the country acquired considerable influence by managing and making loans from the orphans' trust fund.[34] The service of the public guardian was recompensed by "honor" only; it would have been considered improper to receive money for it. The much esteemed former public guardian János Boross administered the affairs of 42 orphans during the 1930s, keeping the children's documents at home in his own chest of letters. In the majority of instances the orphans had little property to be managed. However, in four or five cases of landed orphans he had to supervise the use of the lands.

In addition to the orphans, the poor of the village were also the concern of the public tutor, who made proposals to the body of representatives as to what aid should be given them (such as coverage of the costs of drugs, doctors' bills, and funerals, including the cost of the coffin).

The remaining eight members of the village board were "sworn men" or "aldermen."[35] They were usually elected so as to be representative of all *fertály*-s, and even the larger *zug*-s; thus each of these officials looked after the affairs of the people of his own *fertály* or *zug*. One "sworn man" was always chosen from among the *zsellér*-s or the teamless farmers.

These officials drafted the registers, the one with the best penmanship doing most of the work for all *fertály*-s. If the mayor or the village judge could not go, they were sent to settle inheritance divisions or to measure land. In official duties the council members usually worked in teams of two; the pairs were formed so that one of them should be "more knowledgeable," cleverer, and better versed in the affairs of the village and the matter at hand than the other. It was also the business of the council members to make estimates regarding, for instance, the probable yield of the uncut grain, hay, alfalfa, etc. or the actual quantity that had been harvested, in cases where it was needed in asking bank credit or in preparing forced sale. On occasion they were given the disagreeable task of escorting the bailiff and the police investigators. The "sworn men" also estimated the damages reported by the field guard. Their official visits were financed by allowances for the given occasion.

[34] Szabad, 1965: 178–188.
[35] Before 1912 one member of the administration held the office of a *hadnagy*. This role was allotted to a relatively young but sedate village councillor (the last *hadnagy* was János Boross, cf. Appendix A). It was his duty to keep a continuous watch over public order; he directed the activity of the watchmen and village drummers, visited the tavern on some evenings, and generally kept on the lookout for disorder in the village. He received a modest fee.

Moreover, all proposals were discussed by the council members at the meetings of the village board. Those who had less "talent for words" preferred to remain silent, so usually three or four men took part in the debates. Often these men recalled their participation with self-consciousness later: "I was always the first to speak in the meetings."

The "body of representatives," made up of 24 members, is a higher authority over the twelve-member village board. (The size of both the body of representatives and the village board is proportional to the population of the village.) Twelve of the representatives were elected by the villagers for six-year terms in such a way that every three years half of them came up for re-election. The remaining twelve seats were occupied by the landowners who paid the highest taxes in the village; thus the landlords of Szárazbő, the manager of the Coburg-Koháry estate, and even the Reformed Church and the *Hangya* Consumers' Cooperative were non-elected members, by virtue of their wealth and the high taxes they paid.

Membership in the representative body was regarded as a higher and more illustrious office than membership in the village board, since the representatives only had to attend meetings—"they were not sent to the houses"—in other words they were free from performing disagreeable duties in the homes of the villagers. The representatives were recruited from among the older and wealthier persons, and most of them had already held a position on the village board. Four of the body of representatives were also members of the municipal board of the county. This was a great honor, but it also entailed sacrifices, such as the loss of time and money involved in attending meetings at the county seat.[36]

The body of representatives and the village board were summoned to an assembly by the mayor twice a year. The assemblies were almost always called to discuss the budget and the general finances, though the mayor was also entitled to summon them in case of emergency. The body of representatives, as the higher organ of the local government, supervised the financial matters of the village, the budget, and the management of the community property.

The village (as distinct from the Pasture Associations) owned 24 *hold*-s (34.08 acres) of land, the so-called "village land," which was usually leased out. Furthermore, the community possessed a tavern and two smithies, which it also rented out; the income from these establishments went into the village treasury. In some cases the community made cash loans to local *gazda*-s, to be paid back with interest.[37] The decision to make a loan was made by the body of representatives, which assumed responsibility for the sum before the higher authorities. However, the village met its expenses mainly by means of the surtax, assessed in proportion to the national taxes. At the end of the

[36] They had to drive to Eger in their wagons every month to attend the minor county assemblies. Each trip involved a whole day in town, during which their own labor and that of the team was unavailable for agricultural work. In addition they had to bear the unusual costs of eating and drinking away from home. They were able to communicate the wishes of the community to the county authorities as members of the municipal committee, a body made up partly of the biggest tax payers and partly of members elected by the villages and thus similar in structure to the village government.
[37] In 1896 the capital lent by the village totaled 800 *korona*-s. After 1890 these loans were secured by mortgages on the property of the debtors.

last century the local tax amounted to 5 to 10 per cent of the national tax, but since then it has gradually risen, amounting at times to as much as 75 per cent.

The village also collected a tax on alcoholic beverages. Formerly the administration taxed the wine consumption in the taverns directly, but later the innkeepers commuted the excise into a sum fixed in advance.[38]

The salaries and honorary fees of the officials and the upkeep of the community buildings were included in the budget of the village. At about the turn of the century the local government constructed several important buildings—a large new town hall and new houses for the village secretary and the doctor. Both in the mayor's accounts and in the later budgets, maintenance and repair of roads and bridges and digging and care of community wells were of considerable importance. In order to carry out these tasks, the population of the village had to contribute their labor.[39] In 1902, however, public labor was replaced by a money tax. The appropriation of the public labor and its money equivalent were governed by the body of representatives.

The body of representatives had the power to grant residence rights to outsiders, and thus had control over who was allowed to move into the community. It had jurisdiction in matters of local poor relief. It supervised the work of the village council. It organized the elections and made the nominations. Employees of the community were engaged by the representatives. Running elections and hiring employees were tasks which came up either annually or once every three years. The election of a village secretary, an assistant secretary, a doctor, or a midwife was a much rarer, but much more momentous, task. The right to nominate for the office of secretary belonged to the county; for that of doctor, to the district judge; for the job of midwife, to the doctor.

Thus a considerable proportion of the village officials were elected by the people of the village. The elections were preceded by nominations in the body of representatives and vigorous campaigning, *kortesz* or *korteszolás*, in the village. According to statute, three persons were nominated for each office. It was customary in Átány to renominate the former mayor along with two new candidates for the mayor's office. For other positions the former official was nominated only if he had become popular during his term. The list of candidates was drawn up by the nominating committee of the body of representatives. They then sent the proposed list to the district judge, who approved it and sent it back to the village. In later years the choice of the villagers was restricted, for it became customary to nominate one favored candidate and two other people who stood no chance of getting more than a few votes.

But who were nominated? Among the numerous inhabitants of the village, who were the people who could rise to positions of leadership? The members of the body of representatives regarded it as their duty to give some consideration to their succes-

---

[38] This was a vestige of the traditional right of the villages to keep inns.

[39] The exact obligation varied with social stratum: the team owner (one or two horses) owed one day with his horses; the *zsellér* home-owner three days of manual labor; "the dweller" (a day laborer who did not own his own house) one day of the same. In 1891 the community works required a total of 12 days with one animal, 225 days with two, and 514 days of manual labor. The main task for which public labor was used was repair and maintenance of the roads and ditches of the village.

sion. János Boross summed it up by saying, "As soon as a child left school, the representatives of the village saw what sort he was." As we have mentioned above, the school examinations were held publicly in the church. "One knew about the behavior of a child's father and mother too." If an inappropriate person happened to be proposed, someone would say: "Don't bring him here; he will be of no use. His ancestor was a blusterer, and he is no different." When the representatives looked out the window of the town hall at the bachelors strolling about in bands on Sundays, they could single out those who were disciplined and suited for leadership. A young man who was considered fit to play a role in the life of the community had first to marry and to attain his manhood by reaching the age of thirty or thirty-five. Then the elders would say, "We have no one from this *zug* among us; let us have him. Perhaps he will be good." However, not all young men agreed to take a position, even if they were deemed worthy by the administration.[40] Many high-ranking families did not participate in the political life of the village at all; they did not vote, but simply "paid their taxes and did not come near the town hall afterward." This was believed to be partly an inherited feature, "in the blood" of some people. Others avoided public office because they believed that "it is impossible to really do justice to people" or because they did not want the responsibilities.[41] At the beginning of this century it was especially difficult to find a *zsellér* who would be willing to serve on the village council. One year a certain *zsellér* was visited by the personal representative of the mayor every day for two weeks before he was finally persuaded.

With other families, interest in public affairs and the ambition to take part in them were recurrent traits. Thus the Bedécs-s, descended from a noble family, regarded active participation in public life as a family characteristic. Károly Bedécs, sixty-six at the time of our field work, was married at the age of twenty-two. Even before that he used to attend the meetings of the Pasture Associations, the hiring of herdsmen, and the rendering of accounts by the pasture *gazda*-s; thus even during his bachelor-hood he was already interested in public affairs. As he says: "I was picked out early. I became a controller, the next year I advanced to the post of treasurer. Having served my term of office, I was a village board member for six years, and finally a representative." Until 1940, when he was called up for military service, he was without interruption "a man of the community." When he was first elected village council member, his predecessor, the aged Samu Madarász, grasped his hand happily; "he always knew that someone would rise to fill his place as I did, when I became his successor." These politically oriented people generally continued to play a role in the

---

[40] The offices of a village mayor, a judge, and representative were filled by *gazda*-s. Medium-holders presented themselves for positions on the village council and similar offices. Since the beginning of this century two *zsellér*-s have also been elected to these offices.

[41] A person elected mayor had to accept the post; he could resign only by paying a heavy fine or after serving at least one year in office. Sometimes a *gazda* was afraid to hold office, believing himself unsuitable for it. This was the case of S. B., who was elected village mayor in the 1890s. "He did not dare accept the office. He gave his *sógor* [the former mayor] a heifer-in-calf, saying, 'Take the mayor's office, *sógor;* I won't be a mayor.' " However, he was not allowed to resign, so he accepted the office with the intention of serving only for the required year, but he got accustomed to it and stayed in office for the whole three-year term.

government of the village throughout their active lives, generally until about the age of sixty; "as long as he is a man, he is in the town hall."

Months before the election date the candidates began to compete with one another and to campaign for votes. It was said that "the whole election was made by thirty or forty people," whose favor had to be gained if a candidate was to succeed. Treating the voters to brandy was an important part of the campaign. The candidates began treating the influential people to drinks weeks before the elections, and their assistants visited all the voters[42] with brandy or brandy coupons a few days before the voting. In the Átány value system the distribution of drink was not regarded as bribery, and a person who accepted it from a candidate was not necessarily obliged to vote for that candidate; one could accept brandy from several candidates for the same office. It was merely a sort of traditional nomination fee, which the voters had a right to expect from all candidates. However, if someone gave the voters anything else, he was considered guilty of corrupt campaign practices. For instance, if a candidate for mayor treated his adherents to food, he was referred to with scorn: "He bought his office with sausages." Worst of all, the candidate who was accused of giving away money was morally stigmatized.

A candidate for the office of mayor usually treated his voters to drinks twice. For each occasion 52 liters of brandy were distributed among the *tanyakert*-s by the candidate's assistants. An exact record was kept of how many people frequented each *kert* and also of which men did not visit any *kert*, and thus had to have their brandy brought to their homes. Three liters were usually offered to a group of ten or twelve people, two for a group of six or eight. György Szórád, who held the office of mayor off and on for twenty-seven years, was defeated by his *nász* on two occasions when the latter distributed more brandy and it was his turn to treat the voters last, immediately before the elections. After the event, at the *áldomás*, the conversation went like this: "Well, *nászuram*, the colt is gone, isn't it?" (i.e., the value of a colt was spent on brandy for the campaign). The defeated candidate answered: "Never mind, Pejkó [his brood mare, known all over the village] will have another. But *nász-uram* has spent a granary of wheat." His answer was: "Never mind, new wheat will grow."

The elections were usually held in November, after the harvests; people voted first for the members of the body of representatives, then for the mayor and the village council. A few days before the date the elections are announced in the village by means of the drum. They used to be held in the market place, in "the center of the market," where platforms were erected for the district judge and the village secretary. There were not usually many voters; the majority of the people who were qualified to vote would stay at home. The electioneerers invited those who turned up to have another glass of wine or brandy into the nearby tavern, repeating the names of their

---

[42] Legally, the right to vote belonged to all men over twenty years old and domiciled in the village who had paid direct taxes on their property or income for at least two years in Átány. Servants, soldiers, prisoners on trial, people serving terms of imprisonment, etc. were deprived of this right. At the end of the last century there were 612 voters in the village.

candidates to them. The candidates had to be present; their names were called out one at a time by the secretary, leaving time for the public to voice their opinion of each one. If the people were in favor of the person named, they would shout, "That is the right one"; "All right, hurrah!"; if not, they would cry, "Not the right one"; "Out with him"; "Throw him out"; or similar expressions of disfavor. If the voters were divided, the secretary asked for a show of hands and proclaimed the winner on the basis of majority. The elected officials were sworn in by the district judge, who was also present on the day of the voting. In 1929 the ballot was introduced, and since then the elections have been held indoors.

The new administration offers *áldomás* in one of the taverns after the elections. Each voter is treated to a glass of wine. Half of the expense is covered by the new mayor, a quarter by the village judge, and the other quarter by the remaining members. The elected council also celebrates a private *áldomás* in the assembly room of the town hall; each member contributes as much wine as he wants to for this occasion. An official elected for the first time usually brings 25 liters.

Those who were elected were held in high regard on account of their offices. The mayor was the most highly esteemed, and the honor was also extended to the members of his family. He occupied the first seat in the town hall and in church, and his wife also occupied a distinguished pew. Everyone lifted his hat to the mayor; "the children took off their hats from a distance too." The other officials "were not so elevated; other people esteemed them as their fellow-men." Only the terms by which they were addressed changed; even those who would otherwise have used the more familiar "my *báty*," "my *öcs*," now addressed them as "*uram*," adding this word to the name of their office—"sworn man" *uram*, council member *uram*, treasurer *uram*— or to their names—"Bedécs *uram*." A person who held an office for a long time retained the honorable form of address even after his term had expired. Thus János Boross was addressed as "guardian *uram*" or "uncle guardian" for several years after his resignation.

The symbols of the mayor's office were also honored. No one would touch the staff of the mayor, not even the bachelor whose back had suffered under its blows. It was forbidden to carry a stick into the church, but the mayor's staff had a special place in his pew, since he attended the service with the token of his office. In the eighteenth century insolence toward the mayor's staff was regarded as a serious offence against the community and against general public order. An ancient record relates the indignation of a peasant toward a sergeant who had hit him with a rod: "I belong under a different rod" (i.e., under the mayor's rod, the jurisdiction of the civil authority). Nor would anyone but the mayor occupy his seat; anyone who ventured to do it was fined two liters of wine. Decency demanded that people enter the town hall in their dress suits and behave properly. "We sat decently there, as in church," with heads uncovered[43]—this is how the old peasants remember it. No one

---

[43] In Átány etiquette does not demand that men take off their hats to enter a house; the *gazda* often wears a hat or a lambskin cap in his own house. Men are expected to take off their hats at meals, however, and also in church.

was allowed to smoke; the mayor himself went into the drummer's room if he wanted to light his pipe.

The twelve members of the village council were called "sworn men" or "council members," and the 24 members of the larger body "representatives." Upon inquiry about the behavior expected of them and the norms they followed, we discovered a special set of "public morals." It is said that "all of them were anxious about their honor, not their fortune; honor was the main point with them." "If anyone sought his own profit instead of the common weal, he lost his honor in the eyes of mankind," said József Kakas. János Boross revealed the secret of the popularity he enjoyed for the 27 years of his community service: "I was a friend of everyone. I gave way to everyone, I didn't encroach on the rights of anybody, and I offered my seat to an older person. I answered everybody who sought my advice. I explained what he ought to do, and I mentioned it to the secretary if it was necessary. This is how one rises. I tried through all my life to help my fellow man according to my power." Boross and other people often expressed the rule that an official ought to be "just," saying that they had adherents because they were just.

"Righteousness" and fairness toward other people were also the standards of the officials in religious affairs: "Let each one keep the faith in which he was born, whether Catholic or Calvinist. It is not worth anything unless it is genuine. We, being just men, were of the view that we have one God, and everyone has to follow his own creed," János Boross continued.

In addition to governing with justice and righteousness, the administration was expected to protect the interests of the citizens. The journals of the assemblies bear witness to the courageous resistance shown by the village council members toward their secretary (who frequently represented the wishes of the higher administrative organs) or the Átány landlords, in order to avert increased financial burdens on the villagers. The members of the village council, anxious about the unjustified increase of already heavy state burdens, were constantly on the alert and practised caution in dealing with the propositions of the higher administrative organs. This fear and mistrust induced the body of representatives to pass decisions which hindered the "progress" which they otherwise advocated zealously. In the early 1890s they opposed the connection of the village with the telephone system, and they refused to join a corporation which planned a railway branch line with a station at Átány, but they also refused the demand of the secretary for a higher salary with the justification, "We cannot increase the burden of the people." After World War I and in the 1930s the village was deeply in debt. The secretaries sought to remedy the situation with long-term loans, but they met with the resistance of the body of representatives, who were unwilling to entangle the parish in new debts which could be avoided. (After World War I this spirit of opposition in the village government and the readiness of the administration to challenge higher authorities gradually decreased, as has the jurisdiction of the local government.)

During the seasons when the most intensive agricultural labor was required and at times when there was no urgent community business to attend to, the mayor and the members of the village council did not meet on weekdays, but under no circumstances did they give up their Sunday meeting. The mayor sent out the town criers on Sunday mornings to invite the "sworn men" to church. The messenger arrived at the houses of the village council members early in the morning, saying, "My lord the mayor greets Károly Bedécs *uram* and asks him to appear in the town hall at half past nine, in order to go into church." Accordingly, the council members arrived in their dress suits at the council chamber, where they were received by the mayor and the village secretary. Here they briefly discussed the business and events of the past week and the agenda of the next. When the church bell was rung for the second time, they rose and marched to the nearby church in pairs, the mayor and the secretary leading the column, then the village judge and the treasurer, the public guardian and the first council member, and finally the remaining "sworn men." In the churchyard they fell into single file and marched to their places. After the service they waited for the other people to leave before making their own exit. If there was not much business to be done, they returned to the town hall and dealt with it before lunch; if they were not finished by lunchtime, they reassembled in the council chamber after the afternoon service.

The mayor also maintained friendly relations with the council members outside of matters of official business. If one of them celebrated a wedding at his house, all of his colleagues were invited. If a member of the village board built a house, the others did not wait to be asked, but sent their sons and servants with their teams to help; then in the afternoon they all visited the new house and exchanged a friendly word with the owner. More than anyone else, the mayor was expected to participate, and therefore he never failed to appear at the housebuilding of a council member. The members of the village board also helped each other with smaller jobs by contributing a team or manual labor. If a respectable person died in the village or on any of the neighboring estates, the mayor had the town crier invite the magistracy, and they attended the funeral as a body.

Besides attending each other's family ceremonies, the members of the village council and the body of representatives liked to get together informally for a friendly conversation and a few glasses of wine. After the meetings on Sunday afternoons, one or another of them would have wine brought from his house, or they would take a collection and send out to the tavern for it. Often the members of the church council would join them, and they would all sit around and talk together, the younger ones staying on to sing until late in the evening. They celebrated name-days, Christmas, and New Year's Eve by drinking together, but none of these occasions was as lavish as the election celebration.

In addition to their elected officials, both the village council and the body of representatives had paid employees, engaged for a year—such as the two town criers, the two night watchmen, and the coachman.

In selecting the two town criers (drummers) the administration looked for intelligent, well-behaved bachelors who wrote a good hand and knew the village well. "We looked around to find out what sort of man he was and what his abilities were; the administration of livestock ownership papers was also their task," states an old village board member. The job was sought by poor bachelors, as "the son of a *gazda* was bound to the handles of the plow." This office was an honor for its holder; "he was advanced" in public opinion.

The occupation of town crier was time-consuming. Generally one of them had to spend the night in the town hall, in the town criers' room, as guard and policeman of the building; this is why bachelors were preferred for this post. One of them was from the Lower End, the other from the Upper End, and their tasks were also divided on this basis. In 1943 a third one was engaged, primarily as "an outside town crier" for the job of delivery man in the *tanya*-s.

The town criers had to clean up the town hall and the surroundings and the market place, care for street lighting (only two kerosene lamps in 1910), deliver the official announcements, and summon the members of the village council and the body of representatives to meetings. They were also supposed to keep order in church (on holidays), on the streets, and in the tavern. They had to accompany the mayor to the tavern when he went to check up on a noise or a light burning after hours. He also had to go alone to restore order whenever he heard the noise of fighting.[44] On market days the town criers had to keep order and clean up afterward. Before World War I the town criers used to patrol their *fertály*-s on the evenings when courting was to take place. If they saw a bachelor and a girl together in a house after nine o'clock, they escorted him to the town hall and locked him up for the night.

Making public announcements with the drum was an even more important part of their job. There were two drummings a week in Átány: on Tuesdays and Fridays early in the morning, before people started out for the fields. Formerly there were 26 spots in the village where the town crier had to stop, beat his drum, and cry out whatever announcements the administration had given him; later, due to the expansion of the village, the number of stops was increased to 56 (see Fig. 34).

The village coachman was also hired by the community for a year. This post was sought by owners of a *fertály* who possessed a wagon and good horses. Their only duty was to be on call with their carriage to drive the mayor or a council member to Heves, to the *tanya*-s, or to the estates. Thus they were not occupied constantly, and they had time left over to work on their farms. The post of "village coachman" was instituted in Átány in 1891; formerly team owners were ordered to take turns doing this task as a sort of public service.

Other paid employees engaged for a year were the night watchmen, recruited from among the elderly poor people. They used to patrol the streets of the village from 8 P.M. till 6 A.M. From November to March, four additional "winter watchmen" were "pressed out of the community" to serve. This meant that each *fertály* had to send one man per night to help keep watch. The obligation rotated among all the men in the *fertály*. If anyone could not go, he sent his servant or hired a poor man as a substitute. In summer, the period of most intensive labor, the peasants were too

---

[44] The town crier János Barna was killed at such an effort to restore order.

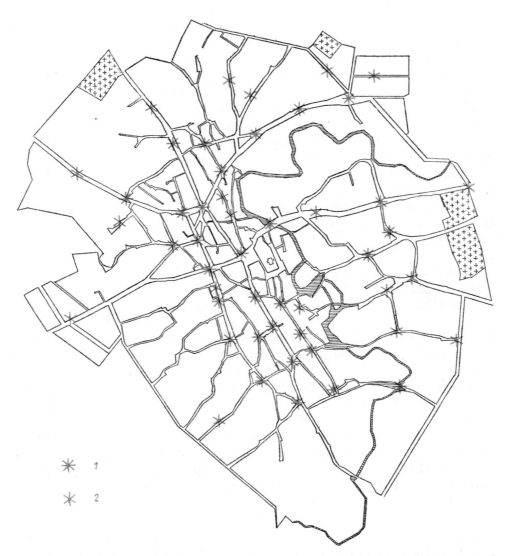

34. Public announcements. The places where the two town criers stopped, beat their drums, and announced the notices and orders. Key to symbols used: (1) Traditional places of drumming. (2) Additional places of drumming, which became necessary after World War I owing to the expansion of the village.

busy to perform this duty, so the community engaged two additional summer watchmen to help the regular guards. The hired and the "pressed" watchmen patrolled the village by *fertály*-s. No one was allowed to know their route (especially that of the regular watchmen) beforehand; "no one was supposed to know where they went, since they had to find out whose property was being stolen." The watchmen's second duty was to assist people in trouble. "If a light was burning somewhere at night, they would ask what was wrong. If they saw a light, they went in and inquired whether help was needed. They had to stay there until the light was put out."

Postal service for centuries has been a "reserved right" of the Hungarian state. The Átány post office was established in 1939. Before this date, the village was served by a "postal agency" led as a subsidiary occupation by one of the teachers. Mail for Átány arrived in Heves, the district capital, and was carried regularly every day between Heves, Átány, and Kömlő by a one-horse mail cart. The agency at Átány employed a postman, who sometimes was aided by the watchmen in delivering the mail. In 1893, the local board entered into negotiations about the installation of telephone service, and in 1901, the postal agency opened telephone and telegraphic service as well.

Written records from the last hundred years mention the existence of from two to five smiths in the village at a time. Two of them were "village smiths" working in smithies rented from the community, one of them in the Lower, the other in the Upper End.[45]

The midwife was also an employee of the community. After making a call for applicants, the district physician proposed a name, and the body of representatives appointed the midwife. She received a modest yearly salary in return for which she was bound to give free service to the poor; however, the majority of the inhabitants paid her for her services. Lodging for the midwife was also supplied by the community.

Before Átány had a doctor, death certificates were issued by special persons authorized to do so. These officials were informed of their duties by the district physician, the duties being simply the ascertainment of the demise. The entry in the death register was made solely on the basis of the "slip," the certificate written out by this official.

The villagers built a house for a community doctor on the site of the old secretary's house in 1935, but not until after World War II did a physician settle in Átány. Prior to the arrival of a physician in the village, the people of Átány were cared for by a doctor who lived in the town of Heves but serviced Átány and two smaller villages. He used to visit the village twice a week. Illnesses were reported to the town crier beforehand, and he took the doctor to the patients' houses.

In summary, the following officials were active in Átány during the 1930s: 3 educated persons from outside the village at the head of the administration (a secretary-in-chief, an assistant secretary, and another assistant secretary for fiscal matters), elected by the local body of representatives on the basis of nominations made by the county and the district judge, respectively; 2 qualified persons from outside the village (the physician and the midwife), elected as hygiene officers by the local body of

---

[45] In Átány the community provided the smith with a workshop, expecting him to perform high quality work for the villagers in return. Each customer entered a yearly agreement with the smith (see Chapter 12, "Non-peasants in the Village") or paid by the job. In other villages another way of engaging the "community smith" existed: the artisan was obliged to perform certain jobs for all inhabitants of the village (or a part of it), for which he received a fixed yearly wage, which was assessed from the *gazda*-s in proportion to the area of their holdings or the number of their teams, or both. Thus the employment of the smith resembled that of the village herdsmen at Átány.

representatives on the basis of nominations made by the district judge and the district physician, respectively; 6 educated persons from outside the village who performed various duties in the church and the school (the minister, the choir leader, the school-masters, and the assistant minister), elected by the congregation on the basis of nominations made by the local church council; 36 peasants from the village (who had completed from four to six grades in the elementary school), elected by the people of the village to deal with secular administration; 24 peasants from the village, elected by the people of the village to deal with ecclesiastical administration; 6 persons of partly alien (the minister and the teacher), partly local origin, elected by the church council for the management of education; 18 peasants from the village, elected by those inhabitants who possessed grazing rights, for the management of the common pasture; 1 local peasant, the vineyard elder, elected by the vine-owning *gazda*-s for the surveillance of the vineyards.

In addition, there were: 6 community employees, engaged for an annual salary; 1 church employee, engaged for an annual salary; 9 herdsmen and 2 field guards (assisted by 11 boys), engaged by the *gazda*-s who possessed pasture rights, for the task of watching the livestock and the arable land, respectively; 3 vineyard guards, engaged for an annual salary by the *gazda*-s who owned vineyards; 2 craftsmen from outside the village (smiths), engaged by the local government to be "village smiths."

Thus the offices of the community and the church were held by 13 educated people from outside the village, 81 uneducated elected locals, and 22 uneducated hired locals. The 6 members of the school board have been left out of the enumeration, since they were appointed by the church council from its own membership.

Thus there were about 110 offices or jobs available in the civil and ecclesiastical administration of a village of 2,600 inhabitants. However, this does not necessarily imply that there were actually 110 different officials in Átány at the same time. Running through the lists of the local officials who have served in the past decades, one finds the same names recurring in the various bodies. As we have mentioned already, only the village mayor and the churchwarden were prohibited from holding two offices at once; the other officials of the government and the church council were allowed to serve on several bodies simultaneously. In fact, this was the case. The village council members and the members of the body of representatives were also elected to the church council and the pasture associations. Thus in 1934 Károly Bedécs was a "sworn man" in the local government, a member of the church council, and the secretary of the Great Pasture Association. János Boross was public guardian on the village board, member of the church council, and president of the Great Pasture Association at the same time. Gábor Varga, the community treasurer, was a member of the church council and treasurer of the Great Pasture Association.

The *gazda*-s acquired grazing rights in the pasture of the *zsellér*-s, so they were eligible for the leadership of that association too. And in fact they were elected, so the *zsellér*-s were usually under the direction of the *gazda*-s even in this body. In practice, the approximately eighty offices which could be obtained by the local *gazda*-s were held by not more than thirty or forty persons in any given period.

23

The lowest ranking official positions were those of the Pasture Associations, of which the lowest was the post of controller. Young people twenty-two to twenty-four years old could be elected to this position if they were interested and intelligent. The next step in the career of a rising official might be the post of treasurer or secretary of a Pasture Association, followed by positions in community and ecclesiastical administration. The presidents of the associations were usually elderly persons who had gained experience in the village government or the church council and had become honored and respected men.

The leadership of other community organizations consisted of: 14 (later, 19) peasants from the village, as officials in the *Hangya* Consumers' Cooperative; 5 peasants from the village, as the leaders of the Cooperative Dairy; 1 educated person from outside the village and 5 villagers, as the leaders of the Volunteer Firemen's Association; 2 educated leaders from outside the village and a varying number of local committee members, as directors of the Reading Circle, and later the *Gazda* Circle; the Civic Readers' Club, after it had separated from the other, was directed by 3 peasants from the village.

Although the names of the leaders of these community organizations also appear on other lists, the frequency of simultaneous office-holding is much reduced. The leaders of the Firemen's Association and the *Gazda* Circle often served on the village council or the body of representatives too, but in the *Hangya* Consumers' Cooperative new names occur, though the long-time president, János Ötvös, was a member of the body of representatives and of the church council at the same time, and the administrative director, Imre Fuder, was also the bell ringer. Most of the names that occur only once were leaders of the relatively new Civic Readers' Club, but even this association endeavored to get its leaders on the boards of church and village administration.

The higher administrative authorities of Átány were the district (the *szolgabíró*, the district judge) and the county.[46] The increasingly specialized branches of the national administration also reached the village through county and district offices. Eventually only a rather narrow range of affairs could be settled directly by the local authorities. As the people of Átány would say, "We dealt with the minor matters in our village, we brought the larger ones to Heves, and the more important ones to

---

[46] The counties are the regional organs of Hungarian public administration, established at the time of the founding of the state. The boundaries of Heves county have been fixed since the Middle Ages. Prior to 1848 the county was an organization of nobles living in its territory; it had jurisdiction over the serfs and it served as the organ through which the legal privileges of the nobles were defended against the king and the government. After the organization of legislation and village administration on a representative basis, the county lost its nobiliary character; it became the organ of territorial self-government, but only within certain limits, since it also served as an intermediate unit of national administration. Its advisory and deliberative body was made up of elected representatives of the villages (thus of Átány too), besides the members who belonged by right of their office or wealth.

The county was divided into districts, each headed by a *szolgabíró*, "district judge." Being a secondary administrative authority, the district had no self-government. The *szolgabíró* exercised supervision and control over the villages, and most of the orders from the government and the county reached them through him. He directed the renewal of the village government, through the election of the local officials. In some matters he even made decisions at the village level (some questions of public order, permissions to assemble, hygiene, animal health protection, etc.) (Magyary, 1942: 266–296). This administrative system was reorganized in 1949–1950, when the direction of villages, districts, and counties was entrusted to the councils and their executive committees.

Eger, but there were problems that could be settled only in Budapest." On the whole this simplified statement is right. The treatment of a sick man is almost symbolical. His mild diseases would be cured in the village by the district physician or later by the village doctor; if he needed a specialist, he saw one of the physicians in Heves, where the nearest pharmacy was also located. Serious cases were treated in the Eger hospital; quite special ones in Budapest.

The local government decided quarrels which were called "below the limit" or "bagatelle" disputes in official language. A lawsuit above a certain value had to be brought before the district court at Heves. The superior court was located in Eger, and the highest ones—the Supreme Court and the Court of Appeals—in Budapest. Litigants from Átány knew that they should grant powers of attorney to a Heves lawyer in lawsuits of minor importance and to an Eger advocate in more momentous ones. In quarrels over old boundaries and balks, they could find the title deeds from the 1890s in the Átány town hall. On the basis of these they were able to demand a remeasuring of the debated plot. Land registers were kept at Heves, however, and if anyone looked for the ancient distribution or qualitative classification of the fields, he had to visit the Eger County Archives.

The task of keeping order in the village fell to the town criers and night watchmen. The nearest police station was at Heves. In cases of unsolved thefts or major damages, the police had to be called in to investigate.[47]

The roads, bridges, and wells of the village were kept in good repair by the community; this was the object of the public labor force. The ballasting and repair of the so-called "vicinal" roads were the tasks of Átány and the neighboring villages together. Only the causeway, which crossed the fields but not the village, enjoyed the rank of a "county road"; accordingly its repair fell to the county. Wells that were dug by hand were ordered by the Átány magistracy, but the drilling of an artesian well was carried out with the financial help of the county.

[47] Around the turn of the century several horses were stolen in the village. The administration asked for a local policeman. The district constable agreed on the condition that the village provide a suitable lodging to go along with the position. Frightened by the unusual expenditure, the administration dropped the idea of a policeman in the village.

CHAPTER 18. ÁTÁNY IN THE COUNTRY

ÁTÁNY AMONG THE NEIGHBORING VILLAGES

Nine communities (Heves, Vezekény, Tarnaszentmiklós, Kisköre, Kömlő, Mezőtárkány, Besenyőtelek, Tenk, Erdőtelek) are the neighbors of Átány. There are a number of differences between these villages, to the extent that they might almost serve as illustrations of the various possibilities of historical development. Besenyőtelek was inhabited by petty nobles who owned their own soil and had no landlord. Tenk (formerly administered as a part of Erdőtelek) was, like Szárazbő, a manorial settlement, inhabited by the hired men and domestic servants of the estates. Tarnaszentmiklós and Kisköre are the results of a planned resettlement in the middle of the eighteenth century; this action was preceded by removal of the original Calvinist population from the latter village. The character of a planned settlement is most conspicuous in the case of Kömlő. This *puszta* (uninhabited site of a former village) was repopulated by the Archbishopric of Eger in 1770. Its streets were measured out by engineers at right angles, like a chess board, in striking contrast to the irregularity of other villages. Heves, being the seat of the district and a center of administration, commerce, and local industry, far surpassed the other villages in population and development.

Few relationships are established with the inhabitants of the neighboring villages merely on the basis of a shared common boundary. Only the Átány people who owned vineyards within the Heves borders felt that they had neighbors there. With these they could establish continuous and intimate connections, just as with their Átány field neighbors.[48]

Otherwise the boundaries effected a strict separation of the villages. There was even a prohibition against going across the borders to pick up fallen kernels of grain or gather camomile (acts which could be freely performed in the fields within the village *határ* without the owners' permission); the field guards would chase away women who tried to do so. Near the border the sense of certainty experienced on the land of one's own village was diminished. During the last century, whenever herds spent the night

[48] In the winter of 1944–1945, when the front line came near Átány, the Soviet military command ordered the evacuation of Heves. Some of the inhabitants came to Átány and were given lodging there. The family of József Kakas invited the family of their vineyard neighbor to their home on their own initiative.

342

near a boundary, the herdsmen would lie awake near the animals in order to keep the inhabitants of the neighboring village from stealing one or two.[49]

Owing to its Calvinism, Átány was somewhat set apart from its neighbors. The people of the Catholic parishes of the vicinity would call the Átány people "ravens" or "crows" because of their dark attire, since women over thirty and men over forty hardly ever dressed in any other color than black. The people of Átány admit that "there were more feasts," "there were more customs" in the Catholic villages—for instance, all of them celebrated the day of the patron saint of the village—but they add, "No village knew the art of merrymaking better than Átány." "In other places as many as seven dishes were served at weddings, but people could eat their fill better at Átány, where only three were given."

These religious differences influenced the marriage connections of the Átány people, which extended to more distant Calvinist parishes, bypassing the Catholic villages of the immediate vicinity. These connections are illustrated by Table 12 and Figure 35.[50]

The decrease in exogamous relations since the end of the eighteenth century is conspicuous. Through the middle of the eighteenth century, while the large migration of the peasants of the Great Plain was still going on (see Chapter 1, "The Past") and the Calvinists had not yet been displaced from several of the neighboring villages, about a third of the marriages entered in the registers of the Átány Reformed Church were contracted between an Átány resident and an outsider. The village had lively exogamous connections with the mountainous regions of the north, probably owing to the fact that many Átány residents had originally come from there. Toward the

---

[49] The moral standards regarding theft were looser when it was a question of animals and crops belonging to the inhabitants of other villages. In the course of their travels in distant regions, the Átány horse dealers would pilfer a few sheaves of grain or a small bundle of hay or fodder to feed their horses, or they would let their cattle graze in a forbidden place at night. At home, too, the people of Átány could reckon with similar damages caused by passing strangers. On the other hand, it also happened that when flocks of sheep from another village were driven through Átány, mainly by night, the bachelors would pull a sheep into a *kert* in places where the road narrowed between *kert*-s and hedges and the flock became scattered.

[50] Our data are based on the registers of the Reformed church of Átány. One may ask how inclusively the registers record the marriage relations between Átány and the other villages. If a girl married into another parish, the marriage was usually celebrated in her native village. The wedding was also held in her native village if a *vő* married into the house. Consequently, the data of the registers contain the marriages of Átány girls to men from other villages in all probability, regardless of whether the young couple settled in Átány or somewhere else. It is less certain that the marriages of Átány men who brought their brides from other villages or settled there themselves—marriages contracted in other parishes in most cases—were entered on the Átány registers. Presumably the keeping of registers was not necessary, although it was customary to record weddings held in other parishes if the couple then was domiciled in Átány. A similar custom prevailed in the registers of other Calvinist parishes (Pataki, 1937: 14–15).

The marriage registers of Átány date back to 1727, but they are very defective in mentioning the domiciles of people from other villages before 1750.

The proportion of the marriages between Átány people and people from other villages is very low when compared with the data available on other regions or parishes of the country. Let us take as an example the marriages of four villages, similar in size to Átány, situated on the Danube in the Sárköz, the southern part of the country. At the turn of the eighteenth and nineteenth centuries, about 60 to 70 per cent of these were contracted with people from other villages; the proportion of all exogamous marriages between 1770 and 1935 is 45 per cent in these southern villages (Pataki, 1937).

We owe the data on the marriages contracted with inhabitants of other villages to the kindness of the assistant minister Márta Szabó, who gathered it from the registers.

Table 12
Marriages Contracted with Parties from Other Villages Registered
at Átány Reformed Church, by Decade, from 1751 to 1940

Decade	Total of marriages	Contracted with an alien man	Contracted with an alien woman	All marriages contracted with alien parties	
				number	percentage
1751–1760	133	20	24	44	33.0
1761–1770	150	20	34	54	36.0
1771–1780	90	12	18	30	33.3
1781–1790	179	26	33	59	32.9
1791–1800	192	24	28	52	27.0
1801–1810	220	28	19	47	21.6
1811–1820	205	11	24	35	17.1
1821–1830	200	11	21	32	16.0
1831–1840	270	16	20	36	13.3
1841–1850	261	22	22	44	16.8
1851–1860	198	12	13	25	12.6
1861–1870	296	17	17	34	11.5
1871–1880	280	6	6	12	4.2
1881–1890	243	14	16	30	12.3
1891–1900	252	27	9	36	14.2
1901–1910	250	25	9	34	13.6
1911–1920	221	11	10	21	9.5
1921–1930	263	26	6	32	12.1
1931–1940	205	15	21	36	17.5

end of the nineteenth century these relations were severed; the area within which marriages were contracted with inhabitants of other villages became more restricted, and the numbers show a proportional decrease.[51] Around the middle of the nineteenth

[51] On the map we have marked the villages with which at least ten marriages were contracted over the whole period, as recorded in the Átány registers from 1727 to 1940. However, these marriage relations were not simultaneous. As further information, we add the following table on the chronological division of these marriage relations.

Number of Marriage Relations with Átány

Name of Village	1731–1800	1801–1850	1851–1900	1901–1940
Tiszanána	72	46	23	21
Poroszló	32	25	30	3
Maklár	22	28	6	2
Jászkisér	22	19	9	5
Szárazbő	5	10	10	11
Heves	2	8	7	15
Egerlövő	15	10	2	4
Tenk	8	3	3	5
Tiszabura	7	7	5	—
Noszvaj	15	—	—	—
Gyöngyös	11	—	1	—
Andornak	8	3	—	—
Bükkzsérc	9	1	—	—
Sum total	228	160	96	66
Other localities	23	34	41	57

The decrease is a remarkable feature, even in the case of the stable tradition of intermarriage with Tiszanána. In the case of Szárazbő and Heves, there were growing Calvinist minorities which belonged to the Átány ecclesiastical organization. The growing proportion of marriages from "other localities" is conspicuous too. Besides the waning of the connections with the traditional partners and the general dwindling of the number of exogamous marriages, this ever-growing "dispersion," the appearance of new villages and towns in the second half of the nineteenth and mainly in the twentieth centuries, may be the result of the increasing mobility of the Átány folk, manifested in out-of-town jobs, military service, and the like.

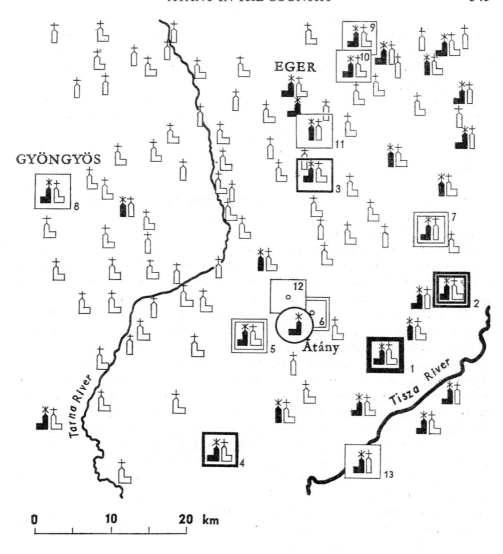

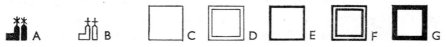

35. Marriage relations of Átány with other villages between 1731 and 1940. We have marked the parishes according to whether they had a Catholic or a Calvinist church, or both, in 1910. (At this time there were also Evangelical and Jewish churches in the area depicted, but almost exclusively in the larger towns.) The boxes around the symbols represent the frequency of marriage relations with Átány. Key to symbols used: (A) Calvinist mother-church or affiliated church. (B) Catholic parsonage (or affiliated church). (C) 10 to 20 marriage connections with Átány. (D) 30 to 40 marriage connections. (E) 50 to 60 marriage connections (F) 90 marriage connections. (G) 162 marriage connections. The serial numbers identify the parishes as follows: (1) Tiszanána; (2) Poroszló; (3) Maklár; (4) Jászkisér; (5) Heves; (6) Szárazbő; (7) Egerlövő; (8) Gyöngyös; (9) Bükkzsérc; (10) Noszvaj; (11) Andornak; (12) Tenk; (13) Tiszabura.

century the proportion of exogamous marriages was 10 to 12 per cent, and in one decade it fell below 5 per cent. We witness the development of a certain "reserve" in marriage customs; it may well be that Átány also became "reserved" towards its neighborhood in other respects at this time.

In the eyes of the present-day Átány people, a marriage contracted with the inhabitant of another village is of less value than an endogamous marriage; one has to be sorry or ashamed about it. Átány girls who have married out of the village are mentioned with compassion. "The strange village is never like one's own. She is homesick all the time. She cries a lot; her life is different from that at home. She would like to be here with her sisters and brothers and relatives." The story of the innkeeper Bedécs is also recalled. He gave his daughter into marriage to Tiszanána in the years preceding World War I, but he was so sorry for it that when the wedding party from Nána started off with the bride, "his heart was broken" by sorrow and he died.

A marriage with an outsider cannot link two kinspeople in the way a village marriage does, owing to the distance. One of the two semicircles which represent the relatives of the husband and those of the wife is missing in the case of a family founded by an exogamous marriage. This is a serious drawback in a village which regards numerous relatives as an advantage and a source of pride. When a girl wanted to marry a bachelor from a distant region (beyond 15 or 20 km.), her mother would tell her, "You may go, my daughter, but you must know that I won't be able to fulfill my duty as a mother." This meant that she could not assist her daughter in the case of childbirth or take care of the young mother and the baby. Among the villages entering into exogamous relations with Átány, only Tiszanána was situated near enough to allow regular relationships with both kin groups. With the people of Nána, even the traditional visits of both wedding parties could be celebrated during the wedding ceremonies. The Tiszanána kinsfolk would come to ask for the bride in several carts, and the Átány people would drive to Nána to dance with the bride at midnight, though they had to drive fourteen kilometers and back.[52] Relatives living in both villages would visit each other for weddings, funerals, and sometimes christenings and illnesses; they would drop in on the other family if they passed their house on the way to the fair. If no special occasion arose, they would pay a call on each other at least once a year anyway.

Átány wedding parties setting out for another village regarded the journey as a sort of research expedition by which they could observe the unfamiliar customs of the outsiders. Such trips are often mentioned when a conversation turns to the differences between the neighboring villages and Átány. People in other villages serve different dishes—for example, beef with horseradish, which is unusual in Átány; they sing different songs; they have the bride jump over a fire at dawn, and so forth. The Átány party also took great care to arrange an impressive entrance to the other village. The bachelors would march in followed by a retinue of gypsy musicians, all singing

---

[52] In recent years, now that the wedding party goes to the other village in cars and trucks, the possibilities have been extended. During a wedding in 1963 the people from Átány covered a distance of nearly 50 km. in order to dance with the bride.

appropriate songs, such as one about a rose grown in this alien place being plucked by an Átány bachelor and stuck in his hat.

In addition to the ties created by intermarriage, common military service created friendships between the men of Átány and those of other villages. This is like a special kind of *koma*-ship. Before and during World War I recruits from Átány joined the 60th Eger regiment, which included soldiers from the southern part of Heves and Borsod counties. These lasting personal connections were often established by the comradeships formed during active duty in World War I, less frequently in World War II, when the Átány soldiers were more scattered. "When people spend eight or ten months beside each other in the front line, it is a real friendship." These ties were not affected by religious differences; Átány veterans would often visit their comrades from Catholic villages on saint's days, for instance. Differences in wealth counted for more, however. *Gazda*-s and *zsellér*-s chose their friends from among those of similar standing. The war comrade was invited to weddings and came to pay his last respects and attend the funeral when a member of the family died. His house was also a stop on the way to the fair.

There are several signs by which the villagers are able to distinguish an Átány person from an outsider—for example, the shape of the face (according to local opinion, the real Átány man or woman has a round, ruddy face), the gait (a person from Átány moves more briskly and is lighter on his feet; the young woman "makes twenty steps in the dance in the time it takes the Kömlő girl to make one"), etc. (see Chapter 15). In almost all villages the women wear their kerchiefs tied under their chin, but the way the cloth is folded may mark a local difference. Likewise, while the men all wear similar fur caps, clues to residence may be gained by observing whether the cap is convex on the top and concave on the sides or vice versa.

Some villages are richer than others. Átány is regarded by its neighbors as a wealthy one. The Heves craftsmen often remark on what demanding customers the Átány *gazda*-s are, and the saddler used to manufacture the finest ornamental harnesses for them. The shopkeepers complain about the fastidiousness of the Átány women in selecting fabrics. The wealth of Átány was not due to an outstanding number of rich *gazda*-s. There were more wealthy *gazda*-s in the villages along the Tisza and, for instance, in Besenyőtelek. "But there the rich man was awfully rich, the poor one awfully poor." Átány was "wealthier" in that the average standard of living was higher; there was a relatively higher number of more or less self-sufficient farms and a relatively lower number of indigents than in most other villages of the region. An elderly *zsellér* related the following: "Once I worked as a reaper in the Heves fields with people from Heves. Three out of the thirty had bacon; the others brought onions and all sorts of vegetables with their bread. In another year I was reaping with Átány men at Szárazbő; there only two out of the thirty were without bacon." (It is a sign of extreme poverty if one has no bacon for the time of the year's most exhausting work, the harvest.)

The people of Átány are proud of the long history of their village and they rather despise the "riff-raff," "motley," or "gypsy" population of the other villages, settled more recently by people from many different regions. They acknowledge that they are more old-fashioned and conservative than some of their neighbors. The irregular layout of the village is "old-fashioned" too, and many of them would like to exchange it for regular, straight streets; they regard the custom of having the stables on the outskirts of the village as a legacy from their "Hungarian ancestors." In house design and dress they recognize that the people of both Kömlő and Tiszanána are more fashionable than they are, but they point out that the women have no fine reserves of linen like the Átány women's. The people of Átány also regard themselves as better at doing strenuous work. They say of some Budapest employers, "As long as they could get an Átány man, they would not hire any other." The other thing they are most proud of is the Átány friendliness and hospitality. "If a craftsman came to Átány, he grew old here, whether he was a shoemaker or a wheelwright" (meaning that he was at ease in the village and did not want to leave). The inhabitants of Kömlő are regarded as especially "wild ones," lacking friendliness. "Even among the soldiers of that village one could hardly find a friend; of all the villages, Tiszanána is the most similar to us."

ECONOMIC RELATIONS BETWEEN ÁTÁNY AND OTHER AREAS

Although in the eyes of the peasants the main object of farming is to provide for the family, the household, and the livestock, people cannot remember a time when none of the produce left the village. During the period of serfdom a part of the crop had to be paid to the landlord,[53] and the state also demanded taxes. Some produce was also exchanged for goods which the village lacked. This exchange of products, goods, and services established lasting links between Átány and its close and more distant neighbors.

The primary mechanism for buying and selling goods is the market. In Átány the market place is at the center of the village. Here people can sell their goods (in an order regulated by the local board, by paying a fee) on the market day, Thursday. Marketing is almost exclusively the business of women, and the products exchanged are those of female husbandry—eggs, poultry, milk, butter, curd, vegetables, fruit, seeds, and the like; grain is traded rarely and in small amounts. The local market serves primarily the needs of the village. However, it is also visited by merchants who buy poultry, eggs, and dairy products to sell in the towns, and by craftsmen or farmers who come from other regions to market their goods.

The Átány market is quite small, since the larger town of Heves is nearby, and even the villagers themselves prefer the lively Heves market. The Átány trade is important for Heves as well, since it far exceeds that of the other villages. The people of Heves

---

[53] In 1770 (before the standardizing national settlement) the Átány serfs of Sámuel Haller gave one-seventh of their spring and autumn crops, besides which each *gazda* "of six oxen" (using 24 *hold*-s of arable land) owed the lord one and a half *forint*-s as hearth tax, four chickens, fifty eggs, one woven sack, and about 1²/₃ pounds of butter; the 84 serfs and *zsellér*-s of Sámuel Haller were as a group bound to give him 24 geese and twelve ducks (Soós, n.d.).

say, "Were it not for Átány, there would be no market in Heves." The goods brought to Heves are poultry, eggs, dairy products, and vegetables, but the men also send wheat, barley, and sometimes maize. The grain is bought by Heves craftsmen and landless day laborers as well as by grain merchants.

The importance of the Heves market has grown considerably since the turn of the century, especially since World War I. Formerly the people of Átány preferred to frequent Eger instead of Heves. If the household needed something but there was no money, the woman would bake a few loaves of bread and take them to the Eger market. A *gazdasszony* whose husband failed to fully provide for her by giving her money "from the hand" would help herself in the same way. The Átány women sold butter in earthen vessels. If a carter was momentarily unemployed, he might purchase a load of straw in Átány and market it in Eger. The difference in price between Átány and Eger made it worth his while.

Women would take sunflower oil and dried apples, plums, and spices (saffron and red pepper) to the neighboring Catholic villages. Catholics "jumped for Lenten fare," trading it for a low grade of hemp which the Átány women spun and wove into canvas or sackcloth and then sold at the Eger market.

Such immediate relations of exchange and purchase extended to other products and villages as well. Átány's supply of hay and fodder, for instance, was intermediate between that of the villages along the Tisza, where a great deal of hay was grown, and that of the western villages, which were poorly supplied. In winter the *gazda*-s of the western villages would come to Átány looking for hay and alfalfa for sale. In lean years the Átány *gazda*-s drove to the Tisza region to buy feed. People of the Jászság, where geese were fattened for the market on a large scale, came to purchase maize for this purpose. The artisans and professionals of Heves and Eger looked for pigs. When the tobacco growers made their delivery to the state monopoly and received their money, they came to the village from Tenk, Szárazbő, and the manors along the Tisza inquiring for wheat for sale.

A more extensive network of face-to-face exchange relationships was represented by the routes of merchants who came by cart or foot from regions which produced specialized wares and from industrial centers. These routes, radiating from one or another of these centers, frequently spread across an area of several counties. The merchants brought fruit from the villages in the vicinity of Gyöngyös and Eger, cabbage from the Tápió (50 km. west of Átány), and dried fruit from the mountain district north of Átány (today a part of Czechoslovakia). The villages of artisans in the northern mountain and woodland region sent wooden tools, pitchforks, rakes, brushes, various tool handles, thorn bush harrows, implements of spinning and weaving, grain bins, and collapsible wooden pigsties, as well as quicklime for whitening. Potters came by cart from three directions, bringing fire-proof cooking vessels from Gömör, and bowls, plates, and lead-glazed ware for wine, milk and water from Mezőtúr and Gyöngyös. (The potters of the two latter towns used different colors and decorations on their products; the choice between them was a matter of taste.)

The carts arrived in the village according to a fixed schedule. Pitchforks, rakes, and shafts of the scythes were brought in spring, in time for the work with hay; brakes and spindles were brought in autumn, in time for the hemp. The goods were paid for in kind—for example, the earthen vessels were exchanged for the amount of wheat they could hold. All of these artisans and ambulant merchants traded their wares for wheat, since they came mainly from districts where an unbalanced economy resulted in a scarcity of that commodity, such as the hill country or the vineyard region.

Some factory products were brought by middlemen to the village from various industrial centers in a similar way. Faience plates, mugs, and brandy pitchers came by wagon from Hollóháza and Bélapátfalva. Cambric was brought from the Szepes region (today located partly in Czechoslovakia and partly in Poland). The "scythe Slovak" came with a collection of scythe blades tied on his back. At the beginning of the last century scythe blades came from the forges of North Hungary, later on from Silesian, Austrian, or Hungarian factories. The "glazier Slovak" set glass in window frames and sold glass night lights. Every year at about the time the maize was harvested a peddler appeared selling needles, yarn, and buttons; as he passed by the fields along the cart road, he exchanged his wares for maize. In addition to the peddlers, there were itinerant craftsmen such as the scissors grinder, the tinker (who fixed broken pottery with wire), and the tinman, and also entertainers, such as the bear trainers. The visits of peddlers became less frequent at the end of the last century and increasingly so after World War I. Even in the 1950s and 1960s, however, we could still see carts in the village bringing fruit or quicklime to exchange for wheat.

The widest range of opportunities for buying and selling was at the fairs (see Fig. 36). On the calendars which gave the dates of the various fairs, one would find the following note: "In such and such a locality: national livestock and unpacking fair." The description "national" meant that animals and goods could be brought to the fair from anywhere. (There was an old term for the fair which also meant "liberty.") The "monthly" fairs held in the larger parishes had a smaller volume of trade and were less important than the national ones. The name "livestock and unpacking fair" referred to the two main features of these occasions. A part of the market place was fenced off by wooden bars for the various kinds of animals; horses, oxen, cattle, swine, and sheep in separate pens were bought and sold there. In the "unpacking fair" the booths and tables of the artisans and merchants were set up in rows according to craft—one row was occupied by the tailors; another by the furriers, bootmakers, and haberdashers; a third by the saddlers, cord makers, and coopers, and so on. Toolmakers also "unpacked" their products at the fair; they made pyramids of tool handles, rakes, and pitchforks and piles of brooms. Short-order shops offered cooked meals; fly-by-night bars served drinks; and showmen and fortune tellers entertained the public.

The right to hold fairs was granted by the state, formerly by the king. At one time it belonged to the privileges granted to the cities. Over the last hundred years, however, the network of fairs has extended rapidly, and an increasing number of villages

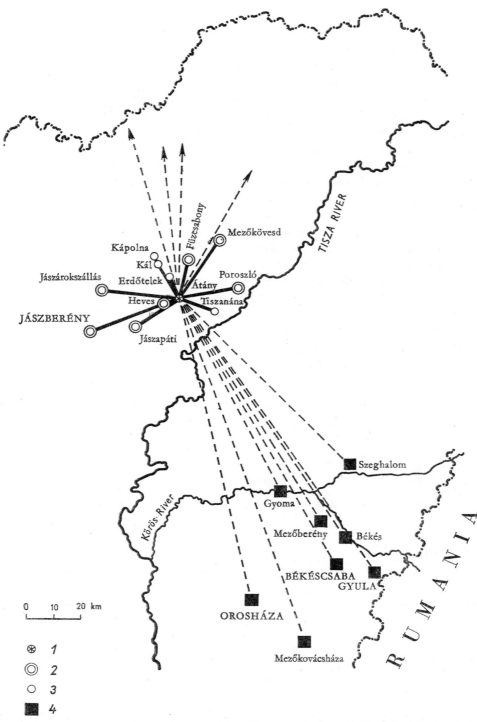

36. Fairs most frequented by the Átány peasants. Key to symbols used: (1) Átány. (2) Much frequented "big" fairs. (3) Less frequented fairs of minor importance. (4) The distant fairs from which the Átány dealers used to bring horses. The arrows indicate the regions in the northeast where they sold the horses.

have acquired the right to hold them.[54] Thus in the neighborhood of Átány, not only Heves, but also Erdőtelek, Kömlő (though only for a few decades), and Tiszanána possessed this right. The scope, the popularity, and the attendance at the various fairs differed markedly. "Good fairs" were those which attracted a large crowd of people, many vendors and many buyers. The fairs held at Jászberény, Jászapáti, Füzesabony, and Mezőkövesd were generally considered "good fairs." People from Átány often visited them, though these towns were so far away that the people had to start out on the eve of the fair and drive all night or spend the night away from home. Formerly they were more mobile; in the middle of the last century they went to the Pest and Debrecen fairs, and often to those of Gyöngyös and Hatvan.

Owing to the characteristic features of the various regions, different sorts of things were traded at the different fairs. Thus fine colts could best be sold in the Jászság, a region of intensive agriculture where good horses were needed. A beautiful animal could be sold for a good price here; those of a lower quality, however, could be sold more advantageously in the villages along the Tisza, where fewer demands were made of the horses. The goods traded also varied seasonally. For instance, the "green fair" at Füzesabony, held before the harvest (when the crops were still green), offered the largest choice of implements and handles. When artisans no longer visited their village with laden carts, the Átány people traded with them at this fair.

All farms which raised livestock regularly sold or exchanged the offspring.[55] Poor *gazda*-s would sell their draft animals in the autumn (if possible at plowing time, when prices were highest) and purchase new ones in spring. Even if the farmer was not dealing in livestock, he would customarily visit at least four fairs each year.[56]

[54] In 1741 Átány itself (its landlords) made an unsuccessful attempt to acquire the right to hold fairs.

[55] Chapter 12, "Varieties and Levels of Subsistence," points out that only a few wealthy peasant farms used draft animals of their own breeding and could keep a horse or an ox from birth to death. The value and working power of the animals varied with age, and the different grades of peasant farm required the use of livestock of different ages and values. The poorer team owners used to work with relatively cheap, untrained young animals and then sell them after one or two years. This was a profitable but also necessary transaction; as the working power of the full-grown animals was more than they needed and its care proved to be too expensive. On the other hand, the large estates and the carters needed strong animals. Some of the *gazda*-s who bred horses had to sell the foals quite young, as they lacked sufficient fodder to raise them, but others were able to market them fully grown. In most instances the peasant farms exchanged their draft animals and sold and bought pigs and cows without the intervention of middlemen or dealers. Consequently a small holder with a horse that was too valuable for his needs had to look every year for a more wealthy *gazda* who would purchase it. Likewise he had to find another horse-breeding *gazda* who would sell him a new colt. These transactions took place at the fairs. Vendors and buyers often had to visit several fairs before they could make a bargain suitable for their special demands.

Without the fairs the traditional structure of peasant farming can be preserved only with difficulty, for many obstacles arise. This is shown in the case of some villages which avoided collectivization in 1958–1959, such as Szarvaskő, situated north of Átány in the mountain region. This community has little arable land and is unsuited for mechanized, large-scale farming. There the peasants try to continue to farm in the old way, but their efforts are in vain because no draft animals have been bought and sold at the fairs since the establishment of the nation-wide cooperative farms. The people have to keep using the oxen which they ought to have exchanged for younger animals long ago, to name just one of their many problems.

[56] The bartering is performed with certain rituals. When the buyer and the seller make their offers, they strike each other's hands with a broad gesture. When they reach an agreement after a series of hand strikings, they shake hands. The agreement becomes binding with this handshake and the advance payment. After the purchase of an animal the license has to be written out. When the full

These fairs were the main occasions for the purchase of manufactured articles. Thus fine new "*jász* carts" could be bought at the fairs of the Jászság, where also the "marketing smiths" (see note 18, Part Four) sold their cultivators, root cutters, etc. In winter, after the tobacco was delivered to the station, the tobacco grower purchased clothes for all the members of his family at the stall of the tailor.

The fair is one of the great sights of rural life, appearing as a colorful whirl to the onlooker. Here one could survey the differences between the farming and customs of various regions—the quality of the horses, carts, and harnesses, and the attire, behavior, and speech of the people. To a considerable degree it was through the fairs that the people of Átány gained their knowledge of the surrounding regions.

In the early morning of a market day one cart would follow another down the road; by the time they approached the fair the road was so clogged they could hardly move along. Pedestrians drove their oxen or cows between the carts. The roads were equally crowded after the fair. A wagon may be towing two empty ones behind, since the horses had been sold. On the other hand, six or eight horses would be tied to the carts of the dealers. At any moment one might find a fellow villager whom he could greet loudly. "Half of Átány" went to the spring fairs at Jászberény. People watched each other on the way back, trying to ascertain which of them had succeeded in selling what he wanted to, what sort of purchases were made, and what kind of mood various individuals were in. Many carts are drawn up around the roadside inns; those who had had a "good fair" drank a repeated *áldomás*.

The fair-going of the horse dealers was more adventurous. They might travel 200 km. or more, by train, cart, or even by foot, beyond the circle of well-known fairs within a radius of 20 to 30 km. They traveled through rain and storm, often looking for the right road in unknown regions at night. As they became acquainted with strange people and customs, the horse dealers were links between distant regions which were too far away from each other to be able to meet at a common fair. They bought horses from the parts of the southeastern Great Plain which specialized in rearing the Nonius breed in order to sell them in the villages of the northern regions, where no horses at all were raised.[57]

During the second half of the last century Átány was self-sufficient in most respects, though it relied entirely on the outside world for certain commodities. As regards male costume, the linen was woven and sewn at home by the women, and the sheep-

price is paid and the animal is led away, both parties exchange good wishes: "I wish you good luck with the horse"; "I wish you good luck with the money." A very important transaction is finished by an *áldomás*, usually paid for by the person receiving the money.

[57] Later on dealers made use of the railway network, traveling to fairs and bringing the purchased horses home by train. Although horse dealing began to flourish only about the turn of the century, livestock trading had old traditions in Átány. Judicial records of the eighteenth century mention peasants trading in cattle. In the last hundred years livestock marketing has dwindled to insignificance; one or two *gazda*-s have experimented with it for short periods of time, nothing more. The butchers of the village would purchase a whole flock and fatten it in the Átány pasture for slaughtering.

In the 1930s and 1940s trading in goslings and "dry geese" suitable for fattening proved to be a profitable enterprise. The geese were purchased in the Jászság, where they were raised on a large scale. The people of Átány covered long distances in order to make a profit on the goslings and geese. We know peasants who joined the goose business with fixed assets and calculated a "dividend" in proportion to their capital.

skin coats (*suba*) and jackets were manufactured by the furriers of the village. Men's broadcloth suits and boots had to be purchased outside the village for the most part. As for the women, they were dependent on sources outside the village for factory-made cloth, silk kerchiefs, and bonnets ornamented with artificial flowers, while their linen costumes were made at home. The basic foodstuffs were provided by the fields of the village: flour, bread, meat, lard, eggs, dairy products, wine, spices such as paprika and saffron, etc. However, salt, sugar, brandy (at least in part) and tobacco had to be imported. Of the building materials, the adobes were made near the village, and thatching was done with reeds which grew in the village. On the other hand, the beams, the wood for doors and window frames, and the stone used to line window niches and wells came from other regions. When the oldest villagers alive today were still children, pine wood used to be sent down the Tisza on rafts, and the villagers who wanted to buy wood went to the landing place on the bank of the river. They purchased stone from the quarries of the nearby mountains, paying the stonecutter in kind. The tools that were imported were scythes, hoes, plowshares, and other iron tools as well as a large proportion of the wooden ones. They had to order harnesses and all varieties of rope from outside craftsmen, but often an Átány *gazda* would bring the hemp, processed by his wife, for the rope maker to use.

Thus Átány was for the most part a self-sufficient society in which not only the individual households endeavored to live on their own provisions, but also the community, as in the case of the local furriers making coats and jackets for the villagers out of the skins of their own sheep. Articles the community lacked were secured from exchange relations between regions, itinerant artisans and craftsmen, and finally the fairs.

These traditional exchange relations between peasants and between peasants and craftsmen or artisans were gradually supplanted by a more impersonal commercial network. As early as 1828 there were two merchants in Átány, but they were of the lowest, poorest sort. Later, with the spread of factory products, the role of the shops became more important. As earthenware vessels came to be replaced by ironware and enameled pots and pans, the potters' wagons ceased to frequent the village. The size and significance of the "unpacking fairs" decreased; after selling his livestock at the Heves fair, the *gazda* would no longer go to the booths of the Jászság smiths to buy a plow or a harrow but would patronize the ironmonger's shop instead. Within the village the main dealer in industrial products was the *Hangya* Consumers' Cooperative, founded in 1892. At that time it sold nothing but salt, sugar, matches, and kerosene, but by the beginning of this century its merchandise included textiles, ironware, pots and pans, and even sowing machines; and in the case of larger purchases, it sold its goods on the deferred payment system.

The system of marketing Átány products also changed. During the second half of the last century, Átány grain was sent not only to the markets and fairs, but also to the mills of Eger and Miskolc. In the meantime the system of buying-up was gaining ground in the village; from the 1870s on, large-scale grain merchants were active in Heves, and at the beginning of this century they began to station agents and middlemen in Átány. In 1913 a cooperative dairy was founded, resulting in a decrease in the production of butter and curd for the local and the Heves markets and the discontinuation of the marketing of clarified butter.

One aspect of this change in agricultural trade is that the rural farms have come into closer and closer contact with national and international markets (see Chapter 2, "Agriculture," and Chapter 13, "Mobility in the Last One Hundred Years"). The exchange value in wheat of a flax brake, a thorn bush harrow, or an earthen jug had been fixed for generations, but now the Átány *gazda*-s who marketed grain would check on the daily prices of the Budapest produce exchange by telephone. Thus the booms and the depressions of the national market were quickly reflected in individual rural farming operations. The rotation plan of the peasant farms was not changed fundamentally, although to a limited extent new commercial-industrial crops which were not used in the rural households were introduced into the agricultural round, such as sugar beets, seed grains, and peas. Since the 1930s the *gazda*-s have entered into production and marketing contracts with the Hatvan sugar factory and various seed companies.

With the new expansion of commercial relations, the circulation of money in Átány has also steadily increased. Wages and prices which were formerly paid in kind are more and more being replaced by their cash equivalents. This change is far from being complete or fully internalized, however. For one thing, the people of Átány have twice witnessed the devaluation of money and the introduction of new currency, once after each World War. Even today the *gazda*-s tend to define prices and values in relation to wheat: "One could buy a fine *jász* cart for the price of four *mázsa*-s of wheat"; "One pair of boots was always cheaper than a *mázsa* of wheat," etc.

Credit in the form of mortgage loans was introduced at an early date. Even during the 1866 consolidation of serf holdings several peasants purchased land with the help of such loans. Later many people were induced to borrow on account of a bad harvest, disastrous weather conditions, heavy taxes, or investments such as the purchase of land, construction, or the acquisition of a threshing machine. Owing to the burden of mortgage loans, a considerable amount of the produce of the Átány fields left the village in the form of interest.[58] Several *gazda*-s even went bankrupt; "the debt twisted itself around their necks."

In the period of serfdom a significant amount of Átány manpower was demanded by the landlords of the manors in the form of both manual and yoke (team of draft animals) corvée. Even before the abolition of serfdom the numerous teams of the peasant farms provided sufficient horsepower to take part in transport operations

---

[58] The amount of Átány resources consumed by mortgage payments rose rapidly during the second half of the last century. People in the lowest category of landed property, those who owned between zero and ten *hold*-s (14.20 acres), incurred especially heavy debts. According to two different nation-wide calculations, in 1905, 37 per cent or 39 per cent of the market value of the peasant holdings was owed. Investigations of peasant households made at that time reveal that 10 to 12 per cent, and in certain families as much as 24 per cent of the income had to be used to make interest payments. Almost one-quarter of the new loans were raised in order to amortize old ones. Contemporary bank records show the following additional reasons for making loans to the peasantry: indigence, poor crops, the purchase of additional land, and payments to other family members after the division of an inheritance (Szabad, 1965: 238–240).

along the "Great Road" and to undertake threshing for wages or for a part of the produce in the eastern part of the Great Plain. After the liberation of the serfs, Átány men and women would go to work on the large estates as harvesters, day laborers,[59] and later *summás*-s, and some hired themselves out as farm hands on the manors. The threshing of grain by team owners came to an end with the general expansion of the threshing machine at about the turn of the century, and the opportunities for wagon transport decreased with the construction of railroads. Nevertheless, even in the period between the World Wars carters could count on a regular income from transporting building material, firewood, or tobacco from the tobacco growers on the estates. But in general such job opportunities for the villagers became fewer and fewer. Therefore some people had to go beyond the traditional spatial limits to find a job, contracting as *summás*-s to work on distant estates for a period of months or years. Others left the traditional orbit of rural work to look for jobs in the towns, at construction sites, and in factories (see Chapter 13, "Mobility in the Last One Hundred Years"). Thus the Átány economy reached a new balance, which includes and requires the income of poor people (mostly, but not exclusively, men) working far from their families in towns, at construction sites, in industrial plants, and on far-away estates. The prosperity of Átány then depended not only on the quantity of the crops, but also on whether the teamless farmers could find work in other regions, and if so,what kind of work.

Similarly, there was very little chance for outside labor to come into the village. Some Heves people worked as servants for the Átány *gazda*-s, and at about the turn of the century some inhabitants of Eger came to their fields as harvesters. Day laborers from the vineyards of Eger came to the plain regions in order to acquire wheat by reaping.

THE SCHOOL

In 1878 the Átány minister noted that the recruiting commission would not believe a bachelor of Átány who claimed to be illiterate. Illiteracy was exceedingly rare, with the possible exception of the children of hired men who lived outside the village. Átány was widely renowned because its population knew how to read and write and its schooling was much better than the regional average. (The national average proportion of people who knew how to read was slightly below 50 per cent in 1869; this average had risen to over 80 per cent by the beginning of the twentieth century.)[60]

---

[59] The Átány people who worked on the large estates saw a different type of farming from what they knew at home; namely, large-scale cultivation of commercial and industrial crops with correspondingly different agricultural methods. They regarded this as a separate world, and generally did not try to imitate it at home. Nevertheless, several innovations from the estates were adopted on the peasant farms of Átány, chiefly through the harvesters and day laborers who worked there. Examples are the cultivation of fodder-turnip and sugar beets. The sharecroppers were paid in wheat, barley, or maize from the large estate, often different varieties from those grown in the village. In this way new types of plants came to Átány; the peasants would exchange their grain for the wheat or maize the reapers brought from the estate and use the new varieties as seed grain.

[60] These figures refer to people over six years old. Elementary education was reorganized by Act 38 of 1868, at which time 80 per cent of the elementary schools were owned by the churches (Balogh, 1965b: 523–531).

The amount and type of knowledge is strikingly uniform among the people of Átány. The legends about the development, the survival, and the struggles of the community, known by only a few people in other villages, are generally known and transmitted with slight variations in Átány. The outstanding figures and events of national history are known in the same manner; the memory of historical days is recalled by different informants with quotations from the same poems.

Many people are fond of reading, gazda-s and poor men alike. In about 1860, László Szatmári Király, a landowner who lived alone, donated a library of eight hundred volumes to the community.[61] Most of the books were historical and literary works, and the villagers borrowed them eagerly. Episodes from some of the library's novels and short stories, such as the story of the origin of the gypsies and the story of the mysterious wedding of a neighboring landlord, have become "popular tradition" and everyone knows them. In the second half of the last century there was also an Átány gazda who owned a more modest library of about forty volumes. This collection also included works of history and literature, as well as books on agriculture and works which were meant to popularize agricultural machines. An Átány house without a Bible is exceptional, and the majority of the homes have several editions of the Old and New Testaments, besides hymnals of various ages and books containing religious stories and prayers. (One of the functions of the Bible in family life is to preserve on its inner cover the recorded dates of the births, deaths, and occasionally weddings of the members of the family.)

Reading newspapers is a winter occupation. Subscriptions to weekly papers were favored; the men used to read them aloud in the tanyakert-s. As the period of the summer agricultural work set in, the subscription was allowed to lapse. At the beginning of this century a few craftsmen of outside origin, influenced by Socialist doctrine, began to show some interest in politics, and consequently they subscribed to daily papers.

Each family purchased an almanac if it could afford it; the horse dealers' families also bought special calendars showing the dates of the national fairs.

Although reading is considered an easy task in Átány, that cannot be said of writing. Villagers living in America, soldiers in service, and more recently workers who spend a considerable amount of time in town are the people who usually write letters. It is unusual to mail a letter to Átány people who have moved to other villages; people prefer to send messages. Patients in hospitals far from the village also send messages in preference to writing letters, and within the village the oral message is by far the favorite means of communication.[62]

Reading and writing were taught in the old and excellent parochial school, whose

---

[61] This library was located in the town hall until 1896, when the new town hall was constructed. Then the library was transferred to the large rectory. All the books were destroyed in World War II.

[62] The Átány people begin and close their letters with standard formulas which recall letters of Hungarian gentlefolk in the seventeenth and eighteenth centuries. Let us quote a letter sent to Edit Fél as an example: "My letter is dated the 15th of February 1952. Dear Miss. I hope to God that this my line of writing may find all the family in the best of health. We are all right too; thank Goodness there is nothing the matter with us either. I received the letter addressed to me, I have understood it..." etc.

long tradition of schooling produced a certain educational homogeneity among the villagers. This tradition does not extend to the secular school, however, which was founded in the 1900s for the Szárazbő *tanya*-s and maintained by the village and the estates, since this institution was frequented by the children of Roman Catholic hired men who had come from other villages.

For more than two centuries (as far back as we have the relevant records), the Calvinist school of Átány has drawn its teachers from Sárospatak, the outstanding center of Calvinist instruction in Hungary. During the eighteenth century and the first half of the nineteenth they were third- and fourth-year divinity students, several of whom had visited a Protestant theological school in the Netherlands or some other Western country before coming to Átány. The teacher was chosen by the members of the Átány church council and brought to the village for a term of three years. After this term the majority returned to the academy to finish their studies and become clergymen. Those who did not return for further studies or who failed their final examinations sought employment as "rectors" (teachers) or secretaries in rural villages.

School records from the middle of the eighteenth century mention two teachers at the same time at Átány: the rector and the assistant schoolmaster. By 1801 a separate girls' school existed in the village. An Átány minister is mentioned as early as in 1596, "but one cannot tell whether there was a rector, since neither the rector nor his salary are mentioned. It is more probable that the office of rector was held by the ministers themselves, as may be guessed from their salaries. ... However, the visitation of 1754 shows that there was a rector in Átány in that year. ..." The above is quoted from the school records of the 1760s.

At the end of the eighteenth and the beginning of the nineteenth century the year's teaching was divided into two terms; at the start of our field work we found people in their eighties who had attended the school under this system. The winter examination fell on St. Paul's day (January 25), and the summer one coincided with the harvest.

Instruction took place in a single long building, with boys and girls in separate classrooms. During the winter term the children spent the whole day in school, since the deep mud prevented them from returning home for lunch. In the lofts of some Átány houses one can still find small ornamental mugs in which the children used to carry milk or sour cream to school for lunch. The first large school building was also the place where the teacher lived. Later two such buildings are recorded, although the date of construction is missing for the second. One was for the boys, the other for the girls, and the two teachers lived in their respective buildings. In 1887 a third school building was constructed and a third teacher was invited to the village at the same time. One building served for the instruction of the "small ones," boys and girls in the first and second grades; the second one held the boys and the third one the girls of the third and fourth grades. During this period the classrooms were heated in winter with the help of the children themselves. Each of them had to bring two turf bricks from home for fuel. Cleaning up was also done by the children. As recently as the period between the two World Wars the father of each schoolchild made or had made a small broom, which the child took to school during the week when it was his turn to clean up. After World War I the church engaged a "cleaning woman" to clean the classroom and light the fire in winter, but sweeping at noon is still the duty of the children.

In the eighteenth century the number of pupils was between 110 and 120, each entering class containing from 20 to 23 new ones. Few children completed all four grades; the majority left after the second or third grade. Notes made by the teachers —"he has left school in holy simplicity"; "he kicked the school in the side like an ass"; "necessity called him away"; "poverty called him away from school"—allude to the fact that some of the children were put to work at an early age. This phenomenon is still noticeable in the present century. A class starting out with sixty pupils in 1910 had dwindled to twelve by the time it reached the sixth grade. In 1813 the higher church authorities ordered that children should attend school between the ages of six and ten; nevertheless one finds several children who were enrolled for the first time at the age of eight, nine, or even ten.

In the eighteenth and the nineteenth centuries it was customary for two or three —sometimes as many as five—of the best pupils to leave annually for further studies in Sárospatak. According to the records of the Sárospatak secondary school, there were usually many pupils of peasant origin; in the mid-nineteenth century the proportion oscillated between 15 and 25 per cent. Since the 1870s, however, peasant children have practically disappeared from Sárospatak.[63] None of the Átány peasant boys registered at Sárospatak in this period succeeded in finishing his studies at "the school." After passing the examinations of the fourth year of secondary school, the boy was sent or brought home for one reason or another. Such a "learned" youth could fill the post of secretary in another village or get a job as a supervisor on an estate. During this period Átány produced only one "great man," General Ötvös, after whom a street is named. Tradition holds that he never finished his schooling either.

In the eighteenth century the main subjects taught were reading and writing. Children began writing with their fingers in dust sprinkled on the table; only later were they given slates. The curriculum also included singing psalms and memorizing prayers and chapters of the Old Testament, this instruction being called "the history of the saints." The boys attended church every morning and afternoon from the third grade on. From among them the choir leader picked ten or twelve good singers to sing with the choir at funerals. One of them also eventually became the church "diktás," who (until 1946) recited the lines of the hymns one at a time for the congregation to repeat.

The records of 1811 show that the subjects of instruction were standardized.[64] They indicate that there was a difference between the curriculum of the boys and that of the girls, but unfortunately they do not describe what it was: "Although the girls' school

---

[63] Balogh, 1965b: 545.
[64] We publish the 1811 curricula for the four grades of the Átány Boys' School in Appendix C.

should educate its pupils in almost all the skills that are taught in the four grades of the National School [the boys' school], nevertheless there are some subjects which are not as necessary for female children as they are for the males; for this reason the division of the National Schools into Male and Girls' Schools has been approved. It was deemed necessary too that instead of such sciences which affect only the Male Children and not the Daughters, other sciences should be entered in the Curriculum for the latter, which will serve the purpose of their education." The records of the school contain the curriculum of the boys by grades. The first grade studied reading, writing, and the Roman and Arabic numerals; the second learned religion, reading, arithmetic, "Natural History by pictures," and the correct use of the "Planisphere" and maps (which may help to explain the astonishing ability of older Átány men to orient themselves quickly on maps they have never seen before); the third grade adds a short history of Hungary, a summary of Hungarian law, the "physics" of the general properties of masses, and the geography of Europe; the fourth grade was occupied with the "Rules of Health," a "Compendium of the Science of Agriculture," a "Compendium of the Science of Craftsmanship," drawing, practical geometry, and mechanics.

The Golden Alphabet first appears in the records in 1828 and continues as an obligatory subject of instruction until 1904.[65] (After it was dropped from the school curriculum, it was taught by parents to their children at home. In 1953 we met a young woman who was teaching it to her husband in the evenings because he had never learned it.)

Copies of one or another edition of the Golden Alphabet (the last one dates from 1912) can be found in the lofts of numerous Átány houses, these rooms being the general repositories for unused objects. The Golden Alphabet is a collection of moral rules and good manners, arranged in alphabetical order, which represent the traditional ideal of Átány behavior. Most people over forty years old know at least a few lines of it, and old people quote it with resignation, feeling that the behavior of the younger generation is guided by new principles. "He did not learn the Golden Alphabet" means that the person referred to does not behave the way the villagers do. He does not greet older people; he does not honor his parents; he does not give his seat to an older person; he does not esteem the worker in his employ; and he disagrees with the principle, "Do not do to your neighbor what you do not want to have done to you." These "rules of life," as some editions call themselves in the subtitle, were known and quoted by everyone for more than a century; their smooth or clumsy lines were used as warnings for young people and children, and also as a justification by elderly people: "I lived a good life, I behaved and acted according to the rules in the Golden Alphabet."

In 1870 the higher authorities began to promote adult education as well: "... a strict ordinance of the Minister for Culture and Education was read, enjoining not only young people from twelve to fifteen years of age, but also all adults who lack basic

---

[65] Several variations of the Golden Alphabet are known, one of which is given in Appendix D.

education, and especially the recruits and soldiers, to go to school." The instruction was arranged for two evenings a week; judged by the fact that the school bought the required three lamps for the classroom, adult education was initiated.

From the early 1800s we find records of a school "library." In the early years the number of books varied between two and eight, these being the manuals of the teachers. Later all the works used in the curriculum were included, and from time to time a donor would contribute some new ones. For instance, the aforementioned László Szatmári Király gave a book on gymnastics in 1853. (Copies of these books can be found in the lofts of Átány houses, since the peasants bought and read them as adult literature later on. They were relegated to the lofts in the last decades.)

In the early 1830s the church authorities wrote an inquiry as to "whether there exists some land or holding donated to the school on which the children ... might acquire some practice in gardening, silk production, or fruit growing." The answer is found in the later community assembly journals, where mention is made of an existing nursery garden.

In 1828 authorities warned the teachers of the ecclesiastical school that "the Teacher is a member of two societies, the Church society and the Civic society ... and is subject to the laws of both." The influence of the "civic" society was felt by the church school more and more every year. In 1854 only those books could be used for teaching which "were declared admissible by the Imperial and Royal Ministry of Culture and Education."

The year 1887 saw a major reorganization of the Átány school system. The third schoolmaster was invited to the village at this time, and the salaries were readjusted. Up till then the "rector" had enjoyed the use of 66 *hold*-s (93.72 acres) of church property, a house, a garden, and an annual payment of one *véka* of wheat and half a *véka* of barley from each pupil. Out of his wages he had to pay the assistant (or girls') teacher, who was given only one pair of "summer chickens" by each pupil annually. After 1887 each schoolmaster received separate land for his own use— the "rector" 44 *hold*-s (62.92 acres), and the two assistants 25 *hold*-s (35.60 acres) apiece, and each received a *kert*. The pupils brought one *véka* of wheat and half a *véka* of barley to each of them separately. The rector received an extra salary for his activity as choir leader.

The immediate authority in matters concerning the school was the school board of the village, the founding date of which we could not ascertain. Headed by the minister of the village, it included also the headmaster, the churchwarden, and three experienced members of the church council. Its duties were the direction and maintenance of the schools. Twice a year the members of the school board visited the classes in pairs and then reported on their findings at the meeting of the church council. It was their task to keep the school buildings and equipment in good repair, and when necessary to purchase new school supplies.

During this same period the public election of schoolmasters was introduced. The school board called for applicants, asking them to write out offers that would then be considered and to demonstrate their talents for singing and playing the organ in front of the community in church. The election was made on the basis of these two qualities.

In 1932 the number of teachers rose to four, and another readjustment of salaries took place, in which it was revealed that the church paid its schoolmasters less than it should according to new state regulations. Salaries were raised, but since the state assumed only a small part of the cost, the church became involved in heavy debts. Thereafter the state provided an increasing proportion of the teachers' salaries, in the meantime gaining more and more control over the curriculum and the instruction. In 1940 a new school building was erected, paid for with state funds, and the number of teachers was increased to six. In 1948 the school was nationalized entirely. Religious instruction, formerly the central task of the school, was restricted to one hour a week for those who asked for it.

The new two-story school building, which was the second two-story construction ever built in the village (the other was the mill), was finished in 1955. Eight years of schooling are obligatory, now taught by a staff of twelve.

In the journals of the community assembly from the 1890s on are recorded various attempts of the state to found a day-nursery in Átány. The villagers, not wanting to bear the costs of construction and maintenance, put up a staunch resistance against the institution, emphasizing that no child in the village received inadequate supervision from its parents. As a result, it was not until 1952 that the state managed to establish a day-nursery.

THE LAW OF THE LAND IN ÁTÁNY

As Hungarian citizens, the villagers are subject to the law of the land. The law has an especially direct influence on the life of Átány in the areas of ownership, inheritance, village administration, labor relations, and the punishment of crimes.

In the judgment of József Kakas, the prescriptions of law "are always just, since what would have become of the world without laws? The trouble is that they are not always executed properly." A similar view prevails in the village as a whole. The law is not to be censured, but it is a strange thing, its actions not always entirely predictable; one does well to avoid it. "Beware of these three things—the lawyer, the pharmacy, and the inn; they ruin everybody." "A man who visits the lawyer, receives a visit from the doctor, or frequents the pub will perish." A bad family life is implied when brothers cannot agree on the division of the inheritance by themselves or with the help of the village magistracy and have to resort to a lawsuit. At the same time it is dangerous, since the property in question may be absorbed by the court costs.

The community has its own ideas of "justice," law, and crime—sometimes identical with the rules of law, sometimes stricter, and sometimes more lenient. It is not considered a theft to pick a grape in the vineyard or a fruit from someone else's tree for consumption on the spot, or to cut a stick from another's fence to use as a switch. The thefts of bachelors from the granaries of their fathers and the pilfering of someone else's pantry or loft are not judged in the same way. In the opinion of the villagers, the fights between bachelors are acts of *virtus*, manly prowess; though the court may punish them, it is considered more shameful to run than to participate. On the other hand, manslaughter brands the culprit for all his life, regardless of the motive, and the same fate befalls the man who has performed repeated acts of arson or theft.

There are immediate means of gaining revenge or retaliation for a personal injury. Bachelors who are beaten up try to return the blows on another occasion; a *gazda* who finds that someone has been stealing from his orchard lies in wait in order to knock the thief on the head personally with a pitchfork. In such cases there is no need to set the wheels of justice in motion. Finally there is a class of minor injuries which are settled by the reconciliation mechanisms described above (see Chapter 9, "Neighborhood").

Nevertheless there are crimes which have wider implications than those involving simply the offender and the injured person—namely, those crimes which are considered transgressions of the universally accepted moral order, such as murder or robbing an orphan of his inheritance. These acts cannot go unpunished, and their punishment is meted out almost with the severity of the principle of an eye for an eye and a tooth for a tooth. This retribution is exacted by divine justice, which, according to the Átány view, does not hurry but it never forgets (see Chapter 16, "The Calvinist Reformed Church"). Whether or not the criminal is found guilty and punished by law, he cannot avoid the judgment of God. Thus S. O. served his term of imprisonment for the murder committed in his youth and afterward married and went back to work on his farm, living a life of exemplary industry and self-denial. However, the villagers always shrank from him and never entered his house. When his fingers were contracted by arthritis in his old age, the general opinion in the village was that this represented a divine punishment, and it was said that his hands had frozen into the same position that they had long ago assumed when he pointed the revolver at his grandfather. G. V., Jr., though never brought to trial, was reputed to have killed his brother, albeit unintentionally. Everyone regarded it as divine retribution when he died a violent death.

Once we asked Gábor Varga why it was that people talked so much about petty offences (such as failure to return the correct change after being sent to buy something, keeping a neighbor's stray chicken, or having a disorderly footpath in front of his house) but were silent about major crimes. He explained that it is the affair of divine justice to avenge major crimes but that it is up to relatives, neighbors, and acquaintances to take care of the small ones. In the case of a real criminal, man's only responsibility is to avoid relations and interactions with him. It would be improper either to bring about legal punishment or to call for divine retribution with a curse. The people of Átány believe in the power of a curse, especially a curse called down upon a close relative, but they also believe that to use this power would be to interfere with divine judgment, which is rightfully outside the scope of man. One who is cursed says to himself, "From your mouth to your bosom," i.e., may your curse revert to yourself. There are many stories about curses which have returned to the initiator, such as that of the estate overseer who habitually cursed people. A common phrase with him as he inspected the work of the women bent over to hoe turnips was, "the lightning should strike your back rather than your head," meaning that they should remain in their bent position without interrupting their work even to stretch. During a summer storm his little boy was struck dead by a bolt of lightning. "The little boy had to die so that his father would be shaken," they say in Átány.

The legal system is seen as dealing with more or less the same crimes as those which the villagers feel should be left to divine justice, though without the trusted omniscience and impartiality of the latter. Although it is improper to bring about the punishment of a villager by cursing him or informing on him, the sanction meted out is generally regarded as just. A term of imprisonment impairs one's honor in any case, even if the Átány moral code does not condemn the criminal act. This is why bachelors arrested for fighting endeavor to have their prison sentence commuted to a fine, and why József Kakas, Sr., paid a large sum to avoid going to prison when he was tried for a political statement during World War II.

Although the legislative machinery has little direct influence on most affairs of Átány life, changes in the law open or close possibilities, thereby effecting a gradual transformation of local customs. The best illustration is the modification of the system of inheritance, with the gradual introduction of female succession (see Chapter 13, "The Order of Succession"). It took two or three generations after the statutes of 1836 and 1840 were passed before the customs of inheritance actually changed. The traditional views against female heirs proved to be so strong that in several cases daughters gave up their part of the inheritance on the request of their brothers. Once accepted, the inheritance of property by daughters influenced other sectors of life: it altered the standards in the choice of a mate; it caused marriage between people of the same economic level to become general; it hastened the division of fortunes into small portions; it modified the opportunities for mobility; and so on.

The chapters above have also enumerated other chain reactions of adaptation initiated in Átány by legal statutes. Act 40 of 1868 introduced the draft, which in practice rearranged the division of male age groups, opened the way for new accomplishments and customs to reach the village via the returning soldiers, and led to the creation of new customs in the bachelor bands and the groups of neighbors and relatives. The activity of the village council and the body of representatives, described above, shows the effects of statutes on village administration passed in 1871 and 1886. Moreover, national laws are executed in Átány with particular local modifications and additions, such as the solemnization of the enlistment of Átány recruits by the donning of ribboned hats.

In the use of the fields and agricultural practices in general, the abolition of compulsory three-crop rotation (1901) and later the consolidation of holdings (1913–1927) represent important landmarks. Each of the innovations was based on an act of Parliament, and in both cases a few years' lag was necessary to break the order of age-old tradition before the change was accepted in actual practice. Both changes affected almost the entire population of the village, since in neither case was it possible for some people to accept the new system while others retained the old. The agitation against the three-crop rotation system was begun by the innkeeper Mihály Bedécs, a member of an old Átány family and a poor *gazda* who read newspapers and was interested in a variety of subjects; he won the battle with the help of a group of other relatively poor *gazda*-s. The Agriculture Act of 1894 allowed a minority of the proprietors to leave the rotation system if they wanted to. An almost formal clash occurred between the reformers and the Pasture Associations, which held to the traditional use of the fields. When Bedécs and his followers planted their fields during the season when land was supposed to lie fallow, the leaders of the Pasture Associations let the village herd graze in their crops. The injured proprietors went to court and won their case, and the Pasture Associations were obliged to pay damages. This judgment practically ended the three-crop rotation system and the fallow period.[66]

As regards the consolidation of individual holdings, a new procedure was introduced by Act 39 in 1908. The initial stages of the process were made easier and the necessary surveying of land holdings was underwritten with an interest-free state loan. In Átány the agitation was begun by the same "unruly" *gazda*-s, those who owned less land and read more newspapers, who had started the movement for the abolition of the rotation system a few years earlier. By 1913 public opinion had turned in favor of consolidation. In this instance another feature deserves to be mentioned. A very small proportion of Hungarian villages made use of the favorable opportunity offered by the Act of 1908, but the villages which did consolidate holdings formed clusters in a few small areas. Eight villages in the vicinity of Átány started the consolidation procedure between 1911 and 1913.[67] Thus not only the newspaper reports and news of the legal decisions, but also the immediate example of the neighboring villages influenced the local decision. The idea of consolidation reached them more or less in the same traditional peasant way by which they learned of several new implements, work techniques, new fashions in costume, and other innovations which they eventually adopted.

MILITARY SERVICE

The people of Átány believe that "one owes allegiance to the fatherland"; "one should serve the fatherland truly." The highest duty toward the fatherland is military service.

The draft was introduced in Hungary in 1868. People still remember that "once"

[66] Fél and Hofer, 1961b: 10–11; 1963: 564. (*Ibid.*: 572, see the contribution of György Szabad on the legal background of the abolition of three-crop rotation.)

According to Act 12 of 1894, if one-tenth of the landowners wanted to give up the rotation system, they could initiate proceedings, but their adversaries had to have a two-thirds majority to continue the old system. In other communities also there were violent clashes on the question of abolishing the old three-crop rotation system. The problem gave rise to heated debates in Parliament. The change was only gradually effected; in 1912, 28.9 per cent of the communities still adhered to the rotation system (Balogh, 1965a: 398–399).

[67] Ozoróczy, Tátray, and Kovách, 1938.

(i.e., before 1848) the army was mustered by the *úr*-s. People explain that "the large estates were not given to the *úr*-s to promote idleness and debauchery; rather they were obliged to equip a certain number of armed men." Old men remember that one of the Átány landlords, Tamás Pappszász, had ancestors who equipped men for the Twelfth Hussars stationed at Gyöngyös. They remember the recruiting too when the commissioners tried to attract the youth of the village to the army with music, drink, and *verbunkos* (a recruiting man's dance), and dragged some of them away by force, in collusion with the village magistracy.[68] They quote the widely known folk song:

> "Impressment goes on in our village,
> The poor bachelor is caught by force,
> Five or six sons of a *gazda* are left behind,
> But even the only son of a poor man is taken."

In this period military service was almost a profession, lasting for twelve years or more. Afterward the ex-servicemen enjoyed personal privileges under the system of serfdom. The 1828 census listed the ex-servicemen under a separate heading. Some people derive the name of the "Katona" (soldier) family of the village from their ancestor, Sámuel Katona, who was impressed into military service and served for twelve years in Klagenfurt, Austria, at the beginning of the last century.[69]

The introduction of the draft interjected a two- or three-year span of military service into the life of the men. During this period they lived far from the village, followed a different system of rules than the traditional mores, and exchanged their peasant attire for the uniform. As mentioned above, joining the service represented the end of the carefree bachelor age, and thus the end of irresponsibility. Military service was customarily followed by marriage. Owing to the importance of this transition, the period of preparation was surrounded by new customs. The draft call became a festive occasion. After their enlistment the recruits were distinguished from the rest of the villagers by their beribboned hats; public attention was thereby focused on them during the period before they actually reported for duty, a date which was marked by another solemn farewell.

In Átány it is unanimously held that the army "turns the boy into a man. The idea of esteem and honor is hammered into him during those three years; he learns how to respect his fellow man." The ex-serviceman is a "tested one"; he faces the vicissitudes

---

[68] According to tradition, Miska Vég was to be enlisted from Átány in 1829, but he fled and hid in the marshes near Kömlő. As a fugitive soldier, he could not return home, so he became a *betyár*. Many stories are told of him. Judging by this tradition, he ought to be as famous a leader of the *betyár*-s as Sándor Rózsa in the southern part of the Great Plain. Tradition has it that Miska Vég and Sándor Rózsa met at Kondoros and agreed that Miska Vég would not operate in the parts south of the Körös river and Sándor Rózsa would not go north of it. On one occasion he was almost arrested. His trail was followed by the police, led by the commissar András Barát. This man was also from Átány. When the pursuers came near enough to recognize him, the commissar gave the order: "Stop, turn back—this is not a *betyár*, but a godson."

[69] The nickname "Katona" was given to János Balog, who enlisted in the 1820s. He returned "from war" wearing a black vest trimmed with braid, decorated trousers, and shiny top boots. He is credited with introducing the braid-trimmed broadcloth suit and hard shiny boots to Átány.

of life with courage, he is not afraid of danger, and he is accustomed to discipline. A reprehensible action (such as suicide) is often explained by the fact that the man was "untested." If he had been a soldier, he would not have done so. To be sure, not everyone was enlisted. Those who were physically or mentally unfit and those who were their family's only source of support were exempted. To be found unfit was a cause for shame. Bachelors who were rejected stood out awkwardly among their companions, for they were allowed to put only a single white ribbon on their hats, while those who were accepted had dozens of ribbons of all different colors.

Military duty itself was not a sad period in the life of the bachelors; nobody was sorry for them, howsoever sadly the farewells were made. They did not have to work in the fields; they were freed from the domination of their parents; they wore a splendid uniform; and they got to see something of the world. At the end of the last century it was customary for most of them to bring home a memorial picture after their military service; it was a colored print which depicted the soldier in the uniform of his regiment, surrounded by military equipment and the portraits of the king and the commanders. Only the face of the soldier was a photograph of the individual, applied to the ready-made print. Those were the first portraits of family members in the Átány houses; hung in the place of honor between the windows, they commemorated the period of military service. Some of the old men were so attached to these pictures that they had them put into their coffins.

The ex-serviceman is conscious of his position and refers with pity to those who were not found acceptable, even if his own period of service involved war or captivity. Thus Ferenc Orbán told us, "I never reproached anyone for not having served a single day while I spent five years in the army. It was not the other man's fault if he was not called up. Thank Goodness, I was always a healthy man, so I was found able-bodied." But those who avoid military service by fraudulent means are despised. During the revolutionary movements in the autumn of 1918 this sentiment resulted in a manslaughter in the village during a fight between a bachelor who was not exempted though he should have been and another who was exempted though he did not deserve to be.

In the words of elderly Átány people, the army is "the splendor of the country." This idea is related to the Átány view of the history of Hungary. Recalling the characteristic scenes of national history which embody the patriotism and the loyalty to the fatherland, the pictures which come to mind are generally war episodes—their ancestors conquering the land by armed forces; warriors fighting the Mongolians and the Turks—soldiers in the struggles for freedom. Many of these wars were fought without the hope of victory, but nevertheless with pride and determination. In the Átány school the children were taught to love their fatherland by the example of Miklós Zrínyi, who, having destroyed all his property, left the demolished Szigetvár fortress and launched a futile and fatal last attack against the overwhelming Turkish majority (1566); or by the story of the defence of Eger castle (1552), whose garrison, badly in need of reinforcements, fought with heroism and held on after all hope seemed to be lost until they were finally victorious. On the wall of the schoolroom was a colored print of Petőfi, the greatest Hungarian poet, dying of a mortal wound on the battle ground and writing with his blood in the dust: "Fatherland forever!" (1849). The ideal of a good soldier and that of a good Hungarian overlapped. During the Austro-Hungarian Monarchy the Hungarian soldiers serving in the common army endeavored to excel among the other nationalities represented in the army or in front of the population of the foreign territory where they were garrisoned. Gábor Varga spent his military service in Vienna as a sergeant instructor in a training school for non-commissioned officers. He told his Hungarian soldiers, "When we go out into Vienna, people should not point at us because we are strangers, but their eyes should fix on you because you are a Hungarian." He and his companions of similar views stuck to their conviction in war captivity as well. "I have my moustache brushed every day [as a sign of neatness]; do not give in!" It is recalled that the Hungarians could be recognized among the war prisoners of the Russian camps during World War I "since the Hungarian was tough; he refused to give in."

Military service, and especially war, took Átány men to various regions, and they returned full of new experience. The first pocket watches were introduced to the village at the beginning of this century by returning soldiers who had bought them with their pay.[70] The methods of tending, caring for, and grooming horses were modified by new techniques learned by the soldiers, and some new methods for curing horse diseases were introduced by ex-servicemen. The soldiers were also able to see how agriculture was practiced in other regions—how people plowed or fertilized the soil in Moravia; what sorts of scythes were used in the western parts of the country; what kinds of barns were built by the Hungarians of Transylvania—but they did not modify their own agricultural practices on the basis of this experience.

Peacetime service, however, cannot be compared with the experiences of war. Almost all able-bodied Átány men took part in World Wars I and II. We do not know how many joined up, only how many died. On the various fronts of World War I, 94 inhabitants of Átány were killed. This number is more than one-tenth of the Átány men who were between the ages of twenty and fifty in 1910. In World War II, 53 died and 39 were reported missing. Those who joined the regiment were no longer escorted with music; some of them were mourned by the female members of their families with laments similar to those used in grieving for the dead.

Men who fought in the war and were held prisoner would say, "Most women cannot even imagine the suffering there." "Man endures more than a dog. He is all right at one moment, then an attack begins and the next moment he does not exist. We said the Lord's Prayer as often as a hundred times. Man becomes wild then. It's unfortunate to have to go to the front." However, one rarely hears men complain of their past sufferings; more frequently this or that episode of the war is recalled and rounded out into a story. Samu Kiss remembered two extremely cold Galician winters in the following way: "For two years I spent the winter in the open. We

---

[70] Pocket watches caught on rapidly and made it possible to tell what time it was (in hours) in the stables and the fields. Formerly people kept track of the hours only in places where the tower clock was visible or in their houses, where large hanging clocks had been a familiar item for some time.

collected leaves until they were covered up by snow. Or, if we saw a thatched roof, we said, 'Let's go and get some straw to lie on.' The man sleeping in his house woke in the morning to find there was no straw over his head."

Even today, at family celebrations, pigsticking, or in friendly conversation, memories of military service or the events of World War I or II frequently come up spontaneously. In these conversations a moral order is revealed, a norm of behavior valid for the soldier in far-away parts and for the members of his family in the village. Wherever the soldier may be thrown by fate, he must not deny or conceal his religion or Hungarian nationality; on the contrary, he should bear them proudly and courageously. He must do his best to create a favorable opinion of Hungarians when he is among foreigners, who are likely to judge the nationality by his behavior. A decent soldier "does not mix with women in a foreign country." He is bound by honor to take care of his comrades. All soldiers are comrades, brothers of war. Friendships formed in the battle line often endured for life, and were almost as important as the *koma*-ships in the village. A soldier may choose a comrade from among his co-villagers or from the inhabitants of other parishes. Even here, however, men looked for comrades of similar backgrounds, since "a gypsy's friend is a gypsy," and "one sticks to his own kind." Károly Bedécs said, "One knew who had been a swineherd and who was a peasant of average means like ourselves." Comrades kept a constant lookout for each other, stayed near each other whenever possible, and helped each other when wounded. They endured captivity and planned means of escape together. A man could become so attached to his comrade-in-arms that he would invite him to pigsticking forty years after the beginning of the friendship. Aside from these very close relationships, an Átány soldier was expected to keep track of other Átány men and to help them, to be of service if any were wounded, and, if necessary, to attend the burial and bring back the news to the family.

It is not easy for the women who stay at home in time of war either. Before joining up, the head of the family takes steps to ease the cares of the woman as much as possible. This is especially necessary when the old *gazda* is already weak and the boy is still small. Thus the man exchanges his horses for oxen, which require less attention and are simpler and less dangerous to take care of. If there is a suitable brother or other male relative, the *gazda* may give him the horse to use, but in exchange he must undertake the tilling of the soldier's land. Some of the women who were left alone during the wars learned to mow and to sow in order to keep the farm going. Women who farmed for four or five years aided only by a ten- or twelve-year-old boy and handed over the estate to the returning soldier without loss or damage are spoken of with esteem. Such women get special, gratuitous help from those who have not joined up.

As long as the husband, son, or father is away in the war, the women wear mourning, changing back to normal clothes only when the soldier is discharged. If he is killed, they remain draped in black. The 39 Átány men who were reported missing during World War II have now been declared legally dead, but their mothers and wives still wait for them, nevertheless. They still wear mourning, and they save the clothes of those who are lost. The wives have not remarried, even those who were young women at the time. Of these women only two have exchanged the black bonnet for a colored one, and they are reproached for doing so.

The soldiers who were fortunate enough to survive the war and to return from captivity will never forget the moment of their liberation. "What a joy it was to tread Hungarian soil again, on which we live, where we were born. . . ."

POLITICS

Prior to 1848 three aristocrats who owned Átány land were entitled by birth to a seat in the Upper Chamber of the feudal diet. They were the prince Coburg-Koháry and the counts Butler and Esterházy. The possessions of these families in Átány consisted only of land, however; their residences were far from the village. The majority of the Lower Chamber was made up of representatives of the petty nobility, two from each county. The deputies were elected by the noble landlords of Szárazbő, Tenk, Heves, etc., and the landless rural noble families, such as the Bedécs, the Madarász, the Galvács, and the Fóra in Átány. The number of voters was considerable. In the 1839 election of the deputies of Heves county to the diet, 6,418 votes were cast; among these 2,072 came from the Tarna district, which included Átány at that time. On this occasion Tamás Pappszász, a landowner at Szárazbő and Tenk, was re-elected as one of the deputies. The serfs had no representation in the legislative assembly.[71]

In the 1839 election mentioned above, the battle was waged between two national parties, the conservatives and the liberals. The elections were preceded by long discussions of party platforms and lively campaigning. On their way to the polls in the district capitals, the conservatives fastened black feathers to their hats, the liberals white ones.[72]

In speaking of the former privileges of the gentry, the descendants of the noble families of Átány recall these elections with pleasure. The petty nobles who farmed on their small *telek*-s could feel themselves equal to the landowners; the lively, colorful assemblies made them imagine that they played a part in running the country.

In June of 1848, after the abolition of the privileges of the nobles, the eight constituencies of Heves county elected representatives to an "assembly of popular representation." But the crushing of the freedom rebellion in the next year was followed by the absolute rule of the Vienna government of the Hapsburgs, and the Átány people could not go to the polls again until the relative independence of the country was restored. The right to vote was no longer granted on the basis of prerogatives at this time; rather, a certain minimum income or capital was required, domicile of at

---

[71] Balássy and Szederkényi, 1890–1897: IV, 380.

[72] Old Átány people still remember elections in which a man's party affiliation was made known by the color of the feather in his hat. The adherents of the left party later wore a red feather and those of the right party a white one.

least two years, and evidence that the elementary school examination had been passed. Owing to these restrictions, only 620 persons were entitled to vote in Átány in the 1870s. The site of the elections remained the seat of the district. They were preceded by animated campaigning; the electioneerers and their assistants spent a great deal of time in the *kert*-s, bringing brandy to the voters and making appeals. The candidates themselves came to "give a program," i.e., to deliver a policy speech. Led by the campaign assistants, the candidate's adherents rode to the border of the neighboring village to meet him and escort his carriage to the center of town. The young men especially enjoyed joining such a mounted escort; bachelors would prepare for the occasion for months, asking their fathers or older brothers to lend them a horse or even a saddle. People no longer remember the promises and declarations, but even today they recall the personal qualities, the bearing, and the voices of long-ago candidates. In 1911, for example, Mihály Diószegi, the minister of Tiszafüred, ran as a candidate for the opposition (the Left); "he had an awfully strong voice, it could be heard near the *kert*-s when he was campaigning in the market place; the wind brought his voice from the Ér." He found support with the Átány people but he lost the election. The next year the villagers took advantage of a vacancy in the rectory and made him their minister.

The people of Átány also saw these elections as the clashes of two parties, the "right party" and the "left party," or the "1867" government party and the "1848" opposition.[73] The villagers held that a good Hungarian had a duty to support the opposition, the party of 1848. The village elders were the only people who were not reproached for siding with the government, since they were considered more or less "official people." A story is told about a *gazda* who "did not enter the house of his younger brother for ten years" after he found out that the brother "had turned the ornamental cloak" *(szűr)*—i.e., was a turncoat and had gotten a job as a campaign assistant for the government.

The choice between the two parties was influenced not only by national sentiment and the memory of the 1848 freedom rebellion, but also by the general mistrust of and opposition to the measures of the government. This constant suspicion of government policies was characteristic even in the proceedings of the village council. The villagers hardly ever envisioned the possibility of a change in their circumstances as a result of the outcome of the elections, though all candidates generally used promises to influence the voters in their direction. During this period the national parliament was concerned mainly with the constitutional relationship with Austria, the relative independence of the Hungarian army, and similar problems rather than with social reforms; therefore the parties were also characterized by their attitudes toward these national and constitutional questions.

On the day before the elections the candidates had campaign flags brought to the village and distributed to those of their adherents who intended to go to the polls

[73] 1867 was the year of the constitutional compromise with Austria and the Hapsburg king; 1848 was the year when the anti-Hapsburg war of independence, led by Kossuth, broke out.

by carriage.[74] The followers of each candidate lined up their carts in a caravan; each cart carried six people and many also sported flags bearing the name of the candidate and the slogan of the party. The whole caravan often included as many as thirty or forty wagons. The flags played an important symbolic role. While en route the chief campaign assistants might stop the caravan at some inn along the road. If the carts of the rival party caught up with them, there was the possibility of conflict. The newcomers whipped their horses into a gallop and dashed past the halted wagons. As they drove by, the members of the rival party triumphantly extended their banners, dragging them over the heads of the persons sitting in the halted wagons, and thereby humiliating them. At the same time they recited mocking poems, such as the following:

> "Kálmán Kovács stuck a dog,
> He treated the Right party to it;
> Mihály Madarász was very angry,
> Because he only got the tail."

(The verse alludes to the quarrel of the two head campaign assistants of the government over their reward.) If the attackers were quick, they could get away unhurt, but often the men of the other party managed to wrench the flags from their hands; not infrequently the result was a brawl with the flagpoles. The road of the opposition voters to Poroszló, where the elections were held, was unsafe in other respects. They had to cross Kömlő, whose population was strongly pro-government. If they wanted to get through the village in peace, or if they saw a superior force by the roadside, the more cautious voters hid their opposition flags inside the carriage.

These elections were by open ballot and were held at Poroszló until shortly after World War I, when the site was moved to Átány and the secret ballot was introduced —which considerably diminished the liveliness of the event. The Átány voters continued to remain faithful to the opposition during these decades, casting their votes for the leftist Small-holders' Party.

Thus Átány was connected to the legislature and the government first of all through its local government and administration, which received orders from the higher authorities and had only a limited opportunity to decide whether to accept or reject them. Secondly, the parliamentary elections were occasions when the candidates of both parties appeared in the village and offered a choice between their programs.

The people of Átány had other sources of information on the affairs of the country. One of these was the newpapers. Political news was read and discussed in the *tanya-kert*-s as early as the end of the last century. Some copies of 1848–1849 newspapers have been found among the documents preserved in peasant houses. Sometimes the people's confidence in the truth of the information in the papers was shaken; for

---

[74] We succeeded in acquiring a few old campaign flags for the Ethnographic Museum. We may say that no other object purchased for the Museum created such a sensation or was greeted with such applause and enthusiasm. Elderly people of Átány beheld them with shining eyes, and they began to tell old election stories.

instance, in 1894 the village council withdrew its subscription to the governmental paper *Pesti Hírlap* with the explanation that "it is a useless expenditure." Nevertheless the reading of newspapers spread, and between the two World Wars it became organized in the form of the Reading Circles (see Chapter 17). These groups were mainly political and read journals representative of their party views. In the 1920s and 1930s Átány had a newsvendor who carried a bundle of newspapers under his arm and shouted out the interesting news as he strolled along some of the main thoroughfares of the village in the evening after the men had returned from work. Peasants looked to the papers partly for information about the acts and intentions of the government which might be related to their own personal welfare, and partly for news of the events of the world, especially wars. Elderly people would speak of the Italo-Abyssinian War, and even of the Boer War and the war between Russia and Japan. One of our acquaintances, an aged teamless farmer, made a habit of asking the newsvendor whether the paper had any news about Chiang Kai-shek that day, because he was interested in the events of the war in China and he always purchased the copies which reported on them.

The idea that other means besides elections might be used to express political demands of the rural people touched the Átány society quite superficially and ineffectually. In the 1870s and 1880s, and more intensively at the beginning of the present century, the Great Plain was the locus of peasants' movements aimed at the improvement of the living conditions of hired men and *summás*-s on the large estates, primarily those of day laborers and reapers. They agitated for shortening the working day to twelve hours, for child labor laws, for wage increases, and for increases in the share of harvesters. These aims had little effect on the team owners or on the majority of the teamless farmers of the villages, though they felt sympathy for them. These social problems were not accentuated in Átány since there were no local estates. In 1905 a march of demonstrators was held in the village with a police escort. No clashes ensued, and the event left no deep traces in the life of the community beyond the fact that it was the first appearance of this form of political expression.

The idea of political organization was introduced to Átány by the laborers employed in Budapest, primarily the factory workers. Some used their time advisedly to get to know the capital as well as possible and attended political meetings organized by the various parties and trade unions. Many of those occupied in the Csepel munitions factory and heavy industry became members of the trade unions or the Social Democratic Party and took part in strikes and political demonstrations, such as the movement for the secret ballot in 1912. They were unable to import to Átány a program that would mobilize the population of the village, since the attitude of the Social Democratic Party toward the agrarian problem was uncertain and equivocal. They declared that the rights of the poor working men should be supported against the large estates, but the hired men lived in scattered *tanya*-s and had no connections with these Budapest factory workers.

In the autumn of 1918, when the republic was proclaimed in the capital and demonstrations for reform movements were common, an Átány teamless farmer who had

25*

received a social democratic party education through the organization of the Budapest factory where he worked was sent home "to make the revolution" in the village. He organized a soldiers' council made up of the soldiers on leave and those returning home in masses from the front lines, and he held a march of demonstrators across the village, cheering the peace. They forced the mayor and the village secretary to pay sums of war relief which they thought had been unjustly withheld. An armed militia was set up. In March, 1919, the dictatorship of the proletariat brought about a further change: the directory, recruited from among the poor who became members of the United Workers' Party organized at that time, took over leadership of the village. However, the family traditions in the village government were not entirely interrupted even then, since István Szórád, the grandson of "mayor Szórád" (who held his post for 27 years), was one of the members of the new directory. The dictatorship of the proletariat brought about favorable changes for the stratum of poor peasants; the large estates were obliged to allot one-eighth of their crops to the harvesters instead of the previous tenth or eleventh, and to give them beef cattle so that they would be provided with meat. The directory also saw to it that every man who needed a reapers' job would get one. There were no movements to take over the land; the agricultural hired men remained quiet, here and in most other parts of the country. The militia was ready to interfere with arms if the people of the neighboring villages planned to divide the property of the large estates which was included within the administrational boundaries of Átány, but the villagers themselves did not touch this property.

In July, 1919, the royal Rumanian Army broke through the front line along the Tisza and brought another political change to the life of Átány.[75] Several members of the directory and the soldiers' council joined the Red Army; besides being an expression of their revolutionary political tendencies, their struggle was regarded as national defense. In a few weeks' time, however, they were forced to flee or to hide: sanctions and punishments for political activities appeared for the first time in the life of Átány.

The teamless farmers who had acquired political training in the movements of 1919 and who continued to work in Budapest renewed their efforts to organize the poor at the end of the 1920s and in the 1930s. This movement was centered primarily in the Reading Circle. Its main object was to unite the forces of the teamless farmers and day laborers employed in Budapest, who together represented the majority of the voters, and thereby to secure positions for the poor in the leadership of both the church and the village. Their careful organization resulted in some successes at the elections, but the movement soon waned, for the teamless farmers elected as leaders were unable to bring about any changes in the village administration, which by that time was strictly regulated by government ordinances and injunctions. In a few village council meetings the "indigenous *gazda*-s" and the teamless farmers engaged in heated debates,

---

[75] One of our impoverished informants recalled the crushing of the revolution as follows: "The Rumanian army came, followed by the Hungarian police. They said: 'Harvest is to be recompensed with a tenth of the crop; the old contract is invalid.' " (The fall of the proletarian dictatorship occurred just at the time of the harvest, before the reapers were able to get the increased share.)

even resorting to blows on one occasion. During this period a few of the Budapest workers who made a practice of reading newspapers voted for the then oppositional Arrow-Cross (National Socialist) Party in the 1938 parliamentary elections. However, World War II brought a number of draft notices as well as increasingly strict control of agriculture, political organization, and the life of the village in general.

THE NATION AND PATRIOTISM

The people of Átány are proud to call themselves Hungarians and feel deeply toward Hungary as their fatherland. The word "fatherland" has both a broad meaning and a specific one. The villagers would explain that "the fatherland is the land where we were born, where we live." For the Átány people, the village and the fields are the "homeland" to which they long to return when they are in strange places. Should they be unable to return alive, they want at least to be buried in the village cemetery. (See Chapter 15.)

The Átány "homeland" is a part of a larger fatherland, Hungary. "If we are out in the *tanya* and we come home, this is also a tiny part of the fatherland." As the land of one's birth and of one's compatriots, the fatherland is distinguished from a "country." József Kakas explained this as follows: "If one feels for the country only, it is all the same to him where he is [i.e., it makes no difference which country he lives in], but there is only one fatherland, where he was born, where he was brought up, to which he constantly longs to return, where he finds everything."

The person who has been taken far from his native soil and lives among strangers especially longs to be at home. Among the Átány people who went to America to find jobs, there were some who could have earned enough money to build their own farms at home if they had kept their American jobs for six months or a year more, but they felt so homesick that they returned to Hungary, leaving everything behind. Those who managed to keep at it repeated over and over again in their letters, "If only we may live to see our return home." When they finally set sail for home, they sent touching letters to their families asking them to pray that "God may help them home across that huge water on this occasion." The soldiers in war captivity also spoke often of their fatherland and longed for home. One Átány peasant interned in a prisoner-of-war camp in Siberia remarked, "Oh how far away is the watering well on the pasture of the *zsellér*." This saying has become a commonly cited expression of homesickness.

The quality of being a Hungarian also involved being a member of the Hungarian nation. In Átány the word *nemzet*, "nation," is used in the traditional local meaning: *nemzetség*, kinship, the circle of blood relatives in the male line. However, it is also used for "nation" in its standard and literary meaning. As a matter of fact, the two meanings are closely related. The Hungarian nation is made up of kinsfolk whose common ancestors, the ancient Hungarians, came on horseback through the eastern passes of the Carpathians and conquered "the fatherland." Being more or less relatives,

Hungarians feel a duty to help each other in a strange country or any other situation where they are faced with aliens. They should stick together, as when the Átány men and the other Hungarian soldiers in the combined army of the Austro-Hungarian monarchy cultivated friendly relations among themselves and endeavored not to disgrace their compatriots and their nation. The same consideration, along with a particular desire to support national industry, led the village magistracy in 1901 to decide to purchase for the community only industrial products "whose Hungarian origin is absolutely unquestionable" and to call on merchants not to sell any other goods.

The villagers feel that various branches and groups of Hungarians participate in a common historical destiny. This attitude is inculcated in the children during their years in the Átány school. They are proud to recall the thousand-year history of their country. In 1896, when the millennium of the Hungarian Conquest was celebrated throughout the country, a memorial grove of long-lived chestnut, linden, and pine trees was planted in the center of Átány, a marble tablet was set in the wall of the town hall, and four Hungarian flags were purchased to be raised on special occasions—one for the town hall, one for the church tower, and two for the school. The Átány magistracy, so unsympathetic and parsimonious regarding appeals of the government on other occasions, contributed to the financial fund of the national celebrations.

In thinking of their nation's history, the Átány peasants have images of times of "ancient glory," periods when the country was strong and flourishing under wise rulers, like King Matthias (Matthias Corvinus, 1458–1490). But what stands out as the main feature of Hungarian history is the long series of hopeless struggles against superior forces. The Hungarian national anthem asks God's blessing for the nation in the following words: "Bring a happy year to the people who have long been lacerated by misfortune." Every Átány schoolchild learns these words by heart. When they sing of "misfortune," they think of the Mongolian invasion, the century-and-a-half struggle with the Turks, and the unsuccessful wars of independence and revolutions for national freedom.

"National liberty," worth fighting for and making sacrifices for, is another of the great concepts instilled in the peasants through the teachings of history. The memory of the 1848–49 freedom rebellion is especially vivid in the minds of the older generation. In the winter of 1848–49, Austrian military units were stationed in the fields of Átány; people still remember that the soldiers even took the grave markers from the cemetery to use as fuel. In the spring of 1849 the first decisive battle between the national army and the Austrians was fought at Kápolna, in the immediate vicinity of Átány. (When József Kakas took tobacco to the state receiving station at Kápolna, he never failed to visit the memorial of the battle.) Kossuth, the political leader of the national movement for liberty, and Petőfi, the freedom fighters' poet, are still the "national heroes" in the eyes of the older people of Átány. Their principles and programs, for which they sacrificed themselves (Petőfi was killed on the battlefield of Segesvár, and Kossuth died in exile), are the ideals of the people to this day.

As mentioned above, "1848" was the slogan which mobilized the people of Átány in support of the parties of the opposition, whereas "1867" referred to those who stood for cooperation with the Austrians on the basis of the constitutional compromise of 1867. March 15, the day of the outbreak of the revolutionary movement of 1848, was a school holiday and a day of celebration. A special service was held in the church, Petőfi's "National Song" was recited in the market place, and a banquet of the Reading Circle finished the day. The other national festival was held on October 6, a day of mourning commemorating the military leaders of the freedom revolt, who were executed on October 6, 1849.

The people of Átány more or less connect the Hungarian tricolor with the fight for freedom and the figure of Kossuth too. "It was Kossuth who unfurled the Hungarian flag in order to bring liberty to the Hungarians and to end the oppression of the peasants." The flag is the symbol of the nation. One of our informants said: "The three colors have an inspiring effect; if one sees them he often raises his hat, like a good Catholic in front of the Cross."

Several families have kept "Kossuth banknotes," paper money issued by the revolutionary government, as national relics of the fight for liberty, though these were supposed to have been handed over to the authorities according to an ordinance issued after the fall of the national cause. In the Átány houses the majority of the engravings and oleographs purchased at the fairs depict Petőfi, Kossuth, the independent Hungarian government of 1848, the martyr generals executed at Arad, the dying Petőfi, and Kossuth bidding farewell to his country at the frontier. The same attitude is reflected by the portraits of Rákóczi, of the galley-slave pastors (condemned to this labor by the Austrian government in the period of the Counter Reformation), and of the princes of Transylvania, who fought for both religious and national freedom.

The national characteristics of the Hungarians are more evident to the villagers when they are compared to strangers. The two World Wars and their attendant war captivities presented many occasions for such comparisons; men from Átány went to Serbia and Italy as well as to the Transcaucasian regions, and they lived among Poles and Czechs. They also had numerous opportunities to compare themselves with the other nationalities included within the Hungarian borders. The horse dealers, who traveled to the fairs, saw the Slovakian and German towns of the southeastern plain and met Rumanian peasants, while Slovakian peddlers came to the village from the north. The villagers find that the Hungarians stand out as superior to those of other nations, just as Átány stands out as superior to the neighboring villages. The consensus in the village is that the Hungarians are firm, tenacious, and long enduring in work, privation, and war, and that they are hospitable. The Rumanians, by comparison, are said "to have walked like old men" instead of having a stately gait and straight backs, a trait supposedly due to the fact that during this period (1900–1910) they wore a sort of moccasin instead of the hard top boots of the Hungarians. The Slovaks of the Great Plain were reproached for refusing accommodation to Átány travelers, in spite of the fact that they were well-to-do *gazda*-s. In the immediate neighborhood of the village the only non-Hungarians were the gypsies, whom the Átány people regarded (as mentioned above) as "having been created different." On the other hand, they are ready to admit that "the ancestral blood which flows in Hungarian veins has also brought the desire to fight and the spirit of strife, so that the Hungarians could not stick together with their own people as those of other nations did."

EPILOGUE: THE "PROPER PEASANTS" OF ÁTÁNY

Seen from the airplane that flies regularly from Budapest to Miskolc, Átány is one of the many villages which form a settlement network made up of units of about the same size. In the study of the history of the Hungarian peasantry, it is one of several thousand similar local units in which essentially the same processes have existed and continue to exist, with more or less important differences of emphasis and pace. In the general study of peasant life, Átány fits into the broad area of "Central Europe beyond the Alps," where the peasants have combined agriculture (mostly cereals) and stock raising for many centuries, where they formerly lived in the bondage of serfdom, and where they have been attempting for several generations to adapt their rural traditions to the conditions of increasingly industrialized national economies and urbanized societies.

For the traveler who comes to the village by road, however, the church tower and the rooftops of Átány present a unique silhouette. Inside the village one notices the uniform whiteness of the whitewashed houses, the dark attire of the older women, the words spoken in a particular dialect, and the antiquated forms of address. The villagers themselves and the people of the neighboring parishes know that Átány has retained the ancient traditions of peasant life more than the other communities of the region. The manager of the Átány dairy, a local peasant who is widely read and who has had some experience in town, told us, "I have read that China encircled itself with a stone wall in order to preserve its own customs. This is the analogy of Átány for me; I only wonder, what is the wall which has preserved the old essence of Átány."

Why are the society and the culture of Átány more homogeneous and integrated than the other villages in the vicinity? This study has suggested numerous factors. Its past was more continuous, and the serfdom of the eighteenth and the nineteenth centuries was less oppressive and restrictive than in most Hungarian villages. The process of polarization which divided the "people of the soil," who had formerly all enjoyed a common legal status and performed similar services, into a class of wealthy independent gazda-s and a class of wage earners was less extreme in Átány than in the other villages. Átány was regarded as a well-to-do village in the neighborhood since it contained fewer "very poor" and also fewer "very rich" people than the surrounding communities. The number of inhabitants is astonishingly stable, having remained almost unchanged over the past hundred years, and the indices of its population trends also show a more even development than is usual in the region. Its peasant population has not been mixed with many people of different occupations. One church stands in the center of the parish; the community is not divided by religious antagonism, unlike the numerous Hungarian villages "with two churches." Furthermore, their Calvinist religion has had a special unifying power and symbolic significance in the predominantly Catholic vicinity. The network of human relations, comprising all the various connections of kinship, neighborhood, friendship, and economic cooperation, is closer and stronger in Átány than in most Hungarian peasant villages. Perhaps it has been this strong, dense network of relations which has acted as a "wall," preserving the uniformity and continuity of Átány's particular local culture. (Naturally this characterization is a relative one, comparing the village in transformation to the constantly changing rural life of the region.)

The strong and homogeneous tradition of the village is represented by such people as Ferenc Orbán, József Kakas, Károly Bedécs, Gábor Varga, János Boross, and Samu Kiss, to mention a few names familiar to the reader. In speaking of them, Károly Bedécs often began his sentences with the phrase, "We proper peasants"; for example, "We proper peasants knew about the horse; we raised the good colts. One could recognize a genuine born peasant by his bearing when driving through the village—by the way he held the whip in his hand." Thus the "proper peasant" is not just a villager who farms, since the soil may be tilled in several ways, and the same is true for driving a horse. The "proper peasant" of Átány can only be a man who drives his horse, holds the whip, and flicks it in a certain manner, so that his horses raise their heads proudly and step delicately. (When the authors tried to record the traditional rules for handling a whip, they took up about twenty pages.) Thus, for the proper peasants, agriculture and work were an art, beyond the practical utility and profit involved. Following the rules of this "art" gave one security and pride and gained him the esteem of the community.

A proper peasant could only be a man who "was born into it," who was brought up in this way of life as a child, playing hide-and-seek under the belly of the horse at the age of four or five and harnessing the team at the age of eight, as Ferenc Orbán did. The land he cultivated was inherited from his ancestors; to keep and work it with care and responsibility was his moral duty to his precursors and successors, and also to the fatherland and God, since the end product of his labors was bread, the basic subsistence food and the material of the Lord's Supper.

In addition to the land and the ancestral house lot, a proper peasant inherits a populous crowd of kinsmen from his ancestors, and also the ties of the *koma* and *nász* relationships, which he multiplies and extends by forming new ties. Thus he not only lives in a village where everyone knows and greets each other, but he also has personal connections with a large proportion of the population.

The Átány *gazda*-s know that their life and that of the community may be influenced by forces beyond their control. The harvest is "in the palm of God's hand." The unpredictable climate of the Hungarian basin may bring frost or drought to the young crops, or floods may cover their fields. But their life is also influenced by national and world events. They have seen more than one foreign army march through their fields and known that the state would extort new taxes from them and drag their sons away as recruits even if they refused to give either. But in spite of being prey to these external forces, these peasants refer to their fields and houses as "castles" and feel sorry for the inhabitants of the towns, who have to obey orders and cannot eat bread made out of wheat grown in their own fields. When, with deep affection, the authors remember their faces, they see marks of assurance and dignity in them. As heads of households, they supported their families, who in turn awaited their orders as to the allotment of work and food. They were members of the village, acting with confidence in public affairs according to their own opinions and beliefs. They had the self-assurance of people who know the difference between good and evil and the rules of behavior toward other people.

Our study deals with the world of these "proper" or "born" peasants.

This world has by no means existed without changes. It suffices to recall the system of the ownership and the use of land. Since the eighteenth century the distribution of the fields and the rules governing their cultivation have undergone changes in the lifetime of almost every generation. The implements in the hands of men, the kinds of seed sown into the soil, and the breeds of animals have changed too. There has also been a great transformation in the country surrounding Átány. Industrialization, urbanization, and widely ramifying public administration have influenced the life of the community. Many people have left the village; some migrated to the towns, while others embarked on a half-rural, half-urban way of life, professing the Átány ideals, but only half-heartedly. But there is no doubt that the center of society was occupied by the "proper peasants," who set the tone of Átány life.

Our field work was begun at a relatively fortunate time. By February, 1951, the damages from World War II were more or less repaired and the peasant farms were profitable. Both the exteriors and the interiors of the snow-covered rural houses followed "the Átány custom," as did the attire of the men and women. Women and girls were spinning and weaving in the houses. The males gathered in the stables to talk. At sunset one could observe the men returning to their homes from the distant *kert*-s, carrying bundles of straw for fuel on their backs. On Sundays the church was crowded, and the villagers sang the psalms with visible satisfaction. National leadership was in the hands of the Hungarian Workers' Party, a Communist government which aimed to reorganize the country according to socialist principles. However, at the level of the local villages, the measures had not affected the majority of the populace. Only a few major *gazda*-s and the church had to hand over their land to the state. The school had been nationalized and the system of village administration had been altered.

In several regions of Europe the rural way of life is but a damaged and diluted vestige of former times; in other regions the peasants themselves feel that it is a burden which has been forced on them and almost suffocates them. Unlike these groups, our Átány informants professed themselves peasants with pleasure and pride. The impending possibility of a change caused them to adhere to the old manner of life of "proper peasants" more self-consciously. When we wrote this study more than ten years later, we endeavored to describe the society of these proud and "proper" people.

It is not the aim of this study to take a position in the international discussion of whether peasant societies are characterized by tension or by harmony. It is the portrait of a Hungarian village during the moments preceding fundamental change, when the institutions were still living and working, but when they were no longer taken for granted as in former times. It was a time when the people were especially conscious of their traditional way of life and sometimes saw it in the rose-colored light of their attachment.

Today this portrait is no longer typical of Átány; it has become a historical document. Events followed each other rapidly. With the compulsory delivery of agricultural products to the state, increased year by year, all peasant economies have in effect been subjected to a strict state supervision. The program of the government to annihilate the social stratum of well-to-do *gazda*-s as such has also been realized at Átány; their houses were confiscated, and several were imprisoned. In 1952–1953 the situation was made worse by an especially poor harvest, so that even the basic subsistence of men and animals became irregular.[1]

In the autumn of 1951 the first cooperative farms were founded; at that time they were primarily associations for the common execution of certain specified tasks. The membership of the cooperative farms varied widely during the following years, owing to changes in the policy of the government and alterations of the burdens weighing on "private" farms, but it never included more than a small fraction of the population. The general collectivization of the Hungarian peasantry was begun in 1958; Átány's turn came in February, 1959. All the fields were put under the management of the cooperative farms, except for 120 *hold*-s (160 acres), which remained private property.[2]

The cooperative farms practice a mixed agriculture similar to that of the peasants; they still raise grain and breed animals. However, plowing is done with tractors, as is much of the harvest in dry years, when combines are able to work in the fields. There are hardly any horses in the village now. The cooperatives pay some rent to the old owners in proportion to their former acreage, but the main income of the members is the share[3] which they receive on the basis of the work they actually perform, calculated in workday units and paid in kind and in cash. The cooperative reallots about one

---

[1] Szakál, 1964.

[2] This land is owned by 35 families. The distribution of Átány land in 1964 was as follows: the two cooperative farms owned 3,934 and 2,304 *hold*-s respectively, the state farm covered an area of 1,468 *hold*-s, and the remaining territory either belonged to private owners or was exempted from land tax.

[3] The workday unit is the basis for calculating the amount of work performed on the cooperative farm, being equivalent to the theoretical work output of one day. The various tasks are categorized and the number of workday units recorded in the members' labor books depends on these categories as well as their actual performance. As soon as the wheat and maize are harvested, they get an advance share of these products according to the number of workday units they have earned up to that time. An advance cash payment is also given, but the members find the amount rather small. Final accounts

hold of land to each member family. The income derived from intensive cultivation of this plot and from livestock raising in private stables nearly equals the income received directly from the cooperative.[4]

Since the beginning of the 1950s the extended families have dissolved rapidly, owing to the burden of progressive taxation and compulsory delivery of agricultural products to the state. Most of these "dissolutions" were purely formal, a smaller number were actual. The traditional organization of labor by families has become extinct in the cooperatives; the members of a family are assigned to different brigades and tasks, according to their age and sex. More and more of the young people turn to industry for employment and move to the towns permanently.[5] The average age of the cooperative membership is 57 years.[6]

The weight of recent events has produced rapid modernization and urbanization of the Átány peasantry. Young persons from the village are now able to adjust easily to an urban environment. Modernization and urbanization have produced many notable benefits for the villagers in the form of better health standards, schooling, ease of communication, and manufactured goods. However, the transition has been possible only at the expense of the traditional way of life.

The goals which motivated the efforts of the Átány people in the old days—the acquisition of land and fine animals and the founding of a self-sufficient farm for one's successors—have lost their meaning. Not only in the material sphere, but also in other respects, the old homogeneous order has disappeared. New houses are built, no longer in the "Átány way," but following allegedly urban models, and often replacing old buildings in good condition and suitable for living in. Mass-produced furniture, radios, and sometimes television sets are seen in the living rooms. In 1958 a cultural center and a new school building were constructed, and eight years of schooling are now obligatory. The members of the cooperative farms are entitled to medical treatment at reduced rates, and many of them take advantage of it. Babies are born in the maternity center at Heves, but the birth rate is extremely low. The old restrictions on marriage and the choice of spouse are gone; young men who work in the towns often do not look for a Calvinist wife, and the young woman is no longer placed under the guidance of her mother-in-law in order to learn the Átány customs.

---

are settled in January or February of the following year; then the value of one workday unit is defined and the payments are completed according to the annual balance.

[4] The house lots of the cooperative peasants also play a significant role in the economic life of the country. In 1961, 26 per cent of the gross agricultural production and 38 per cent of the livestock production were derived from the household plots. In the cooperative farms common farming was responsible for 61.9 per cent of the total production, family plots for 38.1 per cent. In 1960 the Central Statistical Office studied the households of 26,000 cooperative families and discovered that the household plots provided 50.6 per cent of the income of the members of the cooperative farms (Zsarnóczai, 1964: 99).

[5] From 1949 to 1964 about one and a half million of the ten million Hungarians gave up agriculture and looked for industrial or commercial jobs. In 1964 the Átány village council lists contained the names of 313 men who were permanently employed far from the community but whose families lived in Átány (cf. Zsarnóczai, 1964; Lettrich, 1965).

[6] On January 1, 1964, the Átány population totaled 2,407. Among these, 1,588 persons were members of the two cooperatives. However, only 597 of them worked regularly on the farms (i.e., performed at least eighty workday units per year).

The increased demands on people's time and the altered daily schedule leave hardly any chance to cultivate good relations with kinsmen, baptismal *koma*-s, or members of one's age group. The kin group assembles only for the large family ceremonies, the weddings and funerals. Church life is likewise restricted to special holidays; on these days the church is full, but hardly anyone attends the Sunday services.

The young people of Átány dream of learning a craft, of becoming industrial workers, or even "learned men," so as to receive weekly or monthly wages and retirement pay in their old age. The older people try to find a place in the changing Átány world; they have become uncertain, lacking the support of the traditional order. They get their wheat allowance from the cooperative farm, and most of them bake their bread at home, but this wheat is not the same as the wheat they used to grow themselves in the old days. As a former *gazda* put it, "We don't know when it was sown, or the time when it was reaped; the wheat is just brought. One feels there is no summer anymore. Formerly we saw that people were harvesting, meals were being carried out to the fields for the reapers, the crop was gathered in, carts went and returned, stacks were piled in every yard. Now everything is all alike. It seems as if we were not in the same world where we used to live."

APPENDIX A

BIOGRAPHICAL DATA ON SOME ÁTÁNY INFORMANTS AND THEIR FAMILIES

Károly Bedécs (see Plate 26). Of our principal informants, Károly Bedécs is the only one of noble origin. (When in 1959 he resigned his office as member of the church council and left the pew reserved for them, he returned to the pew of the nobles, which was held by his ancestors. His wife has also occupied a seat in the nobles' pew ever since she was led into church as Mrs. Bedécs.) He was born in 1896. His father owned twelve *hold*-s of land (17.04 acres) and also had, besides Károly, two daughters. In 1910, after he had finished school, his father took him to the stable and set him to work in the fields and with the livestock. As he used to say, he was linked to the village for his whole life through the tilling of its soil; he was unable to go on the errands of a horse dealer or to find a job in town. Being an only son, he could not spend much time away from the farm in the village either, as he had to watch his father's horses in the stable.

During World War I he was called up for the first time for front-line service; he was discharged at the end of the war, in 1918. In 1919 he married Julianna Fazekas and had two sons and a daughter by her. In 1920 he spent another half-year in the military service. In the meantime his father died, leaving their small plot to him, albeit encumbered by debt. The inheritance was divided in 1927. Although his father had bequeathed all the land to Károly, overlooking the sisters, Károly followed the spirit of more recent local practice and retained only half of the plot, letting his sisters have the other half. His father's house and the *kert* with its equipment fell to his share. He increased the income of his small holding by profitable use of the land of other peasants too, cultivating it on the half-and-half system. In 1938 further parcelization enabled him to acquire an additional five *hold*-s (7.10 acres) of land with a state subsidy.

In 1932 his wife died, after which his household was run by his mother, who lived with him. In 1937 he married for the second time; his second wife was Erzsébet Együd, widowed but recently and having a ten-year-old daughter by her first marriage. Another daughter was born from the second marriage.

In 1939, K. B. was called up for military duty again; he served for a half-year once in 1940 and again in 1941, and for an entire year in 1945.

In 1948 he built a new house on his ancient *kert*, where his stable was situated. He fulfilled a childhood desire thereby, for he found the walks between house and *kert* several times a day, mostly laden with a burden, very bothersome throughout his life.

In the meantime his children grew up. His eldest son died. When the second son married, Károly thought of their staying and working together as a joint enterprise. But it proved impossible, and before the year was out, his son parted from him, principally because of the changed conditions in family farming after World War II. (As a matter of fact, the son returned in 1965 and built a separate house on his father's plot.) K. B. has given his daughter and his stepdaughter in marriage; they moved into the homes of their parents-in-law as *meny*-s. His youngest daughter, born of his second marriage, celebrated her wedding in 1960; she also moved to the house of her father-in-law.

In 1959, K. B. joined the cooperative farm, where he has performed manual and foot work ever since.

Following family tradition, K. B. played a leading role in the life of the community. From 1927 until his voluntary resignation at the end of World War II, he was a member of the village council and later a member of the body of local representatives. On and off again through the years he was a treasurer of the Great or the Small Pasture Associations. He was elected to the church council in 1947, remaining a member for twelve years, after which he resigned his office voluntarily.

Erzsébet Együd, the wife of Károly Bedécs (see Plate 31), was born in 1909, the only child of Sándor Együd, a poor man owning but a single *massza*. Although Sándor Együd married the daughter of a well-to-do *gazda*, he worked as a teamless farmer throughout his life. Erzsébet Együd was spared by her parents and was not sent to do day labor. She busied herself in the household, weaving and spinning, tending the geese, and preparing her trousseau. In 1926 her parents forced her to marry the wealthy *gazda* János Oláh, by whom she had a single child. János Oláh was a sick man; he died after eleven years of marriage. In 1937, E. E. became the second wife of Károly Bedécs. She is an excellent housewife; she helped to disencumber the poor, indebted farm belonging to her husband; she reared five children in harmony (her daughter from János Oláh, the three children of Károly Bedécs by his first marriage, and their own child). She gave the girls into respectable marriages, helped the son to found his own farm, and has bound them all together to this day: all children return to the paternal house with their respective spouses and children every Sunday afternoon (as well as other holidays), and E. E. treats them all to an abundant meal. When her husband became a member of the cooperative farm, E. E. continued to work wholly in their household plot; she is not a member of a brigade.

János Boross (see Plate 21) was born in 1881, the second of his parents' two children. (The first died in his early years.) His father owned twelve *hold*-s (17.04 acres) of land. He went to school for four years. Then, when he was twelve years old, his father made him a swath-layer at the side of their harvester; this was earlier than was usual in *gazda* houses to send a son to work. But J. B. was a strong boy. He played a lot of tricks with a band of his age-mates, pilfering fruit and the like. A suit of clothes was purchased for him as his first "salary," and this served as an incentive for further work. Both he and his parents took pride in the fact that as a boy of twelve János earned the price of a suit of clothes.

In the following year the harvester asked J. B. to be his stripper. When he saw that the boy wanted to try reaping, he presented János with a scythe. The boy worked for this scythe all that summer.

In this year his mother died and his father remarried. Although his stepmother treated him well, his maternal uncle interfered in János's plans several times. Thus in the first winter when he was left without a mother, the uncle made him hire out to tobacco growers for five weeks. But he earned enough by bundling so that another suit of clothes could be bought for him.

He was called before the recruiting commission when he was twenty-one years old. He served for only two months; in the meantime, his father's hand became crippled, and J. B. was exempted as the only wage earner of the family. Henceforth the work of the farm weighed chiefly on his shoulders. In 1902 he married Erzsébet Kádár, increasing their property by three *hold*-s (4.26 acres). They had three children: two sons and a daughter. In 1914 he joined up and served for four years on the battle fields of World War I.

Until the death of his father in 1922, the two farmed together. János gave his daughter in marriage in 1920. His elder son died in 1927; the surviving younger son brought his wife to the house in 1936. They live working together to the present time. His property increased by seven *hold*-s (9.94 acres) through inheritance in 1932 from a childless relative on the mother's side. His wife died in 1956, and he had a serious stroke himself in 1950. From that time forth, the most he does is look after the animals in the stable.

J. B., a leader of a bachelor band in his youth, served the community for 21 years as a middle-aged man. In 1903 he was elected *hadnagy* and was the last person to fill this post, since it was abolished in 1912. After 1904 he was a substitute member of the body of village representatives. For three years he served as a parish councillor, and then for nine years as a public tutor. He was a member of the church council for eleven years; he resigned this office voluntarily. In the mid-1930s he was the president of the Great Pasture Association for four years.

Sándor Czákó was born in 1900 on a manorial *tanya* close to Átány, the eighth child of a family of tobacco growers. Until his sixth year he lived in the *tanya*, helping his parents in watching the swine. Then his father sent him to his uncle Mihály Czákó in the village in order to attend the Átány school. He spent only the summer holidays with his parents, doing the work of tobacco growers on various manorial farms. In the meantime he studied in the Roman Catholic school at Erdőtelek for a year, something an Átány man would never do. (The people of the *tanya* are frowned upon, not only because of their ignorance and mean education, but also for sending their children to the schools of other faiths.)

In 1910 his father inherited a house in Átány. The whole family left the *tanya* and settled in the village with the express intention "to have a local mating," i.e., that their children should marry Átány children instead of those of the hired men on the estates. From then on the members of the family still worked as day laborers and sharecroppers on various estates, but they went out to work from their home in the village.

When he was seventeen years old, he was summoned before the recruiting commission, but they ruled the underdeveloped and ill-fed boy as being unfit. In 1922 he was called up again and this time performed auxiliary service.

He is a man who is eager to learn and is well-read. He asserts that he read all the books bequeathed by Szatmáry. Among our informants, he clearly was the best-read, although perhaps at the expense of working as hard as the others.

He married in 1923, bringing his wife to his father's house. He constructed a house of his own with a state loan in 1925, on a household plot allotted in the course of the agrarian reforms after World War I. However, he was unable to pay off his debts and so sold the recently built house. He settled in again with his father and put the house into good repair, for which his father made him the proprietor of half of the house. He acquired the other half from his brothers by undertaking to care for their parents and to bury them decently.

His single daughter was born in 1927.

He actually spent most of his time in Budapest gardening, living the life of an Átány teamless farmer. He told us that he always asked for a book if an employer wished to tip him.

In 1945 he was a member of the commission of land claims, assisting in the process of dividing the estates of the Átány landlords. On this occasion he received four *hold*-s (5.68 acres) of land and began independent farming. In 1949 his daughter was married and the *vő* settled in the house of S. Cz. But his new son-in-law spent more and more time working in town and finally left the village with his family in the early 1960s.

In 1951, S. Cz. joined the first farmers' cooperative group of the village, acting first as its president and later as its treasurer for several terms.

József Kakas (see Plate 29) (host to Tamás Hofer) was born in 1906, the only son of a wealthy and esteemed *gazda* family. (For further details about the family, see Chapter 13, "The Careers of Three Families.") During the time of our field work he was the only one of our main informants who still had a separate house and *kert*.

He spent all his life farming together with his father. He attended school for six years and was an outstanding student (and a good singer). In World War I his father served with the military, leaving the chores of the farm to him, then a boy of hardly ten years, and to his mother and his aged grandfather. He suffered hernia through overexertion and was thus later classified as unsuitable for military service. The family cultivated its 24 *hold*-s (34.08 acres) of land with the help of only a few harvesters and did not engage hired men. They reared thoroughbred horses.

In 1915 his parents purchased one of the former houses of their ancestors and settled into it. It was to this dwelling that J. K. brought his wife Zsófi Rózsa in 1927. In 1932 they exchanged their *kert* for another, since the earlier one proved to be too small, and built a new stable on it in 1941.

Their only daughter Katica was born in 1932. Katica Kakas was "a *gazda* daughter" who was given the best of what they could afford and spared from hard work. She attended the higher elementary school at Heves and was employed by the post office there for a year after school. In 1956 she married a teacher of the local school, a boy from a peasant background in Átány. She moved to her husband's house, which was provided for his services.

The elder József Kakas died in 1958. His widow continued in the role of a *gazdasszony* for a few years. In the early 1960s, however, her age began to tell and she surrendered these duties to her *meny*. At present she works with Zsófi, helping her and obeying her orders.

In 1959, József Kakas had to join the cooperative farm, like many others. Since that time he has worked in one of the collective's barns, tending cows.

József realized an old wish in 1961 when he sold his house in the village and constructed a fashionable modern-style dwelling in the *kert*, uniting the house and the stable on the same plot.

He never longed for a role in public life, following the example of his predecessors even in this respect. As he relates, he attended the assembly of a Pasture Association for the first time and was thereupon elected controller. He carried out his tasks faithfully, but he eagerly awaited the end of his term. In 1950 he was elected presbyter; he was glad to have this office and he holds it yet.

Zsófi Rózsa, the wife of József Kakas (see Plate 35), was born in 1909, the first daughter of a *gazda* who owned eighteen *hold*-s (25.56 acres). She is a descendant of the Rózsa family, which still lived as a large extended family at the turn of the century (see Chapter 5, "The Forms of the Family and Its Division of Labor"). She is the daughter of that Sámuel Rózsa who worked for a long time under his elder brother Mihály "as a real hired man."

She went to school for four years. She was not obliged to work in the fields, rather busying herself in the household, spinning and weaving. In 1927 she moved to the house of the Kakas family as a *meny*.

In the early 1960s she gradually took over the duties of *gazdasszony* from her mother-in-law.

She does not work on the cooperative farm; besides household tasks, she busies herself in the family garden and household plot.

Samu Kiss (see Plate 27) was born in 1898, the son of a teamless farmer (his father owned six *hold*-s [8.52 acres] of land). We have dealt with his ancestors in detail (see Chapter 13, "The Careers of Three Families"). He had one sister, Zsuzsanna Kiss, who became the wife of Ferenc Orbán. He did not finish school since he was sent to do day labor on the nearby estates. As a bachelor, he earned his bread as a harvester and day laborer. In 1914 he joined a regiment and fought in various engagements of World War I, spending one and a half years as a prisoner-of-war. He was discharged at the end of the war. In 1919 he married the well-to-do Maris Sárándi, a distant relative, and settled as a *vő* on the well-equipped farm of his wife's family. They had three children, the youngest of which died in 1935.

His wife inherited nine *hold*-s (12.76 acres) of land; S. K. continued working this plot. To supplement his income, he worked as a horse dealer. His father died in 1946, bequeathing him three *hold*-s (4.26 acres). He built a new stable in 1936 and a new house in 1940.

S. K. gave his daughter Eszter into marriage in 1939. Since her husband was called up after only a few months of married life (he returned after front-line service and captivity only in 1950), the son of the young couple, born in his absence, was reared by the grandparents.

János, his son, married Rebeka Balog in 1945; they stayed with the parents, living and working together until their partition of the land in 1964.

In 1959, S. K. became a member of the cooperative farm. He retired in 1965, but on occasion he still performs various light tasks for the group.

In 1946 he was elected parish councillor and was a member of the local board until 1948. During the same time he was elected to the church council, where he remained a member until 1959.

Maris Sárándi, the wife of Samu Kiss, was born in 1898, the daughter of a *gazda* who owned sixteen *hold*-s (22.72 acres) and employed a hired man. She had one brother. Attending school for four years, she learned the Golden Alphabet by heart, together with the stories from the Bible and their rhymed morals; she was our best informant on the subject of the golden rules of behavior.

Her father died in 1914 and her brother was called up for military duty soon thereafter. So she had to learn the men's work in the fields and with the animals and continued to perform it until 1959. She married Samu Kiss in 1919. Their family was troubled by frequent illness, resulting in appreciable expenditure for medical care, as well as calamities (the death of animals). Their son broke his arm as a child and the bones did not knit well so that he could not really perform farm work; he became a mason. Their growing daughter could not help in farming either; because the bad economic situation of the family could not permit accumulation of the expensive trousseau clothes necessary to make her marriage prospects good, they allowed her to work for wages and to earn for her clothing. So wife helped husband in all his work, and her growing children did not ease her burden at all. Whenever her husband went on his frequent errands trading horses, she was obliged to tend the livestock in the stable for days by herself. As she characterizes her role: "I used to be a hired man all the time," alluding to the man's work she had to perform besides the household duties.

In marrying, she exchanged wealth for want and passed from a comfortable girlhood to a woman's life full of hard labor. Nevertheless, even the additional burden of farming could not induce her to drop the fine traditions of managing a home learned in the wealthy house of her parents. Sometimes she had to cook or tidy up until the late hours, but she always kept order.

János Madarász, the son of a hired man, was born in 1887 at Kápolna on one of the manors of an estate owned by the Archbishopric of Eger. His ancestors were herdsmen, which is to say they were poor people (see Chapter 13, "The Careers of Three Families"). The parents had nine children, of whom five lived to maturity. J. M. did not go to school. He had a weak physique, so he was not sent to work until he was eleven or twelve years old: he helped in driving the fattened sheep out and back, watching the piglets, and carrying meals to the workers in the fields. Later he became a hired man for half, later for three-quarters, of the adult wage. His father changed the place of his service repeatedly in order to get nearer to the village; in 1901 he finally moved into Átány and became a hired man there (see Chapter 13, "The Rise and Decline of Individuals and Families"). It was then that J. M. began to learn how to write, taught by an aged field guard; later he completed his knowledge of writing, reading, and arithmetic in an evening class started for the illiterate in the village.

At first he worked as a farm hand with Átány *gazda*-s. In 1908 he came to blows with his drunken and tempestuous *gazda*, injuring him severely, and was sentenced to prison. After he had served his term, he no longer wanted to be a hired man any more; instead he worked in Budapest gardening establishments and had a job as a house porter for a while. When he was twenty-four years old, he married the daughter of an Átány tobacco grower. For two years he worked with his father-in-law as a gardener on the manorial farm. But he was unhappy with the treatment he received here too, so he broke his contract before the appointed time and voluntarily joined the colors in World War I in order to avoid the interference of authorities. He fought in the front line and spent three years as a prisoner of war. He did not return home until 1918. His marriage resulted in three children; his wife died in 1938.

Later he married again and succeeded in buying a house in the village. He lived the life of a teamless farmer, taking on diverse occupations: at various times he was a sharecropper, a day laborer, a roofer, and a carpenter. As a result of the agrarian reform after World War I, he was allotted one *hold* of land. During World War II his second wife died, and he married a third one from Tiszanána.

The agrarian reform which followed World War II provided him with seven *hold*-s (9.94 acres) of land; in his old age he tried to cultivate his plot as an independent *gazda*. In 1959 he joined the cooperative farm, where he works as a carpenter and as a manual laborer.

Ferenc Orbán (see Plate 30) (the host of Edit Fél) was born in 1896. His father was a *gazda* who owned twenty *hold*-s (28.40 acres) of land and employed a farm hand. There were two sons and three daughters in the family. When F. O. finished the fourth grade in school, he became "a real farm hand" on their own plot, as he says himself (see Chapter 6, "Children," "Boys"). His father gradually entrusted him with work in the fields and the use of the horse too. In 1915 he escaped the strong hand of his father by volunteering for the army, in which he served until 1919. In the meantime he spent one and a half years as a prisoner of war in Russia. In 1917 his father died. Since his elder brother was also serving in the army, the land was farmed by the women who were left at home. His brother married at the end of the war, and, being the older son, left the house with his wife. (He worked as a gardener on an estate.) F. O. and his mother worked the farm together. In 1922, F. O. married a young widow, Zsuzsanna Kiss, who had an eighteen-month-old daughter from her first husband. In 1923 they had a son, but he died when he was only a few months old.

The two sisters of F. O. married men from Tiszanána, a more urban and modern village than Átány, where the practice of giving daughters a share of the paternal inheritance equal to that of the sons had been in existence for decades. At the insistence of these two sisters, the family property was partitioned in 1924; this was the first case in Átány where sons and daughters received equal shares of the inheritance. As a consequence of the partition, F. O. became a poor man with neither a house nor land enough to support himself. However, he succeeded in acquiring a house, a stable, and a horse by diligence and hard work (see Chapter 13, "The Order of Succession"), starting in the spring of 1929 to work as a carter. Besides his own plot, he cultivated eight to fifteen *hold*-s (8.52 to 11.36 acres) of land on the half-and-half system. He gave his stepdaughter, Zsuzsi Kálósi (see Plate 34), in marriage to István Gulyás in 1938. The young woman moved to the house of her husband's parents. However, she returned in 1942, since István Gulyás was called up in the course of World War II and he was soon reported missing. The young widow had a small daughter, who was raised as the granddaughter of F. O. in his house. The wife of István Gulyás inherited six *hold*-s (8.52 acres) of land from various relatives, which was henceforth farmed in common.

In 1947, F. O. was elected a member of the church council and was re-elected several times; he holds this office to the present day.

In 1956 he gave his granddaughter, Juliska Gulyás, in marriage; the young woman moved into the house of her husband as a *meny*.

In 1959, F. O. had to join the cooperative farm too, where he did manual work. In 1966 he was pensioned off, but he still performs work in the fields or as a driver almost daily.

Zsuzsanna Kiss, the wife of Ferenc Orbán, was born in 1905 (information about her parents is given in connection with the biography of Samu Kiss). Before she was six years old she was sent to be a nursemaid for the family of a tobacco grower on a nearby estate. (For certain tasks, the tobacco grower cannot dispense with the labor of his wife. If they have a small child or children, they engage a nursemaid for four to six weeks during this period of work.) When she was ten years old, Zsuzsanna Kiss began to perform easy day labor on the estates; when she grew stronger, she became a swath-layer. In 1919 she married István Kálósi and moved to his house, where she worked under the direction of her mother-in-law. They had one daughter. A little over a year later her husband died. The young widow remained with her daughter in the house of her mother-in-law until she became engaged to Ferenc Orbán, when she returned to her parents' house and was given in marriage by them for the second time. She moved in with her second mother-in-law, but when she became pregnant she was in poor health, so she returned to her own mother. There she gave birth to a son, who died a few months later. For a short time she lived with her mother-in-law again, and then after the partition of the Orbán inheritance she and her husband and daughter returned to her own parents' house. She worked there while her husband earned money by taking jobs in Budapest. She was a good *gazdasszony*, able to make ends meet. She saved carefully and purchased useful objects that would be necessary when they started a home of their own, so that by 1929, when Ferenc Orbán returned to the village, she was able to fully equip their house (built in 1926). She rarely did work in the fields, contenting herself with the cultivation of their own plot. She worked in the house and brought up her daughter, who was given in marriage in 1938. Her parents died in 1946, leaving three *hold*-s (4.26 acres) of land to the couple.

The household chores and the raising of poultry and pigs continue to be her jobs to this day.

Gábor Varga (see Plate 28) was born in 1883. His father owned twelve *hold*-s (17.04 acres) of land and had three other children. After going to school for four years, G. V. worked with his father on their farm. He performed his military duty in the Austro-Hungarian army in Vienna and Graz and became a non-commissioned officer. In 1907, after the completion of his service, he married Eszter Sebők, by whom he had two sons. Since his father was still living, he could not have his share of the inheritance, but his father-in-law gave him six *hold*-s (8.52 acres) of land, heavily mortgaged, which he was sure to lose. It was on this plot that he started farming after his marriage. He also took land in *métayage*. He had not yet managed to pay off the mortgage before he was called up in World War I. He fought all through the war and spent a year in Russian captivity. In the meantime both his father and wife died; at the end of the war he found their property laden with debt and in desolate condition. He had to start all over again. As a supplementary income, he started to work as a horse dealer.

In 1920 he married again, Eszter Ötvös, a widow who already had a daughter, Lidi Kaja;
the child was brought up in the house of G. V. from that time on. In 1921 the couple had
a son, László. Soon G. V. purchased a *kert* (in a more suitable place than the one he had
inherited) and constructed a stable in it. In 1935 he received five *hold*-s (7.10 acres) of land
from a distribution with state subsidy.

One of the sons of the first marriage died a violent death in 1927; the other got married
in 1929. Being the elder son, he left the Varga house and became a *vő* in that of his in-laws.

In 1940, G. V. constructed a new house next to his stable, thus uniting house and *kert* on
the same holding. His wife died the following year. His youngest son was married in 1942
and brought his wife, Zsófi Mérten, to the house. They lived and farmed together till the
death of G. V. in 1961.

Being a man of much experience and good understanding of world affairs, G. V. played
an active role in the life of the village: in 1928 he was elected village treasurer (skipping the
lower grades), a post which he held for nine years. Then, until 1947, the date of his voluntary
resignation, he was a member of the body of representatives. He served as a treasurer of the
Great Pasture Association for several years and as a member of the church council for twelve
years.

APPENDIX B

A DESCRIPTION OF ÁTÁNY PLACED IN THE FOUNDATION OF THE OFFICIAL RESIDENCE OF THE VILLAGE SECRETARY, 1901

(Excerpts from the copy entered on the community journal)

"Dear Brethren, Beloved Friends!

"You who are reading these lines and remembering the past, think of transience and recall to your minds that all of us have come from dust and shall return to dust; nothing can last forever!

"While you are razing this building, we who were alive at the time of its construction will be mouldering in the grave in eternal sleep—and if the existence of a nether world is true, we shall be watching you from above, silently observing your work and pondering over the all-inclusive power of time—that this secretarial residence, built in the year 1901, was unable to last forever; perhaps it has been ground down by the ravages of time, or perhaps the spirit of the age, the requirements of progress and of the era, demand its demolition. Whatever the motive of your work may be, we utter a blessing on your labors; that you may fully realize your desired objective and that you may prove by this activity that the village of Átány has never resisted the idea of progress but has understood the warning of the times. The demands of society have ever renewed achievement and it (the village) avoids no sacrifice in its endeavor to occupy a place among the first.

"As I have mentioned before, this dwelling was constructed to be a secretarial residence in the year 1901. The building costs amounted to 7,200 *korona*-s.

"The construction was performed by Soma Reiner, domiciled at Füzesabony, as building contractor; József Rab and Ferenc Zachetty, domiciled at Eger, as masons; Gáspár Merczel, domiciled at Eger, as carpenter; and József Mező, domiciled at Átány, as joiner. The foundations were dug by Gábor Bartók, Sámuel K. Szabó, Sámuel Együd, and Gábor Együd, domiciled at Átány. The work of the construction was begun on Wednesday, the first of May, 1901. The first foundation stone was laid on Friday, the third of May, 1901.

"At the time of the construction our population totaled 3,034; as regards religion there is an overwhelming majority of Calvinists, a small number of Roman Catholics, and even fewer—four or five families—of Israelites. There are four groceries, one of them a 'Self-Help and Consumers' Cooperative.' There are six inns. The occupation of the inhabitants is agriculture. There is an industrial plant to the eastern side of the village: a steam mill, owned by Ede Meister and Mrs. Sámuel Meister.

"...We have a fine social life; we have a Casino and a Firemen's Association. In the current year a soda-water works was founded by the community treasurer János Együd.

[Now the text lists the members of the village council and the body of representatives, the

393

minister, the assistant minister, the three schoolmasters, the superintendent, and the church-warden.]

"The village has a post office; Bertalan Végh being the postmaster.

"The telephone network is in construction.

"I think, dear reader, you are bored by the enumerated details, and therefore I close my lines with:

"May God bless this village with all earthly goods,

"May He give it abundant crops, wine, and wheat; may He bless it with all benefits.

"May this population never know party strife;

"Let its slogans be peace and harmony!

"Given at Átány on the 6th of May in the year 1901, on Monday."

APPENDIX C

CURRICULUM OF THE ÁTÁNY BOYS' SCHOOL IN 1811

(The Journals of the School, pp. 453–454.)

First National Boys' School
1. Spelling, Syllabification, Reading.
2. Rogations: the Lord's Prayer, the rogations in the Morning and in the Evening, before and after Meals, and in addition the Apostolic Creed and the Ten Commandments.
3. Sacred History: the History of the Old Testament, from the Creation of the World to Abraham.
4. The art of writing: the holding of the pen and the formation of the letters.
5. The Rules of good behavior and of decency.
6. Arithmetic: the knowledge, pronunciation, description, and counting of the Roman and Arabic numerals.
7. Training in attention and courage in speech, learning of some moral proverbs and stories by listening and reciting.
8. The Psalms and Hymns usually sung at church: memorization of the notes of the easier ones and training in how to sing them.

Second National Boys' School
1. The concise summary of Christian Religion.
2. The Sacred History of the Old Testament and the New to the end.
3. Rogations: the prayers in Illness and after the recovery of Health, before and after Learning, for Parents and Teachers, in Church both before and after the service.
4. The Psalms of St. David and those of the Hymns which are most often sung in common services, by heart.
5. Practice in reading.
6. Hungarian grammar: declension, comparison of adjectives, pronoun rules, conjugation.
7. The teaching of Natural History by pictures.
8. Geography: the planisphere and the correct use of maps.
9. Arithmetic: addition and subtraction of single digits, multiplication and multiplication tables of the same, division of single digits.
10. The Rules of Health.
11. Training in intelligent speaking.
12. The art of singing and training in the same.
13. The beginning of the art of writing.

Third National Boys' School

1. The Teachings of Christian Religion.
2. The Sacred History of the Old Testament.
3. All school prayers learned so far.
4. Learning the Psalms and Hymns in general use by heart.
5. Training in the location of passages in the Holy Scripture.
6. A short history of Hungary.
7. A summary of Hungarian law.
8. Physics or Natural Science: the learning of the general features of Bodies (Physica Generalis).
9. Natural History: the Compendium of the three realms of Nature.
10. The intelligent continuous reading of printed books and manuscripts.
11. Training in writing a Hungarian text from dictation.
12. Arithmetic: addition, subtraction, multiplication, and division.
13. Geography: All Europe generally; Hungary and Transylvania together with a summary of their Statistics; also the Austrian Dominions and the Holy Land particularly and in more detail.
14. Oral training in good conduct.
15. The Rules of Health.
16. Calligraphy and Orthography: the art of handwriting and correct spelling.
17. The art of singing and training in it.
18. Training in attentive listening to Sermons and examinations on the material delivered.

Fourth National Boys' School

1. Christian Moral Science.
2. The Sacred History of the New Testament.
3. Agenda or the preparation of the child about to partake of the Lord's Supper for the first time, for the Communion Table, together with the relevant prayers.
4. Diverse rogations and prayers.
5. Hymns: those usually sung at festive and other occasions shall be learned by heart, together with their notes.
6. The History of the Reformation and the difference between Christian denominations.
7. Physics or Natural Science: the Special Physics to the end.
8. The Compendium of Universal History.
9. Compendium of the Science of Agriculture.
10. Compendium of the Science of Craftsmanship.
11. Drawing.
12. Geometria Practica.
13. Mechanica.
14. Of Arithmetic: the Fractio Aurea Regula and training in Columnal addition.
15. Hungarian Composition: training in writing, e.g., Letters, Quittances, Contracts, Reports, Petitions.
16. Geography: everything which has been taught in the three preceding years.
17. Training in the reading of printed Hungarian books and manuscripts.
18. Calligraphy and Orthography.
19. The art of singing and training in it.

APPENDIX D

ARANY ÁBÉCÉ — ÉLETSZABÁLYOK

(Pálóczi Czinke István: Imádságos Vallástételek, 2. bővített kiadás, é.n. Lévai Izsó, Rimaszombat.)

A *Atyádat* anyádat tiszteld,
  Hogy Isten áldását megnyerd

B *Becsüld* meg az embereket
  Úgy nyersz te is becsületet
  Nyájas szíves; ne légy kevély
  Mindenkivel békében élj
  Amit nem kivánsz magadnak
  Te se tedd embertársadnak

Cz *Czélod* mindig nemes legyen
  Foltot ne tűrj a lelkeden
  A tiszta lelkiismeret
  Bizonyosan mennybe vezet

D *Dolgos* gondos szorgalmas légy
  Minden munkát jó kedvvel tégy
  Amit véghez kell vinned ma
  Sose halaszd azt holnapra
  Minden gonoszság kezdete
  A henyélés szeretete

E *Erős* lélek legyen benned
  Nem kell mindent szívre venned
  Ne csüggedj el ínségedben
  Folytasd tiszted s bizz Istenben

GOLDEN ALPHABET — RULES OF LIFE

(István Pálóczi Czinke: Professions of Faith in Prayers, 2nd enlarged edition, no date. Izsó Lévai [ed.], Rimaszombat.)

Honor thy father and thy mother,
In order to obtain the blessing of God.

Esteem every man
And you will be esteemed yourself;
Be kind and friendly, not proud;
Live in peace with everybody;
Do not do to your neighbor anything
You would not have done to yourself.

Let your aim be always noble—
Don't bear a stain on your soul.
A pure conscience
Will surely lead you to heaven.

Be busy, careful, and industrious,
Perform every task willingly;
What you have to do today
Never put off till tomorrow.
All wickedness begins
With a liking for idleness.

Have a strong soul;
Don't take everything to heart;
Don't lose courage in your need;
Go on with your business and trust God.

F *Fogadást* csak okosan tégy
   De aztán szódnak ura légy
   Esküvést ritkán végy szádba
   Soha ne esküdj hiába
   Ha esküdni mersz hamisan
   Megver Isten bizonyosan

Make vows thoughtfully,
But keep your word afterward;
Swear an oath but rarely;
Never make an oath in vain;
If you dare to forswear yourself
Be certain of God's punishment.

G *Gondolj* mindig jó lélekkel
   Az elhagyott szegényekkel
   Ha megáldott Isten téged
   Nyújts másoknak segitséget
   Mert nem tudod te is végre
   Nem szorulsz-e segitségre

Remember always with a kind heart
The poor and destitute;
If you are blessed by God,
Lend a hand to others,
For you don't know if sometime
You will need the help of others.

H *Ha* valaki jót tett veled
   Te azt soha el ne feledd
   A rosszért is jóval fizess
   Hogy Istennél kedves lehess

If somebody does a good turn for you,
Never forget it;
Repay an evil deed with good ones
In order to endear yourself to God.

I *Istent* féljed
   Istent szeresd
   Reménységed őbenne vesd
   Ő mindnyájunk édesatyja
   Oktalan, ki ezt tagadja

Fear God,
Love God,
Set your hopes on Him;
He is the Father of us all;
It is stupid to deny it.

J *Járj* el az Isten házába
   Oda sosem jársz hiába
   Öntsd ki szíved Isten előtt
   És nyersz tőle áldást erőt
   És míg ott vagy légy csendesen
   Viseld magad figyelmesen
   Ne suttogj és ne szunnyadozz
   Szemeiddel ne kalandozz
   Épülj a jó tanításon
   Ne járjon az eszed máson
   A templomban maradj végig
   Az utolsó éneklésig

Attend the house of God,
There you never go in vain;
Pour out your heart to God
And you will receive blessing and strength;
Be silent when you are there,
Behave attentively,
Don't whisper, don't drowse,
Don't look here and there;
Be edified by the good teaching,
Don't think about anything else,
Stay in the church till the end,
Till the last hymn is sung.

K *Kövesd* a szép igazságot
   Kerüld a rút hazugságot
   Aki egyszer hazudni mer
   Hitelt többé nem igen nyer

Follow the beautiful truth,
Avoid the ugly lie;
One who dares to tell a lie
Will rarely be trusted thereafter.

L *Legjobb* örökséget vettél
   Ha okosan neveltettél
   A ki tanulni nem szeret
   Felnőtt korában bánja meg

You receive the best inheritance
If you are brought up to be smart;
One who dislikes to learn
Will be sorry as an adult.

M *Megbántódon* ne állj bosszút
   Békességre ez legjobb út
   Kész légy jussodból engedni
   Mintsem mással perlekedni

Don't take revenge on an injurer,
This is the best way to peace;
Be ready to cede your right,
It is better than turning to the law;

Csekélységen fel ne akadj
Éktelen szókra ne fakadj
A rossz vétkét megvesd
De magát mint embert szeresd

Don't worry about a pittance,
Don't utter foul words,
Despise the sin of an evildoer,
But love him as a man.

N *Nincs* jobb a rendes életnél
Megbánnád, ha mást követnél
Oda lenne kedved erőd
Elhervadnál idő előtt
Mert a mértéktelen élet
Nem ér tartós öregséget

There is no life better than a decent one;
You'd be sorry for living otherwise;
You'd lose your spirit and strength;
You'd waste away before your time
Since an immoderate life
Does not lead to a long old age.

O *Oh* félj az első vétektől
Csakúgy lehetsz ment többektől
Akármely rejtekhelyen légy
Lát az Isten, rosszat ne tégy

Oh fear the first sin
So you can avoid later ones;
Wherever you may hide
Do no evil, for God sees you.

P *Pénzt* csak igaz uton szerezz
Lopni, csalni nagy vétek ez!
S magadra csak átkot hoznál
Ha emiatt elkárhoznál

Get money only in a rightful way;
It is a grave sin to steal or cheat!
You would call down curses on yourself
If you were damned for such acts.

R *Rendetlennek* száz a dolga
Ő a legnagyobb rabszolga
Tarts mindent a maga helyén
Tégy mindent kellő idején
Dolgod csak úgy mehet rendben
S többre boldogulsz mindenben

A disorderly man has a hundred tasks,
He is the greatest slave of all;
Keep everything in its place;
Do everything at its proper time
And everything will be all right,
And you'll be more successful in everything.

S *Se* ne dicsérd, se ne gyalázd
Magadat, hanem megalázd
Megdicsérnek erényeid
Ha mások is megismerik

Do not praise and do not blame
Yourself, but be humble;
Your virtues will praise you
If they become known to others.

Sz *Szívből* szeresd magyar hazád
Ez második édesanyád
Munkád után ez ad neked
Kenyeret és becsületet

Show heartfelt love for your
    Hungarian homeland,
She is your second mother;
After your work she gives you
Bread and honor.

T *Tanitód* legjobb barátod
Javadra van tudod, látod
Légy hát neki szófogadó
Minden tisztességet adó

Your teacher is your best friend,
You know; you see; he means well by you
So be obedient to him
And give him all esteem.

U *Úgy* szólj mindig, hogy meg ne bánd
Nevelt ember senkit se bánt
A Jóistent ne káromold
És senkire átkot ne mondj
Ha látnál is rosszat mástól
Őrizkedj az utánzástól

Speak always in a way you won't
    regret later;
A well-bred man doesn't hurt anyone;
Don't swear against the Godhead
And don't call down a curse on anybody;
Even if you see an evil deed done

Figyelmezz a kisebbekre
Ne tanítsd őket vétekre

Beware of imitating it;
Be careful with the little ones,
Do not teach them to sin.

V *Vén* emberből csúfot ne tégy
Inkább szolgálatjára légy
Gondolj arra, hogy majd egyszer
Te magad is megöregszel

Don't ridicule an old man,
Rather be of service to him;
Think of the fact that some day
You will grow old yourself.

Z *Zabolázd* indulatodat
Hagyd holnapra haragodat
Őrizkedés a haragtól
Megment a késő bánattól

Curb your temper,
Leave your anger for the morrow;
Refraining from anger
Will save you from a later sorrow.

APPENDIX E

THE FAREWELL OF THE BRIDE
FROM HER FATHER'S HOUSE AND HER ENTRANCE
INTO THE HOUSE OF HER FATHER-IN-LAW

(Recited by Katalin Galvács at her wedding in 1947)

[Farewell as she starts for the church for the wedding ceremony:]
"The hour has come to start out on my road,
To reach the goal with my beloved mate,
That we may be linked with the chain of love
In the house of God, that we may have one another.
My dear parents, your tears spring from
The painful feeling in the parental heart.
Although I was a flower blooming in your garden,
I desired an even greater happiness than that.
Let me go on my road now,
I leave you in the protection of the Lord,
     I greet you with all my heart."
[Farewell as she leaves her father's house for good, together with the bridegroom, after the
ceremony in church:]
"My provident and beneficent God,
I entreat you for a few words of farewell.
When the migrating bird sets out in autumn,
It too bids farewell to its old abode.
So I, taking leave of my father's house,
Entreat the help of the Lord of Heaven.
My dear father, I know your heart is aching
As your beloved daughter bids farewell to you;
I have felt so much of your paternal goodness,
My dear father, God bless you.
My dear mother, your tears spring from
The painful feeling of the maternal heart.
Your eyes are full of tears as you behold my departure,
Wondering if I shall find my happiness.
Don't cry, my good mother, I am going now,
But your faithful providence is written in my heart.
God bless you, my dear mother, you
Who took so many pains for me.
My dear grandmother from the father's side, the fate of the widow is sad,

401

However much she may be blessed with goods.
I thank you too for your nursing,
May God bless your old days.
My dear grandfather and you grandmother from the mother's side
Who are standing here deep in sorrow,
Your hearts are bleeding; you are bereaved;
Inimical hands have grieved you,
Since you do not know whether your dear son
Is alive in a strange country or is dead.
Trust in God, he will help you,
Aching hearts are cured by Him alone.
God bless you for all your labors.
My dear brother, let's shake hands for farewell,
May brotherly love continue between us.
May brotherly devotion, the flower of love,
Never be withered, may its branch stay green.
My dear guests who are present here,
Forgive me all of you, if I have wronged you.
Let me go on my road now,
I leave you in the protection of the Lord,
   I greet you with all my heart."

[Entering the house of her husband's father:]
  "My dear mother, I wish you good evening,
I stand at the door of your house with fear.
As the migrating bird leaves her nest,
So I left that of my dear parents.
So does a single bird fly about alone
Until it finds its mate at last.
But your dear son is no longer alone,
Having found his loving mate already.
I have become a companion to your dear son today,
Receive me as your daughter now,
Therefore I ask you whether you receive me,
Whether I may cross the threshold,
   I greet you with all my heart."

APPENDIX F

FORMS OF FAMILY UNITS AT ÁTÁNY
BETWEEN 1942 AND 1945

The Source

The data given below are taken from the family files prepared in the early 1940s by the pastor of Átány to register the social status and church-tax payments of his congregation. A separate file was drawn up for each family. These files contain the names of the heads and of all members of the families, often their dates of birth and marriage, their relationship to the head of the family, data concerning deceased members of the family or those who had moved to another house or to another community, the house property and landed estates, together with other sources of income of the family. In a smaller portion of the files some columns are blank, while other files were withdrawn from use and replaced with less detailed ones.

Altogether the exact composition of 495 families, a total of 2,033 persons, was established. Of these families, the financial status of 433 was stated with certainty. According to the 1941 census, the Calvinist population of Átány numbered 2,432 persons. But these two figures cannot be compared because the census indicates only the population actually present, while the Church records include those whose families and houses were in Átány and who paid church-tax there but were temporarily away for some reason or other (seasonal industrial work, military service, etc.).

Beside the names of quite a number of men in the family files, we find the remark: "in war service." Nearly one hundred of them have never returned home: they were killed in action or are missing. Our calculations regard persons in military service as living members of the family. Later (until 1950–1952), various changes were noted in the files. Out of the overlapping items, we have sampled those corresponding to the early 1940s; although it appears that full synchronism among the families could not have been reached. When determining financial status, we have not taken into consideration the land granted within the framework of the 1945 land reform.

Of the 433 families where financial status could be established, 426 are "peasants," while 7 belong to the category of "others" (craftsmen, intelligentsia, and tradesmen). The classification according tot he size of property of the 426 peasant households is as follows:

	No. of families	No. of persons	No. of persons as percentage of sample
Indigent holders (0–5 *hold*-s, 0–7.10 acres)	237	930	51.75
Small holders (5–10 *hold*-s, 7.10–14.20 acres)	89	397	22.09

	No. of families	No. of persons	No. of persons as percentage of sample
Medium holders (10–20 *hold*-s, 14.20–28.40 acres)	73	330	18.37
Well-to-do *gazda*-s (over 20 *hold*-s, 28.40 acres)	27	140	7.79
Total	426	1,797	100.00

Accordingly, the strata within the peasant population of Átány are proportionally represented in the sample. A subrepresentation of some degree can be found in the cases of family fragments or of single widows and widowers; namely, that single persons with no property whatsoever over the age of seventy were exempted from paying the church-tax. The files also are not appropriate for determining whether closely related nuclear families dwelling in the same house lived in a complete community or partially separated as far as farming and household are concerned.

Size of Households

No. of persons in household	No. of households	No. of persons	No. of persons as percentage of sample
1	22	22	1.08
2	74	148	7.28
3	81	243	11.95
4	128	512	25.18
5	93	465	22.87
6	57	342	16.82
7	25	175	8.62
8	10	80	3.94
9	4	36	1.77
10	1	10	0.49
Total	495	2,033	100.00

Average Household Size

For the whole sample, the average number of household members is 4.11. Within peasant households there is a gradually increasing difference according to financial standing. For these households the average size of household is: indigent holders, 3.92; small holders, 4.46; medium holders, 4.52; and well-to-do *gazda*-s, 5.18 members.

Forms of Family Units

When grouping the data we aimed at ascertaining the numerical ratio in Átány for the major family types (joint family, stem family, nuclear family) as described in Chapter 5, "The Forms of the Family and Its Division of Labor." However, considering that a large number of transitory and incomplete forms appear, our categorization requires some explanation.

Within the nuclear families we listed as "parents with children" nine families where a brother or sister of either parent also belonged to the household.

In drawing the limits of stem family, the decisive criterion was that a family so listed should include at least two nuclear families of subsequent generations after the pattern of either "parents + married son" or "parents + married daughter." (In one case we had "parents + married son + married grandchild," while in two instances "parents + widowed child + married grandchild.") Furthermore, the families where the two couples lived together with children, with one widowed grandparent, or with one or more unmarried brothers or sisters, have also been listed here.

There are several families however where the extension in the direction of the ascending or descending line is conspicuous, without being consistent with the above requirements. Such family patterns are the following: married couple + widowed parent; parents + children + widowed grandparent; parents + children + widowed grandparent + widowed great-grandparent; parents + widowed child + grandchildren, etc. These variations occur also complemented by brothers and sisters. All of these household types have been listed into the category of "incomplete stem families."

Joint family, without exception, means two married children—in five cases, two married brothers, while in two cases one married brother and one married sister—who live with their parents (in one case with one widowed mother only). The two cases where one married sister and one married brother kept joint household with their parents seem to be of transitory character. In the first instance the sister's husband had been away for years in military service and the wife must have moved to her father's home for the period of her husband's absence, while in the second instance there was a transitory post-marriage situation.

	No. of households	No. of persons	No. of persons as percentage of sample
Family fragments			
Bachelors	3	3	
Single widows or widowers	19	19	
Widowed persons + other members of the family	21	63	4.19
Nuclear families			
Married couples	65	131	
Married couples + children	169	691	40.35
Stem families			
Incomplete	95	433	21.33
Complete	116	642	31.57
Joint families	7	52	2.56
Total	495	2,033	100.00

Meny-s; Võ-s

In the sample there are altogether 228 married couples who live with the parents or with one widowed parent of one of the parties. (In one case the mothers of both husband and wife are members of the joint household.) There are 154 couples living together with the man's parents (89 with both of them and 65 with one of them), while 74 couples live together with the wife's parents (38 with both of them, 36 with one of them).

Accordingly 89 wives belonged to the household of their mothers- and fathers-in-law, while 49 belonged to that of their widowed mothers-in-law. Three widows lived with the parents of their deceased husbands and three with the mothers of their deceased husbands. If the fact of living in joint household with the mother-in-law is regarded as the criterion of being a *meny*, the number of *meny*-s in our sample totals 144.

The 38 husbands living with the parents of their wives are termed "married-in võ-s." So are sixteen husbands out of those who live with one widowed parent of the wife, where it could be ascertained that the majority of the property comes from the wife's family. Thus, the total of "married-in *vő*-s" can be estimated at 54.

The considerably high number of *vő*-s is due to the fact that at that time, in addition to the former tradition of marrying-in poor *vő*-s, it had become customary for firstborn *gazda* sons (who had to leave the paternal house) to marry into *gazda* families where there was a single daughter. On the other hand, many *vő*-s lived in landless or indigent families (nineteen out of fifty who could have been identified according to financial standing).

Interrelations between Family Type and Financial Standing

With the exception of the joint family, which does not occur in the indigent category, all of the described major family types can be found in all strata of Átány peasants. Considering that among the seven joint families the small holders are represented by the two examples that are non-typical and of transitory character, it can be stated that the category of joint families in the 1940s was restricted to peasants possessing holdings of over ten *hold*-s (14.20 acres).

The ratio of frequency for the other family types varies considerably when the different strata are taken into consideration. The simple forms predominate in the less prosperous strata, while the complex ones are mainly found among the well-to-do peasants. To illustrate this numerically, we have compiled a table giving the percentage of persons within the strata according to major family types. (Stem families and joint families are indicated in the same column, because in both groups more than one couple is living together in the same household.)

	Family fragments (%)	Nuclear families (%)	Incomplete stem families (%)	Stem and joint families (%)
Indigent holders	4.62	49.25	21.50	24.63
Small holders	2.01	31.74	22.67	43.58
Medium holders	3.33	23.03	21.52	52.12
Well-to-do *gazda*-s	—	4.29	30.00	65.71
Full sample (non-peasants included)	4.20	40.32	21.34	34.14

When studying the ratio of the nuclear families it must be noted that, according to the system of inheritance and the domestic cycle in Átány, at the time of obtaining the heritage, several indigent nuclear families entered a higher category of wealth and thus with some probability, became extended. In other words, a portion of the nuclear families of well-to-do *gazda*-s, still in expectance of the heritage, were hidden in lower categories.

The above table agrees with the statement that in this period the values and the traditional culture of Átány were largely homogeneous, but this world-view and this culture were practiced by the landholding peasants in a more concentrated form and by the poor in a thinner, more or less diluted form. Full conformity with the rules and customs of traditional life could have been attained in families where several married couples of subsequent generations formed the household. Some 25 per cent of the most indigent people had this extended family pattern. In the *gazda* stratum, however, the ratio of this family type was as high as 65 per cent.

GLOSSARY

ág	— lineage; a more or less extensive group of the descendants of a common ancestor in the male line; a subordinate unit of a larger group of blood relatives
ágazat	— *ág*
áldomás	— a ritual in which wine is drunk together by the persons involved to celebrate the success or completion of an enterprise, or to solemnize an agreement, usually a bargain made at a fair
Alvég	— the Lower End, southern half of the village
ángy	— the wife of an older brother, uncle, or other older blood relative
ángyomasszony	— the more honorable form of *ángy*. Used in conversation (1) for the wife of a close relative (within three *íz*-s); or (2) if the person mentioned or addressed is more than ten or fifteen years older than the speaker, even though she is the wife of a more remote relative
atyafi	— the looser variety of the term *atyámfia;* this term refers not only to the kinsmen on the paternal or the maternal side, but also to people from the same region when they are in a foreign environment
atyámfia	— "the son of my father"; all the people who are counted as blood relatives on both the paternal and maternal sides; also an old-fashioned, endearing expression used in addressing a younger kinsman
atyafiság	— (1) all the blood relatives of a person or a family, reckoned on both the paternal and the maternal sides; (2) the relationship between *atyafi*-s
báty	— older brother; more generally any older male blood relative
bátyám	— "my *báty*"; the term of address for a *báty*
bátyámuram	— the more honorable form of *bátyám* (cf. *ángyomasszony*)
bejáró	— the mandatory of the bereaved household in preparing and conducting the ceremony of the funeral; he is usually the *keresztkoma*, or if the *keresztkoma* is no longer living, the godson, or even the *nász* or brother-in-law, but never a blood relative
betyár	— highwayman; in the eighteenth and nineteenth centuries the career of *betyár* was chosen by many villagers who came to

loggerheads with the state or the seignorial administration or did not want to "eat the Emperor's bread" as soldiers; they are generally regarded sympathetically in the peasant tradition

cékert — a *kert* (farmyard) whose stable was the habitual gathering place of men of the neighborhood for friendly conversation, *tanyázás* around the fire

cívis — a peasant who was a citizen of one of the peasant towns of the Great Plain, especially Debrecen; a descendant of a well-to-do indigenous family

család — (1) family (the notion of the family is not restricted to members living in the same household, because descendants who eat "a separate bread" are also included in it; thus it is often used in the sense of "a restricted group of blood relatives" (see footnote 8, Part Two); (2) child

cseléd — (1) servant; (2) child (see footnote 8, Part Two)

csikós — the herdsman for the horses

diktás — the song (primarily hymns) leader, especially for a bereaved household; he (she) starts the singing and recites each line for the others to sing after him (her)

eladó — "for sale"; a girl of marriageable age

fajta — "race" or "breed"; an indefinite term which is used for a group of descendants similar to the *ág*, but which has slightly pejorative connotations, generally related to inherited mental or physical qualities

família — like *fajta*, an indefinite term used for a group of descendants

fél — "one half"; a group of neighbors larger than the group of four or five "close neighbors"; usually those who live on the same side of the road

félhely — "half place"; in the period of serfdom the term referred to half a feudal *telek*, its extention in 1866 was 18 *hold*-s

félódal — see *ódal*

Felvég — the Upper End, northern half of the village

fertály — "one quarter"; (1) a holding equivalent to one-quarter of a feudal *telek*, or to 9 *hold*-s in the 1866 survey; (2) a quarter of the village as a territorial unit of community administration

földes — "possessing land"; a term more or less equivalent to *igás ember;* a peasant with enough land to be able to own a team, whether or not he actually does own one

forint — historical monetary unit; new monetary unit introduced in 1946, used in place of the *pengő*

főszolgabíró — up to 1945 the chief administrative officer of a Hungarian county-district

gallér — uninvited bachelors or sometimes young married men who lounge about and watch the evening festivities at a wedding; it is proper to treat them to wine and cake and to order the gypsy musicians to play dance music for them

gatya — linen trousers, either underwear or (with wider legs) outer clothing

gazda — (1) a peasant owning a farm which enables him to support his family without additional income (at least 15 to 20 *hold*-s of land); (2) a farmer by birth, upbringing, and experience;

(3) the head of a family—e.g., "the woman is *gazda* in that house"; (4) an elderly man, a well-to-do head of a family who lets his son or a servant do the work while retaining direction for himself; (5) in labor bands, the entrepreneur, organizer, leader—e.g., carter *gazda*, harvester *gazda*, *summásgazda*

gazdasszony — "*gazda* + woman"; (1) the wife of the *gazda,* who directs the other women in the household chores; (2) close kinswoman (elderly) invited to the marriage ceremony to prepare the festive meals; the wife of the *násznagy* is the chief *gazdasszony*

gazd'uram — "*gazda* + *úr*"; a term of address for a *gazda* which expresses esteem, generally used by a hired man, day laborer, or craftsman; the term is unusual in Átány

gyalogember — "pedestrian man"; translated throughout the book as "teamless farmer"; a villager who does not own a team of draft animals, and so must earn his living by manual labor, going by foot

had — a group of descendants in the male line; a term used rarely, sometimes with a pejorative tint

hadas settlement — common term in Hungarian ethnography for a settlement pattern in which the houses of families derived from a common ancestor in the male line, stand near each other, forming the subordinate units of the village

hadnagy — (1) lieutenant; (2) in the Átány local board, a relatively young councillor who kept public order

hancsikolás — "digging up"; the customary vandalism of May Day Eve, when the bachelor bands break up and demolish the earthen seats in front of the houses, or unhinge the gates at houses where there are marriageable daughters, etc.

Hangya Szövetkezet — "Ant Cooperative Society," a national organization made up of rural consumers' cooperatives

határ — (1) the territory belonging to a village, including its fields, meadows, forests, etc.—a precisely delimited area under the control of the local magistracy; (2) boundary line

ház — (1) house; (2) family unit living in the same house
háznép — "the people of the house," members of a family living in the same house

hold — square measure equal to 1.42 acres; the so-called "small *hold*" or "Hungarian *hold*," measuring 1.08 acres, is also common at Átány

hőrísz — a phase of the wedding celebration during which the guests of the bride's house set off for the groom's house at midnight or later in order to visit the newly-weds

hóstya — a wide neighborhood unit, including sides of a road leading out of the village, together with the *köz*-s and *zug*-s forking off from the road

igásember — "man with a yoke," translated throughout the book as "team-owner"; a peasant who owns a team of horses or oxen; in order to keep a team, a man must own a certain amount of land; thus the term has status connotations

íz — "finger joint"; a measuring unit for genealogical distance; the first *íz* is the child, the second the grandchild, the third the great-grandchild; in collateral reckoning the first *íz* includes the brothers and sisters, the second the children of the father's or the mother's brother or sister, etc.

jobbágy — serf (not exactly the same as the Western European serf), (see Chapter 1, "The Past")

jegy — a wedding present exchanged between the prospective bride and the bridegroom in a traditional ritual at the betrothal

kelmed — "your worship"; archaic term of address expressing honor

kert — "a fenced-in place"; a farmyard situated on the periphery of the settlement, at some distance from the house and containing a stable, a stack yard, and sometimes a kitchen garden

keresztkoma — "baptismal *koma*"; in Átány a symmetrical connection between two men of similar age who are godfathers of all of each other's children

kisebbik uram — "my minor husband"; term by which a wife addressed her husband's younger brothers and younger cousins

koma — a man belonging to the same age group and bachelor band as the speaker; men may also become *koma*-s by common military service, in which case they are called "soldier *koma*-s" or "war *koma*-s"; can also be used to mean *keresztkoma* (cf. *keresztkoma* or baptismal *koma)*

komámuram — term of reference and address for one's *keresztkoma*

komaasszony — term of reference and address for the wife of one's *keresztkoma*

korona — "crown"; the monetary unit of Hungary before 1925

kortesz, korteszolás — electioneering, campaigning

köböl — a dry measure for corn = 4 *véka*-s

köz — side street, usually a winding and irregular one

közkoma — friend of the bachelor years invited to the christening along with the real *keresztkoma;* this act does not create a *keresztkoma* relation but it strengthens the ties of regular *koma*-ship

kukás — a tobacco grower hired by an estate for a year on the half-and-half system

kukásalja — the piece of land allotted by the estate to the *kukás* according to the half-and-half system, usually 4 *hold*-s

kurátor — churchwarden

lakzis — people who participate in a wedding festival

massza — the dwarf-holding of a *zsellér* (see below) measured out in 1866: 600 square fathoms of arable land and the right to use the same amount of the undivided pasture of the *zsellér* commonage

mátka — a woman belonging to the same age group and girls' band as the speaker; this is the female counterpart of the *koma* relationship between males

mázsa — a measure of weight equal to 100 kg. or 1 quintal

ment — "going"; a large neighborhood unit, similar to *fél* and *ódal*

meny — daughter-in-law

nagyobbik uram — "my major husband"; term by which a wife addressed her husband's elder brothers and elder cousins

nász — in its more restricted sense, the term used by the parents of one spouse for the father of the other; in a wider sense, the father of the spouse of a male or female cousin

násznagy	— marriage sponsor; the godfather of the groom or the bride, the official witness, and the most honored role in the ceremony
nászos	— people connected by the *nász* relationship
nászuram	— the term of address for a *nász*
nászasszony	— the wife of the *nász*
nemzet	— (1) *nemzetség;* (2) a member of the *nemzetség*—e.g., "my nemzet" = my *nemzetség* or a certain member of my *nemzetség;* (3) nation
nemzetség	— a group of descendants in the male line, including both the living relatives and the deceased ancestors
néne	— older sister; more generally, any older female blood relative
néném	— term of address for a *néne*
nénémasszony	— the more honorable form of *néném* (cf. *ángyomasszony*)
ódal	— "side"; a large group of neighbors, similar to *fél* and *ment*
ólaskert	— "*kert* with a stable" = *kert*
öcs	— younger brother
pados	— a functionary at a wedding who divides up the cake and pastry collected in the loft and directs the serving of them
párbér	— "tax of the couples"; church tax paid by all married couples
pengő	— the monetary unit of Hungary from 1925 to 1946
perenge	— a simple merry-go-round (a revolving beam fastened horizontally to a post with simple seats hanging at both ends; it is turned round by hand)
pitar, pitvar	— small room in front of the kitchen in the old, traditional style of house (see Fig. 12)
pite	— a flat, sweet cake
pogácsa	— a fat, rich cake, baked in small pieces cut to a round shape
porta	— a comprehensive term for the house, the yard, and the out-buildings
rész	— "part"; a large neighborhood unit, similar to *hóstya*
rétes	— strudel, a kind of puff pastry, stuffed usually with cheese, apple, cabbage, or poppy seed
rokon	— traditionally an affine; more recently it has been extended to include blood relatives too
rokonság	— all the *rokon*-s of a person or a family
sógor	— brother-in-law; the husband of a sister or a female cousin; in a broader sense, any man related to the speaker by marriage
sógorom	— "my brother-in-law"
suba	— a long sleeveless cape, made of wooly sheepskin
summás	— an agricultural seasonal worker who is hired as part of a labor gang for a long period fixed in advance and is paid a lump sum for the whole job
summásgazda	— the contractor who organizes and directs the *summás* labor gang
szolgabíró	— the district judge before 1945
szüle	— grandmother, great-grandmother; in general, term used by both family members and outsiders for the old woman of the house
szűr	— a long overcoat made of thick, coarse woolen cloth
tagos	— landowner peasant who in 1866 did not join the three-field rotation system and received all his holdings in a single lot
tanya	— (1) a separate, isolated dwelling outside the village on one's

own land; (2) a manorial farm, outbuildings and farm labor-ers' dwellings outside the village; (3) a short-term abode for people who live a wandering life

tanyasi
— a person living in a *tanya*, mainly a hired worker on a manorial farm; less frequently a peasant dwelling in a *tanya* erected on his own land

tanyakert
— a *kert* (farmyard) whose stable was the habitual gathering place of men of the neighborhood for friendly conversation *(tanyázás)* around the fire

tanyázás
— a prolonged, friendly social gathering; conversation; speci-fically, a male gathering in a *tanyakert* or *cékert*

telek
— piece of land; building site; in the period of serfdom the legally fixed unit of plowland, meadow and *porta* allotted to the serf; by the 1866 reorganization of holdings, one *telek* in Átány contained 36 *hold*-s (as measured by the survey) and the right to use 10 *hold*-s of pasture

tőke
— "capital"; the money of the farm as contrasted to that of the housewife; money for the *tőke* comes from the sale of livestock and produce and may be used for farm investment, land, and clothes and boots for the men

úr
— "lord"; referring to a member of a social stratum regarded as superior to the peasants; primarily landowners and by exten-sion "learned men" and administrative officials such as the village secretary, the minister, and the teacher

uram
— "my lord"; the term of address for an *úr;* a wife uses this term to address her husband, and the ordinary citizens use it for the members of the village magistracy—e.g., "mayor *uram*"

véka
— dry measure for wheat, containing about 30 liters (in the past centuries the capacity of the *véka* has oscillated over time and from one region to another; the *véka*-s used in Átány contain about 30 liters)

verbunkos
— originally a "recruiting dance"; in a wider sense a dance of the men without female partners

vérem
— "my blood"; the old-fashioned term of endearment for a blood relative (whereas the term "*atyámfia* is used mainly by men, *vérem* is common among women as well)

virilis
— a wealthy member of the body of representatives of the village, who occupies this office by virtue of his property, specifically by the direct state tax paid on his property instead of by election

virtus
— self-confident, audacious, competitive, manly behavior; ba-chelors and young men are guided by the value of *virtus*, for instance, in the fights of bachelor bands, or in the undertaking of outstanding, strenuous feats of labor

vő
— son-in-law

zug
— a by-road or a dead-end lane

zugosi
— a person living along the same *zug*

zsellér
— in the period of serfdom a villager who owned less land than one-eighth of a *telek* (or no land at all) and was subject to the jurisdiction of the lord; there were two categories: the "*zsellér*-s without a house" paid rent to the proprietors;

the "*zsellér*-s with a house" had a right to use the grazing fields of the village, and consequently each of them received a *massza* after the abolition of serfdom; in recent usage the word *zsellér* is similar to *gyalogember*—a landless villager or a dwarf-holder earning his living as a day laborer or wage earner

BIBLIOGRAPHY

ARENSBERG, CONRAD M.
1963. "The Old World Peoples: The Place of European Cultures in World Ethnography." *Anthropological Quarterly*, 36: 75–99.
BACSÓ, NÁNDOR.
1959. *Magyarország éghajlata. (The Climate of Hungary.)* Budapest.
BALÁSSY, FERENC, and NÁNDOR SZEDERKÉNYI.
1890–1897. *Heves vármegye története. (The History of Heves County.)* 4 vols. Eger.
BALOGH, ISTVÁN.
1947. *Cívisek társadalma. (The Society of the "Cives.")* Budapest.
1965a. A paraszti gazdálkodás és termelési technika. (Peasant Agriculture and Techniques of Production.) In *A parasztság Magyarországon a kapitalizmus korában 1848–1914*, István Szabó (Ed.), vol. I: 349–428. Budapest.
1965b. A paraszti művelődés. (Peasant Culture.) In *A parasztság Magyarországon a kapitalizmus korában 1848–1914*, István Szabó (Ed.), vol. II: 487–567. Budapest.
BÁTKY, ZSIGMOND, ISTVÁN GYÖRFFY, and KÁROLY VISKI.
n.d. *A magyarság néprajza. (The Ethnography of the Hungarian People.)* 4 vols. Budapest.
BOROVSZKY, SAMU (Ed.).
1909. *Heves vármegye. (Heves County.)* Budapest.
BULLA, BÉLA, and TIBOR MENDÖL.
1947. *A Kárpátmedence földrajza. (The Geography of the Carpathian Basin.)* Budapest.
CSAPLOVICS, JÁNOS.
1822. Ethnographiai Értekezés Magyar Országról (An Ethnographic Study of Hungary). *Tudományos Gyűjtemény*, vol. VI (no. 3) 37–65; (no. 4) 3–90; (no. 6) 79–92; (no. 7) 45–51.
DEN HOLLANDER, A. N. J.
1960–1961. "The Great Hungarian Plain: A European Frontier Area." *Comparative Studies in Society and History*, 3: 74–88, 155–169.
ELEK, PÉTER, BÉLA GUNDA, ZOLTÁN HILSCHER, SÁNDOR HORVÁTH, GYULA KARSAY, GYÖRGY KERÉNYI, ÁKOS KOCZOGH, IMRE KOVÁCS, FERENC PÓCSY, and LÁSZLÓ TORBÁGYI.
1936. *Elsüllyedt falu a Dunántúlon: Kemse község élete. (A Sunken Village in Transdanubia: The Life of the Village Kemse.)* Budapest.
FÁY, ANDRÁS.
1854. *Adatok Magyarország bővebb ismertetésére. (Data for a More Detailed Description of Hungary.)* Pest.
FÉL, EDIT.
1944a. *A nagycsalád és jogszokásai a komárommegyei Martoson. (The Extended Family and Its Legal Customs in Martos, Komárom County.)* Budapest.

1944b. *Egy kisalföldi nagycsalád társadalom-gazdasági vázlata. (A Socio-economic Outline of a Joint Family in the Small Hungarian Plain.)* Érsekújvár.

1959a. "Some Data concerning Kinship Institutions among the Szeklers of Bukovina." *Acta Ethnographica*, 8: 85–97.

1959b. Fejezetek Tiszaigar társadalmának megismeréséhez. (Contributions to the study of the society of the village Tiszaigar.) *Néprajzi Közlemények*, 4 (nos. 1–2): 70–114.

FÉL, EDIT, and TAMÁS HOFER.

1961a. A parasztember szerszámai, Beszámoló az átányi monografikus eszközvizsgálatról. (The Tools of the Peasant. Report on the Monographic Research on Átány Implements.) *Ethnographia*, 72: 487–535.

1961b. Az átányi gazdálkodás ágai. (The Branches of Agriculture in Átány.) *Néprajzi Közlemények*, 6 (no. 2): 1–220.

1962. Der Átányer Scheffel. Ein Beitrag zu den Beziehungen Mensch und Gerät. *Schweizerisches Archiv für Volkskunde*, 58: 102–124.

1963. Egy monografikus néprajzi gyűjtés történeti tanulságai. (Lessons from an Ethnographic Research Monograph for the Historian.) *Agrártörténeti Szemle*, 5: 558–577.

1964. A monografikus tárgygyűjtés. Az átányi példa. (The Monographical Collection of Objects: The Example of Átány.) *Néprajzi Értesítő*, 46: 5–89.

1965. Über monographisches Sammeln volkskundlicher Objekte. In *Festschrift Alfred Bühler. Basler Beiträge zur Geographie und Ethnologie. Ethnologische Reihe*, vol. 2, pp. 77–92. Basel.

FÉNYES, ELEK.

1836–1840. *Magyar Országnak s a hozzákapcsolt tartományoknak mostani állapota statisztikai és geográfiai tekintetben. (The Current Statistical and Geographical Position of Hungary and the Annexed Provinces.)* 4 vols. Pest.

FÜR, LAJOS.

1965. Jobbágyföld–parasztföld. (From Serf Holdings to Peasant Land.) In *A parasztság Magyarországon a kapitalizmus korában 1848–1914*, István Szabó (Ed.), vol. I: 33–153. Budapest.

GÖNCZI, FERENC.

1914. *Göcsej és kapcsolatosan Hetés vidékének és népének összevontabb ismertetése. (A Concise Description of Göcsej and the Land and Folk of Hetés in Relation to It.)* Kaposvár.

GYIMESI, SÁNDOR.

1965. A parasztság és a szövetkezeti mozgalmak. (The Peasantry and the Cooperative Movements.) In *A parasztság Magyarországon a kapitalizmus korában 1848–1914*, István Szabó (Ed.), vol. II: 616–653. Budapest.

GYÖRFFY, GYÖRGY.

1959. *Tanulmányok a magyar állam eredetéről. (Studies on the Origin of the Hungarian State.)* Budapest.

GYÖRFFY, ISTVÁN.

1928. *Takarás és nyomtatás az Alföldön. (Harvesting and Threshing in the Great Plain.)* Debrecen. (Published also in *Néprajzi Értesítő*, 20: 1–47.)

1941. *Nagykunsági krónika. (Nagykunság Chronicle.)* Budapest.

1942. *Magyar nép, magyar föld. (Hungarian People, Hungarian Soil.)* Budapest.

1943. *Magyar falu, magyar ház. (Hungarian Village, Hungarian House.)* Budapest.

HOFER, TAMÁS.

1965. Eine eigenartige ungarische Siedlungsform und ihre europäischen Parallelen. In *Europa et Hungaria, Congressus Ethnographicus in Hungaria*, pp. 95–100. Budapest.

HOFFMANN, TAMÁS.

1963. *A gabonaneműek nyomtatása a magyar parasztok gazdálkodásában. (Threshing of Cereals in the Agriculture of the Hungarian Peasants.)* Budapest.

HULTKRANTZ, ÅKE.
1960. *General Ethnological Concepts. International Dictionary of Regional European Ethnology and Folklore*, vol. I. Copenhagen.

ILLYÉS, ENDRE.
1936. *A magyar református földművelő ifjúság lelkigondozásának története. (The History of the "Cure of Souls" among the Rural Calvinist Youth of Hungary.)* Debrecen.

ISTVÁNFFY, GYULA.
1898. Újabb adatok a palóczok ethnográfiájához. (Additional Data on the Ethnography of the *Palóc*-s.) *Ethnographia*, 9: 305–315.
1911. A borsodmegyei palóczok. (The *Palóc*-s of Borsod County.) *Ethnographia*, 22: 162–166, 222–232, 292–303, 363–395.

JANKÓ, JÁNOS.
1902. *A balatonmelléki lakosság néprajza. (The Ethnography of the Population of the Balaton Region.)* Budapest.

JUHÁSZ, LAJOS.
1936. *A porta története 1526–1648. Jobbágygazdálkodásunk egysége és az adóegység. (The History of the "Porta" from 1526 to 1648. The Land Unit of Serf Agriculture and Taxation.)* Budapest.

KISS, ISTVÁN (see: N. KISS, ISTVÁN).

KISS, LAJOS, and BENJAMIN RAJECZKY (Eds.).
1966. *Siratók — Laments. A Magyar Népzene Tára — Collection of Hungarian Folk Music (Corpus Musicae Popularis Hungaricae*, vol. V.*)* Budapest. (Hungarian and English text.)

KNIEZSA, ISTVÁN.
1955. *A magyar nyelv szláv jövevényszavai. (Slavonic Loan-words in the Hungarian Language.)* vols. I/1 and I/2. Budapest.

KOVACSICS, JÓZSEF (Ed.).
1963. *Magyarország történeti demográfiája. (The Historical Demography of Hungary.)* Budapest.

LETTRICH, EDIT.
1965. *Urbanizálódás Magyarországon. (The Process of Urbanization in Hungary.)* Földrajzi tanulmányok *(Studies in Geography*, 5.*)* Budapest.

MAGYARY, ZOLTÁN.
1942. *A magyar közigazgatás. (Hungarian Public Administration.)* Budapest.

MAKKAI, LÁSZLÓ.
1958. Pest megye története. (The History of Pest County.) In *Pest megye műemlékei (Monuments of Art in Pest County)*, Dezső Dercsényi (Ed.), vol. I: 89–169. Budapest.

MENDÖL, TIBOR.
1943. Die Stadt im Karpatenbecken. *Földrajzi Közlemények*, 71: 31–148.

MÉRI, ISTVÁN.
1952–1954. Beszámoló a Tiszalök-rázompusztai és Túrkeve-mórici ásatások eredményeiről. (Report on the Results of the Excavations at Tiszalök-Rázompuszta and Túrkeve-Móric.) *Archaeológiai Értesítő*, 79: 49–67, 81: 138–154.

M. SOMLYAI, MAGDA.
1965. *Földreform 1945. (The Land Reform of 1945.)* Budapest.

N. KISS, ISTVÁN.
1960. *16. századi dézsmajegyzékek. (Sixteenth Century Tithe Rolls.)* Budapest.

OROSZ, ENDRE.
1939. *Heves s a volt Külső-Szolnok vármegye nemes családjai. (The Noble Families of the Counties Heves and the Former Exterior Szolnok.)* Eger.

OROSZ, ISTVÁN.
1965. A differenciálódás és kisajátítás. (Differentiation and Expropriation.) In *A paraszt-*

ság Magyarországon a kapitalizmus korában 1848–1914, István Szabó (Ed.), vol. II: 9–145. Budapest.

OZORÓCZY, ERVIN, ISTVÁN TÁTRAY, and ELEMÉR KOVÁCH.

1938. *Tagosítás és egyéb birtokrendezések. (Consolidation and Other Redistributions of Land.)* Budapest.

PATAKI, JÓZSEF.

1937. *Adalékok a Sárköz népességének történetéhez. (Data on the History of the Population of the Sárköz.)* Pécs.

RÁCZ, ISTVÁN.

1965. Parasztok elvándorlása a faluból. (The Emigration of Peasants from the Village.) In *A parasztság Magyarországon a kapitalizmus korában 1848–1914*, István Szabó (Ed.), vol. II: 433–484. Budapest.

RADÓ, SÁNDOR (Ed.).

1963. *Magyarország gazdasági földrajza. (The Economic Geography of Hungary.)* Budapest.

REDFIELD, ROBERT.

1956. *Peasant Society and Culture.* Chicago.

RÉVÉSZ, IMRE.

1925. *A magyarországi protestantizmus történelme. (The History of Hungarian Protestantism.)* Budapest.

1938. *Magyar református egyháztörténet 1520–1608. (Hungarian Reformed Ecclesiastical History from 1520 to 1608.)* Debrecen.

SCHRIKKER, SÁNDOR.

1943. A sommások alkalmazásának és kereseti viszonyainak üzemi vonatkozásai. (The Operative Relations of the Employment and Wage Conditions of Seasonal Contract Workers.) *Magyar Gazdák Szemléje*, 134–183.

SOMLYAI, MAGDA (see: M. SOMLYAI, MAGDA).

SOÓS, IMRE.

1955. *Heves megye benépesülése a török hódoltság után. (The Repopulation of Heves County after the Turkish Occupation.)* Eger.

1958. *A jobbágyföld helyzete a szolnoki Tiszatájon 1711–1770. (The Situation of the Serf Holdings in the Tisza Region near Szolnok from 1711 to 1770.)* Szolnok.

n.d. *A jobbágyföld sorsa Heves megyében a XVIII. században. (The Fate of the Serf Holdings in Heves County in the Eighteenth Century.)* Eger.

SPIRA, GYÖRGY (Ed.).

1952. *Tanulmányok a parasztság történetéhez Magyarországon 1711–1790. (Studies in the History of Peasantry in Hungary from 1711 to 1790.)* Budapest.

STEFANOVITS, PÁL.

1963. *Magyarország talajai. (The Soils of Hungary.)* Budapest.

SZABAD, GYÖRGY.

1965. Hitelviszonyok. (Credit Conditions.) In *A parasztság Magyarországon a kapitalizmus korában 1848–1914*, István Szabó (Ed.), vol. II: 184–245. Budapest.

SZABÓ, ISTVÁN.

1940. *A magyar parasztság története. (The History of Hungarian Peasantry.)* Budapest.

1941. Nemesség és parasztság Verbőczi után. (Nobility and Peasantry after Verbőczi's Time.) In *Úr és paraszt a magyar élet egységében (Lord and Peasant in the Unity of Hungarian Life)*, Sándor Eckhardt (Ed.), pp. 44–80. Budapest.

1947. *A jobbágy birtoklása az örökös jobbágyság korában. (The Tenure of the Serf in the Epoch of Permanent Serfdom.)* Budapest.

1948. *Tanulmányok a magyar parasztság történetéből. (Studies in the History of Hungarian Peasantry.)* Budapest.

1963. Magyarország népessége az 1330-as és az 1526-os évek között. (The Population of Hungary between 1330 and 1526.) In *Magyarország történeti demográfiája*, József Kovacsics (Ed.), pp. 63–114. Budapest.

1965a. Jobbágyság — parasztság. Terminológia, fogalom, társadalomszerkezet. (Serfdom and Peasantry: Terminology, Concept, Social Structure.) *Ethnographia*, 76: 10–31.

1965b. (Ed.) *A parasztság Magyarországon a kapitalizmus korában 1848–1914. (The Peasantry in Hungary in the Age of Capitalism from 1848 to 1914.)* 2 vols. Budapest.

SZAKÁL, PÁL.

1964. Mezőgazdaságunk fejlődése 1945–1956. (The Development of Our Agriculture from 1945 to 1956.) *Agrártörténeti Szemle*, 6: 233–265, 488–508.

SZILÁGYI, LÁSZLÓ.

1951. *A mezőgazdasági szövetkezeti értékesítés Magyarországon a felszabadulás előtt. (Cooperative Agricultural Marketing in Hungary before the Liberation.)* vol. I, 1867–1918. Budapest.

THIRRING, LAJOS.

1963. Magyarország népessége 1869–1949 között. (The Population of Hungary between 1869 and 1949.) In *Magyarország történeti demográfiája*, József Kovacsics (Ed.), pp. 211–412.

TÓTH, DEZSŐ.

1941. *A hevesnagykunsági református egyházmegye múltja. Az egyházi élet hétköznapjai. (The History of the Reformed Church District of Heves-Nagykunság: The Workdays of Church Life.)* 2 vols. Debrecen.

VÁCZY, PÉTER.

1958. A korai magyar történet néhány kérdéséről. (On Some Problems of Early Hungarian History.) *Századok*, 92: 265–345.

VARGA, JÁNOS.

1964. Öreg Gyüker József krónikája 1787–1866. (The Chronicle of Old József Gyüker from 1787 to 1866.) *Agrártörténeti Szemle*, 6: 453–472.

VISKI, KÁROLY.

1932. *Hungarian Peasant Customs.* Budapest.

WARRINER, DOREEN.

1939. *Economics of Peasant Farming.* London, New York, Toronto.

WELLMANN, IMRE.

1952. Az 1753-i alföldi parasztfelkelés. (The peasant upheaval on the Great Plain in 1753.) In *Tanulmányok a parasztság történetéhez Magyarországon 1711–1790*, György Spira (Ed.), pp. 141–220.

1961. Földművelési rendszerek Magyarországon a XVIII. században. (Agricultural Systems in Hungary in the Eighteenth Century.) *Agrártörténeti Szemle*, 3: 344–370.

ZAGOROFF, S. D., JENŐ VÉGH, and ALEXANDER D. BILIMOVICH.

1955. *The Agricultural Economy of the Danubian Countries 1935–1945.* Stanford.

ZSARNÓCZAI, SÁNDOR (Ed.).

1964. *Tanulmányok a mai faluról. (Studies on the Village of Today.)* Budapest.

1. A view of the church at the center of the village. In the foreground is one of the places where the Hanyi brook spreads out to form a small pond.

2. A snowbound street in the Lower End of the village.

3. Men wearing *suba*-s among the *kert*-s. Unlike those in the crowded interior of the village, the holdings in the region of the *kert*-s are spacious and the stables and recently built houses are relatively far apart.

4. Houses in the Upper End of the village. An example of the old-fashioned pattern of settlement, with houses standing irregularly and close together.

5. A house constructed in the traditional local style, with a thatched roof and a veranda with stone pillars.

6. The double door of a traditional house: the outer is the latticed summer door, the inner is the "boarded door." To the right of the doorway stands the bent walking stick of the aged owner.

7. Living room: the table and the corner bench.

8. Living room: an ornamental bed with a tall stack of bed clothes on display.

9. Living room: the stove (the oven door is in the kitchen.)

10. Loft: on the floor ears of maize are spread out, and from the rafters pork and sausages are hanging.

11. Pantry: at the right is a ladder leading to the loft, with flour sacks, a scoop, and the corner of the grain-chest behind it. At the top is a rack for the bread.

12. Team of three horses. In the background is the old stable of János Kusper (cf. Figs. 19 and 20).

13. Footpath leading to the *kert*-s. The path crosses an earth dam at one of the places where the Hanyi brook spreads out into a pond. The water flows through a small opening in the dam. In the background are stables in the *kert*-s.

14. *Ólaskert*. In front of the stable and the cart shed is a well, and farther back are a poultry pen, a shed for chaff, and a shed for drying tobacco.

15. Stacks of provender in the *kert*.

16. The stable of a well-to-do *gazda*, large enough to hold 16 to 18 horses and cows.

17. The stable of a *zsellér*, large enough for only 1 or 2 cows.

18. The interior of a stable. Behind the horses are two plank-beds where the men sleep.

19. In the stable of József Kakas. On a winter morning the old and the young *gazda* and their sharecropper light up, having done the morning's chores.

20. Men at *tanyázás* in the stable of the Szilágyi family (cf. Fig. 26) on a winter morning. In the card game the loser has to remove his fur cap.

21. Men at *tanyázás* in the stable of József Szilágyi (cf. Fig. 26).

22. Kindling a fire in the stable (János Boross).

23. The community pasture: a well with a watering trough and a herdsman's reed hut.

24. A grazing herd.

25. A well-to-do sheep farmer, István Rózsa, wearing a *suba* turned inside out and holding a shepherd's crook.

26. Károly Bedécs.

27. Sámuel Kiss.

28. Gábor Varga.

29. József Kakas.

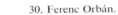

30. Ferenc Orbán.

31. The wife
of Károly Bedécs,
Erzsébet Együd.

32. The wife of László Varga, Zsófia Mérten.

33. The wife of Károly Kusper, Julcsa Kusper.

34. The wife of István Gulyás, Jr., Zsuzsanna Kálosi (the step-daughter of Ferenc Orbán).

35. The wife of József Kakas, Zsófi Rózsa, reads the Bible on a Sunday afternoon.

36. Girls out walking on a Sunday afternoon.

37. Enlisted bachelors with ribboned hats, waiting for the church service to start.

38. Old women in front of the church.

39. Making fuel out of dung: a family arrives to help in the work, the *gazda* first, and the women behind him.

40. Making fuel out of dung: preparations for the work.

41. Making fuel out of dung: the men take the dung from the dunghill and carry it to the site of the work on a wheelbarrow.

42. Making fuel out of dung: the dung is spread out, and the women stamp it into a solid layer of uniform thickness.

43. Making fuel out of dung: the men sharpen the spades in order to cut the stamped dung.

44. Making fuel out of dung: the men cut the layer of stamped dung into squares.

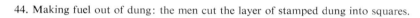

45. Making fuel out of dung: having finished the work, the women are treated to a meal in the yard first, since their work is over sooner, and then the men are similarly treated to a meal.

46. Making fuel out of dung: the helpers go home, carrying the tools they have brought for the work party.

47. Wedding: an invited family carries presents to the bride's house; the man is bringing chickens and wine, the women pastry, cake, and eggs.

48. Wedding: on the eve of the wedding the "bed" (bedclothes) of the bride is carried to the groom's house.

49. Wedding: the *gazdasszony*-s plucking fowls in the court of the bride's house.

50. Wedding: the *gazdasszony*-s are treated to mulled wine and the roasted blood of the slaughtered sheep.

51. Wedding: before going to church people dance in the court to the tunes of gypsy musicians; a bachelor commands the musicians to play his favorite tune.

52. Wedding: singing men.

53. Wedding: the *násznagy*-s chatting at the corner of the table.

54. Wedding: the bride takes leave of her parents after the marriage ceremony in church, before she follows her bridegroom (the young man reading from the paper) to his house; the two best men (one chosen by the bride, the other by the groom) are standing on either side of the couple.

55. Publishing a death: after tolling the bells to announce the bereavement, the bell ringer "cries out" the name of the deceased in front of the church.

56. A bereaved house: the men sing funeral hymns in the *pitar;* in the center is the leader of the singing, or "*diktás*," Sámuel Jámbor.

57. Mourning the dead: the widow, the daughters, and the *meny*-s stand up to sing the improvised lament and make caressing movements with their hands.

58. A bereaved house: close female relatives around the bier, with the widow at the head of the deceased.

59. Burial: in the yard of the bereaved house the participants form groups according to age and sex.

60. Burial: in the yard of the bereaved house the religious ceremony of valediction is going on; in the center the coffin is surrounded by the relatives; a wider circle is formed by the remaining guests, males and females forming separate groups.

61. Burial: in the funeral procession men walk ahead of the carriage which carries the coffin, the immediate kinsfolk follow it, and the women come last.

62. Burial: before letting the coffin down into the grave, the widow and the daughters mourn the deceased *gazda*, prostrating themselves on the coffin.

63. Burial: at the completed grave the widow continues to lament her deceased husband.

64. Burial: at the completed grave the widow continues to lament her deceased husband.

65. The cemetery of the Lower End.

INDEX

I

L

N

T